The Center Could Not Hold

Congressman William H. English and His Antebellum Political Times

Elliott Schimmel

THE CENTER COULD NOT HOLD: CONGRESSMAN WILLIAM H. ENGLISH AND HIS ANTEBELLUM POLITICAL TIMES

1405 SW 6th Avenue • Ocala, Florida 34471 • Phone 352-622-1825 • Fax 352-622-1875
Website: www.atlantic-pub.com • Email: sales@atlantic-pub.com
SAN Number: 268-1250

Library of Congress Cataloging-in-Publication Data

Names: Schimmel, Elliott, 1948- author.
Title: The center could not hold : Congressman William H. English and his antebellum political times / by Elliott Schimmel.
Other titles: William H. English and the politics of self-deception, 1845-1861
Description: Ocala, Florida : Atlantic Publishing Group, Inc., [2019] | Revision of author's thesis (doctoral)—Florida State University, 1986, titled William H. English and the politics of self-deception, 1845-1861. | Includes bibliographical references and index. | Summary: "The story of a self-deceived congressman who believed, from his misreading of the Southern mind, that Civil War could be prevented"— Provided by publisher.
Identifiers: LCCN 2019028442 (print) | LCCN 2019028443 (ebook) | ISBN 9781620236604 (paperback) | ISBN 1620236605 (paperback) | ISBN 9781620236611 (ebook)
Subjects: LCSH: English, William Hayden, 1822-1896. | United States. Congress—Biography. | Democratic Party (U.S.)—History—19th century. | Legislators—United States—Biography. | United States—History—Civil War, 1861-1865—Biography. | United States—Politics and government—1853-1857. | United States—Politics and government—1857-1861. | Indiana—Biography.
Classification: LCC E415.9.E64 S44 2019 (print) | LCC E415.9.E64 (ebook) | DDC 328.73/092 [B]—dc23
LC record available at https://lccn.loc.gov/2019028442
LC ebook record available at https://lccn.loc.gov/2019028443

Printed in the United States

PROJECT MANAGER AND EDITOR: Katie Cline
INTERIOR LAYOUT AND JACKET DESIGN: Nicole Sturk

For Gretchen

For Gretchen

Table of Contents

Maps:

Author's note:

I have chosen to dispense with the use of "sic" in direct quotes throughout and have allowed the original spelling, grammar, and emphasis through underlining and italicization to be maintained. Furthermore, for the sake of brevity, within the footnotes, I have abbreviated "William H. English" and "Congressional Globe" to "WHE" and "CG," respectively.

Introduction

At certain points in American history, perhaps all too few, a significant portion of the nation allows itself to address a fundamental injustice. Such was the period immediately prior to the Civil War, when the institution of slavery came under final attack. Afraid that this attack would disrupt the Union and the prosperity it had fostered, many conservative politicians fought a losing battle to contain the agitation. In the North, most of these politicians were Democrats, and many of the most conservative came from the border region close to the Ohio River where the division of the Union was most genuinely feared. One of these border politicians was William H. English, an Indiana congressman whose name today is all but forgotten. Intelligent, patriotic, and politically prescient in general, he nevertheless misunderstood the nature of the debate over slavery, thereby committing himself to positions that were ultimately untenable.

English belonged to a class of antebellum figures who considered the Democratic Party the vessel through which the experiment in republican government could best be validated. He believed, in other words, that the Party's success and survival were essential to national happiness. He rather literally inherited his faith in the Democracy from his father, an early settler of the state of Indiana who himself was a Democratic politician. The younger English quickly rose to prominence in the Party, eventually serving in Congress during the eight years directly previous to the outbreak of Civil War. From this position, he preached the importance of party harmony, genuinely attempting to reconcile northern and southern Democrats in order to defeat what he considered the predictably devastating effects of anti-slavery 'agitation'. A polite, civil, conservative, and generally gracious politician, he was a Democrat to the core of his being, rising to the top tier of his party in Congress by the time of his retirement. Yet, despite his partisanship, he was generally considered fair-minded, open to compromise while navigating the growing political maelstrom swirling into disaster during the youthful decade of his 30s.

A natural compromiser, English has often been portrayed as a "doughface," a northerner too eager to accommodate the beleaguered South over the slavery controversy. But he should more charitably and realistically be described as a moderate politician, who, as one historian has put it, "believed there must be limits to political controversy, and that civility, rational discourse, and attachment to procedure were the most important determinants of those limits." Indeed, there is an essential humility to English's political posture that conformed to the constitutional framers' belief that people are fallible and too often failed to act in a properly republican disinterested manner. Compromise, thus, often derided, may be elevated to a principle intended to moderate the destabilization of arrogance, often masquerading as moral or cultural imperatives. It represents the central crucible of politics, whereby passions are cooled and reflection is advanced. But its strategy broke down when it was applied to the slavery controversy brought on by the success of the Mexican War in a time when slavery itself was fast becoming an anachronism of western civilization.[1]

In his eventual failure to apply the liniments of compromise and mutual affection to the passionate issue of slavery, he, and like-minded statesmen, failed, largely due to premises that turned out to be misconceived. There were two major misconceptions that English held with regard to the central issue of slavery's expansion into the federal territories. First, he incorrectly believed that the southern Democrats would willingly adopt the northern Democratic conception of popular sovereignty, i.e., that a majority of a territory's electorate had the right to decide the legality of slaveholding within its territorial boundaries. It was with this policy that English hoped to unite the party, defeat the Republican agitators, and maintain the harmony between the sections. But the southern Democrats never truly accepted the northern formula. Instead, they consistently, if somewhat surreptitiously, maintained that only a state government had the sovereignty to limit the property rights of its citizens. As time went on, English was forced to admit that he had deceived himself—that southern Democrats did not share his enthusiasm for majoritarianism—and he resorted to old political methods of ambiguity, delay, and racism to hold the Party together. With a sense of fatalism, he ultimately watched helplessly as the Democracy fell apart. At any rate, English's position on all these matters was arguably located in the "center" of the national Democratic Party.

1. For a discussion of the importance of moderation and compromise to the efficiency of our constitutional framework, see Peter B. Knupfer, *The Union As It Is: Constitutional Unionism and Sectional Compromise, 1787-1861* (Chapel Hill and London: The University of North Carolina Press, 1991). The quote in this paragraph is taken from the preface of that work, p. x. On the importance of "republican disinterestedness," see Gordon S. Wood, *Revolutionary Characters: What Made the Founders Different* (New York: The Penguin Press, 2006), 16.

English's second misconception was that slavery could be treated similarly to any other political issue. Fundamentally racist, perhaps even a bit more than most northerners of his time, English was immune to ethical appeals made in favor of abolition. His opposition to slavery, such as it was, stemmed solely from reasons of political economy. Unaffected by moral arguments, he could not understand why a significant portion of northerners refused to acknowledge that slavery could not survive in the climate of the West, and thus agree to simply allow nature to determine its antislavery course. Essentially cerebral and conservative, he not only underestimated the growing sense of impatience in the North, but also the growing sense of impotence in the South. By the mid-1850s, slavery did not lend itself to dispassionate compromise. Whereas English stressed majority rule, or the means of government, as the solution to the slavery question, increasing numbers of northerners and southerners favored the more revolutionary concept of natural rights, whether in liberty or property. As the controversy raged toward its denouement, the middle ground of compromise shrunk to its essentially meaningless core: no program but the Union; no principle but the Constitution.

This book does not focus exclusively on slavery; rather, it is a political biography of the first half of one man's life in the context of his times. But as a contemporary newspaper editor noted, nothing in this period could be discussed without discovering "a negro in the woodpile." The political infighting of the Indiana Democratic Party, the commercial and economic composition and needs of English's congressional district, the twists and turns of national legislative politics—all were somehow related to the great distracting question. It is what gave the era its lasting significance, and each politician was eventually defined in relation to it. In the end, I hope this study of this one politician's struggle with the key political issue of his day will shed some light, however small, on the great question of how irrepressible the Civil War actually was.

I would like to recognize and acknowledge the assistance of those who were particularly helpful in making this work possible. The staffs at the Indiana State Historical Society and the Indiana State Library showed considerable patience with my many requests in locating material germane to my subject. Especially helpful was Monique Howell, Indiana Division Supervisor at the State Library. From my college, I would like to thank David Reeves, Library Specialist, for performing the duties of acquiring for me primary sources and secondary works from other libraries and institutions while I could not leave Kansas City. And, finally, I would like to thank Katie Cline, my editor and project manager at Atlantic Publishing, for, with unfailing grace, reading the original manuscript, suggesting what were necessary changes, and guiding this work to publication in a remarkably timely and efficient manner.

CHAPTER ONE

Youth and Apprenticeship

W illiam Hayden English was not a self-made man—he was raised in modest wealth and around political influence. The truly self-made man was William's father, Elisha Gale English, one of 14 children, who left his parents' farm when he was 20, crossed the Ohio River from Kentucky, and established a homestead in southeastern Indiana. As one local newspaper later put it, Elisha "was cast in the wilds of the West."[1] Through simple common sense and an eye out for local opportunities, he speculated in land, got elected to the state legislature five times, and left behind a wealthy estate at the time of his death. Because of Elisha's pluck, his son William possessed early advantages that the father himself had not had.

Elisha English's story, of course, was not dissimilar to that of many Americans in the period subsequent to the War of 1812. Partly because of the diminished Indian threat but more fundamentally because of the availability of relatively cheap land, tens of thousands of citizens migrated to the old Northwest. The path most frequently followed was the Ohio River, many of the migrants settling just north of it in the territories of Indiana and Illinois. By 1816, the year Indiana became a state, it had already organized 15 counties, all of them bordering the Ohio or just adjacent to those that did. In 1820, Indiana boasted a population of almost 150,000 souls, an increase of 125,000 residents in the 10 years following the 1810 census. These early Hoosiers, later referred to as the "Old Settlers," were venerated at county fairs until none remained. Coming into the state early in its history, they entered the financial and political fortunes of Indiana at its ground level, in the most literal sense of the term.[2]

Although they arrived from all sections of the nation, these early settlers were primarily southerners. They came predominantly from Kentucky, Virginia, Tennessee, and North Carolina, and as both the Northwest Ordinance and the state

---

1. *Madison Courier,* March 24, 1851.

2. Howard H. Peckham, *Indiana: A Bicentennial History* (New York: W.W. Norton & Co., 1978), 38, 49-50.

of Indiana had forbidden slavery, they generally represented the yeoman farming and tradesman element. Elisha, himself, was first a trader and then a farmer. As his name suggests, he was of British stock, his great-grandfather having come directly from England to Delaware in around 1700. Elisha's own father, also named Elisha, was born in Delaware in 1768, and 20 years later married Sarah Wharton, the daughter of a captured and executed Revolutionary War privateer. In 1790, the couple crossed the Appalachian Mountains and rode the Ohio River to northern Kentucky, outside Louisville. There they settled to help farm the land and populate the region, producing those 14 children who all went on to marry and produce another batch of descendants. Elisha Gale, born to them in 1797, was perhaps the only one of this brood to leave for Indiana. He was barely removed from his teenage years when he set out from Kentucky.[3]

Arriving in Lexington in 1818, a town in southeast Indiana about 30 miles from the Ohio River, Elisha came more than a decade after the first American citizens settled in the area. By the time he reached it, the region was sufficiently organized to inhibit squatting, and he bought an undetermined number of acres from one John Kucks for a not inconsiderable sum of $140. Since public land sold for at least $2 an acre, Elisha's private purchase probably netted him over 50 acres. It may have been more, however, for in 1825, Elisha English sold part of his land for $200. These transactions were just the beginning of a lifetime of speculative activity that was fundamental in producing the $40,000 estate he owned by the Civil War.[4]

In 1817, the citizens of Lexington and the surrounding townships petitioned the state legislature to allow them to separate from Jefferson County and form their own county government. They claimed that the 15–20 mile journey eastward to the Jefferson County seat at Madison created an unnecessary hardship. The legislature granted the request, and Scott County was organized in February 1820 with Lexington as its capital. It began with only 2,334 inhabitants and, throughout the century, remained one of the least-populated counties in the state. It boasted little urbanity—as late as 1850, the Lexington census maintained that

3. Nicole Etcheson, *The Emerging Midwest* (Bloomington: Indiana University Press, 1996), 2-3. The Northwest Ordinance was a federal law passed under the Articles of Confederation in 1787 (and reaffirmed under the Constitution in 1789) that outlawed slavery in the federal territory east of the Mississippi, north of the Ohio River, and, essentially west of the Appalachian Mountains. Although, thus, technically illegal, slavery continued for a few decades under a territorial law, allowing lifetime contracts between masters and servants. In 1820, Indiana contained 190 of these contract slaves. Jacob P. Dunn, *Indiana and Indianians*, vol. 5 (Chicago: The American Historical Society, 1919), 2154. John H. B. Nowland, *Early Reminiscence of Indianapolis* (Indianapolis: Indianapolis Sentinel, Inc., 1870), microfiche, Indiana State Library, LH 11832, 422. William Wesley Woolen, *A Biographical History of Eminent and Self-Made Men of the State of Indiana*, vol. 2 (Cincinnati: Western Biographical Publishing Co., 1880), District 7, 209.

4. Mary Wilson and Sharon Y. Asher, *Lexington*, (typed manuscript in Indiana State Library, Indianapolis), 1-2. Peckham, *Indiana*, 28. Indiana Land Records, Scott County, Indiana State Archives, Indianapolis. 1860 Census, Lexington Township, Scott County, Indiana State Archives, Indianapolis, 54.

425 of the 586 working residents were occupied in farming. Most of the rest (110) were artisans. There were only two lawyers, three schoolteachers, and 14 others who could be classified as merchants.[5]

Having bought land and become one of the many propertied farmers in this young agricultural community, Elisha had accomplished the primary goal he'd set for himself when he left Kentucky. But in the course of this development into what may be described as responsible manhood, he had not yet fulfilled the attendant responsibilities of husband and father. In 1821, he discharged the first when he married Mahala Eastin. Exactly how he met Miss Eastin is unclear, but it is not likely that she resided in Lexington, because, upon her parents' death, their estate was settled in Clark County. What *is* clear is her pedigree. She could trace her maternal ancestry to Joseph Hite, a German who was granted 100,000 acres of Blue Ridge, Virginian land from Great Britain's first Hanoverian king. There, he settled fellow German émigrés. On her other side, Mahala's father was descended from Louis Dubois, a Huguenot patentee and colonizer of Kingston, New York. Both these parents bore some marks of distinction. Her father, Philip, served in the American Revolution as a lieutenant in the 4th Virginia Regiment, a fact to which his grandson would often later refer. Her mother, Sarah Smith, had the more prosaic distinction of being very rich, her family having remained on the original patented lands. Mahala was born to this pair not in Virginia, but in Fayette County, Kentucky, during a stopover on the family's journey to southern Indiana.[6]

Some evidence suggests that Mahala could not offer Elisha the financial help that her mother probably was able to offer her father. On her mother's tombstone, it is written that "the prosperity of her early life gave place in old age to poverty," and, while this might have resulted from the death of her husband in middle age, it was also no doubt furthered by having 17 children. Elisha did receive $50 from one of Mahala's brothers in December 1821, but this has been listed as a land transaction, the amount of acreage sold unknown. Any financial help that Mahala could have tendered Elisha, however, was probably not as important to him as her ability to offer *cultural* assistance. Elisha's background was common—he was an uneducated, frank, quick-tempered man who could use a little reflective breeding to improve his character. Mahala had retained a vestige of landed aristocracy and

5. Wilson , *Lexington*, 14. J. H. Colton, *The State of Indiana Delineated* (New York: J. H. Colton, 1838), 35-36. Lexington's occupational statistics may be gotten from *Indiana Census Records 1820- 1850*, at https:// **indianagenealogy.org**/census, accessed May 3, 2017: 1850, Scott County, Lexington Township and Town of Lexington, 340-343. Statistics for Indiana aggregate population by county are in *1850 Census: The Seventh Census of the United States* (1853), accessed at www.**census.gov**/library/publications/ 1853/dec/ 1850a.html: 755-757.

6. Assignment of Eastin Estate, November 11, 1847, William H. English Papers, Indiana Historical Society, Indianapolis, Indiana. Dunn, *Indiana and Indianans,* 2154-2155. Woolen, *Eminent Men*, vol. 2, District 7, 209.

military respectability. She would trade this off for Elisha's drive, strength, and native intelligence that could provide her with financial security.[7]

The *Scott County Assessor's Book* for 1839 illustrates that Mahala had not misplaced her faith. Elisha English was listed as owning 744 acres of land valued at $4,870. He had made 30 real estate transactions since their marriage, debits amounting to $4,170 and sales to $2,650. He, thus, essentially owned land valued at over $3,000 more than the amount he had invested. Moreover, while he probably farmed a good portion of the land surrounding his homestead (about 450 acres), he most likely collected rents from the rest. His speculative activity had propelled him toward the top rank of wealth in the county.[8]

Very little of this fervid activity, only three transactions, took place before 1828, and therein lies a connection between money and politics. In that year, Elisha English was appointed Scott County sheriff, a post he would hold until 1832. During his tenure, he purchased four major parcels of land, the initial parcel being bought directly from Scott County in November 1829. No evidence exists to prove that Elisha obtained this land through the undue influence of his office, but his position as primary legal officer of the county could only serve to ease his acquisitions. From this point on, his buying and selling of real estate became constant, as did, in the main, his office holding. In 1832, he was elected to the first of two consecutive terms in the state legislature.[9]

Elisha probably owed these early electoral successes to his ebullience, down-to-earth nature, and lack of artifice. Although posthumous assessments almost always described him as opinionated, he was also known to be honest, charitable, warm, and loyal to his friends. One appraisal noted that he had "a heart instead of a gizzard, which is very rare amongst politicians," and another testimonial in the middle of his career pointed to his "sound practical mind, true heart, and thorough knowledge of human nature." His first public position, major in the Indiana militia, actually preceded his selection as sheriff by a couple of months, and, coupled with these noted assessments of his character, illustrates his frontier personality. He seems to have had, in large degree, that admixture of roughness and chivalry that characterized the president-hero after whom the age is named.[10]

---

7. *Ibid. Indiana Land Records, Scott County*, Indiana State Archives, Indianapolis. Nowland, *Early Reminiscences*, 378.

8. *Scott County Assessor's Book, 1839*, Indiana State Library, Indianapolis, Indiana. Also see: *Scott County, Indiana Assessor's Book for 1839*, transcribed by Jane Eaglesfield Darlington, Indiana State Library, Indianapolis, 1981.

9. Rebecca A. Shepherd, et al., eds., *A Biographical Directory of the Indiana General Assembly*, vol. 1 (Indianapolis: Indiana Historical Society Bureau, 1980), 119. Indiana Land Records, Scott County, Indiana State Archives.

10. Nowland, *Early Reminiscences*, 378. *Indiana State Sentinel*, November 11, 1874. Joseph P. Milliken to WHE, May 4, 1848, English Papers. *Madison Courier*, March 11, 1851. Shepherd, *Biographical Directory*, 119.

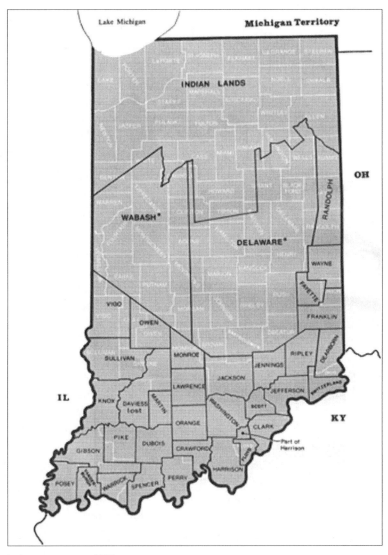

Indiana counties in 1820

Elisha's entrance into state government occurred at a time when politicians were dividing into Jacksonian Democrats and Clay-Adams National Republicans, the latter of which would soon morph into the Whigs. Democrat Andrew Jackson had carried Indiana by landslide proportions in both 1828 and 1832, but the opposition remained a majority in the state legislature. As befit his frontier mien, Elisha aligned himself firmly with the Jacksonians, and he became one of the early active leaders of the fledgling state Democratic Party. One politician later noted that Elisha "knows how to legislate better than many who claim for themselves great wisdom," and his rugged artfulness helped produce friends from both parties. He would serve with politicians who would be influential during the entire antebellum period. Probably because of the state custom limiting legislators to two consecutive terms, Elisha did not seek re-election in 1834. But his popularity was so great that he was elected Sergeant at Arms for the State Senate, after which he temporarily retired from public service for four years to concentrate on developing his own financial resources.[11]

In Elisha's absence, the legislators worked to develop the state's resources. Between 1820 and 1830, Indiana's population had more than doubled, and 26 new counties had been created. The capital had been moved from Corydon near the Ohio River to Indianapolis in the center of the state to anticipate and stimulate migration northward, but little had been done to ease transportation and communication. Unremoved land bars, dangerous eddies, and fallen trees obstructed all the interior rivers. There were no extensive canals or turnpikes, and only two often-impassable stage routes ran to Indianapolis. In 1836, in a frenzy of better-late-than-never activity, the state legislature passed a "mammoth" internal improvements act that allocated $13 million, one-sixth of the state's wealth, toward developing transportation. Two large canals were planned to crisscross the state, a railroad was to run from Madison on the Ohio River through Indianapolis and north to Lafayette, and a few macadamized roads and smaller railroads were to be constructed in different sections of Indiana. Even though only one of these projects came anywhere close to completion, and four years later, overextended Indiana had to default on its bonds, the bill did illustrate the state's willingness to proceed apace from a frontier community to a modern commonwealth. It predicted the frenetic later development of the 1850s, and it presaged a time when rustic politicians would have to give way to those more polished.[12]

11. Peckham, *Indiana,* 133. W. J. Van Der Weele, "Jesse David Bright: Master Politician from the Old Northwest" (PhD diss., Indiana University, 1958), 12. Joseph P. Milliken to WHE, May 4, 1848, English Papers. *Indianapolis State Journal,* January 16, 1874. Shepherd, *Biographical Directory,* 119.

12. Ernst V. Schockley, "County Seats and County Seat Wars in Indiana," *Indiana Magazine of History,* 10, no. 1 (March, 1914), 45. Logan Esarey, *Internal Improvements in Early Indiana* (Indianapolis: Edward J. Hicker, 1912), 51, 101. Peckham, *Indiana,* 63.

2.

Elisha English did not wait until the 1830s to fulfill his fundamental filial responsibility. On August 27, 1822, a little more than a year after his marriage to Mahala, the couple produced their first and only child, William Hayden. A detailed announcement of the boy's birth would not have listed his height, weight, or color of eyes. None of these factors was as germane to his entrance into the world as the one noted by a friendly journalist over 30 years later:

> He was born a Democrat; he inherits it from his father who is a democrat before him and is as good a one as ever breathed the democratic air of democratic Indiana—he was reared a democrat, and has known no change in his political faith from his boyhood to his manhood, and down to the present hour.

There was no greater vital statistic of William English's birth. Formal religion played little, if any, part in his upbringing, but his "political faith" ran deep. He was born contiguous with the birth of the Democratic Party and was raised under the immediate tutelage of his father and the more distant but no less compelling influence of Andrew Jackson. As he would put it himself years later during his first term in Congress, "the Democratic party, sir, is the political party of my father, my father's father—a love of whose creed constituted a goodly portion of my patrimony."[13]

Whether or not William's parents envisioned for their son a future in partisan politics, there is little doubt that they wished to provide him with the rudimentary tools and helpful environment that would make that life possible. His formal education, merely by being formal, was markedly better than his father's, and, as elementary education in Indiana was at that time unmandated and often privately funded, his parents had to make the conscious choice to school their son. It is highly likely (though not certain) that William was first sent to Salem Grammar School about 10 miles from Lexington, as it was the leading educational institution for young boys in his part of the state. Its curriculum was composed of arithmetic, grammar, and spelling along with typical religious instruction. For the latter, William never showed any great affinity, and, later in life, he did not attach any elevated importance to matters of faith. Minimal, as well, were the few months per year of instruction, but, in total, his early education was enough to earn him entrance into Hanover College at the rather typical age of 14.[14]

---

13. William H. English Scrapbook of Newspaper Clippings, Indiana State Library, Indianapolis, Indiana, 66. *Congressional Globe, 33-1, Appendix*, 606.

14. Scott Walter, "'Awakening the Public Mind': The Dissemination of the Common School Idea in Indiana, 1787-1852," in William J. Reese, ed., *Hoosier Schools: Past and Present* (Bloomington and Indianapolis:

The village of Hanover was located 20 miles east of Lexington and a few miles southwest of the Ohio River town of Madison, Indiana. The college was placed on a high bluff that enabled one to view the flow of the river for 20 miles. Of all the lessons English was to learn there, none might have been so useful as the firsthand observations of the river's importance to the region. In the 1830s, Madison was the greatest commercial center in the southeastern part of the state, and young English could not have failed to be impressed by the constant flow of flatboats before him. It was here, too, that he would have made the acquaintance of the sons of Madison's merchants, bankers, and lawyers, and his subsequent life was closely attached both to that city and those occupations. The company of such boys would most likely have broadened English's outlook, for he exhibited a certain urbanity and moderation later in life not given to his father.[15]

This formal curriculum served English in other ways as well. Although it was established as a Presbyterian seminary in 1827 and was originally envisioned to prepare students for the ministry, early on in its history Hanover also taught courses in literature, math, and science. The college was not subject to ecclesiastical control, and a great deal of its liberal-arts curriculum was intended to crank out teachers for the frontier community. By the mid-1830s, its curriculum also offered much to a future secular politician, including courses in logic, classical literature, geography, rhetoric, and moral philosophy. William probably took classes in history as well and learned at least a smattering of Latin and Greek. In 1839, after three years of attendance, he was granted a Certificate of Teaching, which validated his ability to "teach youth in reading, writing, arithmetic, and geography, history, grammar, natural philosophy, and surveying." However, English's name has never appeared among a list of formal Hanover graduates, and all the biographical sketches of him merely mention the fact of his attendance. It is difficult to explain this shortcoming in one who was later known to have carried through to a satisfactory conclusion all that he began. Perhaps he may have simply been impatient to enter the more practical realm of men's affairs.[16]

Indiana University Press, 1998), 5. Woolen, *Eminent Men*, vol. 2, District 7, 210; vol. 1, District 6, 95. Wilson, *Lexington*, 34-35, 39. Richard G. Boone, *A History of Education in Indiana* (1892; repr., Indianapolis: Indiana Historical Bureau, 1941), 22. *History of Orange, Warwick, and Washington County, Indiana* (1884; repr., Paoli, Indiana: Stout's Print Shop, 1961), 836. Minnie B. Clark, "The Old College at Livonia," *Indiana Magazine of History*, 23, no. 1 (March, 1927), 75-76. Harvey L. Carter, "A Decade of Hoosier History" (PhD diss., Univ. of Wisconsin, 1939), 320. Henry C. Hubbart, *The Older Middle West, 1840-1880: Its Social, Economic, and Political life, and Sectional Tendencies before, during, and after the Civil War* (1884; repr., New York: Russell & Russel, 1973), 38.

15. Ralph D. Gray, "Thomas Hendricks: Spokesman for the Democracy," in Ralph D. Gray, *Gentlemen from Indiana: National Party Candidates, 1836-1940* (Indianapolis, Indiana Historical Bureau, 1977), 123. Fasset A. Cotton, *Education in Indiana* (Bluffton, Indiana: The Progress Publishing Co., 1934), 29.

16. William Alfred Willis, *The History of Hanover College from 1827-1927* (Hanover, Indiana: Hanover College, 1927), 19, 90, 154, 184-186; accessed July 14, 2017 at https://history.hanover.edu/texts/millis/millistc.html. The famous Presbyterian divine, John Finley Crowe was the founder and leading light of the college

In the spring of 1839, English resided not at Hanover or Lexington but at Madison, probably with the intention of exploring vistas of social and professional opportunity. He was only 16, and part of his sojourn may have been nothing more than a late-adolescent adventure. He entered the city's society sufficiently enough to have written that he almost "received religion" there, but he might have gone to church primarily to meet young women. The meager evidence that exists for this period suggests that he was indeed actively in pursuit of romance. Sometime during his final year at Hanover, he won the affections of a local girl named Lane Campbell. While in Madison, he consistently wrote her romantic missives, to which she increasingly began to reply in kind. The affair is significant not only for its own sake but also because it illustrated English's political abilities. While traveling between Madison, Lexington, and Hanover in the summer and fall of 1839, English deftly kept the affections of Miss Campbell while slowly distancing himself from another young woman to whom he had previously committed his devotion.[17]

English's adventures on the romantic front coincided with exploration on the professional one. After receiving his general teaching certificate, he procured favorable recommendations from three of his professors. He returned to Lexington to pass the teaching examination, which allowed him to be employed in Scott County common schools. These exams were generally not difficult; in some cases, a college certificate made them all but superfluous. No evidence suggests that English was ever actually employed as a teacher, and, by the time he passed his examination, his activities appear to have turned decidedly political. In the 1839 fall canvass, his father was elected for a third time to the Indiana House of Representatives, and, for a few days, English joined him in Indianapolis as a delegate from Scott County to the Democratic State Convention. This should not be interpreted as an honor granted to him by the citizens of his home county, as it was common for all who wished to make the hard journey to be invited to attend as delegates. But, at the precocious age of 17, he would be introduced at

---

until the Civil War. *Ibid.,* 19. See also John W. Holcombe and Hunter M. Skinner, *Life and Public Services of Thomas A. Hendricks* (Indianapolis: Carlon and Hollenbeck, 1888), 68-69, 75. English attended Hanover for part of the time that Hendricks (future governor, senator, and vice-presidential candidate) also was enrolled. Certificate of Teaching from Hanover College, September 13, 1839, English Papers.

17. William received the following letter from the young woman he jilted: "I have heard of you and that girl. Now William if that is the case I want you to tell me when you come down. I don't think you are so deceitful as that with one who loves you. If you love me as you say you do don't have anything more to do with her for my sake, but if you love her better than me let me know and I [will] try to bare it as well as I can." Elizabeth to WHE, August 8, 1839, English Papers. Later in that year, "Elizabeth" married someone else, and she asked English to send her ring back. Elizabeth to WHE, December 1839, English Papers. Lane Campbell to WHE, February 20, March 18, October 1, October 9, October 18, November 12, 1839; Elizabeth to WHE, July 31, 1839. English Papers.

the state capitol to the many Democrats and Whigs who were well acquainted with his father.[18]

What it meant to be a Democrat in the 1830s and 1840s revolved around a few key issues and principles.[19] In a philosophically political sense, Democrats were generally more likely than Whigs to harbor greater suspicion of governmental power, both because they believed that those who governed had a strong tendency to chip away at the liberties of the citizenry ("power corrupts") and because the privileged classes had greater access to power in the first place. Thus, both liberty and equality were constantly threatened by government. These corruptive tendencies were especially prevalent with respect to the *Federal* Government, as its distance from most of the people made the citizenry's vigilance over these threats to liberty and equality difficult. Such distance also made it difficult for naked financial corruption to be discovered—a central government with a large budget and extensive bureaucracy was always susceptible to hidden financial chicanery. For example, a high protective tariff that necessitated a plethora of paid customs officials was regarded, for this reason among others, as a measure tending toward political and financial corruption. So, too, were laws calling for federally funded transportation improvements and a nationally chartered central bank. Protective tariffs, public assistance to transportation improvements, and specially chartered banks also had the tendency, Democrats believed, to assist the privileged economic classes. Again, according to Democrats, the proper center of political power should be the state and local governments, whose expenditures and governmental appointees could be closely watched by the people so any public corruption, either political or economic, could be more easily discovered.

The Whigs, on the other hand, had a much more positive view of government. It may fairly be said that the Whig Party began as a reaction to what many believed to be the executive overreach and general coarseness of Andrew Jackson. And, as Michael Holt argues, the Whigs originally trumpeted their "republican" ideology by noting that such Jacksonian overreach threatened the constitutional

---

18. Recommendation of E. D. McMaster, Thomas W. Hynas, John Finley Crowe, September 23, 1839, English Papers. Certificate of Examination, Scott County, September 30, 1839, English Papers. Boone, *Education*, 25. Woolen, *Eminent Men*, vol. 2, District 7, 210. According to Woolen it took three days to travel by horseback from Lexington to Indianapolis in the 1830s.

19. There are numerous historical works concerning the differences between Whigs and Democrats and the exceptions to these general differences geographically and socially. But three works to me of special interest and incisiveness are Major L. Wilson, *Space, Time, and Freedom: The Quest for Nationality and the Irrepressible Conflict, 1815-1861* (Westport, Connecticut and London, England: Greenwood Press, 1974), esp. chapter 2; Daniel Walker Howe, *The Political Culture of American Whigs* (Chicago: University of Chicago Press, 1970); and, of course, Michael F. Holt, *The Rise and Fall of the American Whig Party: Jacksonian Politics and the Onset of the Civil War* (New York and Oxford: Oxford University Press, 1999). Short good summaries of differences can also be found in Daniel Feller, *The Jacksonian Promise: America, 1815-1840* (Baltimore and London: The Johns Hopkins University Press, 1995), 167-168, and Bruce Collins, "The Ideology of the Antebellum Northern Democrats," *Journal of American Studies* 11, no. 1 (April 1977): 105-120.

framework of the Unites States, and, indeed, liberty itself. But, by the late 1830s, during the time that William English began to embark on a political career, many Whigs had begun to focus on particular policy positions that were based on the concept that government could be effectively used to advance society. And it was this belief in that role of the government that ultimately distinguished Whigs from Democrats. They believed, for example, that a national bank, financed transportation improvements underwritten by central and state governments, and even a protective tariff promoted the general welfare of the country by stimulating expansive economic opportunities for Americans. An influential historical work written in 1974 maintained that, while the Democrats believed the simple migration of Americans westward would create prosperity and opportunity, the Whigs tended to argue that government needed to help spur advancement through legislation. Democrats, in other words, believed that the nation, when given the opportunity to expand geographically, would prosper naturally without government intrusion, while Whigs maintained that active public stimulus over *time*, regardless of geographical expansion, produced greater opportunity. On social and moral issues, such as promoting publicly funded education, limiting the consumption of alcohol, assisting the ideals of evangelical Protestantism, and, at least among party adherents in the free states, preventing the growth of black slavery, Whigs tended to see a legitimate cause for governmental influence. Democrats, however, tended to view government action in these areas as an intrusion into individual liberty due to its tendency to increase taxes to advance these goals, its tendency to limit the freedom to drink or use one's property (like slaves) as one wishes, or its tendency to affect religious freedom; thusly, such laws "squinted" toward tyranny. Concomitantly, Democrats believed such Whig aspirations to use governmental power to perfect humanity were unnecessary, as the "common man" needed no such assistance. Indeed, the Whig tendency to promote the improvement of humanity was often viewed by Democrats, North and South, as a veiled elitism—an attack on the less educated and less privileged. To Democrats, then, Whigs were the descendants of the aristocratic Federalists. As one historian has put it, "the Whigs wanted to use state and federal government to develop and control the social and economic realm," while "the Democrats stressed individual action to shape outcomes free from government restriction or control."[20]

English carried these Democratic ideals with him almost from his birth, and he certainly carried them back from Indianapolis in early 1840. Indeed, upon his return from the Party's state convention, he spent a respectable portion of his time speechmaking for state and national Democratic nominees. Yet, he also began to attend to his own professional advancement by formally ruminating on the legal

---

20. Holt, *The Rise and Fall of the American Whig Party,* 28-30, 68-70. The work written 45 years ago is Wilson's, see footnote 19. The historian quoted is Joel H. Silbey, *The Partisan Imperative: The Dynamics of American Politics before the Civil War* (New York and Oxford: Oxford University Press, 1985), 61.

giants, Kent and Blackstone. These different tasks entailed another balancing act, as the office in which he read law was that of the formidable Whig attorney and politician of the city of Madison, Joseph G. Marshall. English's political and professional activities became even more incongruous when Marshall, who was called the "Webster of Indiana," was chosen as a state elector for Whig presidential nominee William Henry Harrison. Some amusement may be gained from imagining the callow, aspiring lawyer excusing himself from his respected mentor's law office in order to go make a speech for Democratic nominee Martin van Buren. Fortunately for English, perhaps, the Whigs were successful in the state and presidential races, as well as in Madison and Jefferson county as a whole.[21]

For another less-dissonant reason, it is significant that William read law in Marshall's office. Marshall was so highly regarded that a fellow lawyer said of him, "Indiana never had [his] equal…in breadth and strength of intellect." Others commented that "he was the embodiment of the law," or "if he differed from the books, the books were usually wrong." (Three years later, Marshall would run for governor on the Whig ticket.) Marshall allowing English to benefit from his guidance might have had something to do with the young man's character, but it probably had more to do with the young man's connections. By then, English's father was well acquainted with the leading figures of both political parties in southeastern Indiana; indeed, he was an early colleague and a friend of the just-elected Whig governor of the state. Although Elisha was always a strong political partisan, it is not unlikely that he would want his son to have the best legal instructor available, whether he be Whig or Democratic. That Marshall would take on Elisha's son also speaks to a fellowship feeling among the early settlers of the state. This is another early example of the way in which Elisha's political success smoothed the path for his son, a pattern often repeated for over a decade.[22]

By the summer of 1841, having just turned 19, English spent studying legal precedents for hours, enabling him to pass the examination that would allow him to practice in Indiana's circuit and inferior courts. Although not destined to practice for long, young English did open an office in Scott County and received appointment as a county commissioner in bankruptcy the next year. One brief biography glowingly maintains that "English had all the elements of great success at the bar had he continued in the practice."[23] But he did not continue. Having

21. Woolen, *Eminent Men,* vol. 2, District 7, 210-211. Gerald F. Handfield, Jr., "William H. English and the Election of 1880," in Gray, ed., *Gentlemen from Indiana,* 87. Woolen, *Eminent Men,* vol. 1, District 4, 47-48. Carter, "Hoosier History," 345. Dorothy Riker and Gayle Thornbrough, eds., *Indiana Election Returns, 1816-1851* (Indianapolis: Indiana Historical Bureau, 1960), 30, 32, 34, 36, 149, 150, 253.

22. Woolen, *Eminent Men,* vol. 1, District 4, 47-48. Nowland, *Early Reminiscences,* 422. Thomas Smith to WHE, 1854, English Papers.

23. Certificate to Practice in Indiana Circuit and Inferior Courts, August 14, 1841, English Papers. Appointment as Commissioner in Bankruptcy, August 19, 1842, English Papers. Woolen, *Eminent Men,* vol. 2,

been certified as both a teacher and lawyer by his 19th birthday, and having received a decent upper-level education with his father's support, English was ready to dismiss the strict academic or legal worlds for the occupation for which all these formalities had only helped prepare him: politics.

3.

The first political patronage job that William H. English actually held dated back to 1837, when he was barely 15. Appointed a deputy clerk of Scott County, he received for his services a third of the circuit court and records departments' fees. In a certain sense, this was a type of apprentice position, which he no doubt owed to his father's prominence. With this position, he could smartly reward his father by keeping a close watch on the county's real estate. When the Whigs regained control of Scott County the next year, English was promptly replaced.[24]

To English's advantage, the Democratic Party began a resurgence in Indiana soon after he was admitted to the bar. The Party had suffered a humiliating defeat in 1840 when the state's voters had not only selected the presidential electors pledged to Whig William Henry Harrison but had also elected a Whig governor and a Whig state legislature. Over the course of the next year, the Indiana Democrats lost six of seven congressional races; the only congressional seat they won was because two Whigs ran and split the majority Whig vote. To try to revitalize the Party, a new, hard-hitting state organ, the *Indiana State Sentinel,* was introduced in the summer of 1841. For a full year, the *Sentinel* hammered away at the opposition by, not completely unjustifiably, placing the blame for Indiana's current state of indebtedness and sluggish economy on the Whig's internal improvements bill passed a few years earlier. This strategy bore fruit in the state elections of 1842 when the Democrats captured the state House of Representatives and a majority of legislators (including Elisha English) on a joint ballot.[25]

The Democratic success in Indiana was also assisted by the split in Whig ranks nationally. William Henry Harrison, the Whig president elected in 1840, had died in April 1841, one month into his term. Harrison had been a rather orthodox Whig and had been supportive of the general party programme calling for the reinstitution of a national bank, enactment of a protective tariff, and appro-

---

District 7, 210. By 21, English was admitted to practice in the Indiana Supreme Court and, two years later, in the U.S. Supreme Court. There is no evidence that he ever partook in these privileges.

24. Appointment as Deputy Clerk of Scott County, December 15, 1837, English Papers. Riker, *Indiana Election Returns,* 243.

25. Roger van Bolt, "Sectional Aspects of Expansion," *Indiana Magazine of History* 48, no. 2 (June 1952): 119-120. *Indiana Biography Series,* vol. 21, Indiana State Library, Microfilm, 19. Michael J. Dubin, ed., *United States Congressional Elections, 1788-1997* (Jefferson, North Carolina and London: McFarland and Co., Inc., 1998), 128. Van Der Weele, "Jesse Bright," 20-21.

priations for national transportation projects. Despite some unpleasantness and rivalry between him and the towering Whig leader, Senator Henry Clay, the two of them had essentially been in agreement on these Whig policies. However, Vice President John Tyler of Virginia, Harrison's successor, was a former Democrat. He had joined the Whig Party only several years earlier after breaking with Andrew Jackson over what Tyler believed were Jackson's unconstitutional assertions of presidential and federal power. Tyler had never truly abandoned the Democratic Party principles that saw the Whig economic measures as tending toward a bloated federal bureaucracy and governmental corruption. (He had been nominated as vice president by the Whigs to help them win in the southern states.) When Tyler succeeded to the presidency, the Whig leaders had rather hoped that "his accidency" would allow Henry Clay to push their measures through Congress, Tyler acquiescing in their adoption. But the new president chafed under Clay's imperious attitude and reverted to his Democratic politics, vetoing bills on the tariff and the United States Bank. Thereupon the Whig leaders essentially read Tyler out of the Party, his Cabinet resigning *en masse*.

This Whig split not only helped the fortunes of the Democratic Party in general but also promoted the political career of William English in particular. As Tyler moved back toward the Democrats, hoping to somehow receive *that* Party's presidential nomination in 1844, he began to replace the Whigs holding the federal patronage with Democrats. On August 20, 1842, over the objections of Indiana's Second-District Whig congressman, Tyler replaced the Whig postmaster of Lexington with the 20-year-old English. A letter written to English from the state's lone Democratic congressman, Andrew Kennedy, illustrated that the young politico had solicited the position in July, one month earlier. Kennedy had been a state legislative friend of Elisha's, and, although he was unsure of his influence with the "powers that be," he wrote a letter to the administration in support of the appointment. As he later wrote English, he was "proud to aid any of my Democratic friends whom it is within my power." Federal postmasters were considered key local political leaders of their party, and English would hold this position for another two and a half years.[26] His father's connections continued to work for him.

Even before the ambitious English embarked on his new duties, the peripatetic youngster attempted to test his political fortunes in Indianapolis. With his father having just been elected a member to the state House of Representatives, English began a campaign to procure for himself the House's minor position of enrolling clerk. Although he would ultimately fail in this attempt, its pursuit resulted in an early correspondence with his future political mentor, Jesse David Bright. Bright, who would eventually become Indiana's most powerful senator between 1845 and

---

26. Certificate of Appointment as Lexington Postmaster, December 2, 1842, English Papers. Andrew Kennedy to WHE, July 9, 1842, English Papers. Wilson, *Lexington*, 55.

1861, managed, along with his brother Michael, the Democratic Party of Jefferson County, home to the city of Madison. In 1842, he was one of the few Democratic state senators in Indiana. In early November of that year, English invited Bright to attend a meeting of the senator's "Democratic friends" in Scott County. Bright wound up not attending, but, four days later, the *Madison Courier*, the Democratic organ of Jefferson County, endorsed English's bid for House enrolling clerk.[27]

The tone of Bright's reply to English's invitation to the Scott county gathering indicates that the two were not yet well acquainted with each other, though they most certainly had met.[28] English no doubt sought the assistance of other Democrats as well, but no other elected Democrat would become as powerful an asset, or, eventually, as cumbersome a liability to English, as Bright would. Their correspondence, which lasted until Bright's death in 1875, though always replete with politics, was clearly that of close, if not fully intimate, friends. As their connection intensified over the years, they looked out for each other's fortunes: Bright clearly the mentor and advisor; English the efficient assistant. In the end, it was the pupil who proved himself politically superior to the master.

English's nascent association with Bright was well timed. At the Democratic State Convention of January 1843, Bright was nominated lieutenant governor. English attended that convention, and, as befitted a patronage appointee of the Party (as Lexington postmaster), he went back to Scott County to assist the Party's fortunes. The 1843 campaign was pivotal for both the political future of Indiana and the political development of 20-year-old English himself. The Democratic Party was testing whether its gains in the previous election reflected a real shift in popular sentiment, and the new postmaster was testing his skills at political organization and manipulation. The race for Congress in his district gave English the opportunity to exhibit his political acumen. The incumbent was the Whig who had opposed English's appointment as postmaster the previous year; to help defeat him would be personally and politically satisfying. In pursuit of this objective, English continued to correspond with Bright, who was impressed by English's "deep interest in the Democratic cause." Bright counseled his rising acolyte to concentrate on the young men of the district, whose energy controlled elections.

---

27. John L. Robinson to WHE, November 2, 1842; Jesse Bright to WHE, November 18, 1842, English Papers. Van Der Weele, "Jesse Bright, 13-18. *Madison Courier*, November 18, 1842.

28. Bright's reply to English's invitation read: "Your polite note…is received. It will afford me much pleasure to be with you on that occasion, and unless I am unavoidably detained in Kentucky [Bright owned a slave plantation in Kentucky], I shall certainly be on the ground." Bright to WHE, November 18, 1842. Bright's brother, Michael, studied law with Joseph G. Marshall, as English did. And Jesse Bright himself was recommended to the bar by Marshall. Furthermore, Bright was the primary Democrat in Madison in 1840 when English studied in Marshall's office and made speeches for the ticket. William Wesley Woolen, *Biographical and Historical Sketches of Early Indiana*, (Indianapolis: Hammond and Co., 1883), 450. Van der Weele, "Jesse Bright," 8. It is also likely that English's father was acquainted with the Brights before William was, as the three of them had all served in the legislature around the same time. Shepherd, *Biographical Directory,* 37-38, 119.

He clearly understood that English was a useful ally: "You have it in your power to do much in Scott Co. Your long residence there together with an extensive acquaintance gives you a decided advantage over most men."[29]

In the end, English's congressional district indeed elected its Democratic candidate, Thomas Henley, by almost 1,000 votes. And Henley's smashing victory was just one example of the remarkable success of the Indiana Democracy in 1843. The Party elected its first governor, held on to its recent majority in the state House of Representatives, captured the state Senate, and won eight of the state's now 10 congressional seats. Jesse Bright, too, was elected, outpolling the vote for the Democratic gubernatorial candidate. The magnitude of the victory was such that a Democrat would remain the state's chief executive until the eve of the Civil War almost two decades later, and during the same period, the Party would only briefly lose control of one branch of the legislature or the other. Democrats called it the "Revolution of 1843," and it marked a point from which the Whigs would never recover until they merged themselves into another affiliation.[30]

Soon after this election, Henley wrote English thanking him for "the services you so kindly rendered me, at the time the most important of all others in my life, [which] cannot be easily reciprocated."[31] Earlier, when Scott County Democrats had held their meeting to nominate local candidates, English was appointed one of the convention's secretaries, and when his father saw fit to decline nomination to succeed himself as state legislator, citing "circumstances of an unavoidable character," the convention briefly turned to his son. Though quite literally a generational shift, it may not have been universally perceived as in accordance with what was meant by the "new" Democracy. Certainly, it would open the local Democrats to the Whig charge that the post had become an undemocratic hereditary bailiwick. It was probably also resented by other aspiring Scott County Democrats who hardly wanted the local Party to become the provenance of one family. Moreover, English would no doubt have faced the charge that his father's rejection of the nomination was part of a premeditated scheme to promote the son. In any event, "in a few brief remarks," English asked the delegates to withdraw his name. The convention proceeded to nominate instead David McClure, a 28-year-old transplanted easterner who had resided in Scott County for only four years.[32]

There was little doubt now that English had embarked on a political career. And, as it turned out, he would enter the state legislature through another door.

29. J.G. Read to WHE, February 3, 1842, English Papers. Van Der Weele, "Jesse Bright," 20-22. Jesse Bright to WHE, March 4, April 21, 1843, English Papers.

30. Dubin, *Congressional Elections*, 133-134. Riker, *Election Returns*, 106, 155, 272-78, 105-109. Van Der Weele, "Jesse Bright," 25. Van Bolt, "Sectional Aspects," 119-120.

31. Thomas J. Henley to WHE, December 19, 1843, English Papers.

32. *Madison Courier*, July 22, 1843. Shepherd, *Biographical Directory*, 247.

Warmly supported by congressman Henley and increasingly becoming a political friend to Lieutenant Governor Bright, the still very young postmaster got himself elected principal clerk of the Indiana House of Representatives on the first ballot. This was the earliest position to which he had actually been elected, and but for one impossible attempt late the next year, it inaugurated a string of victories that would continue down to the Civil War. As in all his positions, English carried out his duties with what eventually would be seen as his characteristic aplomb and competence, for at the end of the session he received the unanimous thanks of the House for "the able and impartial manner" with which he performed his responsibilities.[33]

4.

Lest it be inferred that English's focused pursuit of political preferment blocked out the natural inclinations of youth, it should be noted that he rather consistently continued to exhibit keen interest in the young ladies around him. Upon his return from Indianapolis in December 1842 from his failed attempt to gain the position of House enrolling clerk, he had received a letter from a state senator with whom he had made his acquaintance that noted that his "female friends make many inquiries about you."[34] A few months earlier, on a visit to his uncle in New Liberty, Kentucky, English had caught sight of a local beauty named Elizabeth Payne. When he returned to Indiana, he encountered a male relative of hers and struck a bargain with him: English would campaign for the fellow as he ran for political office, if, in return, Miss Payne's relative would campaign on English's behalf for Elizabeth's good graces. The relative obviously carried out his end, for in the same week that English received his postmaster's appointment, he also received a surprise letter from his uncle who'd heard the story of the bargain from Elizabeth herself. English's chances were good: "They have heard that you are sprightly and that your father is rich," his uncle wrote, "I know you can succeed if you try."[35]

Try he did. He wrote Elizabeth a letter, and, as postmaster, mailed it forthwith. Her return missive, however, was not prompt at all, and, when it finally arrived, it caused English more anxiety than pleasure. She simply wrote, "I have no objections to a further acquaintance with you, my not returning your letter might have convinced you that I had none. Nothing more at the present." It was signed "respectfully, M. Elizabeth Payne." To a man of romantic inclinations, this terse reply was not especially satisfying, and he worried about it in a letter to his

33. *Journal of the House of Representatives of the State of Indiana during the Twenty-Eighth Session of the General Assembly* (Indianapolis: Dowling and Cole, 1843), 6, 553.

34. James G. Read to WHE, February 3, 1843, English Papers.

35. John B. English to WHE, August 13, 1842, English Papers.

uncle. Uncle John tried to "assure" English that "it was a very encouraging note… strictly in accordance with propriety. I know that you expected a long letter, but she would have acted wrong to have written anything else than she did. You must remember that you are a stranger to her." The elder English continued to encourage his nephew and counseled him to appear at the Paynes in person, "for it is evident that they are expecting you from what has happened, and if you do not come soon they will think that you are tampering with them."[36]

Duly encouraged, English took up the challenge. Within the week, he was off to New Liberty. Exactly how the encounter went is unclear, but it did not seem to increase intimacy to any measurable degree between the pair. Moreover, at Eagle Station, Kentucky, on his return to Indiana, English was thrown from his horse and landed in the mud. A few weeks later, he received another short note from "MEP" inquiring about the effects of his fall. This letter is revealing if only because of its atrocious verb usage ("when I last seen you"; "my reasons was"). New Liberty Lizzie's education may not have equaled her beauty and wealth. Cause and effect may not be fairly inferred, but, after this communication, English's ardor for Miss Payne appears to have waned.[37]

In truth, English's declining affections for Elizabeth may also have been caused by the lure of another woman. Not long after he returned from New Liberty, he received an ethereal letter from Woodford, Kentucky. The writer was Ann Warren Offit, an apparently educated woman whom English met adventitiously in an inn after his fall at Eagle Station. They corresponded at least fitfully for the next two years, and, as was made apparent by her letters, English visited often. Yet, there were obstacles to any consummation of their affections. As she stated herself, "my father is the only one who has my hand and heart," and his recurrent illnesses prevented her from truly considering any other profound personal relationship. Another drawback was the state of her finances. Though previously wealthy, her family had evidently fallen into desperate straits. Indeed, upon hearing of English's relations with Miss Offit, English's Kentucky aunt, still politicking for Lizzie Payne, explained the case distinctly: "The pernicious influences of decayed fortune is too shockingly visible about her father's domain to secure her more than a passing tribute of a complimentary letter from her Hoosier beau."

---

36. Elizabeth Payne to WHE, September 10, 1842; J.B. English to WHE, September 16, 1842, English Papers. English's romantic nature is fully evident from a poem he wrote to an unrequited love earlier that year: WHE to ?, July 15, 1842, English Papers.

37. J.B. English to WHE, October 6, 1842; Elizabeth Payne to WHE, October 21, 1842; J. B. English to WHE, September 26, 1842, March 17, 1843, English Papers. English also received at least a few letters from one Martha Johnson who appears to have been a friend of Payne's. In one letter, dated April 21 [1843], she refers to a young woman named Elizabeth, and remarks to William that "I guess you never told her that you loved her but I am afraid you deceived her." She continues: "now you want to deceive another but that's not possible—there's not a man in the world who could deceive me." There are also a series of letters around the same time from one "Alice," though she is careful to address them "my dear friend." English Papers.

Yet, English refused to be dissuaded. In the fall of 1844, around his 22nd birthday, he formally proposed marriage to Ms. Offit.[38]

However, it was not to be. Her rejection letter, evincing a touching yet hardheaded melancholy, deserves to be printed at length:

> He [her father] objects to me marrying any gentleman unless he is of his choosing. My father is *old* and *infirm* and I feel that it is my duty as a dutiful child and a Christian to remain with him. His kind and affectionate appeals to me have won me completely, and his reasoning so simple and plain that I could not do otherwise than promise him solemnly that if he did not insist on me marrying a certain gentleman that I would remain with him at least for three years. If you have the same feelings we will talk on this subject more wisely. We are too young to give the subject the thought that it requires, and another great objection I have to our *union* is this: I am too proud to marry *at* the *present time* due to my temporary financial condition, and I would not be induced to marry and then be entirely dependent on my husband's exertions or his relatives.

She wrote that if in one year English's affections had remained constant, he was welcome to direct a letter to her. He should not attempt to see her now, however, as "it would be useless."[39]

It was as useless a full year later when he wrote her again. Her reply contained little but details of her father's illness. No evidence exists of any further correspondence between the two of them.[40]

5.

Ann Offit's rejection letter had come at the height of the 1844 presidential campaign. Perhaps this was good timing for English, for he was able to distract himself from his disappointment by tending to his first love, politics. In truth, he had been involved in the politics of the 1844 presidential sweepstakes as soon as he was appointed postmaster in 1842. It was then that he began to correspond with one D. Vanderslice, secretary and political advisor to former vice president of the United States Richard Johnson. A Kentuckian reputed to have killed Tecumseh in the War of 1812, Johnson was a mercurial figure who had served in both houses of Congress before he became Martin Van Buren's successful running mate

---

38. Ann Offit to WHE, November 7, 1842, September 10, October 6, December 18, 1843, January 16, 1844; Mrs. J.B. English to WHE, February 16, 1844; Ann Offit to WHE, October 15,1844, English Papers.

39. Ann Offit to WHE, October 15, 1844, English Papers.

40. Ann Offit to WHE, October, 1845, English Papers.

in 1836 (and unsuccessful one in 1840). His performance as vice president was passably competent, but he did not have any real influence with the president. Indeed, he was often absent from Washington. The most remarkable thing about him was that he had once boldly cohabitated with a mixed-race woman, siring two daughters by her, both of whom he presented socially. Though the mother was deceased by then, these social indiscretions made Johnson a controversial figure to say the least. Still, English, who was searching for a suitable Democratic presidential candidate by which to advance his political fortunes, continued his correspondence with Vanderslice for more than a year. For his part, Vanderslice unctuously solicited English's support for a Johnson candidacy, though he never appears to have clearly promised anything in return. Yet Vanderslice's attentions paid off. At the same Party congressional convention that nominated Thomas Henley in May 1843, English introduced and put through to passage a resolution favorable to Johnson. It instructed the as yet unselected district delegates to the 1844 Democratic Presidential Convention to cast their first ballots for the former vice president. According to the New Albany *Democrat,* the resolution was adopted by "an overwhelming majority."[41]

The success of his resolution illustrates English's growing influence in the district, but less clear is why he used such influence to assist Johnson instead of others. Perhaps he realized that there were fewer competitors for influence in the Johnson camp than in the other more supported candidates' organizations. Perhaps their shared Kentucky affiliation had something to do with it as well. But what was probably more significant was Johnson's resemblance to Andrew Jackson. Like Jackson, the Indian-fighting Johnson was an instinctive man who was unconcerned with custom, supportive of equal opportunity and rights among white men, and unafraid to take an unpopular position. Furthermore, like Jackson, Johnson exhibited the strength and manliness of the western man of action.[42]

Although not the favorite, Johnson's chances for nomination were good enough for the delegates to the Indiana Democratic Convention, in January 1843, to include him among a list of presidential possibilities. Along with Lewis

---

41. D. Vanderslice to WHE, September 26, January 29, 1842, May 17, 1843, English Papers. This Vanderslice may well have been the superintendent for tuition, boarding, clothing, and medical attendance for a portion of Choctaw students educated in Federal schools set up for Native Americans. *Report of the Secretary of Interior in Compliance with a resolution of the Senate of March 10, 1853 [CG*, 33-3. Special Session of the Senate, 257] *calling for a statement of the amounts paid as annuities, under the different treaties with the Choctaw Indians,* Executive Document No. 64, 33-2, 32. Eugene H. Roseboom, *A Short History of Presidential Elections* (New York: Collier Books, 1967), 50, 55. Carole Chandler Waldrup, *The Vice-Presidents: Biographies of the Forty-Five Men Who Have Held the Second Highest Office in the United States* (Jefferson, North Carolina and London: McFarland & Company, Inc.), 1996. Earl Smith and Angela J. Hattery, *Interracial Intimacies: An Examination of Powerful Men and Their Relationships across the Color Line* (Durham, North Carolina: Carolina Academic Press, 2009), 44-45. *New Albany Democrat*, May 13, 1843.

42. This frontier character of Richard Johnson comported well with characteristics that appealed to many Hoosiers, especially those of southern extraction. See Etcheson, *Emerging Midwest,* p. 9, chs. 3 and 6.

Cass, James Buchanan, John Calhoun, and Martin Van Buren, he had been so-licited to submit opinions on the questions of the day to a committee of Indiana Democrats. But Cass and Van Buren had the deepest support in the state. In July, Cass visited Indiana to help celebrate the completion of the canal linking the lower Wabash to Lake Erie, and his western-flavored speech created the favorable impression he sought. Although the 1844 state convention did not instruct its presidential delegates as a whole, by the time it adjourned, Cass was clearly the Party's favorite.[43]

English continued to correspond with Vanderslice as late as two months before the Party's National Convention, and evidence suggests that he may have gone to the gathering in Baltimore as a non-delegate. But, despite the resolution of the previous May, the Second-District delegates did not go for Johnson. All Indiana's initial votes at the Convention were split between Cass (9) and Van Buren (3), and, by the fifth ballot, all but one went to Cass. Nevertheless, in the end, the nomination went to a relative dark horse, James K. Polk of Tennessee, who rather stampeded a deadlocked convention on the ninth ballot. Polk was an expansionist, and he ran on a platform that called for the annexation of Texas, which had become an independent republic in 1836 when Americans there had revolted against Mexico. He also called for the annexation of the Oregon country, whose boundary then comprised today's states of Oregon, Washington, and parts of Idaho, as well as part of today's western Canada. In 1844, this area was jointly occupied by Great Britain and the United States, so full American claim to it would put the United States at odds with the British. This Democratic platform reflected the popularity of the principle of Manifest Destiny, wherein the United States was destined by providence to expand across the continent. Although the Indiana delegates remained loyal to Cass almost to the end, they, too, fell in line and voted for Polk on the final ballot.[44]

Had Richard Johnson miraculously carried the Party and later the nation, English might well have been assured of some political advancement. Wisely, he did not rely on this outcome, for, early in 1844, he had begun to consider other political options. His father and Jesse Bright advised that he try to move up to the position of state representative, but the incumbent Democrat, David McClure, showed no signs of giving way. Thomas Henley suggested that English offer him-self once again as the Indiana House's Principal Clerk, maintaining that that po-sition was "a better situation than representative in every point of view." English

---

43. Van Bolt, "Sectional Aspects," 126-127. Van Der Weele, "Jesse Bright," 30-31. T.J. Henley to WHE, May 11, 1844, English Papers.

44. D. Vanderslice to WHE, March 28, 1844, English Papers. Van Bolt, "Sectional Aspects," 127. Willard Carl Klunder, *Lewis Cass and the Politics of Moderation* (Kent, Ohio and London: The Kent State University Press, 1996), 139-141. Richard Bain and Judith H. Parris, *Convention Decisions and Voting Records* (Washington, D.C.: The Brookings Institution, 1973), 36-40, Appendix D. John Seigenthaler, *James K. Polk* (New York: Henry Holt and Company, 2003), 82-84.

decided to do this, and, by the late summer, he had lined up enough support to have apparently become the Democratic nominee for the post.[45]

This all hit an unexpected snag in August. The "New Democracy," fully intending to increase its margin in both chambers of the state legislature, actually lost control of the House. This was especially problematic for the Party because the new legislature was to choose a United States senator on joint ballot; for English, the chances of re-election as the House's Principal Clerk appeared hopeless. He was, however, committed to try, and even though the Whigs had a majority of 10 in that body, he rode to the capital in late November. By the time the legislature convened on December 2, the Democrats had decided to stand firm behind him. A bevy of Whigs aspired to the position, and on the first ballot English ran well ahead of them, gaining one more vote than there were Democrats in the House. For six ballots English's total ran between 46 and 48, all greater than the number of Democratic legislators. No Whig came closer to him than 15 votes. The *Madison Courier* later attributed English's popularity to his "gentlemanly manner and the ability by which he discharged his duties at the last session." After the sixth ballot, the House adjourned.[46]

That night, the Whigs caucused and appeared to agree to throw their strength behind one candidate, Austin W. Morris. But on the next morning's first ballot, six Whigs refused to vote for Morris and at least one voted for English. This result repeated itself on the next vote, and, after eight ballots there was still no principal clerk. For some reason, perhaps to diffuse Morris's vote, or perhaps to gracefully accede to the majority party, English withdrew his name on the succeeding ballot. The move produced confusion; the Whigs again split their vote and the Democrats balloted freely. Two ballots later, with the House still without a Principal Clerk, the Democrats re-nominated English, and on this 11th tally, he more than doubled the total of his leading Whig competitor. He continued to gain, and by the 15th ballot he had come one vote shy of election. But, by that time, the Whigs had united behind a new champion, John Farquar, whose vote total had risen to be equal with English's. Having come to the realization that he could not get elected, English withdrew. On the last ballot, Farquar was elected on a strict party-line vote, the Democrats casting their votes for multiple other suitors.[47]

45. D. Vanderslice to WHE, March 28, 1844; T. J. Henley to WHE, April 3, 1844; W. J. Otto to WHE, September 11, 1844, English Papers.

46. *Journal of the House of Representatives of the State of Indiana during the Twenty-Ninth Session of the General Assembly* (Indianapolis: J.P. Chapman, 1844), 8-9. *Madison Courier*, in *Indiana State Sentinel*, December 17, 1844. Although there were 100 seats in the House, only 98 votes were ever cast on any one ballot. One uncast vote belonged to George P. R. Wilson, a Whig friend of English's who did not take his seat until later in the month. The full breakdown in the House was Whigs, 55, Democrats, 45. Shepherd, *Biographical Directory*, 488-490.

47. *Journal of 29th Session of Indiana House*, 10-11.

Although the *Madison Courier* claimed that English would have been elected had he remained in the field, it is difficult to believe when push came to shove that the majority Whigs would have allowed a Democrat to be elected Principal Clerk. Despite his ability to gain from one to five Whigs on any given ballot, English had never been able to get that sixth opposition party member to elect him. Several Whigs, dissatisfied with their own party's candidates, allowed themselves to vote for the talented English so long as he could not be elected. But, of course, that much was a great compliment. He had certainly achieved an outstanding poll, and it is hard to disagree with the *Courier's* assessment that he had very much impressed legislators at the last session.[48]

An apparently respected politician, English was nevertheless an underemployed one. He quickly attempted to remedy that situation. By the time of his defeat in the House, the state patronage had already been dispensed or promised away, and because most of it was beneath the level of the Principal Clerk anyway, he turned instead to the federal government. Although the Democrats had lost the Indiana House in the 1844 state election in August, their aggregate state vote had actually topped the Whigs. This was repeated in the presidential election, enabling the Democratic candidate, James K. Polk, to closely carry Indiana as he did the nation. Before December was out, Polk received an earnest recommendation

---

48. *Ibid.,* 11. *Madison Courier,* in *Indiana State Sentinel,* December 17, 1844. The full ballot was as follows:

	1	2	3	4	5	6	7	8
English	6	48	46	47	48	47	46	46
Morris	24	24	31	28	28	26	47	47
Ward	12	13	9	8	8	6	2	2
Higgins	9	9	9	12	10	10	1	0
Pierce	5	3	3	3	4	5	0	1
Farquar	—	—	—	—	—	1	0	0
(Others)	1	0	0	0	0	3	2	2

	9	10	11	12	13	14	15	16
English	—	—	43	47	48	49	49	--
Morris	41	35	20	9	2	0	0	0
Ward	32	36	5	0	0	0	0	0
Higgins	6	9	7	1	1	0	0	0
Pierce	13	13	1	1	0	0	0	0
Farquar	0	5	21	38	46	48	49	54
(Others)	5	0	1	2	1	0	0	44

from the Indiana Democratic electors to bestow upon English some position in the incoming government. The testimonial claimed that "the Democracy of Indiana is deeply indebted to Mr. English for his exertions on its behalf during the late political canvass," and considered him "fully worthy [of] the confidence and patronage of the Democratic Administration." Subsequent to that encomium, Polk was deluged with solicitations for the young Hoosier. Practically every important Indiana Democrat beseeched the president-elect on English's behalf.[49]

The struggle for the patronage of the new federal administration was very competitive, and, to enhance his chances, English decided to leave for the nation's capital. His patron there, Congressman Henley, actually might have been the one to suggest he come. Yet, by Polk's inauguration in early March, English had still either not been tendered any appointment at all or had not been offered a satisfactory one. Henley, thus, recompiled the copious testimonials on English's behalf and sent them under a cover letter directly to the president's brother and close advisor, Colonel W. R. Polk. Henley evidently knew the Colonel personally, and he strongly suggested that the presidential sibling bring English's recommendations to the attention of the president. The letter itself was signed by all 10 of Indiana's congressmen (including the two Whigs), who claimed that a position for English would be considered "a most special personal favor." Two of these congressmen sent their own separate recommendations. One of them wrote:

> Members of Congress are compelled, frequently, to sign recommendations (or offend friends) in cases where they had rather not do so. As to the application of Mr. English, however, I wish to say, *in all sincerity*, that I think he is worthy and would make a good officer—and I should join his numerous list of friends in regarding his appointment as a *personal favor. No earthly doubt exists as to his merit and qualifications.*[50]

The position most requested on English's behalf was recorder of the land office, a natural niche for Elisha's son. But Polk had already promised that office to a Virginian. Indiana congressman Andrew Kennedy thus suggested to the administration that a clerkship of the first or second grade in one of the Executive Departments would be acceptable. But it was another Indiana congressman, New Harmony's Robert Dale Owen, who took it upon himself to forward some general pro-English

---

49. These recommendations may all be found in the English Papers. The state electors did not send separate letters; rather, all signed one note of recommendation. The other list of supporters included Bright (now United States senator-elect), all the elected state officers, the State agent, the president of the State Bank, the State printer, the State librarian, the Supreme Court justices, the Canal superintendent, the State's Indian agent, a United States district attorney, land office registrars, the editor of the *Indiana State Sentinel*, two ex-governors, and even some citizens of Kentucky and Illinois—including Stephen A. Douglas.

50. T.J. Henley to WHE, January 20, 1845; T.J. Henley to Col. Polk, March 6, 1845; John Pettit to president Polk, March, 1845; Andrew Kennedy to president Polk, March 6, 1845, English papers.

recommendations to the Treasury Department, and it was from there that an appointment ultimately came. After having spent two months in Washington, English finally received notification of his appointment in a formal letter from Treasury Secretary Robert J. Walker (somewhat presciently, as it was English, 13 years later, who would stand by Walker's vindicated position in the Lecompton controversy). As of April 8, 1845, he was to be employed as "clerk" in the Treasurer's Office of the Second Auditor. The designation probably refers not to the chief clerk but to the second rank, which carried with it an annual salary of $1,400. Those newspapers in Indiana that took notice of the appointment heartily approved. Two weeks later, the industrious young politico resigned his position as Lexington's postmaster and prepared to fully ensconce himself in his new surroundings.[51]

6.

During the four years English toiled in his new position, the nation sustained a full recovery from the depression of the late 1830s. Land sales rose, railroad building accelerated, and banks returned to a policy of liberal credit. Immigration also increased significantly, and native-born Americans from the East again began to push westward. Accompanying the return of prosperity was an expansive and optimistic national mood. Newspaper editors and politicians throughout the nation confidently celebrated America's grand future. They extolled the concept of Manifest Destiny, beseeching the nation to spread what they perceived as the blessings of liberty. At the time this attitude was summed up in two words: "Young America."[52]

An essential part of this outlook was its bellicosity, and the United States's declaration of war against Mexico in May 1846 was clearly an outgrowth of this impulse. During the interregnum between Polk's election and his inauguration, President Tyler was able to get congress to jointly resolve to approve the annexation of the independent Republic of Texas into the United States. The Mexican government, which never formally agreed to the independence of Texas, and at the least considered the Republic's declared southern boundary too far south, took a bellicose stand toward United States annexation. Polk used Mexican threats of military action and its unwillingness to negotiate to promote a conflict of which the real animus was the desire for more Mexican territory, specifically California. A military skirmish in the boundary area under dispute allowed Polk to get

51. Andrew Kennedy to President Polk, March 6, 1845; Robert Dale Owen to the Secretary of the Treasury, March 10, 1845; Robert J. Walker to WHE, April 8, 1845, English papers. Horace Greeley, ed., *Whig Almanac and United States Register for Year 1845* (New York: Greeley and McGrath, 1846), 36. *Brookville Independent*, April, 1845; *Crawfordville Review*, May 3, 1845, in English Scrapbook, 13. T.J. Henley to WHE, April 20, 1845, English Papers. Wilson, *Lexington*, 55.

52. Frederick Merck, *Manifest Destiny and Mission in American History* (New York: Alfred A. Knopf, Inc., 1963), chapter one, *passim*.

Congress to declare war, claiming that the Mexicans had "spilled American blood on American soil." Most Democrats in Indiana and elsewhere enthusiastically supported the war. On the other hand, the dour Whigs, especially in the North, sniffed at a conflict of territorial conquest and suspected that the war's real purpose (begun by a Tennessee president and strongly supported by the South) was to extend slavery. But, in August 1846, Indiana voters illustrated their support of expansion by re-electing their Democratic governor and allowing the Party to re-capture the state's House of Representatives.[53]

But the same month that produced the triumphant Democratic state results in Indiana also produced the troublesome introduction of the historically ultra-significant Wilmot Proviso. It would be this measure that would rekindle the debate of the future of the expansion of slavery in the United States, a debate that little ceased until the Civil War. English, like all antebellum politicians, would not be able to escape the revival of this dangerous question, and he essentially functions on the national and Indiana stage within the context of it. Thus, an extensive discussion of the Wilmot measure and its consequences is necessary if English's course as future congressman is to be at all intelligible.

The Wilmot Proviso was introduced as an amendment to a Polk administration's appropriations bill. Introduced by a Pennsylvania Democratic congressman, David Wilmot, it made the bold proposal to prohibit slavery in any land the United States should conquer from Mexico as a result of the war. Commonly regarded as a strict anti-slavery measure, the Proviso has also been interpreted as an intraparty protest against certain earlier measures of the Polk administration. Some historians have argued that pro-tariff northeastern Democrats were upset over the administration's forceful passage of the low Walker tariff while Midwestern Democrats were dissatisfied with Polk's geographical compromise with the British over the Oregon territory and his veto of a federal bill intended to improve inland rivers and harbors. But, for northern Democrats, besides registering sectional intraparty strength, the Proviso could be used to counter Whig charges that the Mexican War was primarily fought to extend slavery.[54]

The Proviso's backers envisioned a western land of opportunity for white men, unencumbered by aristocratic slaveholders and their black serfs. Although north-

---

53. Donald F. Carmony, *Indiana, 1816-1850: The Pioneer Era* (Indianapolis: Indiana Historical Society, 1998), 627-630. Riker, *Election Returns*, 301-309, 153-155. See also William J. Cooper, *Liberty and Slavery: Southern Politics to 1860* (New York: Alfred A. Knopf, 1983), 215-217 on the dilemma of the southern Whigs and general opinion on the war.

54. The standard treatment of the proviso is Chaplain Morison, *Democratic Politics and Sectionalism: The Wilmot Proviso Controversy* (Chapel Hill: The University of North Carolina Press, 1967). See also Eric Foner, "The Wilmot Proviso Revisited," *Journal of American History* 56, no. 2 (September, 1969): 262-279; Clark Persinger, "The Bargain of 1844 as the Origin of the Wilmot Proviso," *AHA Reports, 1911*, vol. 1 (Washington, D.C.: Government Printing Office, 1913), 189-195; Richard R. Sternberg, "The Motivation of the Wilmot Proviso," *Mississippi Valley Historical Review* 18, no. 3 (March, 1932): 535-541.

ern anti-slavery sympathy within the two political parties is most often primarily attributed to so-called Conscience Whigs, who tended to stress the immorality of the institution, the Democratic Party contained within it a not insubstantial number of politicians who were opposed to slavery largely because slaveholders appeared similar to other privileged anti-egalitarian groups. Party harmony had kept such northern Democrats in check, but they had begun to expand their numbers as a result of official measures the Party had supported to appease its southern wing. The House "gag rule," for example, which prohibited the House of Representatives from receiving anti-slavery petitions, had been adopted in the name of national harmony through a combination of northern and southern Democratic votes in 1837. It was finally rescinded in 1844, but the postmaster general's authority to remove abolitionist literature from the mail still stood. Many northern Democrats, even those not as bothered by compromises made to maintain southern support, viewed slavery as a backward socio-economic institution. In its failure to develop a diversified economy in the South, slavery showed it inhibited economic development. And slavery's expansion would prevent the west from becoming lily-white. The Proviso was, in fact, both anti-slavery *and* racist. As its author himself noted:

> I plead the cause of white freemen [and] I would preserve to free white labor a fair country, a rich inheritance, where sons of toil of my own race and own color, can live without the disgrace which association with Negro slavery brings upon free labor.[55]

Yet, in general, northern Democrats had been more sensitive than northern Whigs to southern demands for the federal government to respect the South's "peculiar institution." Indeed, many northern Whigs, though by no means actual abolitionists, used anti-slavery appeals as a wedge issue to gain votes among the northern electorate. Indiana Democrats, along with other northern members of the Party, were challenged by the Proviso: voting for it would blunt Whig appeals to anti-slavery opinion, but such a vote would also create a troublesome cleavage between northern and southern Democrats. In Congress, Indiana Democrat Robert Owen sought to delay a vote. He argued that the Proviso disrupted the purpose of the appropriations bill, which was to achieve peace. William Wick, first term congressman from Indianapolis, maintained that the amendment was "precipitous" and in bad taste: it attempted to regulate land that the United States did not yet own. When the Proviso eventually came up for a direct congressional

---

55. Jonathan H. Earle, *Jacksonian Antislavery and the Politics of Free Soil, 1824-1854* (Chapel Hill and London: The University of North Carolina Press, 2004), 4. Earle's book is convincingly devoted to reviving the recognition of the anti-slavery element in the Democratic Party during the Jacksonian era. Eugene H. Berwanger, *The Frontier against Slavery* (Urbana: University of Illinois Press, 1967), Wilmot quotation from pp. 125-126.

vote, the Indiana Democracy split on it. Owen, Wick, and senators Bright and Hannegan all voted against it; five Democrats, including Henley, voted for it. In the elections of 1847, the Indiana Democracy, faced with a unified Whig Proviso Party, lost the state House of Representatives and three seats in Congress. Only the power of the federal patronage prevented worse.[56]

Most Hoosiers' attitudes on the subjects of slavery and race made an unalloyed pro-Proviso position attractive. Both those who came to Indiana from the southern states, as well as those who had migrated from the northeast, agreed that slavery was not a progressive institution. The *New Albany Ledger*, a Democratic newspaper representing an area stocked with southern ancestry, noted that Pennsylvania, with almost three times the population of Virginia, had over 30,000 fewer illiterates; it asked its readers to draw its own conclusions. The Indiana state Constitution, framed largely by southern-born pioneers, not only prohibited slavery, it disallowed any attempt to legalize it in the future. Though generally opposed to slavery, Hoosiers did not, however, promote racial equality. Benjamin Kavanaugh, the man behind the revitalization of the Indiana Colonizationist Society in the 1840s, declared that a major purpose of the group was to rid the state of its black population. In 1848, the Indiana legislature would resolve that "while we should rejoice in the universal emancipation of the slave, we can never consent that Indiana shall be made the receptacle of manumitted negroes of other states." In the next session, a committee of the Indiana House prophesied "internecine warfare" unless the races were separated by colonization. Referring to increasingly harsh restrictions on free blacks recently passed by northern states, Indiana's governor would later urge his state to follow suit "in this great struggle for the separation of the black man from the white." As Indiana's congressmen repeated *ad nauseam*, they had "no sickly sympathy with the Negro."[57] The Proviso, then, mirrored this Hoosier combination of anti-slavery and anti-black outlook, so one could predict that Indiana voters would support it.

Nevertheless, as the calendar turned to the presidential election year of 1848, Indiana Democrats continued to divide over the Proviso. (It had passed the national House several times, but the even division between free and slave states in the Senate made passage there impossible.) Along with other northern Democrats, they sought a solution that would effectively prohibit slavery from the new west without disrupting the nationality of the Party. In January, they found a temporary

---

56. *CG*, 29-1, 1216. *CG*, 29-2, 425, 555. Roger H. Van Bolt, "Hoosiers and the Western Program, 1844-1848," *Indiana Magazine of History* 48, no. 3 (September, 1952), 264. Carmony, *Indiana*, 627, 629. Riker, *Election Results*, 320, 114-117.

57. Emma Lou Thornbrough, *Indiana in the Civil War Era, 1850-1880* (Indianapolis: Indiana Historical Society, 1965), 13-26. *New Albany Ledger*, January 21, 1856. Carter, "Hoosier History," 95. The 1816 Indiana Constitution may be found at *www.gov/history/2875.html*, Article VIII. Berwanger, 55-56. Emma Lou Thornbrough, *The Negro in Indiana* (Indianapolis: Indiana Historical Bureau, 1957), 81-82.

resolution when the Democratic state convention resolved it "improper...under present circumstances [for Congress] to bind the future inhabitants of any portion of our territory as to their local institutions or internal affairs."[58] The phrase "present circumstances" is the key one. The Indiana Democracy was essentially hoping that a congressional measure restricting the expansion of slavery into any lands gained from Mexico might well be unnecessary to prevent such expansion. Mexico had already outlawed slavery in its country, so any land the United States gained from Mexico would continue that prohibition unless overturned by positive legislative law. In any event, the matter was not yet ripe for definitive adjudication.

Less than a month after the Indiana Democracy passed this resolution, peace was made with Mexico. As a consequence, Mexico ceded to the United States what later would become the states of California, Nevada, Utah, Arizona and parts of Wyoming, Colorado and New Mexico, about a third of its territory. (Mexico also recognized American sovereignty over Texas, which at this point claimed what would become the rest of Colorado and New Mexico.) This was thus the territory that the Wilmot Proviso anticipated would be closed to slavery. What had been an abstract question previously now became a real one: would slavery be allowed in these new lands acquired from Mexico?

The general question of slavery's legal existence in the federal territories, recently gained or not, was hardly a completely new one, and, to put this late-1840s state of the debate in perspective, it is necessary to examine some of its antecedents.[59] It may fairly be said that historical practice in the early republic appeared to confirm that the absence of any actual congressional prohibition of slavery in a federal territory confirmed that slaves could be owned in such territories. Such was the case in the Southwest Territory out of which came the states of Kentucky and Tennessee as well as in the Mississippi Territory that eventually produced Alabama and Mississippi. Congress did act, however, to prohibit slavery in the Northwest Territory, whose boundaries were north of the Ohio River, east of the Mississippi, south of the Great Lakes, and west of the Appalachians. This prohibition was contained in the famous Northwest Ordinance of 1787, which was actually passed when the Articles of Confederation was the Constitution of the United States, but reaffirmed in 1789 by the first Congress that met after the new Constitution was ratified. From this territory came the states of Ohio, Indiana, Illinois, Michigan, and Wisconsin. Essentially, the Ohio River, which flowed from Pittsburgh into the original western boundary of the United States (the Mississippi River), was the demarcation line between territories (and states) that allowed slavery and those in which slavery was congressionally prohibited.

---

58. *Indiana State Sentinel*, January 13, 1848.

59. These next five paragraphs are based upon Don E. Fehrenbacher, *The Dred Scott Case: Its Significance in American Law and Politics* (New York: Oxford University Press, 1978), ch.4, *passim*

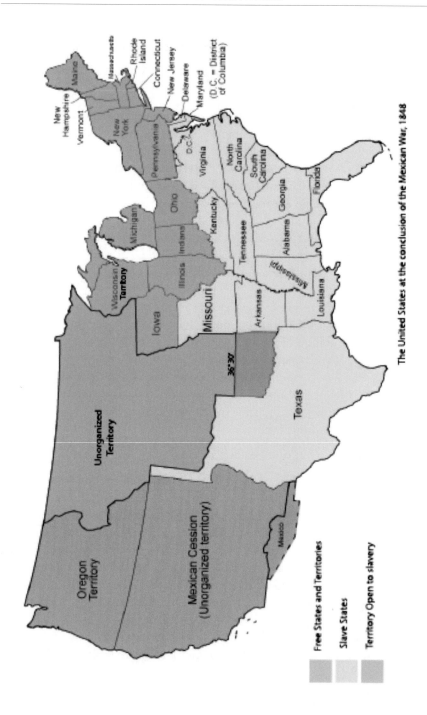

The United States at the conclusion of the Mexican War, 1848

Free States and Territories

Slave States

Territory Open to slavery

With the Louisiana Purchase in 1803, which almost doubled the size of the United States, the relatively calm national determination of what territory would be free of congressional restriction of slavery and what would not did not appear to change at first. The whole purchase was originally organized as the Louisiana Territory with no congressional prohibition of slavery, though some northern congressmen unsuccessfully introduced various amendments that essentially sought gradual emancipation. In 1804, the area around New Orleans, already populated under French and Spanish administration, was organized into the Orleans Territory with no congressional prohibition of slavery and relatively easy acceptance of the fact. When Louisiana was admitted as a slave state in 1812, most of the rest of the Louisiana Purchase was declared the Missouri Territory, also with no prohibition of slavery.

This Missouri Territory was most quickly settled along the Missouri River, spilling westward from St. Louis and the Mississippi and well northwest of the mouth of the Ohio. Its fertile land had attracted slave owners, and, by 1818, there were nearly 10,000 slaves in the territory. In that same year, having sufficient population to apply for statehood, the Missouri territorial legislature did so, confirming, in their proposed state constitution, the right of its citizens to hold slaves. (This new state, with its boundaries the same as today, would be sliced out of the rest of the original Missouri Territory.) But, at this point, some northern congressmen in the Senate and the vast majority in the House of Representatives refused to allow the admittance of Missouri as a slave state. A number of factors played into their position, but, in general, it was the growing opinion in the northern states that the existence of slavery tended to slow economic diversification, debase free-labor wages, raise land prices, and, thus, reduce opportunity for white settlers. (These concerns were not much different from those of David Wilmot 28 years later.) That the state of Missouri was the first one to be carved out of the vast expanse of the Louisiana Purchase (excepting the already heavily settled Louisiana), with its rather northern geography (almost wholly bordering on the state of Illinois—see map on next page), threatened the whole rest of the original Louisiana Purchase with slave-culture domination.

Southern representatives were rather taken aback by this strong northern opposition, some darkly alluding to secession should Missouri be denied admission as a slave state. After two years of debate, within which the United States' union itself seemed to be threatened, an agreement was fashioned generally known as the Missouri Compromise. Under this agreement, Missouri would indeed be admitted as a slave state, but all of the rest of the Louisiana Purchase territory north of latitude 36°30' (the southern boundary of the new state of Missouri) would be closed to slavery. This area where slavery would be prohibited comprised the vast majority of the remaining Purchase territory, and, presumably, as slavery was restricted from that territory by this congressional prohibition, states carved from it would be free states, and the West would be spared the deleterious effects of the slave economy.

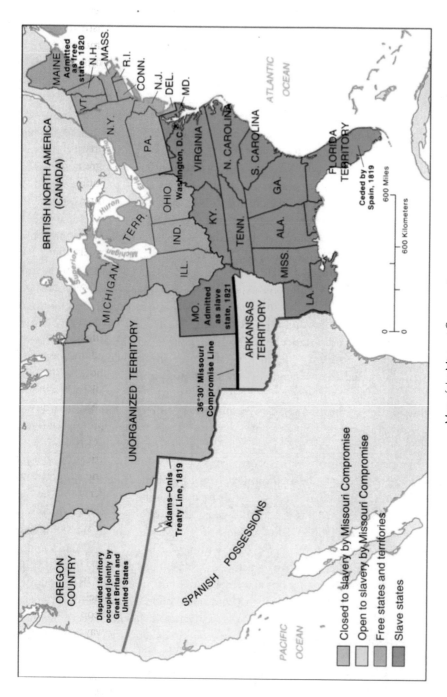

Map of the Missouri Compromise

The Missouri Compromise, after the Northwest Ordinance, was the second time Congress used its power to prohibit slavery from a federal territory. During the crisis, some southerners expressed disagreement with this constitutional right of Congress to restrict slavery—but their dissent was relatively muted; after all, the South's main concern during the crisis was the immediate acceptance of Missouri as a slave state. But as it became clear that the free states with their greater population would continue to control the House of Representatives, and, perhaps, the Senate when the northern non-slavery part of the Louisiana Territory would become settled and produce a plethora of free states, many southerners began to more stridently argue that the rights of private property (in slaves or otherwise) in a federal territory could not be restricted by Congress; only states had that sovereign power. A growing opinion in the South maintained that the Missouri Compromise restriction was unconstitutional and the threat of the Wilmot Proviso increased the South's attachment to that opinion.

Between the Wilmot assertion that Congress certainly had the power to prohibit slavery from the federal territories and should indeed assert that power in relation to the Mexican Cession, and the increasingly southern position that congress did not constitutionally have that power at all, existed somewhat of a middle ground widely circulated by Michigan senator Lewis Cass in his so-called Nicholson letter of 1847. As a northern Democrat, Cass was willing to accommodate the South to a point; certainly, he believed that the Wilmot restriction was unnecessarily extreme. Southerners had fought at least as gallantly as northerners in the Mexican War, and to so presumptively deny slaveholders the fruits of settlement into the lands thereby gained was unnecessarily disrespectful and discordant. In a letter to staunch Tennessee Democrat A. O. P. Nicholson, Cass went so far as to deny Congress's constitutional power to prohibit slavery from a territory (implying both the unconstitutionality of the Northwest Ordinance and the Missouri Compromise restriction), maintaining that the Article IV grant of power to Congress, allowing it to make all needful rules respecting property, was meant to apply to United States property but not private property. In the end, Cass argued that only a *territorial* electorate, through their representatives in their territorial legislature, had the power to restrict the institution of slavery in their jurisdiction. As Cass put it, Congress

> should be limited to the creation of proper governments for new countries, acquired or settled, and to the necessary provision for their eventual admission into the Union; leaving in the meantime, to the people inhabiting them, to regulate their internal concerns in their own way. They are just as capable of doing so as the people of the States.[60]

---

60. A copy of the "Nicholson letter" may be found in *http://elektratig.blogspot.com/2010/06/lewis-casss-nicholson-letter.html.* It was originally printed in the *Washington Daily Union,* December 30, 1847. Its significance

This formulation, soon to be labeled "popular sovereignty," held a number of advantages. It apparently removed from Congress the contentious issue of slavery's legality in a territory. It also had the advantage of endorsing the principle of local majority rule, a decentralized concept of governmental authority that appealed to Democratic federalism. Cass had also made his method palatable to northern Democrats at one point by obliquely noting that, since Mexico had previously abolished slavery in the Cession lands, it could only be introduced there by positive law; in other words, slaves could not be owned there unless a territorial legislature passed a law allowing it.[61]

As the national party conventions met in the summer of 1848, the Proviso issue hung over the proceedings. On the Democratic side, Cass's position held some promise of acceptance by Party leaders. By the time of the National Democratic Convention, Indiana Democrats were comfortable enough with Cass's formula (and particularly loyal to a fellow northwesterner) to once again support him for the Party's presidential nomination. It sent 27 delegates to cast 12 votes, and among these delegates were both English and his father. William's job at Washington probably contributed to his selection. Bright, Hannegan, and Henley were also there, along with other Washington Hoosiers. The delegation stood solid for Cass throughout the balloting. Equally solid did it stand against a set of minority resolutions generally called the Alabama Platform. While these resolutions agreed with Cass that the federal government had no constitutional authority to prohibit slavery in the territories, they also denied the right of a territorial legislature to do the same. The resolutions argued that a territorial legislature was a creature of Congress, created when Congress passed a federal enabling act to organize the territory. Thus, it, too, like Congress itself, had no power to prohibit slavery. In that assertion, northerners were not willing to acquiesce. Not one northern delegate, including not one Hoosier, voted for it.[62] Indiana Democrats may have come to believe that the Wilmot Proviso may be unnecessarily provocative, but

---

is noted in most secondary works on the politics of the 1850s. George Dallas, vice president of the United States, may have been the first to publicly suggest Cass's territorial principle in relation to the Mexican Cession. Cass consulted at least with Daniel S. Dickinson before writing his Nicholson Letter. Christopher Childers, "Interpreting Popular Sovereignty: A Historiographical Essay," *Civil War History* 57, no. 1 (March, 2011): 49, 52-53.

61. *Ibid.*, 60. Klunder, *Lewis Cass,* 169.

62. *The Campaign*, May 31, 1848, in English Scrapbook, 14. Roger H. van Bolt, "The Hoosiers and Eternal Agitation, 1848-1850," *Indiana Magazine of History* 48, no. 4 (December, 1952), 334. Woolen, *Eminent Men,* vol. 2, District 7, 211. Bain, *Convention Decisions,* Appendix C. Eric H. Walther, *William Lowndes Yancey and the Coming of the Civil War* (Chapel Hill: University of North Carolina Press, 2006), 102-103, 109. The resolutions that Yancey introduced to the Convention did not include the more extreme ones in the full "Alabama Platform" passed by his state's Democrats. One of those extreme resolutions called for the Democratic Party to deny support for any Democratic candidate who didn't adhere to the two brought up at the National Convention; the other maintained that the Federal Government had the responsibility of protecting an owner's slave property in the federal territories. *Ibid.*, 102-103. The latter resolution, of

they certainly viewed the popular sovereignty formula as it applied to the Mexican Cession more than fair toward their southern compatriots.

A revealing vote at the Convention illustrates that Indiana Democrats were not all fully satisfied with popular sovereignty. The New York Democrats were fiercely divided into two groups: the Barnburners, who generally supported the concept of "free soil" implied by the Wilmot Proviso, and the Hunkers, who were more willing to accommodate possible slavery extension. These two groups had sent separate delegations to the Democratic convention. The credentials committee had recommended the seating of the Hunker delegates, but a resolution equally splitting the seats between the two factions passed the full convention by two votes. Indiana voted seven-to-five in favor of the successful substitute.[63] Indiana's division predicted the intraparty division of the coming years. While the Indiana Democracy was rather united in resting itself on the basic gist of the Nicholson letter, underneath it was conflicted over its devotion to that formula should it fail to preserve the West for freedom.

In the end, Cass was nominated on a platform that, though not explicitly endorsing the theory of popular sovereignty, did label "all efforts...to induce Congress to interfere with questions on slavery calculated to lead to the most alarming and dangerous consequences." This statement was clearly a repudiation of the Wilmot Proviso. In consequence, the New York Barnburners walked out of the convention. Along with other Wilmot Democrats, and united with abolitionists and so-called Conscience Whigs, they formed the new Free Soil Party. Its platform asserted that it was the "duty of the Federal Government to relieve itself from all responsibility for the existence or continuance of existence of slavery wherever that Government has the constitutional power to legislate on that subject" (which would include Washington, D.C. as well as the federal territories). They, then, went ahead and nominated former national chief executive and present Barnburner Martin Van Buren for president. The loyal Whigs, for their part, trying, like most Democrats, to keep their northern and southern wings united, simply nominated Zachary Taylor, hero of the Mexican-American War. Although a Louisiana slaveholder, Taylor was not a southern extremist on slavery expansion, and the Party adopted no formal platform at the Convention. In a later brief statement of principles the Whigs completely ignored any reference to the slavery/territorial issue. In the general election, Taylor defeated Cass by the

---

course, is the principled genesis of the later insistence on a federal slave code, a proposal hardly congruent with 'states rights'.

63. Joel H. Silbey, *Party over Section: The Rough and Ready Presidential Election of 1848* (Lawrence, Kansas: The University Press of Kansas, 2009), 62-63. Bain, *Convention Decisions*, 36-38, Appendix C. Both factions of the New York delegation refused to accept the convention's compromise, and New York never cast a vote during the presidential nomination. Joseph G. Rayback, *Free Soil: The Election of 1848* (Lexington: The University of Kentucky Press, 1970), 190.

electoral count of 167-to-123. Each candidate won an equal number of states and ran well against each other in both North and South. The Free Soil Party, though not coming close to actually capturing any states, polled 13.5 percent of the free state popular vote, clearly holding the balance of power in most of those states.[64]

Indiana gave Free Soil Van Buren his lowest percentage of votes from any northern state save Iowa and Pennsylvania. The Indiana Democracy remained relatively united for Cass, carrying the state by a comfortable margin.[65] William English vigorously campaigned for Cass. His speeches apparently ignored the slavery issue, concentrating instead on Taylor's inexperience in politics and his criticism of the performance of Indiana troops at the battle of Buena Vista.[66] About to embark on his own exploitation of the Mexican Cession, English was one of those Americans who believed that "agitation" of the slavery issue only served to disrupt the proper destiny of the nation. Thomas Jefferson had argued that the republic needed to expand to make available private property for its burgeoning citizenry, and "Young America" was most eager to open the now vast domain of the west to private exploitation. At each stage of his career, as the slavery issue forced its way into prominence, English sought to minimize its importance. He began here by ignoring it.

---

64. Silbey, *Party over Section*, 158 (Appendix A, Democratic National Platform) 72-73, 165 (Appendix C, Free Soil National Platform), 70, 162-163 (Appendix B, Whig Party Statement of Principles). Walter D. Burnham, ed., *Presidential Ballots, 1836-1892* (Baltimore: Johns Hopkins University Press, 1955), 887, 246, 248, 250.

65. *Ibid.*, 246, 248, 250.

66. *New Albany Ledger*, August 10, 1852. Woolen, *Eminent Men*, vol. 2, District 7, 211. In his report of the battle of Buena Vista, General Taylor claimed that "except for a handful of men...under [their] gallant Colonel Bowles," the bulk of Indiana's Second regiment had unaccountably retreated from the action. In fact, apparently, quite the opposite was the case. In an inquiry convened at the insistence of Indiana brigadier-general Joseph Lane, it was fully revealed that Bowles, "ignorant of the company, battalion, and brigade drills, [and] manifest[ing] a want of capacity and judgement as a commander," mistakenly ordered the retreat. Although confronted with this evidence, general Taylor refused to amend his report. Indianan Lew Wallace, the later author of *Ben Hur*, some years afterward wrote that Taylor's position "dishonored the whole state," and, in that appraisal, he seems to have echoed the sentiments of Indiana. R. Carlyle Buley, "Indiana in the Mexican War," *Indiana Magazine of History* 16, no. 1, (March, 1920), 46-66. Logan Esarey, *History of Indiana*, vol. 1, (Indianapolis: B.F. Bowen, 1915), 447. 483. Lew Wallace, *An Autobiography*, vol. 1, 1906; (repr., New York and London: Garnett Press Inc., 1959), 177-180. Taylor also ignored the rather gallant performance of the Indiana Third regiment while praising his son-in-law, Mississippian Jefferson Davis, for bravery in the wake of Hoosier cowardice. Ian Michael Spurgeon, *Man of Douglas Man of Lincoln: The Political Odyssey of James Henry Lane* (Columbia, Missouri: University of Missouri Press, 2008), 20. It is significant that the Indiana Whigs, aware of the attractiveness of having a Mexican War general at the head of the ticket, preferred Winfield Scott to Taylor. Van Bolt, "Eternal Agitation," 334.

7.

From his post in the U.S. Treasury Department, English had a close view of these political consequences of the Mexican War. When he had first come to Washington in February 1845, he shared a boarding room with then-congressman Andrew Johnson of Tennessee. Whether English had previously known Johnson is unclear, but the two became at least sufficiently acquainted for the future president to have added his name to the list of those who had recommended English for a federal appointment. Very early in his stay, English gained a certificate allowing him to practice before the Supreme Court, and he was importuned by the editor of the *Indiana Sentinel* to help the state Democratic organ secure the advertising of the Post Office department. But nothing appears to be extant in his correspondence concerning the official transactions of this patronage position.[67] And little in his surviving correspondence even makes allusion to the Mexican War or the Wilmot Proviso. The cause of these omissions, perhaps, is due to an unofficial and apolitical chapter in his life: with Ann Offit having firmly closed the door to matrimony, English began a new pursuit of a Virginia belle named Emma Mardulia Jackson.

Miss Jackson had arrived in Washington sometime in the early part of 1846 with the intention of continuing on to New York and thence westward. Soon after she came to the nation's capital, English began to court her. A later letter he received from her suggests that, during her time in Washington, English had expressed sentiments to her bordering on everlasting love. Other later letters also illustrate an educated and sophisticated young woman who wrote clearly and engagingly and possessed, at least at 19, an adventurous spirit. After remaining in Washington for a couple of months, she pressed on as intended, and, though smitten with English, her generally attractive and accomplished personality gained her other suitors along the way. (Her sister, perhaps jealous, labeled Emma "a great flirt.")[68]

Not long after Miss Jackson left Washington, she wrote English from New York City. Receiving no reply, she wrote him a second time, wondering if he had "changed [his] mind." Clearly, she thought him honorable and would only be angry if he did not inform her of any alteration in his affections. Any inattention English was guilty of was quickly remedied. One epistle he sent her was composed of four quatrains, each stanza bracketed by "Come Home!" ("Come to the heart that loves thee, to the eyes that beam in brightness but to gladden thee.") In the late summer of 1846, he apparently left Washington for a while and went home to

---

67. F. Gerald Handfield, "William H. English and the Election of 1880," in Gray, *Gentlemen,* 88. Andrew Johnson to President Polk, March 1845; Certificate to Practice before the United States Supreme Court, February 20, 1845; J.P. Chapman to WHE, June 23, 1845, English Papers

68. Emma M. Jackson to WHE, April 14, 1846; May 15, June 3, June 22, 1847; Ada F. Jackson to WHE, April 12, 1846, English Papers.

Lexington. Emma had reached northern Indiana by that time and had intended to travel south to meet him. But illness in her family delayed her, and, instead, she wrote English a revealing letter outlining the state of their affections. She was depressed at not being able to visit. She wrote of her dashed expectations, not only of horseback rides and conversations, but for other desires contained cryptically in the phrase "I can't begin to tell you how far I allowed my imagination to go." But she would not fully commit herself, primarily, it seems, because she believed he was holding back from her. His letters to her, though filled with affection, were nevertheless qualified with attachments as well to "freedom." Together they struggled to maintain their intimacy without fully addressing the ultimate question.[69]

Distance and time were beginning to threaten any real hope of a lifelong union. Their letters to each other became less frequent. William tried to excuse himself by referring to the "wonderfully increased war business here" (the only mention of the Mexican War in his letters), but it seems to have been Emma who wrote more inconsistently. In April of 1847, having not received a letter from her for a month, English plaintively asked, "Have you entirely forgotten me?" Having learned from Miss Jackson's brother that she was to visit Madison in the early summer, he resolved to meet her there. In reply to this plan, she returned an ambiguous response. Although clearly wanting him to come, the letter's tone was less romantic than her previous missives. She addressed him throughout as "Mr. English," and spoke only of friendship and never of love. Frantically, English wrote back two letters in the space of four days, assuring her that he would come to Madison, despite learning that she would be back at Washington as early as June 10. On the eve of his departure, he received a note from her that reeked of secrecy and ended mysteriously "I shall expect you very soon…I have something to tell you."[70]

When he got to Madison, all became clear. Somewhere in her Indiana sojourn, she had met a Dr. Fields; he had proposed marriage, and she had accepted. But there was a complication: she did not love him—or so she told English. Quite possibly, it was her family that had promoted the match. It is likely that Fields was wealthy, as English noted the doctor presented to her "a suitable opportunity" to achieve security. There is also the possibility that Miss Jackson may have become disenchanted with English's procrastination in matters concerning marriage, and she used the engagement to test his true intentions. Indeed, he, too, was not bereft of other interests. At any rate, learning of her situation, English penned a note to her declaring his readiness to substitute for Dr. Fields: "In a word I want you to be happy and if your marrying Dr. Fields will not make you so and to marry me

69. WHE to Emma Jackson, September 5, 1846; Emma Jackson to WHE, September 8, 1846; WHE to Emma Jackson, October 11, 1846, English Papers.

70. WHE to Emma Jackson, February 18, April 29, 1847; Emma Jackson to WHE, May 15, 1847; WHE to Emma Jackson, May 25, May 29, 1847; Emma Jackson to WHE, June 3, 1847, English Papers.

will then I am ready to take you to my bosom to love, cherish and protect you forever and forever." At the end he wrote, "my heart aches, my hand trembles, my eyes are swimming in tears."[71]

No further letters between the two unattached lovers exist. Perhaps they were not necessary. In a December, 1847, number of the *Vincennes Sun,* the following small notice appeared: "William H. English, of Lexington, Scott Co., was married on November 17 in Baltimore by the Rev. Mr. Slicer, Chaplain of the U.S. Senate. The bride was Emma Mardulia Jackson, of Farquier Co, Virginia."[72]

His youth was over.

---

71. WHE to Emma Jackson, June 22, 1847, English Papers. As to English's dalliance with other women, it may be inferred from the part of this letter where he maintains that "there is no one within my range of acquaintance who would more likely receive the offer of my hand hereafter. Further than this I could not, at this time in justice go, for I would prefer falling short of what I could in truth say, than to say one word more than I considered entirely reliable. I will however add that if I had met with any one since our intimacy that I preferred to you that I would have frankly acquainted you with the fact, and I would do so still if you would remain single."

72. *Vincennes Sun*, December 1847, in English Scrapbook, 14.

CHAPTER TWO

Persistent Factionalism and the Road to the House

The election of Whig Zachary Taylor to the presidency about a year after English got married put into jeopardy the federal offices held by hundreds of Democrats. Their removals could come as early as Taylor's inauguration in March 1849, but most of them would not be replaced until some months after the new administration began its tenure. About six weeks before the new president was to be inaugurated, William English received a letter from Horatio J. Harris of Mississippi, a former Hoosier who had served in the Indiana legislature with Elisha. Harris had just accepted a position with the outgoing Polk administration in the Treasury department. He wrote English that his family connections with president-elect Taylor would prevent his own removal when Polk's term expired, and he assured the young clerk that he had it in his own power to guarantee the continuance of English's position as well. Harris, a Democrat, indeed remained in office as part of the new Whig administration, although he was transferred to the Justice department by the middle of Taylor's term. English, however, decided against accepting the protection of his friend. On the last day of the Polk administration, he wrote the president the following:

> Sir: Having opposed the election of General Taylor to the presidency, and differing with his party in principle, I do not feel disposed to hold office under his administration, and therefore respectfully resign the situation I have for some years held in the Treasury Department.

Somehow, the letter found its way into the *Washington Union*, the national Democratic organ, and from there it was copied into other Democratic newspapers throughout the nation. In an era when many critics were beginning to argue that politics was a mere chase after office, English's letter was received with much satisfaction. For a time, he was hailed as a Democratic hero.[1]

English's independent spirit in this matter must not be considered apart from his financial station. His father had become quite wealthy, and as early as 1843 he had helped his son acquire a parcel of land in Scott County worth $800. English himself speculated in the stock of Indiana's pioneer railroad, the Madison and Indianapolis, which, after 1847, began to yield him a tidy sum. He had learned the speculative art well, and while in Washington he continually sought investment in real estate on both an individual and partnership basis. Throughout his life he was able to use money to make money. By 1850, English would be listed as the richest man in Scott County, possessing $8,000 worth of real estate, $1,000 more than his father. Clearly, he did not depend on his position in the Treasury Department for his livelihood, and, indeed, he might have been very willing to resign in order to free himself to pursue more lucrative areas of opportunity.[2]

Three days before he resigned, English renewed his subscription to a local Indiana newspaper in flamboyant fashion. He had recently received "a quarter eagle, coined out of California gold," and he decided he "could not make a better disposition of it than to send it to some clever fellow in payment for a good Democratic paper." Here was a clear example of how Young America's war directly aided the American economy. Little could be more of a direct economic stimulus than a gold rush. Many young men, of course, seeking opportunity were drawn to California. Those who had little capital came in the main as prospectors; others sought to capitalize on those prospectors' needs. Hotels, saloons, gaming houses, and supply stores created cities in the wilderness almost overnight. English decided to join in the adventure. Less than two weeks after he mailed the California gold to the *Madison Courier*, he entered into a partnership designed to flood his own treasury with quarter eagles.[3]

The enterprise embarked upon was based on the reasonable assumption that many of the gold diggers would remain to live in California. English and his partners, including Thomas Henley and English's brother-in-law, William S. Jackson, ventured to supply these settlers with the materials to build their houses and establishments. The other two partners were Henry Howison, an Indiana businessman then residing in Washington, and one George B. Field. Each was to contribute $2,000 and to divide equally the assets and liabilities. The agreement was

1. Horatio J. Harris to WHE, January 23, 1849, English Papers. Shepherd, *Biographical Directory,* 168. *Washington Union*, March 15, 1849. Woolen, *Eminent Men,* vol. 2, District 7, 211.

2. Scott County Land Records, Indiana State Archives, Indianapolis. Handfield, "Election of 1880," 91. Thomas L. Hamer to WHE, July 19, 1846; Joseph L. Dunn to WHE and Mr. French, October 24, 1847, English Papers.

3. *Madison Courier*, March 18, 1849. *Henley and English v. Field, Howison, Warbuss, Morse, and Heyl*, 6th Judicial Circuit of Sacramento County, May 23, 1850, English Papers.

signed on March 13, 1849. Three of the partners initially traveled to California to set up shop; Howison and English remained back east to purchase additional supplies and convert the gold coming out of California into bank notes and coin. By August, the business was in full operation, and the California partners alerted English that the first shipment of gold was on its way. Presently, Field implored Howison to come out to California, claiming his "*personal* labor" was required. English, on the other hand, was instructed to move his headquarters to New York City where the firm had a special relationship with familiar financiers.[4]

Field had written Howison that California is "the place to make money." Had the business been managed competently and honestly, it could hardly have failed. But fail it did, under circumstances not altogether clear. Apparently Field, allowed the primary management of the firm, deceived Henley and Jackson on its operation and attempted to use the company for his private gain. In January 1850, Jackson wrote his sister that Howison, who had arrived in California the previous November, "got rid of Field by purchasing him out." This was good news to Jackson, as he labeled Field a "contemptible scoundrel." He elaborated later in a letter to English:

> I have been greatly deceived in Field, as a businessman or as an *honest one*. Before I left St. Louis I found out he was indebted $3,000. We had several altercations on the prairies, also Thomas Henley and Field. On our arrival here, Field stated to us his great experience in the Saw Mill business and requested that he should have entire control of the Mills. This was granted him, feeling great superiority to transact business. He was not satisfied with this. He wanted to control everything. Thus he would persist or have a fit. Everything Henley done for the good of all would be undone by Field. Th. H., wishing to get along without difficulty yielded, and I am sorry to say to our detriment of $30,000.

Consequently, on January 10, 1850, the firm was dissolved, but, even after the dissolution, Field continued to defraud his former partners. The terms of the divestment gave Jackson "the power to take charge of the assets of the firm and close up its affairs." But upon doing so he found that Field had sold $20,000 worth of property belonging to the company three months after dissolution. Outraged, Henley and English sued him.[5]

---

4. *English v. Field*, May 23, 1850, English Papers. George Field to Henry Howison, March 31, April 5, August 30, 1849; Thomas Henley to WHE, August 30, 1849, English papers.

5. George Field to Henry Howison, August 30, 1849; William S. Jackson to Juliet, January 30, 1850; William S. Jackson to WHE, April 28, 1850; George Field to WHE, June 25, November 11, 1851; *English v. Field*, May 23, 1850, English Papers. There is no evidence that this Field was the earlier paramour to Emma Mardulia Jackson English.

Because he was physically removed from the action, English was at a great disadvantage. He knew little of Field; only with Henley was he truly intimate. In fact, English appeared, for the most part, to put the blame on Henley for the failure of the enterprise. Throughout the year, the two formerly close friends angrily corresponded. For his part, Henley admitted that the company began with "good prospects, and could have made money," but he blamed its failure on the fact that "Mr. F. was looked upon by both you and Mr. Howison as the head of the firm. I had no authority and no power until all the harm was done." The disagreement between the two became great enough for their common friend, Jesse Bright, to intervene. Bright wrote English that "mutual explanation will restore former friendly relations." In the political language that they both could understand, he noted that "you have been of mutual service to each other and may often be again." But it does not appear that English and Henley remained close.[6]

No statement exists illustrating how much the company lost, but the sale of its assets seems to have paid for much of the firm's debts. Thomas Henley remained in California and later served as a state representative. Franklin Pierce, for whom he was an elector, appointed him Postmaster of San Francisco and then U.S. Superintendent of Indian Affairs for the state. Upon Senator Broderick's murder in 1859, Henley was rumored to be in line for the vacant seat, but another Democrat was appointed instead. The subsequent Republican ascendency in the state ended his political career. Henry Howison died soon after the company did, and his wife had great trouble clearing up his estate. As with many speculators, her husband appears to have left numerous legal entanglements. One of these concerned land that Field claimed was his on account of some promise of payment unfulfilled. Tangled in this web as well was an outstanding loan that Howison had made to Jackson earlier. English was also Jackson's creditor, and he became enmeshed in a legal suit concerning all of these parties for the next 10 years. The wily Field proved himself a worthy, if unscrupulous, adversary; the eventual settlement satisfied none of the parties completely. By the end of it all, English might have been better able to appreciate the difficulties with which Henley had to contend in his management of the firm with Field.[7]

The company lasted only 10 months, but its effects spanned a decade. And, what's more, it sharpened English's natural tendency toward caution.

---

6. Thomas Henley to WHE, April 29, October 27, 1850; Jesse Bright to WHE, September 2, 1850. English papers. I assume a future lack of closeness between Henley and English on the fact that there is no further extant correspondence between them.

7. *English v. Field,* May 23, 1850, English Papers. Shepherd, *Biographical Directory,* 179. *New Albany Ledger,* May 2, 1856; October 21, 1859. George W. Jackson to WHE, December 4, 16, 21, 23, 1858; January 6, March 2, 30, July 20, August 18, November 14, 23, 24, December 20, 1859; Field and English Agreement, March 3, 1859, English Papers. The full case involving Jackson did not get completely adjudicated until at least the Fall of 1859, as Field wrote English on September 29th of that year that the Jackson case would soon be resolved. English Papers.

2.

During the time that English had served the California concern, the national argument over slavery's status in the newly acquired territories had become more acute. The Democratic Party in particular was at war with itself. Early in 1849, many southern Democratic congressmen signed John Calhoun's "Address of the Southern Delegates in Congress to Their Constituents," which enumerated northern aggressions against the South. Intended to unite southern Whigs and Democrats behind the rights of slaveholders, it specifically demanded, among other things, that these slaveholders have equal access to the new territories gained from Mexico. All but two of the 48 signatories were Democrats. On the other hand, northern Democrats, responding to the almost 15 percent vote the Free Soil Party had received from the free states in the 1848 election, began to more closely embrace the Wilmot Proviso. Despite the state's low Free-Soil vote, Indiana was no exception. The Democrats had retained control of both houses of the state legislature in the August 1848 elections, and the first act of the Party's representatives in December was to elect James Whitcomb, who had since resigned as governor, as United States senator to replace Edward Hannegan. While Hannegan had voted with Jesse Bright against the Wilmot Proviso, Whitcomb had gone on record maintaining that the Mexican Cession territory "has come to us free, it is now free, and in my opinion it should remain free, and that every constitutional and legal means should be adopted to continue it free." A month later, at the January 1849 Democratic State Convention, the Party went beyond its qualified support of the Proviso a year earlier. It repeated its claim that the Cession territories were at the moment free by existing Mexican law, but it went on to announce that it was opposed to any change in this status. The Convention called on Congress to use its constitutional power to prohibit forever any introduction of slavery into the area. Essentially, the Indiana Democrats of 1849 had now found that the "present circumstances" of early 1848 had changed. It was now necessary "to bind the future inhabitants" of the territory to freedom.[8]

---

8. John Calhoun's "Southern Address," accessed December 27, 2016, eweb.furman.edu/~benson/docs/calhoun. htm. Michael F. Holt, *The Political Crisis of the 1850s* (New York: John A. Wiley and Sons, 1978), 69. David Potter, *The Impending Crisis: 1848-1861* (New York, Hagerstown, San Francisco, London: Harper and Row, 1976), 85. It, perhaps, should be noted that the 15 percent Free-Soil vote, despite the fear it caused Democrats and Whigs, may have been overestimated. It had not a little to do with the Barnburner secession in New York and the fact that a former President led the ticket. The 1852 Free-Soil candidate received only 5 percent of the vote; it would take the Kansas-Nebraska Act to rekindle Free-Soil fervor. George Julian, *Political Recollections: 1840-1872* (Chicago: Jansen, McClung, & Co, 1884). 132. Shepherd, *Biographical Directory,* 498-500. Thornbrough, *Civil War Era,* 27. Carmony, *Indiana,* 632. Logan Esarey, *History of Indiana,* vol. 1 (Indianapolis: B.F. Bowen, 1915), 483-84. Van Bolt, "Eternal Agitation," 339, 345. Riker, *Election Results, 134.* Philip H. Crane, "Onus with Honor: The Political History of Joseph A. Wright, 1809-1857" (Master's thesis, Indiana University, 1961), 145-148. The Indiana Democracy's growing support for the Proviso in this period occurred during the same time that two later famous avowedly Free-Soil candidates were elected to the United States Senate with Democratic support. In Ohio, Salmon Chase promised Free-Soil state legislators

The year 1849, indeed, witnessed the height of free soil sentiment among Indiana Democrats. Several of the Party's congressmen during the lame duck session either took pro-Proviso stands or chided the South's attachment to slavery. In the same period, the state legislature, with its clear majority of Democrats, helped pass a resolution requesting Congress provide for the prohibition of slavery in any law made to organize the Mexican Cession. (The vote for this resolution was 80-16; the 16 naysayers were free-soilers who believed restricting abolition to just the Mexican Cession, instead of all new territories, was too conservative.) In east central Indiana, George Julian, running as the Free-Soil candidate in the Fourth District, defeated his anti-Proviso Whig congressional opponent with Democratic support. Even in relatively conservative southeastern Indiana, in English's congressional district, an avowed anti-slavery Democrat won the congressional nomination and election. And in the gubernatorial race that summer, the Democrats nominated and elected Joseph A. Wright, an acolyte of Whitcomb's, who helped draft the State Convention's pro-Proviso resolution of the previous January.[9]

But a curious episode at the end of 1849 began the drift of the Indiana Democracy away from the Proviso. When the United States House of Representatives convened in December, neither the Whigs nor the Democrats held a majority of seats, and nine Free-Soil congressmen held the balance of power. The Democratic caucus had agreed to support Howell Cobb for the speakership. Cobb was a Georgian amenable to northern Democrats for his generally conservative stance on slavery extension: he had not, for example, signed Calhoun's "Southern Address." But the inability to elect Cobb (or anyone) forced the Democratic caucus to look elsewhere. As it happened, the Party settled on Indiana's William J. Brown. Brown was neither new to the House nor to national politics in general. He had already been elected to Congress in 1843 and had later been appointed second assistant postmaster general by president Polk. A week after the caucus rallied around him, he received 112 votes in the full House, more than any other candidate had polled or would poll. He was just three votes shy of election. But, at this pinnacle, his hopes were dashed. For, immediately after that vote, he was forced to produce a letter he had written to David Wilmot. It promised the author of the Proviso that should Brown become Speaker he would so constitute the committees on the Judiciary, District of Columbia, and Territories to the "satisfaction" of Wilmot and his free soil "friends." Moreover, it contained the following sentence that

---

would vote for Democratic control of the lower house in return for Democratic votes for him as senator as well as the repeal of Ohio's repressive black laws. And in Massachusetts, Free Soiler Charles Sumner was elected senator in 1850 through a combination of Conscience Whigs, antislavery Democrats, and Free-Soil legislators. Earle, *Jacksonian Antislavery,* 184-186.

9. Van Bolt, "Eternal Agitation," 341-345. 338. Woolen, *Eminent Men,* vol. 1, District 5, 322. *Madison Courier,* March 18, 1849. Crane, "Joseph Wright," 140.

destroyed his support among southern Democrats: "I am a representative of a free state, and have always been opposed to the extension of slavery. I believe the federal government should be relieved of its responsibility for slavery, where they have the constitutional power to abolish it."[10]

Although Brown was simply politicking for Free-Soil support, southern congressmen would have none of it. He was quickly dropped from consideration as speaker. After some peevish dalliance, the Indiana Democrats all returned to the orthodox fold and solidly voted for Cobb on the final poll under the plurality rule.[11] Brown's embarrassing failure had taught them a lesson: perceived strong anti-slavery positions may win elections in Indiana, but they will get nothing accomplished in Washington. Indeed, Jacob P. Chapman, who expressed a strong pro-Wilmot attitude as editor of the Party organ, the *Indiana State Sentinel,* withdrew from the newspaper in early 1850.[12] As the U.S. House of Representatives organized itself and president Taylor's territorial programme came under scrutiny, the state's Democratic delegation began to reconsider the political sagacity of adhering to the Wilmot formula.

The apparent wisdom of moderation was, then, reflected in the ensuing first session of the Congress that elected Cobb House speaker right before Christmas in 1849. This 31st Congress is most famous for the so-called Compromise of 1850 that adjusted several questions concerning slavery. English followed the great debates that fashioned the Compromise first as a congressionally recognized reporter for the *Indiana State Sentinel* and later from his position as clerk of the Senate Claims Committee, an appointment he gained from the influence of newly elected Indiana senator Whitcomb, a member of the committee. (This was another example of English's ability to keep on friendly terms with Indiana Democrats of differing opinions.) Among the issues in dispute in these debates was whether slavery should be abolished from the nation's capital, whether California could skip the territorial stage and enter the union directly as a free state, whether the Fugitive Slave Act of 1793 should be strengthened to make it easier for slaveholders to recapture their escaped slaves, whether Texas's boundaries should include all land westward to the Rio Grande (which would have included two-thirds of today's state of New Mexico and part of today's Colorado), and,

---

10. *CG, 31-1,* 3-8. Holman Hamilton, *Prologue to Conflict: The Crisis and Compromise of 1850* (1964; repr., New York: W. W. Norton & Co., 1966), 35. Potter, *Impending Crisis,* 90. Nowland, *Early Reminiscences,* 320. Shepherd, *Biographical Directory,* 42. *CG, 33-1,* 18, 21-22.

11. Van Bolt, "Eternal Agitation," 356. *CG, 33-1,* 31, 65-66.

12. Mildred C. Stoler, "Insurgent Democrats of Indiana and Illinois in 1854," *Indiana Magazine of History* 33, no. 1 (March, 1937), 7. William Brown did not long remain, if he ever had been, a Wilmot supporter. Upon Jacob P. Chapman's "retirement" as editor of the *Indiana State Sentinel* in 1850, Brown ran it for five years as a conservative Democratic sheet. (see p.47). Julian, *Political Recollections,* 117-118.

most significantly, whether slavery should be permitted in the territories organized out of the Mexican Cession. At the end of January, Henry Clay proposed a
series of compromise resolutions. In the middle of April, the Senate established a
special select Committee of Thirteen, chaired by Clay, to consider these matters
and suggest legislation. Jesse Bright was one of its members.[13]

The Committee reported a set of measures. On the one hand, slavery could
only be abolished in Washington, D.C., if Virginia and Maryland agreed; however, slave *trading* was abolished in the capital. Other provisions maintained that
Texas's northwestern boundary would not include all the land westward to the
Rio Grande, but about half of what it claimed. As well, Texas's debt, incurred
while it was an independent republic (and most of which was held by northerners
and Englishmen) would be assumed and paid for by the Federal Government.
California would enter as a free state, but the Fugitive Slave law would be markedly strengthened. When it came to the question of slavery's status in the Mexican
Cession outside of California, the Committee of Thirteen noted that "the legitimate power of the Territory shall extend to all rightful subjects of legislation...
but no law shall be passed...in respect to African slavery." For those who believed,
like Cass and many northerners, that Mexican law ran until overturned by United
States positive law, and, since Mexico had abolished slavery, this restriction on
territorial legislation appeared to make it impossible for the territory to legitimize
slavery. On the other hand, if one did not believe Mexican law still ran, and the
territories were naturally open to all property, the territorial legislature could not
abolish it. In the final law, this provision was amended to simply read that any
territory carved out of the non-California Mexican Cession "shall be received into
the Union [as a state] with or without slavery, as their constitution may prescribe
at their time of admission." There were no restrictions put on the power of a territorial legislature to pass laws concerning slavery. Many northerners understood
this to mean popular sovereignty, that a territorial legislature could abolish (or,
actually, legitimize) slavery, but most southerners disagreed, arguing that only a
truly sovereign state (at the point of writing its constitution) could exercise such
power. Southerners continued to believe that, as property, slaves could not be re-

---

13. Speaker Howell Cobb to WHE, January 16, 1850: B.B. French to WHE, February 9, 1850; Moser Morris
to WHE, March 9, 1850, English Papers. *CG, 31-1,* 247, 280. General works containing studies of the
Compromise of 1850 include Hamilton, *Prologue to Conflict,* Potter, *Impending Crisis,* 96-105, Fehrenbacher, *Dred Scott.* 157-177, and Mark J. Stegmeier, *Texas, New Mexico, and the Compromise of 1850* (Kent,
Ohio: Kent State University, 1996). While historians have traditionally lauded Clay for his statesmanship
and criticized Zachary Taylor for his inability to understand sectional tensions, newer histories of the 1850
Compromise often castigate it as one-sided, primarily favoring the South. For a very good, though over-
stated, repetitive, and sometimes unfair example of this position, see Paul Finkelman, "The Appeasement of
1850," in Paul Finkelman, ed., *Congress and the Crisis of the 1850s* (Athens: Ohio University Press, 2012),
36-79.

stricted by a territorial government. In any event, the Wilmot Proviso restriction was not enacted.[14]

The day after Clay reported the Committee's original proposals, Jesse Bright made a speech in support of them. In its most significant passage, the senator argued that the Indiana legislature erred when it instructed its congresmen to vote for the congressional slavery restriction principle of the Proviso. Adopting the line earlier enunciated by others, Bright claimed that an explicit prohibition of slavery in the new territories was both unnecessary and injudicious: unnecessary, presumably, because the climate there prohibited plantation agriculture anyway, and injudicious, presumably, because it superfluously insulted the South. He noted that other northern legislatures had recently rescinded similar pro-Proviso resolutions. Had Indiana better understood the tense state of affairs, exemplified by constant threats of secession should the South be disrespected and treated unfairly, it, too, would repeal its instructions. He maintained that, as for him, duty to the Union impelled him to disregard those instructions and vote for a territorial bill that would not include the exclusion of slavery.[15] In a sense, he intended to lead, not follow, public opinion back home.

The Indiana Democrats in the House, almost to a man, fell in line behind Bright. Seven of eight sustained his position on slavery in the new territories, and five of those seven voted for all the Committee of Thirteen's measures, including the fugitive slave act. Senator Whitcomb, too, abandoning his erstwhile endorsement of the Proviso, followed Bright's lead.[16] Southern threats to secede should Wilmot be insisted upon and the South be denied a fair adjustment appear to have been the deciding factor. As one Indiana congressman, Wilson Gorman, put it: "I am solemnly impressed with the belief, that if we persist in passing the Wilmot Proviso, that the Senators and Representatives of six states will leave the halls of Congress." Gorman and others were willing to let themselves believe that, even without Wilmot, the Mexican Cession territories would remain free,

14. CG, 31-1, 944-948. The quote from Clay's speech on the bill concerning slavery in the Mexican Cession territories is on p. 945. The actual, final provisions of the 1850 compromise may be found at http://www.ourdocuments.gov/doc.php?flash=true&doc=27&page=transcript. Michael F. Holt, *The Fate of Their Country: Politicians, Slavery Extension, and the Coming of the Civil War* (New York: Hill and Wang, 2006), 50-83, though by no means a complete rendering of the congressional maneuvers producing the Compromise of 1850, is a very fine summary of the politics surrounding it.

15. *CG, 31*-1, 956. Van Der Weele, "Jesse Bright," 68-70. Bright's understanding of how the Proviso dishonored the South is well supported in Cooper, *Liberty and Slavery,* 220-221: "Whether or not the insistence of the southerners of their right to take their slaves into the territories also meant they wanted or expected to remains a vexing question. [But] the possibility or probability of actually taking slaves into the territory, however, was not the crucial issue in the debate…[It was] the right to take slaves into the new territories, or, at the least, to prevent the denial of that right."

16. Hamilton, *Prologue,* appendix C, 195-200. The Democratic congressmen from Indiana voted to abandon the Proviso principle and support the Compromise measures at a higher rate than northern Democrats as a whole.

because settlers there will not agree to slavery's legality. They hoped that the courts would declare that previous prohibition of slavery under Mexican Law be recognized, making it illegal for slaveholders to take their slaves without a territorial law allowing for them to do so, but they didn't insist on it. As Gorman noted, he "would not apply the incendiary torch to the magazine."[17]

Senator Bright worked hard to support the notion that the Compromise measures, and, implicitly, then, the turning back from the Wilmot Proviso, were essential actions. He maintained that "the public mind is wearied and worn out with this eternal agitation [and] it is due alike to the Union, to our constituents, and to ourselves to settle these questions." In May, the senator smoothed the way for Indiana Democrats to accept the Compromise by engineering a politically friendly purchase of the *Indiana State Sentinel*. The publisher of the *Sentinel*, the aforementioned Jacob Chapman, a Free-Soil Democrat, had at first intended to sell the paper to likeminded buyers. In order to prevent this transaction, Bright financially backed the higher bid of Austin H. Brown, son of the congressman. (He made his father the editor.) Immediately upon the transfer, the *Sentinel*, which had been pro-Proviso, changed its tune. It pronounced the Democratic Party a "national party," and offered to "quarrel with any man who attempted to make it sectionalist." Alluding to its shifted ground on the Proviso, the *Sentinel* noted that though "we are opposed to extending slavery into any territory now free…we may differ with many Democrats upon the mode by which this is to be done."[18]

There was, to be sure, great opposition in Indiana to the new Fugitive Slave Law enacted along with the other Compromise measures. The *Lafayette Courier* called it "atrocious," labeling Democrats who voted for it "doughfaces" (northern men with southern principles). Even the *Madison Courier* wrote that the Act "was repugnant to all the feelings of a man living in a free state." But the pro-Compromise Democrats fought back through the pages of the *Sentinel*. Tellingly, the *Sentinel* labeled anyone who opposed the law "an abolitionist not a Democrat." Most Democratic editors, again, tired and fearful of agitation, took the position that although the act was unjustly harsh, it was the price necessary for peace. The *Logansport Pharos*, for example, admitted that "in many of its provisions the fugitive slave law is unjust," but it was "opposed to forcible resistance [or] anything that looks at a violation of law."[19]

---

17. W.A. Gorman to WHE, January 17, 1850, English Papers.

18. Van Der Weele, "Jesse Bright," 71. Van Bolt, "Eternal Agitation," 356-357.

19. Thornbrough, *Civil War Era*, 48-49. Van Bolt, "Eternal Agitation," 357. Van Der Weele, "Jesse Bright," 83. The 1850 Fugitive Slave Law created new federal commissioners specifically empowered to issue writs for the arrest of alleged runaway slaves and to oversee their possible return to their owners; charged these commissioners to act as judges in the trial of alleged fugitives for which the commissioner would receive $5 for an innocent verdict and $10 for a guilty one (the discrepancy claimed to be necessary because a guilty verdict required more paperwork); assumed the veracity of an affidavit from the owner as to truth of the al-

By the end of 1850, the Indiana Democracy had, thus, shifted its position. Democratic governor Joseph Wright, never an extreme free soiler but representative of that faction of the Party less compromising on the slavery issue than senator Bright, announced that Indiana "knew no North, no South, nothing but the common brotherhood of all." He denounced sectional partisanship, and declared that Hoosiers should "not be alarmed at the word 'compromise'." Although many Democrats remained uneasy over the Fugitive Slave Law, Party support for the 1850 Compromise provisions grew. By the election of 1852, it would reach the proportion of sanctified party doctrine.[20]

3.

As noted earlier, William English had witnessed firsthand the great debates over the Compromise measures during the first nine months of 1850 from his patronage post in the Senate. But, when the historic congressional session adjourned on September 30, he was once again a politician without a political job. In a sense, his political career was at a crossroads; he could continue to rely upon the federal patronage or he could reestablish himself on the ground in Indiana. In the end, English chose the latter course, as an opportunity presented itself when the Indiana electorate voted to authorize the state legislature to call for a convention that would revise the 1816 state Constitution. The Convention delegates were to be elected in August of 1850, too early for English to abandon his duties in Washington in order to campaign for a seat, but he found another way to be part of the action. As soon as it became clear that the Democrats would have a strong majority of the delegates, he assiduously began to solicit support for the post of principal secretary.

His relation to his father, who was back in the state legislature serving his second consecutive term as state senator, continued to play an essential role in English's political success in Indiana. One Whig delegate agreed to support William for the post, because he "esteem[ed] Elisha highly, [and] would do anything to advance his wishes of self or family." Another delegate called Elisha "one of the noblest specimens of humanity." Christopher Columbus Graham, who served with Elisha in both houses of the state legislature, wrote that it was "highly probable" that he would vote for William, despite not having "the pleasure of an intimate

leged fugitive's existence and physical characteristics; did not allow the alleged fugitive to testify on his or her own behalf; and charged the commissioner with the right to deputize citizens for the capture of the alleged fugitive, denial of service to result in stiff fines. One may access the act at https://www.ourdocuments.gov/doc.php?flash=true&doc=27&page=transcript#no-5.

20. Thornbrough, *Civil War Era*, 47. Dale Beeler, "The Election of 1852 in Indiana," *Indiana Magazine of History* 11, no. 4 (December, 1915), 302.

acquaintance with [him]." He gave as his reason his "high regard for [his] worthy father, whom [he was] proud to call [his] friend."[21]

Of those who responded favorably, Michael Bright, Jesse's older brother, deserves special mention. An Indiana contemporary historian labeled the elder Bright "the best party manipulator in the state." His influence extended throughout Indiana as a railroad promoter and financial wizard, and he used his wealth and standing for the Indiana Democracy in general and his younger brother in particular. He had served with Elisha in the state House of Representatives as early as 1832, and it is quite likely that his relationship with William antedated that of his brother's. In a letter from Madison to his senatorial sibling in December 1845, Michael inquired about English, who was then serving in Washington as Treasury clerk. He reminded Jesse, "Bill English is a young man of talent, and deserves to be noticed. I hope you will treat him with marked respect which he merits." Two weeks after English was selected clerk of the Senate Claims Committee, Michael wrote William cryptically about the nature of certain Mexican claims. Whereas Jesse recognized English's political energy and loyalty, Michael appears to have been genuinely impressed with English's speculative and financial acumen and general intellect. Acknowledging English's letter asking for his backing as principal secretary, Michael replied, "No one in the state could more certainly get my support than yourself for the place you name." The elder Bright was himself a delegate to the Convention, and he promised to "go for" English "with all my heart." He even pledged the support of a Whig delegate from Jefferson County, Milton Gregg, and concluded his letter by telling English, "I think you can be elected."[22]

English was indeed elected, though not without competition from some fellow Democrats. His primary task as principal secretary was to superintend the daily recording of the Convention's business. He was eventually authorized to compile such records into three separate volumes—two of them a journal of debates and the other a straightforward journal of official proceedings. Additionally, he was responsible for relaying all official communication to and from the convention, and he had the final honor of overseeing the printing of 55,000 copies of the new constitution, 5,000 of which were to be in German. Three assistant secretaries, elected by the Convention, served under him, as did a few stenographers. For all his services he received the same salary as that of the secretaries of the state Senate and House, $4 a day.[23]

---

21. Thomas D. Walpole to WHE, September 7, 1850; James W. Borden to WHE, August 29, 1850; C. C. Graham to WHE, September 12, 1850, English Papers.

22. Woolen, *Historical Sketches,* 452, 450. Michael G. Bright to Jesse Bright, December 28, 1845; Michael G. Bright to WHE, March 22, August 23, 1850, English Papers. Riker, *Election Returns,* 379, 385.

23. *Journal of the Convention of the People of the State of Indiana to Amend Their Constitution, Assembled at Indianapolis, October 1850* (Indianapolis: Austin H. Brown, 1851), 11-12, 118, 878, 922, 16, 1023-1024. *One Hundred and Fifty Years: An Exhibit Commemorating the Sesquicentennial of Indiana Statehood* (Bloom-

The Convention met from October 7, 1850 to February 10, 1851. In general, it made the tenets of Jacksonian Democracy the organic law. It attempted to decrease the amount of future legislation by reducing legislative sessions to every other year and limiting special sessions to 40 days. Further, a majority of the whole membership of each House, not just those present and voting, was required to pass a law. Distrust of too much government was complemented by trust in the electorate. Many state offices, including Supreme Court judgeships and cabinet posts, were changed from appointive to elective positions. No longer appointive, too, were a host of local offices, including sheriff. Governors, although having their terms increased from three to four years, were no longer eligible to succeed themselves. And a certain egalitarianism was evident in provisions that allowed all males to practice law and decreased the residency requirements for alien suffrage.[24]

Democratic Party ideology similarly prevailed on economic issues. The state was prohibited from going into debt "except to meet casual deficits of revenue, or pay interest on the present debt, or suppress invasion or insurrection." Banking was freed from the dominance of a favored state bank, all local banks were required to redeem their notes in specie on demand, and all stockholders were held individually responsible for twice the amount of their stock. The legislature was specifically forbidden to pass a law allowing banks to suspend specie payment. In other areas, the only organic reform that was more Whig than Democratic was committing the state to the financial support of common schools, but even that was supported by Democrats who favored secular over seminary education.[25] Just as the Federal Constitution reflected the state of republicanism at the end of the 18th century, the new Indiana Constitution reflected the triumph of the frugal, common, Jacksonian farmer—the updated Jeffersonian ideal.

It was to this ideal that one had to bow in order to be successful in Indiana antebellum Democratic politics. One did not need to be a farmer, or small entrepreneur, but anyone seeking office as a Democrat was wise to praise the ideals of less government and trust in the so-called common people. A certain skepticism toward any institutional concentration of wealth was also advantageous. In many ways, William English was not the epitome of this egalitarian model. He was privileged from the start, both economically and politically, and, throughout the 1850s, he rather constantly speculated in land, railroad stocks, and state bonds.

---

ington: Indiana University, The Lilly Library, 1966), 8. Israel G. Blake, *The Holmans of Verustau* (Oxford, Ohio: Mississippi Valley Press, 1943), 59.

24. The text of the constitution, article by article, may be found at http://secure.in.gov/history/2838.htm. A thorough discussion of the main actions and tenor of the convention is in Carmony, *Indiana,* chapter 8. Discussion of legislative session changes may be found in pp. 410-414; on gubernatorial term changes, 424; on appointive judgeships, 430; on requirements for lawyers, 433; on common schools, 439-441.

25. Carter, "Hoosier History," pp. 58-63. Van Bolt, "Transition",136. Carmony, *Indiana,* 437-438, 439-440.

By the end of the decade, he was a very rich man preparing himself to enter the banking business. But, in almost all his political speeches, he was careful to praise the wisdom of the common (white) man and to evince a proper distrust of the governmental institutions through which he practiced his occupation. As a good Jacksonian, he downplayed his own privileged status and convinced voters that any success he achieved was due to hard work, frugality, and making the most of his individual opportunity. After all, Jacksonian Democrats were not opposed to success and upward mobility as long as it was perceived to be fairly and honestly achieved. The ascent from Elisha to William was regarded as properly respectable as long as the electorate believed sincere the son's espousal of the fundamental shibboleths.

Two other related facets of the convention's deliberations need to be mentioned. By a 90-to-25 vote, the delegates endorsed the 1850 Compromise in its "general features and intentions" and commended it for its tendency to promote the "perpetuity of our glorious union." And Article 13, section 1 of the new Constitution declared that "no negro or mulatto shall come into or settle in the State after the adoption of this Constitution." Both a majority of Democrats and Whigs supported this article, but Democrats at a much higher rate. This so-called "Negro Exclusion Clause," had to be separately ratified by the Indiana voters at the same election the following summer when the full Constitution would be submitted for an up or down vote. It actually passed with a higher percentage (83.8 to 80.4) than the full Constitution itself.[26]

The convention adjourned the second week in February. The delegates gave English the full authority "to select any office [he] may deem it expedient to secure [the] faithful execution" of the printing of the 55,000 copies of the new Constitution. For this task, English bypassed the *Sentinel* and chose the publishers of what had become the most influential Democratic sheet of his own congressional district, the *New Albany Ledger*.[27] One of the publishers, Phineas M. Kent, a combative and wily Democrat (and also a convention delegate) would soon become the closest thing to a campaign manager that English would ever have.[28]

---

26. *Journal of the Convention*, 323-324, 328-337. Carmony, *Indiana*, 447. Riker, *Election Returns*, 390. The "Negro Restriction" clause appears to have been enforced. According to census records, in 1850 Indiana had a black population of 11,262, an increase of 57 percent from 7,165 in 1840 (the state population as a whole increased 44 percent). In 1860, Indiana's black population stood at 11,428, a paltry increase of 1.04 percent from 1850 (the state population increased 36 percent). Carol O. Rogers, "Black and White in Indiana," *Indiana Business Review*, accessed July 16, 2017, at www.ibrc.indiana.edu/ibr/2005/summer/article1.html. The 1850 exclusion clause may be seen as an extension of "black codes" already in place, such as the illegality of blacks testifying against whites in court and the fact that black segregated schools could not receive state funds into which they as well as whites contributed. Julian, *Political Recollections*, 115.

27. *Journal of the Convention*, 995. P.M. Kent to WHE, February 16, 1851, English Papers.

28. In Thomas Henley's original contest for Congress, Kent had called Henley's Whig opponent a "perjured villain" while on the same stage with him. The affronted Whig, in response, brandished his theretofore

The other, John B. Norman, would turn out to be English's chief correspondent from the district during the whole time William was in Congress. Norman would also become, in essence, English's closest political advisor and somewhat of an alter-ego. The soon-to-be unemployed principal secretary was cleverly tending to his political future.

4.

In the spring of 1851, while English considered his next move, his father made a second attempt to move up from the state senate and into the United States Congress. Two years earlier, one might remember, Elisha had attempted the same jump, but he was thwarted by one Cyrus Dunham, a much slicker politician. While in Congress, Dunham had flip-flopped on the Wilmot Proviso, first supporting it and then abandoning it to support the 1850 Compromise. Perhaps Elisha believed that example of tergiversation made Dunham vulnerable. The Bright brothers backed Papa English in part because they did not yet trust Dunham's conversion, but mostly because of their long friendship with Elisha. So did *Madison Courier* editor Michael Garber, but for the politically opposite reason that Dunham had voted in favor of the Fugitive Slave Act. (Phineas Kent, too, was working for Elisha behind the scenes.) In the end, however, the clever and accomplished incumbent beat back the challenge: at the district Democratic nominating convention in April, reluctantly realizing that only Scott County was for him, Elisha withdrew his name, and Dunham was easily re-nominated.[29]

It is quite possible that Elisha's defeat actually redounded to his son's benefit, for, when Scott County Democrats convened later that spring to nominate a state representative, William was selected. To some degree, his county may have chosen him in order to compensate for his father's defeat, but William's talents and accomplishments were by now well recognized not only in the county but

---

concealed pistol and aimed it at Kent. As John B. Norman would later remember it, "wild confusion ensued for a few moments. Pistols, knives, and bludgeons by the hundred leaped from their hiding places in an instant." No one, however, was seriously injured. *New Albany Ledger*, February 13, 1861. Upon hearing that Austin Brown "grumbled" upon being bypassed by English for the right to publish the Constitutions, Kent dismissed him as a man "without sense, tact, or influence." PM Kent to WHE, February 16, 1851, English Papers. Kent had also been one of those who supported English for principal secretary. PM Kent to WHE, August 21, 1850. English Papers. Riker, *Election Returns,* 384.

29. Van Bolt, "Eternal Agitation," 357. M.G. Bright to WHE, March 27, 1851; PM Kent to WHE, April 11, 1851, English Papers. *Madison Courier*, March 11, 18, 24, 1851. On March 24, the *Courier* reprinted a comment from the *Salem Democrat* that noted that perhaps Elisha, though a good, honest Democrat, was not "a man of any very brilliant capacity." Commenting upon that statement, Garber acknowledged Dunham's lawyerly "fluency" but attributed it to socio-economic advantages that the pioneering Elisha did not have. What Elisha did possess (and, by implication, Dunham didn't) was sympathy "with the people, know[ing] their interests, and the nerve and ability to defend their rights when necessary." The District Convention Minutes are in English Scrapbook, p. 31.

statewide as well. Oddly enough, William's opponent in the general election was Aaron Hubbard, who, three years earlier, had been defeated by Elisha for state senator (representing Jackson as well as Scott County). Elisha had actually lost Scott in that election, but, in the present contest, William carried the county with 53 percent of the vote and, thus, swept into his first elected legislative position. In the county, he also outpolled both the Democratic congressional candidate and the Democratic candidate for the state senate.[30] At barely 29 years old, English was bound for the state legislature.

Statewide, the Democrats increased their majorities in both houses of the General Assembly. In some measure the Democrats' increasing success may be attributed to their more accommodating stance on the 1850 Compromise. Although there was still certainly some deep Indiana anger over the Fugitive Slave Act (even within the Democratic Party itself), most voters apparently believed that the whole Compromise's tendency to alleviate sectional discord was the greater good. The Whigs had not won a statewide election for eight years now and were becoming a rather permanent electoral minority.

On the same day that English and many other Democrats were successful, the new Indiana Constitution (a substantially Democratic Party document) was also overwhelmingly ratified.[31] Outside of Scott County, the general public probably did not closely identify English with this Constitution, but the state's politicians were well aware of his fundamental role at the convention. A mere perusal of the journal of the Convention's proceedings is enough to illustrate the constant activity of its principal secretary. Taking advantage of this momentary political limelight, in a remarkably bold move, English tried to parlay it into a quick climb up the political ladder. As soon as it became clear that the Democrats would have a large majority in the new Indiana House, English let it be known that he was in the running for that body's leading position, the Speakership.

He might very well have achieved that goal if the competition had not been so formidable. For some reason, Dr. John W. Davis, who had not only already served as Indiana House speaker but also as speaker of the national House, desired the position again. Davis was literally from an earlier generation—he was 23 years older than William and a political contemporary, in fact, of Elisha's. He had held numerous federal appointive positions, including United States Commissioner in China, and would later go on to be appointed governor of the Oregon territory. English had apparently tried to discourage Davis from re-seeking the speakership, but the doctor replied cryptically that while the young challenger had "made some very cogent suggestions why I should have withheld my name for that place,

30. *Madison Courier*, August 15, 1851. *Indiana Statesman*, August 13, 1851. Riker, *Election Returns*, 333, 360, 123, 363.

31. *Ibid.*, 390.

there are some peculiar circumstances which would hardly permit me to do so at present." Davis had taken quite a long time to respond to English's letter, almost a month, and his tone was rather patronizing. At one point he "kindly assured" his rival "that whatever be my position I shall not fail to exercise all proper means to promote your political and private advancement."[32]

English was not pleased by Davis's refusal to withdraw. Senator Whitcomb, too, wondered why the venerable politician should want the position at all after having received "the frequent and liberal manifestations of favor at a higher grade. How gracefully he could have stepped aside," Whitcomb continued, "and suffered a young and deserving man to occupy the place without impairing his own worth or position in the slightest degree." Perhaps Davis reasoned that the first legislature after the new constitution would need an experienced hand at the helm, or perhaps he was beholden to some special interest, but whatever Davis's reasons, English was unwilling to surrender without a fight. He, too, refused to withdraw, and the House Democratic caucus was forced to choose between them. In the end, Davis did prevail, but by the surprisingly narrow margin of 31-to-22; this was especially surprising when one considers that English had never before served in the House and was only older than five of its present members.[33]

Jesse Bright, an ally of both Davis and English, directly counseled his young friend to reach an honorable reconciliation with the caucus's choice. Not one to act rashly, English probably did not need this advice, and, of course, he did not challenge Davis in the full House. (Although considering English's friendship with and respect held by at least several Whigs, a floor fight may have yielded immediate results, even if damaging to English's future within the Democratic Party.) For his part, once he became Speaker, Davis was more than willing to give English his due, appointing him to three important committees and often requesting he take the chair in Davis's own absence. Meanwhile, there was much work to accomplish. Ignoring the rift over the speakership, the *New Albany Ledger* remarked that "a more harmonious body has never met at the Capital for many years." If true, it was probably the effect of lopsided Democratic majorities in both

---

32. J.W. Davis to WHE, October 3, 1851, English Papers. Davis served as Indiana House speaker in the sessions of 1831-33 and 1841-43. Shepherd, *Biographical Directory*, 94. He served as the speaker of the United States Congress from 1845-47. *Biographical Directory of the United States Congress, 1774-2005*, (United States Government Printing Office, 2005), 929. Davis was appointed commissioner to China in the last half year of the Polk Administration but informed Zachary Taylor's secretary of state, in a letter written in September of 1849, that he intended to resign that position. John M. Clayton to James Whitcomb, February 26, 1850, *James Whitcomb Papers, Indiana Historical Society, Indianapolis, Indiana*. Davis actually formally resigned on May 25, 1850. http://history.state.gov/departmenthistory/people/chiefsofmission/china. Accessed May 30, 2019.

33. James Whitcomb to WHE, December 29, 1851, English Papers. Woolen, *Eminent Men*, vol. 2, District 7, 212. *Indiana Statesman*, December 3, 1851, in *English Scrapbook*, 19. Shepherd, *Biographical Directory*, 506-508, *passim*.

houses, and they methodically set about to shape into law the Jacksonian dictates of the previous year's state constitutional convention.[34]

One of the fundamental issues that divided Democrats from Whigs during the second party system was the relation of government to banking. On the state as well as federal level, Democrats were more suspicious than Whigs of banks in general but especially of banks whose stock was partially owned by the government. Since 1834, the only permitted banking institution in Indiana was the state bank, composed of 13 branches. In 1851, it had capital of $2 million, half from the state and half from private investors. It had been generally well managed; the only exception being a brief time in the early 1840s. Yet Democratic opponents of the bank viewed it as Andrew Jackson had the Bank of the United States, some arguing that it showed favoritism to stockholders, others claiming that it unduly restricted credit within the state. Those critics dominated the Party at the 1851 Constitutional Convention, but they were divided over whether to abolish all banks or to allow for many banks outside the state system. Eventually, most of them supported the latter position called "free banking," while a few Democrats and most Whigs continued to support the state-bank-only concept. Accordingly, the delegates rather compromised. The Constitution allowed the state bank to continue its operations so long as the state did not hold stock in it. Secondly, it authorized the legislature to pass a general banking law permitting the creation of banks outside the state system, but they must be closely regulated as to currency on hand, liability, and charter life. It would be the task of the ensuing legislature to fill in the details.[35]

The regular standing committee on banking, of which English was a member, would ordinarily have reported such a bill, but many legislators suspected it of hostility toward free banking. Consequently, the House passed a resolution requiring the speaker to appoint a select committee to frame a general banking law. English (who, true to his moderate inclinations, had gone on record as being in favor of "a well-guarded system of free banking") was appointed to this select committee. He served with four Whigs and eight other Democrats. On February 9, the committee reported a bill. All banks had to be completely secured by United States bonds or state bonds deposited with the state auditor, and, if a bank defaulted on its notes, the holder could redeem them from these securities. Moreover, banks had to have 12 percent of their notes in specie on hand, and refusal of specie payments was ground for immediate loss of a bank's charter. Additionally,

---

34. Jesse Bright to WHE, December 16, 1851, English Papers. Woolen, *Eminent Men*, vol. 2, District 7, 212. *Indiana State Sentinel*, December 6, 1851, January 7, 1852. *New Albany Ledger*, December 12, 1851, January 7, 1852, December 18, 1851.

35. Logan Esarey, *State Banking in Indiana: Indiana University Studies* no. 15 (Bloomington: Indiana University Press, 1912), 251-253, 271, 178. Carter, "Hoosier History," 242. William G. Shade, *Banks or No Banks: The Money Issue in Western Politics, 1832-1865* (Detroit: Wayne State University Press, 1972), 139-141.

all banks had to make semi-annual reports to the state auditor, and the state was in no way pledged to redeem a bank's currency.[36]

A moderate bill, it received general bipartisan support outside the legislature. Although most conservative creditors had been satisfied with the old system, many of them properly realized that the state possessed inadequate lending facilities. This had generally caused deflation, and, in truth, was hardly suitable during the expansive period in which they lived. In essence, "Young America" demanded free banking. During debate on the bill, a bipartisan group of Indianapolis supporters resolved that passage was necessary for the ends of "growth and prosperity." The legislative opponents of the bill were comprised of a strange coalition of inveterate supporters of the old state bank, and, more dangerously, hard-money-only advocates. In the end, the strange bedfellows were unable to kill the bill, and it passed by the thinnest of margins, 51-to-30. (According to the new constitution, all substantive bills needed a majority of the full number of legislators to pass.) Throughout the debate, English supported the measure and employed a number of parliamentary tactics to prevent the bill's derailment.[37]

It was the Whig vote that passed the measure. The Democrats split evenly, 25-to-25, while the Whigs voted for the bill overwhelmingly, 26-to-5. Most of the Democratic opponents came from the hard money southern part of the state, so that English probably voted against many of his own Party constituents.[38] His vote reflected his fundamental departure from the ultra-Jacksonian approach to currency matters. In general, he was not a great advocate of an inflated currency, but he was financially wise enough to understand the need for easier credit by which to develop both the nation's wealth and his own. Although he was never a great proponent of governmental intervention into the economy in general, his approach to strictly currency matters reflected the stance of both Whigs and later Republicans, even to the point of eventually supporting the national banking institution during the Civil War. English's banking policy represented the one great area where he was at odds with the majority of his Party but at one with many other wealthy Democrats.

Another significant issue that came before this legislature deserves some attention. During the previous year's constitutional convention, 29 Democrats and 15 Whigs had voted against the Jeffersonian maxim that "all men are created equal, and that they are endowed by their creator with certain inalienable rights."

---

36. *Indiana State Sentinel*, January 13, 1852. Esarey, *State Banking*, pp. 279-281. *Journal of the House of Representatives for the State of Indiana during the Thirty-Sixth Session of the General Assembly*, vol. 1 (Indianapolis: J. P. Chapman, 1851), 803-808.

37. Crane, "Joseph Wright," 184. Shade, *Banks*, 171. *Indiana State Sentinel*, February 26, 1852. *Journal of the House, 36th, vol. 2*, 1054-1058.

38. *Ibid.*, 1058. Shepherd, *Biographical Directory*, 506-508. Shade, *Banks*, 171. Thornbrough, *Civil War Era*, 195, 286, 317.

Lest any doubt be attached to the meaning of this opposition, debate on the resolution revealed that those who voted against it were loath to include black Americans under the most fundamental rubric of American democracy. Although these opponents lost that vote, as earlier noted, the Convention did pass an article later separately ratified by the Indiana electorate excluding black or mixed race peoples from subsequent settlement in the state. Any individual fostering such immigration was to be fined between $10 and $500 upon conviction. Additionally, the Constitution ordered the legislature to appropriate these collected fines for "the colonization of such Negroes and mulattoes as are now in this state and may be willing to emigrate."[39]

Consequently, on January 24, 1852, the Indiana House took up a Senate bill that limited the fines to $50 but said nothing about colonization. Representative Oliver Torbet, assistant editor of the *Indiana State Sentinel*, believed the Senate had not fully accommodated the constitutional directives. Maintaining the accepted notions of the day, Torbet argued that the Constitution's provision for colonization complemented that of future black exclusion. He also noted that the sooner the races were separated, the better it would be for both of them. When Torbet finished, English rose to concur. He moved to add to the referred bill "instructions appropriating a reasonable amount out of the State Treasury for the purpose of sending to Liberia such Negroes and mulattoes in this state, as may desire to emigrate to that country and have not the means to defray the expense of going." The amendment was adopted by a voice vote. The legislation that later passed strictly followed the constitutional mandate, directing the state to use the fines collected under the exclusion clause for colonization. On the racial elements of these matters, English agreed with the majority of Hoosiers.[40]

In order to align state legal codes with the new state constitution, the legislature would pass a great many new laws. But there were also many existent laws that had to be tweaked to properly conform to the new organic law. Accordingly, both houses adopted a resolution authorizing a Joint Committee of Revision to meet during a six-week adjournment when the bulk of this legislative work would be done. In the House, there was some question of whether the Speaker had the power to appoint the House's members to this Committee or if that power resided with the full body. In the ensuing discussion, English moved a resolution that passed granting such power to the speaker. In execution, Davis appointed two Whigs and two Democrats, one of whom was English himself. But, the next day,

---

39. *Journal of the Convention*, 349. *Reports of the Debates and Proceedings of the Convention for the Revision of the Constitution for the State of Indiana, 1850* (Indianapolis: Austin H. Brown, 1851) vol.1, 964; vol. 2, 1791. Carmony, *Indiana*, 442-445. *Journal of the Convention*, 652, 753, 754, 756-757, 760.

40. *Journal of the House, 36*[th], vol. 1, 613. Shepherd, *Biographical Directory*, 394. John W. Miller, *Indiana Newspaper Bibliography* (Indianapolis: Indiana Historical Society, 1982), 274. Crane, "Joseph Wright," 213. *Journal of the House, 36*[th], vol. 1, 612-613; 631; 67, 68, 182-183.

this resolution that had authorized the speaker to make those appointments was decided to be reconsidered, 52-to-21.[41]

During this reconsideration debate, English led the fight for the speaker to exercise the power of appointment. Wishing to make clear that his support for Davis was not one of self-interest, he had early on requested (and received) permission to be excused from Davis's appointment of him to that Committee. In the end, only 13 Democrats, English, of course, among them, voted to allow the speaker to keep his power of appointment. The full vote to adopt the reconsidered motion to allow the full House to elect its committee's members then passed, 50-to-27, but Davis ruled that such a vote needed a two-thirds majority. The speaker's ruling was appealed, and he was then defeated, 31-to-15. Immediately after this tally went against Davis, the abashed speaker called English to the Chair. There, apparently humiliated (one historian noted that for the first time in Davis's life his "character for impartiality had been impeached: it was the severest stab ever aimed at him"), the chastened speaker handed English his letter of resignation. Davis later said that, had he continued as presiding officer, "he should be wanting in every sentiment of self-respect."[42]

For the moment, the House had no speaker—just William English as presiding member. It quickly adjourned. That afternoon, a Democratic caucus tried, and failed, to convince Davis to resume his duties. When the House reconvened, with English still in the chair on the motion of Robert Owen, it proceeded to hold nominations for a new official speaker. One Whig and three Democrats were so nominated, William English among them. By 40-to-35 the House again voted to adjourn, to reconvene two days later on Monday, March 8. At 9 a.m. on that appointed day, on recommendation of the Democratic caucus, English was elected, receiving 52 of the 76 votes cast. He gained 49 of the 64 Democrats who cast votes and even picked up the support of three Whig legislators.[43] Though some members may have disapproved of his position during the appointment debate (and may have even suspected some quid-pro-quo in his support for Davis),

41. Justin E. Walsh, *The Centennial History of the Indiana General Assembly, 1816-1978* (Indianapolis: Indiana Historical Bureau, 1987), 246. *Journal of the House, 36th*, vol. 1, 67-68; vol. 2, 1182-1183. Woolen, *Historical Sketches, 237.*

42. *Journal of the House, 36th*, vol. 2, 1195-1197. Woolen, Historical *Sketches,* 238. In his fine Centennial History of the Indiana General Assembly, Justin Walsh argues that Davis resigned his position because the House overturned his ruling against the necessary adjournment for the special committee to conform previous laws to the Constitution. He also maintains that English, out of continued animosity toward Davis, engineered the House vote that overturned that ruling. *Centennial History,* 230-231. But the House Journal makes clear that not only was the issue over who would appoint the members of the special committee, but also that English was a steadfast supporter of the speaker's power. How English or any other specific member felt about the speaker's ruling that a 2/3 vote was needed to reconsider the passed resolution granting the speaker the power to appoint is unrecorded, as no individual roll was recorded on the matter.

43. *Journal of the House, 36th*, vol. 2, 1199-1200

his eventual election both in caucus and in the House appears to illustrate that he was not much hurt by the association. The circumspect manner by which he gained the position that he had unsuccessfully sought more than three months earlier may fairly be considered quite fortuitous. But it was partly made possible by the pubic magnanimity with which he handled that earlier setback. It was also, certainly, a reflection of his standing in the House.

Upon taking up his duties, the new speaker made a short speech, now admitting his inexperience and humbly asking for the House's "forbearance" and "indulgence." He reminded the legislators of their remaining task to enact "a full and complete code of laws, general in their application, corresponding with and carrying out the principles of the constitution [and] adapted to the spirit of the age." And he combatively criticized those "miserable time serving demagogues who hope to make political capital by the cry that the session is being protracted to an unnecessary and ruinous length."[44] In the future, English would mix the same humility with a similar fighting spirit when in battle with Republicans. Because of the necessary law revisions, the session did not technically end until June 21. The *Sentinel* had earlier predicted that English would make "a most excellent presiding officer," and, indeed, the mostly rump rest of the session seemed to pass uneventfully. On the last day of House business, English received the perfunctory, unanimous thanks of the members, and, in his final address to the legislators, he boasted that "no harsh word had passed between any member and the Chair, nor, as far as I have heard, a murmur of complaint from any quarter."[45] In all, it may be said to have been a successful few months for the rising Democrat.

5.

Important intraparty activity occurred at the same time that English served as member and speaker of the state House. Although the Indiana Democracy resolved at its State Convention in February 1852, that the "Compromise measures...should, under no pretense be disturbed," the Party had not completely healed over its earlier differences concerning the Wilmot Proviso and the Fugitive Slave Act. In Indianapolis, E.W.H. Ellis, a relatively free soil Democrat, had inaugurated the *Indiana Statesman*, a competing sheet to the more pro-Compromise *Indiana Sentinel*. Even in Jesse Bright's hometown of Madison, editor Michael Garber of the *Madison Courier*, an erstwhile grand supporter of the senator, was generally critical of Bright's role in the passage of the Fugitive Act.[46]

---

44. *Ibid.*, 1201-1202.

45. *Indiana State Sentinel*, March 9, 1852. *Journal of the House, 36*th, vol. 2, 2208.

46. *Indiana State Sentinel*, February 26, 1852. Van der Weele, "Jesse Bright," 98-99.

Underneath these differences over issues surrounding slavery was the personal rivalry for Party leadership between the Machiavellian Bright and governor Joseph A. Wright. (The similarity in their names is quite comical.) Bright had a deserved reputation for keen political manipulation and fiery combativeness; he once shouted at a free soil editor, "God damn you—I wish you were in Hell!" He viewed Wright as presenting a challenge to his state Party supremacy, and, as the governor became a greater and greater force in the Party, Bright's hatred of him grew. Wright had a more prosaic, down-to-earth reputation. As a youth, he labored as a bricklayer to support himself and his widowed mother, and, in order to finance his later education, he took a number of odd jobs from bell ringer to janitor. As he became involved in Democratic politics, Wright made it a rule to study the needs of Indiana husbandry closely. Compared to his rival (a slicker denizen of the Ohio River city of Madison), Wright seemed to exude the rustic republican values of frugality, integrity, and hard work. One biographer of Wright's labeled one of his chapters "Bright is not right and Wright is not bright."[47]

Like most Indiana Democrats, Wright ran hot, then lukewarm, on the Free-Soil issue, and he fully supported the 1850 Compromise for its tendency to promote sectional peace and national Democratic harmony. But, unlike Bright, he did not castigate as abolitionists Democrats who had a less-favorable view of accommodation with the South. In return for his greater magnanimity, and his generally honest character, the more free soil elements of the Party, like Ellis and Garber, were drawn to Wright. Bright also distrusted Wright, as he was too closely associated with Whitcomb, and he mildly tried but failed in 1849 to deny him nomination as Whitcomb's successor as governor. By 1852, with the threat from Wright to Jesse's hegemony growing, the senator began to view any Indiana Democrat who had a kind word to say about the governor a personal enemy. Though he tried again to get the Indiana Democracy to deny Wright renomination in 1852, the governor's popularity was too strong to make that possible.[48] As sitting

---

47. Woolen, *Historical Sketches,* 224. Van Der Weele, "Jesse Bright," 93. Crane, "Joseph Wright," 152, xii. Before he became governor, Wright had a long political pedigree, having served as a circuit prosecuting attorney, three terms as a state legislator, and one term in Congress. He had won his term in Congress, in 1843, in a Whig District, by three votes, but lost the next two elections by, albeit, less than 200 votes. Shepherd, *Biographical Directory,* 431. Riker, *Election Returns,* 107-108, 112, 116. Wright sarcastically recognized that Bright and his Democratic followers were more cosmopolitan than he was when he wrote Henry Wise a few years later that these Indiana men were looking with "anxious eyes" about investing in any Pacific Railroad project. Joseph Wright to Henry Wise, November 25, 1856, Joseph Wright Papers, Indiana Historical Society, Indianapolis, Indiana.

48. Crane, "Joseph Wright," 45-149, 143-144, 159-167, 226-227. Beeler, "Election of 1852 (part 1)", 311-312. Van der Weele, "Jesse Bright," 118-119. As an example of the loyalty that Bright received, an acolyte of his, one Hamilton Hibbs, refused to serve with Michael Garber as part of a receiving committee for Louis Kossuth, the Hungarian revolutionary. Hibbs reputedly maintained that he would rather serve with a "buck nigger." This comment precipitated a later scuffle between the two where Garber was said to have hit Hibbs

governor when the new constitution prohibited gubernatorial re-election, Wright was exempted from that restriction.

Intraparty disputes are generally unwanted minefields for young politicians. They often necessitate choosing sides, and a wrong choice has destroyed many a fledgling career. Rare is the young politician who is able to safely choose and still retain the respect and support of all factions. By this time, of course, William English had become an intimate correspondent with the Bright brothers, and he shared their general antipathy toward anti-slavery rhetoric. As the 1850s would progress, English began to have reservations about too closely accommodating himself to southern interests, but, for most of the decade, he supported Bright as a close political associate and prominent pro-Compromise senator. While he rather successfully steered clear of Bright's bitter feuds with Indiana free soil Democrats, English certainly acted as a trusted lieutenant in the senator's intraparty battles with Governor Wright. In late 1850, while he was serving as principal secretary to the Constitutional Convention, English had written Bright that the governor was angling for the caucus nomination to replace the Madison boss as senator. In reply from Washington, Bright directed English to "counteract" the "movements" of the Wright "machinery." Bright also contacted Elisha, William's father (who, as state senator, was part of the Democratic legislative caucus), and suggested that he "give Joseph [Wright] your special attention." In the end, the anti-Bright forces let Robert Owen formally challenge Bright instead, and only Bright's hurried trip from Washington prevented Owen from carrying the caucus and denying Bright his renomination.[49]

English apparently escaped unscarred from this battle. In December 1851, immediately after his failed challenge to Dr. Davis for the House speakership, Ellis's anti-Bright, Free-Soil *Statesman* called the vote for English "flattering," claiming that "no other man in the state could have mustered so many votes against that man." The *Statesman's* friendly attitude apparently worried senator Bright, for, two weeks later, he wrote English to "beware of that moral putrefaction Ellis." Bright was hoping to prevent Wright's gubernatorial renomination the coming February, and he wanted to keep his corps intact. He had been upset by English's competition with Davis, for the doctor was not only an ally of Bright's but the man whom Bright had been promoting to defeat Wright as the Democratic nominee for governor. Bright had earlier implored English to "let no temporary jar between Dr. Davis and yourself drive you from his support. He can beat Wright for the nomination if the sound Democrats of the party take hold of him." Perhaps

---

with his cane; Gibbs retaliated by stabbing Garber three times with a chisel. No one was criminally charged. Woolen, *Historical Sketches,* 482.

49. Jesse Bright to WHE, December 21, 1850; Jesse Bright to Elisha English, December 23, 1850. English Papers. Van der Weele, "Jesse Bright," 113, 117. Roger H. Van Bolt, "Indiana in Political Transition, 1851-1853," *Indiana Magazine of History* 49, no.2 (June, 1953): 143.

this explains English's cordial relationship with Davis so soon after Davis defeated him for speaker.[50]

The 1852 Democratic State Convention that renominated Wright for governor (which Jesse Bright did not attend) seriously attempted to harmonize the Party. To promote pre-Convention unity, the *Statesman* agreed to merge itself into the *Sentinel*. For almost a year, prominent Democratic politicians had been involved in negotiations to combine these two Democratic newspapers in Indianapolis, a move of which English approved. Indeed, he was among those who signed the merger statement that appeared in the *Sentinel*. At the state convention itself, the delegates overwhelmingly endorsed the 1850 Compromise. Then they balanced out Wright's gubernatorial nomination by choosing Bright men for most of the other state offices. The Bright men were also given a slight majority of the state-selected delegates to the 1852 National Presidential Nominating Convention in Baltimore.[51]

Indiana's course at this 1852 National Convention would prove to be a curious one. Curious, too, was that John W. Davis was chosen as permanent president of the convention, effectively salving any wounds from his lost Indiana speakership. Many Indiana Democrats favored one of their state's own favorite sons, Joseph Lane, for president. Lane had won fame as Indiana's only brigadier general in the Mexican War; in 1852 he was serving as the Oregon Territory's delegate to Congress. He was supported by both Phineas Kent and Michael Bright, though, significantly, Jesse was not as keen on the general as his brother was. Other Indiana Democrats were drawn to the rising senator from Illinois, Stephen Douglas, who had become the preferred candidate of Young America and had shown his parliamentary skill in guiding the 1850 Compromise into law. The State Democratic Convention had wound up resolving that Lane was its first choice, but it did not go so far as to formally instruct its national delegates to vote for him. Michael Bright, though believing that a majority of the state delegates to the national convention supported Lane, nevertheless confided to the general that "we have done the best we could but not as well as I have wished."[52]

---

50. *Indiana Statesman*, December 3, 1851, in English Scrapbook, p. 19. Jesse Bright to WHE, December 16, 1851, English papers. In this letter to English, Bright appears to put Phineas Kent in the group that favored Ellis and the free-soilers. If Kent was so consorting, he pulled back later.

51. *Indiana State Sentinel*, February 23, 1852. Van der Weele, "Jesse Bright," 119. *New Albany Ledger*, February 27, 1852. *Indiana State Sentinel*, February 26, 1852.

52. Bain, *Convention Decisions*, 45. Joe Lane to P.M. Kent, June 20, 1847, in Oran Perry, ed., *Indiana in the Mexican War* (Indianapolis: William H. Buford, 1908), 197. *Indiana Democrat*, August 24, 1848, in *English Scrapbook*, 32. Van der Weele, "Jesse Bright," 123. Michael G. Bright to Joe Lane, January 28, February 24, March 3, 1852; J.P. Chapman to Joe Lane, February 20, 1852, Joseph Lane Papers, Oregon Historical Society, Portland, Oregon, accessed Xerox copies at Lilly Library, University of Indiana, Bloomington, Indiana. As an example of Lane's popularity, William Williams, the publisher of the *Washington Democrat* in English's congressional district, promoted the general's name for president on his paper's masthead as

Because of the excessive length of the state legislative session in 1852, the last three months of which English was speaker, it turned out that although he had been selected as a national delegate at a meeting of his district delegates to the state convention, he was unable to attend the gathering. But he nevertheless appears to have been most impressed by Stephen Douglas. The previous December, English had written Douglas that after the Indiana delegates had fulfilled their filial obligation to Lane on the early ballots, they would switch to the Illinois senator when the time was ripe. As it would be unwise to bring Douglas into direct "collision with General Lane," English promised to try to get the state Democratic convention to instruct for Douglas as its second choice. Douglas wrote back appreciatively, asking English to keep him apprised of "how things stand."[53]

English's somewhat secret support for the Illinois Senator is noteworthy for a couple of reasons. In the first place, most of the Hoosiers who backed Douglas were identified with the Wright wing of the Party. English's support, therefore, ran contrary to the fortunes of his mentor. Indeed, Jesse Bright was to develop an inveterate hatred for the "Little Giant," and, even in 1852, the two had become rivals for the distribution of the federal patronage in the Northwest.[54] It is possible that English feigned his support for Douglas to better serve Bright, but none of the evidence supports this thesis. More likely, English's actions illustrate an ability to consult his own mind while maintaining cordial relations with Bright and others. Throughout his career English would illustrate this innate characteristic to re-

---

early as January 18, 1851, a year before the Democratic State Convention. On the other hand, Douglas's popularity is also clear: the editor of the *Indiana Sentinel,* the state Democratic organ, wrote to Douglas in the summer of 1851 of his support for the Illinois senator. In writing back, Douglas showed he was certainly aware of Lane's popularity, but that did not stop him from flattering the *Sentinel* editor nor shy away from promoting said editor's continued support. "[Y]ou can do more for me than any man in the country," he told him. "Your intimate acquaintance with all the public men of this country and your knowledge of the true state of politics in each State give you peculiar advantages." Stephen Douglas to W.J. Brown, June 21, 1851, *Douglas Letter, Indiana Historical Society, Indianapolis, Indiana.*

53. *Washington Democrat,* March 6, 1852. Stephen A. Douglas to WHE, December 29, 1851, English Papers. Douglas had been acquainted with English at least as far back as the early 1840s, and, as earlier noted, had written a letter of recommendation to President Polk that followed hard upon the letter written to Polk by prominent Indianans (see p.25, Chapter 1). In this 1845 letter at the beginning of the Illinoisan's second term in the House of Representatives, Douglas noted that he "intended to join the delegation from Indiana in recommending the appointment of William H. English Esq of that state to be recorder of the General Land Office, but having been deprived of the opportunity at that time, I hope you will pardon me for troubling you with a letter in his behalf." Douglas also noted he had "some personal acquaintance with Mr. English and know him well by reputation," and added that English would "make an active, attentive, and faithful officer." As the letter notes, Douglas beseeched Polk on English's behalf as a personal favor to him, considering that the Hoosier had a "large number of relatives" in Illinois, "principally in my district." Douglas to James K. Polk, March 10, 1845, in Robert W. Johannsen, ed., *The Letters of Stephen A. Douglas* (Urbana: University of Illinois Press, 1961), 109-110. English burnished his relationship with Douglas, under probable constraints as a Bright acolyte, especially as the Little Giant became more prominent.

54. Van Der Weele, "Jesse Bright," 123. Roy F. Nichols, *The Democratic Machine, 1850-1854* (1923; repr, New York: AMS Press, Inc., 1967), 199.

main on friendly relations with those who were unfriendly to each other. He had earlier suggested this ability when he was able to keep the support of the free soil wing of the Party while campaigning hard for Bright's renomination as senator. Secondly, English's support of Douglas appears to have been a genuine preference for the ideals of Young America, most represented by its Illinois champion. By supporting Douglas, he supported the vigor of the West, "a region which," English said two years later, "will probably one day govern America and possibly the world—a region contemplating the future."[55]

Unlike Bright, who, at the top of his mountain, felt threatened by any vigorous movement underneath, English was not completely averse to dynamic impulses. Although cautious by nature, he had not yet achieved sufficient success to cause reflex resistance to energetic efflorescence. A letter from an old friend of his father's, major John S. Simonson, appears to confirm that English and Bright were not of one mind concerning the Party's presidential preference. Simonson wrote English that he was "clearly with you in relation to the nominee," and noted that "it will require two of us to give the vote of the [congressional] district to suit ourselves and friends provided Bright is determined for another." At one point, Simonson refers to Bright's choice as "J.B.," probably referring to James Buchanan, but there is no hard evidence to show that Bright favored the venerable Pennsylvanian in 1852. Bright appears to have had everyone guessing, but he did not favor Douglas.[56]

Part of Simonson's purpose for writing English was to convince him to attend the convention in his company. Three weeks later, Bright, apparently unaware of English's dalliance with Douglas, wrote him to "come to the convention if possible, we need delegates to Indiana who feel and act upon the great questions of the time as you do." But Bright's imploration may not have been especially sincere, for he quickly added, "if, however, you cannot come, send me a letter asking me to act in your stead. This will be ratified, I know, by the other delegates, and I feel quite sure would be acceptable to the great body of our party."[57] Without further available correspondence, it is difficult to interpret the full meaning of Bright's words, but from all other evidence they appear to connote both agreement and disagreement between the two friends. Both certainly agreed that the Party should not sully itself with freesoilism. On the nomination, they both probably agreed that Lane was not possible to nominate, and that Indiana, should, in historian Roy Nichols's words, "use him only until the winner should appear."[58] They dis-

---

55. *Appendix to the* CG, 33-1, 607-608

56. John S. Simonson to WHE, April 22, 1852, English Papers. Van der Weele, "Jesse Bright," 123-124. P.M. Kent to Joe Lane, June 3, 1852, Lane Papers.

57. John S. Simonson to WHE, April 22, 1852; Jesse Bright to WHE, May 15, 1852, English Papers.

58. Nichols, *Democratic Machine*, 134.

agreed, of course, on the next favored nominee. English, again, did not attend the convention, but whether he gave Bright his proxy is a mystery.

In any event, for 30 ballots, Indiana cast its full 13 votes for Lane, but not one delegate from any other state so complied. On the second day of balloting, as Douglas slipped into the lead, Bright looked for a way to head off the Illinois senator. A victory for Douglas, he reasoned, was a victory for the Wright faction in Indiana, and he was loath to allow that. In his attempt to slow down Douglas, Bright, by a slim margin, was able to get the state's delegation to switch its 13 votes to the Party's 1848 nominee, Lewis Cass. Within two ballots, this move had had the desired effect, and Cass gained at Douglas's and others' expense. Bright had accomplished his goal but no doubt at the price of further alienating the Wright faction. In the end, Cass could never compile the 2/3 vote necessary for nomination, and, on the 49th ballot, the exhausted convention nominated dark horse Franklin Pierce of New Hampshire. Indiana eventually lined up behind him and behind the so-called "finality" resolution that pledged the Party to resist all attempts to renew agitation over slavery and to "abide by and adhere to" the 1850 Compromise measures. For the moment the Wright and Bright factions decided to unite for the upcoming canvass and to regain the federal patronage.[59]

6.

William English probably reacted to Pierce's nomination as most Democrats did: with surprise and little enthusiasm. He and his fellow partisans soon found enough virtues in the nominee to allow them to praise him from every podium, and they needed to praise him often merely to raise him from obscurity. When news of the nomination reached Indianapolis, the state legislature had almost completed its business. In two weeks, it would adjourn, and, once again, English would have to decide what future political course to follow. Earlier in the session, he had hopes that Jesse Bright would take care of him. Since December 1851, Bright had tried to get the Senate to amend its rules concerning the selection of its secretary, doorkeeper, assistant doorkeeper, and sergeant-at-arms. Before 1847, these officers had been elected, but excessive electioneering had led the Senate

---

59. Bain, *Convention Decisions*, 45–46, Appendix D. Beeler, "Election of 1852", part 1, 318. P.M. Kent to Joe Lane, June 3, 1852, Lane Papers. Van Der Weele, "Jesse Bright," 124. Bright's use of Cass to blunt Douglas brings to mind one contemporary's observations of the two contenders' behavior while in the senate where they sat "opposite each other, and each watched the other's movements with more interest than rival bidders at a great auction sale." Josiah B. Grinnell, *Men and Events of Forty Years: Autobiographical Reminiscences of an Active Career from 1850 to 1890* (Boston: D. Lothop Co., 1891), 64. Another autobiographer recounted that Franklin Pierce was acceptable to the South as he had "never given a vote or written a sentence that the straightest Southern Democrat could wish to blot." Indeed, it was Virginia that first brought Pierce's name up for nomination. Ben Perley Poore, *Perley's Reminiscences of Sixty Years in the National Metropolis, vol. 1* (Philadelphia: Hubbard Brothers, 1886), 414, 423.

to allow the then existing officers to hold permanent tenure unless removed by a specific vote. Bright moved that the original rule be reinstated. He wrote English a few days later, "I intend to keep moving [the resolution] until I move you where you desire to be, at any rate until we restore the old rule, and come back to biennial elections and then you can take your chances." Always the deceiver, Bright had told the senators that he had "offered this resolution without at all being influenced by the consideration of who are now, or who may hereafter be the officers of this body." Although, the next February, Bright had assured English that he was on the "look out" for him and had him "in my eye all the time," he was never able to get the Senate to consider his resolution. The young politico would have to look elsewhere.[60]

Despite Bright's false promises, English must have believed that he would have little trouble in managing a federal appointment should Pierce be elected president. On the other hand, he could also attempt to seek reelection to the state legislature. But neither of these courses would represent political advancement. Should he again be elected state representative, only his reelection as speaker would be acceptable, and he could hardly be certain of this. As for a federal appointment, he could not be sure how "honorable" a position he could claim. Because these routes offered no real political progress, English instead decided to take a calculated risk. On June 19, the *New Albany Ledger* listed six men who were seeking the Democratic congressional nomination from Indiana's Second Congressional District. The third name on the list was "William H. English."[61]

There was no incumbent in the mix, for the latest federal census granted Indiana an additional congressional seat, and Cyrus Dunham decided to run in the Third District which now contained part of the old Second. James Lockhart, the incumbent congressman from the First District, part of which was now moved to the new Second, was retiring. Because the old Second lost three counties to the new Third (Jefferson, Jackson, and Jennings) and gained four counties from the First (Orange, Crawford, Perry, and Harrison) it essentially shifted southwestward. The Bright clan, incidentally, was moved out of the Second, as Madison was in Jefferson County. The new Second, thus, was prime hunting ground for any ambitious native politician.[62] Note that the 1851 Indiana Constitution moved

---

60. Beeler, "Election of 1852," part 1, 319. *CG, 32-1,* 41, 62-63. Jesse Bright to WHE, December 16, 1851, February 16, 1852, English Papers.

61. *New Albany Ledger,* June 19, 1852.

62. Stanley B. Parsons, William W. Beach, and Michael Dubin, *United States Congressional Districts, 1843-1883* (New York, Westport, Connecticut, London: Greenwood Press, 1986), 10, 56. Shepherd, *Biographical Directory,* 108. *Biographical Directory of the United States Congress,* 1460. The redistricting had been done by the just adjourned 36th General Assembly. English had, at least initially, not favored the new composition, very likely because it excluded both the city of Madison as well as Democratic stronghold Jackson County. *Washington Democrat,* December 24, 1851.

Indiana Congressional Districts, 1853 - 1861

congressional elections from the odd-numbered years to the even-numbered ones. Dunham and Lockhart, who were elected in August 1851, had taken their seats in December of the same year. The first year of the new even-yeared elections was 1852; congressman who would be elected that year, now in the month of October, not August, technically would begin their terms in March 1853. They would not typically, however, fill their seats until the following December, 13 months after their election, the month when the first session of most new congresses convened.

This reshaped Second District was composed of some of the oldest settled regions in Indiana. Its most significant characteristics stemmed from the fact that five of its eight counties bordered on the Ohio River, and the other three bordered on the first five. Geographically, economically, and, to a great degree, culturally, it was linked to the South. The Second's long border along the river made it a way station for Indiana produce bound for southern plantations. Hogs, for example, were driven down to the district from as far away as Bloomington. Allowed to fatten up in Crawford, Harrison, Floyd, and Clark counties, they were butchered, pickled, and smoked, then shipped along the Ohio and down the Mississippi. By the 1850s, much of the produce into the district found its way to New Albany and, from there, either across the river to Louisville or westward to the Mississippi. Indeed, much of the antebellum commercial history of southeastern Indiana revolved around the competition between Madison and New Albany for the premier shipping and distribution point along the Hoosier Ohio. Madison, having been established earlier, was the major commercial center of southern Indiana until 1850. The Madison and Indianapolis Railroad, completed in 1847 but operational as early as 1840, allowed the city to maintain its position even after New Albany surpassed it in population and shipping facilities. In order to overtake its upriver rival, New Albany persistently sponsored efforts to build turnpikes and railroads out from itself. Under the same internal improvements bill that established the Madison and Indianapolis Railroad, macadam roads were sanctioned to run to New Albany from Vincennes and Crawfordville, supplementing the small plank roads built in the district in the 1820s and 1830s. Yet these largely uncompleted roads could not compete with the Madison and Indianapolis, which offered the shortest route to the Ohio River from the interior.[63]

Finally, in 1848, a project was approved that resulted in the preeminence of New Albany during the 1850s: the New Albany and Salem Railway. Originally

---

63. Hazen Hayes Pleasant, *A History of Crawford County, Indiana*, (Greenfield, Indiana: William H. Mitchell Printing Co., 1926),164. *One Hundred and Fifty Years*, 47. Victor M. Bogle, "New Albany: Reaching for the Hinterland," *Indiana Magazine of History* 50, no. 2 (June, 1954), 163, 145. Arthur L. Dillard, ed., *Orange County Heritage* (Paoli, Indiana: Stout's Print Shop, 1971), 77. Frank F. Hargrave, *A Pioneer Indiana Railroad* (Indianapolis: W.M. Burford Printing Co, 1932), 36. *New Albany Ledger*, December 8, 1851, June 11, 1855. N.N. Hill, *History of the Ohio Falls Cities and Their Counties* (Cleveland: L.A. Williams and Co., 1882), 153. Elmer Duane Elbert, *"Southern Indiana Politics on the Eve of the Civil War,"* (PhD diss., Indiana University, 1967), 7. Crane, "Joseph Wright," 213-214.

conceived by some Salem businessmen who wished to facilitate travel to the river, it quickly expanded into a million dollar project that envisioned a track running the length of the state. The citizens of New Albany enthusiastically supported the enterprise, allowing the city council to subscribe the initial $100,000. By 1851, the railroad reached Salem where it veered westward through Orleans and then directly North. Although not fully completed until 1854, it pulled the produce of much of southwestern and west central Indiana into New Albany as early as 1852.[64]

In general, the decade preceding the Civil War was New Albany's golden age. Between 1840 and 1850, it had nearly doubled its inhabitants, becoming the largest city in the state. Although its population was eclipsed by Indianapolis shortly after mid-century, New Albany continued to prosper greatly on the strength of its shipping industry. Peculiarly located two miles below (west of) the Ohio falls, directly opposite the west end of Louisville, it rested on a plateau overlooking the river. Many ships traveling from the east avoided the falls by unloading at Jeffersonville and carrying their shipment overland to New Albany. There, they would put their cargo back on boats. Other shippers, however, transshipped their goods on the Kentucky side, producing a natural rivalry between New Albany and Louisville. As there were no interstate east-to-west railroads around until shortly before the Civil War, the trade along the Ohio was great enough for both towns to feed off of it abundantly. The extent to which New Albany prospered from and depended upon the river trade is exemplified by the fact that both its newspapers, the *New Albany Ledger* and the *New Albany Tribune*, filled their pages with extensive shipping reports.[65]

Commercially, New Albany served as more than a mere transshipment point. Between 1849 and 1860, its shipyards built over 155 steamboats, placing it behind only Pittsburgh, Louisville, and Cincinnati as far as the nation's interior cities were concerned. Most of the steamers that New Albany constructed were larger and longer than those built elsewhere and were destined for use on the Mississippi. In this respect, as in its function as an entrepôt for goods crossing to and from Kentucky, the city's prosperity was closely tied to the southern economy. As the hub around which the rest of the district revolved, New Albany fastened the Second to the southern market. Madison and the Third District bordered on the state of Ohio as well as Kentucky; Evansville and the First had Illinois as much

---

64. Hargrave, *Pioneer Railroad*, 15, 39, 44-45, 136-137. Carter, "Hoosier Decade," 270-271. *New Albany Ledger*, December 11, 1855.

65. Esarey, *History of Indiana*, vol. I, 506. *Biographical and Historical Souvenir for the Counties of Clark, Crawford, Harrison, Floyd, Jefferson, Jennings, Scott, and Washington* (Chicago: Chicago Printing Co., 1889), 72-76. Victor M. Bogle, "New Albany's Attachment to the Ohio River," *Indiana Magazine of History* 49, no. 3, (September, 1953), 255.

as the South for a neighbor. Only New Albany and the Second faced completely toward the slave states.[66]

The geographic and economic southern orientation of the district was augmented demographically as well. All parts of Indiana were composed of many citizens of southern ancestry, but the Second District had far and away the highest proportion of them. In 1850, 39 percent of the population of the state as a whole was of southern ancestry, but in the Second District it was 59 percent. No other District had over 50 percent; only two had 40 percent. Incidentally, Indiana had the greatest proportion of citizens of southern ancestry than any other state north of the Ohio.[67] This southern orientation was often expressed culturally in the form of suspicion and disdain for the Yankees flooding into the northern and central counties of the state. To many Hoosiers of southern origin, these transplanted New Englanders and New Yorkers were cold, parsimonious, pinched, and arrogant meddlers. Their tendency to promote social reforms threatened the frontier independence and more easygoing ways of the transplanted southerners.[68]

Reserved for special condemnation was anti-slavery "agitation." The District's great hostility toward it exemplified how its citizens felt about slavery and race. Apart from degrees of disapproval over the Fugitive Slave Law, sympathy with the anti-slavery movement before 1854 was quite limited in the Second. In the most recent electoral test of anti-slavery sentiment, the gubernatorial contest of 1849, this fact was made abundantly clear. Excluding the Second District, an abolitionist, running on the Free-Soil ticket, gained 2,809 votes statewide, or 2.1 percent of the whole. In the redistricted Second, he received a total of seven of 14,376 votes cast, or a minuscule 0.05 percent. In other words, the rest of the state voted over 40 times as much for the anti-slavery candidate as did the Second District.[69] When, afterward, the *New Albany Ledger* learned that the American Anti-slavery Society saw promise in northern Indiana, it remarked that this meant that "we may therefore shortly look for the invasion of Indiana by a gang of crazy abolitionists." And, indeed, there was some organized anti-slavery activity among the Quakers of Orange County, and temporary "stops" on the Underground Railroad in New Albany, Jeffersonville, and Salem. These were more than merely isolated instances, with free

---

66. Hill, *Ohio Falls Cities,* 170-171, 156. Hubbart, *Older Middle West,* 82. Bogle, "New Albany's Attachment," 265-266, 257-258.

67. Carter, "Hoosier Decade," 12-13, 33-36, 15-18. John D. Barnhart and Donald F. Carmony, *Indiana: From Frontier to Industrial Commonwealth,* (New York: Lewis Historical Publishing Co., 1954), vol. 2, 607-609. Kenneth Stampp, *Indiana Politics during the Civil War* (Indianapolis: Indiana Historical Bureau, 1949), 2. Hubbart, *Older Middle West,* 6.

68. Many historians have commented on this "anti-Yankeeism" of southern Midwesterners. A nice, brief description of the animosity may be found in James M. McPherson, *Ordeal by Fire: The Civil War and Reconstruction,* 2nd ed., (New York, et al.: McGraw-Hill, Inc., 1992), 22. A deeper discussion may be gained from Nicole Etcheson, *The Emerging Midwest.* chapter 1; esp. pp. 6-9.

69. Riker, *Election Returns,* 178-180.

blacks working on, for example, the wharves of New Albany assisting the fugitives. Some church leaders were involved as well, as one elder of the Second Presbyterian Church of New Albany who was powerfully the president of the New Albany and Salem Railroad apparently gained free passes on the railroad for fugitives. Actually, Madison to the east and Evansville to the west were even greater centers of activity. But, in total, anti-slavery activity was low in the Second District. As the owner of the *Harrison County Democrat* understated to English, "abolitionism is very unpopular in these parts." Writing to the *New Albany Ledger* a few years later, a citizen of the district put it more crudely: "Nigger wool in Crawford is not worth picking."[70]

All district politicians refused to become identified with anti-slavery activity. The district's leading anti-Democratic (Whig, Know-Nothing, Republican) newspaper of the 1850s, the *New Albany Tribune,* consistently feared being accused of friendliness toward black people. Unlike all other districts, the Second would never possess an orthodox Republican sheet before the Civil War. The *Tribune* would consistently try to distance itself from the decreasingly racist state Republican organ, the *Indianapolis Journal.* It likened the difference between the two newspapers to that of "ebony and topaz." In the main, like its crosstown Democratic rival, it tried to position itself far away from abolitionism, never remarking kindly on the character of black people. For its own part, the Democratic press went further. The *Paoli American Eagle* of Orange County printed the following remarkable comparison of the races:

> It is but fair to consider the purely white race as the most noble and elevated of God's earthly creation, while the Negro, if not the lowest, is at least considerably inferior to the white. The skin of the white race is fair and crystal like, ornamented by a slight tinge of scarlet red, the features smooth and well arranged, the eyes intelligent and mildly bright, the hair of soft and silky material, the frame is delicate and well-proportioned, the voice participates of the properties of some winning and melodious sound, all of which go clearly to indicate the superior nature of the being. In addition to these, his taste of living, his inventive genius, his love of science and art, his never dying exertions to reach the highest pinnacle of usefulness, must likewise be taken into account. But what is seen in the Negro?—a clumsy clunk of 'flesh and blood' sure enough, ill proportioned and repulsive in manners, emitting a nauseating scent, a little like a sheep and a little like a dog, with legs struck nearly in the middle

---

70. Thornbrough, *Negro in Indiana,* 40, 41. Esarey, *History of Indiana,* vol. 2, 623, 129. Fergus M. Bordewich, *Bound for Canaan: the Underground Railroad and the War for the Soul of America,* (New York: Harper Collins, 2005), 202, 219, 364. Pamela R. Peters, *The Underground Railroad in Floyd County, Indiana,* (Jefferson, North Carolina and London: McFarland and Co., 2001), 49, 81-82. S.K. Wolfe to WHE, July 21, 1856, English Papers. *New Albany Ledger,* August 24, 1858. The Ledger's advice to abolitionists was to "go to Hayti or England or some other country where they can find a government and constitution to their mind." September 15, 1853. Julian, *Political Recollections,* 115.

of the feet, a hide as black as smoke could make it, a badly shaped and detestably looking face, lips like two segments of a black snake, a nose resembling the back of a large toad, eyes which are fearful in the extreme, a head as flat as the top of an anvil, and covered with a heavy coating of coarse and bushy wool, a voice somewhat resembling the broken and smothered sounds of a poorly constructed bass trumpet. In addition to these his mode of living is careless and slovenly, he possesses little or no inclination to refinement, and, in short, in the scale of nature at some remote point between the human and the ape species.

Admittedly, the *Eagle* tended politically toward the 'doughface' persuasion. The *New Albany Ledger*, however was rather in the mainstream of the Indiana Democratic Party, and its opinion in this matter equally reflected the District's proclivities:

However beautiful may seem the theory, or laudable may be the motive that impels the effort in favor of the general equality of human races and their indiscriminate dispersion throughout the earth, and that of their adaptation to all climates, it is plainly ascertainable that such a state of existence is an absolute violation of the original ordination of nature.

As the Orange County Democrats resolved in 1857, echoing *Dred Scott v. Sanford*, the Constitution's guarantee of liberty has "no reference to the Negro."[71]

The Democratic press often used Haiti as an example of the incapacity of black people to self-govern. The *New Albany Ledger* argued that the black monarchy there, created after the slave revolt, "relieved" the blacks "from all cares of government—a state of things very grateful to so imbecile and degraded a race." The newspaper encouraged a white rebellion, upon whose side of the island "was found nearly all the intelligence and talent," and claimed that "the sooner the Negroes are placed under the tutelage of those more capable of exercising power, the better it will be for them as well as their neighbors." This fundamental belief that black people could not govern themselves democratically produced an inconsistent attitude toward slavery. As earlier noted, the *Ledger* did argue that the *system* of slavery was regressive for southern society as a whole, yet, in its effect upon blacks alone, the paper interpreted slavery as almost desirable. Typical is its following comment: "Although all admit that the taking of the original stock from Africa was contrary to right yet, under the disadvantages of slavery, the race has made much progress, and collectively, now rank, intellectually and morally, much higher than the native blacks now in Africa." Such a position greatly tended

---

71. *New Albany Tribune*, February 15, 1858. *Paoli Eagle*, November 5, 1857. *New Albany Ledger*, July 29, September 22, 1857.

to temper any animosity claimed toward slavery; it fundamentally ignored its existence as a great evil and allowed for its toleration.[72]

What clearly underlay the Second District's lack of concern for the fate of slaves was the great antipathy its citizens held for any association with the black race. Of the 11 congressional districts in Indiana, the Second polled the greatest number of votes for the constitutional provision excluding black people from the state. Its attitude was clearly represented by headlines in the *New Albany Ledger*. One cried, "Unparalleled Depravity—a White Woman Deserts Her Husband and Elopes with a Nigger." Another announced, "More Negro Insolence," which referred to a black man who refused to change his seat on a boat and "take a position less offensive to the ladies." For this insolence, he was beaten.[73] These assumptions, not merely of black inferiority, but of black depravity, were at the core of the district's national politics in the decade before the Civil War. Although its citizens differed more in degree than kind from the rest of Indiana, the degree was significant, for, unlike in other districts these notions had no concentrated opposition in the Second. Politicians disregarded them at their peril.

The Second District's southern orientation was well represented by the candidates for the Democratic congressional nomination in 1852. Three of the six men seeking the post were born in Virginia, a fourth could trace his ancestry to the Old Dominion (though he, himself, was born in Pennsylvania), another came to Indiana by way of Baltimore and Kentucky, and the last, English, was the son of a Kentucky migrant. The most politically accomplished of the six was Nathaniel Albertson, a 52-year-old transplanted Virginian who had most recently served as the First District's congressman from 1849 to 1851. His rather undistinguished efforts in the national House led the district to deny him renomination. When he moved to Indiana, he had first resided in Harrison County, for which he served in the state legislature in the late 1830s, but he had since moved to Greenville in Floyd County. A "Nicholson letter" popular sovereignty man on the territorial question and a staunch Lane supporter at the national convention, he had many friends among the moderate men of the district. He was clearly the favorite, and, if he had any shortcoming, it was probably that he had been defeated for political office more times than he had been elected.[74]

Should Albertson falter, two men appeared likely to defeat him. One was state senator James G. Athon. Also born in Virginia, Athon roamed north and

---

72. *New Albany Ledger*, February 1, February 26, 1856.

73. Riker, *Election Returns*, 388-390. *New Albany Ledger*, August 10,1857, August 2, 1858.

74. *New Albany Ledger*, June 19, 1852. Shephard, *Biographical Directory*, 3, 10, 84, 284, 424. Woolen, *Eminent Men*, vol. I, District 3, 41; vol. 1, District 6, 95. Woolen, *Historical Sketches*, 478. *Indiana Biography Series*, vol. 3, Indiana State Library, Indianapolis, Microfilm, 3. *Paoli Eagle*, May 2, 1851. M.G. Bright to Joe Lane, February 18, 1852, Lane Papers. Albertson was also, like English, chosen as a delegate to the 1852 Democratic National Convention by the district's state delegates. *Washington Democrat*, March 6, 1852.

south of the Ohio until he finally settled in Clark County. In 1834, a year before he made Indiana his home, he graduated from Kentucky's Medical College, and, during the Mexican War, he served as a surgeon to both the Third and Fifth Indiana regiments. A man of charitable social concerns, he was recently chairman of the Committee on Benevolent Institutions in the state Senate. Already in 1852, he had been selected presidential elector for the district by the Democratic state convention, and, at 41, he clearly intended to parlay his present political visibility into a congressional seat. Albertson's other strong challenger was John I. Morrison, a former professor of Ancient Languages at Indiana University, and, in 1852, one of its trustees. Greatly respected as an educator, he was appointed the chairman of the Constitutional Convention's Committee on Education in 1850. For some years, he had been one of the most active of the District's Democrats, having early founded the very partisan Washington County *Salem Democrat*. He had also served as Washington County's state senator from 1847 to 1850 and at 46 could truthfully claim not to have failed in all his diverse endeavors.[75]

As it turned out, two early candidates, entrepreneur John B. Winstandley and soldier-farmer James A. Cravens, decided to drop out of the race by the end of June. This left only William English to contend with Albertson, Athon, and Morrison. At 29, English was 11 years younger than any of his rivals. Yet, unlike Athon, a physician, and Morrison, primarily an editor and educator, English was a professional politician. And, unlike Albertson, he did not carry with him a load of electoral defeats to weigh down his prospects. English's youth, perhaps his greatest liability, could also be positively used as a refreshing characteristic or to illustrate how far he had come in such a short time. From postmaster to house speaker, his inexorable rise as an Indiana politician had been equally matched by his clear competence.

English formally entered the contest late. Unable to leave Indianapolis until the legislature completed its business, he did not begin to seriously campaign until July. He was further at a decided disadvantage because Albertson, Athon, and Morrison were likely to gain the full support of "favorite son" counties (Harrison, Clark, and Washington, respectively) that were far more populated than English's Scott. In search of more votes, he first intended to concentrate on Floyd County, the home of New Albany. The Democrats of Floyd had planned a rally for the evening of July 16, one day before they were to meet in county convention. Believing this an opportunity to present his case, English gained a spot on the program. But, at the appointed hour, he failed to show. In the next day's *New Albany Ledger*, John Norman wrote that English had failed to appear because he was "detained at Salem by severe indisposition." In antebellum Indiana, "severe indisposition" was a catch-all phrase used to excuse any and all absences, and, from subsequent events, it can

---

75. Shepherd, *Biographical Directory,* 10. Woolen, *Historical Sketches,* 478-479. *New Albany Ledger,* December 13, 1851. Woolen, *Eminent Men,* vol. 2, District 6, 95. Shepherd, 284.

be gleaned that English was "detained at Salem" because he was working out a deal with John Morrison. It might also serve to note that he was well enough, evidently, to speak to the Democrats of Salem the previous evening at a county rally. The deal was of such importance that he apparently found it necessary to delay his journey to Floyd until the day of its actual county convention. On that day, he attended that gathering in Galena and was "called upon" to address the county's Democrats. In what the *Ledger* called "an able and eloquent speech" (a stock phrase of the era used to connote approval of the principles of the speech but not necessarily the person of the speaker), English briefly testified his adherence to the Democratic creed: limited government, opposition to "class" legislation, and faith in unmanipulated popular judgment. The *Ledger* reported that his effort "elicited the frequent applause of the [county] convention," but, when it came time to resolve upon a candidate to support for Congress, the Floyd Democrats became mute. The Baltimore and Indianapolis platforms were approved, and a prominent citizen of New Albany was promoted for state senator, but nothing was decided about Congress.[76]

As the district convention approached, only Albertson picked up the committed votes of counties outside his own: Crawford and Perry. The only real hitch in Albertson's possibilities was the action of Orange County, which, like Floyd, could not decide on its choice. Consequently, by the day of the convention, the following appears to have been a breakdown of the vote.

COUNTY	ALBERTSON	ATHON	MORRISON	ENGLISH	UNCOMMITTED
Clark		15			
Crawford	4				
Floyd					12
Harrison	11				
Orange					10
Perry	3				
Scott				5	
Washington			17		
TOTAL	18	15	17	5	22

[77]

76. *New Albany Ledger*, July 17, July 19, 1852. *Washington* Democrat, July 23, 1852. WHE Campaign Speech, 1852, English Papers.

77. *Paoli Eagle*, July 9, 23, 1852. *New Albany Ledger*, July 12, 21, 30, August 5, 1852. The counties were allocated one vote for every 100 votes cast for Cass in 1848 and an additional vote for every fraction over 40. Thirty-nine votes, a simple majority, were necessary for nomination.

Because Morrison and Athon held large chunks of delegates as "favorite sons," the uncommitted votes of Floyd and Orange appeared to be the key to nomination. If both counties voted together, either Albertson or Morrison could win on the first ballot; if they split, it could be a long contest.

The convention assembled at Corydon, Harrison County, on the morning of August 4. According to the *Cannelton Express*, it "was the largest assemblage of the kind ever held in the State." While such hyperbole was commonplace for the time, the rather large number of candidates, the lack of an incumbent, the closeness of the contest, and the high hopes of the Party probably brought out more Democrats than usual. On the first ballot, it was clear that the contest would not be over quickly:

COUNTY	ALBERTSON	ATHON	MORRISON	ENGLISH
Clark		15		
Crawford	4			
Floyd				12
Harrison	11			
Orange	7	3		
Perry	3			
Scott				5
Washington			17	
TOTAL	25	18	17	17

78

By picking up the bulk of the Orange County delegation, Albertson had taken a nice lead, but the real coup was the vote of Floyd. Why the county went solidly for English is not entirely clear, but back when English was principal secretary of the Constitutional Convention, it may be remembered that he chose the *New Albany Ledger* over the *Indiana Sentinel* to publish the 55,000 copies of the Constitution. The leading political manipulator of New Albany was Phineas Kent, the co-editor of the paper. Kent and his partner, John B. Norman, may have

---

78. *Cannelton Express*, August 21, 1852. *New Albany Ledger*, August 5, 1852. *Salem Democrat*, August 13, 1852. For the concerted action among English and many New Albany Democrats see the rest of the chapter. English made New Albany his first general campaign stop, and spoke to the Democratic Club of Floyd even though "suffering under [the ubiquitous] severe indisposition." *New Albany Ledger*, August 6, 1852.

worked to pay English back, and both of them would heretofore turn out to be his very loyal supporters and political confidants. Their alliance may, indeed, have begun with the favor English granted them a year and a half earlier.

Only slight movement occurred on the second ballot, but it was in a direction significant enough to determine the eventual outcome. While Athon and Morison held fast, two Orange County votes slipped away from Albertson and into English's column. The vote now stood as follows: Albertson 23, English 19, Athon 18, and Morrison 17. Although Albertson still led the vote, he was declining, and English had now proven his ability to pull in Democrats from three counties. It was at this point that whatever deal English made in Salem came to bear fruit, for, on the next ballot, Morrison released his delegates and evidently instructed them to go for Scott County's favorite. The third ballot thus stood as follows:

COUNTY	ALBERTSON	ATHON	MORRISON	ENGLISH
Clark		15		
Crawford	4			
Floyd				12
Harrison	11			
Orange	5	3		2
Perry	3			
Scott				5
Washington				17
TOTAL	23	18	0	36

79

Morrison had served in the Indiana House with Elisha English during the 1839–1840 term, but his withdrawal here in favor of William was probably caused more by the son's competence than the father's influence. Having also been a member of the Constitutional Convention, the young principal secretary may well have favorably impressed Morrison; he would have at least gotten to know English well. It is also possible that Morrison knew English much earlier, when the latter was a young boy, for the older man was principal of the Salem grammar

---

79. *New Albany Ledger*, August 5, 1852. The *Washington Democrat*, August 13, 1852, had English's total as 35, but if that's the case one county did not report its full vote.

school in the late 1820s when William may very well have studied there.[80] At any rate, the agreement between English and Morrison, struck at Salem, probably maintained that one of them would withdraw in favor of the other should either show the greater strength. The deal may have been expressly aimed to stop Albertson. Be that as it may, the switch still left English three votes shy of election. He gained them on the fourth ballot—but just barely. Crawford County made the difference, and the final tabulation read as follows:

COUNTY	ALBERTSON	ATHON	ENGLISH
Clark		15	
Crawford			4
Floyd			12
Harrison	11		
Orange	1	7	2
Perry	3		
Scott			5
Washington			17
TOTAL	15	22	40

[81]

On motion, the nomination was made unanimous.

Upon receiving the prize, it was imperative that English thank the Convention. This he did in a short, unrecorded speech. After the delegates concurred in all the national and state resolutions of the Party, they adjourned *sine die* to take to the hustings. While English planned his canvass, the disappointed unsuccessful nominees worked for him and the Party in the hope that success would bring them the much-desired patronage. While Athon and Morrison would remain fixtures in Second District politics for decades to come, Albertson's disappointment was keen. After failing to gain a federal appointment, he moved to Iowa in 1853 and made his livelihood as a dry goods merchant. Relocating repeatedly, he eventually settled in Colorado during the Civil War. In 1863, soon after he lost

---

80. Shepherd, *Biographical Directory*, 284, 119. Woolen, *Eminent Men*, vol. 1, District 6, 95.

81. *New Albany Ledger*, August 5, 1852. *Washington Democrat*, August 13, 1852.

almost all his possessions in a steamboat accident, he died, a forgotten man in southern Indiana.[82]

7.

As soon as the Democrats had selected English as their nominee, the Party's organization took over. Besides the candidate himself, the district Democracy possessed three somewhat-overlapping nerve centers. First, there was the district central committee, formed to handle correspondence, confirm appointments, and direct the campaign in general. The four men who composed the committee at the time represented four different counties; all of them would be correspondents of English's throughout the 1850s. Three of these men, Benjamin P. Douglass, Samuel S. Crowe, and Amos Lovering, were lawyers; the other one, John L. Menaugh, was a venerable Democrat of Washington County who had established the first Democratic newspaper in the district in 1839. Menaugh was currently Washington County treasurer, Douglass the auditor of Harrison County, and Lovering the candidate for Clark's Court of Common Pleas. Crowe was the son of John Finley Crowe, renowned Presbyterian divine and founder of Hanover College. He was a close associate of English's, having moved to Lexington in the early 1840s and having served as Scott County surveyor from 1843 to 1844.[83]

The second locus of the campaign, supplementing the work of the central committee, was the ubiquitous *New Albany Ledger*, tirelessly edited by the transplanted Englishman, John B. Norman. In 1852, the whole district's Democratic press consisted of four newspapers; the Whigs had three, and one claimed to be independent. The *Ledger*, the only Democratic daily in the district, served as both a source of news and comment for the smaller Democratic weeklies as well as a focal point for the dissemination of collected tidbits from the same newspapers. It was at least the second largest daily in the state and, along with the Third District's *Madison Courier*, was the leading Democratic sheet in southern Indiana. Hard upon English's nomination, the *Ledger*, though noting the candidate's youth, strongly endorsed him for having exhibited in his previous positions "talent of the highest order and capacity for legislative business attained by few of much longer

82. *New Albany Ledger*, August 5, 1852. The *Washington Democrat*, August 13, 1852, reported that Athon and Albertson offered their "cordial support." Woolen, *Historical Sketches*, 479, 3. Woolen, *Eminent Men,* vol. 1, District 6, 95. Shepherd, *Biographical Directory,* 284. Nathaniel Albertson to Joe Lane, January 10, 1853, Lane Papers. *New Albany Ledger*, April 20, 1854. *Indiana Biography Series*, vol. 3, 3.

83. *New Albany Ledger*, March 1, 1852. *Washington Democrat,* March 6, 1852. Donald D. McDonald, *A History of Freemasonry in Indiana From 1806 to 1898* (Indianapolis: Grand Lodge, 1898), 90-91. Woolen, *Eminent Men*, vol. 1, District 3, 8. Leander J. Monks, ed., *Courts and Lawyers in Indiana*, Vol. 3 (Indianapolis: Federal Publishing Co., 1916), 998. Shepherd, *Biographical Directory,* 86, 104, 268. Hubbart, *Older Middle West,* 123. *New Albany Ledger*, September 21, 1852.

experience."[84] Henry Comingore's *Paoli American Eagle* and William Williams's *Washington Democrat* also contributed much to the cause, but, without the *Ledger*, the Party would have suffered greatly.

The third center of importance was what could be called the New Albany regency, a set of city politicians whose skillful manipulation allowed them the control of a party whose population was overwhelmingly rural. Foremost among these manipulators were Norman, Kent (who, besides having served in the Constitutional Convention and state legislature, had also been the city's attorney from 1850 to 1851), three-time mayor Alexander S. Burnett, city clerk William W. Tuley, and banker John B. Winstandley. By the liberal use of their money and influence, they attempted to control the tone and course of the campaign and bring out the maximum vote. A special task of theirs was to insure that the significant German population of New Albany be apprised of its right to vote and its duty to vote Democratic. Another function was to integrate the city with the surrounding countryside. Often, one of them would accompany English on his appointments to smooth over any problems in the provinces. Although New Albany, like most Indiana cities, was primarily a Whig stronghold, the energy and wealth of the regency produced a large Democratic vote that radiated into the more favorable hinterland.[85]

Early in the campaign Phineas Kent wrote to Joe Lane that "the canvass in this portion of the state looks more flattering for the Democratic party than for many years," and, throughout the campaign, the Party served English well. The *New Albany Ledger* began by issuing a sketch that described him as "a man of action rather than words," a description intended to appeal to the no-nonsense Indiana farmer. When Norman elaborated by noting that English's "efforts as a debater partake more of the practical common sense than the brilliancy or the flowers of rhetoric," he pushed the point into some inaccuracy. But English was, indeed, relatively modest, if not ingenuous, and these were respected traits on the recent frontier. Realizing these facts, Norman capped his portrayal by claiming that "in personal intercourse he is inclined to be retiring and reserved," which was not an unfair assessment. While the *Ledger* attempted to package English attractively, the candidate pressed his senators for help. Whitcomb responded by wishing English a "pleasant canvass" and a triumph, but, because of poor health, he could do little directly—he would be dead in six weeks. On the other hand,

---

84. Miller, *Indiana Newspaper Bibliography*, 45, 108, 109, 143, 155, 344, 355, 483. *New Albany Ledger*, August 5, 1852. A few years later, Williams, responding to the *Paoli Eagle's* assertion that it was the *Louisville Democrat* that was actually the most popular Party newspaper in southern Indiana, countered that the Kentucky newspaper may have exerted a "greater influence in southern Indiana than any other publisher in or out of the state—excepting the *New Albany Ledger.*" *Washington Democrat*, March 13, 1858.

85. Roger H. Van Bolt, "The Hoosier Politician of the 1840s," *Indiana Magazine of History* 48, no.1 (March, 1952): 30. Shepherd, *Biographical Directory*, 219, 47, 397, 424.

Bright responded heartily and flooded the district with franked speeches and documents. Although unable to promise a personal appearance, he did offer the advice and encouragement of a tested politician: "'Continual dropping will wear a stone'. Adopting this motto and working up to it, I believe you can be elected by a thousand majority."[86]

The prospects for Democratic success were good not only in the Second District but throughout Indiana. This was partly the result of having the very popular Joseph A. Wright at the head of the ticket. Continually stressing the needs of agriculture and the evils that had accrued from profligate Whig schemes, Wright struck the proper chords for Hoosiers. That his merchant opponent, Nicholas McCarty, was reputed to have been a "noteshaver" when earlier employed by the Indianapolis Land Office, only served to augment Wright's appeal. As to organization, the Whigs were far more divided among themselves than their opponents currently were, especially on the "finality" of the 1850 Compromise; they made no reference at all to the slavery question in their state platform. So divided, lacking any real pressing issue, unenamored of their presidential candidate (General Winfield Scott of Mexican War fame) and their rather weak gubernatorial candidate, the Whigs were in no shape to dislodge the Democrats from their entrenched position in the state. James Slack, a former fellow legislator, wrote English from northern Indiana that "our political firmament looks bright. If you ever wished to make something betting on elections, now is your chance I solemnly think."[87]

Sensing certain victory, the *New Albany Ledger* sarcastically advised the Whigs to "stay home and attend to their own business." Refusing to heed this advice, the district Whigs nominated a young lawyer from Clark County, John D. Ferguson, to oppose English. Ferguson, a very talented attorney, had served two terms in the Indiana House before he turned 25. The *Ledger* admitted that he was a "clever gentleman [and] a man of honor." His greatest liability was his health, for he was exceptionally frail and tended to be consumptive. As respectable a candidate as Ferguson was, English and the Democrats were fortunate that the Whigs were

---

86. P.M. Kent to Joe Lane, August 1852, Lane papers. *New Albany Ledger*, August 10, 1852. James Whitcomb to WHE, August 19, 1852, English Papers. Whitcomb's long-term ill health is attested to in a letter from Miriam H. Kenneth to him on July 11, 1850, Whitcomb Papers. Jesse Bright to WHE, August 22, 1852. English Papers.

87. Beeler, "Election of 1852," part 2, 35-37, 52, part 1, 307-308. Charles Zimmerman, "The Origin and Rise of the Republican Party in Indiana from 1854 to 1860," *Indiana Magazine of History* 13, no. 3 (September 1917): 217. James Slack to WHE, July 19, 1852, English Papers. Winfield Scott did not make for a good presidential candidate for the Whigs. Besides insisting on making some of his own campaign speeches, "some of which did great harm," he was personally vain, and southerners were suspicious of his views on slavery. He might have been born in Virginia, but Zachary Taylor, too, had been a southerner—and he turned out to be anything but loyal to his section. In truth, the Whigs' northern wing was both too infected with antislavery sentiment and badly divided between "cotton" and "conscience" members to long exist as a successful national party even in the North. Poore, *Perley's Reminiscences,* 419. Holt, *American Whig Party,* 673 737-738.

unable to nominate their first choice, John S. Davis. One of the richest men of New Albany, Davis had gained rather widespread fame as a criminal lawyer. He had held various governmental positions, from city attorney to state senator (1843–1849), and was presently a New Albany councilman. Having served on the commission that sold stock for the New Albany and Salem railway, he was thoroughly identified with the commercial interests of the Second District. Earlier in the year, he had seriously intended to be the nominee, but "the bad health of [his] wife, and the nature of [his] professional engagements," caused him to bow out in favor of Ferguson.[88]

The congressional contest of 1852 was not the first time Ferguson did battle with the English family. During the legislative session of 1848, as a lawyer for one John Zulauf, Ferguson felt the wrath of the state senator from Jackson and Scott counties, Elisha English. The altercation revolved around the disposition of a large estate of land in Jackson County. The deceased had willed it to his nieces and nephews, and they sold their title to Zulauf. Elisha, noting that the will had bypassed the brother and sister of the testator, claimed that the lands were in escheat, and should thereby devolve to the county. He was able to get the state Senate to pass a bill declaring the title to the lands open, and inviting those who claimed it to sue in Jackson County. Hoping the county would disallow Zulauf's claim, Elisha argued that it should, then, use the lands to subsidize its school fund. But, after much lobbying by Ferguson, the House refused to concur in the Senate's bill, and, instead, repudiated it by passing a substitute that released the land to Zulauf. As Ferguson put it, "English was very enraged at the defeat [and] he came to me and vowed hostility to me hereafter."[89] It was now up to the son to avenge the father.

Although the Democrats had the clear advantage, Ferguson was not without organized support. Foremost among his champions was Milton Gregg, the editor of the Whig *New Albany Tribune*. Gregg had been editing newspapers since 1830. In Ohio, he edited the *Western Statesman*, and, when he moved to Lawrenceburgh, Indiana, he edited the *Palladium* and the *Beacon*. In 1848, he transferred to Madison to engage in manufacturing, but when his establishment was destroyed by fire he returned to publishing and brought out the *Madison Tribune*. He had mixed his publishing career with an active political one, serving twice as Dearborn County sheriff and continually using his newspapers to organize the Whig Party. In 1850, he was elected a Whig delegate to the Constitutional Convention, where

88. *New Albany Ledger* August 11, 1852. Shepherd, *Biographical Directory,* 124. *New Albany Ledger*, May 26, 1856, August 31, 1852. *Paoli Eagle*, September 24, 1852. Woolen, *Eminent Men*, vol. 1, District 3, 9. Shepherd, 94. Hargrave, *Pioneer Railroad*, 17. *New Albany Tribune*, August 18, 1852.

89. John D. Ferguson to John Zulauf, January 27, February 10, February 18, 1848, Zulauf Papers, Indiana Historical Society, Indianapolis. *Indiana Biography Series*, vol. 22, 9. John Zulauf later became president of the Jeffersonville Railroad. *New Albany Ledger*, May 22, 1855.

he apparently voted for English as principal secretary (see p.49), and, for the next two years, he promoted Winfield Scott for the presidency. As Madison was not large enough to support two Whig newspapers (the *Banner* being the other), he agreed, in 1852, to suspend publication and move his equipment to New Albany. Within a few days, he bought out the city's *Bulletin* and merged it with his own presses to begin the publication of the *New Albany Tribune*, the *Ledger's* great rival.[90]

For the next seven years, Gregg and Norman would do daily battle for the allegiance of New Albany and the Second District. In their rivalry, Gregg was handicapped by abolitionist sentiment in both the state Whig and later state Republican Parties, but the *Tribune* gave the *Ledger* all it could handle. The congressional race of 1852 was the first contest in which the two grappled, and Gregg indicated his partisanship early when he labeled the Democratic congressional gathering the "Locofoco Convention," and English the "Locofoco candidate." One week later, he beseeched the Whigs to take advantage of what he believed was a favorable redistricting, which he claimed reduced the Democratic majority from 1,000 to 536. "This advantage," he wrote, "together with the weakness and bitterness of the Democratic nominee, will insure success if we but do our duty."[91]

As the above quote suggests, the campaign did not revolve around substantive issues. The *Tribune's* basic strategy was to attack English for want of character. The "bitterness" to which Gregg referred concerned English's unwarranted personal attacks on Winfield Scott. Most notably, Gregg maintained that English had called Scott a coward. And Gregg also accused the Democratic nominee of falsely charging that the General "had embezzled funds belonging to his soldiers" during the Mexican War. The *Tribune* argued that English assailed Scott as part of a venal and unpatriotic strategy to prove that Franklin Pierce was a better general, even claiming that English went so far as to berate the Whig commander for signing a premature armistice in 1847. In truth, the relative military ability of the two presidential candidates *was* a campaign issue, and it is quite possible that English criticized Scott's military prowess in some form. The *Ledger* denied that English ever called Scott a coward, and Gregg was only able to offer an eyewitness who heard the young Democrat refer to the general as "not a gentleman or at all qualified for President." The *Tribune* concluded that, compared

90. Shepherd, *Biographical Directory*, 152. Hill, *Ohio Falls Cities*, 181. *New Albany Ledger*, January 5, 1859. Miller, *Indiana Newspaper*, 200, 107.

91. Shepherd, *Biographical Directory*, 152. *New Albany Tribune*, August 5, 13, 1852. The term "locofoco" generally referred to the extreme *laissez-faire*, anti-banking interest, hard-money-men faction of the Democratic Party. Their perceived extremism led Whigs for a time to try to tar the whole Democratic Party by using this title as synonymous with all Democrats.

to Ferguson, who "bore the unmistakable stamp of a gentleman," English was a "blackguard."[92]

The most compelling conflict of the canvass concerned an aspect of English's performance as principal secretary of the Constitutional Convention, specifically his duties after the Convention adjourned. As earlier noted, English had been ordered by the delegates to remain at Indianapolis to superintend the printing and binding of the journals and debates of the convention. For this service, he received his four dollars per diem. He remained at the capital until the printing was completed on June 19, 1851, charging the state 129 days of service, or $516. While English was campaigning for the state legislature later that year, Gregg, from Madison, began to accuse him of cheating the state out of most of that money. He argued that only "three or four days" were required to transcribe completely the journals and debates, and that English had little to do with the subsequent printing. Gregg also charged that it was improper for English to collect any pay for Sundays. These charges were generally ignored when made, but, in April 1852, after English became Indiana House speaker, Gregg reprinted them and implicated not only English but also the president of the Constitutional Convention, George W. Carr. Upon reading the reprint of these accusations in the *Indianapolis Journal*, Carr responded in the *State Sentinel*. In the course of defending himself, he angrily noted that the completion of the transcribing and printing of the journals and debates could hardly have taken only half a week. Carr called Gregg's statement to that effect "either pitiable ignorance or a reckless disregard for the truth," preferring to believe the latter, because Gregg himself was a member of the Convention. As for English's Sunday pay, Carr not only noted that this was customary but also that Gregg himself had received such compensation, as well as pay for days he traveled home to be with his family.[93]

Despite Carr's reply, Gregg for a third time brought up the charges during the congressional campaign. This time, the primary thrust of his argument was that, although English might be *legally* entitled to the $516, he was *morally* culpable because he, himself, had done none of the work. According to Gregg, the two official copies of the Constitution were enrolled by one W. B. Chase, who received $400 for the task; Chase also transcribed the journals, and the German translation of the Constitution was done not by English but by A. Owen. It was Phineas Kent who took care of the printing of the 55,000 copies of the Constitution, and Austin Brown who did the same for the journals and debates. The *Tribune* further claimed that English did not do any real "superintending":

---

92. *New Albany Tribune*, September 15, 1852. *New Albany Ledger*, July 22, 1852. *New Albany Tribune*, September 25, 1852.

93. *Indianapolis Journal*, April 12, 1852. *New Albany Ledger*, April 24, 1852 (reprint of Carr reply from the *Indiana State Sentinel*).

After the manuscript copy of the journal and the enrolled constitution were deposited in the Secretary of State's office, which took place fifteen days after the adjournment, Mr. English had nothing under heaven to detain him at Indianapolis, but the reading of a few proof sheets. And these Mr. [Austin] Brown tells us were sent to him at Lexington.

Gregg also maligned English for an unnecessary trip to Cincinnati (where Kent was printing the Constitution), costing the state $82.57, and for receiving $200 extra for indexing the journals.[94]

The *Ledger*'s defense of English was mundane and legalistic: the convention had ordered him to remain at Indianapolis, and it was his responsibility to insure that all the aforementioned tasks were properly completed. Although Norman was correct that English, indeed, had the legal authority to collect from the state, clearly his labor was far from onerous. By peeking behind the façade of the Convention's resolution, Gregg had caught this truth and embarrassed the candidate. The *Ledger* contained the damage by ridiculing Gregg's newfound role as censor. It proved that the *Tribune* editor, while a delegate to the Constitutional Convention, had charged the state for five weeks of service while he remained at home in Madison. Additionally, Norman reprinted letters to the *Sentinel* from Austin Brown, state auditor E.W.H. Ellis, and the chairman of the Convention's Committee on Accounts, J.P. Chapman, defending English and ridiculing Gregg.[95] In the end, English may have been somewhat tarred by the whole imbroglio, but he had previously no reputation for public dishonesty, so Gregg's rather petulant charges most likely cost him few votes.

Counterattacking, the *Ledger* attempted to impeach the morality of the Whig candidate. It claimed that Ferguson had received $150 from the recent legislature for a task not nearly worth that much. The ever-wily Gregg, doing a bit of research, used this charge against Ferguson to implicate English. Pointing to the Legislative Journal, he showed that English had voted for the resolution allowing Ferguson the money. The *Ledger* countered that English voted against the allowance in the Committee of the Whole and only acquiesced in it as part of a full appropriations bill. Each newspaper produced affidavits supporting its side of the story. The *Tribune* printed the written evidence of the resolution's sponsor, Andrew J. Hay, who stated that he "did not recollect any opposition was made to it either in the House or when the bill was under consideration in the Committee of the Whole." The *Ledger* countered with representative Thomas W. Gibson and printed his response to a letter from English requesting him to state whether English "had not, during the pending of the specific appropriation bill, expressed

94. *New Albany Tribune*, August 31, 4, 16, 1852.

95. *New Albany Ledger*, August 28, 30, September 1, 1852.

[himself to Gibson] as opposed to the allowance of the $150 appropriation to Mr. Ferguson." Gibson dutifully replied, "I remember your expressing to me your disapprobation of that item at the time." The *Tribune*, however, had the last word. It quite correctly noted that Gibson's letter failed to state that English had actually *voted* against the measure, and Gregg cleverly argued that Gibson's testimony only imperiled English's character further by illustrating that "he had not the moral firmness to offer any opposition [despite] believing the allowance *wrong* in itself." Such was the stuff of this campaign.[96]

In truth, more substantial issues were not completely ignored. Of the two candidates, it appears that Ferguson, the underdog, was more interested in promoting them. During the joint canvass he consistently argued for two traditional Whig proposals: a protective tariff and federal appropriations to improve Ohio River shipping. Piling on, the *Tribune* cavalierly argued English was the "avowed enemy" of improving the river. Ignoring most charges made against him and, in general, any specific issues, English, instead, concentrated on scurrilously attacking the Whig Party as a whole. At every stop, he tried to identify it with the Federalists, claiming that they obtained power by "false pretenses, and when in power they betrayed their constituents." He repeatedly maintained that the Whigs had never sponsored one measure that promoted the nation's prosperity. Raised as a dyed-in-the-wool Democrat, English no doubt believed these charges, but neither of them was weighted with specifics. When he labeled Winfield Scott an "aristocrat," he betrayed his deep-seated belief that the Democrats were the Party of "the people" and the Whigs of the rich and well born, a perhaps ironic position for him to take.[97]

For its part, the *Ledger* accused Ferguson of refusing to support proper measures to relieve the state of its continuing indebtedness. But Norman's attack was mild, and, in general, it is hard to disagree with one Indiana historian's assessment that, in this campaign, "the politicians fought over the carrion of extinct political questions. Office was the real issue, and its cause was championed by Whigs and Democrats alike." The *Indiana Weekly Express*, in Perry County, noted the same phenomenon:

[In the 1840s] the issues dividing the two political parties were enveloped in no cloud of doubt. The Tariff, National Bank, Distribution of

---

96. *New Albany Ledger,* September 16, 28, October 7, 1852. *New Albany Tribune,* September 16, October 7, 8, 1852.

97. *New Albany Ledger,* July 31, 1852. *Paoli Eagle,* September 17, 1852. *New Albany Tribune,* October 12, 1852. *Washington Democrat* in English Scrapbook, 37. *New Albany Tribune,* October 8, 1852. As Joel Silbey makes clear in his *The American Political Nation, 1838-1893* (Stanford, California: Stanford University Press, 1991), 94-97, English's charges against the Whig Party were made across the nation by Democrats during the 1840s and early 1850s.

the Proceeds of Public Lands, &c., were great dividing questions. Now, these questions in the progress of events, seem to be entirely done away with, and it would require a microscopic vision, not possessed by even the keenest sighted political observer, to ascertain what the differences between the Democratic and Whig parties really were.

Ferguson's occasional criticism of the naturalization laws may be interpreted as an indication of a possibly new divisive issue, but an examination of the *New Albany Tribune*'s list of "Whig Principles" two years later illustrates that the two parties had achieved a great measure of convergence on their traditional differences. On expenditures, Gregg listed "an economical administration of the general government"; on the tariff, he promoted a "revenue one with suitable discrimination in favor of American industry"; concerning the 1850 Compromise, he claimed Whigs adhered to "all compacts and compromises made by Congress, having as their object the adjustment of existing differences between the states." The Bank of the Unites States was not even on the list, and Midwestern Democrats would agree with Gregg's call for "just and liberal" appropriations "for the improvement of our rivers and harbors." As the *Cincinnati Gazette* argued in the summer of 1853, there was "but little difference between Democrats and Whigs," the latter "having abandoned all the means which they formerly so zealously advanced."[98]

On the issue that would eventually tear the nation asunder, both parties were studiously silent. The Whig gubernatorial candidate, Nicholas McCarty, did mention that he disapproved of particulars of the fugitive slave law, but he did not advocate its repeal, declaring that it should first have a "fair trial." The Whig state convention had refused to resolve on the 1850 Compromise one way or another. Some Whigs supported "finality," others hedged, but only the free-soilers harshly criticized the Compromise. In the single reference to slavery in the Second District, the *Tribune* attempted to distance itself from Conscience Whigs by adversely commenting that Van Buren's support for the Democratic presidential nominee made Pierce an abolitionist. The *Ledger* did not deign to respond.[99] Until the Kansas-Nebraska Act, the Second District Whigs were just as disgusted with anti-slavery rhetoric as the Second District Democrats. Only the lure of political advantage would change that.

The joint canvass in the district lasted from the end of August to Election Day in early October, about six weeks. Despite one newspaper's conclusion that

---

98. *New Albany Ledger*, September 7, 1852. Beeler, *(part 2)*, 51. *Indiana Weekly Express*, September 11, 1852. *New Albany Ledger*, August 31, 1851. New *Albany Tribune*, September 12, 1854. *Cincinnati Gazette* quote in *New Albany Ledger*, June 20, 1853. The classic work noting the "convergence" of Whigs and Democrats by the early 1850s is Michael Holt, *The Political Crisis of the 1850s*, esp. chapter 5.

99. Beeler, "The Election of 1852" (part 1), 307-308. *Indianapolis Weekly Journal*, March 16, 1852. *New Albany Tribune*, September 24, 1852.

the two candidates' stump speaking "was productive of far more harm than good" and "unmistakable humbug" ("[t]he passions are inflamed and one neighbor is arraigned against the other"), in general, English spoke forcefully, and Ferguson acquitted himself well through his gentlemanly behavior and clear illustration of his competence. English made his last speech a sole effort before the citizens of Scott County. He, then, retired to Lexington to await the outcome. One year earlier, the counties that, in 1852, would compose the new Second District gave the Democratic congressional candidate 53.1 percent of the vote. In 1852, English had the added advantage of Joseph Wright literally at the head of the Indiana Democratic Party ballot. If a citizen wished to vote for Wright and not English, he had to cross English's name out before he handed in the Democratic printed ballot. Strict party voting was common, for, to do so, all one had to do was "cast" the Democratic ticket unedited. Because the ballots were shaded a different color depending upon the party, intimidation was clearly possible. Democrats often accused Whigs of physically threatening farmers; Whigs countered that Democrats illegally brought scores of transient Irish railroad workers to the polls.[100] Election Day was rough business.

As the returns were compiled, it quickly became clear that the Democrats had achieved a great victory throughout the state and nation. Nationally, Franklin Pierce defeated General Scott for president by a 7 percent popular vote margin, 51 to 44, and carried 27 of the 31 states, including Indiana by 8 percentage points. Wright was reelected by the largest margin ever given an Indiana gubernatorial candidate up to that time; he received over 56 percent of the vote, a plurality of 20,000. Only one Indiana Whig was elected to Congress and that was incumbent Samuel Parker, who revolved his campaign around his constant support of the Compromise of 1850. In the other 10 congressional districts the Democrats swept into power—none of them received less than 52.8 percent of the vote. As for English, he defeated Ferguson by over 1,500 votes (far more than even Jesse Bright had predicted), improving on the Democratic tally of 1851 by 2 percent. Floyd County, which had trickled into Dunham's column in 1851, broke the dikes for English a year later. Even in normally Whig New Albany, English outpolled Ferguson by 112 votes. Only in Clark County did the Democrats suffer any significant loss from the previous year, and that can clearly be traced to the fact that Ferguson, born in Jeffersonville, was very popular there. Outside of New Albany no decent-sized town supported English, so his victory depended upon

---

100. *Indiana Weekly Express*, September 11, 1852. *New Albany Tribune*, October 12, 1852. *New Albany Ledger*, August 31, 1852. Riker, *Election Returns*, 122-123. George Julian noted how Samuel Parker had completely flipped on his anti-slavery positions of 1849 to get reelected, *Political Recollections, 117*. Howe, *Political Culture of Whigs*, 14.

the great vote of the surrounding countryside. His final full-district proportion was 55 percent.[101]

As great as English's victory was in the district, Wright's was even greater. He outpolled the congressman-elect in every county and wound up with a remarkable 57.5 percent of the district's vote. Both Wright's popularity and Ferguson's respectability probably accounted for this unfavorable comparison as far as English was concerned. In truth, English's victory was more for party than for himself. Over the course of some years, Indiana had effectively become a safely Democratic state.[102] The opposition would need to find new issues and new personalities if it hoped to again become competitive. New issues would indeed shortly arise, morphing the Whigs into a different organized coalition and causing English and Indiana Democrats to look back to 1852 as their high point of dominance. In the meantime, the Whigs could always depend upon Democratic infighting to give them an opening.

8.

As earlier noted, congressmen elected in the fall of 1852 did not take their seats until the new Congress, the 33rd, began its proceedings in December 1853. In the intervening time, English was kept politically busy, navigating the waters of persistent factionalism in the Indiana Democracy, attending to party patronage requests, and shoring up his personal political support. The primary factional dispute soon after his election concerned Indiana's choice of a senator to replace the departed James Whitcomb, who left this life in October 1852 with two years remaining on his term. Both the Wright and Bright factions agreed that, because Jesse Bright came from the southern part of the state, the replacement for Whitcomb should come from the northern part. As usual, Bright wished to secure a loyal acolyte for the post. He finally decided on Graham Fitch, a professor of medicine and veteran Democrat from Logansport. Fitch had just completed two terms in Congress where he had neatly trimmed his free-soil sails, becoming a loyal supporter both of the 1850 Compromise measures and the person of Jesse Bright. He was also an intimate friend of Lewis Cass, another reason for Bright to support him. The Wright forces opposed Fitch, with many supporting John Pettit, who, as an admirer of Stephen Douglas, was anathema to Bright. In order to get Fitch selected, Bright depended upon English among others. He wrote the newly elected congressman that Fitch was "a man of superior talents" and assured

---

101. Crane, *"Joseph A. Wright,"* 152. Robert J. Pitchell, *Indiana Votes* (Bloomington: Bureau of Government Research, 1960) 6-7. English Scrapbook, 39. Dubin, *Congressional Elections,* 164. The recent influx of German immigrants may have accounted for the turnaround in Perry County. Thomas de la Hunt, *Perry County: A History* (Indianapolis: W. K. Stewart Co., 1916), 187.

102. Pitchell, *Indiana Votes*, 6-7.

English that he was "your friend and my friend." From Washington, Bright urged English to "give this matter your attention," hoping the congressman-elect would go to Indianapolis to help influence the Democratic legislative caucus.[103]

Fitch directly solicited English's help on his own behalf. Writing to English in late November, Fitch argued that "your position in our party enables you to wield an influence second to that of few in our State." This was not merely idle flattery. Although no one could dispute English's fundamental loyalty to Jesse Bright, he had also remained on good terms with key Democrats outside the senator's camp. E.W.H. Ellis, late of the *Statesman*, whose free-soil views made him undesirable even to the Wright forces, continued to correspond with English over financial matters. Phineas Kent, whom Bright distrusted for his over-friendliness with some in the Wright camp, was, of course, English's close confidante. The last three *State Sentinel* editors all respected English, and, as he was with Ellis, English was connected to many politicians through speculative transactions and straight moneylending. This is quite possibly what Fitch meant when he referred to English's "influence."[104]

But, when the Democratic legislative caucus met on January 10, Pettit defeated Fitch by almost 10 votes. Bright was not happy. He wrote English that he was "greatly disappointed at the defeat of [their] mutual friend, Doct. Fitch, and if one half of the men for him had done their duty half as well as you and I the result would have been different." English had, indeed, sent Bright a list of those who had betrayed him. Bright warned English to "set your house in order. We are to have a war, but it will be a short one. Such creatures as Jo Wright, Bill Brown [the pro-Wright editor of the *Sentinel*] and their tools cannot prevail…"[105]

In his letter to Bright informing him of the caucus vote, English expressed concern that he may have impaired his position in the Party by so zealously advancing Fitch's cause. Bright assured him that, on the contrary, his behavior no doubt

---

103. Van Bolt, "Indiana in Transition," 155-156. Crane, "Joseph Wright," 227-228. Van der Weele, "Jesse Bright," 119-120. Whitcomb's death was caused by surgery for a kidney-stone ailment. Crane, 226. *Biographical Directory of United States Congress*, 1056. David Turpie, "Typewritten Copy of "Sketches of My Own Time," Indiana State Library, Indianapolis, Indiana. Jesse Bright to WHE, November 21, 1852; Michael Bright to 'Dear Sir,' November 21, 1852, English Papers. Michael Bright offered that "Pettit with all his goodness, is too much identified with the Douglas faction to receive my cordial support. On the other hand, Fitch is a real gentleman—known to be right, and as true as steel." Shepherd, *Biographical Directory*, 313, 127.

104. G.N. Fitch to WHE, November 22, 1852; E.W.H. Ellis to WHE, January 20, 1854, English Papers. *Indiana Statesman*, April 28, 1852. *New Albany Ledger*, December 15, 1852. Thorton Triplett to WHE, May 1852; Samuel B. Morison to WHE, February 9, 1853; E. G. Whitney to WHE, July 6, 1853; Jesse Bright to WHE, November 21, 1852, October 15, 1853, English Papers.

105. Van Bolt, "Indiana in Transition," 155-156. *Indiana State Sentinel*, January 13, 1853. *New Albany Ledger*, January 12, 1853. Jesse Bright to WHE, January 25, 1853, English Papers. Pettit was well aware of Bright's enmity toward him. On the evening of his election, some "warm words passed" between him and Michael Bright during which Pettit informed the senator's brother that he would challenge Jesse for control of the appointing power in Indiana, and sarcastically added that he intended to support his senior senatorial colleague for a position as "minister plenipotentiary to the Guano Islands." Woolen, *Historical Sketches*, 455.

made him more friends because he had advocated the "right" and denounced "the wrong."[106] To Bright, it was very simple: if you were for him, you were in the "right," and, if you were against him, you were in the "wrong." But English took a more balanced view of the factions. He was, after all, in principle drawn to Douglas and in no way shared Bright's antipathy toward the Illinois senator. English's support of Bright was primarily caused by personal loyalty to a respected mentor as well as attendance to his own political advancement. Intraparty infighting, while often necessary, did not suit his temperament. He clearly enjoyed denouncing the Whigs and criticizing what he considered their meager achievements, but his political instincts made it difficult for him to attack other Democrats. In fact, as his career progressed, "harmony" in Party councils was his byword.

Besides the senatorial contest, there was also Indiana's quadrennial push for a Hoosier to be nominated to the president's cabinet. At one point, an English correspondent, believing Jesse Bright's appointment was imminent, counseled English to hurry to Indianapolis to vie as Bright's senatorial replacement. Jesse Bright's law partner, Joseph W. Chapman, in a letter to Joe Lane, listed English as one of the five serious contenders for Bright's possibly vacant seat. But Bright apparently believed that he would be better served by remaining in the Senate, especially in terms of power within Indiana. As he wrote English, "I dismiss the Cabinet from my mind. Nothing could tempt me now to resign my place in the senate, this would be suicidal to both myself *and friends.*" Even if Pierce considered nominating a Hoosier, the persistent factionalism among Indiana Democrats would make any presidential choice poison to the faction that did not receive the appointment. As Norman noted later that spring in the pages of the *New Albany Ledger*, "[A]t home there was an interest hostile to Mr. Bright, who supposed that in the event of a Cabinet appointment, he would use his influence to reward his friends and punish his enemies. They therefore went to work to prevent the appointment." So, no Hoosier entered the Cabinet.[107]

The *Ledger* dismissed any disappointment Indiana might feel about not receiving a Cabinet post by noting that "the principles of the Democratic Party are worth contending for without the incentive of office." But, without the incentive for office, the Democratic Party could hardly survive. During the long interregnum between the end of one Congress (March 1853) and the first session of

---

106. Jesse Bright to WHE, January 25, 1853, English Papers.

107. S.S. Crowe to WHE, February 13, 1853, English Papers. J.P. Chapman to Joe Lane, January 17, 1853, Lane Papers. Van der Weele, "Jesse Bright," 137-138. Jesse Bright to WHE, January 25, 1853, English Papers. Roy Nichols, *Franklin Pierce: Young Hickory of the Granite Hills*, 2nd edition (Philadelphia: University of Pennsylvania Press, 1958), 228, 303. *New Albany Ledger*, April 12, 1853. Michael Bright summed up the situation of Bright going into the cabinet: "In the first place the position will not be offered to him; in the second place I think that it would be inexpedient, under the circumstances, to accept if were offered. He can be of as much service to his friends and more to himself by remaining where he is." M.G. Bright to "Dear Sir," November 21, 1852, English Papers.

the new one (December 1853), English was besieged by applicants for federal appointments. One applicant, requesting assistance in securing a consulship in Europe, wrote emotionally of revisiting "the land of my nativity"; another, seeking a postmastership, reminded English that he "used to nurse you on my knee"; a third wrote that "my son died on the 6th of January and my brother John of Charlestown died on the 11th of January." One applicant refused to stoop to such personal devices—instead, he put his case in unabashed Party terms: "I have been of some service to my party for I have spent the flower of my life in her ranks, and if the victor belongs to the spoils [sic?] I am entitled to no more than I ask."[108]

In two special patronage cases, English carefully sought to exert his influence to his best advantage. One concerned the financial stability of the two most important Democratic newspapers in his congressional district. Four weeks after Pierce's election, the editor of the *Paoli American Eagle*, Henry Comingore, wrote English that his "financially distressed" newspaper would greatly appreciate the coveted contract to publish the nation's laws. Knowing that English would soon be traveling to Washington to oversee patronage matters in general, Comingore asked him to add this request to his list. Had the *New Albany Ledger* made the same request, English would have found himself in a difficult situation. Fortunately, the new co-owner of the *Ledger*, Lucienne D. Matthews, applied for a different contract. Claiming the paper was in great debt, and could not meet its obligations "unless we get some aid from some other source than our office," Matthews petitioned English for the post of mail agent on either a railroad or steamboat line that passed through New Albany. He promised "to relinquish the post to some other one" after the debts were paid. He ended his letter by baldly stating that "should you succeed in getting me the place, you will place us under an obligation to you which shall be discharged whenever the opportunity shall offer." This quid pro quo hardly needed to be mentioned. Within three months, Matthews had gotten the position he desired, and, for the spring of 1853, the *Eagle* was entitled to publish the laws.[109] These two small appointments should not be underestimated. From the moment English stepped into Congress, the *New Albany Ledger* would effectively serve as his political organ, and the *Paoli Eagle*, though less constant, would rally to his standard at very important moments.

The other significant patronage matter concerned the New Albany postmastership. This was the most important appointment in the district, as far as elections were concerned, and English needed to choose a Democrat both loyal and competent. By March, he had decided upon a close friend of the family, Martin

108. *New Albany Ledger*, April 12, 1853. A.D. Gaily to WHE, December 18, 1852; J.G. Read to WHE, February 25, 1853; Elias Long to WHE, February 24, 1853, L.T. Keogatt to WHE, February 12, 1854, English Papers.

109. H. Comingore to WHE, November 29, 1852; L. G. Matthews to WHE, February 1, May 19, 1853, English Papers. *Paoli Eagle*, February 10, 1854.

Ruter, whose cousin owned farmland adjacent to the English estate in Lexington. Ruter was a respected elder New Albany politician, and the choice satisfied Democrats generally. But, before the postmaster-designate could actually take possession of his office, he suddenly died. No sooner had he been laid to rest when a mad scramble occurred to gain his vacant position. At least five Democrats vied for it. Of these five, only three—Alexander S. Burnett, James M. Morrison, and Phineas Kent—stood any possibility of succeeding. Morrison, a member of the New Albany Regency, wrote English directly, stating that his friends proposed he seek the position. The *Ledger's* Lucienne Matthews, however, writing English on the same day, argued that Morrison was unreliable politically—he had not shown any special loyalty to English during the recent campaign, and, at the "first opportunity," Matthews maintained, Morrison would "weaken your influence." Matthews, instead, favored Kent, albeit reluctantly. At least Kent could be relied upon "as your friend against the field." English was inclined to agree. It was Kent who first suggested Ruter, and it was also probably Kent who had much to do with New Albany's recent course in the congressional convention. Moreover, as previously noted, Kent had served in the state legislature, in the Constitutional Convention, and, probably most significantly, as New Albany's city attorney; he had many contacts.[110]

English sent Kent's name to postmaster general James Campbell late in May, but his recommendation did not go unchallenged. Burnett, twice previously postmaster of New Albany, personally journeyed to Washington to present his own credentials. An old Jacksonian, Burnett had run for lieutenant governor twice, served in 1832 as a Jackson elector, and soon after was selected director of New Albany's branch of the state bank. He was regularly chosen the city's mayor (three times) and sheriff (twice), and served as a commissioner of the New Albany and Salem Railroad. Kent feared him as an opponent. He wrote English thrice in the span of four days, apprising him of Burnett's machinations. On May 28, Burnett returned to New Albany and informed his friends that he had failed to dissuade Campbell from making the appointment upon English's recommendation. There was a certain changing of the guard here, for Burnett had apparently been counting on the support of Senator Bright, but Bright recognized the greater future usefulness of the young English than the elderly Burnett. Bright refused to countermand his protégé despite his suspicions concerning Kent.[111]

It is quite possible that Kent offered himself for the position simply to prevent Burnett from getting it, for, in mid-July, he wrote English of his "determination" to resign. He argued that "our future interests" demanded that he take this course.

---

110. P.M. Kent to WHE, March 4, May 19, 1853; James Morrison to WHE, May 19, 1853; L.G. Matthews to WHE, May 19, 1853, English Papers. Shephard, *Biographical Directory*, 218.

111. P.M. Kent to WHE, May 24, 1853. English Papers. Shephard, *Biographical Directory*, 47. Hargrave, *Pioneer Railroad*, 20. P.M. Kent to WHE, May 28, 1853, English Papers.

From subsequent events, it is clear that Kent saw himself as English's principal political confidante, and the public office of postmaster did not leave him enough latitude in the long run to apply his political skills more privately. In his stead, he offered the name of Frank Gwin, a young, affable Democrat whose brother owned the largest newsstand in New Albany. Gwin had worked diligently for English's election, and he could claim the backing not only of Kent, but of the most prominent New Albany Democrat of all, Lieutenant Governor Ashbel Willard. Gwin's popularity was partly a result of his exploits during the Mexican War, when, at 15, he lied about his age in order to volunteer. Later he received a medal for bravery. Upon English's recommendation, Pierce appointed Gwin in late July. Kent later wrote English that Gwin's selection "gives almost universal satisfaction. He is much more popular than his intimate friends ever imagined." Gwin would serve as New Albany's postmaster until he prematurely died in 1861. Always loyal to English and the Democrats, he diligently distributed the campaign material coming from Washington for the full eight years that English would serve in Congress. As Kent remarked later in 1853, "a more propitious appointment could not have been made."[112]

One last example of English's general political and administrative skill should be mentioned. As a western congressman, he was well aware that the regular and efficient handling of the mails was a very important matter. Gwin's appointment was a good one, but there was more to be done. One major problem for the Second District was that it was dependent upon the post office in Louisville, Kentucky. Mail boats along the Ohio were required to drop off their parcels there for distribution into southern Indiana, causing what Hoosiers considered an unnecessary delay. Another problem was the too-infrequent passage of the mails into the interior. When English was elected, mail traveled within the district but twice a week, and direct routes between many towns were unestablished. To the delight of his constituents, English tackled both these problems before the year was out. In April, he announced that he would attempt to get New Albany "on the list of mail landings," thereby reducing its dependence on its Louisville rival. By June, he had succeeded, no doubt assisted by an administration seeking to reduce the influence of Louisville, a Whig city in the midst of a Whig district. Later in the year, when Congress actually convened, he proposed bills to establish two new routes into his district's interior and to increase the flow of mail on other routes already extant.[113]

---

112. PM Kent to WHE, July 11, July 30, August 7, 1853, English Papers. Gwin's Mexican-War story is detailed in *CG, 33-1*, 1990. He was granted 160 acres by congress for his service, thanks to English. *CG, 33-1*, 1995.

113. *Cannelton Express*, April 16, 1853. *New Albany Ledger*, April 22, June 21, 1853. *New Albany Tribune*, December 28, 1853. *Paoli Eagle*, January 13, 1854.

For all these efforts he was praised not only by district Democratic sheets, but by the *Corydon Argus, Washington Sun,* and *New Albany Tribune*—all Whig newspapers. The *Argus,* owned by the very influential Harrison County Whig Thomas C. Slaughter, put it this way:

> We differ widely from Mr. English in general politics, but we never intend to withhold our approbation from any good thing done by a political opponent, and so long as Mr. English conducts himself with the modesty and propriety he has so far done, and exhibits the same industry he has hitherto exhibited, we should take occasion to refer to it with approbation.

The *Cannelton Express,* an independent newspaper in Perry County, early lauded English for his energy, and pronounced him "a working man [who] will render good service."[114] In these months of 1853, few could argue with that assessment. But energy and industry are often foiled by unexpected political events. If English wished to be an effective congressman, he would need to position himself where the political winds would cause him little damage. From the beginning of the first session of his first Congress, he would have to navigate carefully.

9.

Besides the landslide victory of Franklin Pierce the previous November, the Democrats also gained great majorities in both houses of Congress: over two-thirds of the House of Representatives were Democrats and three-fifths of the Senate. The Party's enormous success was, at least in the North, partly the result of its resolutions of 'finality' concerning the Compromise measures of 1850. Even in the South, many Democrats had become disposed to these measures. Yet despite, or perhaps because of, this success, continued factionalism plagued the Democratic Party in both Indiana and nationally. The source of this factionalism was Pierce's patronage policy. In making his federal appointments, the president wished to essentially forgive those Democrats, like the New York Barnburners, who had gone Free Soil four years earlier but had come back to the Party in 1852. Many Democrats who had remained loyal throughout, and, like the New York Hunkers, were less anti-slavery believed Pierce's policy was too "soft" toward the apostates. After all, the bolters may well have cost the Democrats the presidency in 1848. At the least, these 'loyal' Democrats believed that they deserved far more of the spoils than the 'traitors'. But Pierce tried to distribute the patronage impartially,

---

114. *New Albany Tribune,* December 28, 1853. *Corydon Western Argus,* January 24, 1854, in English Scrapbook. Miller, *Newspaper Bibliography,* 355. *Cannelton Express,* April 16, 1853.

thereby enraging some of the Hunkers or "Hardshell" faction along with many southerners.[115]

In the Indiana Democracy, the Bright forces believed in a "hard" policy and the Wrights in the "soft" one. As Pierce's patronage policy often followed the generous "soft" line, it was not surprising that the president worked more through Wright than Bright in its Indiana distribution. This was additionally galling to Bright because the Wright faction held a favorable attitude of Stephen Douglas, Bright's great rival for the patronage of the Northwest as a whole. In truth, Douglas, too, was left relatively unconsulted by Pierce over patronage matters; indeed, Pierce's forgiving and rather balanced appointment policy, though conceived to bring harmony to the Party, actually had the opposite effect. For example, when he offered the lucrative post of collector of the port of New York to leading Hunker Daniel Dickinson, he did so with strings attached. Should Dickinson accept the position, he was required to do so with the understanding that all New York factions would be equally represented in Dickinson's own appointments. Dickinson declined under this condition. When Pierce then went ahead and nominated the then-leading Barnburner of New York, John A. Dix, as assistant treasurer of New York City, six Democratic senators, composed of five southerners and Jesse Bright, voted against the nomination to make a point. And this was in the first month of Pierce's presidency![116]

When the 33rd Congress convened in December 1853, English's initial month as a sitting congressman, the first order of business was the election of a speaker. In Party caucus a few days earlier, House Democrats were presented

115. In the House there were 157 Democrats, 70 Whigs, 5 Free-soilers, and 1 Independent. Dubin, *Congressional Elections*, 168; in the Senate there were 38 Democrats, 22 Whigs, and 2 Free-soilers. https:// www. **senate.gov**/history/partydiv.html. The factionalism arising out of the patronage situation during Pierce's presidency is nicely summarized in Michael F. Holt, *Franklin Pierce* (New York: Henry Holt and Co., 2010), 66-70. See also chapters 1 and 2 in Peter A. Wallner, *Franklin Pierce: Martyr for the Union* (Concord, New Hampshire: Plainswede Publishing, 2007). Also see Roy Nichols, *Franklin Pierce*, chapter 36. A New Hampshire innkeeper, upon being informed that Pierce had won the Democratic presidential nomination in 1852 remarked that "he's a pretty considerable fellow . . . But come to spread him out over the whole country, I'm afraid he'll be dreadfully thin in some places." Poore, *Perley's Reminiscences*, 421.

116. Roger van Bolt, "Fusion Out of Confusion, "*Indiana Magazine of History*, no. 4 (December 1953), 374. Robert W. Johannsen, *Stephen A. Douglas* (New York: Oxford University Press, 1973), 375-381. Van der Weele, "Jesse Bright," 139. Nichols, *Franklin Pierce*, 254-255. Holt, *Franklin Pierce*, 69-70. The saga of John A. Dix is quite complicated. According to Dix's son, soon after the election Pierce had actually offered his father the position of secretary of state, but after Dix accepted the offer, once it got out, the Hardshell northern Democrats and many southerners so vociferously protested it that Pierce had to abashedly withdraw the offer. The State position then went to William Marcy, a rather softshell Hunker. To atone for having to take back his offer to Dix, Pierce then offered him the French mission, which Dix again accepted. Anticipating possible problems with this appointment, the president appointed Dix temporarily to the Treasury position with the knowledge that he would resign if the French appointment went through. But, as anticipated, the French appointment hit a snag with the same aforementioned political opponents, and in pique and frustration Dix resigned the Treasury position in late August. Morgan A. Dix, *Memoirs of John Adams Dix, vol. 1* (New York: Harpers and Brothers, 1883), 271-274.

with a choice of three men: David Disney of Ohio, a confidante of Lewis Cass and the Hunker favorite, James L. Orr, a relatively moderate pro-Compromise South Carolinian (from a rather immoderate southern state) who was generally considered the administration's favorite, and Linn Boyd of Kentucky, the previous speaker. English had written Boyd earlier in August to discover whether the Kentucky congressman intended once again to seek the speakership. Boyd responded that he was indeed interested, but confessed that he had "no means of judging the temper of the members-elect" toward him. He then noted that he left it to his "friends" to discover such disposition, "no one of whom I hope will ever have cause to regret any service they may feel disposed to render me." What "service" English may have performed for Boyd is unknown, but, when the Democratic caucus took its first vote for speaker, English was one of only two Indiana Democrats to go for him. This vote was indicative of English's penchant for compromise, Party harmony, and, in truth, avoiding a difficult decision. One might say it indicated his political prescience as well, for Boyd was selected by a majority of Democrats on the second ballot of the Party caucus. Easily elected speaker, thus, in the Democratically controlled House, Boyd rewarded English by placing him on the ultra-important Committee on Territories. Except for Cyrus Dunham, all other Democratic Hoosiers were given insignificant committee appointments.[117]

At the beginning of the congressional session, the "Hunker" opposition to Pierce's "soft" patronage policy was fully illustrated in the battle over congressional printer. Robert Armstrong, publisher of the *Washington Union*, and favorite of president Pierce, had held the post in the last Congress. He clearly wished to be reselected for so lucrative an office. But his editor, Alfred O. P. Nicholson (of Cass's Nicholson Letter fame), had made enemies among the "hards" by strongly defending Pierce's policy of treating the "softs" as equal to them. Consequently, when the House voted for printer, 20 Democrats bolted from Armstrong and voted for Beverley Tucker, editor of the recently established *Washington Sentinel*. These dissenters were composed of the New York Hunkers and southern hard pro-slavery men. Three other Democratic congressmen also did not vote for Armstrong, among them William English, who cast the sole vote for John G. Rives of a third newspaper, the *Washington Globe*. He was the only Hoosier Democrat to defect from the administration's preference for Armstrong.[118]

---

117. *New York Tribune*, December 1, 2, 3, 1853. R.S. Sproule to WHE, September 19, 1853, English Papers. Nichols, *Democratic Machine*, 90-91. Nichols, *Franklin Pierce*, 307. Linn Boyd to WHE, August 21, 1853, Boyd Papers, Miscellaneous Manuscripts, The Filson Club, Louisville, Kentucky. Wendell Holmes Stephenson, *The Political Career of James H. Lane* (Topeka: Kansas State Printing Office, 1930), 34-35. *New Albany Ledger*, December 5, 9, 1853. *New Albany Tribune*, December 5, 1853. *CG, 33-1*, 33-34.

118. Nichols, *Franklin Pierce*, 315. L.G. Matthews to WHE, December 26, 1853. *New Albany Ledger*, January 16, 1854, December 17, 1853. *CG, 33-1*, 15. *New Albany Ledger*, December 29, 1853.

English's defection, combined with the 22 other Democrats who voted for Tucker, did not deny Armstrong the House's selection as printer; the Democrats, after all, had an 85-vote majority. But the rationale for his vote was revealed nine days later, when the Senate expressed its own choice for printer. In that body, Jesse Bright led nine senate Democrats, in league with almost all the Whigs, to elect Tucker over Armstrong by a healthy margin. As Joe Lane explained the "bolting" Democrats' vote, they "have on all occasions supported democratic principle, but [they] are unwilling to see the democratic party *abolitionized*…and will not go for the confirmation of unsound men." Bright's course in the matter made English's refusal to vote for Armstrong in the House all too clear. The *New Albany Tribune* baldly accused "this protégé of Bright's" of more loyalty to the senator than to the administration. The *Washington Star* took the same line more circumspectly:

> We can have no idea that Mr. English, of Indiana, would have voted against General Armstrong had he supposed his vote for that gentleman to have been necessary for his election. Mr. E. is very young in the Hall, and is supposed to council with a more experienced gentleman, to whose (*sub rosa*) advice the political world attribute the irresponsible attack made on individual members of the administration in Indiana Democratic papers. It is thought that with Mr. English 'the spirit is willing, but the flesh is weak, —that he is disposed to act in full communion with the Democracy during the present session, and yet hesitates to incur the displeasure of his friend by doing so.[119]

As the *Star* more than merely implied, English was essentially caught between his loyalty to Bright and his loyalty to the Democratic administration. Knowing Armstrong did not need his vote, and wishing to maintain some independence from Bright, he solved his dilemma by giving neither Armstrong nor Tucker his support. Charitably, one might say his vote illustrated not fear of confrontation but commitment to compromise and Party harmony. English's vote for Rives allowed the *Ledger* to defend his course by arguing that "some gentlemen not caring to identify themselves in the quarrel existing between the 'Union' and the 'Sentinel,' the organs of the two sections into which the Democracy are, to some extent, unfortunately divided, voted for neither of the leading candidates." Norman hailed Rives as "a man of high character, not mixed up with the 'hard' and 'soft' divisions, and perhaps better prepared to execute the public printing with neatness [!] and dispatch than any of them." By explaining the matter in this fashion, the *New Albany Ledger* equated the presidency with mere party faction, and,

---

119. *CG, 33-1,* 15. Van der Weele, "Jesse Bright," 138-39. Nichols, *Franklin Pierce,* 315-316. Wallner, *Franklin Pierce,* 87. Joe Lane to Nesmith, December 13, 1853, Lane Papers. *New Albany Tribune,* December 16, 1853. *Washington Star* in *English Scrapbook,* 48.

according to the explanation, so did English. Such a neutral attitude toward the administration could hardly be interpreted as loyal Democracy, prompting the *Ledger* to add that the votes against Armstrong were also to protest his "premature" selection outside caucus. The *Washington Star*, noting that caucus selection on the printing was unorthodox, questioned the *Ledger's* argument and dismissed it with the comment "so the political world wags."[120]

Because John Pettit, Indiana's other senator, remained loyal to Armstrong (and thus to Pierce), English and Bright stood alone in Hoosier opposition. But this breakdown did not mean that all the Indiana congressmen favored Wright over Bright. While only English could be classified as definitely in the Bright camp, only congressman Jim (not "Joe") Lane was probably considered more of a Wright man, even though he represented a district that bordered on Bright's. The other eight Democratic representatives maintained a general degree of independence, yet they shaded their allegiances somewhat along the lines of geography. The four Hoosiers from the northern districts, Norman Eddy, Ebenezer Chamberlain, Andrew J. Harlan, Daniel Mace, had all exhibited, to some degree, free soil proclivities, and they were not considered loyal to Bright in a showdown. On the other hand, Dunham, Smith Miller, and Thomas A. Hendricks, were all, at this point, more allied with Bright than Wright. John G. Davis, though by no means unfriendly to Bright, was a longtime friend of the governor. As a group, the 10 Democrats were well experienced in politics.[121]

Most interesting among them was Jim Lane, a Mexican War veteran noted both for his courage and violent temper. During the war, as colonel of Indiana's Third Regiment, he nearly got into a duel with his immediate superior, General *Joseph* Lane. Singled out for bravery at Buena Vista, he returned to Indiana a great hero and was put on the ticket with Joseph Wright in 1849. Many Democrats distrusted him—Joseph Chapman called him "dishonorable," and John L. Robinson, a Bright politico from southern Indiana, labeled Lane the "prince of scoundrels." Yet, he proved himself popular with the people, whether they be troops in Mexico, voters in Indiana, or, later, vigilantes in Kansas.[122]

As the previous lieutenant governor to Joseph Wright, Lane appeared to favor the governor over the senator. Any antipathy between Bright and Lane was markedly enhanced by a curious episode in 1853. During the period between Franklin Pierce's election and his inauguration as president, word got out that Pierce intended to appoint Jefferson Davis as secretary of war. Lane opposed this nomination because during the Mexican War (see p. 40, fn 66) General Taylor

120. *New Albany Ledger*, December 17, 1853. *Washington Star*, in *English Scrapbook*, 48.

121. *New Albany Ledger*, December 15, 1853. *CG, 33-1*, 15. Crane, "Joseph Wright," 146.

122. Stephenson, *James H. Lane*, 28-33. For Lane's volatility in this period, see Spurgeon, *Man of Douglas Man of Lincoln*, 21, 22-24. J.P. Chapman to Joe lane, January 17, 1853, Joseph Lane Papers. J.L. Robinson to WHE, February 28, 1854, English Papers.

had unfairly disparaged Indiana troops at the battle of Buena Vista and had instead given Davis (Taylor's own son-in-law) undeserved praise for stiffening the Hoosiers' backs. Davis never corrected this false impression that essentially dishonored the Indiana boys. Lane and other Indiana Democrats thus signed a petition of protest concerning Davis's rumored appointment and sent it to Senator Bright to show to the president-elect. But Bright not only failed to forward the petition to Pierce, it was discovered later that he surreptitiously showed it to Davis instead, enraging Lane. From then on, Lane was particularly an enemy of Bright's, and, to some degree, by extension, of the senator's political friends.[123]

As an example of Lane's antipathy toward the coterie of Bright and his loyalists, he was the only Hoosier congressman to oppose the selection of the *New Albany Ledger* to publish the federal laws in Indiana once the congressional session began. Bright had written secretary of state William Marcy requesting that the *Ledger* be given the contract along with any Wright sheet. English, too, of course, pushed the *Ledger's* claim. Despite Lane's opposition (and also Senator Pettit's), the *Ledger* still prevailed. But Norman clearly understood Lane's anti-Bright attitude when he later admitted that he "had no claims upon Lane, and had no other expectation than that he would resist me to the 'bitter end.'" Of Pettit's opposition Norman was more surprised, but such was the nature of politics in Indiana's factionalized Democracy. Lane also forcefully opposed the appointment of John L. Robinson as United States marshal for the state. Robinson had become a real henchman for Bright, and the only way Bright was able to get Robinson appointed was as a tradeoff for his promise not to block the administration's selection of a "soft" for the post of New York City collector. Lane had tried to delay Robinson's confirmation by asking Pierce for all the documents connected with it. In the end, he again failed, but Robinson's interest was clearly piqued when he discovered that, outside of English, no other Indiana Democrat protested Lane's tactics.[124]

Such was the state of the Democracy both in Indiana and nationally in the first months of the 33rd Congress. The *Ledger* might deny that any "unfriendly relations exist between the President and any member of the Indiana delegation of either branch of Congress," and may coo that "harmony" prevailed in the Party, but others knew better. A former Hoosier, then living in Kentucky, warned English of the dangers inherent in intraparty divisions. He advised the first-term congressman "to keep out of it if possible," and he lamented the fact that "the Democratic Party should split to pieces upon a question of the distribution of the

123. Stephenson, *James H. Lane*, 35.

124. Jesse Bright to W.L. Marcy, January 23, 1854, Jesse D. Bright Papers, Lilly Library, Bloomington, Indiana. J.B. Norman to WHE, February 8, 1854; J.L. Robinson to WHE, February 26, 1854, English papers. *New Albany Ledger*, January 18, April 10, 1854.

offices among a set of political gamblers."[125] Lacking any effective opposition from the Whigs, the Democratic Party had raised internal bickering to the first level of concern. Shortly, Stephen Douglas would offer a piece of congressional legislation that would change the nature of both intraparty and interparty squabbling for the rest of the decade. Much more consequential than petty patronage matters, the Kansas-Nebraska bill would require each Democrat to ponder for himself the nature of the Democratic Party. William English would be no exception.

125. *New Albany Ledger*, January 16, 1854, December 17, 1853. T. W. Gibson to WHE, January 6, 1854, English Papers.

CHAPTER THREE

The Democratic Creed

The Washington correspondent of the *New York Tribune*, writing three months into the 33rd Congress, reported that "the prevailing characteristic of a congressional life are nightly conviviality and prolonged revelry, excessive eating and drinking, followed by gross immoralities." No doubt, some representatives lived up to this description, but most of them could hardly burn their candles so brightly in the evening without adversely affecting the performance of their duties on the morrow. One morning, after a night of relatively tepid socializing (during which he was "compelled to drink some liquor") English awoke with a bitter headache. Because it was a Sunday, he was able to suffer his "just punishment" with little interference, but, had it been most any other day, he would have had little time to ail and much less time to ruminate upon it. An effective congressman had to rise and breakfast shortly after dawn, tend to his correspondence and reading before his committee met at 10 o'clock, spend the rest of the day in and around the House overseeing pet projects, and, after dinner, do more than a little bit of lobbying with the Department functionaries. Moreover, back at his quarters late at night, he often had to answer letters that he had failed to reach earlier. As representative Schuyler Colfax later complained, "business at the Depts. is ceaseless, correspondence is a torrent, committee labor is bothersome, [yet] congressional duties is all that one gets credit for."[1]

Because they were at the seat of power, congressmen often received mundane personal requests. English had his goodly share of these. One typical appeal asked him to procure for a constituent the proper land warrant due her as compensation for the death of her son in the Mexican War. The appellant had often been beseeched by lawyers to leave the matter to them, but she wrote English "knowing

1. *New York Tribune's* correspondent summary in *New Albany Tribune*, February 18, 1854. WHE to Mardulia, December 7, 1856, English Papers. Alexander Stephens to Richard M. Johnston, January 26, 1859, in Richard M. Johnston and William H. Browne, *Life of Alexander Stephens* (Philadelphia: J.B. Lippincott and Co., 1878), 342. Schuyler Colfax to Charles Heaton, April 27, 1858, in Willard H. Smith, *Schuyler Colfax: The Changing Fortunes of a Political Idol* (Indianapolis: Indiana Historical Bureau, 1952), 98.

that [he] had a knowledge of obtaining Land Warrants," and she preferred that he attend to the matter. In compliance, he dutifully sent her letter to the Court of Pensions, along with a note briefly describing the heroic death of the deceased and asking the court to send him the necessary forms "in behalf of [the soldier's] good old mother."[2] Other common requests concerned the procurement of seeds, the expansion of mail service, the disposition of private claims, and the incessant appeals for office. In all these cases, it was necessary for a congressman to develop a working relationship with the executive departments and to do a tortuous amount of legwork.

But, as Colfax implied, a congressman's labor directly in the halls of Congress was paramount to all else. It was there that a representative received his widest notice and made his electoral fate. And a politician's effectiveness in the House often depended upon the luck of the draw—specifically the draw of marbles for seats. Because congressmen distant from Washington had complained of the first-come-first-serve basis upon which members had gained their places, the system was changed in 1845 to resemble a lottery. Marbles bearing a corresponding number to a congressman's name were chosen from a box by a blindfolded page, and this prestidigitation determined the order of voluntary seating. In 1853, English was fortunate to be one of be first men selected; consequently, he gained a desk very close to the speaker's podium. Had he not supported Boyd for the speakership, his enviable seat may not have appreciably assisted him, but, because he had backed Boyd, the grateful Kentuckian was alert to recognize the Hoosier freshman when he desired to address the House. A little bit of political foresight and a little bit of political luck had situated English well for the start of business.[3]

He lost little time in taking advantage of his position. Within minutes of Boyd's election, he rose to give notice that he would introduce three bills in the near future. One of these proposed that the federal government donate a portion of the public lands "to aid in the construction of a railroad from the falls of the Ohio River to a point on the Mississippi River opposite the city of St. Louis." This was an ambitious design of some 250 miles, and it was an unabashed attempt to divert the Mississippi/Ohio river trade from Louisville directly to New Albany. As the railroad would cut clear through southern Illinois and would benefit St. Louis as well as points that lay to the south and east, English may have anticipated that other congressmen would rally to his cause.[4] Significantly, this piece of legislation was of a type more commonly identified with Whigs than Democrats. It clearly illustrated how northwestern Democrats, attentive to the domestic side of Young

---

2. Rachael A. Kinder to WHE, January 28, 1854, English Papers.

3. D. Stanwood Alexander, *History and Procedure of the House of Representatives* (1954; repr., New York: Lenox Hill Publishing Co., 1970), 39–40. *New Albany Ledger*, December 17, 1853.

4. *CG, 33-1,* 4

America, were not truly one with their southern counterparts. Northwesterners could argue that the interstate nature of the project made it clearly constitutional, but the extent of the enterprise contradicted the Jacksonian and southern admonitions concerning large governmental schemes. The sectional differences on this issue reflected a rift in the Party that harkened back to Polk's presidency.

Aware or not of the west-south disagreement over internal improvements, English certainly introduced the bill as a simple pork-barrel measure. So, too, did he give notice that he would attempt to get congress to designate Jeffersonville (in Clark County) a port of delivery. Finally, as a good westerner, he stated that he would soon offer a bill "to reduce the price of public lands in certain cases." (Of course English, himself, dabbled in public land procurements.) His swift action on the part of his district pleased his constituents markedly. The Whig *New Albany Tribune* graciously complimented English and wrote that "for the honor of the district, we hope he may win a good reputation as an industrious, working member." The Democratic newspapers naturally concurred. The *New Albany Ledger* argued that his proposals proved that English was "determined to see that the interests of his constituents shall not suffer on his account," and the *Paoli Eagle* saw English's activity as evidence that he "will be no idler in Congress." English was lauded by Whig and Democratic presses outside the district as well. The most poignant commendation came from Jesse Bright's growing adversary, Michael Garber of the *Madison Courier*, who offered the following remarks directly after praising the first-term congressman's efforts (bracketed explanations are mine):

> It would give us much pleasure to record, as it doubtless would our numerous patrons, to read any effort on the part of our immediate representative in the House [Cyrus Dunham], or of our former townsman, who has been designated in a public manner by his friends in this city, the "Roman of the Senate" [Jesse Bright], to increase the business facilities of Madison, where there is more business done in a month than is transacted in Jeffersonville in a year. The warmest supporters of the Senator and Representative we allude to cannot specify a single instance in which the energies of either have been exerted for the benefit of this city or county.

Garber's sarcasm did not go for naught. Dunham introduced a bill the next day promoting the construction of a steamboat canal around the falls of the Ohio River.[5]

---

5. *Ibid. New Albany Tribune*, December 7, 1853. *New Albany Ledger*, December 12, 1853. *Paoli Eagle*, December 23, 1853. *Madison Banner* in *Ledger*, December 17, 1853. *Rushville Jacksonian*, in *Ledger*, January 9, 1854. *Madison Courier*, December 21, 1853. *CG, 33-1*, 87.

English formally introduced his bills by the middle of December. He lobbied with the commissioner of the General Land Office for his railroad proposal and gained from him the necessary geological facts to pursue it effectively. He also sponsored other pork-barrel legislation and was able to gain an amendment to a bill dividing Indiana into two judicial districts, designating New Albany as the center of the southern circuit. But none of these measures ever came to fruition, for, like much other local legislation, his proposals were buried under the volcanic ash of the soon-to-be introduced Kansas-Nebraska Act. Even greater legislation, such as the Pacific Railway proposal and the Homestead bill, succumbed to the battle over the repeal of the Missouri Compromise.[6]

Initially the session gave little indication that slavery would once again become a compelling issue. When Free-Soilers Gerrit Smith and Joshua Giddings tried to inject it into the debate over the nation's response to despotism in Europe, they failed to ignite a fire. In December and early January, it was not slavery but the economic issues of internal improvements, tariff reform, and the Homestead bill that predominated as major questions. The primacy of economic issues was the traditional raison d'etre of the rivalry between Whigs and Democrats, yet it was those issues that first revealed disunity within the Democracy itself. On December 20, Thomas Clingman of North Carolina introduced a bill that was intended to make it easier for foreign ironmakers to import railroad iron into the United States. He argued that the high tariff duties had created a prohibitive price for the sale of foreign iron, and that domestic iron production was insufficient to meet the great demand. When the House voted on another Democrat's motion to table the measure, the Party split almost evenly, 54 to 48, a bare six-vote majority for relieving the high tariff. Strict Democratic principle should have produced a greater margin, but the unanimous votes of New York, Pennsylvania, and Ohio, combined with the near unanimity of New England, completely offset the overwhelming free-trade position of the South and most of the Northwest. Two weeks later, when a Louisiana Democrat attempted to pass a resolution that called for the full repeal of all foreign duties on railroad iron, the Party, along similar lines, split almost dead evenly.[7]

In both of these cases, English supported the traditional low-tariff stance. So did the rest of the Indiana Democracy, except for Hendricks who would not vote to remove all duties on iron. On the Homestead issue, Indiana and the rest of the Northwest continued to act as a unit, but this time they found themselves aligned

---

6. *CG, 33-1*, 38, 46. *New Albany Ledger*, December 17, 1853. *CG, 33-1*, 180.

7. *CG, 33-1*, 89-91, 95. The Clingman bill specifically mandated that importers shipping foreign iron into the United States, "for the use of some railroad [may], instead of paying [duties in] cash, give bonds, with approved security, conditioned to pay the said duties with interest at the end of four years from the date of importation." *CG, 33-1*, 71. The Democratic vote against tabling the Louisiana Resolution was 48 to 47. *CG 33-1*, 114.

with Northeast and border representatives. On a motion to suspend the rules in order to make the Homestead bills the special order of February 14 and each successive day until disposed, the Party split two to one affirmatively. Only six of the 42 votes against the resolution came from Democratic free-state congressmen. English and Indiana again found themselves on the majority side of the Party's vote and could thus claim orthodoxy. Both the tariff and Homestead issues clearly illustrated how the West held the balance of power in the Democracy.[8]

On the question of internal improvements, there initially appeared to be more party cohesion. Resolutions mandating that the federal government construct a railroad to the Pacific were beaten back by all geographical sections of the Party. It is true that the Democratic representatives from those states most likely to benefit from the road, California and Illinois, did vote in favor of the resolutions, but they never mustered more than 20 votes for their position. English and all of Democratic Indiana twice stood with the party majority, and the *New Albany Ledger* explained their position not as one that unilaterally opposed the construction of a railroad, but one that responsibly delayed action until federal surveys could show "that the road is practicable at a moderate comparative cost." Such an explanation was certainly compatible with cautious Jacksonian economic policy, and for good measure the *Ledger* noted its additional fear that "stock jobbers" might reap the primary awards.[9]

But the fundamental reason for party cohesion on this issue was that most Democrats agreed that the present transcontinental plan was essentially too large to be constitutional. Suspicion of the schemes of the federal government was a Democratic shibboleth, and present objections to its involvement in such a vast enterprise were not essentially different from Jackson's objections to the now relatively insignificant Maysville Road. When one examines the Party's vote on river and harbor improvements, this point becomes clearer. In the second week of the session, Democrats voted 98 to 16 to table a resolution instructing the commerce committee "to report a bill, as soon as practicable, for the completion of the public works for which appropriations were made by the last congress." One week later, however, when the words "in the opinion of the Committee are within the constitutional powers of this government" were added, Democrats voted 56 to 50 in favor of the resolution. In this case, the border regions and the Northeast divided evenly while the South still opposed the resolution by a great majority. But the Northwest, Indiana included, supported the motion almost unanimously, and, by their votes, passed it. Long John Wentworth of Illinois, soon to leave the Party, chided the southern position two weeks later by noting that southerners called such improvements "anti-Democratic, although General Jackson signed bills for appropriating more money for harbor and

8. *CG, 33-1*, 71, 114, 179.

9. *CG*, 33-1, p. 38, 42. *New Albany Ledger*, December 20, 1853.

river improvements than all other Presidents, [and though] Cass and Douglas voted for the last harbor and river bill, large as it was." On January 16, when Virginian "extra-Billy" Smith objected to a measure designating Quincy, Illinois as a port of delivery, Wentworth accused the Virginian of being anti-West. The bill passed, and once again the West defined Democratic orthodoxy.[10]

A growing Northwestern-South estrangement, properly tracing itself back to the pre-war Polk administration, was thus evident even before the Nebraska bill came before the House. In truth, Democrats from the Northwest identified not primarily with the free states in general but with the free West and often found as little solidarity with Northeastern Party members as with southerners. At this point, English was clearly among these Northwesterners: a mainstream Democrat who still identified with Young America and its section. Fragmented as it was, the Democratic Party had become greatly influenced by the Northwest, which composed only about 20 percent of the House and had no majority on any committee.[11] Inevitably, it and English would attempt to play a key role in defining Democratic orthodoxy on the question relating slavery to that part of the Louisiana Purchase territory that remained unorganized—a question supposedly already settled by the Missouri compromise.

2.

About five months before Stephen Douglas first introduced the Nebraska bill into the 33rd Congress, an alleged fugitive slave was captured in Indianapolis and tried there under federal law. After a very short time, it became clear that the accused, John Freeman, was clearly not the escaped slave of Reverend Pleasant Ellington who had come all the way from Georgia to claim him. The manner in which Freeman was accused was so specious that even Ellington's friends doubted his guilt, and the case became a cause célèbre among Indiana politicians of all stripes. Over 100 white men, including many prominent Democratic politicians, signed Freeman's bail note. Great indignation was leveled at English's friend John L. Robinson, the new United States marshal for Indiana, for his overzealous attempt to enslave an innocent man; and Freeman, having successfully countersued Ellington, brought charges against the marshal for assault and fraud. As the *New Albany Ledger* euphemistically put it, "the black man has been very hardly used by the white one."[12]

---

10. *CG*, 33-1, p. 45, 76, 138-9, 203-205.

11. Nichols, *Franklin Pierce*, 307.

12. Van Bolt, "Indiana in Transition," 357-359. Thornbrough, *Civil War Era*, 51. John L. Ketcham to Howell Cobb, August 9, 1853, in Ulrich B. Philips, ed., *The Correspondence of Robert Toombs, Alexander Stephens, and Howell Cobb* (New York: De Capo Press, 1970), 332. *New Albany Ledger*, September 5, 1853.

The general effect of the case was to rekindle Indiana's uneasiness over the Fugitive Slave Law. When Freeman was incarcerated, the *Ledger* noted that "northerners voted for the [Fugitive Slave Act] not because it gave them any pleasure to see the panting fugitive hurried back into slavery but because the constitution and the obligations of good neighborhood required it of them." Two months later, Norman sardonically rebuked the southern editor of the *Charleston Standard*. The editor had lashed out at United States Supreme Court Justice John McLean because he stated, after upholding the conviction of a fugitive, that "'it would have been gratifying to have found the defendant was a free man, instead of a slave.'" Norman mockingly agreed that one's "gratitude at finding a man to be a free man instead of a slave is an offense of the greatest magnitude—one which should not be tolerated in the meanest of Uncle Sam's deputies, much less a Judge of the Supreme Court." Hoosiers, even southern Hoosiers, had clearly acquiesced in the Fugitive Slave Law only to promote sectional harmony, and though they had "no sickly sentimentality for the Negro," they resented the implication that they should be as zealous as slave owners in capturing escaped slaves.[13]

In essence, Indiana deprecated any action that rekindled the sectional discord over slavery, and the overly energetic pursuit of fugitive slaves tended to do just that. Abolitionists were still regarded, especially in southern Indiana, as the primary enemies of peace, but all "extremism" was anathema. In the eyes of the *Ledger*, both ends fed upon the middle. A book such as *Uncle Tom's Cabin* was criticized not only for its abstract tendency to inflame passions in the free states but for its more concrete tendency to incite slaves to escape from the slave states. Norman noted that "every debate in Congress has a Negro in it every knotty question has a Negro in it…No election can now be held, from justice of the peace to United States senator, without having a Negro in it. No editorial paragraph can be written upon a political topic, without some jealous contemporary smelling a 'nigger in the wood pile'." It was this tendency that Indiana generally wished to allay, and fugitive slave prosecutions, anti-slavery novels, and suggestive editorials only made the task more difficult.[14]

13. Van Bolt, "Indiana in Transition," 357-359. *New Albany Ledger*, September 5, 1853. John L. Brooke has written an interesting article about the interaction between the public and political sphere in framing northern anti-slavery public policy leading to the Civil War. He maintains that the overwhelmingly northern pubic aversion to the Fugitive Slave Act, while somewhat muted by the political parties between 1850 and 1854, was one of the essential factors in setting the groundwork for the outcry against the Kansas-Nebraska Act. John L. Brooke, "Party, Nation, and Cultural Rupture: The Crisis of the American Civil War," in *Practicing Democracy: Popular Politics from the Constitution to the Civil War*, ed. Daniel Pearl and Adam J. P. Smith (Charlottesville: University of Virginia Press, 2015), 74, 79-81

14. *New Albany Ledger*, October 2, 1852, April 14, April 28, May 12, February 11, 1853.

It was from this perspective that much of Indiana and the North in general initially reacted to the direct reintroduction of the slavery/territorial question into national politics. On January 4, 1854, Stephen Douglas, the chair of the Senate Committee on Territories, introduced his Nebraska bill into the Senate. Primarily a measure to stimulate western expansion and the nation's development, it called for the federal organization of all the remaining unorganized territory of the Louisiana Purchase (see map, p.34). As earlier noted, that territory, lying north and west of the state of Missouri, had been declared free of slavery in 1820 by the famous piece of federal legislation known as the Missouri Compromise. At that time, the South had essentially agreed to this restriction in exchange for Missouri's immediate entrance into the Union as a slave state. Because of this restriction, however, southern representatives had consistently refused to vote for the organization of said territory, as, obviously, such organization would lead to rapid settlement and an abundance of free states and free-state congressmen. Southern congressmen could not prevent the House of Representatives, which, by this time, contained a three-fifths majority of free-state representatives, from voting to organize the territory, but, in the Senate, southern senators held 30 of the 62 seats. Along with a few northern allies (including Jesse Bright, who owned slaves in Kentucky[15]), they prevented territorial organization. In order for Douglas, thus, to get his bill approved, he had to somehow make it palatable to the South without destroying its viability in the northern-dominated House.

In his first version of the bill, then, on January 4, Douglas included a section that maintained that, when any part of the territory should be "admitted as a state or states, [it] shall be received into the Union, with or without slavery, as their constitution may provide at the time of their admission." This language was essentially taken from the Utah and New Mexico bills of the Compromise of 1850. Though this iteration would technically allow slave states to be formed out of said territory, it did not repeal the original Compromise line. That is, it did not repeal slavery's exclusion from the area while it remained in territorial status. The chances that a territory would become a slave state when slavery would still have been prohibited before it became a state was, obviously, more than remote. Consequently, some southern senators withheld their support for the measure. To meet their objection, Douglas maintained through the auspices of the *Washington Union* on January 10 that a clerical error had been made in the original presentation of the bill, whereby a key section had been omitted. Part of that section contained a clause essentially adopting the general understanding of popular sovereignty, which read "all questions pertaining to slavery in the Territories, and in the new states to be formed therefrom are to be left to the people residing

---

15. Van Der Weele, "Jesse Bright," 42-43.

therein, through their appropriate representatives." But the new clause did not fully satisfy the South, because, *before* a territorial legislature met, slaves would still be excluded by the Missouri Compromise restriction, making it unlikely that a large enough pro-slavery interest would travel to the territory in order to elect a pro-slave territorial legislature. Thus, southern senators demanded Douglas include in the bill a specific repeal of the Missouri Compromise restriction, thus allowing slave owners and their chattel equal access to the territory from the beginning. This he did with a third version, formally presented to the Senate on January 23, that declared the Compromise restriction "inoperative," as it was "superseded by the *principle* [emphasis added] of the legislation of 1850, commonly called the Compromise measures." The "clerical error" section, mandating popular sovereignty, was removed, as reference to the 1850 Compromise principle, he argued, already assumed territorial determination concerning the legality of slavery.[16]

Even in its first version, there were rumblings from free-state observers. In English's own district, the commanding *New Albany Ledger* maintained that, in its earlier versions, the bill "in effect, if not in words annuls and ignores the Missouri Compromise of 1820," and Norman expressed the opinion that, "if Nebraska *is* to be organized, of which we see but little necessity at this time, we should much prefer to see the Missouri Compromise applied to it." Immediately before Douglas had introduced his bill, the *Ledger* had maintained that it was indeed about time for the rest of the Louisiana Purchase to be given proper government, but the discovery of a "Negro in the wood pile" had caused it now to change its mind. When Douglas's final version clearly stated that the 1820 Compromise restriction was "inoperative," Norman sardonically wondered, "How long will it be till we shall hear of propositions to repeal the Compromise of 1850?" A week later, the *Ledger* issued its harshest criticism to date:

---

16. Examination of the introduction, course, and consequences of what would eventually be labeled the Kansas-Nebraska Bill appear in many works. For the course of Douglas's bill in the Senate, see Alice Elizabeth Malavasic, *The F Street Mess: How Southern Senators Rewrote the Kansas-Nebraska Act* (Chapel Hill: The University of North Carolina Press, 2017), 87-121. See also Allen Johnson, *Stephen A. Douglas: A Study in American Politics* (1908; repr., New York: De Capo Press, 1970), 223, fn 2, for an interesting evaluation of the "clerical error." Very good for the House procedure is Roy Nichols, *Blueprints for Leviathan: American Style* (New York: Athenum, 1963) 95-103, 106. Also helpful is Potter, *Impending Crisis,* 154-171, and Johannsen, *Stephen Douglas,* 405-418, The January 4th version of the bill, with the "clerical" omission added, may be found at http://memory.loc.gov/cgi-bin/ampage?collid=llsb&fileName=033/lisb033. db&recNum=71, which is from the Bills and Resolutions section of *American Memory: A century of Lawmaking for a New Nation: U.S. Congressional Documents and Debates, 1774-1875,* accessed at memory.loc. gov/ammem/amlaw/lawhome.html.

The attempt to force the administration and its friends into a measure that violates twice-plighted faith [1820 and 1850], for the benefit of a presidential aspirant, will, we think, signally fail. But whether the administration succumbs or not, the PRESS should not hesitate to denounce the scheme. The fear of being "read out of the party" by Washington organs of crafty politicians, "hard" or "soft," should not prevent a free and fearless expression of public sentiment.[17]

The early denunciation of Douglas's bill by the *New Albany Ledger* appeared to reflect the initial feeling of most of Indiana's Second Congressional District. A January letter to Congressman English noted that "49/50 of your constituents intelligent enough to understand the question [are] opposed to its passage." The writer, a "firm adherent of the Democratic Party," beseeched English to "give no vote which directly or indirectly will open any more of that beautiful inheritance which a kind providence has given us to the blighting curse of slavery." A little later, a patronage appointee of English's, J.B.A. Archer, wrote him of the "sentiments" of citizens in the "lower part of your District":

> The popular voice is strong against any and every measure having for its object the repeal of the "Missouri Compromise." While all seem perfectly willing to abide in good faith by the acts of 1850, and give the South all of its benefits no one is willing to add one additional foot of Slave Territory into the Union.

The *Cannelton Reporter* in Perry County, at that time a moderate Whig sheet, succinctly hoped that English "will give his voice and his influence for freedom."[18] No correspondents of English's supported the bill in the first month after its introduction.

---

17. *New Albany Ledger*, January 17, 25, 31, 1854.

18. J.S. Maughlin to WHE, January, 1854; J.B.A. Archer to WHE, February 23, 1854, English Papers. *Cannelton Reporter*, February 18, 1854. The opposition to the bill was not, at least by Democrats, based on the impropriety of the theory of popular sovereignty in general but with the breaking of the "sacred pledge" of the Missouri Compromise. The most-used argument was that of the "dishonorable" behavior of Douglas and his supporters in their repeal of a measure (the Missouri Compromise) that was intended to diminish sectional discord, much as the Compromise of 1850 had been intended to do. To be sure, the argument of an aggressive "southern slavocracy," which accused the South of treating the North as slaves (much as the British were accused of doing to the colonies before the American Revolution) was also made and became paramount as the decade progressed. But the point of view that the North had been betrayed and dishonored, indeed emasculated, was apparently the greater complaint originally. See Mark E. Neely, Jr., "The Kansas-Nebraska Act in American Political Culture," in John R. Wunder and Joann M. Ross, eds., *The Nebraska-Kansas Act of 1854* (Lincoln and London: University of Nebraska Press, 2008), 36-41, 23-26.

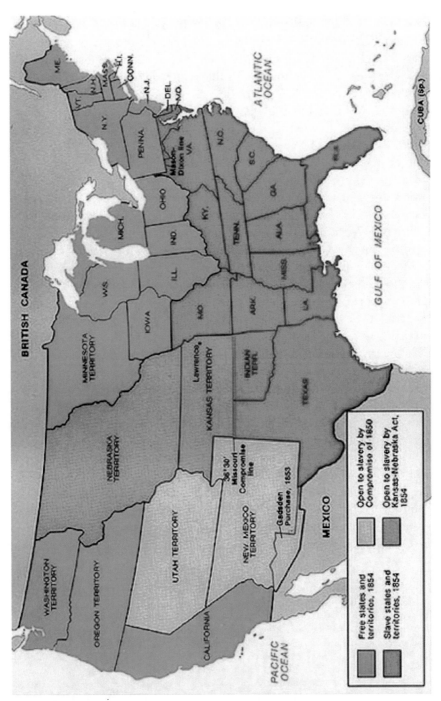

U.S. Map of Proposed Kansas-Nebraska Act

In the House, a simple bill to organize what Douglas labeled the Nebraska territory had been under consideration in the House Committee on Territories since December, but no further action had been taken. On January 23, the same day that Douglas introduced his version of the Nebraska bill that forthrightly repealed the Missouri Compromise, his Illinois ally and chairman of the House Committee on Territories, William A. Richardson, sought the approval of his own committee to substitute Douglas's new bill for any House version. A majority of the committee was disposed to agree, as southerners composed five of its nine members. Richardson, of course, was with them, the two northern Whigs on the committee were opposed, and the ninth member, William English, rather stood in the middle. Abundantly aware of the danger that the bill presented him within his own constituency, English moved a resolution in committee "declaring it inexpedient, at that time, to decide in favor of organizing territorial governments for Nebraska and Kansas." (In the present iteration of his bill, Douglas had divided the territory into two, presumably holding out hope to the South it could win the southern one, labeled Kansas, for slavery.) The resolution was defeated, but Richardson was persuaded to grant his fellow western Democrat a week to prepare a minority report.[19]

English's uncertain position was one in which many northern Democrats found themselves. Whereas most northern Whigs had, especially since the Mexican War, taken a more decided anti-slavery approach to politics, northern Democrats had been more accommodating to the South in an attempt to keep the Party united and prevent crises that could threaten the Union. Consequently, these northern Democrats had left themselves open to the charge that they insufficiently appreciated the immorality of slavery and the stultifying socio-economic effects of the slave system. Again, in presenting his bill, Stephen Douglas had argued that the formula of popular sovereignty, arguably endorsed by the Compromise of 1850 in organizing the Mexican Cession, had superseded the practice of congressional action concerning slavery's legality in the federal territories, making the Missouri Compromise restriction outmoded. But many northerners found that restriction, which had lasted for 34 years, a "sacred compact" as fundamental as the Constitution itself. Two days before the House Committee on Territories

---

19. Roy Nichols, *Blueprints*, 105-106. Gerald W. Wolff, "The Kansas-Nebraska Bill and Congressional Voting Behavior in the Thirty-Third Congress," (unpublished Ph.D. dissertation, University of Iowa, 1969), 174. Malavasic maintains that the presumption that the territory was divided into the southern Kansas and the northern Nebraska to give the South a chance that one of these territories would adopt slavery is false. Instead, the division may have had more to do with unextinguished Indian lands. Malavasic, *The F Street Mess*, 99. She appears to base this on Allen Johnson's *Stephen A. Douglas*, 238-239, who himself cites the *Transactions of Nebraska Historical Society, Vol. II*, 90. That volume II appears to be from the 1887 *Transactions*, from an article by Hadley D. Johnson, an Iowan who was chosen a delegate from the unorganized territory to Washington in 1853 to help secure a bill to organize it. Hadley Johnson, "How the Kansas-Nebraska Line was Established," *Transactions and Reports, Nebraska State Historical Society, Vol. II*, 1887, 87-90.

had voted, by apparently six to three, to report Douglas's Kansas-Nebraska bill to the full House, President Pierce had agreed to make the bill a Democratic Party measure, essentially tying Party members to the repeal of the Missouri restriction. This was an extremely untenable position for a northern Democrat to be in, for, if he chose to support the administration, he was jeopardizing his standing with his direct constituents.

Why Stephen Douglas chose to reintroduce the territorial/slavery question into the national debate at this time has long been a question for both contemporaries and historians. Some in 1854 accused him of currying favor with the South in anticipation of southern support for the presidency in 1856; others believe that Douglas's real estate holdings in Chicago led him to promote that city as an eastern terminus for a transcontinental railroad, and the remainder of the Louisiana territory had to be organized to promote that route. No doubt as an exponent of Young America and continental expansion, Douglas wished to develop the West, but, also, as a key player in the promotion of the Compromise of 1850 and its "finality," it is strange that he would so jeopardize the recently crafted sectional truce. Indeed, his introduction of the bill ran directly counter to the Democrats' 1852 national platform that maintained that the Party "will resist all attempts at renewing in congress and out of it the agitation of the slavery question, under whatever shape or color the attempt may be made." A few historians have actually maintained that leading Democrats hoped that the measure might either serve as a unifying factor in the face of the Party's persistent factionalism, strengthen the Party by purging its insufficiently loyal free-soil and Soft element from its ranks, or simply reinvigorate the differences and rivalry between Whigs and Democrats. In Douglas's defense, it should be noted that he had thought, in principle, that the Missouri Compromise, though beneficial in ending sectional strife in 1820–21, was not good policy. For at least a decade, Douglas had argued that territories should be given wide latitude to frame their own institutions, that territories, like the original 13 colonies, should resist centralized authority over them.[20] But

---

20. Helpful works discussing why Douglas introduced his bill and made his many changes are Robert R. Russel, "The Issues in the Congressional Struggle over the Kansas-Nebraska Bill, 1854," *Journal of Southern History* 29, no. 2 (May, 1963): 199-200; Arthur C. Cole, *The Whig Party in the South* (Washington, D.C.: The American Historical Association., 1913), 286; Avery O. Craven, *The Growth of Southern Nationalism 1848–1861*, (Baton Rouge: Louisiana State University Press, 1953), 175-205; Jon B. Fackler, "An End to Compromise: The Kansas-Nebraska Bill of 1854," (PhD diss., Pennsylvania State University, 1969), 71. See also Roy F. Nichols, "The Kansas-Nebraska Act: A Century of Historiography," *The Mississippi Valley Historical Review* 43, no. 2 (September 1956), 187-212. That Douglas managed a slave plantation in Mississippi with well over 100 slaves would be overstated as evidence that he was pro-slavery or wished to extend the institution. The slaves were actually the property of his first wife, bequeathed to her by her father in his will. Douglas's father-in-law had originally sought to give the slaves and the plantation to Douglas and his wife as a wedding gift, but Douglas had at that time "dissuaded" him from doing so for obvious political reasons. The will, nevertheless, made Douglas the manager of the plantation, for which he was to receive 20 percent of its profits. When Douglas's first wife died in 1853, the slaves and plantation legally went directly to the

whatever Douglas's motivation, he, the southern Democracy, and Pierce had put the northern Democrats in a tough spot.

Early in the week that English had prepared his 'minority report,' the "Appeal of the Independent Democrats" was published in a Washington newspaper. Essentially misnamed (all six of the congressmen who had signed the document were presently Free-Soilers) it was a passionate denunciation of the Kansas-Nebraska bill, one day after it was formally introduced into the Senate. It denounced Douglas as a servant of the "slavocracy," determined to promote his presidential ambitions, who grossly violated the "sacred pledge" of the Missouri Compromise to help foist the "despotism" of slavery on the West. Essentially, it claimed that the bill was part of a nefarious conspiracy to extend the institution of slavery across the nation. Most northern Democrats considered The Appeal incendiary and extreme, and indeed, its signers were fundamentally abolitionist.[21] In his own report, English would take a far more nuanced and measured approach.

On January 30, Richardson informed the members of the Territorial Committee that he would report the bill to the House the following day. English, ready with his own report, gained from the chairman the promise that he would yield to him for an explanation before Richardson moved that the bill go to the Committee of the Whole. Consequently, on the last day of January, Richardson had the title of Douglas's January 23 version of the bill read to the House twice and then yielded the floor to English. Richardson expected only a short statement by his fellow committee member, but the Hoosier congressman had other

young sons of the marriage while Douglas continued to manage it, but, four years later, he sold it and entered into a partnership to which he contributed the sons' slaves to work the land of his partner. Johannsen, *Stephen Douglas,* 208-209, 211, 381, 337-338. The primary exponent of the thesis that Douglas's concern had more to do with party than national policy is Michael Holt, first enunciated in his *The Political Crisis of the 1850s,* 147-148, and later embellished in his *The Fate of their Country,* 97-100. Holt's main thesis is that the genesis of the act was to promote party harmony, in tatters over Pierce's appointment policy. Although a couple of quotes are cited to support this thesis, it does not mean that this purpose was the *primary* rationale. (Allen Johnson in his *Stephan A. Douglas,* 237, does aver that Douglas publicly hoped the Party could ameliorate its "distracted condition" by clarifying its principles. He does not, however, cite any source for that comment.) Indeed, far from being a party unifier, the powerful New York Hards saw the bill as a way of embarrassing their fellow Democratic New York Softs and Barnburners, a point Holt himself also notes. As well as for promoting party harmony, it is also interesting that, when the Nebraska bill was attempting to move through the House in March, a New York Hard, Francis Cutting, proposed and succeeded in passing a temporary roadblock to it. Cutting probably did this to embarrass President Pierce, who had agreed that the Nebraska bill would be presented as an administration party measure. For Cutting's maneuver see *CG, 33-1,* 701-703. For interpretation of this maneuver see Fackler, 78-79 (dependent on a letter to Howell Cobb from Thomas Baylay, May 6, 1854 in Phillips, *Toombs, Cobb, Stephens, 343),* and Nichols, *Blueprints,* 107-108. The resolutions of the National Democratic Party of 1852 may be found in the digitized *American Presidency Project* at www.presidency.**ucsb.edu**/ws/?pid=29575. For Douglas's lack of enthusiasm for the Missouri Compromise and his attachment to local democracy, see Martin H. Quitt, *Stephen Douglas and Antebellum Democracy* (Cambridge, New York, *et al.*: Cambridge University Press, 2012), 113,114-115.

21. The *Appeal* is discussed in most secondary historical works that touch on the Kansas-Nebraska Act. A text of it is in the *Congressional Globe* of January 30. *CG, 33-1,* 281-2.

ideas. He introduced his remarks by directly stating that he wished to present his "objections to the bill so that my position may not be misunderstood by my constituents, and so that their attention may be called to this important question." No doubt he had already read the misgivings of the *New Albany Ledger* and some of his own correspondents and predicted general trouble at home. At this point, his responsibility to the northern democracy in general, and perhaps the nation at large, was inseparable from his responsibility to his own political future. Less than two months into his first congressional session, earlier than all the other representatives, he felt he was forced to make a major political statement on the fundamental issue that eventually led to Civil War.[22]

He began his criticism cleverly and obliquely. Avoiding the contentious issue of slavery, he concentrated, instead, on the boundaries of Kansas and Nebraska as described in the bill. Noting that Douglas had allowed about one-third of the Utah Territory to be included in the two new areas, English proposed that the bill be amended to exclude that land and return to a western boundary at the crest of the Rocky Mountains. He argued quite cogently that such a line was clearly more "natural" and registered surprise that any other should have been considered. As he began to warm to his argument, Richardson rose in protest. He had not expected English to make a "speech," but only an "explanation," and he clearly wished to prevent any real discussion of the bill until it could be printed and sent to the Committee of the Whole for full House debate. English replied that he believed it was due him, as a member of the Committee on Territories, to state his problems with the bill, and, in order to mollify Richardson, he admitted that, perhaps, his "objections to the bill are not of such vital character but I may ultimately vote for it, even in its present shape." Richardson, claiming no discourtesy, still proposed to the Speaker of the House that perhaps English should wait until Richardson completed his business of the bill's disposition; whereupon Boyd answered that the committee chairman could take back the floor any time he wished. But Richardson, perhaps wishing to avoid a major disturbance, did not press his case and allowed English to proceed. The young congressman thanked him and promised not to "extend" his remarks "to any great length." He then kept the floor undisturbed for the next 20 minutes.[23]

He returned to his argument by concluding his points concerning the boundaries. He noted two reasons why there is little "community of interest" between the populations on either side of the Rockies. One, of course, was the difficulty in transportation and communication the mountains presented, but the other was more sociological. Noting that such a boundary would mix Mormons with non-Mormons in the same political unit, he could not understand its necessity

22. Nichols, *Blueprints*, 106. *CG, 33-1*, 294.

23. *CG, 33-1*, 294-295.

considering the geographical limitations. He suspected that the reduction of Utah's land was somehow tied to a widely held prejudice against Mormonism, one that he permitted was "perhaps" justified, but he was not "willing to carry these prejudices to the extent of extending the boundaries of this Territory already too large." He was careful to state that he had "no particular love for the Mormons, nor for their peculiar institutions," but he refused to punish them for their practices. English's position here is significant, as his use of the phrase "peculiar institutions" implies. His fundamental objection to the present shape of the Nebraska bill was clearly going to be what he considered its lukewarm exposition of popular sovereignty, and his reference to Mormonism emphasized the consistency of the argument that territorial citizens should be free to choose morally disputed institutions.[24]

Without directly expounding on the connection of Mormonism to slavery, he nevertheless obliquely connected them as he quickly moved to his main objection. Noting that "there is another question involved in this bill [of] great delicacy," he boasted that, unlike other gentlemen, he was "not afraid to face the music." He began his discussion of "African Slavery" by directly stating that he was "a native of a free state, and [had] no love for the institution of slavery. Aside from the moral question involved, I regard it as an injury to the state where it exists, and if it were proposed to introduce it where I reside, would resist it to the last extremity. I hope the day will arrive when it will be unknown in this free Republic." But these sentiments competed unfavorably with his respect for federalism. Each state was sovereign, "and if the people of Kentucky believe the institution of slavery would be conducive to their happiness, they have the same right to establish and maintain it that we of Indiana have to reject it." (In the use of the word "people," English, as most other congressmen, of course, meant white, adult, males.) This, of course, was his touchstone. For English, the fundamental right "of American freemen to govern themselves" was a principle second to none, and he had little trouble in asserting that it should apply to territorial citizens as well as those of a state.

> A man who has exercised the attributes of a free citizen of Indiana, or any other state loses none of his powers of self-government emigrating to a Territory. Is he less virtuous, less intelligent, less imbued with the spirit of patriotism and love of country because he resides in a Territory and not in a State? Is he less an object of government regard because he has gone into the wilderness to endure the hardships of frontier life, in preparing the way for that tide of population, civilization and empire, which still flows West? [These citizens] are the best judges of the soil and

---

24. *CG, 33-1*, 295. The term "peculiar institution" was often one used to describe southern slavery.

climate, and wants of the country they inhabit; they are the true judges of what will best suit their own condition, and promote their welfare and happiness.[25]

Douglas himself could make little better common-sense argument for popular sovereignty. Both he and English downplayed "the moral question involved" and treated the enslavement of men perceived to be innately inferior as a policy decision to be made by the sovereign "freemen."

But there were subtle differences between the two men that are significant. Here is the part of Douglas's January 23 iteration of the bill, the one Richardson was recommending to the House and the one with which English had differences, which dealt with popular sovereignty and its relationship to the Missouri Compromise:

> The Constitution, and all Laws of the United States which are not locally inapplicable, shall have the same force and effect within the said Territory as elsewhere within the United States, except the eighth section of the act preparatory to the admission of Missouri into the Union, approved March 6th, 1820, which was superseded by the principle of the legislation of 1850, commonly called the Compromise Measures, and is declared inoperative.[26]

And here is English's substitute amendment to that section:

> That nothing in this act shall be so construed as to prevent the people of said Territory, through the properly constituted legislative authority, from passing such laws in relation to the institution of slavery, not inconsistent with the Constitution of the United States, as they may deem best adapted to their locality, and most conducive to their happiness and welfare; and so much of any existing act of Congress as may conflict with the above right of the people to regulate their domestic institutions in their own way, be, and the same is hereby, repealed.[27]

Whereas Douglas, in response to southern pressure, makes the repeal of the Missouri Restriction the driving force of the section and *assumes* the principle of popular sovereignty by reference to the 1850 Compromise, English *specifically* re-incorporates the principle of popular sovereignty into the bill and clearly makes

---

25. *CG, 33-1*, 295.

26. *CG, 33-1*, 222.

27. *CG, 33-1*, 297

the repeal of the Missouri restriction dependent on it. Indeed, in English's version the Missouri act is in no sense specifically singled out—*any* former congressional act that may be interpreted to "conflict" with popular sovereignty in the new territories is voided. Moreover, English's version specifically refers to the notion of *local* democracy, investing popular sovereignty directly with the decentralized political philosophy of the Democratic Party. And English, in his specific use of the terms "happiness" and "welfare," imbues the principle of popular sovereignty with the founding documents of the Declaration of Independence and the Constitution. He disregards Douglas's rather novel and certainly tendentious argument that the Compromise of 1850 "superseded" the Missouri Restriction and instead attempts to ennoble and identify the Kansas-Nebraska bill with fundamental American political doctrine, allowing for the wholly implied repeal of the Missouri restriction as almost a reluctant afterthought.

Finally, some notice must be taken of English and Douglas's assertion that the Constitution of the United States may limit the principle of territorial popular sovereignty. Although it might be deemed obvious and superfluous to state that any legislation is subject to consistency with the Constitution, its use here illustrates an uncertainty with the constitutional status of slavery outside the states. Many southerners argued that slavery, a constitutionally recognized institution, was a species of the general, natural right to property, which could not legally be prohibited by either Congress or a territorial government before the territory became a sovereign state. While southern congressmen would overwhelmingly vote for the Kansas-Nebraska bill because it repealed the Missouri restriction, many of them hoped that one day the Supreme Court might rule that even a positive territorial law outlawing slavery in its jurisdiction was inconsistent with one's right to hold property in any portion of the United States that had not yet achieved statehood. English did not support this southern constitutional interpretation,[28] but his recognition that the Supreme Court, in its duty to interpret the Constitution, *could* find popular sovereignty as applied to slavery an unconstitutional limitation on property rights may be seen as a concession to southern sensibilities and could thus be interpreted as promoting Democratic Party harmony. After invoking his intended amendment, English asserted that its adoption (and another one he offered meeting his boundary requirements) would lead him to vote for the bill. Although offhandedly noting that his vote "should of course carry out the wish of the people I represent," he pronounced himself "ready to act."[29]

---

28. English's two contentions, that slavery is not automatically legal in a territory and, further, that it is not beyond prohibition by a territorial legislature, are contained in this strong and pithy statement in his address: "I am opposed to admitting slavery in these territories and placing it out of the reach of the people until the formation of a state government. And it is in part because the bill is not explicit on this head that I dislike it." *CG, 33-1,* 295.

29. *CG, 33-1,* 295

Richardson had allowed English to speak at length, but, before the Hoosier congressman could formally introduce his amendments, the Territories chairman rose to reply. He began by answering English's boundary objections. It was not true that no common interest tied eastern Utah with western Kansas, he said, as both sides of the Rockies lay "along the same route of travel towards the Pacific Ocean." More significantly, Richardson defended taking a large chunk out of Utah because the "lawless" Mormons "ought not to be encouraged and promoted by this government." He claimed that scores of Utah citizens had petitioned Congress to remove power from the Mormon Hierarchy, and he cited the request of one trader, who was "driven" away by the Mormons after residing there for 30 years. Richardson was either unaware of the negative implications this argument held for popular sovereignty or believed that slicing off a territory with a territorial government in place was not considered federal "intervention." His tone indicated that he was not pleased that he had been drawn into debate on the bill this early.[30]

Before Richardson could continue, another Indiana congressman, John G. Davis, called for the reading of the bill. He reasoned that if the House was now to discuss the measure, it should be read. Discussion was exactly what Richardson wished to avoid, and Davis complied by offering to withdraw his request if debate ceased. But, by this time, the House had become animated, and numerous members wished to offer their own amendments. Richardson, whom Murat Halstead later described as a man who contained within him "that excellent quality which we call *humanity*," was not stern enough to stem the tide. He even went so far as to withdraw his motion to send the bill to the Committee of the Whole so that some members could now read their amendments. At this point, great confusion ensued and business was suspended for some minutes until order could be restored, but even then Elihu Washburne of Illinois shouted that he did "not know who has the floor, or what is going on [because] there is such noise in the Hall." Eventually, with help from speaker Boyd's ruling that amendments to an uncommitted bill could only be received by unanimous consent, Richardson remade the motion to send the measure to the Whole. This was passed by an unrecorded vote.[31]

Having not yet actually read his amendments, English had been one of those who had attempted to get the floor for that purpose. Dunham had come to his aid by injecting a point of order that noted that minority reports had always been graciously received. The ensuing melee, and Richardson's consequential motion to commit, delayed English's proposal, but after the bill was safely on the Committee of the Whole's calendar the speaker asked for any further reports from the

---

30. *Ibid.*

31. *CG, 33-1,* 295-297. William B. Hesseltine and Rex G. Fischer, eds., *Trimmers Trucklers, and Temporizers: Notes of Murat Halstead from the Political Conventions of 1856* (Madison; State Historical Society of Wisconsin, 1961), 45-46. *CG, 33-1,* 295-297.

Territorial Committee, and English rose to read his amendments. After a perfunctory objection by an administration Democrat, English was allowed to enter his amendments as House Report No. 80. As it was seemingly entered as *the* minority report, the Whigs of the Territories Committee, E. Wilder Farley of Maine and John L. Taylor of Ohio, rose to disassociate themselves from its contents. As Taylor remarked, both he and Farley were rather in favor of those proposals in the last Congress that organized the territory in compliance with the Missouri Compromise. After this explanation, the House agreed to print English's "report" and send it to the Committee of the Whole.[32]

English was trying to find some accommodation that would both satisfy his constituents and the northern Democracy as a whole and keep him within the good graces of the Democratic administration and power structure. This modus operandi would be repeated throughout his congressional career, but here his attempt to define the proper niche was rough going. His amendments, after all, did not substantially differ from Douglas's bill or the Party line. He was clever to try to bury his acquiescence in the repeal of the Missouri Compromise in legislative draftsmanship, but with that acquiescence he had put himself in jeopardy of being accused of too willingly accommodating southern sensibilities. Moreover, he had stated directly that he might yet vote for the bill, even if his objections were not met. His attitude was partly a product of his position in the Indiana democracy. On the same day that he made his brief speech, Jesse Bright wrote him from the Senate "not to make any committals against the bills now before Congress for the organization of the territories." Bright, after a couple of weeks of indecision, had begun actively supporting the bill behind the scenes. Besides his natural proclivity to accede to southern wishes (again, it should be noted here that Bright owned a slave plantation in Kentucky), he saw in the bill a way of eliminating the hard-core free soil element from the Democratic Party in Indiana. Opposing the bill too strongly, English consequently realized, would put him in the company of those Indiana Democrats who were most opposed to Bright, something he did not have the courage to do at this early stage in his congressional career. He allowed himself to believe, not irrationally, that popular sovereignty would most likely work to keep slavery out of the new territories and thus believed that the repeal of the Missouri restriction would not make any difference. But it would be a tough sell to his constituents.[33]

The first reaction back home to his early pronouncement rather depended on the political stance of the commentator. The *Madisonian*, the Bright newspaper created to counter Garber's independent course with the *Madison Courier*, wrote

---

32. *CG, 33-1*, 296-297.

33. Jesse Bright to WHE, January 31, 1854, English Papers. *New Albany Ledger*, January 17, 1854. Van Der Weele, "Jesse Bright," 142, 150.

that English "took the ground of a true democrat, in favor of the right of the people to organize, according to their own view, such domestic institution as they desire to live under." Privately, the Bright forces were still uneasy with English's stance. John L. Robinson wrote the Second District congressman that he hoped his objections were "susceptible to obviation in some way, [as] it is important we all stand together on that bill." On the other side, the Whigs ridiculed English's contentions. The *New Albany Tribune* called it a "new and startling doctrine that territorial governments are capable of governing themselves in all things." This was, Gregg argued, hardly the view of the Constitution's framers, and he sarcastically added that "to Young America belongs the honor of discovering their mistake." The *Madison Banner* warned English that he "cannot jockey and speculate in votes on the slavery question as he is fond of doing in plank-road, railroad, and other stocks." Interestingly, however, the Whiggish *Cannelton Reporter* of Perry County simply noted that English had "entered quite actively into the discussion," and rather optimistically held out the hope that "he will give his voice and influence to freedom."[34]

This *Cannelton Reporter*, begun in the same month that Douglas introduced his Nebraska bill, was probably the most anti-slavery sheet in the Second District. It announced its relative nonpartisanship in its first issue, noting that although it generally "believed in Whig doctrines we do not feel bound to think the Whig creed contains all political truth . . . We mean to be independent." Indeed, in its pages it would often allow discussion encompassing widely differing opinions on important political matters. But it certainly had a Whig-like philosophy, a kind of political evangelism, which sprung from its belief that government could be used as a tool to improve society and man. Though not technically abolitionist (it did not believe in interference with slavery in the extant slave states), it was as close as one could get to abolitionism in the Second District. Unlike the racist yet Whig *New Albany Tribune*, it was appalled by the slave system, not just for its tendency to retard material and intellectual progress, but for its direct physical and social effect on black men and women. In its first issue it cryptically derided "many of our country's best men, [who,] jealous of the honor and perpetuity of our glorious Union, and endowed with too cautious conservatism, have deprecated the coming of the time when this country shall be forced into an exhibition of her moral power and strength."[35]

When Douglas thus introduced his Nebraska bill, the *Reporter*, though strongly and consistently opposed to it, also believed it would serve as a needed wake-up call to the free states. Specifically, "Mr. Douglas's . . . shamelessness to

---

34. *Madisonian*, February 8, 1854, in English Scrapbook, 57. J. L. Robinson to WHE, February 6, 1854, English Papers. *New Albany* Tribune, February 9, 1854. *Madison Banner*, February 2, 1854. *Cannelton Reporter*, March 18, 1854.

35. Miller, *Indiana Newspaper Bibliography*, 356. *Cannelton Reporter*, January 28, 1854.

contend . . . that the Missouri Compromise was repealed by the Compromise of 1850" would be the catalyst for the North to exercise their moral power and strength: "It will be found in this contest that the Conservatism, which saved the country in 1850, will be unavailable. Men who then yielded to save the Union, will now be convinced that one concession only leads to another—that slavery continually cries 'give, give, give,' and that forbearance and yielding only make her more arrogant and exacting." The *Reporter* confidently predicted that "there will be such a storm of just and honest indignation aroused in this country within a few weeks that the projector and abettors of this diabolical scheme will tremble at the consequences of their unhallowed temerity."[36]

That the *Reporter's* editor, J.M. Beatty, did not as yet identify William English as one of those 'abettors' of perfidy is a testimony to English's lifelong ability to keep on relatively good terms with those who differed with him politically. Even months after English would ultimately disappoint Beatty by voting to pass the Kansas-Nebraska bill, when the 1854 congressional campaign was in full swing and anti-Nebraska Hoosiers were harshly criticizing pro-Nebraska Democrats, Beatty could not bring himself to cast aspersions on English's character. Though making it clear that he disagreed with his congressman on the measure (and, indeed, writing a series of scathing articles as to English's illogical arguments), the *Reporter's* editor stated that he "personally [had] very kind feelings for Mr. English." He "regard[ed] him as a gentleman [and] as an obliging, energetic, and able man."[37] Alas, however, the very tough and emotional campaign did eventually change Beatty's overall opinion of his representative by the time the voters went to the polls.

English's criticism of the far western boundary of the territory that the bill allowed gave those Democrats who were troubled by the measure something on which to compliment him. The foremost German Democrat of the district, Rudolphus Schoonover, noted that this boundary objection was approved by the farmers of Floyd County. The *Ledger*, too, commended the congressman for his proper construction of the boundary proposal, but Norman's refusal to go any further illustrated that he feared himself at odds with English and the administration on the bill's substance. On February 8, Norman wrote English his matured reflections at length (bracketed italics are my comments):

> It seems to me the Nebraska Bill is a very ill-advised scheme and ought not to have been introduced. I do not think the South asks the annulment of the Missouri Compromise [*here he is wrong*], or think it will thank Douglas for introducing his proviso to that effect. Of course if

36. *Cannelton Reporter,* February 18, 1854.

37. *Cannelton Reporter,* September 2, 1854.

one compromise is annulled another can be, and, the North having the power, possibly *may* be, in some particulars [*Fugitive Slave Law*], before many years. It is certainly news to many that the Compromise of 1850 was intended as an annulment of that of 1820. Certainly no such avowal was made at the time that compromise was pending. The indecent haste of Douglas in attempting to force this bill through the Senate without debate, and the various amendments he has at different times proposed, shows that he himself doubts its propriety or its popularity.

Norman's analysis evinced a genuine frustration. He believed that the bill breached a national contract, but by early February his concern seemed less one of stubborn resistance to the measure and more of a sullen resignation. He ended his missive by noting that he thought English's course "thus far right and proper,"—"thus far" being the operative phrase. On the same day, the *Ledger* ruefully noted that "we have said that we did not think there was any necessity for organizing the Territory of Nebraska at the present time, and that we were opposed to the provision which renders the Missouri Compromise inoperative."[38]

After this pithy statement, the *New Albany Ledger* went silent on the bill until its passage. Gregg had written that the *Ledger's* pronouncements were "irreconcilable" with English's position, and he attributed Norman's silence, probably correctly, to this discrepancy. In truth, the *Tribune's* own criticism of the Nebraska Act was initially rather mild. Indeed, on January 31 it stated that despite "a great fluttering and outcry, we do not believe any serious consequences will occur if the bill passes." Gregg warmed slowly to the political capital to be gained by strenuous opposition. A week later, he still continued to pronounce "the principal features of the bill just and righteous," but now he added that its violation of the "solemn compact entered into in 1820" was reason enough to vote for its defeat. Although he ridiculed Douglas's assertion that the 1850 Compromise had superseded the Missouri restriction, Gregg's main line of argument was practical: the repeal of the 1820 restriction "would reopen the slavery agitation and we would again have the excitement and turmoil that was witnessed in 1850." This stance was not much different from Norman's. The *Tribune*, far from identifying itself with the cause of free soil, represented the typical border-state, Whig position that willingly supported the 1850 Compromise and accommodations made between the two sections generally. It blamed not the South, which, like Norman, it incorrectly believed "has not asked for this measure," but the "political demagogue [who] wishes by the introduction of this bill to curry favor with the South and thereby more easily reach the presidential chair in 1856." In essence, the *Tribune's*

---

38. Rudolphus Schoonover to WHE, April 3, 1854, English Papers. *New Albany Ledger*, February 7, 1854. J.B. Norman to WHE, February 8, 1854, English Papers. *Ledger*, February 9, 1854.

position cogently illustrates how close most Second District Whigs and Democrats were on the slavery question.[39]

The Second District criticisms of the bill were essentially mirrored throughout much of the North, and there was a serious chance that the bill's rather indirect promotion of popular sovereignty, coupled with its essentially direct repeal of the Missouri Restriction, was not satisfactory to enough northern Democrats in the House to allow its passage.[40] Consequently, on February 7, a week after English's observations in the House, Douglas began to see the Hoosier's approach as possessing great merit. Reworking the language, he offered a substitute amendment that re-incorporated a direct endorsement of popular sovereignty among other revisions. Here is the substitute amendment, the stylization of the portion below representing the reworked language:

> That the Constitution, and all laws of the United States which are not locally applicable, shall have the same force and effect within the said territory as elsewhere in the United States, except the eight section of the act preparatory to the admission of Missouri into the Union, approved March 6th, 1820, which ~~superseded by was~~ being inconsistent with the principle of non-intervention by Congress with slavery in the States and Territories, as recognized by the legislation of 1850, commonly called the Compromise Measures, is hereby declared inoperative and void; it being the true intent and meaning of this act not to legislate slavery into any Territory and State, or to exclude it therefrom, but to leave the people thereof perfectly free to form and regulate their domestic institutions in their own way, subject only to the Constitution of the United States.[41]

The re-inclusion of a direct statement endorsing popular sovereignty clearly reflected English's own intent and language. Douglas continued to emphasize that the formula of popular sovereignty was tied to the 1850 Compromise (something English ignored), but he now found the Missouri Restriction "inconsistent with," rather than "superseded by", the later law. And in his speeches in late February and early March defending his bill Douglas adopted English's implied argument that the principle of popular sovereignty flowed more from American fundamental political philosophy than from positive law (i.e. the Compromise of 1850). Indeed the usual phrase allowing Congress to veto a territorial law was excluded from the final draft of the bill, so that this bill actually gave greater sovereignty to its new territories than to any territories previously established, including New

---

39. *New Albany Tribune*, January 31, February 3, February 6, February 9, 1854.

40. Nichols, *Blueprints*, 99-100.

41. *CG, 33-1*, 353.

Mexico and Utah. To be sure, it was not solely English's amendment, of course, that pressured Douglas into reworking his bill, but it *was* English who first formally illustrated how troubled but loyal northern Democrats might possibly be able to support it.[42]

With this new version incorporated into the bill, many leading Democrats in Indiana's Second District were now prepared to argue for it along English's lines of local democracy. Thomas Carr wrote English in Jacksonian terms that he was "not afraid to refer the question of slavery and all other questions to the best and safest of all tribunals, the people." Rudolphus Schoonover argued that it would be wrong "to withhold from the citizens of the U.S. the right (sacred to Americans) of self-government." And Benjamin P. Douglass, the political leader often referred to as the Pope of Harrison County, wrote that "the principle of nonintervention on the subject of slavery is decidedly popular with us at the present." However, some of these politicos, although they believed the Kansas-Nebraska bill a fair measure, worried how it would be perceived by the masses. J.B.A. Archer warned English that a vote for the bill would be "used as a powerful weapon against you in the canvass," and the leading entrepreneur of Perry County believed that "the feeling of your constituents, as far as I can learn, is against the Nebraska Bill."[43]

Had all reports been of a negative nature, English would have been hard-pressed to vote for the bill. As it was, he kept a close counsel, refusing to publicly state his position beyond his January 31 speech. The early indications that many Democrats and most Whigs in the district opposed the measure probably caused him to wait as long as possible before fully declaring himself, and even when the Senate passed the bill on March 4, his course was not certain to many. "Mr. English guards his points with much care," wrote a Washington correspondent, and the *Ledger* could only state that "when the bill shall come up for discussion in the House Mr. English will give his views at more length."[44]

---

42. *The Paoli Eagle* publically recognized English's contribution to Douglas's final bill. In March, when the bill passed the Senate, Comingore noted that besides adopting English's boundary, "the bill was also changed so as to embrace, in substance, the amendment offered by him in reference to the slavery question." *Eagle*, March 17, 1854. Section 6 of the final bill eliminated the clause allowing for congressional veto of territorial laws. For Douglas's final bill, see "Statutes at Large," volume 10, 273ff, in *American Memory: A Century of Lawmaking for a New Nation: U.S. Congressional Documents and Debates, 1774-1785*, Accessed December 2, 2019. memory.loc.gov/ammem/amlaw/lawhome.html. Access same source for New Mexico (vol 9. 446ff), Utah (vol. 9, 453ff), Oregon (vol. 9, 323ff), and Minnesota (vol. 9, 416ff) enabling acts. For Douglas's earlier iteration of the Kansas-Nebraska Act see same source under "Bills and Resolutions," Senate bill 22 of 33rd Congress.

43. Thomas Carr to WHE, March 5, 1854; Rudolphus Schoonover to WHE, April 3, 1854; B.P. Douglass to WHE, April 4, 1854; J.B.A. Archer to WHE, February 23, 1854; Hamilton Smith to WHE, March 15, 1854, English Papers.

44. *Paoli Eagle*, May 5, 1854. *New Albany Ledger*, February 7, 1854.

3.

The version of the bill that finally passed the Senate tacked on an amendment that caused northern Democrats additional trauma. This was the Clayton Amendment, which restricted voting in the new territories to citizens only (some northern states, including Indiana, had at that time permitted immigrants to vote if they declared their intention of becoming citizens). This amendment was illustrative of the fast-growing nativist movement that had especially infected the Whig Party. By denying the vote to unnaturalized immigrants, it also had the support of many southern Democrats because the large German immigrant population, mostly residing in the North and possibly intending to relocate to Kansas and Nebraska, were considered generally anti-slavery. The amendment passed by two votes—all of its opponents, including Douglas, came from the free states.[45] Northern Democrats had counted on the immigrant vote, in reaction to Federalist elitism, since the Party's earlier incarnation as Jeffersonian Republicans and their general support for white, male egalitarianism made the Clayton amendment anathema to them. From Indiana, English received only adverse comments concerning the amendment. The *New Albany Ledger* deplored it, noting that it came at the insistence of southern senators. A close political friend of English's from Logansport, Indiana, supreme court justice William Z. Stuart, viewed the matter in more alarming terms: "This invidious discrimination against foreigners, so different from the liberal policy pursued in Michigan, Wisconsin, Iowa, &C, will not merely kill the men who vote for the bill, it will utterly defeat the Democratic Party in the North and West." And he added directly, "In Indiana here, you know, that without the Germans and Irish we are nowhere."[46]

But even with this provision, Indiana senators Bright and Pettit still supported Kansas-Nebraska. Bright, suffering all session from rheumatism, did not actually cast a formal vote, but it was clear from earlier statements that he approved of it. Pettit, of whom Bright had earlier written he "shall have little or nothing to do with," also voted with the majority. Pettit's support was somewhat curious because he had earlier told the Senate and the press that he believed Congress had the right, if it wished, to prohibit the introduction of slavery into the territories where it did not exist. Completing the remainder of Whitcomb's term and needing the Party's support for his re-election in January, Pettit had apparently decided, perhaps against his own convictions, not to join with those Democratic Hoosiers who opposed the bill. By this time he had realized that insofar as the leadership of the Indiana Democracy was concerned, they would support Kansas-Nebraska. Although there was some significant opposition from the Wright wing, the Gov-

45. Johannsen, *Stephen Douglas*, 428. *CG, 33-1*, 520.

46. *New Albany Ledger*, March 11, 1854. Shepherd, *Biographical Directory*, 377. Woolen, *Eminent Men*, vol. 2, District 10, 37-38. W. Z. Stuart to WHE, March 13, 1854, English Papers.

ernor himself decided not to stake his reputation against the administration's measure. Had Pettit voted against the bill, he would have certainly complicated his re-election possibilities.[47]

The House managers of Kansas-Nebraska realized that the Clayton Amendment would make the bill impossible to pass, but, even without it, time was needed to try to craft a majority. All the northern Whigs would clearly vote against it, and for some time it appeared that more than half the northern Democrats would as well. For over two weeks after its passage in the Senate, S 22, the Senate bill, lay on the speaker's table waiting to take its usual course. In this case this meant referral to the Committee on Territories, whence Richardson believed he could get it favorably reported out to the full House. Granted, he would need time to ensure a pro-Nebraska majority in the full chamber, but once he felt confident that he had one, he would move it forward. But in late March his plans went astray. New York 'Hards' looking to embarrass president Pierce in retaliation for his Soft patronage policy, northern Democrats unreconciled to the repeal of the Missouri Compromise, and all the northern Whigs voted to send S 22, not to Richardson's Committee on Territories, but to the Committee of the Whole. There it would lay behind 50 other bills and would be impossible to reach without a two-thirds House majority. Clearly, this House vote, 110 to 95, was a great defeat for the proponents of the bill and illustrated at this juncture that the Administration did not have the votes to pass it.[48]

Not all the rebellious Democrats were necessarily unalterably opposed to the senate bill, but, considering the political costs in relation to their constituents, they at least wanted more time to consider their course. English, however, did not join them. He voted on the losing side, that is, to sustain Richardson. Though this vote did not necessarily commit him to support Kansas-Nebraska in the end, it was clearly a signal that he was tending in that direction. His evolving course was partly the result of the key changes made at his suggestion, partly the result

---

47. *CG, 33-1,* 532. *New York Tribune,* March 10, 1854. Van der Weele, "Jesse Bright," 142-43. *New Albany Ledger,* April 8, 1854. Jesse Bright to WHE, January 25, 1853, English Papers. *New York Evening Post,* in *New Albany Tribune,* February 24, 1854. Van Bolt, "Fusion out of Confusion," 365-66. The *Indiana State Sentinel* had given its full support to the bill as early as mid-February. Van Bolt, *"Fusion out of Confusion,"* 364. Pettit's movement away from free soilism allowed him to ingratiate himself with Bright for years. As late as 1858, Bright called Pettit "an original and true friend of the [Buchanan] administration," and asked English to endorse his own support for Pettit's appointment as Chief Justice of the Kansas territory. Pettit secured the position. Jesse Bright to WHE, August 30, 1858, English Papers.

48. Fackler, "End to Compromise," 78. *CG, 33-1,* 700-703. Nichols, *Blueprints,* 107-108. Wolff, "Kansas-Nebraska Bill," 175-176. Alexander Stephens, former Georgia Whig Unionist congressman turning Democratic, wrote his brother in the second week in March that "the fate of the Bill in the House is doubtful. The administration [is] nominally for it—but at heart I have no doubt want it defeated. The poor fools believe it will well make Douglas President—Jeff Davis also fears it will make Union men from the South too prominent." Alexander Stephens to Linton Stephens, March 4, 1854, Alexander Stephens Papers, Manhattanville College Library, Purchase, New York.

of Jesse Bright's support, and partly out of simple party loyalty. And one must not discount his sincere attachment to popular sovereignty as a philosophically sound principle of American government. As one of his district newspapers, the *Washington Democrat*, noted,

> "[r]epresentatives need not and should not wait to learn how their constituents will decide. Principles change not nor can the democratic creed. Democratic representatives should not enquire what the opinion of their constituents are upon a well-known principle, that has ever been maintained on the one hand and opposed on the other by the great political parties of the Union."

English also believed that he could convince his constituents that there was no fear that Kansas or Nebraska would adopt slavery, even with the repeal of the Missouri restriction.[49]

Other northern Democrats whose districts bordered on the Ohio River also voted in greater proportion than the northern Democracy as a whole against the party rebels.[50] Anti-slavery sympathy, or more precisely anti-southernism, was clearly greater in the northern sections of the Northwest than in those areas along the Ohio River. In the northern climes the penchant for national expansion was obviously checked by a greater fear that slavery and southern-like society would expand along with the nation. If the Democrats wished to maintain their force in the Northwest, they would have to convince the voters that the Kansas-Nebraska Act would not produce a slave West, or even one more slave state at all. This was the obvious line that any northern Douglas Democrat was forced to take, and English was as aware of this fact as any of them.

From late March until early May, the Pierce administration used patronage promises, threats, and appeals to party unity to try to pull wavering northern Democrats toward the bill. Most of these tactics were relatively common and low-grade—unfilled consulates were dangled, small offices pledged to representatives' family members, promises made to grant federal jobs to House members who might lose re-election for supporting the bill, or, alternatively, threats to cut off patronage to those Democrats who voted against it. Indeed, one reporter maintained how "surprising it was to see what small prices govern members in this market." Richardson also promised that when the bill came up for a vote he would move to strike out the Clayton Amendment; Jim Lane, for example, was thereby induced to support the measure. By the first week in May, the House managers

---

49. *Washington Democrat*, April 28, 1852. English's rationale, outside the Bright connection, may be gleaned from his later speech in support of the bill in *CG, 33-1*, Appendix, 606-610.

50. *CG, 33-1*, 703.

apparently believed that they had finally changed enough votes to proceed with a plan for the bill's passage. Richardson was to move that the House go into the Committee of the Whole, where he would attempt to get successive majority votes to lay aside the 18 bills preceding the old House version of the Nebraska bill (HR 236) and then move to substitute S 22 for it. He began this process on May 8. He was able to get the House to agree to go into the Whole, 109 to 88, relatively quickly. Alexander Stephens, a Georgia congressman who was in the midst of moving from the Whig to the Democratic Party, then hoped that it would take about a week to allow for the necessary procedure and speechmaking to bring the Senate bill to a final vote (though he was under no illusion that that final vote would be as large as a the 21 majority to go into the Whole). But the Opposition's continuous use of delaying tactics (polled motions to adjourn the House, for members to be excused, for tellers to be elected, for having the different bills read, for laying motions on the table, for calling for votes to appeal the Chair's rulings) were used to obstruct Richardson's progress. In one instance, during this two-week process, the sergeant at arms had to be called to the House to break up a melee around representative Campbell of Ohio that had members standing on their desks and shouting. One congressman, representative Edmundson of Virginia, had to be removed from the hall. In the midst of it all, congressmen made grand speeches on their opinions of the measure.[51]

Although genuinely disturbed by the bill's outright repeal of the Missouri Compromise, English had weighed the full impact of Kansas-Nebraska carefully. Increasingly, he began to convince himself that the bill's primary opponents were less interested in anti-slavery than they were in breaking down the Democratic Party. Consequently, between March and May, he took Bright's advice "to go to your *friends* for council always, not your enemies," and he actively began to lobby for the bill's success. As he later put it, he "labored many anxious days and nights as a member of an advisory committee which was called into being by the friends of the bill in caucus." He could well accept the now more palatable Senate version (without Clayton) when confronted with his perceived realization that the Whigs were using the bill to divide his beloved party. As a former fellow legislator wrote him, "vote for it and get it out of the way. If it does not pass before our next election comes off it may annoy us somewhat, therefore I say pass it and get rid of

---

51. Mark W. Summers, *The Plundering Generation: Corruption and the Crisis of the Union, 1849-1861* (Oxford, New York and Toronto: Oxford University Press, 1987), 209-211. Leonard L. Richards, *The Slave Power: The Free North and Southern Domination* (Baton Rouge: Louisiana State University Press, 2000). Nichols, *Blueprints*, 109-111. CG, 33-1, 1125-1130. Alexander Stephens to Linton Stephens, May 9, 1854, Stephens Papers, Manhattanville. Wolff, 177-180. *Washington* (County) *Democrat*, May 19, 1854. *Cannelton Reporter*, May 20, 1954. Joanne B. Freeman, *The Field of Blood: Violence in Congress and the Road to Civil War* (New York: Farrar, Straus, and Giroux. 2018), 93-94.

it, the people will then quit talking about it."[52] Unlike his mentor, Jesse Bright, English was never content to work primarily in the cloakrooms. On the most important issues, he eventually made a major speech spelling out his reasoning to both the House and his constituents. He began this habit with Kansas-Nebraska. On the first day of full debate, May 9, after four other congressmen offered their arguments, English was recognized by the Chair and rose to offer his own full understanding of the bill. He spoke as a key House member, a northern Democrat who initially had reservations concerning the measure. He spoke partly to explain how the revamped Senate bill met his earlier objections, and, primarily, how the passage of the bill was in the best interests of his section, his party, and his country.[53]

He began his effort, therefore, by downplaying his initial qualified opposition of January. He now claimed that in committee he had opposed the introduction of the bill primarily because he believed it was premature, that is, to provide organized government for the few settlers then living in the territory was hardly worth stirring up the sectional agitation that the repeal of the Missouri Compromise would certainly produce. On reflection, however, he now acknowledged that the timing might not have been premature after all, for the theretofore failure to organize this territory might have been the underlying cause for the dearth of its settlers. "It was highly important for the country that settlements should be encouraged along the great line of travel to the golden shores of the Pacific," he now maintained. At any rate, now that the bill has been introduced and agitation already unleashed, his earlier opposition on this score has become superfluous. As for the amendment he earlier proposed that would have circumvented the necessity of directly and specifically repealing the Missouri Compromise, (see p.111), he now argued that the key portion of that amendment was its unequivocal statement of popular sovereignty and that the present Senate bill had fully incorporated that principle. "I, of course, prefer my own proposition, but whenever my vote will secure the passage of any reasonable bill, it will not be withheld. The crisis will justify concession to minor issues."[54] And, in truth, English's amendment would have indirectly repealed the germane portion of the Missouri Compromise anyway; its early diplomatic wording was essentially intended to palliate northern voters.

Having dealt with his early reservations, English proceeded to the heart of his speech, which beat around a favorable interpretation of the principle of popular sovereignty. He praised the principle both theoretically and practically. In the

---

52. *Appendix to CG, 33-1*, 606. Jesse Bright to WHE, January 31, 1854, English Papers. *CG, 35-1*, 1013. James Slack to WHE, February 27, 1854, English Papers.

53. CG, 33-1, 1142.

54. *Appendix to the CG, 33-1,* 605, 606.

first place, he argued, it contained the essence of republicanism. Here he repeated word for word his remarks made to the House in January, adding only a slight addendum:

> A man who has exercised the attributes of a free citizen in Indiana, or any other State, loses none of his powers of self-government by emigrating to a Territory. Is he less virtuous, less intelligent, less imbued with the spirit of patriotism and love of country because he resides in a territory and not a State? . . . Shall he be taxed to support the government and yet not have a full voice in that legislation which is to govern him?[55]

Moreover, popular sovereignty was a principle consistent with the Democratic Party:

> The principle of non-intervention on the part of Congress with the domestic concerns of the States and organized Territories is no interpolation upon the democratic creed. In one shape or other it is as old as the creed itself. From the earliest days of the republic there has been a party favorable to the increase of the power of the federal government, and another based upon the rights of the States and the supremacy of the people. That was the leading division between the federal and republican parties, is, to some extent, an issue between the parties of the present day, and is certainly involved in the bill now under consideration.[56]

This was good rhetoric for the upcoming campaign, and, for the present, it attempted to put the bill in a more positive light. As a good Democrat, English equated democracy (and the people) with state and local government, and he implied that the central government (and the Whigs) consistently sought to reduce the individual's right to govern himself. This further implied that the Missouri Compromise, a product of federal intervention, was rather undemocratic. Appealing to the Jacksonian spirit still shining brightly within northern Democratic breasts, he went on to state that such federal intervention degraded the "rugged men of the frontier," who, though they "may know little of books, and still less of the cold forms and refinements of what is termed fashionable society, have read the great volume of nature [and] have done much to advance the prosperity and glory of the republic."[57] Anti-intellectualism was rather a staple of Jacksonian Democracy.

---

55. *Ibid.*, 607-608.

56. *Ibid.*, 609.

57. *Ibid.*, 608.

Slavery, of course, was just another one of those "domestic concerns" to be referred "to that best and safest of all tribunals—the people to be governed." Like liquor, polygamy, or voting rights, it was simply a "domestic institution," to be regulated according to what the white males of a state/territory "deem best suited to their climate, soil, and condition, and most conducive to their happiness and welfare." English was again now repeating what he had stated, rather word for word, in his first public sentiments on the subject back in January. He noted that despite the fact that "we [Indianians] do not like the institution in its moral, social, nor political bearing," Hoosiers had no "sickly sentimentality [!] upon the subject. It existed in all the states at the formation of the general government... and as a general rule we think Negroes are but little better off in a state of freedom at the North than they are in a state of slavery in the South." English's approach to slavery and the slave well represented the view of his constituents, as he argued that the institution at least served as "a means of Christianizing, civilizing, and regenerating the whole African race—now one degree removed from brute creation."[58]

Yet English was aware that it was one thing to argue the applicability of popular sovereignty to slavery and quite another to allow for the possibility that such an application might actually produce more slave states. Despite its 'undemocratic' features, the beauty of the Missouri restriction was that it was certain to prevent slaves and slavery from dominating the virgin West. Popular sovereignty, on the other hand, lacked that certainty. Thus, English had to illustrate for northern voters that popular sovereignty would effectually produce the same result as the Missouri restriction, that is, beyond its theoretical purity it was pragmatically sound as well. Consequently, after praising popular sovereignty in the abstract, English proclaimed that "in voting for the bill I do not vote to extend slavery . . . The people of these territories will never adopt the institution." He supported his assertion both demographically and geographically, predicting that only 30 percent of the migrants would come from the South and only one-third of those would be pro-slavery. This assertion was largely based upon his understanding that slaveholders had little to gain by relocating into Kansas and Nebraska. Not only was the climate inconducive to the planting of cotton, rice, and sugar, but the distinct possibility that the territory's electorate might vote to disallow slavery in its limits would inhibit slaveholder migration. Those southerners who did migrate, like earlier southern migrants to the Northwest, would do so partly to escape the effects of slavery and would hardly wish to promote the institution in their new land. And, indeed, English averred, 40 percent of the migrants would come from the free states and 30 percent from Europe. "Give the North, with her superior population, free and uninterrupted competition with the South, in the

---

58. *Ibid.,* 606.

settlement of these acquisitions, and slavery will never be extended much, if any, beyond its present limits."[59]

Given a calm, unagitated nature of settlement, English's analysis was essentially reasonable. But the Kansas-Nebraska bill had hardly produced a calm atmosphere. Subsequent events would illustrate that English's conclusions, while in the long-term essentially correct, in the short-term ignored the bill's dislodging effects. It might be unfair to assume that English should have been able to predict the anti-slavery emigrant aid societies and the Missouri border ruffians, but his cool, logical approach lacked a contextual imagination. In a certain sense, this was a function of his political temperament. Lacking any righteous indignation over slavery he was hard-pressed to imagine abolitionist tactics. Drawn personally to relatively moderate southerners, he could not predict the effect of the fire-eaters. As the decade progressed, his attempt to hold on to what he considered the rational middle-ground would slip out from under him as it became harder and harder to stand upon.

To his credit English was not content to let his assertions of superior northern migration stand alone. He also directly enunciated his opposition to one southern argument, by no means the most extreme, that slavery, legally recognized by the Constitution, was automatically legal in any territory prior to any territorial law that might restrict it—in other words, that a territory, previous to any law, was naturally open to slavery. English maintained, contrawise, like northerners in general, that the territories were naturally free, turning the southern argument on its head by asserting that slavery could only exist there by positive law: "Under the Senate bill slavery can have no legal existence unless the legislature chosen by the citizens of the Territory, give it being by legal enactment."[60]

English provided an array of legal precedents to support this essential point. The most impressive of these were Court holdings from southern judges. A citation from the Mississippi Supreme Court read "'the right of the master exists not by force of the law of nature or nations, but by virtue only of the positive law.'" Louisiana and Kentucky courts concurred in almost the exact language. English also cited U.S. Supreme Court justice John McLean, in circuit, who proclaimed that "'where slavery is not expressly established by law, every person, without distinction of color, is presumed to be free.'" McLean, of course, was a Whig and no southerner, but he did represent at least one vote on the high tribunal. Other "precedents" were not so convincing. English cited Henry Clay's belief, in relation to the Mexican Cession, that "'the idea that, upon the consummation of the treaty, the constitution of the United States spread itself over the entire territory, and carried along with it the institution of slavery, is so irreconcilable with any

---

59. *Ibid.*, 609, 610.

60. *Ibid.*, 606.

comprehension, or any reason which I possess, that I hardly know how to meet it.'" Though Clay had had many enemies, especially among Democrats, invoking his name certainly clothed the invoker with moderation and patriotism.[61]

The research that English did in order to support his positive law position illustrated how important this point was to northerners. With slavery disallowed into the territory before a territorial law was passed legalizing it, slave owners would be kept to a minimum, and English's demographic analysis might indeed come to fruition. But the argument went deeper than that, for it was really one that touched the root of national policy: was slavery national or was freedom? And would "the providence of God," as English stated, "some day [cause slavery] to cease to exist in this country," or was it destined to remain long after other nations had eradicated it? English and Douglas fervently believed that popular sovereignty, as interpreted by them, gave the edge to freedom, and the positive law argument was the clincher. Douglas never intended the repeal of the Missouri Compromise to effectuate the spread of slavery. In truth, as the more prescient southerners divined, the repeal held out false hope for slave owners and might later serve as a powerful and harmful disillusionment. Nonetheless, most southerners, like R.M.T. Hunter, pointed to "the moral triumph" of the repeal, which, "although not all that we thought the South entitled to, was a great advance upon the old order of things." Douglas and English were not averse to giving the South their "moral triumph," so long as the Missouri restriction would effectively remain in practice.[62]

It should, however, be pointed out that while English debunked the southern contention that slavery naturally and constitutionally was legal in a territory until it was prohibited by territorial law, he did not deal with the more extreme and increasingly ardent southern view that even a territorial legislature lacked constitutional power to prohibit slavery in its own territorial jurisdiction. The various arguments for this position concerned the limitations to restrictions on one's property under the due process clause of the Fifth Amendment and John C. Calhoun's assertion that one's property could not be prohibited from a territory because federal territories were held in common by all Americans. This southern view, of course, was later essentially upheld by the U.S. Supreme Court in the 1857 decision of *Dred Scott v. Sanford* (discussed below in Chapter Seven). R.M.T. Hunter's point that the Kansas-Nebraska bill did not give the South "all that they thought they were entitled to" is a reference to this contention. English ignored this argument in his speech, though he was certainly aware of it.[63]

---

61. *Ibid.*, 607, 606.

62. *Ibid.*, 606. R.M.T. Hunter to Shelton F. Leake, October 16, 1857, in Charles H. Ambler, ed., *Correspondence of R.M.T. Hunter, 1826-1876* (1954; repr., New York: De Capo Press, 1971), 238. Johannsen, *Stephen Douglas*, 421.

63. For a nice summation of these Southern contentions see Potter, *Impending Crisis*, 60, 276.

Although most of English's speech was devoted to discussing the substantive merits of the bill, he also significantly noted its politically partisan effects. Ever fearful of the possible future triumph of the infidel Whigs, he pointed out that Democrats who opposed Kansas-Nebraska only strengthened "the common enemy." He appealed to his Democratic colleagues

> to consider well whether this is not only a democratic measure, right in principle, but whether, also, there is not, under existing circumstances, a party necessity for its passage. Without intending it, I much fear that [Democrats who oppose the measure] are playing into the hands of those who would glory in seeing the democracy prostrated in the dust.

English brushed aside the argument that it was the passage of the bill itself that would destroy the northern Democracy. When "its principles were discussed and better understood," he said, it would "wear well."[64] These were easy words from one who represented a relatively politically safe district and probably were sardonically received by congressmen representing more frigid climes.

One might argue that it would have simply been out of character for so inbred a Democrat to have opposed this measure. Backed by the administration, by Bright, by Douglas, and by Lewis Cass, it would appear that English could not have failed to support it. But simple party loyalty for party's sake alone should not be misunderstood. While Whigs and Democrats battled over what were essentially issues of economics and federalism during the second party system, their attacks on each other rather appear to have been incommensurate to the issues at stake. That is, each party appeared to be convinced that the success of the other would spell the end of the republic and that virtue and decency were contained only within their group. It was not simply that Democrats castigated Whigs as aristocratic heirs of the Federalists, but it was the employment of excessive rhetoric in doing so. Indeed, each election was cast as crucial to the survival of the republic. This continued identification of the rival party as "traitors" bent on the destruction of true American principles created a political outlook among some Whigs and Democrats that made party success essential to the survival of the nation. It allowed, perhaps, wider support of some of each party's more questionable measures than might have otherwise been expected. From this prism, English's devotion to the Democracy may be better understood.[65]

But of course many lifelong Democrats did not support the Kansas-Nebraska Bill, and in the end it was English's virulently anti-black, anti-abolitionist constit-

---

64. *Appendix to the CG*, 33-1, 608, 609.

65. The surprisingly harsh rhetoric used toward opposing party members during Whig-Democratic elections is cogently discussed in Silbey, *The American Political Nation*, esp. 92-94.

uency that allowed him the luxury of remaining firmly in the Democratic fold. As the *New Albany Tribune* cogently noted, "there would be far greater opposition to the bill if the Abolitionists were not so rampant against it." The apparently democratic appeal of popular sovereignty and of congressional non-intervention into the 'domestic institutions' of territorial citizens also helped. Benjamin P. Douglass remarked that those principles were well accepted in the district, as many believed that they were "the only way we can ever hope to rid Congress of the agitation of the slavery question." English's constituents were willing to trust in the application of those principles and to allow the removal of what their congressman called the "exciting question of slavery" to "the limited and less dangerous sphere of the people immediately interested in its decision."[66]

English's worthy oration lasted about an hour, after which he immediately left the hall. Reaction to his effort depended of course on one's political position, but in all events his speech was not ignored. The administration organ, the *Washington Union*, labeled it "direct and orthodox" and called English "the embodiment of a stem and sterling democracy." Lewis Cass, the essential originator of popular sovereignty, apparently agreed, for he was said to have remarked that "it was the only speech that clearly defined his position relative to the non-intervention doctrine." A correspondent from Ocala, Florida, however, wrote English that while he generally agreed with the first-term congressman's argument, he was "hostile to the 'squatter sovereignty' doctrine which occasionally flashes through the composition."[67] This may be taken to have been typical of the orthodox southern reaction: grateful for the support for the repeal of the Missouri Compromise, but not yet convinced that slavery could be excluded from a new territory before it wrote its state constitution.

Back home, Democrats applauded English's style. The *Paoli Eagle* proudly praised his "nerve" for being "the only member from Indiana that made a speech in favor of the Nebraska bill." Similarly, the *Washington Democrat* called the effort "direct and orthodox" and noted that "it abounded with useful and practical information." J.M. Beatty, editor of the independently Whig *Cannelton Reporter,* though differing with English on the merits of Kansas-Nebraska, complimented him by writing that "his speech displays research, learning, and a more than ordinary ability. As an energetic, working representative, this district has never had Mr. E.'s superior." Michael Bright sent his congratulations and sweetened them by adding that English would be re-nominated by acclamation. "There will be no opposition."[68]

---

66. *New Albany Tribune*, February 6, 1854. B.P. Douglass to WHE, April 4, 1854, English papers. *Appendix to CG, 33-1,* 605.

67. *Washington Union*, in *New Albany Ledger*, June 2, 1854. *Paoli Eagle*, June 2, 1854. D. [Privener] to WHE, June 7, 1854, English papers.

68. *Paoli Eagle*, June 2, 1854. *Washington* (County) *Democrat*, June 2, 1854. *Cannelton Reporter*, July 15, 1854. M.G. Bright to WHE, May 30, 1854, English papers.

Strong opposition was registered, however, by Milton Gregg's *New Albany Tribune*, which printed a series of articles at the end of May commenting adversely on the speech. Gregg ridiculed English's contention that emigration to Kansas would principally come from the North. He pointed out that that the whole eastern border of Kansas was shared with Missouri, and citizens from that slave state had "but to step over the line and take possession of the country." This was to a certain extent remarkably prescient. He also noted that Kansas provided the eastern slave-owner, whose lands were worn out by cultivation, with a perfect spot to resettle with his chattel. The geographical position of Kansas, lying generally on the same latitude as Missouri, was not so far north that it should prohibit the introduction of planation economy.[69] Gregg's criticism on this point recognized that the eastern third of Kansas was much like Missouri in climate and not inconducive to plantation agriculture.

The *Tribune* was also skeptical of English's constitutional argument, as the newspaper maintained that slavery would certainly be introduced into Kansas even without a positive law. "What is there to hinder slavery from emigrating into the territory, and existing there *illegally*, if you please," before the legislature met. "Will the general government establish a line of military posts all along the eastern border? We rather think not, especially under the present ruling dynasty." A few months later, Gregg attacked English's theory more directly. "Slavery is the creature of positive law, says Mr. English. Now suppose we ask him to show us the law establishing slavery in Kentucky—can he do it? Not at all. And yet we all know that slavery exists there…It exists by toleration, by permission, by sufferance, and because it is not directly prohibited." Gregg called popular sovereignty "buncombe." There was really much in the bill that made a mockery of local autonomy, he argued, given that all the major officials, including the governor, were to be appointed by the administration. Gregg conveniently ignored English's outspoken willingness, made even within his congressional speech, to vote for an amendment that would have allowed Kansas and Nebraska the right to choose their own executive officials. Opponents of the bill actually opposed such an amendment because they feared that it would have made the bill more palatable.[70]

With more justice Gregg derided English's argument that the bill's passage would allay further agitation. "It ill becomes the incendiary who fires his own barn," the *Tribune* remarked, "to call upon his neighbor to fire his also that the excitement may soon be allayed." (Presumably that remark was aimed at the argument that debating slavery in the territories was less dangerous than debating it in Congress.) English's optimism, the Whig editor maintained, was woefully misplaced: "the question of *repeal* will be raised by the people." Gregg also had

69. *New Albany Tribune*, May 29, 1854.

70. *New Albany Tribune*, May 29, September 7, May 30, 1854. *Appendix to the CG, 33-1,* 609.

his own explanation for English's eventual acceptance of the bill. Back in January, he argued, English was reacting substantively, "but now, the indignation of the country being aroused, its passage had become *a question of life and death* politically with Franklin Pierce and Stephen Douglas." Gregg did not elaborate on why English would be so concerned with these men's political fate; Gregg's argument may have been stronger if he more directly charged English with blind loyalty to a *Democratic Party* measure than to concern with any specific Democrats. Moreover, Gregg's *own* reason for opposing the bill was partisan—it was primarily to revive the Indiana Whigs from their death-like slumber. This "act of perfidy," he maintained, which repealed "a solemn *compact* entered into between North and South," was to be the catalyst by which the Democracy could be laid low.[71]

In taking on the Indiana Democracy, Gregg had help from Indiana Democrats themselves. During the congressional debates on the bill, Daniel Mace, Democratic congressman from Indiana's Eighth District in the west central part of the state, was conspicuously skeptical that the Kansas-Nebraska bill would work to prevent slavery from extending into the territories. On May 18, convinced that the supporters of the bill had no intention of allowing Kansans or Nebraskans to legislate on slavery until they drew up their state constitutions, Mace offered an amendment expressly giving the territorial legislatures "full power, at any session thereof, to establish or prohibit slavery in said territory." Before a vote was taken on the amendment, English rose to ask Mace if he would vote for the bill if it was so revised. Mace responded that he would, but he fully expected northern "doughfaces" to defeat his amendment, thus obviating that necessity. At any rate, he maintained, even if by some means his amendment should pass, he was fully convinced that southern Democrats would never vote for a measure that specifically allowed a territorial legislature to prohibit slavery. In such a manner Mace made public the sectionally duplicitous interpretation by the bill's supporters. As Mace promised to vote for the bill if his proposal passed, English promised and did vote for the amendment, the substance of which English claimed was "substantially incorporated in the Senate bill." But as Mace predicted, the amendment was defeated with only one of the bill's supporters voting for it: William English.[72]

Alexander Stephens, having predicted two weeks earlier that the Senate's version of the Kansas-Nebraska bill would be brought to the floor for a vote within a week, began to "chafe" at the apparently endless amendments that were being brought forward. On Sunday, May 21, he complained to his brother that the "timid" policy of Richardson and other Democratic "leaders" was getting the bill nowhere. "How

---

71. *New Albany Tribune*, May 25, 1854. The *Corydon Argus*, another Second District Whig sheet, also noted that English was among those Hoosier representatives who "have bartered away to the minions of slavery a great tract of free territory, yielded up to freedom forever by a solemn compromise." In *Paoli Eagle*, June 16, 1854.

72. *CG, 33-1*, 1238.

long we shall be thus occupied," he wrote his brother, "I cannot tell, [b]ut if I had my way not one minute." His plan to get the bill through was to "strike out the enabling clause which will cut off amendments." It would also be tantamount to a rejection of the bill by the Committee of the Whole. But Stephens, knowing the "friends of the bill" had a majority, reasoned that when the report of such rejection would be taken to the House in regular session, that majority would vote down the report and take up the bill for a final vote. The next day, Stephens carried through such a course, and the Kansas-Nebraska bill finally came up for a vote. Administration pressure had done its work, and it rather comfortably passed, 113 to 100. Southerners voted 69 to 9 in favor of it, most of the southern opponents being Whigs. Northern Whigs voted unanimously, 44 to 0, against it. It was the northern Democrats who were most clearly divided over what to do. It is almost too fitting to report that they split just about down the middle: 44 to 43 in favor of the bill. Only in Pennsylvania and Indiana did a majority of these Democrats vote in support of the bill. In Indiana, only two of the nine Democratic congressmen voted against the bill, making the Hoosier Democracy the most supportive northern Democratic state.[73]

Sectional and Party Breakdown of the House Vote on Kansas-Nebraska Bill

	YES	NO
Southern Democrats	57	2
Southern Whigs	12	7
*Northern Whigs	0	48
Northern Democrats	44	43
*Whigs	12	55
Democrats	101	45
South	69	9
North	44	91

*includes 4 Free Soil votes

73. Alexander Stephens to Linton Stephens, May 21, 1854, Stephens Papers, Manhattanville. *CG, 33-1*, 1241-1242, 1254. Dubin, *Congressional Elections*, 163-168.

The 1854 congressional and state election campaigns were less than three months away. How would the northern electorate react to those northern congressmen—all Democrats—who voted for a bill that repealed the Missouri Compromise and allowed the possibility of slavery extending into the territories? How would northern state Democratic politicians reconcile their differences on the bill? Could the Whigs revive themselves in the North by their opposition to this bill? In essence, how deep would this bill change the party structure of the United States? And what effect would it have on the political future of William English?

4.

As the 1854 electoral campaign approached, Graham Fitch wrote English that "the recent review of all the issues against us will give us a fight just sufficiently warm to be interesting."[74] He clearly understated the case, for the heat was great enough to blaze a trail right through the heart of Indiana's Democracy. The traditional Whig opposition in this election was strengthened by three groups, each of which was either new or not previously as prevalent in the earlier battles between the parties. Galvanized by the anger over the Kansas-Nebraska Act, the adherents of these three groups fused with old-line Whigs to form a stronger opposition to the Democratic Party than it had encountered for some time.

The first element of this fusion, temperance reform, would appear initially to have little to do with slavery, and indeed its strength was primarily an outgrowth of the evangelical movement usually called the Second Great Awakening. The national temperance movement slowly gained steam throughout the 1830s and 1840s, and its relation to anti-slavery was to associate the drunkard with the slaveholder: both committed mortal sins and both were in thrall to those sins. In their reliance on slave labor on the one hand and demon rum on the other, neither exhibited republican behavior, that is, neither was truly free and independent. In 1851 temperance reformers in Maine were strong enough to produce a state law prohibiting the sale of alcohol statewide. In Indiana, in January 1854, a few days before the country was even aware of the Nebraska bill, the greatest state temperance convention to date met at the Masonic Hall in Indianapolis. A year earlier, the state legislature had adopted a local option law allowing a majority of voters in each township to regulate the sale of liquor as they wished. The Indiana Supreme Court declared that law unconstitutional, but that only served to spur the reformers to greater efforts. The great 1854 state temperance convention thus ensued. It resolved to use its financial and public influence, connected especially

---

74. G.N. Fitch to WHE, July 18, 1854, English papers.

to Indiana's Methodist churches, to elect only candidates who supported a strong "search, seizure, confiscation, and destruction law."[75]

Prominent among temperance advocates was Democratic governor Joseph Wright, but the bulk of the reformers were Whigs. The Democratic Party was generally wary of governmental regulation of the liquor traffic, for both politically crass and politically philosophical reasons. On the mundane level it feared to alienate the support it enjoyed among Irish and German voters; both of these groups it considered would be opposed to liquor restrictions. But more deeply, Democratic ideology generally abhorred the use of government to enforce individual morality. As English said in another context, "we [Democrats] think it is enough for us to attend to our own business, and let the business of our neighbors alone." This was illustrative of a key difference between the parties. For Democrats, government primarily existed only to keep public order and to prevent powerful men and interests from abusing their power over "common" white men. For Whigs, one of government's purposes was to promote the individual's and society's development to their full potential.[76]

In the main, Democrats were afraid of a heavily regulative liquor bill, which they maintained would threaten their individual freedom. While a portion of Democrats were drawn to temperance reform, many members of the Party believed that it was primarily a "Whig scheme to break up the Democracy." Ideally the Party wished to remove the issue from the political arena, but, as Michael Garber perceived in the spring of 1854, the "temperance men stand with the balance of power in their hands." Some observers in early 1854 even considered the liquor question would be the controlling one in the fall campaign. At their state convention in late May, the Democrats tried to appeal to the temperance vote by labeling "intemperance" a "great moral and social evil," and endorsing "necessary and proper" legislation to "restrain" it. But they could not condone "authorization of search, seizure, and confiscation and destruction of private property."[77] This was too weak a stance for most temperance advocates, and they looked to the opposition party to fulfill their objectives.

By itself the liquor question was dangerous enough to the Democracy, but in concert with other issues it became even more threatening. One of these was

75. Van Bolt, "Fusion out of Confusion," 354. Crane, "Joseph A. Wright," 202-03. Carter "Hoosier History," 88. William E. Gienapp, *Origins of the Republican Party, 1852-1856* (New York and Oxford: Oxford University Press, 1979), 107. T. A. Goodwin, *Seventy-Six Years Tussle with the Traffic* (Indianapolis: Carlon and Hollenbeck, 1883), 9-10. Stoler, "Insurgent Democrats," 12.

76. Crane, "Joseph Wright," 203-206. *Appendix to the CG, 34-3,* 107. Jean H. Baker, *Affairs of Party: The Political Culture of the Northern Democrats in the mid-Nineteenth Century* (Ithaca and London: Cornell University Press, 1983), 144-146. Howe, *Political Culture of the Whigs,* 20, 36.

77. *Indiana State Sentinel,* January 11, 1854. Crane, "Joseph Wright," 206. *Madison Courier,* April 18, 1854. *Indiana State Sentinel,* May 26, 1854.

nativism, which became a national force in the late 1840s as a reaction to the influx of Irish and German immigrants, most of whom were Catholics. By the late 1850s, the movement had coalesced into a rather secretive association, which the public knew as the "Know-Nothings." (Though it had for a long time been generally accepted that this title derived from its adherents denying knowledge of its existence, it was more likely a term fastened onto them by their enemies.[78]) Decrying the increasing political strength in numbers of these immigrants and perceiving them as often unwilling to assimilate to so-called American ways, the Know-Nothings called for such "reforms" as a longer naturalization period, restriction of the franchise to American citizens, allowing only native-born Americans to hold office, and refusing to allow foreign "paupers" to enter the country. The Know-Nothings also espoused a negative attitude toward established political parties, deeming them corrupt and unresponsive to the populace. Adherents came from disillusioned members of both parties, but its supporters were chiefly Whigs, who were clearly frustrated by the Democratic bloc voting of these Irish and German immigrants and more affected by the Protestant evangelism of the Second Great Awakening.[79] Know-nothingism offered a convenient and practical home to those opposed to the Kansas-Nebraska Act, who saw it as evidence of corrupt party politics but were yet unwilling to make the divisive issue of slavery their main talking point.[80]

In February of 1854, political nativism was formally introduced into Indiana when a Know-Nothing lodge was founded in Dearborn County. That year it spread throughout the state. In May of 1854, its leadership claimed 30,000 members; in July, 60,000; in September, 87,000. Especially in the southern part of the state, including New Albany and Jeffersonville, it was difficult to go many days without seeing one of the ubiquitous right-angled triangular pieces of paper strewn about notifying the membership of an impending meeting. Back in 1852, the Whigs had actually attempted to woo the immigrant vote by spreading the

---

78. Tyler G. Anbinder, *Nativism and Slavery: The Northern Know-Nothings and the Politics of the 1850s* (New York and Oxford: Oxford University Press, 1992), 21-22.

79. *Ibid.*, 63-65. Some historians have maintained that those who saw their status declining were drawn to such nativism by locating outsiders as the culprits for their decline. Others have argued that the unresponsive attitude of the Whigs and Democrats to popular frustrations caused resort to other institutional approaches to politics. (As one Louisville newspaper noted the next year, "the rule of old political cliques must be broken and new and reliable men placed at the head of affairs." *Louisville Courier* in *Cannelton Reporter,* June 20, 1855.) For a brief look at the general historiography concerning the Know-Nothings see the Introduction to Anbinder, *Nativism and Slavery,* ix-xii. For a newer study of the Know-Nothings that concentrates on three counties in the United States to draw general conclusions concerning the order see Mark Voss-Hubbard, *Beyond Party: Cultures of Antipartisanship in Northern Politics before the Civil War,* (Baltimore and London: The Johns Hopkins University Press, 2002.)

80. Stephen E. Maizlish, "The Meaning of Nativism and the Crisis of the Union: The Know-Nothing Movement in the Antebellum North," in Maizlish, ed., *Essays on America Antebellum Politics 1840-1860* (College Station: Texas A&M University Press, 1982), 181-182.

fact that Franklin Pierce, when a member of the New Hampshire constitutional convention, had voted for a provision to exclude Catholics from holding office.[81] Spurned at the polls by Irish and German Catholics anyway, two years later they gave up their wooing and spoke of reviving their party with the help of nativist Know-Nothings, including former Democrats.

Although the Know-Nothings espoused a general anti-immigrant programme, it appears the foreigners it most despised were Roman Catholics. The Catholic hierarchy in the United States did not help matters when it appealed for public funds for their parochial schools and attacked the public (or common) schools for their use of the Protestant King James Bible in instruction. The Catholic attack on public schools reminded the Know-Nothings of the medieval Church's reaction to widespread education in general and was presently viewed as an attack on American republicanism. That immigrant Catholics voted as a bloc for the Democratic Party also made them a threat to republicanism, as Know-Nothings argued that these immigrants were not acting as free individuals but were manipulated by their church and the Democratic Party.[82]

Sensing that "every broken down Whig is trying to avail himself of this association," the Indiana Democrats generally took a firm stand against it. In opposing nativism, they not only helped ensure the Catholic immigrant vote but also took the high moral ground against intolerance. The Whig Party had traditionally "sought," as one historian has put it, "moral integration of the community through enforced conformity to Anglo-Protestant norms." It often appeared to promote the goal of a culturally uniform society. Democrats seemed far less concerned with such cultural uniformity. When it came to the private practice of white Americans, Democrats generally appeared to be far more tolerant of individual differences. In their May state convention at Indianapolis, this tendency instructed them to "condemn" all "secret organizations" that aimed to disrobe citizens of political, civil, or religious liberty.[83]

The Know-Nothings did not view themselves as intolerant and neither did the temperance reformers. Catholicism, foreign influence, and liquor, they reasoned, all posed threats to American liberty. Catholics were enslaved by the Church, foreigners by their long acquiescence under monarchy, and drunkards by their de-

---

81. Carl F. Brand, "The History of the Know-Nothing Party in Indiana," *Indiana Magazine of* History, 18, no. 1 (March, 1922), 58-61. Beeler, "Election of 1852" (part 2), 41.

82. Gienapp, *Origins*, 60-61, 92-98, has a nice overview of how the Know-Nothings considered Catholicism as essentially anti-republican.

83. A. Bussy to WHE, July 13, 1854, English papers. Paul Kleppner, *The Third Electoral System, 1853-1892* (Chapel Hill: University of North Carolina Press, 1979), 60. Howe, "Political Culture of Whigs," 20. *Indiana State Sentinel*, May 26, 1854. The use of the word "citizens" in the Democratic resolution is interesting, for, in truth, Know-Nothings were aiming their arrows at immigrants who were not yet full citizens, though many of them could vote.

pendence on drink. Reigning republican ideology held that only a free, independent, and industrious citizenry could perpetuate freedom in any polity. Catholics, foreigners, and 'alcoholics' represented quite the opposite. Like the Whigs, the nativist and temperance reformers perceived freedom not only as individual, but also as organic. Viewing the matter from this angle, it was not necessarily inconsistent for one to be both a Know-Nothing or temperance reformer and an opponent of slavery. Like liquor, foreign influence, and Catholicism, slavery inhibited an independent and industrious citizenry: slave owners slothfully depended upon slaves to perform their labor. In essence, the slave system degraded labor, and by doing so it produced an unrepublican, dependent citizenry. By focusing not on slavery's effect on the black slave but rather its effect upon the white freeman, a Know-Nothing or temperance reformer could make common cause with those opposed to the extension of slavery westward.[84]

Anti-slavery, or more properly "freesoilism," the belief that slavery should be prohibited from the western territories, was then the third idea that led many northerners to oppose the Democratic Party in 1854. It was re-stimulated by the passage of the Kansas-Nebraska Act, and, indeed, those who espoused free soil in Kansas and Nebraska and called for reinstatement of the Missouri Compromise were generally known as a group as "Anti-Nebraskans" in 1854. In this effort both Whigs and Democrats participated more evenly. In Indiana it appealed to the old Wilmot Proviso wing of the Hoosier Democracy, and one correspondent of English's estimated that about one-tenth of party members adhered to it. The Democratic Party leadership knew that the anti-Nebraska Democrats would give them the most trouble at their state convention, and they laid plans to squelch it and other "non-Democratic" sentiment. As the *Paoli Eagle* later remarked, "we never before witnessed such a vast number of the old and steady men of our party in attendance at a state convention." All too clearly leading the old guard was Indiana's senior senator Jesse Bright. A month before the convention met, while still in Washington, Bright had raised money to start a well-financed newspaper outside Indianapolis with the purpose of supporting Bright candidates for state offices. In mid-May, he left Congress to attend the convention personally and maneuvered successfully to get himself elected its permanent president. In that capacity he controlled the Party platform by approving the members to the Resolutions Committee. Besides reporting out the anti-Know-Nothing and anti-temperance planks noted earlier, the Committee framed a resolution that "fully approved of the principles of the Kansas-Nebraska Act." It also "cordially endorsed the actions

---

84. This paragraph follows the general thesis of Maizlish, "The Meaning of Nativism," who, in truth, owes gratitude to Holt, *Political Crisis*, and, ultimately, to Eric Foner, *Free Soil, Free Labor, Free Men: The Ideology of the Republican Party before the Civil War* (London: Oxford University Press, 1970), despite the fact that Foner and Holt disagree with each other on the importance of antislavery in the 1854 Opposition to the Democrats.

of our Senators and Representatives in sustaining the same."[85] This latter part of the resolution was a clear criticism of Indiana's two Democratic congressmen who had voted against the bill.

Bright's pre-convention preparations worked well and the full convention passed the resolution despite vociferous protest by the anti-Nebraska delegates. Immediately afterward, one of the pro-Nebraska delegates introduced a motion to expel from the Party those Democrats who had opposed the resolution. Before the motion could be properly entertained, the anti-Nebraska delegates, led by future Republican governor Oliver P. Morton, walked out of the convention. The remaining delegates then essentially read the opponents of the Kansas-Nebraska Act out of the Party. As pro-Nebraskan Christopher C. Graham wrote English a few days later (English having remained in Washington for the finalization of the House debate over Kansas-Nebraska), "we do not recognize any one as one of us who oppose it." As most of those Democrats who opposed the resolution supported Wright over Bright in intraparty squabbles, their purgation not only rid the Hoosier Democracy of its free soil element but also appeared to illustrate Bright's strength in relation to the governor. (Wright, himself, however, did not publicly oppose Kansas-Nebraska.) Bright may have also wished to 'read out' the delegates who supported temperance reform, most of whom were Wright supporters. But as the governor himself was on record as being rather supportive of temperance efforts, this would hardly be possible. The Convention merely formally condemned "all political organizations based on the single idea of temperance reform as dangerous to our republican form of government [because they] withdrew the attention of the people from the great political principles upon which it is founded."[86]

The Convention's last act was to draw up an "Address to the People of Indiana." It stated that "Aristocracy" was again rearing its hoary head, and was, as usual, "willing to coalesce with any faction, to wed with any popular heresy, and

---

85. George Julian maintained that the anti-Nebraska movement was more about "the duty of keeping covenants and the wickedness of reviving sectional agitation than the evils of slavery." *Political Recollections,* 136-137. Christopher Columbus Graham to WHE, May 30, 1854, English Papers. *Paoli Eagle,* June 2, 1854. Crane. "Joseph Wright," 228-229. *Indiana State Sentinel,* May 26, 1854. *Washington* (County) *Democrat,* June 2, 1854.

86. Van der Weele, "Jesse Bright," 146-147. Van Bolt, "Fusion out of Confusion," 371-374. Christopher Columbus Graham to WHE, May 30, 1854, English Papers. Crane, "Joseph Wright," 229-30. *Indiana State Sentinel,* May 26, 1854. William Gienapp, in his book recounting the origins of the Republican Party, maintains that there is no contemporary evidence supporting the fact that any anti-Nebraska dissident Democrats walked out of the convention, nor is there evidence that a resolution was introduced to read them out of the Party. The only evidence of such events occurred much later. But Gienapp *does* note that the many county and district conventions subsequent to the state meeting did indeed ostracize these dissidents. Gienapp, *Origins,* 108. One piece of later evidence of expulsion appeared in William Dudley Foulke, *Life of Oliver P. Morton, Including His Important Speeches* (Indianapolis and Kansas City: The Bowen-Merrill Co., 1899), vol. 1, 39.

to court any *ism* or vagrant party organization which either directly or remotely promised to strengthen its numbers." As always, the Democrats saw the opposition as a modern version of the Federalists, demagogically and ironically appealing to popular passions in order to gain power. When the Convention adjourned, Austin Brown wrote English that, considering all that might have gone awry, the meeting was "very harmonious." In truth, the high-handedness of the Bright forces was resented by many delegates.[87]

For almost two months after their state convention, the Democratic organization had the field to itself. This did not mean that the opposition was idle; on the contrary, Know-Nothings, free-soilers, temperance advocates, and old-line Whigs were planning to coalesce into one political unit. The Whigs, who still had some semblance of party organization, were reluctant to publicly commandeer the coalition for fear that this would antagonize many anti-Nebraska, pro-temperance, and Know-Nothing Democrats. As Godlove Orth, a young Whig and prominent Know-Nothing, observed, "the Whigs must control…without seeming to do so." The editor of the Whig state organ, the *Indianapolis Journal,* agreed, refusing to allow his newspaper to call for a Whig state convention. He instead prevailed upon discontented and purged Democrats to make the first move. In truth, these Democrats needed little prompting, for almost immediately after they returned from the Democratic convention, they held meetings to select local candidates to oppose their former party affiliates. Michael Garber was the first purged Democrat to suggest all-out state fusion with other anti-Democratic groups, and in this manner, the People's Party was born.[88]

One unifying force of the new party was the Protestant religion. Especially vocal of late were the Methodists, who were not only the largest of the state's religious denominations but the most widespread as well. Many of their ministers had become so anti-slavery that at the Democratic state convention Bright lieutenant and English correspondent John L. Robinson called them "three thousand abolitionists sent out of New England." In retaliation, Reverend Benjamin F. Crary made a "vitriolic" attack on the Democratic Party platform, which was given wide currency in the opposition press. The personal war between Robinson and the Methodists continued throughout June, when Robinson was reputed to have called the ministers "itinerant vagabonds and irresponsible tax evaders." Robinson was probably playing a losing game, for, as one historian has noted, Indiana was in a state of development, between frontier and industrial phases, when religious enthusiasm tended to run high. The relative ease by which the disparate

---

87. *New Albany Ledger*, May 26, 1854. Austin H. Brown to WHE, May 26, 1854, English Papers. Van der Weele, "Jesse Bright," 149-150.

88. Godlove Orth to Schuyler Colfax, July 14, 1854, in Van Bolt, "Fusion Out of Confusion," 377. John Defrees to Schuyler Colfax, June 16, 1854, in Smith, *Schuyler Colfax,* 50. Van Der Weele, "Jesse Bright," 151-152.

members of the opposition coalition came together may well be explained by alliances formed from membership in sympathetic churches.[89]

By the time the People's state convention met in Indianapolis on July 12, the leaders of the new party had decided that its central *public* tenet would be opposition to the extension of slavery. Only a small portion of the delegates were actual abolitionists—the majority was composed of men who believed in both the 1820 and 1850 compromises. They adopted a plank that repudiated the principles of the Kansas-Nebraska Act, promoted the restoration of the Missouri Compromise, and declared "uncompromising opposition to the extension of slavery." Abolitionist and former Free Soil congressman George Julian, already such a prominent anti-slavery spokesman that he had run for vice president on the Free Soil ticket in 1852, had suggested a more extreme plank. It described the Kansas-Nebraska Act "as part of a concerted movement to nationalize slavery" and asserted that the repeal of the Missouri Compromise "exonerated the North from the duty of further acquiescing in and obeying the Compromise of 1850." Julian sarcastically argued that "every doughface in Indiana can [simply] demand the restoration of the Missouri Compromise because he can expound it as the limit of his anti-slavery designs and as a mere rebuke to the Administration for disturbing the 'healing measures' of 1850." But Julian's substitute resolution was defeated, as it went well beyond where the coalition wanted to go concerning slavery, especially if it wanted to win in October.[90]

The Democratic press nevertheless attempted to attach the label of extremism to this anti-slavery plank of the new party. The *Paoli Eagle*, foreshadowing a tactic that would be increasingly used by even more moderate Democratic sheets, argued that the People's Party desired to "repeal or destroy the thirteenth article of the Constitution of Indiana, which prohibits the emigration of free Negroes into the state." Going further, it accused the People's Party of "wishing to see the right of voting extended to Negroes." This scare tactic was not without force, but the convention's defeat of Julian's resolutions and the disappointment of the established anti-slavery press with the People's convention's narrow stance on the issue diminished the credibility of the *Eagle*'s assertions. The extremely anti-slavery *Free Democrat*, for example, called the People Party's anti-slavery resolutions "too tame and too limited for the occasion." And, indeed, compared to other opposition platforms outside of Indiana, they were.[91]

89. Van Bolt, "Fusion out of Confusion," 381. Carter, "Hoosier Decade," 291. Van Bolt, "Fusion," 373. Moore, *Schuyler Colfax,* 53. *Paoli Eagle*, June 30, 1854, from the *Indiana Sentinel.* Carter, "Hoosier History," 285-286.

90. Carter, "Hoosier History," 97. *Indiana Free Democrat*, in *New Albany Tribune,* July 22, 1854. *Indianapolis Journal,* July 14, 1854. Grace Julian Clarke, *George S. Julian* (Indianapolis: Indiana Historical Commission, 1923), 151-152.

91. *Paoli Eagle*, July 28, 1854. *Indiana Free Democrat*, in *New Albany Tribune,* July 22, 1854.

The nature of the strength of the three elements of temperance, nativism, and anti-slavery at the People's convention is difficult to properly ascertain. Added to the free soil resolution was a temperance plank that declared "intemperance a great political, moral, and social evil [and] a legitimate subject of legislation," though this resolution was somewhat ameliorated by noting that any law should be "judicious, constitutional, and efficient." Although the wording appeared not much stronger than the Democratic resolution on temperance, the omission of any disapproval of seizure of property and the fact that two of the four later nominees to state office were considered strong temperance advocates made it clear where the Party truly stood. What at first glance appears even stranger was that there was no plank directly espousing the goals of the nativists. Such omission would seem to argue that the Know-Nothings were not well represented at the convention, but quite the opposite appears to have been the case. During the two days before the People's convention met, a separate gathering of Know-Nothings (including Milton Gregg of New Albany) convened in the same city. The meeting was so secretive that it was physically shuttered. But it turned out that three-quarters of the delegates to the People's Convention had also been delegates to this Know-Nothing conclave. Moreover, the state ticket supported at the Know-Nothing gathering was the same ticket of candidates later selected at the People's convention. Apparently, the Know-Nothings believed that a public People's Party resolution supporting their principles was asymmetric to their clandestine character and anti-Party rhetoric—it was more important and effective to put their partisans in public office than to advertise their precepts. The Know-Nothing strength in the coalition is also illustrated by the fact that every congressional candidate later nominated at district conventions was a member of a Know-Nothing lodge.[92]

The Democrats lampooned the new party by calling it "piebald," "mongrel," and "confusionist." They mockingly predicted that should it ever gain power it would never be able to govern effectively. Only the thirst for office, they asserted, kept the coalition together. One Democratic newspaper went so far as to call the adherents to the new party "the scum and fagends of creation, broken-down politicians, men who never were and never can be anything but apes and instruments in the hands of others." Years later, when Lew Wallace (the author of *Ben-Hur*), then an Indiana Democrat, wrote of this campaign, he likened the Democracy to a "whale assailed at the same time by many boats harpooning it from every

---

92. *Indianapolis Journal*, July 14, 1854. Brand, "Know-Nothing Party in Indiana," 62-63. Gienapp, *Origins*, 109-110. The only remotely nativist resolution "utterly condemned the abusive attacks which have been made on the Protestant ministry." The *Indiana State Sentinel*, on July 22, 1854, maintained that only two of the five People's Party candidates on the state ticket were actually affiliated with know-nothingism. Brand notes the same thing, "Know Nothing Party," 65. This is probably a mistaken assessment, as these same candidates were nominated by the Know-Nothing gathering. It is quite possible that the secretive nature of lodge membership may have caused the *Sentinel*'s mistake.

direction." The People's Party may have been "unassimilated," he said, "[but] they had fighting force in quantity much greater than we were willing to allow them." Contemporary analysts, like former congressman William Wick, did "not see any cause to fear at all," and Jesse Bright believed that the "Indiana Democracy was strong enough to carry any measure," but as the canvass moved into August, the result appeared more heavily in doubt. Attacked from all sides, the best the Democracy could do, Wallace wrote, was to "fluke the water and blow."[93]

5.

While politicians realigned themselves in Indiana, William English completed his first session as a congressman. Although only a freshman, his eventual willingness to stand with the administration on Kansas-Nebraska, his copious attention to detail and research, and his diplomatic mien, all combined to make him a favorite with the Democratic forces. Late in the session, as the House labored to compensate for time lost over Nebraska, Speaker Boyd appointed English as chairman of the Committee of the Whole, a clear act of confidence in his abilities and thanks for his loyalty. Unfortunately, the young congressman initially presided in this position less surely than he might have wished. Early on, he acted incorrectly on a procedural motion and admitted himself "unadvised" on the applicable rule. Later, John Millson of Virginia complained that English had allowed a bill to proceed despite Millson's objection. English claimed that he had not heard the Virginian object, and though not a few members backed Millson, future speaker James L. Orr of South Carolina, a relatively moderate southerner, supported English by noting that "objections are not such if not heard by the chair—it happens all the time." Boyd allowed a vote of the House to decide whether to recommit the 'objected' bill back to the Committee of the Whole (noting that he did so without "reproach cast on the gentlemen who occupied the Chair"). The House then went ahead and overwhelmingly supported English's original ruling.[94]

As if to prove undoubtedly that he was not stigmatized by Millson's demurral, English was reappointed by Boyd as chair of the next session of the Committee of the Whole. Responsive to the confidence shown in him, he presided with greater command than previously. He ruled more often and more confidently, and at the end of the session he rather courageously allowed, against the general hostility of administration Democrats, a renegade anti-Nebraska Democrat to finish his remarks. Subsequently, over the course of one day in August, English actually took

93. *New Albany Ledger*, July 15, 1854. *Paoli Eagle*, July 28, 1854. *Indiana State Sentinel*, July 28, 1854. *Washington* (County) *Democrat*, June 30, 1854. Wallace, *Autobiography, vol. 1*, 237. W.W. Wick to WHE, June 5, 1854, English Papers. Van der Weele, "Jesse Bright," 149, fn. 42.

94. Alexander, *History and Procedure*, 47. *CG, 33-1*, 1990-1995, 2000-2002.

the speaker's chair itself in regular session while 54 bills passed the House. Just as he had earlier impressed Hoosier politicians, he now impressed the parliamentarians in Washington. By his diligence, loyalty, intelligence, and compatibility, he had worked his way clearly into the confidence of the national party. He was so well regarded that he was even able to reverse the administration's decision to remove the federal pension agency from New Albany to Indianapolis. He also successfully shepherded a bill through Congress that granted 160 acres of land to his loyal New Albany postmaster, Francis Gwin, in "consideration of his gallant services" during the Mexican War.[95]

If it were not, then, for the altercations caused by the Kansas-Nebraska Act, he would have been absolutely certain of re-election. Even one self-admitted Whig correspondent from Orange County wrote him, "your course in Congress has made many friends that you had not in the last election…The Nebraska and 'Know-Nothing' spirit will have some effect but self interest will have a greater, and the people know that you will promote their interest at all costs." Benjamin Douglass wrote English in the same vein:

> Your close application to Congressional duties—your prompt attention to any business entrusted to you—and your uniform courtesy, have won for you enviable standing among your constituency. The honorable and high-minded among the opposition join with your friends in paying a just tribute to faithful merit. I see no cloud on your political horizon. I hear no mutterings of distant thunder from which to draw unfavorable inferences. Your sky is bright and cheerful.

At any rate his renomination on the Democratic ticket was never in doubt. Douglass told him that "the confidence reposed in you by the Democracy when measurably a stranger has not been diminished by further acquaintance." County after county, Democrats passed resolutions supporting his vote on Kansas-Nebraska, and no Democrat ever seriously considered opposing him.[96] It was not uncommon for far less successful first-term congressmen to be renominated, and with a real statewide fight on its hands, the Party was not eager to ditch so popular a candidate.

---

95. *CG, 33-1,* 2002-2013. *New Albany Ledger,* June 22, 1854. *CG, 33-1,* 1888, 1990, 1995, 1006, 2033. Apparently Gwin served in the army at fifteen years of age without pay for one year. He fought at Buena Vista, and although left for dead after being run over by Mexican cavalry, he miraculously "sprung up" and joined a renewed attack.

96. A.J. Simfinis to WHE, July 11, 1854; B.P. Douglass to WHE, June 27, 1854, English Papers. *Paoli Eagle,* June 6, 1854. *New Albany Ledger,* August 19, 24, 1854. George W. Carr assured English that Clark County would support his nomination. July 10, 1854, English Papers. Dr. E.L. Sugg, though noting that Washington County farmer James Cravens might contest English for the nomination, he generally discounted that possibility. July 28, 1854, English Papers.

Consequently, when the district convention met in New Albany on August 24, even the *New Albany Tribune* admitted that the gathering was "altogether harmonious" and that "Mr. English was nominated without opposition." English was indeed nominated by acclamation, and the delegates appointed a five-man executive committee that included both the *Eagle* editor Henry Comingore and B.P. Douglass. Only the absence of expected speakers marred the proceedings. Both the *New Albany Ledger* and the *Paoli Eagle* had earlier claimed that Bright, Graham Fitch, Joe Lane, and even Stephen Douglas and Kentucky congressman John C. Breckinridge had accepted invitations to speak to the gathering. Only Fitch actually appeared (probably to advance his own senatorial ambitions), and there was some speculation that the newspapers advertised falsely to secure a large turnout. If that was their purpose, it failed to work, for although (or probably because) the nomination was not in doubt, only 300 people attended.[97]

Predictably, the Democratic press applauded the convention's choice. Norman's *Ledger* continually praised English, especially pointing to the young congressman's persistence on behalf of his constituents. For example, Norman noted that the counties that now made up the Second District never had such an increase in mail facilities as in the past year and a half. The *Paoli Eagle* roughly echoed those sentiments, stating that "no man has ever applied to him [English] to attend to business for him, but what he done so properly." Bright's organ in the Third District, the *Madisonian*, similarly noted that English "was ever at his post, and always ready to seize any opportunity to advance the local interests of his district." Perhaps carried away by its patron's close association with the Second District congressman, the *Madisonian*'s editor characterized English as "noble and fearless…one of the most talented members of the House."[98]

The opposition, of course, was not quite so laudatory. Although earlier in the year the Second District Whigs seemed very pleased by the way English took care of local business,[99] the Kansas-Nebraska Act, increasingly interpreted by the opposition as a breach of the peace of 1850, destroyed any possibility that he would run unopposed. The *New Albany Tribune*, quite uncharitably and unjustly, wrote of English early in September that "during his brief career in Congress he has been partly instrumental in doing more *harm* to the country than he could well atone for in a lifetime of penitence."[100] For some time, however, the opposition

---

97. *New Albany Tribune*, August 25, 1854. *New Albany Ledger*, August 25, 1854. *Paoli Eagle*, September 1, 1854. *Ledger*, August 21, 1854. *Eagle*, August 4, 1854. The *Tribune*'s estimate of 300 attendees was never challenged by the *Ledger*. *Tribune*, August 25, 1854. *Washington* (County) *Democrat*, August 11, 1854.

98. *New Albany Ledger*, September 11, 1854. *Paoli Eagle*, September 8, 1854. *Madisonian*, in *Ledger*, September 2, 1854.

99. C.W. Cotton to WHE, February 4, 1854, English Papers. Henry Comingore believed, as late as June, that the Whigs would support English. Henry Comingore to WHE, June 4, 1854, English Papers.

100. *New Albany Tribune*, September 5, 1854.

was uncertain on exactly who would be English's official opponent. Most often mentioned (again) was John S. Davis. But Davis refused to accept any but a strict old-line Whig nomination, and by the summer it was clear that any serious run at the incumbent necessitated an opposition that also took in anti-Nebraskans, temperance men, and Know-Nothings regardless of political party, a truly fusionist nominee. Whether the opposition would officially organize under the People's Party banner or not, a strictly Whig nomination was out of the question. Some observers thought that an anti-Nebraska Democrat would be the strongest candidate, but there were none prominent enough in the district to defeat English.[101] So the choice finally boiled down to two Whigs: Thomas Slaughter, lawyer and former editor of the *Corydon Argus*, and David Laird, recent state representative for Perry County and former apprentice to Milton Gregg.[102]

The *New Albany Tribune* and other Whig papers advertised August 30 as the date on which delegates "opposed to the [Democratic State] platform of the 24th of May" should gather to nominate a congressman. No specific mention of the Whig Party was made. The gathering was labeled "The People's Convention," and the *Tribune* posted the "People's Party" state ticket on its masthead. In at least two of the counties, Perry and Floyd, the delegates were selected by Know-Nothing lodges. The nativist appeal was especially strong in New Albany and Jeffersonville, and was scattered elsewhere across the district. Slaughter belonged to a lodge, but Laird did not. When the delegates assembled they selected a nominating committee that secretly heard speeches by the two aspirants. After conferring briefly, the committee chose Slaughter, and he was unanimously ratified by the convention. Resolutions were as yet unprepared, but two days later the *Tribune* printed them. They pledged to work for the restoration of the Missouri Compromise and an end to the extension of slavery. Claiming that the Northwest Ordinance mandated "that opposition to the extension of slavery was the fixed policy of our fathers," it regarded "the recent repeal of the Missouri Compromise…a gross violation of the faith of the Union." Neither temperance nor nativism was specifically mentioned.[103]

In Slaughter the opposition had nominated a fusion candidate, who lacked only the element of having been a Democrat. He was a longtime Whig, strong temperance man, leader of the Know-Nothings of Harrison County, and anti-Nebraska. Despite Democratic charges to the contrary, he was never an abolitionist. His greatest liability was his relative political inexperience. Although he had a law

---

101. N.H. Gillevan to WHE, June 19, 1854; E.L. Sugg to WHE, July 28, 1854, English Papers.

102. *Illustrated Atlas and History of Harrison County, Indiana* (Corydon, Indiana: F. A. Bulleit, 1906), 43. Woolen, *Eminent Men*, vol. 1, District 1, 29-30. Slaughter, previously as editor, had been one of those to compliment English on his early congressional efforts–see p.90..

103. *New Albany Tribune*, August 17 to August 30, 1854. *New Albany Ledger*, August 30, September 22. 1854. Brand, "Know-Nothing Party," 70. *New Albany Tribune*, August 31, September 2, 1854.

practice that extended throughout the Second District, (and the *Ledger* admitted he was a "clever enough gentleman"), he had never canvassed for anything higher than county auditor. He appears to have been less comfortable than English on the stump and less familiar with the complexity of certain political issues. He was also of a "delicate constitution," and not an especially effective speaker. The Democrats were not dismayed by his selection. One did not have to agree with Comingore's assessment that Slaughter was "a fifth-rate pettifogger" to nonetheless agree with Norman that he was "no match for our young, talented, energetic representative."[104]

Yet this election, more than other recent ones, turned less on personal appeal and party loyalty than on powerful emotional issues. Temperance, nativism, and anti-slavery had by 1854 fully replaced banking, internal improvements, and tariff reform. The signposts were blurred. Democrats might call Slaughter "an extreme man on questions of politics and morals," but to many constituents, Democratic support of the Kansas-Nebraska act illustrated a slavish obeisance to the South. For all his shortcomings, Slaughter had the advantage of moral indignation and millennial enthusiasm. His side would have little trouble bringing out its vote. The Whig organization was not yet completely shattered in Indiana, and the opposition could also rely heavily on the cohesiveness of the district's Know-Nothing lodges and selected churches. The *Ledger* might have been correct when it noted that the "most ultra men are not the safest legislators," but many citizens wanted action. And, anyway, the repeal of the Missouri Compromise did not argue well for the greater legislative ability of those who followed so-called "moderate councils."[105]

Of all three major issues contained within fusionism, the extension of slavery received the most attention in the congressional campaign. English had predicted in May that "the great mass of the democracy will stand firm by the side of their southern brethren in support of the principles of [congressional] non-intervention and popular sovereignty," and at least among his own district's Democrats he was not completely off the mark. Phineas Kent had written in early June that "the Kansas-Nebraska Act has no democratic opponent in this section of the state." And though Kent certainly exaggerated, Benjamin Douglass concurred from Harrison county that while "many Democrats have regretted to see the ominous

104. The *Paoli Eagle* (September 8, September 15, October 6, 1854) and the *New Albany Ledger* (August 31, September 17, 1854) made occasional references to Slaughter's affiliations. Matilda Gresham, *The Life of Walter Q. Gresham, 1832-1895*, Vol. I (Chicago: Rand, McNally, and Company, 1919), 31. *Ledger*, August 31, 1854. *Washington* (County) *Democrat*, September 15, 29, 1854. *Eagle*, September 15, 1856. *Ledger*, September 11, 1854.

105. For the complete change in issues see Levi McDougle's open letter to the "old-line Whigs" first offered to the *New Albany Tribune*, but printed only in the *New Albany Ledger*, September 12, 1854. McDougle offered his vote to any candidate willing to discuss the old issues. Brand, "Know-Nothings in Indiana," (part 1), 70. *Ledger*, September 19, 1854.

question of slavery agitated so soon, they concur to a man in the principle of non-intervention." The Clark County Democrats put the position succinctly in a resolution passed unanimously at their county convention: "the proper person to decide whether slavery shall or shall not exist in any newly formed territory are the people of that territory."[106]

By the time of the election canvass, the *New Albany Ledger*, the great Democratic organ of the district, had made its peace with the Kansas-Nebraska Act. It had strongly objected to the measure when it was introduced, but it fell into a long silence on the subject until late May. Once the bill passed, it rationalized its early antipathy and got behind the law. Like English, Norman argued that "we have always believed the *principle* on which the Nebraska bill is founded is correct, although we doubted the expediency of the introduction of the bill at the time it was done." The *Ledger's* January opposition, he asserted, had been primarily based on the unfortunate repeal of the Missouri Compromise, but now he claimed to realize that the principle of that Compromise had been both wrong and ineffective:

> The Missouri Compromise was entitled to respect only so far as it temporarily allayed an excitement on the slavery question. That it did not permanently settle that question is evident from the fact that abolitionism has exhibited itself in a thousand different forms from that day to this... *We*, individually, should have had no objection to its being retained on the statute book. But, being placed there as an *apology for allowing the people of Missouri to govern themselves in their own way*, we cannot regret its removal, by which the doctrine of non-intervention has been vindicated.[107]

By "apology," Norman appears to be saying that the only purpose of the Compromise restriction was to compensate northern opinion for the extension of slavery into the state of Missouri and that the congressional prohibition carried with it no greater principle. This was a tortured reading of history. The *New Albany Tribune*, of course, tweaked its neighbor on its "volte-face," but, as so often, it went too far: Gregg claimed that Norman caved in simply so that he might procure a 13-page Navy advertisement.[108] Perhaps Norman *was* afraid that his continued opposition to Kansas-Nebraska would indeed jeopardize any future contract to publish the laws, but the Navy business was all nonsense. The real reason Norman flip-flopped was that he saw what happened at the state Democratic convention

---

106. *Appendix to the CG, 33-1*, 606. PM Kent to WHE, June 1, 1854; B.P. Douglass to WHE, June 27, 1854, English Papers. *New Albany Ledger*, August 19, 1854.

107. *New Albany Ledger*, May 24, May 26, June 16, 1854

108. *New Albany Tribune*, May 27, 1854.

that May. To continue to oppose the law would have meant purgation from the Democracy, and his convictions were not so strong as to allow him to pay that price. So, he rather sheepishly decided that, while he may have opposed the bill in the past, he did not wish to "disturb it now that it has become law."[109]

Lacking a convincing argument for his conversion, Norman tried to obfuscate the matter by going on the offensive. He unjustly charged that the opponents of Kansas-Nebraska were both abolitionists and traitors. He referred to the *Tribune* as part of the "abolition press," and jejunely wrote that Gregg's "highly colored" statements concerning Nebraska reflected the "complexion of some of his newly found abolition friends." He further argued that the ultimate purpose of the opposition was to construct a Northern sectional party, "resulting as it must and is designed to result in a DISSOLUTION OF THE UNION." Gregg answered both these charges by unheroically, but correctly, noting that he had been "too long battling the dangerous and damnable heresies of the Garrison school to be told that we and those with whom we are pleased to act sympathize with a party who are meditating a dissolution of the Union." Norman attacked Gregg's unadmirable defense as being not unadmirable enough. As a Whig, Norman claimed, Gregg had the responsibility to denounce the abolitionist extremists in his coalition to help the people of southern Indiana restore "the friendly relations which have ever existed between us and the people of the South."[110] Norman was not about to allow Gregg to outflank Democrats concerning those treasonous abolitionists.

As for the Democratic candidate himself, he repeated his arguments he had made in Congress: popular sovereignty was congruent with the principles of American democracy; in its localized process it conformed, unlike congressional restriction, to proper American federalism; it is patriotic; in fair competition with and respect for the South, it will prevent Kansas or Nebraska from becoming slave states. His first major speech was made when accepting his renomination, where he said that "popular sovereignty is truly the great American principle—it is to our political system what the sun is to the universe. Self-government, for which our fathers fought in the Revolution, is the leading feature that distinguishes this republic from most other governments of the world."[111] Aside from his imperfect astronomy, English's quote illustrates the main design of his campaign, which was to define the Kansas-Nebraska Act not as a breach of an earlier compromise, but as the true evocation of the American *Weltanschauung*. Its ultimate principle was to hold majority rule sacrosanct: *vox populi, vox Dei.*

---

109. *New Albany Ledger,* August 30, 1854.

110. *New Albany Ledger,* May 26, May 31, 1854. *New Albany Tribune,* June 17, 1854. Gregg's mention of the "Garrison school" refers to the uncompromising abolitionist from Massachusetts, William Lloyd Garrison. *Ledger,* October 2, 1854.

111. Written acceptance speech in English Papers, dated August 24, 1854.

What of course this paean to majority rule omits is that there are certain fundamental individual rights and liberties that are beyond majority rule, which thus no majority may transgress. Beatty's *Cannelton Reporter* criticized English's glorification of the majority, noting that it often represents "unrestrained will and power; it is the tyranny of the mob." Beatty reminded those who extolled popular sovereignty that the principle of natural rights was also part of the American Weltanschaung and also sanctified:

> What sovereignty rules America? Is it not the Constitution? And what are all our Constitutions but a law against the will of the majority—a barrier against the power of the multitude, to protect the few from the tyranny of the many? What is law, but a power setting limits to the acts of the individual and the community, and from what does it derive its authority, but the eternal principles of Divine right—it is the only legitimate sovereign and potentate on earth, for it rules only by a right derived directly from the everlasting principles of Justice and Right established by the Deity Himself.[112]

Beatty's hyperbolic editorial squarely confronted the essential weakness of the Democratic creed: its amorality. Schuyler Colfax during the 1850 Indiana Constitutional Convention contended that "we should take special care to declare and uphold the rights and defend the interests of the poor."[113] He understood, as Beatty did, that justice was not synonymous with simple majority desire as reflected in positive law. And, anyway, as Beatty maintained, "the great majority of mankind admit slavery to be wrong."[114] His argument would have been stronger, however, had he stood on the Declaration of Independence instead of the Constitution as his supporting document of what essentially was his natural rights argument. The Constitution, after all, recognized, though circumspectly, the legal existence of slavery.

For the most part the combatants in the congressional canvass stayed away from these weightier matters concerning popular sovereignty. On the stump, the candidates usually argued the more prosaic point of whether slavery would actually become law in Kansas. English repeated his congressional arguments while Slaughter maintained that slaves had already been transported to Fort Leavenworth. Beatty's *Reporter* made clear as well that the Creek and Cherokee had held slaves in Arkansas territory under no positive law. Slaughter also asserted that slav-

---

112. *Cannelton Reporter*, October 7, 1854. Of course Beatty's "Divine right" evocation here has nothing to do with monarchical absolutism.

113. Moore, *Schuyler Colfax,* 35.

114. *Cannelton Reporter,* April 29, 1854.

ery was "riveted" upon Kansas by President Pierce's appointment of two southern judges and a southern district attorney. He moreover took note of a local meeting in the territory that resolved "that Kansas of right should be and therefore shall be slave territory." At one point English resorted to bluster, offering $500 to anyone who could prove that a slave could be held in Kansas without positive law. If anyone took him up on his offer, it went unrecorded.[115]

In order to defeat his opponent, English simply had to prevent any major attrition of the 1,500 vote majority the Democrats held in the district. Consequently, he concentrated on preserving party unity by attacking the opposition for its demagoguery, dishonesty, hypocrisy, lack of patriotism, and corruption. He reminded prospective Democratic apostates that

> the desperate leaders who control this new pie-bald party care nothing for these things [they profess] except as a pretext to gain their darling object, which is to get those in power *out* and themselves in. This is the true secret of the whole matter. To attain political power they resort to every species of misrepresentation—sacrifice every national feeling of brotherhood—are willing the north should be arrayed against the south—that agitation and discord shall reign—and the Union be shook to its very centre!

Better Democrats remain with the Party that "has no history of alien laws, of sedition laws, of monster banks, high protective tariffs, [or] bankrupt laws." He reprised his charge that the historical connection between former Federalists and the Democrats' present-day opponents was strong, even asserting that those who called for the restoration of the Missouri Compromise did so for the same reason the Federalists precipitated the Missouri crisis originally: "to divide the great parties by geographical lines and by that means to gain the presidency." (Here English plays it fast and loose with history. Though it is apparently true that once the crisis was in full swing some Federalists saw an advantage to reviving their party along sectional lines, the crisis itself was precipitated by two Jeffersonian Republican congressmen, not Federalists.) The *Ledger* used a similar tactic by reminding its readers that "the whole is simply a contest between Aristocracy and Democracy."[116]

---

115. *New Albany Tribune*, July 22, September 30, 1854. *Cannelton Reporter*, September 23, 1854.

116. English acceptance speech in English Papers, dated August 24, 1854. For the Democratic initiation of the Missouri crisis and the Federalist opportunism, see Glover Moore, *The Missouri Controversy: 1819-1821* (Lexington: University of Kentucky Press, 1953), 15-16, 33-36, 66-67. Also, Robert P. Forbes, *The Missouri Compromise and its Aftermath: Slavery and the Meaning of America* (Chapel Hill: University of North Carolina Press, 2007), 35-36, 99-100. *Cannelton Reporter*, September 23, 1854. *Ledger*, August 26, 1854.

As with the opposition statewide, the district's opposition depended heavily on its network of Know-Nothing lodges, especially strong in southern Indiana. New Albany, perhaps due to its relatively large German population, was a hotbed of nativism, and its power there pushed the *Tribune* into ever-harsher positions in relation to immigrants. Slaughter's preeminence in the Order maximized its effect, but its secretive nature in 1854 prevents one from getting a clear picture of how influential it actually was unconnected to temperance and freesoilism. Some significance may be attached to the fact that two years later the presidential candidate of the updated Know-Nothings, Millard Fillmore of the American Party, outpolled the strong anti-slavery Republican, John Fremont, by 3,500 votes in the district. In 1854 even some Second District Democrats were members of Know-Nothing lodges, though the *New Albany Ledger* claimed that they were regularly deserting. Even Luciene Matthews, part owner the *Ledger*, was a member for a short time. In recognition of this, some Democratic county organizations made candidates swear that they were *not* Know-Nothings, and the *Ledger* and the *Paoli Eagle* regularly excoriated "a secret political society whose members are bound together by oaths of the most revolting nature." This stance did not stop Norman, somewhat ironically, from reminding the district's German and Irish immigrants of their "duty and absolute necessity of merging themselves in the great mass of American citizens." And the *Indiana State Sentinel* warned "our Irish Catholic brethren" that "every assault which you make on our common school system puts but another argument in the mouths of the Know-Nothing natives."[117]

English did not originally take much notice of the Know-Nothings, believing them to be not much more than a front for Whiggery. But as the campaign progressed, he began to award more of his speaking time to lampooning them. Because the Know-Nothings were morally the weakest link in the fusion chain, yet also had the greatest organization, other Democrats throughout the state increasingly began to focus their attacks on them. Slaughter, like most Know-Nothings, was unwilling to discuss nativism in public and continued to speak primarily on the repeal of the Missouri Compromise.[118] This subterfuge is interesting because it mirrored what happened at the People Party's state convention, where the Know-Nothings favored getting their members nominated over espousing their ideals in the party platform. This tactic is indicative of a strategy to gain power

---

117. Brand, "Know-Nothings of Indiana," 59. Van Bolt, "Fusion out of Confusion," 359. Carter, "Hoosier History," 25. *New Albany Tribune*, June 8, July 7, August 17, 1854. Burnham, *Presidential Ballots*, 410. *New Albany Ledger*, September 16, 1854. L.G. Matthews to WHE, [1858], English Papers. *Ledger*, August 21, 22, September 4, 1854. *Ledger*, June 1, June 17, 1854. *Sentinel* quote reprinted in *Washington* (County) *Democrat*, July 21, 1854.

118. *New Albany Tribune*, October 3, 1854. *Paoli Eagle*, October 6, 1854. *Tribune*, October 5, 1854.

surreptitiously by stealth. Despite all of English's taunts, he could not draw his opponent out.

In truth, English appears to have been sincerely anti-nativist. Less than a year later, while speaking in Congress at perhaps the height of Know-Nothing influence, he stated he "could not be blinded to the merit of those whose destiny it happened to be to come into the world elsewhere, and especially those who, from choice, have selected this as their permanent home—neither shall I forget how much our own career of greatness and glory has been facilitated by immigration."[119] Indeed, considering his relative urbanity, there is no reason to suspect English of insincerity, but one must remark that the Democratic platform left him little choice, and, at the time he spoke these words in 1855, the Know-Nothings were politically viewed by many Democrats as the greatest threat to their rule. Moreover, it was essential for him to maximize the traditional ethnic and immigrant Democratic vote.

Because he was a seasoned campaigner, English was gradually able, with the help of Norman, Comingore, and the *Washington Democrat's* William Williams, to put Slaughter on the defensive. For example, in mid-September he began to accuse his opponent of extremism, not only concerning nativism but also on the liquor question. A petition Comingore found that contained Slaughter's signature had once been sent to the legislature recommending that Indiana make it "a penitentiary offense for anyone to sell spirituous liquor." Comingore conveniently left off the words "without a license," but the suggested punishment still appeared harsh. Increasingly, Slaughter had trouble shaking the "extremist" tag. The *Cannelton Reporter* admitted that "Mr. Slaughter did not come up to the expectations of his friends. He does not present his points with that force and clearness that makes them tell upon a popular auditory." (A very Whiggish statement, indeed!) Slaughter's shortcomings were partly the result of his unceasing illnesses. At times, he completely missed his appointments, and either George P.R. Wilson, another Harrison County Know-Nothing and seasoned state legislator, or Slaughter's law partner and campaign manager, future secretary of the treasury Walter Q. Gresham, had to fill his spot. Moreover, on September 10 the candidate's 4-year-old son died of scarlet fever, causing Slaughter's absence from the canvass for a week.[120]

---

119. *Appendix to the CG, 33-2*, 284. In early 1855 there was no certainty that antislavery would win out over nativism as the key pillar of the new Opposition party in the free states. In the slave states, nativism was a strong animus for the strength of the opposition to the Democratic Party. For discussion of the relative strengths of antislavery and nativism within the Opposition to the Democrats in the mid-1850s see Gienapp, *Origins of the Republican* Party; Anbinder, *Nativism and Slavery;* Maizlish, "The Meaning of Nativism"; and Darrel W. Overdyke, *The Know-Nothing Party in the South* (Baton Rouge: Louisiana State University Press, 1950).

120. *Paoli Eagle*, September 15, October 6, 1854. *Cannelton Reporter*, September 23, 1854. Shepherd, "Biographical Directory," 421. Gresham, *Life of Walter Gresham,* 59. *New Albany Tribune*, September 20, 1854.

On the other side, as Gresham's daughter admitted years later, "English was a good campaigner." The *Reporter* attributed this to his "sound and fury, and not [to] any great measure of intellectual discernment." Be that as it may (and that judgment turns on the word 'great'), he *was* a solid candidate. Faced with the fierce gales of the prevailing "isms," he refused to trim his sails and headed directly into the wind. Know-nothingism, temperance reform, and freesoilism were all directly challenged. Having the advantage of a good reputation as a working congressman, even, as in Ohio River improvements, against the wishes of the administration, he was not vulnerable on most of the issues attached to incumbency. Had there been no Kansas-Nebraska Act there would be little question of his re-election. To many in the opposition, he may have represented the essence of improper political thinking, but Gresham admitted that "of all the Democrats that Indiana produced, Mr. English was, in my judgment, the ablest."[121]

Democrats in other parts of the state encountered greater trouble. Election Day in 1854 occurred on October 10, but as early as August Jesse Bright predicted that "Indiana [was] lost for the time being to our party."[122] For this result Bright was partially to blame. It was he who controlled the Democratic state convention so tightly that droves of anti-Nebraska Democrats found their way into the opposition. In September, Stephen Douglas came to Indianapolis to rally the troops, but his appearance, as with a lightning rod, may have served to stir the opposition to greater efforts. Some historians argue that "severe fluctuations" in party realignment, from New York to Wisconsin, had already begun to occur at least a year earlier. They assert that to a great degree the "revolution of 1854" was caused by the matured effect of New England emigration, with its puritanical views of sin and penchant to coerce human improvement.[123] There appears to be some truth to this argument, but without the Kansas-Nebraska Act it is quite uncertain if this ethno-cultural change in population (which had been occurring for some time) would have led to political realignment by itself. And the eventual dominance of the anti-slavery element in the Republican Party arising from such realignment also strongly implies that without Kansas-Nebraska politics may have developed differently.

When all the votes were tabulated, the People's Party and the general opposition to the Democrats won a smashing victory everywhere but in the southernmost reaches of the state. Their entire state ticket was elected by about 12,000 votes. They controlled the state House of Representatives by a wide margin and came within two votes of gaining command of the partially elected Senate. In

121. Gresham, *Life of Walter Gresham,* 60. *Cannelton Reporter,* September 23, 1854. Gresham, 60.

122. Jesse Bright to R.M.T. Hunter, September 2, 1854, in Ambler, *Correspondence of RMT Hunter,* 159.

123. Van Bolt, "Fusion out of Confusion", 386. Kleppner, *Third Electoral System,* 49-51. Holt. *Political Crisis,* chapter 5. Hubbart, *The Older Middle West,* 97, 107.

the congressional races, pro-Nebraska congressmen Dunham, Davis, Eddy, and Hendricks went down to ignominious defeat. Another Democrat, Ebenezer Chamberlain, who waffled, was also routed. Lane did not seek renomination. Of the two Democrats who voted against Nebraska, Daniel Mace was re-elected on the People's ticket and Andrew Harlan chose his own successor, former Democrat John Upfold Pettit (no relation to the Senator). Pettit's opponent, Democrat James R. Slack, took "uncompromising ground in favor of Kansas-Nebraska" and was uncompromisingly defeated.[124]

Veteran judge John Law wrote English after the election that a "lack of hard work throughout the State was the primary cause of the overwhelming losses," but most knew better. James Slack had much earlier written English back in June that it would be "rough going, as anti-Nebraska sentiment is high," and it is unlikely that any amount of hard work could have appreciably changed the result. But the southern districts did, however barely, escape the onslaught. Smith Miller, Democratic congressman from the First District in southwestern Indiana, slipped from 59 percent to 52.2 percent of the vote. Law claimed of Miller that "only his political friends prevented him from defeat." The other southern Indiana congressman, in the southeast was, of course, William English. He also escaped defeat, but even more narrowly than Miller. He won four and lost four of his district's eight counties, receiving only 51.7 percent of the vote, down 3.3 percent from two years earlier. His popular vote majority shrank from 1,560 to 586.[125]

Not since 1847 had the counties that now made up the Second District polled such a low percentage of the vote for the Democratic candidate.[126] If these counties had not built up a sizeable Democratic majority over diseased Whiggery in the early 1850s, English might well have gone the way of Dunham, Hendricks, and the rest. The two major factors that made the vote in the Second District much closer than in recent polling were the organization of the Know-Nothing lodges and the emotional strength of the anti-Nebraska attitude. The latter pulled many erstwhile Democratic voters to the People Party's banner—most of them would come home

---

124. Thornbrough, *Civil War Era,* 67. *The Whig Almanac and United States Register for Year 1855* (New York: Greeley and McGrath, 1855), 61 [Bound in *The Tribune Almanac, 1838-1855,* Indiana State Library, Indianapolis, Indiana.] Carter, "Hoosier History," p. 105-108. Shepherd, *Biographical Directory,* 511-513. Dubin, *Congressional Elections,* 107. James Slack to WHE, June 30, 1854, English Papers.

125. John Law to WHE, November 1, 1854; James Slack to WHE, June 30, 1854, English Papers. *Whig Almanac and United States Register for 1855* (New York: Greeley and McErath, 1855), 61; *Tribune Almanac for the Years 1838-1868,* vol. 1 (New York: The New York Tribune, 1868), p. 46 of year 1853. Dubin, *Congressional Elections,* 164, 170.

126. *Tribune Almanac for 1839-1855, vol. 1,* p. 48 in year 1848, p. 49 in year 1850, p. 48 in year 1852, p. 46 in year 1853. The vote was close enough for Schuyler Colfax, Whig editor and successful Fusion congressional candidate from the northwest of the state, to believe as late as October 15 that the "New Albany district [was] close, with odds in our favor." Schuyler Colfax to Jeff Stailey, October 15, 1854, *Schuyler Colfax Papers,* Indiana Historical Society, Indianapolis, Indiana.

in the next two years, but not all. Old Whiggery was dead in the second district, but opposition to the Democratic Party certainly wasn't. How much of its future would lie with anti-slavery and how much with nativism remained yet to be seen.

But one more factor must be discussed in explaining the Democratic decline. One week before the election, the *Ledger* reported a rumor that the Know-Nothing lodge of New Albany had counseled violence in order to ensure victory in the city. On Election Day the rumor was rather substantiated. To deter immigrants from appearing at the polls (again, aliens could vote in Indiana with six months residence and intention to become citizens), Irish and German houses were randomly attacked. Some immigrants were badly beaten in the streets. Apologists for the violence lamely claimed that it was precipitated by immigrants of short residence who illegally attempted to vote. As Gregg put it, they were "punished on the spot." This vigilantism appears to have been mild compared to later Know-Nothing riots in Cincinnati, Philadelphia, and Louisville, but it was ample enough to have affected English's majority. While the district as a whole increased its poll by 10 percent, New Albany added only 39 voters or less than 2 percent. A proper increase would have added 179 more votes, which could have put English very close to what he polled in New Albany in 1852. In Jeffersonville, too, a prominent opposition leader made a speech on election eve inciting the crowd "to keep foreigners away from the polls by force." The next day there was sporadic violence in that city as well.[127]

The Opposition in the Second District, though by no means expectant of victory, was dismayed that they could not defeat the incumbent. Editor Beatty, who was a good example of a free-soiler who also sympathized with the Know-Nothings, claimed that "Mr. English would return to his seat by virtue of doubtful and illegal votes, and by suffrages of men who voted against their heartfelt principles through a blind subservience to party." He concurred with a *Reporter* correspondent who criticized English's demagoguery during the campaign and maintained that in defeat Slaughter "occupied a position much more honorable and far more enviable than his successful opponent." He dismissed Smith Miller as a weak man and perceived that the Indiana Democrats believed they would be able to "retrieve their fallen fortunes" on English's shoulders. But Beatty thought they were misplacing their faith. He now saw English not as the talented gentleman he had previously extolled but as a "shrewd and conceited man," unequal to any of the "newly elected members of Congress from this State in ability as a legislator, public speaker, or man."[128] The political stakes had gone up a notch.

---

127. *New Albany Ledger*, October 3, October 11, October 12, October 17. *Washington* (County) *Democrat*, October 13, 1854. *New Albany Tribune*, October 12, 1854. Lewis C. *Baird's History of Clark County, Indiana* (Indianapolis: B. F. Bowen and Co., 1919), 111.

128. *Cannelton Reporter*, October 21, 1854.

Cong - 1854

Congressional Election 1854

"Considering the vast—the unparalleled array of machinery, secret and corrupt, brought to bear against you, your victory is a far more triumphant one [than two years earlier]." So wrote one correspondent to English, and, indeed, considering the obstacles, his victory was impressive. He outpolled the state ticket in the district by 100 votes and actually increased his vote percentage in Harrison and Scott counties. Yet while other politicians were quick to congratulate the victorious candidate and marvel how he withstood the "hurricane that has swept over Indiana's best men," the fact remained that he primarily owed his win to the self-reliant, anti-abolitionist, southern ancestry of his district. As James Slack boorishly put it, "white men must live there." The Second District voters might no longer fully identify with the South and might dislike slavery as much as their northern Indiana Tenth District counterparts, but they could not ally with what they considered abolitionists and perfectionists. J.P. Chapman, an apostate Democrat now turned Fusionist, might grant to the *New Albany Ledger*, "more than to any one instrumentality, the reelection of Mr. English to congress," but such an analysis merely begged the question. R.N. English may have written his nephew that "nothing but your own personal exertions and popularity in the district could have saved you," but he, too, missed the point.[129] The Democratic creed, with all its inconsistencies surrounding the nature of individualism, majority rule, and laissez-faire, was still strong in the Second District. Once again, English was to find out if it remained strong as well in the national legislature.

---

129. S.E. Platt (or Plate) to WHE, October 20, 1854, English Papers. The *Whig Almanac and United States Register for Year 1853*, 59; for Year 1855, 61 [Both bound in *The Tribune Almanac, 1838-1855*]. J.A. Cravens to WHE, October 23, 1854, James A Slack to WHE, November 1, 1854, English Papers. *New Albany Ledger*, December 27, 1854. R.N. English to WHE, October 30, 1854, English Papers.

CHAPTER FOUR

Hydra-Headed Headaches

few weeks after the 1854 election, John Norman observed that English was going to be "quite a lion this winter…a [northern] Democrat re-elected to Congress." Indeed, of the 41 northern Democrats who stood for re-election that autumn, only 16 were chosen for another term. It mattered little whether they voted for or against the Kansas-Nebraska Bill; eight of each were successful. (Thirteen pro-Nebraskans and 12 anti-Nebraskans were defeated.) When those northern states that held their elections in the spring and summer of 1855 were added (Connecticut, New Hampshire, and Rhode Island), six other incumbent Democrats were defeated. Only two New England seats in total remained in Democratic hands, and one survived only because the opposition split their 58 percent of the vote between a Republican and Know-Nothing candidate. In all the free states the Democratic congressional representation plummeted from 91 seats to 37.[1]

The Know-Nothing, temperance, and anti-slavery coalition even affected old-line Whigs. Ephraim Farley, a Maine Whig and English's fellow member on the Committee on Territories, wrote the Indiana representative that his "head was cut off by a combination of Know-Nothings, Abolitionists, Ramrods, Maine law men, disappointed office-seekers, minorities, and about every other ism we have in these parts." (One of English's district correspondents called the new Democratic opposition "hydra-headed.") As Alexander Stephens wrote his brother, "old parties, old names, old principles, and old organizations are passing away. A day of new things, new issues, new leaders, and new organizations is at hand."[2]

The newly elected representatives, of course, would not take their seats in Congress until December 1855. In the meantime, the second, lame duck session of the 33rd Congress held forth from December 4, 1854 to March 3, 1855. During

1. J.B. Norman to WHE, November 21, 1854. English Papers. Dubin, *Congressional Elections,* 163-173.

2. Ephraim Farley to WHE, October 2, 1854; Benjamin Douglass to WHE, December 9, 1855, English Papers. Alexander Stephens to Linton Stephens, December 31, 1854, in Johnston, *Life of Stephens,* 286.

this period the emboldened opposition spent a decent amount of time defining its principles and goals and attempting to fashion a coherent policy from disparate elements. The strict legislative activity that did occur, with Democrats still for a couple of months in a heavy majority, consisted of transportation bills and private claims. English continued to represent his midwestern section by consistently supporting transportation and communication advancements that reflected the expansive mood of Young America. For example, in opposition to a majority of other pro-Nebraska Democrats, he voted to overturn Pierce's veto of the Rivers and Harbors bill passed at the end of the first session. The measure appropriated $190,000 for improvements on the Ohio River, and English, unlike neighboring congressman Smith Miller, was not about to support even a Democratic president who operated so economically counter to his constituency. He also acted with anti-Nebraska Democrats and Whigs when he cast his vote in favor of authorizing construction of a telegraph line from the Midwest to the Pacific. Another bill he supported, providing for an overland express mail route from St. Louis to San Francisco, gained a majority of pro-Nebraska Democrats from all sections but the South. Though southern Democrats often frowned upon federal spending, probably their overwhelming opposition in this case may be traced to the likelihood that such a bill would extend population into the northern reaches of the Nebraska territory and more quickly create likely new free states. Interestingly, the only internal improvement bill English opposed in this session was a measure granting $160,000 to improve the Savannah River in Georgia. The South had to pay for its intransigence on improvements elsewhere.[3]

But on most issues English was loyal to the general parsimony of the Democratic Party and not unfriendly to the possibility of slavery's expansion. Outside of transportation improvements he consistently opposed expensive federal projects and always voted the low tariff line. Concerning an issue tied to possible slavery expansion, he stood by Pierce when the Opposition tried to embarrass the president by introducing a resolution forcing the administration to divulge all of its information surrounding the confidential diplomatic dispatch concerning its attempt to purchase Cuba from Spain. This dispatch, known as the Ostend Manifesto, approved by the two southern ambassadors to Spain and France and one northern doughface, the minister to Great Britain, went so far as to advocate war with Spain if it refused to sell. Though the administration eventually publicly disavowed the Manifesto's belligerent line, the mere fact that Pierce promoted a policy of extending the United States into the Caribbean, partly to satisfy southern desire for more slave territory, was anathema to the growing anti-slavery opposition. English voted against the anti-administration resolution twice, and

---

3. *New Albany Ledger*, December 31, 1854. *CG, 33-2*, 19. *Ledger*, July 20, 1854. *CG, 33-2*, 504, 692, 1152-1153.

supported the Democratic alternative of getting it referred to the friendly Foreign Relations Committee. To many northern Democrats, like English, the opposition's resolution was an example of unnecessary sectional agitation. (One could also argue that at least the simple purchase of Cuba was in line with young American expansionism.) Even some anti-Nebraska former Democrats voted against the resolution, believing it an invasion of executive privilege. It did not pass.[4]

English essentially believed himself a loyal Democrat. As one Washington journalist wrote, "the fact that he [English] was one of the most active members in securing the passage of the Nebraska act, is justly appreciated by the National Democracy." His partisanship never questioned, he could well be forgiven his occasionally unorthodox vote to further what he considered economic progress. Indeed, so actually partisan was he that he refused to go along with other Democrats when they voted to confirm Winfield Scott as brevet Lieutenant-General of the Army. Such a reward to so recent a Whig presidential candidate was too much for the young inbred Democrat to handle. Perhaps remembering Indiana's perceived mistreatment by another Whig general, Zachary Taylor, during the Mexican War, Hoosier congressmen Dunham, Lane, and Hendricks also opposed the appointment. The subsequent incessant feuding between Scott and secretary of war Jefferson Davis may or may not have illustrated the wisdom of English's vote, and he probably considered the feud satisfactorily ironic considering Davis was Taylor's son-in-law.[5]

The respectable position English held within the party was also the result of an appointment he held since the first month of the 33rd Congress. By December 19, 1853, Speaker Boyd had selected English as one of the three congressmen to serve on the Smithsonian's Board of Regents. Although certainly another reward for his support of Boyd for the speakership, it appears that English may also have been chosen because he was a Hoosier. For the previous 10 years an Indiana congressman had represented the House on the Board. Robert Owen served from 1843 to 1849 and Graham Fitch from 1849 to 1853. English now continued that tradition, and he would eventually serve to the eve of the Civil War. The appointment had delightedly astonished the Democratic press of his district. It was viewed not as recompense for his services to Boyd, but as evidence that "few members, young or old, enjoy a greater share of the confidence and esteem of both houses of Congress or have more influence than Wm. H. English." English did not truly become influential on the Board until after he had clearly illustrated his intelligence and political skill during the Kansas-Nebraska debate and his subsequent successful re-election, but the Smithsonian appointment added to his

---

4. *CG, 33-2*, 12, 15, 17, 816. Nichols, *Franklin Pierce*, 377. *CG, 33-2*, 1157, 1178, 1555, 3, 17, 18.

5. *Paoli Eagle*, January 5, 1855. *CG, 33-2*, 691. Nichols, *Franklin Pierce*, 385-387.

esteem. And, as a Washington observer predicted, it would greatly aid him "in the discharge of his public duties."[6]

For the first seven years of its existence the Smithsonian provoked little controversy. Begun in accordance with the will of James Smithson, son of the first Duke of Northumberland, it used the inheritance of Smithson's estate for, in his words, "the increase and diffusion of knowledge among men." The act establishing the institution, passed in 1846, allocated an initial $242,129 "for the erection of suitable buildings and other current incidental expenses," and it stipulated that 6 percent of the principal bequest of $515,169 would be allocated each year "for the perpetual maintenance and support of said institution." The general responsibility for managing the Smithsonian lay with a Board of Regents composed of the Vice-President of the United States, the Chief Justice of the Supreme Court, the mayor of Washington, D.C., three members each from the Senate and the House of Representatives, and six private citizens appointed by Congress. The real management—that is the day to day running of the institution—lay with a secretary chosen by the Board, who would be regularly assisted by an executive committee composed of three regents.[7]

When English began his tenure, Joseph Henry was secretary. Henry was a mathematician and eminent scientist, specializing in electromagnetics. His original researches in the early 1830s were said to be "indispensable to the commercial development of the telegraph," and for the next decade and a half he had continued his experiments as professor of natural philosophy at the College of New Jersey. Appointed secretary in 1846, he was the only director the institution had since its inception. Technically, he was only an officer employed by the Board, but naturally he functioned as a CEO and was the driving force behind the Smithsonian. Increasingly, he maintained, reflecting his own experience, that the institution especially patronize experimentation and publication of original research, and he became reluctant to expend funds dedicated to other purposes.[8]

Until 1854, the Board had agreed that the Smithsonian's annual income be equally divided between a library and museum on the one hand and "active oper-

---

6. *CG, 33-1, 66. Jeffersonville Weekly Democrat*, January 7, 1854. *Paoli Eagle*, January 13, 1854.

7. *Eighth Annual Report of the Smithsonian Institution* (Washington, D.C.: A. O. P. Nicholson, 1854), 102-103, 107-111. The members of the Board of Regents in January 1854 were Chief Justice Roger Taney; Senators James Pearce (W, Md.), Stephen Douglas (D, Ill.), and James Mason (D, Va.); Congressmen English, James Meacham (W, Vt.), and David Stuart (D. Mich.); John Towers, Mayor of the District of Columbia; private citizens Rufus Choate, Gideon Hawley, John M. Berrien, Richard Rush, A. D. Bache, and General Joseph Totten. The Vice-President, William R. King, was deceased. *Smithsonian Institution, Board of Regents, Minutes, 1854*, accessed March 10, 2019, https://siarchives.si.edu/collections/siris_14323; *Paoli Eagle*, January 5, 1855.

8. *Eighth Annual Report of the Smithsonian*, 75. Richard B. Morris, *Encyclopedia of American History* (New York: Harper and Brothers, 1953), 674-675. Hugh McCulloch, *Men and Measures of Half a Century* (New York: Charles Scribner's Sons, 1880), 263.

ations" (research and publication) on the other. But that year, Henry was finally able to convince the Executive Committee to issue a report that active operations be allocated substantially more funds than the library and museum. Not all Board members were pleased with the proposed change, and it took a year of debate and politicking to come to a vote. In the end the members agreed with the Executive Committee's recommendation, 8 to 6, English at this point voting with the opposition. Secretary Henry was thus victorious, and a final resolution was passed allowing the Board thereafter to apportion its funds "in such a manner as may, in the judgment of the Regents, be necessary and proper for each operation."[9]

This change in policy caused great anger among some of the key losers. Congressman James Meacham, Vermont Whig, offered a further resolution that would have required "a large proportion of the income of the institution [to] be appropriated for the gradual formation of a library." Three other regents supported Meacham's resolution, but English did not. He had apparently come to the conclusion that opposing the Executive Committee and secretary Henry was not politically wise, and from this point on he began to distance himself from the dissidents.[10] He was a relatively new member of the Board, and as three of the four supporters of this new resolution were Whigs, he may have begun to wonder whether there was some political agenda afoot. He also may have thought that it was not wise during his early tenure to oppose Henry while the secretary obviously had the votes. English was generally not one to continue a fight after it was lost—he was no revolutionary, no idealist, and certainly no martyr.

But the dissidents were not done. Rufus Choate, the eminent lawyer and sometime Whig politician, who was one of the private citizen Board members, resigned in protest from the Institution in January 1855 and sent his letter of resignation to House speaker Boyd and others. He cited his "inability to concur or acquiesce in an [improper] interpretation of the act of Congress constituting the actual institution." He argued that the original debates in Congress that led to the establishment of the Smithsonian "unequivocally" illustrated that a library was expected to be its main feature, and the recent resolutions of the Board "practically disappoint that will." A creature of Congress, the Board of Regents, he maintained, has "in effect repealed the law" and has arrogated unto itself the right to administer the institution without limitation. Choate's letter and resignation was the signal for regent-congressman Meacham to force a congressional investigation. On January 17, he moved to refer Choate's letter to a select committee of five "to inquire, and report to the House, whether the Smithsonian Institution has been managed, and its funds expended, in accordance with the law establishing

9. *Eighth Annual Report of the Smithsonian*, 70-97. *Tenth Annual Report of the Smithsonian Institution* (Washington, D.C.: Cornelius Wendell, 1856), 7-12. *Ninth Annual Report of the Smithsonian Institution* (Washington, D.C.: Beverly Tucker, 1855), 72-74. McCulloch, *Men and Measures*, 265.

10. *Ninth Annual Report of the Smithsonian Institution*, 74, 75.

the institution, and whether any additional legislation be necessary to carry out the design of its founders."[11]

English, who later revealed that he believed Meacham's resolution put the whole institution under attack, moved to table it. But his motion was defeated by voice vote. The direct vote on Meacham's resolution then passed by the slim margin of 93 to 91, with anti-Nebraska Democrats generally combining with Whigs to pass it. This vote was a good indication of how willing the anti-Nebraska Democrats were to coalesce with their new partners to embarrass the regular Democrats. In consequence of the vote, Boyd appointed the select committee. As the mover of the resolution Meacham was entitled to be chairman, but he declined the honor because he was a sitting regent. The committee, as it was finally composed, well represented the shifting state of political affiliation. From the supporters of the resolution, Boyd chose Charles Upham, a Whig/Republican from Massachusetts, Richard Puryear, a Whig/Know-Nothing from North Carolina, and Daniel Wells, an anti-Nebraska Democrat from Wisconsin. From the opponents, he chose pro-Nebraskan Nathaniel G. Taylor from North Carolina. The fifth member, a northern pro-Nebraskan from Pennsylvania, William Witte, actually abstained on Meacham's resolution.[12]

The select committee gathered evidence for a month, between January 27 and the last day of February. During most of that time not a word was spoken of the matter in Congress, but on February 27, four days before the committee actually issued any report, William English rose to defend the Smithsonian and preemptively contain any damage that the Committee's report might engender.[13] Exactly why English continued to believe it incumbent upon himself to come to the Smithsonian's aid is not altogether clear, but he most likely viewed the investigation as little more than another fusionist attempt to embarrass the national Democracy. Not only were a majority of the regents Democrats, but, most significantly, so was Joseph Henry, and the House vote on the resolution to investigate marked the controversy as partisan. As the most active House Democratic regent, English may have believed that he had the primary responsibility of leading the Party against the opposition's attack. Even if defeated, his service could only enhance his reputation both in the eyes of the Democratic leadership and the Smithsonian institution itself. In other words, the political advantages of strong advocacy were clear.

The speech itself was not one of his best efforts. The first part of it used a red herring argument, i.e., that the Smithsonian itself was under attack. "The present

---

11. *CG, 33-2,* 282-283.

12. *Ibid.,* 283, 313.

13. *CG, 33-2, House report no. 141. Appendix to the CG, 33-2,* 282. The Senate Judiciary Committee reported tersely that the Regents acted properly, and recommended no congressional action. *CG, 33-2, Senate Report no. 285.*

condition of the Institution is not only encouraging," he averred, but a subject of congratulation rather than of censure. "[Its] management has been such, in all material respects, as to elicit commendation." To support his point, he referred to two pages worth of lectures, library acquisitions, and letters of praise from eminent scientists. He also praised the sound financial position of the Smithsonian, maintaining that its funds and property were worth twice the amount of the original bequest. In proper Democratic form, he asked, "[w]here, sir, in this age of extravagant expenditure of public money, and deficiency bills, will you find a parallel to this?" In contrast, the investigating committee was a clear waste of the government's time and expense. At so late a date in the session it could hardly be justified.[14]

After he finished praising the institution and declaring suspect the motives of those who supported the investigation, English defined what he saw as the nub of the controversy:

> [W]hether the income should be used to build a library, as the paramount object, or whether it should be applied not only for a library, but for such other purposes 'to increase and diffuse knowledge' as would, in the judgement of the Regents, best accord with the will of Smithson, and the law of Congress organizing the Institution.

The manner by which English phrased the question was disingenuous because the dissidents of secretary Henry's redistribution of the Smithsonian's funds merely wished to return to the *equal* funding between library and research. But more politically to the point, English went on to tackle the meaning of Smithson's direction to "increase and diffuse knowledge among men." As the Hoosier viewed it, a library hardly diffused knowledge among men in general, but rather primarily benefitted the local citizens of the District of Columbia and the "fortunate few" who could travel to it. On the other hand, scientific researches clearly added "to the sum total of knowledge *now* existing in the world and diffused it, rather than [merely] scattering more widely that which is already accumulated."[15] This definition of the words "increase," "diffusion," and "knowledge" was by no means shared by all the others involved in the controversy, but it did align well with the values behind Young American Democracy. Original research, for example in agriculture, electricity, or machinery, was practical. Its fruits stimulated the progress of the nation through their everyday application. The collection of "old truth" from a distant place had much less practical value for a farmer or manufacturer. It catered instead to the intellectual dilettante, of whom we have noted before

---

14. *Appendix to the CG, 33-2*, 282-285.

15. *Ibid.*

English was not very fond. According to this reasoning, the adherents of more expenditures for "active operations" were democrats, while those who favored the library, like Rufus Choate, were impractical aristocrats. This was English's essential implication.

English's speech did not go unchallenged. Congressman Meacham, on the last day of the session, the same day that the investigating committee submitted its reports, offered his own remarks that characterized English's argument as both misinformed and, indeed, bombastic. Meacham declared "the gentleman from Indiana…eulogize[d] the Institution before it had been attacked here." In a tone harshly resentful of English's imputations, Meacham argued that his call for an investigation was not motivated by any hostility to the Smithsonian. On the contrary, it was caused by an "attachment [and] devotion" to it, by a desire to see that its proper object was not sullied. When English lauded the institution for the "augmentation of its capital," Meacham claimed that the Hoosier had raised a point that was highly "irrelevant."

> If the object of the institution were the increase of its wealth, this would indeed be just cause for satisfaction. But, sir, this establishment was created, not to hoard money, not to speculate upon it, not to increase its income, but to expend money 'for the increase and diffusion of knowledge'. We want knowledge more than gold.

This would not be the last time English was criticized for overstating the importance of financial gain. In the end, Meacham claimed that English had incorrectly defined the point of controversy. It was not over the proper way to expend the funds of the Institution, but rather it was over the propriety of annulling the 1847 compromise resolution on the even allocation between library and research. To Meacham and the other dissenters, that compromise had the same relation to the enabling act that the Bill of Rights had to the United States Constitution.[16]

The final denouement to the whole matter was anticlimactic indeed. The regular Democrats on the committee, Taylor and Witte, filed a report upholding the action of the Board of Regents to amend the funding allocation. Upham, the Republican, filed his own report supporting the inviolability of the 1847 compromise. Puryear, the Know-Nothing, and Wells, the anti-Nebraska Democrat refused to concur with either report and filed none of their own. Thus there was no truly majority report, and no action was ever taken to upend what the Board had done. Congress then adjourned *sine die* a few hours later.[17]

---

16. *Ibid.*, 341, 342.

17. *House Report no. 141, 33-2, passim.*

English's efforts, however, proved practical. A week after Congress adjourned he received a letter from Joseph Henry thanking him for his aid. The secretary, still under attack, was determined to distribute English's speech "as widely as possible." It was, he believed, a speech that "redounded to your credit and to the advantage of the Institution." (Well might Henry have thought so.) From then on, English became a real power on the Board of Regents, first as the leading member, ironically, of the Building Committee, and later as the chairman of the all-important Finance Committee. Like the Kansas-Nebraska bill, this Smithsonian controversy could have engulfed a less nimble politician, but English remarkably improved his standing, both in the House and the Party, and did so while avoiding the risks involved with forthright exposition. And he seemed to know how to tack at the right time.[18]

2.

While English attended the second session of the still Democratically dominated 33rd Congress, the Indiana legislature convened in Indianapolis. Although holdovers allowed the Indiana state Senate to barely remain in the hands of the Democrats, the House had an Opposition Fusion majority. In selecting its officers, the Fusionists in the House tried to satisfy all of their parts, choosing a blend of old-line Whigs, anti-Nebraska Democrats, Know-Nothings, and temperance advocates. For United States senator they nominated Godlove Orth, a mildly anti-slavery old-line Whig and the president of the Indiana Know-Nothing order. He had already been suggested for the post by the Know-Nothing state council. He had also been rather paramount behind the scenes in guiding the fusionists to victory in 1854. The state Know-Nothings also supported Milton Gregg for state printer. Gregg's *New Albany Tribune* had been a strong apologist for the Know-Nothings in southern Indiana, and he had been very active in helping to elect a number of People's Party candidates. But while the House majority took little exception to Orth, it gave the state printing not to Gregg, but to Jacob Chapman, the former *Indiana State Sentinel* editor who had noisily broken with his party over the Nebraska Act and effectively rallied anti-Nebraska Democrats to fuse with other opposition elements. Chapman's free soil views, his experience in Indianapolis, and his great early success as an editor had already made him temporary chairman of the People's Party convention in 1854. Gregg, on the other hand, may have been considered insufficiently committed to anti-slavery to properly serve the coalition. The *Paoli Eagle*, looking to stir up trouble in the

---

18. Joseph Henry to WHE, March 10, February 26, 1855, English Papers. *Tenth Annual Report of the Smithsonian, passim. Annual Report of the Smithsonian Institution for 1856* (Washington, D.C.: A. O. P. Nicholson, 1857), 86-88.

opposition's ranks, called the selection "strange," arguing that the mature Gregg "should have certainly been selected in preference to a *brainless* boy." But this criticism merely reflected the anger of the orthodox for the apostate. In essence, Chapman's victory indicated, to some degree, that the Know-Nothings could not dictate the policy of the new party without respecting its free soil element.[19]

On a joint ballot of the two houses the People's Party had an 18 majority, thereby fully expecting that they could elect Orth as Indiana's junior senator. But the Democrats, although soundly defeated in the recent canvass, considered the election results only a temporary aberration of the true popular will, and they refused to be saddled with Orth for six years. Consequently, the Senate, where the Democrats still had a majority (of a slim two votes), simply refused to go into joint convention to elect a United States senator. This was not the first time the Party employed such a tactic. In 1845, with the Senate evenly divided between Whigs and Democrats, lieutenant governor Jesse Bright cast the deciding vote against convention, arguing that the Whigs' gerrymander of 1841 had defiled the people's will. In that year the Whigs had not believed that the Democrats would adhere to their questionable tactics, but they did, and they did so again in 1855. The Senate majority simply would not allow an anti-slavery Know-Nothing to become a United States senator. The People's Party, unwilling to change its choice, hurled epithets at the Democrats and stuck to Orth. As a consequence, Bright was the only U.S. senator who represented Indiana in Washington from March 4, 1855 to February 3, 1857.[20]

Although successful in preventing the election of a Fusion senator, the Democrats could not avert the passage of a strong prohibitory temperance law. In the Senate, seven Democrats broke party ranks to vote with the opposition. The law allowed the manufacture and sale of "intoxicants" only for "medicinal, chemical, and mechanical purposes, and pure wine for sacramental use." Any person convicted of selling liquor was subject to fine and incarceration and was also subject to future search and seizure "upon the complaint of any three persons of good moral character." Any person arrested for public intoxication was required to testify how he obtained the liquor, on pain of indefinite imprisonment. It was this last clause that prompted much of the Democratic press to compare the law to the "heyday of the Spanish Inquisition." Taking note of the commercial drawbacks of the bill, the *New Albany Ledger* predicted that Louisville would reap the benefit to the disadvantage of Indiana's river towns. "They cannot get it *here*; hence they go to Louisville for it, and while there buy their goods." In the main the law,

---

19. Roger van Bolt, 'The Rise of the Republican Party in Indiana 1855-1856," *Indiana Magazine of History* 51, no. 3 (September, 1955): 184. Brand, "Know-Nothing Party in Indiana," 78. *Paoli Eagle,* February 9, 1855.

20. Shepherd, *Biographical Directory,* 511-513. *Paoli Eagle,* March 16, 1855. Woolen, *Biographical and Historical Sketches,* 433. Van der Weele, "Jesse Bright," 33-34. Godlove Orth to Schuyler Colfax, February 5, 1855, in van Bolt, *Rise of the Republican Party,* 186. *Biographical Directory of United States Congress,* 151, fn 17.

which went into effect on June 12, 1855, was rather well complied with. Fusion supporting newspapers especially noticed that one of its effects was to markedly reduce crime. But if one wished badly enough to drink in Indiana, the deed could be accomplished. Liquor was easily obtainable by way of Cincinnati or Louisville. John L. Robinson regularly received shipments from Ohio and Kentucky by rail; he had the kegs marked 'lard oil' to avoid seizure by Indiana agents. The success of such devices probably contributed to the ostensible "compliance" with the law.[21]

The seven Democratic senators who voted for the bill all came of course from the Wright faction of the Indiana Democracy. This fact, and especially Wright's refusal to veto the bill, angered the Bright element that had been strengthened within the Party by the defection of many temperance and free soil Democrats in 1854. By the end of the 1855 legislature, Wright had also angered many Bright Democrats when he opposed a bill, subsequently passed over his veto, replacing the Second State Bank with a new one. The charter of the Second State Bank was due to expire before the next legislature met in 1857, but instead of simply attempting to extend it, the principal investors decided it would be more advantageous to seek a fresh legislative charter for a new institution. Aside from increasing the number of branches, augmenting the amount of capital allowed to each branch, and including a clause that prohibited the state from owning any stock, the charter of the new state bank was exactly the same as the old one. Nevertheless, Wright believed that since the issue was not discussed in the recent campaign, the legislature should have refrained from acting upon it. Moreover, he believed that the manner of stock subscription was unfair and invited corruption.[22]

While old-line Whigs and even free-soilers were heavily involved in the new bank, the principal prospective investors were Bright Democrats. The largest shareholders initially included Phineas Kent, Graham Fitch, John L. Robinson, and Michael Bright. New Albany Democrats were also among the large shareholders. Except for Fitch, these men formed the core of the Indiana Democracy south of the national road, and they resented Wright's opposition. In order to ensure that the legislature passed the bank bill over the Governor's veto, they bribed many legislators with promised shares of the proposed bank's stock. Even the *Indiana State Sentinel* publisher, Austin Brown, was offered 200 shares to stay clear of reporting these machinations. As an investigating committee revealed a couple of years later, the birth of the third Indiana State Bank was midwifed by corruption. On the day of subscription, when the books were to be open to the public for initial stock-buying, the subcommissioners of each city kept them open

---

21. *Paoli Eagle*, March 16, 1855. Goodwin, *Tussle with the Traffic*, 80-84. *New Albany Ledger*, February 13, July 5, 1855. *Indiana State Sentinel*, June 15, 1855. *Indianapolis Journal*, December 21, 1855. *Indiana Locomotive*, December 23, 1855. Woolen, *Biographical and Historical Sketches*, 318. Goodwin, 20.

22. S.T. Ensey to Joseph Wright, July 20, 1854, in Crane, "Joseph Wright," 210-211. Crane, 199, 233. Thornbrough, *Civil War Era*, 425-426. Hugh McCulloch, *Men and Measures,* 128. Esarey, *State Banking*, 288.

for only 10 to 15 minutes, enough time merely to record preselected subscribers. These, of course, included the principal investors named above. Many of them turned around and sold their enormous shares (Kent had 1,700; Michael Bright almost 2,000) for tidy profits.[23]

The bank business is only one example of how the leading Bright Democrats were heavily involved in financial speculation. This is not to suggest that the Wright Democrats were not at all participants in railroad promotion and the procurement of land warrants, but their schemes were generally less ambitious than the ones of their rivals. Bright's close association with the Washington banking house of Corcoran and Riggs had much to do with this. Jesse Bright's daughter was married to George Riggs's son, and W.W. Corcoran was one of the senator's closest friends. In partnership with Corcoran, Bright became one of the leading Democrats who heavily invested in Superior City, Wisconsin, a speculative scheme engineered largely by Stephen Douglas. Other Democratic investors included congressmen Richardson and Breckinridge, senator R.M.T. Hunter, Robert J. Walker, and house clerk John Forney. A coterie of Democrats from southeast Indiana contributed to Bright's end of the venture, but it appears, strangely, that William English had nothing to do with it. He was, however, certainly connected to Bright in other ventures. Michael Bright constantly succeeded in involving English in one scheme or another, and after the state bank bill passed over Wright's veto, English became a stockholder in the branch at Jeffersonville. The *Madison Banner* wrote of English having gained "celebrity as an operator in stocks, having become wealthy in operations of various kinds." He held 400 shares of Madison and Indianapolis Railroad stock worth $20,000, and while in Washington, he consistently bought and sold land before it was developed. He was also, like Bright, heavily involved in Texas bonds, using his voting power in the House to help ensure their payment by the federal government.[24]

The Bright Democracy's greater proclivity for land speculation and financial maneuvering illustrated its tendency to put commercial matters before all else. It was bothered by the "immorality" of intemperance and the "sin" of slavery

---

23. Esarey, *State Banking*, 290-295. *Biographical and Historical Souvenir*, 86. *New Albany Ledger*, November 3, 5, 1855, January 4, 1856. *New Albany Weekly Tribune*, January 2, 1856.

24. Roy F. Nichols, *The Disruption of American Democracy* (New York: The Free Press, 1948), 19. Van der Weele, "Jesse Bright," 160. William C. Davis, *Breckinridge: Statesman, Soldier, Symbol* (Baton Rouge: Louisiana State University Press, 1974), 120-121. Frank H. Heck, *Proud Kentuckian: John C. Breckinridge, 1821-1875* (Lexington: The University Press of Kentucky, 1976), 159. John H. Hinks to WHE, November 30, 1855; B. J. Crary to WHE, April 11, 1855; W. W. Wick to WHE, August 23, 1855, English Papers. *CG, 33-1,* 2100. M.G. Bright to WHE, October 27, 1854, English Papers. *Madison Banner*, March 1, 1854. J.H. Barnes to Schuyler Colfax, January 7, 1855, English Papers. Washington, D.C. deed, April 15, 1854, English Papers. W.S. Holman to WHE, August 26, 1855, English Papers. Davis, *Breckinridge*, 128. Holman Hamilton, "Texas Bonds and Northern Profits: A Study in Compromise, Investment, and Lobby Influence," *Mississippi Valley Historical Review* 43, no. 4 (March, 1957), 589. Wilson, *Lexington*, 117. *CG, 33-2*, 618, 619, 866.

much less than was the Wright faction, partly because slaves produced cotton and intemperates bought liquor. Unlike Wright Democrats, many in the Bright faction, to a great degree including English, deprecated any criticism of other men's behavior or peculiar institutions because of the tendency of such criticism to destabilize the market. As reputedly later noted by our 30th president, "the business of America is business." Tender consciences should be prevented from killing the golden goose.

3.

The primary reason why the two factions of the Indiana Democracy did not break out into another full round of open political warfare in early 1855 was the common threat of the Opposition. Of the three basic elements of which it was composed—anti-slaveryism, temperance reform, and nativism—it was the nativist Know-Nothings on whom the Democrats concentrated their fire. Nativism could not only be righteously attacked as intolerant, but it was also a political necessity for a party so dependent upon German and Irish voters to strongly oppose it. Unlike temperance reform and anti-slavery, opposition to nativism strongly united the whole party, and some Democrats also hoped that a crusade against the Know-Nothings would bring back Party members who had left in 1854. Such sentiment was evident in a Democratic Crawford County resolution declaring their party "open to all who abjure allegiance to the doctrine of Know-Nothing fusion," and an Indianapolis one declaring as "Democrats in good standing all those...who are willing to act with us, upon the platform laid down by the National Convention of 1852 [not the state one in 1854]." The bitter divisions of 1854 were to be healed by resolutions proclaiming that "secret political organizations under a republican form of government, [were] an abomination in the sight of God and man."[25]

For their part the Know-Nothings tried to increase the palatability of their organization by eliminating their secrecy and even going so far as to open their doors to Protestant foreigners. These two reforms allowed them to more easily dominate fusionist local politics in the early spring of 1855, when the anti-slavery issue was awaiting how popular sovereignty would work in Kansas and the temperance reformers had already achieved their state legislative victory. The more narrow exclusion of only Catholic aliens appealed to old-line Whigs, who generally espoused Protestant norms, and it more firmly cemented the alliance between Know-Nothings and the more anti-papal Protestant denominations. Especially successful within the fusion movement were the Know-Nothing lodges in the virulently anti-abolitionist Second District of Indiana. In Jeffersonville and New

---

25. *Paoli Eagle*, April 6, March 23, 1855.

Albany, they dominated the so-called People's Party. Milton Gregg, nativist editor of the *New Albany Tribune*, constantly feared that the state Opposition would succumb to abolitionism; he held a running battle with northern fusionist anti-slavery editors who wished to tear the Party from its nativist roots.[26]

The leading Know-Nothings in the Second District were primarily old-line Whigs, assisted by a smattering of discontented Democrats. Heading the list were Gregg, Thomas Slaughter, and David Laird, but the most venerable of them all was George Patrick Rice Wilson, a longtime Harrison County resident of Scots-Irish Protestant ancestry. A Kentuckian by birth, he had served six terms in the Indiana House during the 1830s and five more between 1842 and 1850. Those were the years of the second party system's greatest intensity, and Wilson was a typical Whig of the old school—friendly to individual opponents in the Democracy (including the Englishes) but an inveterate enemy of what he would call their 'loco-foco' principles. Typical, also, was his opinion of the abolitionists, whom he especially condemned for their many denunciations of his idol, Henry Clay. Caught between what he feared were the extremes on the question of slavery, he found comfort in the conservative avoidance of the issue that the Know-Nothing order appeared to offer.[27]

In their struggle to distance themselves from advanced anti-slavery while at the same time attacking the Democracy and furthering nativism, Gregg and Wilson often charged that the new German immigrants tended to be militant abolitionists. Despite this ploy, they were, unfortunately for them, constantly saddled with evidence that it was actually the Know-Nothings in the free states who were most often allied with abolitionists. The most damaging acts came from the Know-Nothing legislature in Massachusetts, which passed one law prohibiting aliens from holding office and another requiring, as the *New Albany Ledger* put it, "nigger children to be admitted to the public schools on terms of equality with white children." Norman continually used Massachusetts as an example of what could be expected in the way of race equality in Indiana if the state Senate ever fell to the opposition. Despite cries to the contrary from Gregg and others, all Norman had to do was to point to the Garbers, Chapmans, and Julians in the fusion ranks to make his argument.[28]

---

26. Brand, "Know-Nothings in Indiana," 192. Howe, *Culture of American Whigs*, 13, 19. *New Albany Weekly Tribune*, May 16, 1855.

27. Brand, "Know-Nothings in Indiana," 203. Shepherd, *Biographical Directory*, 420. Gresham, *Life of Walter Q. Gresham*, 63.

28. *New Albany Weekly Tribune*, April 25, 1855. *New Albany Ledger*, April 16, May 1, 1855. The Massachusetts 1855 law concerning public schools may be accessed online at State of Massachusetts Archives, accessed July 23, 2018, https://archives.lib.state.ma.us/bitstream/handle/2452/297079/1855acts0256.txt?sequence=1&isAllowed=y

To further counter the strength of the Know-Nothings, "Sag Nicht" or "Say Nothing" organizations were formed throughout the border region. Originally making their appearance in northern Kentucky, they spread to Jeffersonville and New Albany by early spring. They primarily functioned as a vigilante group intent on protecting the voting rights of aliens and Catholics, and in this manner they may be considered an arm of the Democratic Party. In April and May 1855, Hoosiers throughout the state went to the polls to elect city and township officials, and the Democrats in the Second District were determined to prevent the violence that they believed decreased their vote in 1854. Besides taking the precaution of protecting the foreign voter, New Albany Democrats put together an attractive ticket, consisting of a popular merchant, an up-and-coming attorney, and an old-line Whig who detested the Know-Nothings. Yet despite these preparations, two weeks before the election these candidates abruptly withdrew. In separate letters they each claimed that the fear of a repeat of violence at the polls had forced them to leave their races. But the real reason they withdrew was no doubt the certainty of defeat, and, indeed, throughout the state the People's Party repeated the gains they made in 1854. It seems certain that the New Albany regency decided to withdraw its candidates only to reduce the total vote of the opposition. The orchestrated nature of their withdrawals leads one to believe that the Party wished to simply deprive the Know-Nothings of a significant victory.[29]

The continued strength of the fusionists alarmed the Indiana Democracy, and the party appeared determined to do all it could to avoid defeat in the county elections in October. Never one to stand idly by while his beloved party was under attack, William English took an active part in this effort. In Congress, he used his Smithsonian speech to castigate what he considered the inanity of nativism. Recalling that James Smithson himself was not an American, he used that fact to illustrate how foreigners could make a significant contribution to the United States. Moreover, perhaps in conflict with his own Young American exceptionalism, he used the example of Smithson to argue that the most enlightened individuals understood themselves less as members of one nation than as part of a world community. Noting that "the wild Indians and the roving Tartars consider[ed] the customs of their respective tribes the perfection of human life," he proceeded to lampoon and criticize the narrow perspective of the nativists:

> Every savage and most all half-civilized people think that within the boundaries of their own country are to be found all virtue, intelligence, heroism and happiness. They are ever jealous of strangers, deny them all political rights, and sometimes persecute them to death...I shall not be

---

29. Brand, "Know-Nothings in Indiana," 184. *New Albany Weekly Tribune*, March 27, 1855. *New Albany Ledger*, March 27, April 23, 1855. Brand, 185, 186-187. *Ledger*, April 3, 4, 5, 7, May 1, 2, 3, 1855. *Weekly Tribune*, April 11, 18, May 9, 1855.

blinded to the merit of those whose destiny it happened to be to come into the world elsewhere, and especially those who, from choice, have selected this as their permanent home—neither shall I forget how much our own career of greatness and glory has been facilitated by emigration.

English and the Democrats did seem more comfortable with cultural differences in the United States (if not racial ones) than did the Whigs and their progeny. Though by no means modern cultural pluralists, they appeared to have more faith in the power of 'Americanism' to assimilate even religious differences.[30]

English also voted against bills introduced by Know-Nothings that were sometimes nativist on steroids. One measure, for example, designed to "prevent the importation into the United States of foreign criminals, paupers, lunatics, insane, idiots, and blind persons," gained the vote of only one northern Democrat. But the second session of the 33rd Congress saw little real debate over nativism, and English made his greatest contributions to the anti-Know-Nothing cause during the long adjournment between March and December. He was in New Albany on the day the *Ledger* printed the withdrawal letters of the three Democratic candidates, and while there he must have gained a clear picture of the fusionists' strength. He remained in Indiana to witness the Democratic losses throughout the state in early May. But later that month, good news came from a closely watched election in another state. In Virginia, Henry A. Wise, erstwhile Tyler Whig, but for the last decade back with the Democrats, defeated erstwhile Whig and present Know-Nothing Thomas S. Flournoy for governor. English was in New York City when the news arrived and celebrated with party chieftains at Tammany Hall. Wise's victory was optimistically, but not incorrectly, interpreted by many Democrats as the beginning of the end for the Know-Nothings.[31]

The New York celebration partly consisted of politicians, large and small, making speeches well into the night. By the time English got to speak, the hour was indeed late; nevertheless, enough of the press remained (perhaps because of the spirits that were no doubt flowing) to record his words for the New York newspapers. Echoing the sentiments of the Party in general, English stated that Wise's victory had "sounded the death knell of the party of proscription and religious intolerance." He noted that in "all times, and under all circumstances, when the vital principles of this government have been assailed, or the country been in danger, the rock of defense has been [the] indomitable Democracy." It was the Democratic Party, he recalled, that had saved the country from the Alien

30. *CG, 33-2*, 284. Howe, *Culture of American Whigs*, 38. Kleppner, *Third Electoral System*, 60. John B. Norman's warning that immigrants still had to assimilate (see p.177) illustrates that Democrats were by no means cultural pluralists.

31. *CG, 33-2*, 1187. *New Albany Ledger*, April 3, June 6, 1855. Allan Nevins, *Ordeal of the Union*, vol. 2 (1947; repr., New York: Charles Scribner's Sons, 1975), 397.

and Sedition acts, the doctrines of the Hartford Convention (secession-like activities), and the "monster" United States Bank. It was the Democracy now that could be relied upon to resist all "religious and sectional fanaticism." These actions represented the greatness of the Party: its resistance to extreme ideas, and its commitment to moderation. "We have but to stand firm by our principles—by the Constitution and the Union—discarding all sectional prejudice, and all bickering among ourselves, and victory is certain to perch upon our standard."[32]

A celebration of the Party, English's words were also a warning to it. That he used the word "sectional" to modify both "fanaticism" and "prejudice" suggests that he considered strict Know-Nothingism, which by itself was not sectional, to not be the greatest threat to the nation. Near the end of his speech he argued that "the result in Virginia has demonstrated that the Know-Nothing organization cannot exist as a national party. It must inevitably dwindle to a mere sectional Abolition concern."[33] Although nativism was strong in southern Indiana, English understood that even there the cause of anti-slavery inflated the number of Know-Nothing adherents, and the rumored electoral shenanigans and sectional legislation of the pro-slavery partisans in Kansas territory during the spring and summer of 1855 only threatened to stir Indiana and northern free-soilers to greater efforts. To English, the greatest threat of Know-Nothingism was not primarily its nativist doctrine, which he correctly believed by itself did not appeal to a majority of voters almost anywhere, but its ability to act in concert with forces that promoted discontent over slavery.

4.

Indeed, around the time of Wise's victory in May 1855, the anti-slavery element in the Opposition's coalition was clearly becoming dominant. Events in Kansas, beginning a few months after the passage of the Kansas-Nebraska Act and running through the summer and fall of 1855, markedly promoted this phenomenon. Essentially, the on-the-ground application of the Kansas-Nebraska Act's principle of popular sovereignty miserably failed to reduce the political conflict over slavery. Even before the bill had become law, realizing that the nature of popular sovereignty rewarded strength through numbers on the ground, anti-slavery partisans from Massachusetts organized the New England Emigrant Aid Society. The group proposed to help resettle to Kansas New England opponents of slavery. This planned relocation was clearly not an example of the type of "natural," orderly emigration that the Democratic northern sponsors of Kansas-Nebraska foresaw, and they believed it could only hurt the cause of a free Kansas by promoting a pro-slavery backlash. As the *New Albany Ledger* had put it in June of 1854,

---

32. *New Albany Ledger*, June 6, 1855.

33. *Ibid.*

"we know of no manner in which slavery could more surely be established in [Kansas] than by throwing into the country a gang of red-mouthed Yankee abolitionists." According to Norman that was exactly how manumission was prevented in Kentucky and Maryland, and the only effect the "rantings of these men" had was to "tighten the chains of slaves everywhere."[34]

Although the Emigrant Aid Society had only collected $20,000 by even the end of 1854, it had earlier stated its intention to raise $5 million more. Its primary organizer, Eli Thayer, traveled throughout the North seeking subscriptions. As the *New Albany Ledger* predicted, this activity did spur the Missouri slaveholders into action, but Emigrant Aid Society or not, Missouri politicians had already determined to reserve Kansas for slavery. Senator David Atchison, for one, had repeatedly staked his political future on it. It was he who had been one of the southerners instrumental in forcing Douglas to combine the organization of Nebraska with the repeal of the Missouri Compromise, and even months before the act was introduced Atchison had apparently stated that he "would rather see Nebraska in hell than have it admitted as a free state." Should northerners attempt to "take up those fertile prairies," he averred, Missourians would protect their fair inheritance, "if necessary, with the bayonet and with blood."[35]

At any rate, the organization of the Emigrant Society certainly accelerated the pace of the conflict. Forewarned of what they considered an imminent invasion of free-state interlopers, Missourians began to organize "mutual protection" committees, vigilante groups that promised to "assist in removing any and all emigrants who came [to Kansas] under the auspices of the Northern Emigrant Aid Societies." In early and mid-1854, the application of this rhetoric limited itself to the promotion of southern settlers in advance of the great northern waves. Even before the Kansas-Nebraska Bill was passed, many hundreds of Missourians had already eased across the border, and many of the other initial immigrants were from the upper South. Toward the end of the 1854 summer and into the fall, on the other hand, St Louis anti-slaveryites fed hundreds of free soil pioneers along the Missouri River into Kansas. Believing, thus, that they were soon to be outnumbered, pro-slavery southerners in the territory pushed for an early election to the territorial legislature. When that move was vetoed by newly arrived governor Andrew A. Reeder, a moderate Democrat from Pennsylvania, they were forced to settle for a November 1854 election for a territorial delegate to Congress. It was in this election that the Missourians first illustrated to what lengths they would go in order to insure that Kansas remained open to slavery. Unsure that the pro-slavery

---

34. On the Massachusetts and New England Emigrant Aid Societies see Nicole Etcheson, *Bleeding Kansas: Contested Liberty in the Civil War Era* (Lawrence: University Press of Kansas, 2004), 35-38; Nevins, *Ordeal of the Union, vol. 2*, 306-311; Potter, *Impending Crisis*, 199-200. *New Albany Ledger*, June 3, 1854.

35. Nevins, *Ordeal of the Union*, vol. 2, 306-311. Atchison quote from *Lawrence Herald of Freedom*, February 21, 1857, in Nevins, 306.

force of settlers constituted a majority in Kansas, Missourians crossed the border on Election Day and fanned out to vote. According to a later congressional investigation, over 1,700 votes were illegally cast by these "border ruffians." This ensured the election of pro-slavery candidate John W. Whitfield, a political and personal confidante of senator David Atchison.[36]

Subsequent charges of electoral fraud were not limited to the Opposition press. Afraid that such chicanery might again be repeated when Kansans went to the polls to choose a territorial legislature in the spring of 1855, even the *New Albany Ledger* cautioned that "the people of Kansas—those who intend to make their permanent home there—should be left to settle this question [of slavery] themselves." In the short second session of the 33rd Congress, Hoosier Democrat turned Oppositionist (and later Republican), Daniel Mace, had sarcastically noted that "the people of Missouri had manifested a good deal of interest in the election of General Whitfield as delegate to Congress." He went on to directly protest the interference into Kansas politics by residents across the border. Missouri Democratic congressman Andrew Oliver countered with the orthodox Southern claim that his fellow Missourians were merely responding to the impropriety of interference from New England. At that point English gained the floor. He informed the House that Mace himself "was one of the originators of that emigration society—one of the pioneers of that cause." According to the printer of the *Congressional Globe* (an orthodox Democrat) English's statement was followed by "Great Laughter." One Democratic newspaper, resorting to hyperbole, claimed that "members on all sides—Whigs, Democrats, Northerners, Southerners, Free Soilers, and Know-Nothings—were seen holding their sides and wiping away tears flowed from excess of merriment."[37]

Obviously, English and most Democrats wished to place the blame for the fraud on overzealous New England free-soilers, and they hoped to stereotype the promoters of the emigrant aid societies as counterproductive and dangerous abolitionists. But the circumstances surrounding the election of a territorial legislature in March 1855 made it very difficult for them to hold to this line of argument. Once again, on the appointed day of the election, thousands of Missourians crossed the border to vote for the pro-slavery candidates. Subsequent investigation showed that of the 6,310 votes cast, 4,908 were illegal. A contest that should have been very close was turned into a rout in favor of the pro-slavery forces. Moreover, there was physical intimidation, for as Atchison wrote Senator R.M.T. Hunter, "the hickory was used on the most impudent of them." He re-

36. Nevins, *Ordeal of the Union, vol. 2,* 309-313; Etcheson, *Bleeding Kansas,* 32-36, 53-54. *St. Louis Republican,* June 24, 1854, in *New Albany Weekly Tribune,* July 8, 1854.

37. *New Albany Ledger,* December 7, 21, 1854. *CG, 33-2,* 47, 50. English Scrapbook, 53. As Allen Johnson points out, when earlier territories were established, many clear residents already lived there, but as Kansas had been designated for Indians, few American citizens actually resided there in 1854, thus allowing for ambiguity on who could be a voter. *Stephen A. Douglas,* 284.

joiced that the Missourians had saved Kansas for slavery: "Now let the southern men come in with their slaves. Ten thousand families can take possession of, and hold every acre of timber in the territory of Kansas, and this secures the prairie."[38]

The census taken earlier that year indicated that Kansas contained about 8,500 residents. Of these, about 800 had indeed been sent by various emigrant aid societies, but the greatest percentage by far of non-southern settlers came not from the upper North but from the border regions of Indiana, Ohio, and Kentucky. According to almost all accounts, their attitude resembled those of Indiana's Second District: slavery was detrimental to a republican society and economy, but it was most undesirable because it brought in black folks. Many of the migrants from Kentucky, like their ancestors who left for the old Northwest, had fled to Kansas at least partially to escape the slave system, and so, probably, did many of the immigrants to Kansas from Arkansas, Tennessee, North Carolina, and even Missouri. And even many of those southern settlers, who favored slavery, were often not extreme about it or were unconvinced that in the end the pro-slave population would outnumber the free-soilers. As the *Louisville Democrat* had remarked before the election, "emigrants from the slaveholding states do not carry their slaves with them." It believed that such settlers were no fire eaters, and the newspaper predicted that when the "territorial legislature meets…slavery will be prohibited in the territory."[39]

Atchison's irregulars apparently spoiled that prediction, but the injustice of their behavior was all too manifest. The *New Albany Ledger* counseled that the fraud be undone, for it made a mockery of popular sovereignty. When the *New Albany Tribune* taunted the *Ledger* and English for their now evidently false campaign promise that Kansas would remain free under the Kansas-Nebraska Act, Norman responded by arguing that he "never dreamed the rights of the actual settlers would be crushed by armed mobs from Missouri, not possessing, nor even claiming, the rights of citizenship." Governor Reeder, under heavy pressure to allow the result to stand, threw out most of the free soil challenges because they were not received within five days of the election, an inordinately short time for appeal. But even he, by April, had come to understand the elementary fraudulent nature of the election, and he left Kansas that spring to convince the Pierce administration of that fact.[40] As a northern Democrat he could hardly endorse this distorted application of the Kansas-Nebraska Act.

---

38. Nevins, *Ordeal of the Union, vol. 2*, 418-432. Etcheson, *Bleeding Kansas*, 57-59, 61. Potter, *Impending Crisis*, 201. David Atchison to R. M. T. Hunter, in Ambler, *Correspondence of R.M.T. Hunter*, 160-161. Atchison claimed that "we had 7,000 men in the territory on the day of election, and one-third of them will remain there."

39. Nevins, *Ordeal of the Union, vol. 2*, 381-383. Etcheson, *Bleeding Kansas*, 29. *Louisville Democrat*, quoted in *Paoli Eagle*, November 10, 1854.

40. *New Albany Ledger*, April 15, 1855. *New Albany Weekly Tribune*, April 18, 1855. *Ledger*, April 15, 1855. Nevins, *Ordeal of the Union, vol. 2*, 386-388. Etcheson, *Bleeding Kansas*, 60-61.

Pierce received Reeder well, but in the end, he failed to support him. When Reeder arrived back in Kansas he became involved in dispute after dispute with the pro-slavery legislature. That legislature clearly showed that it intended to foist slavery on Kansas by passing laws that not only declared slavery legal in the territory but sentenced to at least two years imprisonment anyone who suggested that slavery's existence in Kansas was, in fact, accomplished against the law. The legislature also made it a capital crime to assist a fugitive slave to escape his bondage. In the end, Pierce, unwilling to confront the southern wing of the Democracy, and still convinced that the emigrant aid societies were at the root of the problem, removed Reeder on the request of Atchison, secretary of war Jefferson Davis, and the Kansas legislature. He used Reeder's indelicate speculation in Indian lands as his public rationale.[41]

As a consequence of these events, the Kansas territory's free soil residents met in Topeka in September 1855 to set up an alternative territorial government and to begin the process of writing a state constitution outlawing slavery. The Democratic administration in Washington naturally considered these actions completely illegal and labeled the participants "outlaws," but, for its part, the Indiana Democracy was at first unsure how to react to the Topeka operation. As the Topeka constitution when written did indeed outlaw slavery, it supported the prediction of the Indiana Democracy that Kansas would become free, and as the same constitution prohibited black immigration into the proposed new state, it mirrored the law and general racism of Indiana. The initial two-month long absence of any condemnation of the Topeka movement by the Democratic press of Indiana illustrated its confusion over events.[42]

The Fusionist opposition in Indiana (and elsewhere) was also roiled by the events in Kansas. Ever since the 1854 elections, the Know-Nothings had hoped to avoid division over slavery, and the delegates to their first national convention that November had adopted a resolution pledging the Party "to defend and maintain the union of the States against all assaults from every quarter." So conservative and innocuous a statement had not been well received by the more committed anti-slavery delegates, and in northern Indiana it caused some loss of membership in the lodges. Later led by the new editor of the *Indiana State Journal*, Berry Sulgrove, Know-Nothings north of the national road refused to be silent on the issue of slavery extension. This dissension frightened the southern Indiana leadership, for it was just such sentiment that laid them open to the charge of abolitionism in

---

41. Nichols, *Pierce*, 413-415. Nevins, *Ordeal of the Union, vol. 2,* 387. Etcheson, *Bleeding Kansas,* 61. Roy Nichols maintains that even at their meeting in Washington, before Reeder retuned to Kansas, Pierce wanted Reeder to resign.

42. Nevins, *Ordeal of the Union, vol. 2,* 391-2. Etcheson, *Bleeding Kansas,* 70-75. No comment was made in the Democratic state organ, the *Indiana State Sentinel,* until November. The Second District newspapers similarly avoided comment on Topeka.

their very anti-abolitionist districts. The *New Albany Tribune*, for example, fresh from its spring victories in 1855, declared that "he who expects to make [the order] subservient to the interests of slavery on the one side or of abolitionism on the other, is but reckoning without his host. The order in Indiana *never can and never will become abolitionized.*"[43]

Such was the situation in Indiana when the Know-Nothings—now formally organized as the American Party—met in national convention in June 1855. The Hoosier delegation, seven in all, represented all sections of the state. They included Godlove Orth and Schuyler Colfax, from the North, and Thomas Slaughter, from the South. All of them readily agreed to the Party's nativist resolutions: the exclusion of foreign born citizens from office, a 21-year period before naturalization, and resistance to the "corrupting tendencies of Catholicism." But when the platform committee brought forth its resolution concerning slavery, the famous Twelfth Section, the feared division occurred. This resolution, claiming that "experience has shown it impossible to reconcile opinions so extreme as those which separate the disputants," resorted to the old tactic of finality, resolving to "maintain the existing laws upon the subject of slavery as a final and conclusive settlement." Such a statement supported, for all intents and circumstances, at least for the moment, the Kansas-Nebraska Act. The resolution also refused to commit itself as to whether Congress had constitutional power to legislate upon slavery in the territories, and it positively stated that "it is the sense of the National Council that Congress ought not to legislate upon the subject of slavery within the Territory of the United States." These opinions were unacceptable to the vast majority of the convention delegates from all the free states save California and New York. They were countered with a minority report demanding the restoration of the Missouri Compromise, or, failing that, the exclusion from the Union of any state formed above the Missouri Compromise line that tolerated slavery.[44]

Despite heroic attempts by some delegates to bridge the gap, the convention foundered. Upon the adoption of the majority report, 80 to 59, the Indiana delegates joined 11 other northern delegations in withdrawing from the convention. None of the Hoosiers voted for the majority report, although two did abstain, and all of them signed the dissenters' declaration of principles incorporating the anti-slavery minority report. When the Indiana delegates returned home, their action was formally endorsed by all the Know-Nothing newspapers in the northern part of the state; nearer the Ohio River, however, unanimity was hardly achieved. In the Second District, the two leading Fusion newspapers, the *Cannelton Reporter* and the *New Albany Tribune*, while both equally lamenting the fact that

---

43. Brand, "Know Nothings in Indiana," 80, 182-183. *New Albany Weekly Tribune*, May 15, 1855.

44. *Paoli Eagle*, July 6, 1855. Overdyke, *Know-Nothing Party*, 131-132. Brand, "Know-Nothings in Indiana," 187. Nevins, *Ordeal of the Union*, vol. 2, 11, 399. Brand, 189-190. Potter, *Impending Crisis*, 254.

the convention didn't simply ignore the slavery question altogether, were not one concerning their opinion of the Twelfth Section. The *Reporter,* trimming its anti-slavery sails, reluctantly but unequivocally supported the convention's work. It refused to maintain that the Twelfth Section was pro-slavery and chastised the northern delegates for continuing their agitation over the Kansas-Nebraska Act. "The contingencies of the times," it declared, "demand that attention be paid to some other momentous matters beside 'the nigger question'." On the other hand, the *Tribune* believed the Twelfth Section went too far—Gregg maintaining that the "finality" provision should have been amended so as to say that the present laws concerning slavery should be upheld "until the same shall or may be constitutionally amended or appealed, so far as it applies to the territories." But the *Tribune* did not explicitly disavow the convention's work, and it, like the *Reporter,* at least partly blamed northern extremists for the disruption.[45]

The sectional divergence within Indiana continued to manifest itself when the Know-Nothing state council met in July, just previous to the state Fusion convention. The Council formally approved the course of the Indiana delegates and boldly declared itself independent of the national organization. It adopted a platform not only calling for the restoration of the Missouri Compromise, but also completely opposed any extension of slavery at all. It even softened some of its nativist positions, most notably reducing its citizenship requirement to only a five-year wait. These planks, especially the one removing Indiana from the national organization, were unacceptable to 15 southern counties, including Clark, and they promptly seceded from the State order. While most of the Second District lodges remained, they no doubt did so with grave misgivings. Indeed, the *Cannelton Reporter* refused to even take notice of the state meeting.[46]

The extent of southern Indiana defection from the growing northern dominated opposition to the Democracy became clear when the next day the People's Party held a convention to devise "a more complete system of organization than now exists." The 5,000 delegates who attended were overwhelmingly from the northern and western sections of the state, where anti-slavery was stronger than nativism. Fewer than 50 delegates came from the Second District, despite the fact that Milton Gregg was appointed one of the vice presidents. Though some other state fusionist parties that were dominated by their anti-slavery element had

---

45. Nevins, *Ordeal of the Union, vol. 2,* 399-400; Potter, *Impending Crisis,* 254-255. Brand, "Know Nothings in Indiana," 190-194. Congressman Colfax, a delegate to the American convention, spoke for northern Indiana in general when he wrote a fellow delegate that "[y]ou must allow me to thank you...for the gallant manner in which you...endorse[d] the action of the Northern Delegates at Philadelphia... If the pro-slavery platform had been acquiesced by us, our constituents would have shit on it and us too when we returned and there would have been no hope of success in 1856." Schuyler Colfax to Friend Stettins, July 6, 1855, Colfax Papers. *Paoli Eagle,* July 6, 1855. *New Albany Ledger,* June 30, 1855. *Cannelton Reporter,* June 29, July 18, 1855. *New Albany Tribune,* June 16, 20, 1855.

46. Brand, "Know-Nothings in Indiana," 187-201. *Cannelton Reporter,* July through October, 1855.

begun to call their organizations "Republican," the Indiana fusionists did not. The convention shied away from so changing the party label for fear that it would open the Party up to the charge of supporting abolitionism, but opposition to the extension of slavery was nevertheless clearly its major concern. By this time, most northern Indiana anti-Nebraskaites and northern Indiana Know-Nothings were Republicans in all but name. As dissatisfied as Second-District delegates Gregg, Slaughter, and G.P.R. Wilson were with the People's Party emphasis on anti-slavery, there was nowhere else they could go if they wished to be part of an organization that had any chance of defeating the Indiana Democracy statewide. Acting with it on the state level, the opposition leaders in the Second District adhered to their own agenda at home. This would prove to be a tricky endeavor.[47]

That they tried to do so, however, is clear from the local fall campaign of 1855. Although the *New Albany Ledger* did charge, after the two opposition gatherings of July, that "so far as Indiana is concerned, the Know-Nothing party has been converted into an abolition party," the canvass in the entire Second District was fought not on the issue of slavery but rather on that of nativism. Not only does this confirm the continued strength of Know-Nothingism there, but, perhaps because of the mounting troubles in Kansas, the district Democrats believed they were vulnerable on the territorial question. But for whatever reason the Democrats did not force Gregg and company to deal with the anti-slavery slant of the People's Party state convention. Instead, the Democratic Party's tactic was to form county coalitions of anti-nativist Whigs and Democrats. As early as June 25, such a coalition was formed in Floyd County. William Weir was made chairman of the first meeting, and John B. Norman was its secretary. The three politicians making speeches were traditional Democrat Phineas Kent, Whig John S. Davis, and Whig-turned-Democrat Simeon K. Wolfe. Democratically controlled mass meetings in other parts of the district were often billed as "Democratic/Anti-Know-Nothing" rallies, and county tickets often included one former Whig to guarantee the widest appeal.[48]

In the midst of this canvass, William English performed significant service. Traveling sometimes with Wolfe, sometimes with Cyrus Dunham, or John L. Robinson, or his constant supporter (and hopeful successor) James A. Cravens, he crisscrossed the district on a continuous speaking tour. The Democratic press, of course, described his speeches as "eloquent," but it was his energy that was most impressive. In between his stops within the district he attended a couple of "Grand Democratic" rallies, the most important of which was in Indianapolis on August 29. This meeting occurred three weeks after the great 1855 election riots

---

47. Willard H. Smith, *Schuyler Colfax: The Changing Fortunes of a Political Idol* (Indianapolis: Indiana Historical Bureau, 1952), 61. *New Albany Ledger*, July 16, 1855. Carter, "Hoosier History," 108.

48. *New Albany Ledger*, July 19, June 25, October 5, September 25, 1855. *Paoli Eagle*, August 31, 1855.

in Louisville, and Know-Nothing violence there allowed the Democrats to reiterate strongly how "monstrous" and "lawless" Know-Nothingism was. No fragment of English's effort at Indianapolis or elsewhere remains, but a half year later, when discussing the effects of Know-Nothingism, he listed them as

> armed mobs placed as judges in the elective franchise; quiet, inoffensive, and respected citizens brutally assaulted for daring to exercise in a peaceable manner rights secured to them by the Constitution and the laws; race against race, neighborhood against neighborhood, and religion against religion; men driven by prejudice, intolerance, and passion, to deeds of violence and bloodshed which sicken the heart—sparing neither age nor sex, and extending even to the sanctuary of God.

This was probably the rhetoric, not altogether undeserved, of the Democratic campaign against Know-Nothingism in 1855.[49]

One of the Party's constant reasons for anger was the role of the Methodist clergy in the opposition's cause. Especially obnoxious was the *Western Christian Advocate*, a popular Methodist sheet. The *New Albany Ledger* claimed the *Advocate* had "no moral right to take sides in politics while professing to be a religious newspaper," and Norman advised Democrats to discontinue their subscriptions. Later he asked the Methodist clergy as a whole "to purge the Church from such poisonous ministers [in] its system." Of course what bothered the Democrats was not the fact that the ministers preached politics, but that they preached the wrong politics. For what especially galled them was that, before 1854, the Methodists were overwhelmingly Democratic, extolling the Party's principles not only from the pulpit but also from the professional chairs of Indiana University. It is no wonder then that Norman labeled them "Judas Iscariots" and "political traitors"—a formerly well-oiled source of the Democratic Party's machinery was now arrayed against it. Exasperated by the Methodists' constant sermonizing in the cause of nativism, the *New Albany Ledger* hypocritically wondered "how long will the[se] political preachers continue to disgrace their high calling by dabbling in the pool of politics?"[50]

As earlier noted, the Democracy's defense of the rights of Catholic immigrants was not untainted by its own religious bigotry. Perhaps to defend himself from charges of being too submissive to popery, Norman stated more than once that "all our sympathies are with the Protestant cause in its conflict with Catholicism." It was with the *extremism* of their anti-Catholicism that he disagreed with the Know-Nothings. Walking this line as far as the Irish vote was concerned, the

---

49. Fred W. Matthis to WHE, July 14, 1855, English Papers. *New Albany Leger*, July 31, 28, 1855. *Paoli Eagle*, August 3, 7, 1855. John L. Robinson to WHE, September 24, 1855, English Papers. *Ledger*, August 7, 8, 9. 10, 1855. *Eagle*, August 17, 1855. *Appendix to the CG, 34-1*, 292.

50. *New Albany Ledger*, May 1, 1855. Carter, "Hoosier History," 87. *Ledger*, September 15, 19, 1855.

English-born Norman even went so far as to write that "it will be a happy day for Ireland when she becomes a Protestant country, devoted to the cause of the true religion." Reworking the familiar southern mudsill theory, the *Ledger* argued that the Catholic immigrants were a fundamental part of the nation's economy: "In every busy, prosperous, active community, there must of necessity be a class of persons to do the drudgery, and if there are no Irish and Germans to do it, it must be done by the natives." Many Know-Nothings would not disagree with these sentiments, but they also desired these "papist miscreants" be deprived of the sacred franchise.[51] Had the immigrants voted Whig rather than Democratic, it is arguable that party sympathies may have been reversed.

When the voters finally went to the polls, the second district Democracy celebrated a great victory. The small Democratic majority of 586 in 1854 increased markedly to 2,701. Admittedly, Democrats were traditionally stronger in county elections than in congressional ones, but the overwhelming vote could not be denied. Only Floyd county gave a majority to the opposition, and that a bare one of 62. The Know-Nothings charged that the Democrats had deceived the voters by printing their New Albany ballots on paper similarly colored to their opposition's, but the Democracy countered that this was done to protect the privacy of the voter and thereby to avoid violence. Although this response may not have been completely honest, the fact is that peace reigned throughout the district. Considering the assaults in Louisville only two months earlier, this was particularly gratifying to the regency of its rival city of New Albany.[52]

In the state as a whole, the Democrats also polled a majority of voters for the pivotal central region returned to the fold. But in the northern counties, where the People's Party was most anti-slavery, the Democracy continued to fare poorly. The only proper analysis, borne out by the election a year later, was that the appeal of nativism was not as strong in the southern part of the state as the appeal of anti-slavery was in the northern part. Even the *New Albany Ledger* admitted that "the abolitionists of this state with a full nominated ticket would poll more votes than the American Tory party [presumably meaning the Know-Nothings]." Nativism apparently reached its peak in Indiana in the spring of 1855, while anti-slavery sentiment continued to grow. The third major element of the 1854 coalition, temperance advocates, had lost ground partly because the legislature had already passed a liquor law and partly because their cause once again languished in the courts. Without the anti-slavery element, temperance advocates and nativists could win few local elections, and it was clear (increasingly because of events in Kansas) that they would simply become the tails of the anti-slavery kite. In the Second District, where a strong anti-slavery stance was considered impossible to

---

51. *New Albany Ledger*, August 18, 21, 1855.

52. *Ibid.*, October 19, 11, 10, 1855.

success, the opposition voters could only add to the aggregate state vote against the Democracy; only rarely could they hope to win an election at home.[53]

With the Know-Nothings in retreat in the state, and the opponents of slavery gaining strength, the Indiana Democracy could only hope that events in Kansas would take a turn that allowed them to successfully support the Pierce administration in its territorial policy. In this regard northern Democrats in general were assisted by the so-called Kansan "Wakarusa War" that occurred in late November and early December. This event began as a quarrel over land ownership that resulted in the murder of a free-soiler by a pro-slavery Kansan late in November. Fearing retaliation, the murderer fled to Shawnee Mission, the home of the legislature and a pro-slavery stronghold. In his absence, threats were made against his life, and his cabin was burned to the ground. The sheriff of the county thereupon arrested one of the free soil arsonists, but before he could secure him in jail, he was ambushed by an armed band of free-staters who rescued the prisoner. In order to recapture him, the sheriff convinced the new territorial governor, Wilson Shannon, to call out the territorial militia. Believing he was faced with thousands of armed free-staters, Shannon called for a force of 3,000 men, intending not merely to re-arrest the prisoner but to break up the Topeka movement. As it turned out, many of the volunteers were Missouri citizens intent upon an all-out invasion of the town of Lawrence, a free-state citadel. As forces massed on both sides and skirmishes on the outskirts of Lawrence led to a number of deaths, Shannon reversed himself and ordered the volunteer "militia" disbanded, avoiding a full-scale bloodbath. But the free-staters active resistance to a legal official (the sheriff) was all the Indiana Democratic press needed to get in line with the national Democracy and label the Topeka movement the source of unlawful activity and controlled by abolitionists. The *Paoli Eagle* called the free-staters "rebels" and began to argue that the whole movement was illegal. The *New Albany Ledger*, though admitting that the Missourians in the past had committed unjustifiable acts, excused them on the ground that they acted as but a "few *individuals.*" On the other hand, the Topeka men had created a political and military machine: "It is evidently the design of abolitionist leaders to fan the flames of discord and arouse the passions to such an extent as to produce a collision in Kansas, if possible." Norman now called their leaders "outlaws" and noted that "if in running away from the Missourians, their horses should stumble and break the riders necks, there would be little occasion for the shedding of tears among those who love country more than party." The Hoosier Democracy now firmly took the line that the free soil movement in Kansas was abolitionist, and that, consequently, it was primarily responsible for the violence in the territory.[54]

---

53. *Ibid.*, October 10 through October 17, 1855: notification of county totals; October 23, 1855.

54. Etcheson, *Bleeding Kansas*, 79-86. *Paoli Eagle*, December 27, 1855. *New Albany Ledger*, February 11, 1856. The *Ledger* and the *Eagle* generally gained their Kansas reports from the proslavery press. See the *Ledger's* account of the Wakarusa War on December 20, 21, 1855, and the *Eagle's* account on December 6, 1855.

5.

It was within the context of these Kansas events and their partisan interpretations that the new Congress convened in December 1855. Not long after the disastrous defeat of 1854, Smith Miller sardonically wrote English that the two of them "will have a pleasant time of it in the thirty-fourth congress." Gone were Dunham, Eddy, Davis, Chamberlain, and the rest of the Democrats from Indiana—leaving the two Ohio River congressmen to face a hostile state delegation. Of the nine fusionists, Daniel Mace, John U. Pettit, and Lucien Barbour were former Democrats. Except for Will Cumback, who was 26, the rest were seasoned Whigs. They included two editors, David Holloway of the *Richmond Palladium* and Schuyler Colfax of the *St. Joseph Valley Register*; one retired Methodist minister, Samuel Brenton of Fort Wayne; and two venerable lawyers who did not trust the anti-slavery wing of the coalition: George G. Dunn of Bedfore and Harvey D. Scott of Terre Haute (see the following map). Colfax would go on to become the most renowned of the group, but, in 1855, Dunn was the most respected. He had already served in the 30th Congress, and while there, partly owing to his master use of invective, he had shown a marked ability in debate. In 1855, he quickly became a leader of the most conservative faction of the northern Indiana oppositionists.[55]

Although they well outnumbered the Democrats in the Indiana delegation and held almost two-thirds of the House as a whole, the Opposition was too fragmented to control business effectively at the outset of the 34th Congress. Of their 151 members, 30 were elected as southern Know-Nothings or Americans. The northerners were more difficult to classify, as many were elected on fused tickets. Yet by analyzing their votes for speaker, it is possible to determine that 13 of them were more nativist than anti-slavery, leaving 108 whose primary concern was to prevent the extension of slavery. Although these committed 108 free-soilers clearly composed the largest bloc in the House, they were still 10 representatives short of a majority. Partially because they realized their weakness and partially because a number of them wished to become speaker, they did not attempt to force a choice for the presiding officer at the anti-administration caucus held the night before Congress convened. Derailing any attempt by the nativists to do so, they convinced the caucus to make no nomination at all. They hoped that after a few ballots their strongest nominee would emerge, and then they would caucus again to try to get the rest of the coalition to support him.[56]

55. Smith Miller to WHE, November 11, 1854, English Papers. *Biographical Directory of United States Congress*, 151, 1484, 1729, 607-608, 904, 1270, 854, 703, 989, 1878. McCulloch, *Men and Measures*, 50.

56. Fred H. Harrington, "The First Northern Victory," *Journal of Southern History* 5, no. 2 (May, 1939), 189. Schuyler Colfax to Charles Heaton, in van Bolt, "Rise of the Republican Party," 199. Temple R. Hollcroft, ed., "A Congressman's Letters on the Speaker Election of the Thirty-Fourth Congress," *Mississippi Valley Historical Review* 43, no. 3 (December, 1956), 448. It is very difficult to classify the members of Congress who were anti-Democratic. Many of them ran as Whigs or in Fusionist combinations in 1854 or the summer of 1855, but by the time Congress met in in December the Whig Party had rather completely disintegrated and the northern Know-Nothings were mostly anti-slavery. See Dubin, *United States Congressional Elections, 1788-1997*, 174.

Congressmen and Their Districts,
1855-1857

Well in the minority, the Democrats had little trouble remaining unified. In October, there had been some talk among the northwesterners of focusing on Howell Cobb of Georgia for speaker, as his reputation as a southern moderate combined with his renowned parliamentary skills made him an attractive candidate. William Richardson urged his nomination, and a sycophant of Jesse Bright's, Robert S. Sproule, claimed that both Smith Miller and English favored him as well. But what made him strong in the northwest—his Unionism—weakened him with the states-rights faction in the South, and his nomination was never seriously considered. When the Democrats formally caucused on December 1, they instead chose Richardson himself, a clear endorsement of Kansas-Nebraska and popular sovereignty. English, a secretary of this caucus, evidently had no trouble acquiescing in the choice. Nor did he complain when the party caucus adopted a resolution severely denouncing the Know-Nothings.[57]

The first ballot for speaker occurred shortly after the House convened on the morning of December 3. Twenty-six different congressmen received votes. Leading the pack easily was Richardson, who garnered 74 of the 78 Democratic ballots. The primary challengers from the opposition were Lewis D. Campbell of Ohio (53 votes), Humphrey Marshall of Kentucky (30), Nathaniel Banks of Massachusetts (21), and Henry M. Fuller of Pennsylvania (17). The Kentuckian, Marshall, was clearly the favorite of the southern Know-Nothings, gaining the votes of all but one of the southern American Party members who voted, as well as three nativist votes from New York. Henry Fuller received the other southern American vote, but the rest of his supporters were all from his Pennsylvanian home state. Neither of these candidates had any strength among the anti-slavery representatives of the coalition, most of whom either chose Campbell or Banks. Campbell was something of an old-line Whig, now a strong Know-Nothing from southern Ohio who, like Thomas Slaughter, English's opponent in 1854, was sufficiently anti-slavery to have been unable to accept the Twelfth Section. He had been a congressman since 1849 and had helped lead the fight against Kansas-Nebraska in the 33rd Congress. Almost three-quarters of his support came from three states: Ohio, New York, and Indiana. All of the fusionist Hoosiers, having caucused earlier, decided to support this fellow westerner. On the other hand, Nathaniel Banks received only three votes from states that did not touch the Atlantic. A former Democrat from Massachusetts, Banks was a member of a Know-Nothing lodge, but he was also the staunchest anti-slaveryite among the four. Essentially the favorite son of Massachusetts, he split New England with Campbell.[58]

---

57. Thomas D. Harris to Howell Cobb, October 15, 1855, in Phillips, *Correspondence of Toombs, Stephens, and Cobb*, 356. *New Albany Ledger*, December 3, 1855. Harrington, "First Northern Victory," 188.

58. *CG, 34-1*, 3. *Biographical Directory of United States Congress*, 776, 605. James G. Hollandsworth, Jr., *Pretense of Glory: The Life of General Nathaniel P. Banks* (Baton Rouge: Louisiana State University Press, 1998), 20-24. Nevins, *Ordeal of the Union*, vol. 2, 414.

Throughout the first two days, the tally remained rather constant. English and Miller dutifully joined almost all the other Democrats to keep Richardson at around 75 votes, while Campbell continued to lead the opposition. But by the third day it was clear that Campbell, although he could overtake Richardson, could not nearly obtain a majority himself. Too many former Democratic members of the opposition refused to vote for him, and on December 6 he bitterly withdrew. After once again spreading their ballots thinly, the fusionists soon concentrated on two candidates in opposition to Richardson: Fuller and Banks. Fuller replaced Marshall as the unofficial nominee of the Know-Nothing American Party, and Banks, effectively, was the choice of the committed anti-slaveryites, or, essentially, "Republicans." All of the Indiana fusionist congressmen (and anti-Nebraska Democrat Daniel Mace) switched to Banks when he was made the authoritative nominee of an "anti-Nebraska" caucus on December 14. But a couple of days later, Hoosier fusionists Dunn and Harvey Scott abandoned Banks, apparently because the nascent Republicans had reneged on their promise to honor Campbell by giving him a sizeable departing vote. They chose instead to cast their votes for other northern fusionists for the remainder of the contest.[59]

By December 15, the vote settled into a position from which it would remain relatively unchanged for a month: Banks at around 105, Richardson hovering near 74, and Fuller anywhere from 29 to 41. Such a situation was perfect for cloakroom bargaining, and rumors of deals appeared in the press constantly. Even earlier, Republicans had offered to support southern Know-Nothing William Cullom of Tennessee for clerk in return for American support for Banks. But the southern Know-Nothings were not yet ready to admit defeat, and instead they had approached the Democrats with a scheme to endorse that party's candidate for printer and clerk, if they would switch from Richardson to Fuller. The Democrats, however, believing the opposition could never reconcile its differences, refused to bargain. Opposed to both free soilerism and nativism, the Democrats took increased pride in their principles and clearly reveled in the opposition's predicament.[60]

---

59. *CG, 34-1,* 3-4, 4-5. Harrington, "First Northern Victory," 192-194. Schuyler Colfax to Charles Heaton, December 25, 1855, in Smith, *Schuyler Colfax,* 68. *CG, 34-1,* 6-8, 11. When Lewis Campbell took himself out of the running he noted that "he could not be elected without either repudiating his well-known American and anti-slavery principles or making pledges regarding formation of committees that would justly expose him to public contempt." Horace Greeley, *Recollections of a Busy Life* (New York: J. B. Ford and Company, 1868), 346. *CG, 34-1,* 11-12, 243-244.

60. *CG, 34-1,* 29ff. *New Albany Ledger,* December 3, 5, 1855. Edwin Morgan, 'Republican' from New York, noted that if the Democrats united with the South Americans they may have been able to forge a majority. He claimed that for some time they were unable to do so because the southern Democrats and southern Americans "are vying with each other in their devotion to the Slave Power." Hollcroft, "A Congressman's letters," 453-454.

A few anti-Nebraska Democrats who remained in the Party, claiming to want to end the deadlock and get the House organized, began toying with ways to drop Richardson, but they were indeed very few and hardly represented the full party or administration. In general, the Party's position was well represented by a speech William English made in support of Richardson. He argued that it was not the Democracy's fault that the House had remained unorganized for so long. It was instead the fault of an incompetent majority, "who are manifesting to the country their peculiar fitness to administer the offices of this great government." In contrast to the blundering forces of the opposition, the Democracy radiated unity and purpose. "And why?" he asked. "Because the Democratic party is a national party, with clear and well defined principles [based on] the Constitution and the Union." It should not be asked, English continued, to abandon its principles, which were well represented by its nominee. Right does not compromise with wrong: "The opposition may come to [our] platform—but I shall not go to theirs, nor shall I meet them on any middle ground." And he grandiloquently invoked that "even if the twelve Apostles differed with me in this instance, I should hesitate about compromise with them unless they subscribed fully to the Democratic creed."[61] On what he would do if Jesus Christ himself came to him, he did not say.

With the Democrats intransigent and the opposition divided, the contest dragged on into the middle of January. English adhered to Richardson throughout, and for his loyalty he appeared to receive the unanimous commendation from his fellow Democrats back home. "Yield not an inch," John L. Robinson wrote him from Rushville, "let the opposition take you if they can, *but never capitulate.*" Alexander F. Morrison, Indiana's representative on the Democratic National Committee, informed English that "we are all well pleased with the manly stand taken by the Democrats in the House in the Speaker's election. Compromise no principle—give no encouragement to vandalism or sectionalism." In January, the state Democratic Convention passed a resolution extolling "that gallant band of Democrats in Congress who have so nobly illustrated the National Character of the Democratic party by their unanimous adherence to principles," a clear endorsement of English's course. To Hoosier Democrats, as argued in English's speech, the inability of the anti-administration forces to choose a speaker "exhibited to the country" the "moral" of opposition incompetence. "It would all be lost," Robinson wrote, "if any portion of our friends should help the opposition out of their unenviable dilemma." Though John B. Norman did lament the fact that the deadlock had the nonpartisan effect of tying up federal business (and, perhaps, printing contracts for himself), he nevertheless remarked that he did

---

61. *CG, 34-1,* 27, 28, 29.

"not think that the House remaining unorganized will do the country any harm, while it *will* do the Democratic party good." As Alexander Morrison bluntly put it, "let the fusionists shoulder all responsibility and let the country judge them by their works."[62]

The deadlock, only made stronger by advice like the above, was not without its mirthful moments. One of these occurred when English offered "that no member be allowed to indulge in the use of meat, drink, fire, or other refreshments, gas-light and water only excepted, until an election of a Speaker be effected." Perhaps he believed that the 'manly' Democrats could withstand these conditions better than their effete opponents. Not to be outdone, Daniel Mace offered a resolution to keep all the doors locked until a candidate was selected. Both resolutions were laid on the table, as was one calling for each member to continually ballot in alphabetical order until one candidate secured a majority. Although tempers did occasionally flare and a couple of fights occurred outside the hall, general civility prevailed. The greatest harm was probably caused by the inability of the members to receive their pay while the House remained unorganized. The sergeant-at-arms, Adam J. Glossbrenner, was reported to have lent various congressmen the total sum of $28,000 for living expenses, and no doubt the richer members, like English, did the same. What connection these debts had to the eventual settlement of the contest has never been investigated.[63]

As the stalemate continued into mid-January, the southern Americans, completely at odds with the "Republican" anti-slavery position, decided to try to get the Democrats to present a congressman more to their liking. To embarrass Richardson, they maneuvered the House into asking questions of the three prominent nominees hoping that Richardson's replies would not satisfy southern Democrats. These "catechisms" began on January 12 and lasted for three days. Whereas Fuller clearly stated that he believed that the Constitution carried slavery into the territories, the preferred southern position, Richardson not only denied that contention, he even implied that Congress could constitutionally prohibit slavery there if it wished. At first, the effect of these disclosures merely cost Richardson three South Carolina votes, but pressure from the White House to organize combined with increasing southern dissatisfaction with Richardson's answers forced the Democrats to abandon the Illinois nominee two weeks later. His replacement, James L. Orr, a moderate from South Carolina, fared no better, and the admin-

---

62. John L. Robinson to WHE, December 23, 1855; A.W.F. Morrison to WHE, January 1, 1856, English Papers. *Indianapolis Journal*, January 9, 1856. J.B. Norman to WHE, December 25, 1855.

63. *CG, 34-1*, 72, 139. Harrington, "First Northern Victory," 197, 200. *New Albany Ledger*, December 13, 27, 24, 1855. Journalist Perely Poore noted that Glossbrenner got the money to loan by gaining his own loan from a bank in Pennsylvania, which essentially insured his re-election as Sergeant at Arms. Poore, *Perley's Reminiscences,* 448.

istration, fearing that the country was clearly "getting tired of the play," began to counsel surrender.[64]

Once again, as in the desperate hours of the Kansas-Nebraska struggle, Alexander Stephens came forward with a strategy. Believing that a plurality resolution was destined to pass shortly, he advised the Democrats to be ready for it. If, as he expected, the southern Americans continued to refuse to come over to Orr, the Democrats should drop one South Carolinian and substitute another, to wit, William Aiken. Aiken, like Howell Cobb, was essentially a southern Democratic Unionist; he was also appealing to the southern Know-Nothings because he had never attended Democratic caucuses and had never gone on record as either for or against nativism. "From my knowledge of the House," Stephens wrote, "its present tone and temper, knowledge of Aiken and the estimation he was held in by several of the scatterers, I believe he would beat Banks." Not taking any chances, he "sounded out" some of the important Americans and concluded that they would indeed support Aiken to defeat Banks. Only a few key Democrats, not including English, were informed of the plan. But before it could fully mature, W.R. Cobb of Alabama, one of those informed, offered a direct resolution simply to make Aiken speaker. The subsequent vote showed Aiken did well, polling one more congressman than Banks had on a similar resolution, but he was still defeated 110 to 103. And the secret plan was now out. In a letter to his brother, Stephens called W.R. Cobb a "fool" for plucking "the melon before it was ripe," but he still hoped that Aiken would win in a strict plurality vote.[65]

In gaining his 103 votes Aiken picked up all but two southern Know-Nothings. He also gained 5 of 13 northern Americans, including Fuller. Hoosiers Dunn and Scott refused to go along, but Stephens and the Democrats could count on them to oppose Banks as well. When Aiken called at the White House that evening, Pierce triumphantly addressed him as "Mr. Speaker," predicting his election. The Republicans, determined "not to yield to the 'doughfaces,'" stuck by Banks, and when the plurality resolution passed the next morning, they presented him as their candidate. As the resolution directed, three ballots were first taken under the orthodox rules. As expected, no candidate received a majority on these, and a plurality vote was then taken. Soon after Felix Zollicoffer cast the last ballot, the result was tabulated: Banks, 103; Aiken, 100; the rest, 11. Predictably 'betrayed' by anti-Nebraskan John Hickman of Pennsylvania, who remained a Democrat

64. Harrington, "First Northern Victory," 198-199. *New Albany Ledger*, January 24, 1856. Hollcroft, "A Congressman's Letters," 455.

65. Harrington, "First Northern Victory," 200-201. *CG, 34-1, 334, 335.* Alexander Stephens to Linton Stephens, February 21, 1856, in Johnston, *Life of Stephens*, 305-306. Matthew A. Byron, "William Aiken, Jr.," *South Carolina Encyclopedia*, http://www.scencyclopedia.org/se/entries/aiken-william-jr/, accessed July 19, 2018. *CG, 34-1*, 335. According to New York Republican Edwin Morgan, Aiken still professed loyalty to states' rights, and, more to the point, owned about 1000 slaves. Hollcroft, "A Congressman's Letters," 456-457. Perley Poore also notes that Aiken was a large slaveholder. Poore, *Perley's Reminiscences,* 448.

after being elected as one in 1854, Aiken also failed to gain the votes of southern Americans Henry Winter Davis of Maryland and Elisha Cullen of Delaware. These two voted for Fuller, as did four northern Americans. Dunn, Scott, and two Ohioans voted for Campbell, and the only North American to vote for Aiken was none other than Fuller himself. Banks had won with only one American vote, Edward Ball of Ohio, but he did not even need that.[66]

Back in early December, the *New Albany Ledger* had predicted that the next speaker would be "half Sam, half Sambo," but even granting that Banks had belonged to a Know-Nothing lodge his victory was much Sambo and little Sam. Although the Republicans appear to have promised some lesser posts to the Americans, they steadfastly refused to substitute for Banks a milder opponent of slavery. In a congressional session replete with political and even physical altercations, Nathaniel Banks would prove to be an able and dignified presiding officer. One contemporary, admittedly partial to anti-slavery, maintained that Banks "won laurels [for] displaying a thorough acquaintance with the intricacies of parliamentary rules and prompt action in those cases when excited Representatives sought to set precedents at defiance."[67] Essentially, the outcome of the contest was less a defeat for the Democracy than it was a defeat for the Know-Nothings. It proved once again, decisively validated later in the year with American Millard Fillmore's poor showing as presidential candidate in the free states, that nativism had become a lesser force than anti-slavery, to which the future belonged.

6.

Completely out of touch with these developments was the opposition to the Democrats in southern Indiana. As late as January 23, Milton Gregg was complaining of Horace Greeley's (anti-slavery editor of the *New York Tribune)* "unreasonable opposition to Campbell [for speaker] and pertinacious adherence to Banks, [and] constant abuse of the American order."[68] As a conservative where slavery was concerned, Gregg was finding it difficult to remain on good terms with the mainstream of the opposition. This presented the Hoosier Democrats with a real opportunity to divide and conquer, but first, they had to put their own house in order. From as early as the day after the disastrous 1854 election, the Hoosier Democracy had vowed that it would soon regain its rightful position as the majority party of Indiana. Democrats had labeled the 1854 result a temporary

---

66. *CG, 34-1*, 335. Harrington, "First Northern Victory," 201. E. D. Kent to Israel Washburn, December 15, 1855 in Gallard Hunt, *Israel, Elihu, and Cadwallder Washburn: A Chapter in American Biography* (New York: MacMillan & Co., 1925), 39. *CG, 34-1*, 335-337.

67. *New Albany Ledger*, December 13, 1855. Greeley, *Recollections*, 453. Poore, *"Perley's Reminiscences,"* 448.

68. *New Albany Weekly Tribune*, January 23, 1856.

aberration, and they eagerly awaited the contest two years later for governor, leg-islators, congressmen, and the whole array of state offices. The local autumn victo-ries of 1855 had been helpful, but 1856 was a presidential year; with the troubles in Kansas and uncertainty as to who would be the Party's national candidate, the Democracy would have to project an image of unity and vitality. Consequently, the clear course for the Democrats was to exploit any disunity among the oppo-sition while avoiding any recurrence of Bright-Wright factionalism in their own ranks, a problematic endeavor.

Essential to this task was a healthy and well administered *Indiana State Sen-tinel*. As the state party organ, the *Sentinel's* functions were to state the orthodox Democratic position on various issues, attack the opposition's weak points, and defend the Democracy. Important, too, was its ability to help keep any division within the Party to a minimum. As editor for five years, William Brown was not especially successful in this latter endeavor. Perceiving this, he had actually wished to leave his duties as early as 1852, but his publisher/son was unable to find a pro-spective buyer, and Brown was forced to remain for another two years. After the Democratic defeat in 1854, he tried again, writing English cryptically that "the peculiar state of the party in Indiana makes me desirous to withdraw from the pa-per." Brown might have considered English a prospective buyer, for he gave him, "as promised, a statement in writing: $16,500, $5,000 down and the rest over two years." However, these terms may have been sent to others as well, and English's interest in the *Sentinel* was most likely strictly political—he did not wish it to fall into the hands of Jesse Bright's enemies. In the end, all factions agreed to support a deal that allowed Jacob Walker and C. Windy Cottom, respectively publisher and editor of the *Laporte Times*, to buy the *Sentinel*. As Walker wrote, "the leading men of our party," including Wright, Lieutenant Governor Ashbel Willard, and Bright, were willing to lend him "all the funds needed on reasonable terms." With these assurances Walker went ahead and borrowed $12,000 from the state bank to pay the initial purchase and costs.[69]

But Walker and Cottom did not prove to be a capable team, and after the spring 1855 elections went against the Democrats in Indianapolis and Marion County, Walker had trouble collecting the assured financial help from party lead-ers. In June he wrote English of his position, asking him to help make up the difference by assisting "to the amount of one thousand dollars due in three years at six per cent interest." Others may have received the same appeal but to little avail, for a month later Walker, too, began to advertise for a buyer.[70] Delightfully bemused by the *Sentinel's* problems, Milton Gregg playfully suggested that John B.

---

69. W.H. Brown to WHE, January 20, 1855, English Papers. *New Albany Ledger,* January 12, 1855. Jacob Walker to WHE, May 24, 1855, English Papers.

70. Jacob Walker to WHE, June 24, 1855, English Papers. *New Albany Ledger,* July 28, 1855.

Norman come to its rescue. Norman took notice of his rival editor's teasing only to deny any interest. He refused to elaborate, but perhaps the recent death of his child had something to do with his initial lack of enthusiasm. Or, perhaps because he presently held an official position as Surveyor of the Port of New Albany, a post that English had obtained for him in order to ensure that the *New Albany Ledger* remained financially stable, he believed he was obliged to remain at home. He also somewhat modestly maintained that he did not possess "the genial and social qualities necessary to success at the capital"; his personality being more suited to the less pressured atmosphere of New Albany. But as the summer waned and no buyer came forward, Norman apparently began to change his mind. It would be both exciting and worthwhile to edit the Democratic state organ, and perhaps a change of scenery was just what his family needed. As for the surveyor post, he could ask English to have it transferred to the other proprietor of the *Ledger*. Though still fearing that Indianapolis was not suited to his tastes, he decided to go ahead, and in partnership with John S. Spann he made an offer to Walker in mid-September. It was evidently satisfactory, for Noman quickly sold his interest in the *New Albany Ledger*, asked English to transfer the federal post to Luciene Matthews, now the sole proprietor of the paper, and made preparations to relocate at the capital. On December 7, 1855, he edited his first edition of the *State Sentinel*.[71]

Back in New Albany, Matthews remarked that Norman's "correct judgment, deep and bold intelligence, and remarkable fund of general information [would help him] more than meet the expectations of the Democracy." Apparently acceptable to both the Bright and Wright factions, Norman's first assignment was to help promote a harmonious state convention, due to assemble on January 8. This was not going to be an easy task. No sooner had Norman arrived in Indianapolis than there was "a fresh breakout of the Wright and Bright business." Apparently Bright's advance suggestions for the party platform did not square with the governor's faction. More pointedly, the senator's partisans had begun to promote Bright fixer John L. Robinson for governor, when, by all accounts, lieutenant governor Ashbel Willard had long been considered the Party's proper choice. Willard was a crafty politician and a powerful orator, and, although he was perhaps too fond of liquor for the more temperate of Wright's partisans, he was clearly preferable to "lard oil" Robinson. Moreover, not only was Robinson, as a Rushville editor and United States Marshal, an unabashed sycophant of Senator Bright, he was politically tainted by his overzealous prosecution of John Freeman a few years earlier. Matthews's *Ledger*, which under Norman had always tried to steer a moderate course between Wright and Bright, was greatly angered by what it considered a breach of harmony. In the fall of 1855 Matthews firmly reiterated his support

---

71. *New Albany Ledger*, July 28, July 18, December 12, 1855. J. B. Norman to WHE, January 15, 1856, English Papers. *Ledger*, December 4, 1855.

for Willard, and as the convention approached he even noted "that there may be room for saying somewhat against [Robinson's] course as U. S. Marshal, but we forbear. We might even go behind the Marshalship and find fault with his votes in Congress, but we'll let that pass."[72]

Norman, too, was disappointed with Bright's machinations. In December he had written English of the senator's shabby behavior. Besides the Robinson challenge, Norman was angered by Bright's influence over C. Windy Cottom, the former editor who stayed on at the *Sentinel* as an assistant. Apparently Cottom, on direct orders from Bright, was writing articles in the *Sentinel* on the senator's benefit. One such article was a thinly veiled attack on governor Wright, which Norman had removed from the paper but only after a score of issues had already left the presses. Miffed, Norman wrote English that only he and Spann "have any right to dictate what shall go into [the *Sentinel*] or be kept out...I feel kindly disposed to Bright, like him personally, but do not wish to be treated as though I am a dog rather than a man." It was just this type of high-handed behavior that had injured the Democracy in 1854, and Bright's continued use of it would eventually cost the senator dearly. Although he had not yet lost control of the Party, events at the state Democratic convention would prove that his mastery would not go unchallenged.[73]

A week before the convention met, Alexander Morrison wrote English that he feared sharp conflict over the nomination for governor. And this was not the only issue in question, for the Party also had to instruct its delegates to the Democratic National Convention. For half a year Bright had been packing the county gatherings, so that they recommended him for the presidency, not primarily because he wished to be a candidate, but because it would give him control of Indiana's votes at Cincinnati. In the Second District both Floyd and Harrison counties so resolved, and even the *New Albany Ledger* expressed its satisfaction at the possibility of a favorite-son Bright nomination. At the time of the state convention, it was not entirely clear who Bright actually favored for president, but the supporters of Stephen Douglas, primarily Wright men, suspected correctly that it was not the Little Giant. Consequently, besides opposing Robinson, the Douglas-Wright clique was determined somehow to limit Bright's control of Indiana's presidential delegation as much as possible.[74]

72. *New Albany Ledger*, September 10, December 8, 1855. J. B. Norman to WHE, December 25, 1855; J.L. Robinson to WHE, December 23, 1855, English Papers. Van der Weele, "Bright," 167. Van Bolt, "Fusion out of Confusion," 358. *Ledger*, November 24, 26, 1855, January 4, 1856.

73. *New Albany Weekly Tribune*, January 2, 1856. J. B. Norman to WHE, December 25, 1855, English Papers. Crane, "Joseph Wright," 231.

74. A.W.F. Morrison to WHE, January 1, 1856, English Papers. *New Albany Weekly Tribune*, January 16, 1856. *New Albany Ledger*, December 31, 1855, January 2, 1856, December 19 1855. Crane, "Joseph Wright," 231-232. Van der Weele, "Jesse Bright," 166. Wallace, *Autobiography*, 248. Gregory Peek, "The True and

Anticipating rebellion in the ranks, Bright had made sure his lieutenants were active. Because the national House was still deadlocked over the speakership, he had no trouble attending the state convention in person, and behind the scenes he tried to direct the show. His first and most important victory was the selection of senator Pettit as permanent chairman. Ever since his orthodox stand on Kansas-Nebraska, Pettit had drawn himself closer to Bright, and by 1856 he was clearly in his fellow senator's camp. No sooner had he taken up the gavel then Pettit played his appointed part by selecting a committee on resolutions favorable to Bright. But after that, things went awry. In the first place, the Robinson challenge never materialized. Although Bright probably had greater command of the county delegations than Wright did, Robinson was just too unpopular to be able to defeat the genial Willard. Realizing this, the resourceful Marshal tried to gain the nomination by convincing Willard's choice for lieutenant governor, John C. Walker, to abandon him. If Walker would so treacherously agree, Robinson promised to drop his own "running mate," judge Robert Lowry, and if nominated with Walker's help, Robinson would insure that the convention selected Walker for lieutenant governor by acclamation. To his credit, Walker declined the offer, forcing Robinson to sheepishly withdraw before the convention voted, resulting in the easy nomination of Willard.[75]

Although the aborted Robinson challenge was a setback for Bright, the nomination of Willard was not unexpected, and, in truth, Willard was not any more identified with Wright than he was with Bright. The real test came when the convention decided on instructions for the presidency. At least a plurality of the delegates probably preferred to endorse Stephen Douglas, but they settled for a resolution that simply left the delegation uninstructed and subject to the unit rule by majority vote. It expressed "undiminished confidence" in Bright and agreed to "present" his name to the convention. But the delegates were not compelled to vote for him, nor was it clear that his name would ever actually be put into nomination. In essence, the resolution deferred the question to the delegates themselves. Of those whom the convention appointed, delegates friendly to Douglas appeared to have had a slight majority. But that was offset by the respect the delegates were compelled to pay their senior senator, who was generally known not to be fond of his Illinois rival. It was also almost certain that Bright would attend

---

Everlasting Principle of States Rights and Popular Sovereignty: Douglas Democrats and Indiana Republicans Allied, 1857-1859," *Indiana Magazine of History* 111, no. 4 (December, 2015), 390.

75. Wallace, *Autobiography,* 248. Charles Kettleborough, "Indiana on the Eve of the Civil War," *Indiana Historical Society Publications, vol. 6* (Indianapolis: the Bobbs-Merril Co., 1919), 145. Jesse Bright to WHE, August 30, 1858, English Papers. (Bright here called Pettit a "true friend.") Woolen, *Biographical and Historical Sketches*, 317. Never a man to forgive and forget, Robinson later that year brought forth documents to show that Walker was too young to constitutionally hold office. The State Central committee agreed, and requested Walker to withdraw. He did so, and the Committee selected Abram Hammond in his stead. *Ibid.*, 317-318. *New Albany Weekly Tribune,* April 23, 1856.

the convention himself, further diminishing the prospects that Douglas would get Indiana's vote.[76]

With difficulty, then, the Bright forces were able to maintain some control over the Indiana delegation. But the Wright faction was hardly in retreat. The convention adopted a resolution applauding the governor's administration, and all the state nominees were either Wright men or basically uncommitted. Moreover, according to the opposition press, the enthusiasm for Bright as a presidential aspirant "was not as strong as usually accompanied the endorsement of a favorite son."[77] Indeed, if the convention proved anything, it proved that Bright's control of the Party was top-heavy, that it rested on the old-line leadership, and that it tended to resort less to reason than to political manipulation in order to keep the rank and file from defecting.

One man who had seen enough was John B. Norman. As editor for the *Sentinel,* he had observed at close range the bickering between the two factions and the expectations that both had from the state organ. He realized that he could not work effectively in that atmosphere. In a letter to English he wrote that being

> [a]ccustomed to write from the impulse of the moment and to express my own conviction of right and wrong, without considering the immediate bearing they may have on the position of this or that politician, or how each prominent member of our party may be affected by the expression of my views, this restraint is to me particularly annoying.

Therefore, after a little more than a month on the job, Norman decided to sell the newspaper, and he inquired of English if he knew of any prospective buyers. "We have no fault to find with the financial prospects of the concern," he wrote, "of the capacity of it to make money there can be no doubt. We wish to sell because our tastes, habits, and inclinations are unfavorable to making this paper such a one as it ought to be during the canvass." Whether through English's assistance or otherwise, there was little delay in the changeover. Professor William C. Larabee, the state superintendent of public instruction, quickly came forward with the cash, and by January 26 the *Sentinel* had new owners. Larabee announced that the new editor would be Alexander Morrison, a choice satisfactory to both factions. As for Norman, he returned to New Albany and took up his old position, Matthews gladly relinquishing the reins in favor of his more experienced friend.

---

76. Wallace, *Autobiography,* 248. William O. Lynch, "Indiana in the Douglas-Buchanan Contest of 1856," *Indiana Magazine of History* 30, no. 2 (June, 1934), 123. Van der Weele, "Bright," 169.

77. *New Albany Weekly Tribune,* January 16, 1856. *Evansville Daily Journal,* February 13, 1856, in Elbert, "Southern Indiana Politics," 13-14.

Norman had come back, Matthews had written in his last *New Albany Ledger* as chief editor, to his "heart-love."[78]

A few weeks after Norman returned from Indianapolis, English officially saluted him by giving him the only vote the editor ever received for House printer. Gestures such as these helped make English so successful a politician. Perhaps in this case it was just that the congressman was glad to have his talented, Democratic friend back in southern Indiana. It was certainly good for the Second District Democracy, and while English had often stated his desire to observe the unwritten two-term rule and not stand for a third election, there was always the possibility, as he would write in a fortnight, that circumstances might alter that decision.[79] If so, Norman's presence would be both politically and personally advantageous. Indeed, it might be indispensable.

---

78. *Indiana State Sentinel,* January 23, 1856. J. B. Norman to WHE, January 23, 1856, English Papers. Norman also took back his old job as surveyor, as the administration had not yet replaced him. Perhaps English had an idea he would be back. J. B. Norman to WHE, January 15, 1856, English Papers.

79. *CG, 34-1,* 397. *New Albany Ledger,* February 28, 29, 1856

CHAPTER FIVE

The Democracy Survives

Norman's return to New Albany essentially coincided with the end of the speakership contest in Washington. Fresh from this great victory, breathing the fire of revolution, the anti-Nebraska coalition was eager to right the wrongs of Pierce's Kansas policy. From the time of the Kansas legislative election in March 1855, through the aborted Wakarusa War at the end of that year, Congress had been unable to deal with the fast moving events in the territory. Adjourned between March and December, it had then been deadlocked over the speakership until February of 1856. Not until later that month did the House finally begin to grapple with the problems resulting from the fraudulent elections, dual territorial governments, and threats of new outbreaks of violence. A particular matter gave the anti-Nebraska House majority a united way to intervene in territorial affairs. In October 1855, both the irregular free-state Topeka government and the official pro-slavery Shawnee Mission legislature had held separate elections for congressional delegate. Not surprisingly, the results were quite different. While John Whitfield was re-chosen under the election run by the pro-slavery forces, former governor Reeder was selected by the free-soilers. As soon as the House was formally organized, Whitfield presented his credentials and was duly admitted, but this was done with the knowledge that the Reeder forces would contest his seat. Fundamentally, Reeder charged that no acts of the Shawnee Mission legislature were legal, including the law authorizing the election of a congressional delegate, because the election of the legislature itself earlier that March was replete with fraud. (Reeder also stated, of course, that fraud penetrated Whitfield's election as well.) It was through this contest, then, that the House began its investigation into all elections held in the territory.[1]

It must be noted that by the time the House was ready to deal with the affairs in Kansas, the national fusionist opposition, though still united in their political enmity toward the Democracy, had predictably formally divided on the slavery

---

1. Etcheson, *Bleeding Kansas, 73-74. CG, 34-1,* esp. 451-464.

issue. The American Party national council, again meeting in Philadelphia, had held a national presidential nominating convention a few weeks after the speakership contest in the House was concluded. At that conclave, almost 50 northern anti-slavery delegates bolted the convention when the majority defeated a resolution to restore the Missouri Compromise. The bolters proceeded the next evening to call for a separate northern Know-Nothing convention in June, while the remaining delegates—a combination of southerners, old-line "cotton" northern Whigs, and mild anti-slavery nativists—nominated ex-president Millard Fillmore to run at the head of their ticket in the fall. Fillmore, who in 1850 supported and signed the bills that made up the famous Compromise measures, ran not only on typical nativist planks passed by the convention but on a territorial plank that supported popular sovereignty fairly executed. When he was nominated, another 20 northern delegates bolted, intending to attend the June "Northern American" convention.[2]

And as Congress began to grapple with the increasingly contentious events in Kansas in 1856, it turned out that most Northern Opposition representatives, elected on some sort of fusion ticket in the fall of 1854, began to increasingly prefer to accent their anti-slavery credentials over their nativist ones. And most of these men by the end of the session began to affiliate with the untainted anti-slavery political organization that called itself the Republican Party. These factors created a northern anti-slavery majority in the House, even without including (though often it did) the recalcitrant, mainly nativist, northern Know-Nothings who supported Fillmore. Thus, on March 5, the anti-slavery controlled Elections Committee submitted a resolution to the House empowering itself to send for any persons and papers in its examination of Reeder's charges. For the next two weeks, congressmen debated whether or not to sanction this essentially plenary investigation of Kansas politics. The Democrats, of course, realized that any such wide investigation was bound to hurt their party, and it could ill afford such bad publicity in a congressional and presidential election year. The Democratic minority report of the committee, drafted and presented by Alexander Stephens, slyly attempted to narrow the scope of any investigation. The Georgia congressman's report assumed the legality of the Shawnee Mission legislature, and thereby tried to narrow the issue simply to the question of whether Whitfield fairly won the election called by that lawmaking body. Locating the burden of proof on the contestant, Stephens argued that Reeder had not proven that he received more legal votes than Whitfield, and thus the general's election must stand. In a letter

---

2. A good, detailed discussion of the American/ Know-Nothing February 1856 convention is in Gienapp, *Origins*, 260-262. Briefer good discussions are Nevins, *Ordeal, vol. 2*, 467-468, and Potter, *Impending Crisis*, 255. The 1855 Twelfth Section was softened to avoid the word slavery by simply noting that the territories could "regulate their domestic affairs in their own mode." *New Albany Tribune*, July 22, 1856.

to his brother on the same day he presented his report, Stephens boasted that it had "made a decided hit in the House."[3]

On March 18, one day before the House was scheduled to vote on the competing resolutions, William English delivered one of the last speeches for the Democracy. He transparently noted right in his first paragraph that the "pending question" had been "ably and thoroughly discussed" and "the minds of gentlemen are fully made up," but for "the eye of my constituents [I have decided] to indicate the votes I shall give, and some of the reasons that influence me." Actually, by the time that English spoke the pending question was not simply a choice between the majority and minority resolutions, but rather one between two substitute resolutions that both allowed for some investigation. The Democratic proposal, submitted by Hedley Bennett of Mississippi, authorized the appointment of two southern lawyers from the District of Columbia, Joseph and Sydney Baxter, to take depositions in Kansas, collect documents, and report back to the House. This resolution appeared to allow a greater investigation than Stephens's original minority report, but, of course, the choice of the investigators made it suspicious to the anti-slavery congressmen. It was countered by George Dunn, one of the fusion congressmen from Indiana, who, interestingly, proposed an even stronger resolution than the original majority one. It would give the speaker the right to appoint a select committee of three to investigate "all violent and tumultuous proceedings in [Kansas] at any time since the passage of the Kansas-Nebraska Act." The appointed committee was furthermore to be granted full subpoena powers of arrest and contempt.[4]

Theoretically, then, English's speech should have concentrated upon the choice of substitutes presented him, and he did devote a part of it directly to those two proposals. But in the main his argument more broadly attacked Reeder's position and the man himself, and it also anticipated by two days the main line of argument used by Stephen Douglas as the definitive position of the northern Democracy. In his initial paragraph English restated Stephens's contention that Reeder had failed to prove "by competent proof in the manner prescribed by law, and in accordance with the usage of this body," his right to Whitfield's seat. Not only had Reeder garnered even fewer votes than Whitfield's untainted count in the 'official' election, but no matter how suspect the Shawnee Mission legislature was, the Topeka government, which sanctioned Reeder's selection, had "not even a shadow of legal foundation and [was] in defiance of all law." English maintained that these facts alone substantiated Whitfield's *prima facie* right to his seat. Yet he understood that it was not enough simply to show that Reeder's *legal* position was

---

3. *CG, 34-1*, 475-476, 593. Rudolf von Abele, *Alexander H. Stephens: A Biography* (New York: Alfred A. Knopf, Inc., 1946), 153-156. Thomas E. Schott, *Alexander H. Stephens of Georgia: A Biography* (Baton Rouge and London: Louisiana State University Press, 1988), 202. Johnston, *Life of Stephens*, 307.

4. *Appendix to the CG, 34-1*, 289. *CG, 34-1*, 601. Nevins, *Ordeal of the Union, vol. 2*, 422-424.

poor; he further felt he had to illustrate that the ex-governor's challenge was based not on high-minded principles but on naked politics. To do so, English analyzed Reeder's political actions as Kansas governor and concluded that his present position was both hypocritical and opportunistic.[5]

As English understood it, Reeder never argued that the territorial legislative election was fraudulent until "he had been removed from office by the President, and had tied his fortunes to the emigrant aid society." A bold charge, indeed, and, unfortunately, it greatly disregarded the facts. For not only, as we have seen, did Reeder present his misgivings to Pierce only three months after the March 1855 legislative election, but on his trek from Kansas to the White House, he made many speeches complaining that the vote totals were illegally manipulated. English must have been aware of this, yet he continued to argue that, since Reeder had only overturned 7 of the 18 electoral district returns, he had implicitly validated the other 11, thereby granting a certified legal majority to the pro-slavery forces. By this assertion, English tried to show that Reeder's later claim of gross fraud in almost all the districts was politically motivated. In truth, a close reading of the Kansas-Nebraska Act illustrates that the governor only had the power to invalidate votes that were formally contested by citizens. Perhaps Reeder could have been more assiduous in promoting protests within the five days allowed by law, but his reluctance to take it upon himself to declare wholesale fraud immediately subsequent to the election does not indict him of hypocrisy—caution and even lack of courage, perhaps, but not hypocrisy.[6]

English's other arguments held somewhat more validity. He charged that Reeder had no quarrel with the legislature at all until the representatives decided to move themselves from Pawnee City to Shawnee Mission. It was this act, and not any fraudulent election, that promoted the breech between legislature and governor resulting in Reeder's subsequent charges. According to English, Reeder was upset with the removal to Shawnee Mission because he had heavily invested in real estate at Pawnee City, implying that crass, vengeful, material considerations, not high-minded, positive principles, lay at the heart of the governor's challenge. Indeed, Reeder *had* accumulated interest in much real estate in Pawnee City, and he was so angered by the legislators' independent removal from that place that he refused to recognize their subsequent legality. While he had already made clear his convictions regarding vote irregularities, it is conceivable that he might not have continued his criticism had the legislators not changed their meeting place. Indeed, Reeder's misgivings concerning the popular vote for the legislature had not prevented him from presenting the legislators with various proposed laws in

---

5. *Appendix to the CG, 34-1,* 289.

6. *Ibid.,* 290. Nevins, *Ordeal of the Union, vol. 2,* 366. *CG, 33-1,* 2229. Potter, *Impending Crisis,* 202.

the few days they convened at Pawnee City, nor from calling for a special session later in July.[7]

Impugning Reeder's motives and character, however, was essentially an argument *ad hominem*. It did not speak effectively to the question of whether fraud was widespread and which investigative proposal was most beneficial to the nation. What it did do, and what it was intended to do, was to illustrate to English's constituents that the Republicans were animated less by democratic principle than by base self-interest and pure partisanship. This was the real theme of English's speech, and, as he proceeded to discuss the Bennet and Dunn substitutes, he fully warmed to it. He argued that the Republicans (and their northern Know-Nothing allies) were not primarily interested in ascertaining what the true facts were in relation to the Kansas elections, but rather in agitating the slavery issue so as to reap "political capital to keep themselves in power." This was why they supported the Dunn substitute: it put the power of appointment in speaker Banks's hands and allowed for an open-ended inquiry intended to reflect the "extreme views of my political opponents." On the other hand, English maintained, the Democratic substitute selected "distinguished lawyers of this city," and intended to limit their investigation "to the pending question [Whitfield v. Reeder] with a proper regard for economy." English added that, although the Baxter brothers were perfectly acceptable to him, he was "willing that any other name be substituted, provided they be gentlemen of integrity, of proper legal attainments, and not partisan or prejudiced in reference to this case."[8]

But very few intelligent citizens were not "prejudiced in reference to this case." English revealed his own predilections when, after maintaining that both the Missouri interlopers and the New England "abolitionists" were to blame for the problems in Kansas, he placed the primary guilt upon the "people of the North through their agency of emigrant aid societies." According to the Indiana Democrat, "the abolitionists and the free soilers violated the principle of the Nebraska Act by an unjust interference, which provoked retaliation by the citizens of Missouri." This was the orthodox Democratic line, and it was intended to somehow connote that free soil, abolitionist Republicans, reflecting their aggressive, excessive Yankee personalities, did not play the game of settlement honorably. As in other cases, they manipulated the natural course of events to produce an artificial crisis and an extremist response. The Dunn substitute was just another example of overreaction. "Free and easy characters with rather belligerent qualities are to be found in all new countries," English maintained, and only the Republican penchant for hyperbole has made this particular settlement of Kansas qualitatively

---

7. *Appendix to the CG, 34-1*, 290. Nichols, *Franklin Pierce*, 407-415. Etcheson, *Bleeding Kansas*, 67.

8. *Appendix to the CG, 34-1*, 290, 291.

different from others. He wryly added that if congressmen wished to investigate electoral fraud, they should inquire into the Know-Nothing riots of Louisville and Cincinnati: "for unprovoked atrocity and cold blooded and deliberate outrage, [they] are without parallel, and greatly exceed anything that has transpired in Kansas."[9]

In the main, English wished to present a picture of Democratic conservatism and patriotism in contrast to Republican fanaticism and partisanship. Democrats, he tried to illustrate, refused to stoke fires to create controversy; Republicans, on the other hand, for their own political or private gain, risking great conflagration, fanned the flames of the slavery controversy. (Of course, one could argue that the Kansas-Nebraska Act was a flame-fanner as well, especially in the face of 'finality'.) Abolitionists and Republicans (one and the same to many) had abused and distorted the proper application of popular sovereignty (which, it must be said in the Republicans' defense, was a formula with which they did not agree), had flagrantly formed extra-legal associations, and in general had flouted the law of the land. This was not the party to be trusted to keep peace in the country and allow for its brilliant development.

Democrats like English attacked the Republicans and the emigrant aid societies partly because they could not comfortably defend the "popular sovereignty legality" of the Shawnee Mission legislature. In reality they were on the defensive. Wishing to avoid a comprehensive investigation into Kansas politics, English and the Democrats tried to limit the controversy to the narrow question of who was the proper territorial delegate, and on that issue they did not think it necessary to assist Reeder in meeting the burden of proof. Democrats tended in this case to interpret popular sovereignty, originally intended to allow territorial citizens to frame their own institutions, to mean general non-interference by the federal government into the affairs of a territory. English himself avoided this transition when he said that he did "not choose on this occasion, to go into the question of whether we would not be justified, under certain circumstances, in inquiring into the validity of election of the members of the Kansas legislature." The opposition anti-slavery majority in the House was not so undecided. Dunn's resolution defeated Bennett's by 13 votes and was then adopted by the full House, 101 to 93. Northern Know-Nothings voted 9 to 3 in its favor, and even three northern Democrats bolted the Party to join the majority.[10] The Republicans had won a

---

9. *Ibid.*, 291. There was certainly chicanery and violence in American politicking before the elections in Kansas. Tracy Campbell, *Deliver the Vote: A History of Election Fraud, an American Political Tradition—1742-2004* (New York: Carroll and Graf Publishers, 2005), 17-20, 22.

10. *Ibid.*, 290. *CG, 34-1*, 691-692. The Democrats who bolted were John Hickman and David Barclay of Pennsylvania, and Augustus Hall of Iowa.

significant victory, for the fruits of the investigation promised to embarrass the Democracy throughout 1856. And this was only the beginning of the session.

2.

Soon after the House voted to send a full investigating committee to Kansas, it became evident that the territory was a powder keg waiting to explode. Great numbers of new settlers had poured in once the ice on the rivers had melted. Although most of them probably wanted only to stake out a claim and better their lives, many nevertheless began their journeys with mass rallies that instilled in them the political importance of their resettlement. Whether they came from the North or the South, these settlers were armed, and in some cases gifts of rifles accompanied them to Kansas. So prepared, they entered a territory that had suspended violence only for the winter season—and even at that not for all of it. The House began to deal with this reality on May 16 when a member moved to suspend the rules to enable the body to vote on a resolution requesting that Pierce furnish information on the winter murders of four free-soil settlers. The motion failed to gain the necessary two-thirds approval by eight votes, yet, significantly, 21 of 58 Democrats voted for it. Among the southerners these included the more responsible voices of Stephens, Williamson R. Cobb of Alabama, John Millson and Thomas Bocock of Virginia, and Thomas L. Clingman of North Carolina. Among the northern Democrats these included English. When a choice had to be made on slavery-related issues between supporting his southern-dominated party and supporting the Kansas free-state position, English usually chose the Democracy. But in cases such as this one in which slave-state Democrats disagreed among themselves, English gratefully followed the southern moderates, which contradicts describing him as a doughface. Smith Miller, a real doughface, joined seven similar northern Democrats in voting to kill the resolution.[11]

Although Democrats did not wish to hand the Republicans more campaign material, the more responsible among them realized that Pierce had let events in Kansas get out of hand. At the same time that the House investigating committee was in Kansas feverishly collecting evidence of election fraud, violence in the territory had not completely abated. In thus voting to pass the above resolution, these 21 Democrats hoped to prevent the territorial civil war that was about to commence—a civil war, they believed, that would only further damage Democratic hopes in 1856. And, indeed, five days after the resolution was sidetracked, the territorial war began in earnest when a group of Kansas pro-slavery forces ransacked the free-state town of Lawrence, pillaging many homes, burning down the Free

---

11. Nevins, *Ordeal of the Union, vol. 2,* 418-432. *CG, 34-1,* 1255.

State Hotel, and destroying two of its newspaper presses. Somewhat exaggerated Republican accounts of this "sack of Lawrence" served to galvanize anti-slavery opinion in the North, and for the next 15 weeks newspapers carried lurid, over-stated reports of strikes and counterstrikes across the territory. (One of these, of course, was the famous Pottawatomie massacres carried out by abolitionist John Brown and his companions.) Not until late September, after about 200 persons were killed and $2 million dollars in property was destroyed did the new governor, John W. Geary, restore the peace with the aid of federal troops.[12]

One day before the Lawrence raid, on May 20, Massachusetts Republican abolitionist senator, Charles Sumner, delivered his "Crime Against Kansas" speech, a scathing attack against slavery and southern culture, in which he personally and obnoxiously insulted a number of senators, including, most savagely, Andrew Butler of South Carolina. Two days later, congressman Preston Brooks of South Carolina, a second cousin of Butler's, assaulted the Massachusetts Republican while he was sitting at his Senate desk stamping copies of his speech to be sent to admirers. After Brooks made a short statement to the effect that Sumner had dishonored Brooks's family in particular and the South in general, the Carolinian beat the Senator repeatedly with his cane even after it broke from five or six blows. Sumner, bloodied about the head, collapsed on the Senate floor as Brooks was finally restrained. That Sumner's speech and Brooks's assault were sandwiched around the Lawrence raid was altogether eerily fitting—violence in Kansas had begotten violence in Washington. No more striking example was needed to illustrate how the Kansas-Nebraska Act had failed to relocate even the venue of controversy. Brooks's attack was so barbaric that mainstream northern Democratic newspapers like the *New Albany Ledger* were forced to criticize it. Norman called it "one of the most dastardly, most cowardly, and most ruffianly acts that ever disgraced the halls of Congress," and, while the *Ledger* abhorred Sumner's repellent expression of his sentiments, it acknowledged that his speech was certainly an example of the "guaranteed right of every Senator to express his opinion in the Senate chamber." Even the *Paoli Eagle*, fundamentally a pro-southern sheet, denounced the attack as "a great outrage."[13]

---

12. Etcheson, *Bleeding Kansas*, chapter 5, *passim*. Nevins, *Ordeal of the Union vol. 2*, 435-437. Potter, *Impending Crisis*, 208-209.

13. The most recent full-length book account of the Brooks-Sumner affair is Williamjames Hull Hoffer, *The Caning of Charles Sumner: Honor, Idealism, and the Origins of the Civil War* (Baltimore: The Johns Hopkins University Press, 2010). *New Albany Ledger*, May 23, 1856. *Paoli Eagle*, May 29, 1856. Another interesting work that focuses on a large period of congressional violence is Joanne Freeman's *Field of Blood*, which makes abundantly clear that the Brooks-Sumner affair was just one of many violent activities between congressmen, in and out of the Capitol, in the 20 years leading up to the Civil War. Brooks's assault was still, however, the most violent inside of Congress itself.

In the House, congressmen quickly convened the next day to consider the assault, and after a short time debate began to center on the question of whether or not to investigate it. A resolution offered by an anti-slavery northern Know-Nothing cited Brooks, Lawrence Keitt of South Carolina, "and other members" as "principals or accessories" to the "violent assault on the person of the Honorable Charles Sumner." (Keitt had accompanied Brooks to the caning after a night of drunken discussion between them on its necessity. Henry Edmundson of Virginia was also aware that the attack would take place.) The resolution called for a select committee of five to be appointed by the speaker to investigate and suggest what remedies "may be proper and necessary for the vindication of the character of the House." Democratic objections to this resolution revolved around the speaker's designation of it as a privileged matter, thereby superseding all other House business. The Democrats claimed that it was unprivileged because it concerned an altercation between a member of the House and one of the Senate and not between two members of the House itself. On a vote to appeal speaker Banks's designation of the resolution as privileged, the House instead upheld him, 85 to 71, with all but three northern Democrats voting for the appeal. The other objection of the Democrats was the resolution's presumption of Brooks's and Keitt's guilt and the vague insertion of "other members" into its preface. Concerning these objections, the resolution's originator, Lewis Campbell, yielded to taking Keitt's name out but not to removing the phrase "other members." When the more southern-friendly resolution then came up for a vote, the southern Democrats still voted against it, along with 8 of the 13 northern Democrats who cast a ballot. But five northern Democrats voted *for* the investigation, two more than voted to uphold the speaker's ruling of privilege, and, interestingly, four northern Democrats who had voted against the speaker's earlier ruling, abstained from this final vote on the resolution. William English was one of those four.[14]

English held an interesting position within the northern Democracy. By this vote and, as we have seen, a couple of earlier ones, he could not be labeled an unadulterated doughface. He certainly parroted the Party position in relation to Kansas, but there were lines he was loath to cross. He admired the gentility and courtesy he received from his southern brethren, no doubt more than he admired many of the northeastern men, but he was not willing to fully excuse the lack of objectivity they took when it came to slavery. It was hard in the end for English to understand how the southern men he respected and believed reasonable, such as Stephens, Thomas Bocock of Virginia, or James L. Orr of South Carolina, were not outraged by Brooks's assault and voted solidly with their more radical southern brethren. Not yet willing perhaps to vote against them, but no doubt

---

14. *CG, 34-1*, 1289-1292.

also unwilling to vote against an investigation to uphold the honor of the House, English simply abstained.[15]

The Brooks committee appointed by the speaker completed its investigation around June 2, but the three presidential conventions of that month and the con-

---

15. Remarking on English's non-vote directly on the resolution, the *New Albany Tribune* later remarked that "English was present in the House not five minutes before the vote was taken on the resolution, and voted against the call of the previous question, but he was afraid to face the vote on the direct question and just dodged into the lobby." *Tribune,* June 13, 1856. Indeed, almost *immediately* after the House passed the resolution, English was on the floor moving to print 10,000 extra copies of the Smithsonian Annual Report. *CG, 34-1,* 1293.

   In an admittedly rough attempt to break down which northern Democrats in the 34th Congress voted as what might be called doughfaces, I selected the 23 voting opportunities during the first session, which may be classified as slavery-related. The greater the percentage each congressman voted according to the southern position, the more doughface I would label him. The list is as follows:

Congressman	Anti-Southern votes	% of southern votes
J. Clancy Jones (PA)	0 (of 16)	100%
John Cadwalder (PA)	0 (of 15)	100%
Thomas I. Harris (IL)	0 (of 15)	100%
Philomen Herbert (CA)	0 (of 11)	100%
John Wheeler (NY)	0 (of 11)	100%
Smith Miller (IA)	1 (of 22)	96%
Sam Marshall (IL)	1 (of 20)	95%
Thomas Florence (PA)	1 (of 18)	94%
John Kelly (NY)	1 (of 17)	94%
Augustus Hall (IW)	1 (of 10)	90%
James Denver (CA)	2 (of 19)	89%
William Richardson (IL)	1 (of 9)	89%
James C. Allen (IL)	2 (or 13)	85%
William English (IA)	4 (of 21)	81%
Thomas Fuller (ME)	3 (of 15)	80%
George W. Peck (MG)	4 (of 18)	78%
George Vail (NJ)	3 (of 12)	75%
John Williams (NY)	6 (of 18)	67%
Asa Packer (PA)	5 (of 13)	62%
David Barclay (PA)	7 (of 10)	30%
Daniel Wells (WS)	11 (of 15)	27%
John Hickman (PA)	11 (of 15)	27%

tinuing civil war in Kansas combined to delay a vote on the matter until July. In the meantime, after all the presidential conventions had completed their business in late June, the coalition majority in the House was able to defeat a compromise on Kansas it feared would have solidified the continued control of the territory by the pro-slavery forces. This compromise was the Toombs Bill, named after the senator from Georgia, Robert Toombs, one of many southerners who had left the Whig party and become Democratic. Faced with competing governments in the territory, continued conflict, and a state constitution for Kansas already submitted to Congress by the irregular Topeka government, Senate Democrats framed this measure that authorized President Pierce to appoint five commissioners to take a census of Kansas and oversee the registration of voters. This census and registration was to be the basis for an election to a constitutional convention in November; the delegates were to convene one month later. Important Republican senators, including William Seward of New York and John Hale of Maine, were impressed by the measure's fairness, but House Republicans, distrustful of Pierce, local Kansas pro-slavery judges, and the ever-present power of the "border ruffians," refused to take so positive a view of it. The Republicans in particular did not wish to contradict their national platform that called for the immediate admission of Kansas as a state under the "free" Topeka constitution.[16]

Though given only modest attention in most books dealing with the 1850s, the Toombs Bill—or rather its eventual defeat—may be considered a lost opportunity to markedly reduce tensions and perhaps prevent the looming Civil War itself. The Republicans' fear that Toombs's provisions were still not foolproof enough to prevent pro-slavery chicanery may be understandable considering the electoral history of Kansas in the past year, but it is difficult not to argue that many Republican politicians believed Kansas needed to remain "hot" to help them in the 1856 election. Toombs had tried in a number of ways to mollify Republicans. For one thing, the bill purposely scheduled the elections to the Kansas constitutional convention in November, as that was the same month that Mis-

---

(Francis Spinner of New York was elected as a Soft-shell Democrat in 1854, but by the time Congress convened in December, 1855 he was caucusing with the Opposition.)

By this chart, at least, and from his many other expressions on political matters, English could actually be labeled in the middle of the northern Democratic bloc. For what I understand is an alternative view of English's position on the Doughface spectrum, see Michael Todd Landis, *Northern Men with Southern Loyalties: The Democratic Party and the Sectional Crisis* (Ithaca and London: Cornell University Press, 2014).

16. *CG, 34-1*, 1348-1352, 1438. The best discussions of the Toombs bill, in chronological order of their publication, are James Ford Rhodes, *History of the United States from the Compromise of 1850 to the McKinley-Bryan Campaign of 1896, vol. 2*, (Port Washington, NY: Kennikat Press, Inc., 1892), 145-152; Ulrich B. Phillips, *The Life of Robert Toombs* (New York: Burt Franklin, 1913), 123-126; Johannsen, *Douglas*, 524-527; John Burt, *Lincoln's Tragic Pragmatism: Lincoln, Douglas, and Moral Conflict* (Cambridge, Mass., and London: The Belknap Press of Harvard University Press, 2013), 150-157. See also Nevins, *Ordeal of the Union, vol. 2*, 472, and Potter, *Impending Crisis*, 215. The Senate debate on the Toombs bill was on July 2, 1856, mostly contained in *CG, 34-1, Appendix*, 750-804. Bain, *Campaign Decisions*, 54-55.

souri voted, which would hopefully work to diminish the possible effect of the "border ruffians." And Toombs agreed to a Republican inspired amendment that rendered the Shawnee Mission legislature's more "obnoxious" pro-slavery laws null and void. (A remarkable concession considering the Democratic policy of non-intervention.) Moreover, Lewis Cass made a public statement that he had been assured that the five commissioners appointed by the president (with Senate approval) would be men of objective honor. Toombs also repeatedly asked Republican senators to offer any other concessions to perfect the bill—but they still voted solidly against it.[17]

In some sense, the real question may be why, in the end, no southern Democratic senator voted against a bill that quite likely would have led to an anti-slavery victory in Kansas. Perhaps the answer lies in information Toombs received a few days before he introduced his bill that there was still a majority of pro-slavery voters in Kansas, however slight. For southerners, then, this may have been considered, at the time, the last and best chance to make Kansas a slave state.[18] But it was a gamble. If Republicans had been more imaginative, when, after all, they believed that Kansas at that moment had a free state majority, they may have taken up the bet and voted for the bill despite their continued opposition to popular sovereignty. In the end, due to the heavy Democratic majority in the Senate, the bill passed there, 33 to 12.[19]

The politics of the moment would nevertheless doom the Toombs Bill when it reached the anti-Democratic majority opposition in the House. In the first place, the bill had the possibility of contradicting the Republican 1856 platform that called for Congress to prohibit slavery in the federal territories. And no doubt, again, it was helpful to the Party to keep the slavery pot boiling. It must also be admitted, however, that the Democrats had their own naked political reasons for promoting passage of the bill and that was conversely to cool tensions in Kansas that would play in their favor in the upcoming elections as well.[20] When the Toombs Bill reached the House floor, as it turns out, it did so as a substitute to a Republican measure intended to admit Kansas under the Topeka constitution. But Toombs never came to a direct vote because, before it could be voted upon, it was amended 109 to 102 to provide for the restoration of the Missouri Compromise line. This proposal was sponsored by the northern Know-Nothings. No Democrat, North or South, voted for it, and neither did any southern Know-Nothings, but it passed because every northern Know-Nothing joined 99

---

17. Rhodes, *History*, 146, 148, 149. Phillips, *Toombs*, 125. Burt, *Lincoln's Tragic Pragmatism*, 151. Johannsen, *Douglas*, 526. *CG, 34-1, Appendix*, 805.

18. *CG, 34-1, Appendix*, 805. Rhodes, *History*, 146-7.

19. *CG, 34-1, Appendix*, 805.

20. Rhodes, *History*, 149. Burt, *Lincoln's Pragmatism*, 151.

Republicans in supporting it. This was an effective example of how the northern majority could control the slavery issue in the House. Thus amended, the Toombs substitute then polled only two votes: northern Know-Nothings Dunn of Indiana and John S. Harrison of Ohio; 210 congressmen voted against it. Three days later, the original House bill, providing for the admission of Kansas under the Topeka constitution, passed 99 to 97. Only four Know-Nothings voted for it, so the Republicans owed their victory to the two anti-Nebraska Democrats who supported it: Hickman and Barclay of Pennsylvania.[21]

As did almost all northern Democrats, William English favored the un-amended Toombs substitute and voted against the Republican Topeka measure. From the northern Democracy's perspective, the Republicans were unreasonable in their demands. The Toombs Bill was eminently fair, and Republicans, as Senator Douglas maintained, refused to approve it because they wished the disturbances in Kansas to continue as fodder for campaign material. The *New Albany Ledger*, ever close to Congressman English's viewpoint, put it this way:

> They [the Republicans] have all along contended that at least three-fourths of the resident citizens and legal voters of Kansas are free-state men, and if they could have an opportunity of giving a free expression to their views and be protected in the exercise of the right of suffrage, they would so decide. But now that it is proposed to give them this opportunity and to protect them in this right, they turn round and say that the object of this bill is to fasten slavery upon Kansas. This confirms us in the opinion we have often expressed that these agitators have no wish to see peace restored to Kansas…Discord, confusion, blood, passion and hatred are their capital stock in this canvass, and it is only by these means that they have the faintest hope of success.[22]

This analysis, while substantially accurate, nevertheless ignored the fact that Republicans, though forced to compete for a majority in Kansas, were fundamentally opposed to the theory of popular sovereignty. To vote for any bill that baldly sanctioned that odious doctrine would implicitly reject the preferred and formerly used route of congressional restriction. Holding the greatest number of seats in the House, they were not about to surrender that point to the Democrats in 1856.

A week after they forced through their own Topeka Kansas Bill, a measure destined to scant consideration in the Democratic Senate, the Republican leadership in the House allowed the Brooks matter to come up for final debate. The six

---

21. *CG, 34-1,* 1468-1472, 1488-1490, 1491, 1501, 1503-1505, 1512-1515 1541.

22. *Ibid.* Nevins, *Ordeal of the Union, vol. 2,* 472. Potter, *Impending Crisis,* 215. *New Albany Ledger,* July 11, 1856.

weeks since the Brooks assault had witnessed a deepening polarization between the Republican and Democratic press. In Indiana's Second District the *New Albany Ledger* argued that while "abolition newspapers pretend to be very indignant and to be greatly shocked at the assault of Brooks on Sumner, no man can read their articles without being convinced that they secretly rejoice at the transaction." Their attitude, Norman reasoned, was governed by the fact that Brooks's actions confirmed their claims concerning southern barbarism, and attainted the northern Democracy by association. Besides accusing the Republicans of hypocrisy, the *Ledger* also became skeptical over the extent of physical injury to Sumner. In late June it stated that "from the testimony of his attending physician, there has not been a day since the assault has been made in which he [Sumner] was not able to attend to his business in the Senate if he wished to do so." As usual, the *Paoli Eagle* was more blunt. Any injuries Sumner suffered, Comingore wrote, were directly caused by his own speech, "the most violent and insulting philippic that ever was made In the Senate." "The man who could make it," Comingore went on, "and not hold himself personally responsible, should not be allowed to sit in that body. Such a wretch should be driven beyond the pale of civilized society."[23]

Norman wrote English in mid-June that there was no sympathy for Sumner in southern Indiana. Yet this attitude did not connote approval of Brooks's assault (as the *Eagle* would have it). Rather, Norman wrote, southern Hoosiers "generally disapproved of the attack because it is calculated to increase the angry feeling between the two sections." As usual, conservative northern Democrats and conservative oppositionists were caught between what they considered extremism on both sides. Wanting only to preserve the Union, and the prosperity that it promoted, they deprecated the passionate outbursts that the slavery issue so often produced. A perfect example of this stance was the House vote on the printing of the reports of the Brooks-Sumner investigating committee. The Republican motion to print called for 100,000 copies. Howell Cobb of Georgia, fully aware that the Republicans planned to use these copies for the campaign, offered an amendment that reduced that number to 10,000. The vote on Cobb's amendment showed that 14 of 16 northern Democrats and 6 of 7 northern Know-Nothings joined 75 southerners to pass it. Having reduced the amount of reports to be circulated, 10 of 17 northern Democrats and 11 northern Know-Nothings, who had voted against the larger number of copies, then voted with the Republicans (and against

23. *CG, 34-1*, 1575. Nevins, *Ordeal of the Union, vol. 2*, 445-449. *New Albany Ledger*, May 30, June 26, 1856. *Paoli Eagle*, June 5, 1856. Two years later the *Ledger* continued to deride Sumner. Upon hearing that he was going to Paris to have an operation performed on his back, Norman maliciously quipped "we had supposed that Mr. Sumner would have been satisfied with the operation upon the back performed by Brooks, without being willing to try another." *Ledger*, July 6, 1858.

the southern Democrats) to help pass the resolution as amended. William English was among those who rode the middle course and switched.[24]

Two days later, on July 10, the House considered the question of whether and how to punish Brooks and his accomplices. The investigating committee's majority report recommended that Brooks be expelled from the House and Keitt and Edmundson be censured. The minority report declared that the House had no jurisdiction over "the assault alleged to have been committed" by Brooks, primarily because it had occurred outside the chamber. It therefore believed it "improper to express any opinion on the subject." These were the orthodox Republican and southern positions, and neither was acceptable to William English. A couple of weeks earlier the *New Albany Ledger* had argued that Brooks should indeed be punished, but to expel him would make him a martyr, and this would hardly diffuse the rancor that the affair had produced. The article recommended censure instead, which, considering the provocation of Sumner's speech, was deemed by Norman a more fitting penalty. Whether English agreed with the "martyr" reasoning or not, the *Ledger*'s suggested course presented a *via media* that appealed to him. Consequently, before any votes were held, he attempted to present to the House a completely new substitute resolution:

> That this House hereby declare its disapprobation of the assault made by the Hon. Preston S. Brooks upon the Hon. Charles Sumner, in the Senate chamber, on June 22, 1856; and the House deem this a fit occasion to express its disapprobation of the use of language, in debate, of a character personally offensive to individual members of Congress, or to any of the States of the Union.[25]

While English's substitute may appear to have offered much to those members who were seeking some sort of compromise, in this, as in other cases, he naively underestimated the culturally passionate attitudes that the Brooks-Sumner affair had unleashed. In almost hackneyed Ohio River border-state fashion, he thoroughly misapprehended the situation. To most northerners, Brooks's assault symbolized the arrogant barbarism of the "slavocracy." For them, to equate Sumner's speech with Brooks's physical attack would be to give up the fight for justice completely. To southerners, Sumner got what he deserved. All Brooks did was to uphold the honor of his state, section, and family, especially as they argued that all Brooks had intended for Sumner was a good "thrashing," something they believed the senator's own barbaric behavior deserved. In English's mind, his

---

24. J.B. Norman to WHE, June 12, 1856, English Papers. *CG, 34-1,* 1575-1576.

25. *CG, 34-1,* 1597. Alexander, *History and Procedure,* 140. *New Albany Ledger,* June 26, 1856. *CG, 34-1,* 1613-1614.

substitute offered northern conservatives the advantage of focusing some guilt upon the Republican Sumner while freeing them from having to vote on the tender question of expelling a colleague. For southern conservatives, English believed, the substitute offered the opportunity of moderately chastising fire-eating Democrats without admitting any more southern guilt than northern. Two of English's steadiest Know-Nothing opponents, George Dunn of the Third District and Humphrey Marshall of Louisville, supported him. Indeed, a majority of northern Democrats (10 to 8), northern Know-Nothings (7 to 4), and southern Know-Nothings (17 to 10) voted for the substitute. It was certainly an apt illustration of English's attempt to discover common northern and southern ground between the ever-increasing extremes.[26]

But it failed miserably. English probably never thought it could have passed. Yet the margin of defeat, 174 to 35, was particularly distressing. Republicans voted solidly against it for its moral equation, something English must have expected. But more distressing was that the substitute failed to muster even one southern Democratic vote.[27] Considering Brooks was certain to at least be censured, English must have wondered why his southern brethren did not support a resolution that also accorded Sumner half the blame. The solidarity of the southern Democracy was portentous, for it clearly signaled that the northern Democratic position of neutrality on the slavery question was not enough for the southern majority. Votes like these predicted the split over Lecompton 18 months later and the final one at the 1860 Democratic national convention.

After the defeat of English's substitute, the minority pro-southern report was easily defeated by 79 votes. Nine northern Democrats, including English, refused to vote for it; the seven who supported it were all doughfaces. Seventeen southern Know-Nothings also voted against it. With its defeat, the part of the majority report calling for Brooks's expulsion became the next order of business. Because an expulsion required a two-thirds vote of the members, there was really little hope that it would pass. In the end, outside of the northern Democracy, only two congressmen broke ranks with their section. Among the northern Democrats, 12 voted against expulsion and six for it. The six were all at the low end of the orthodox (administration's) Democratic scale (see footnote 26). Of the 12 who voted against it, English was the least "doughfaced." Whether he voted against expulsion because of the aforementioned reasoning of the *Ledger* or because he believed it was simply a bridge too far in support of his political enemies is not entirely clear. He continued to vote with the southern and administration Democrats when he

---

26. The differing northern and southern attitudes concerning the Brooks-Sumner affair, and their geneses in different cultural attitudes are well discussed in Hoffer, *The Caning of Sumner*, 17-31. *CG, 34-1,* 1628.

27. *Ibid.*

subsequently voted against Keitt's and Edmundson's censure resolutions, the first along with 13 other northern Democrats and the second with all of them.[28]

Although the Republicans had failed to expel Brooks despite a 121 to 95 vote for the resolution to do so, Keitt's censure, needing only a majority, did pass, 106 to 96. The attempt to censure Edmundson failed, 136 to 60. Brooks and Keitt, both admitting no improper behavior, resigned their seats: Brooks on the same day of the vote on his expulsion and Keitt one day after his censure. They essentially stood on some higher law, and, indeed, both were overwhelmingly re-elected to the House later that year. At least temporarily chastened by the ignominious failure of his substitute resolution, English voted the doughface administration line for the rest of the session. In fairness, so did almost all other northern Democrats. When the House committee investigating Kansas election fraud returned with its reports the Elections Committee submitted to the House the majority report's conclusion that Reeder should be admitted as the legal delegate of the territory because he had received more votes of the *bona fide* territorial residents than Whitfield. The resolution presented to the House was divided into two parts, one unseating Whitfield and the other replacing him with Reeder. Six northern Democrats agreed with the Opposition that Whitfield should be removed, but only one also cast his vote to seat Reeder. Neither man was eventually seated. English, still believing that Whitfield was elected according to law and preferring to follow the minority report of the investigating committee that detailed plenty of violence on the free-state side and real doubt that Reeder received more legal votes, voted with the bulk of the northern Democracy against both Election Committee's resolutions. He later called the select committee the "Kansas-Investigating Committee humbug."[29]

Obviously, when push came to shove English would support the Democratic administration, which at the moment was tantamount to voting the general southern line. We can see by his attempt to diffuse the Brooks-Sumner matter that his heart was not completely in accord with their position, and events would soon show that he could only be pushed so far. Not an essentially passionate man, he continued to believe that some reasonable solution could be found on the slavery issue to allay disunion. Yet he certainly possessed the typical white racism of his time, and his Democratic fealty made it difficult for him to label the Republicans anything but reckless abolitionists who threatened the Union for the benefit of a lowly, degraded, unfit people. With these attitudes, he left Congress a few days

---

28. *CG, 34-1*, 1628-1641. The two non-Democratic congressmen who broke with each of their sections over Brooks's expulsion were John Scott Hamilton, a Know-Nothing from Ohio, and Henry W. Hoffman, one from Maryland. The six Democrats who voted for expulsion were Hickman, Wells, Packer, Williams, Vail, and Peck. Hickman, Wells, and Williams also voted to censure Keitt.

29. *CG, 34-1*, 1628, 1641. *Appendix to the CG, 34-1*, 831. *CG, 34-1*, 1646. *CG, 34-1*, 1859. Schott, *Stephens*, 210-211. *CG, 34-1*, 1873. *Appendix to the CG, 34-3*, 105.

before its first session adjourned in mid-August and went home to support the Indiana Democracy in its state and national campaigns.

3.

By the time the first session of the 34th Congress had ended, the fall political campaign had already begun. In Indiana the positions to be filled included the governorship, the cabinet, all state House members, one-half of the Senate, and all 11 congressmen. The Democrats were fortunate that they were able to avoid any serious breach in their ranks at their January convention. Not so for the Opposition. As already noted, since the summer of 1855 the People's Party fusion had begun to unravel. Districts south of the national road, the First and Second especially, fought against placing anti-slavery above nativism as partisan concerns. By early 1856, both the *Cannelton Reporter* and the *New Albany Tribune* had put Fillmore on their mastheads—the *Reporter* having done so since July 1855, well before the New Yorker became the official nominee. (Two other important southern Indiana newspapers, the *Evansville Journal* and the *Vincennes Gazette*, had done the same.) But in northern and central Indiana only the Laporte fusionists formally supported the former Chief Executive. Other northern counties were waiting for the results of the June meetings of the northern Know-Nothing convention called by the bolters at Philadelphia and the Republican Party get together in the same city. John B. Norman put it directly when he commented that "it has become quite evident that Fillmore has no place in the hearts of the great mass of the Fusion party in Indiana," and the state organ of the opposition, the *Indianapolis Journal*, refused to back the ex-president because he had signed the Fugitive Slave Law and was running on a set of principles that effectively included popular sovereignty.[30]

In most northern states in 1856 the Opposition to the Democrats was similarly divided, but in all of them the anti-slavery element would eventually win out. Indiana was a little slower than some of them to formalize the breach. Whereas Know-Nothing delegates from eight free states bolted from the American Party convention in February that nominated Fillmore and called for that separate northern Know-Nothing convention in June, the Indiana delegation had remained in Philadelphia and initially refused to join the northern call. When the Indiana People's Party held its state convention in May, having invited all opposed to the Kansas-Nebraska Act and the Democratic national administration in general, the split between the primarily anti-slavery northerners and the

---

30. Brand, "Know-Nothing Party in Indiana," 267. *Cannelton Reporter,* July 25, 1855. *New Albany Tribune,* February 26, 1856. *New Albany Ledger,* March 1, 2, 3, 1856. Van Bolt, "Rise of the Republican Party," 211. *Ledger,* March 1, 1856. *Indianapolis Journal* reprinted in *New Albany Weekly Tribune,* April 2, 1856.

more conservative southern Indiana strict nativists could hardly be concealed. The ever-present desire to defeat the Democracy harmonized the convention at the outset, but congressional candidate David Kilgore's resolution calling for delegates to be sent to the Republican convention in June stimulated a breach. Easily passed, the resolution directly repudiated Fillmore, and it led a number of Know-Nothings to repudiate the fusion. The People's Party then passed a platform that included only minor concessions to nativism and temperance, while anti-slavery concerns composed the bulk of their resolutions. Oliver Morton, a clear anti-slaveryite, was nominated for governor, and only one strong nativist, John W. Dawson, was put on the state ticket. By June, even he, along with the northern national Know-Nothing convention, wound up supporting Republican presidential candidate John C. Fremont over Fillmore. As the Democratic press spared no effort to point out, the Indiana People's Party had become "abolitionized."[31]

The disillusioned nativist state Know-Nothings held their own convention in July. Whereas a few thousand had attended previous Indiana gatherings, fewer than 400 came to this one. No more than 10 counties had properly selected delegates, and one-quarter of the counties were not represented at all. This essentially southern Indiana old-line Whig rump of the fusionists endorsed Fillmore's nomination, opposed sectional struggles for the presidency, and refused to endorse the People's Party state ticket. It did not, however, make its own state nominations, leaving individual county organizations free to decide their own course on the Indiana election. Evidently, most nativist energy would be directed toward swelling the vote for Fillmore, which, if large enough, could lead the fusion away from a Republican course in the future. Richard W. Thompson, the most respected old-line Whig in the state, led this campaign, and his speeches that summer and fall condemned the Republicans for their disunionist tendencies.[32]

The split in the opposition was a godsend for the Indiana Democrats. They had been steadily regaining the ground they had lost in 1854, and in 1856 they sensed victory. Yet they were not completely without their own problems. Generally harmonious on the great national questions, before June they were still divided on who should be the Party's presidential candidate. In part this reflected a

---

31. Apparently the First and Second District delegates to the Indiana People's convention did not actually reside in those districts. Van Bolt, "Rise of the Republican Party," 204. Brand, "Know-Nothing Party in Indiana," 268, 269, 272-275. Potter, *Impending Crisis,* 257. *New Albany Ledger,* May 2, 1856. The People's Party nativist plank only noted "that the right of suffrage should accompany and not precede naturalization," and its temperance plank, referring to problems in the Indiana courts, called for "a constitutional law which will effectively suppress the evils of intemperance." On the other hand, the Party resolved that it would resist "by all proper means the admission of any slave state into the Union, formed out of the territories secured to freedom by the Missouri Compromise." It also called for "the immediate admission of Kansas," as, thus, a free state. *New Albany Tribune,* May 5, 1856.

32. Brand, "Know-Nothing Party in Indiana," 278. Carter, "Hoosier History," 119. Thornbrough, *Civil War Era,* 74-75.

division between Wright and Bright followers, but more fundamentally it reflected one between the leadership and the rank and file. That ever-perspicacious observer, Phineas M. Kent, wrote English in March that between Pierce, Buchanan, and Douglas, the main contenders, it was the Illinois senator who appeared to have the strongest support among Hoosiers. Essentially, this had also been the sentiment at the state convention in January, and mass local meetings held during the spring appeared to confirm Kent's analysis. These local Democratic gatherings gave heart to the Indiana district delegates to the National Convention who tended to favor Douglas anyway, and by the time they had left for Cincinnati they were cautiously optimistic that they could institute the people's will.[33]

Just as at the state convention, the Bright machine was at odds with the mass of the Party. Despite assurances of friendliness and even support for Douglas, Bright was working closely with fellow senators John Slidell and Judah P. Benjamin of Louisiana and James Bayard of Delaware, along with banker-friend W.W. Corcoran, to win the nomination for Buchanan. Appropriately safe and willing to follow southern leadership, Buchanan's chief asset was that he was more electable than either Pierce or Douglas. Rather reluctantly, the Party regulars who preferred to support Douglas could hardly disagree. Former congressman William Wick, a close correspondent of all the major Democrats in Indiana, admitted two years later that he only supported Buchanan because Douglas was not "available." William Z. Stuart, former Indiana prosecuting attorney and House member and a Supreme Court Judge in 1856, even two years earlier observed that Douglas "has been too long and too prominently before the public to ever be president." And John B. Norman wrote English two weeks before the convention that "Douglas is regarded by thousands as the author of the Kansas trouble...In a purely *party* sense I think it is probable that the nomination and election of Judge Douglas would be the greatest triumph, but the country needs a more peaceful, less combative leader." Norman also noted that thousands of Know-Nothings wanted to vote for the Democratic nominee, "and will do so if [it is] Buchanan. They would

---

33. The October 1855 election results can be located in the *New Albany Ledger* between October 10 and October 17. Most southern and central counties in Indiana showed considerable Democratic gains. Carl Brand recounts the Democratic trend in the spring municipal elections of 1856. Brand, "Know-Nothing Party in Indiana," 276. In the Second District, New Albany and Jeffersonville remained in Know-Nothing hands. *New Albany Weekly Tribune*, April 16, 1856. P.M. Kent to WHE, March 7, 1856, English Papers. William O. Lynch, "Indiana in the Douglas-Buchanan Contest of 1856," *Indiana Magazine of History* 30, no. 2, (June, 1934), 129. An example of a strong endorsement for Douglas in English's home district was publisher William Williams's note in his newspaper that he believed "Douglas to stand on the topmost round of the ladder in regard to talent and statesmanship, and to be a sound, consistent and patriotic Democrat, one we had rather support for President than any man now living." *Washington Democrat*, April 25, 1856. Although the "Wright men" preferred Douglas, Wright himself early understood that he was not really available because he was so closely connected to the Kansas-Nebraska Act. Joseph A. Wright to James Buchanan, November 14, 1854, partial quote in James L. Huston, *Stephen A. Douglas and the Dilemmas of Democratic Equality* (New York, Toronto: Rowman and Littlefield Publishers, Inc., 2007), 116.

rather not cast their first Democratic vote for a man so conspicuous as a violent opponent as Douglas and I can appreciate their feeling." Around the same time, the *New Albany Ledger* publically came out for Buchanan. Trying to soften the blow, Norman noted that Douglas was young and could "afford to wait," adding ingenuously that his "presence in the Senate can illy be spared at this time."[34]

Although apprised of Norman's cogent analysis, English, like so many other Hoosiers, was loath to give up on the Little Giant. Only three days before the opening of the convention, he wrote a note to Douglas that said "you are my first choice, and [I] have said so to all our delegates." English had now served more than three full years as a congressman, and on almost every issue he had agreed with Douglas, not only on the final yea or nay, but also on the principles than underlay those votes. In a real sense, Douglas was no less a hero to English than he was to many Democrats of the northwest, and there is little doubt that the Hoosier wished to see him as president. But English had another allegiance much closer to home and much more personal. At the end of his letter he wrote Douglas that "I rather think the vote of Indiana will be cast for you but… much depends upon Gov. Bright who, I have just learned will attend the convention." The hold that Bright had on the Indiana delegation as a whole was no less strong than he had on the young Second District congressman. In a showdown between the political loyalty English had for Douglas and the personal loyalty he owed Bright, the Illinois senator was likely to be bested. English was obliquely warning Douglas that the arguments the Indiana 'favorite son' might make concerning availability, coupled with both the personal loyalty that many owed him and the political threats that Bright might make toward those who defied him, might conceivably persuade the delegation to vote against its wishes. Reading between the lines of his letter, it was apparent that among those who could probably be so persuaded was English himself.[35]

It was a seven-hour trip between Indianapolis and Cincinnati by rail. In March, the Ohio and Mississippi Railroad had struck an agreement with the newly formed Jeffersonville Railroad to run two trains daily between the cities, and this was the route that the Indiana district delegates took to the convention. They had all arrived by late May, and there they met their fellow Hoosiers who had come from Washington, including Bright, Pettit, and English. Senator Pettit was a delegate, English and Bright were not. But their status allowed them to attend Indiana's caucus, and Bright was in Cincinnati to ensure that Douglas would not receive the state's support. Not the least of his motivation was that he was promised control of the northwest patronage should Buchanan be elected. When

---

34. Nichols, "Disruption," 18-20, 25. Van der Weele, "Bright," 172-173. W.W. Wick to WHE, February 24, 1858, W.Z. Stuart to WHE, March 13, 1854, J.B. Norman to WHE, May 23, 1856, English Papers. *New Albany Ledger,* May 13, 1856.

35. WHE to Stephen Douglas, March 30, 1856, in Van Der Weele, "Jesse Bright," 171.

the Hoosiers convened on the night of May 31, two days before the convention was scheduled to commence, the result of their discussion illustrated that Bright had done his job well: 16 delegates voted for Buchanan and 10 for Douglas. Compelled by the state convention to vote as a unit, this meant that the 13 votes allocated to Indiana would be cast for Buchanan on the first ballot at least.[36]

There does not seem to be any direct evidence of exactly how each delegate voted in this caucus. Senator Pettit, who seems to have had considerable influence both in the delegation and on the floor of the convention as well, was most certainly for Buchanan, and a handful of Douglas supporters can be identified. As for William English, almost two years later, during remarks made in Congress on the Lecompton controversy, he averred that Buchanan was "my first choice at the Cincinnati convention." Perhaps, if we believe his sentiments expressed to Douglas, these words were carefully chosen to allow for an interpretation that it was only *at the convention* that he abandoned the Illinois senator. Like some Hoosier delegates, at any rate, it was probably Senator Bright's influence that was instrumental in changing his preference, but English's desertion of the Little Giant in 1856 forever foreclosed his acceptance into the inner circle of Douglas Democrats in antebellum Indiana. Defeated for the moment, it was these Democrats who would soon gain control of the Party, and by refusing to stand firm against Bright at Cincinnati, English went a long way toward destroying his chances for future preferment at the state level.[37]

But all this was hardly apparent in June of 1856. English had risen to become a useful party member somewhat esteemed in national councils partly by his association with Senator Bright. It would have taken a great amount of political prescience and personal disloyalty to oppose his mentor now; so conservative a nature as English's did not unduly possess either of these characteristics. Most recently, probably, his friendship with Bright had enabled him to sit as Indiana's representative on the National Democratic Committee. Although he was only substituting for committeeman Alexander Morrison, he was nevertheless elected by the committee as a secretary at the meeting he attended.[38] These were honorable positions, and English apparently was unable to see, at least in 1856, how his political future could be enhanced by aligning himself with insurgents who as yet had gained him nothing.

---

36. *New Albany Ledger*, March 13, 1856. *Official Proceedings of the National Democratic Convention Held in Cincinnati June 2–6, 1856* (Cincinnati: Enquirer Company Steam Printing Establishment, 1856), 7. Lynch, "Douglas-Buchanan Contest," 126, 129. Van Der Weele, "Jesse Bright," 174-176.

37. Hesseltine, *Trimmers*, 27, 28, 41, 45. *CG, 35-1*, 1016. Peek, "The True and Everlasting Principle," 390. For English's political future within the Indiana Democratic Party see the rest of the book, including the Epilogue.

38. A.W.F. Morrison to WHE, January 1, 1856, English Papers. *New Albany Ledger,* January 15, 1856. *Paoli Eagle,* January 24, 1856.

At 10 a.m. on June 2, the convention was called to order. One of the decisions made at the national committee meeting English attended designated him to read the call of the convention on its opening day. This represented another honor for the second-term congressman, and he began to carry out his task minutes after the gathering was formally convened. But only a few short seconds into his reading there occurred a great disturbance on the floor. It was caused by Thomas Hart Benton delegates from Missouri who had not been recognized by the National Committee and who were thus denied access to the proceeding. (Benton was an inveterate enemy of former U.S. senator David Atchison of border ruffian fame. An old Jacksonian, his pro-slavery credentials had become suspect.) Unwilling to meekly abide by the decision excluding them, the Bentonites pushed past the doorkeepers and violently shoved the official Missouri delegates out of their seats. For five minutes, the floor remained in an uproar as the Bentonites held off the convention's verbal and attempted physical chastisement. When order was finally restored, English finished his call, and he then receded for the next four days into the background. (The full convention eventually supported the decision of the Democratic Executive Committee to exclude the Bentonites).[39] The episode fairly illustrated the political violence of the time and the notion that frontier justice was still very much part of the nation's culture. Both, of course, had recently been evoked in Kansas and Congress around this same time. Both, too, did not generally reflect the character of English, and at the moment of the melee, William symbolically represented the opposing forces of civilization and decorum.

It was not until June 4, the third day of the gathering, that the platform resolutions were read and voted upon. All the domestic planks were adopted unanimously, the most salient among them containing a clause that was capitalized and said that the Party supported "NON-INTERFERENCE BY CONGRESS WITH SLAVERY IN STATE AND TERRITORY OR IN THE DISTRICT OF COLUMBIA." This sentence was ambiguous enough to support the northern version of popular sovereignty—that territorial legislatures had control over the legality of slavery in their territory—,as well as the southern version—that slavery is a natural right of a territorial settler. The Democrats explained in further detail that they welcomed

> [t]he cooperation of all who regard the preservation of the Union under the Constitution as the paramount issue—and repudiating all sectional parties and platforms concerning domestic slavery, which seek to embroil the states and incite to treason and armed resistance to law in the territories; and whose avowed purposes, if consummated, must end in civil war and disunion—the American Democracy recognize organic laws es-

39. Hesseltine, "Trimmers," 27, 28. Johannsen, "Douglas," 517. Bain, "Convention Decisions," 57.

tablishing the territories of Kansas and Nebraska as embodying the only sound and safe solution of the "slavery question" upon which the great national ideal of the people of this whole country can repose in its determined conservation of the Union.

And, importantly, especially considering future events, a resolution maintained

that we recognize the right of all the territories, including Kansas and Nebraska, acting through their legally and fairly expressed will of a majority of actual residents, and whenever the number of their inhabitants justifies it, to form a Constitution with or without domestic slavery, and be admitted into the Union upon terms of perfect equality with the other states.

This was the closest the convention came to any mention of possible fraud in Kansas. They also criticized abolitionist activity "that intended to diminish the happiness of the people, and to endanger the stability and permanency of the Union." Another resolution took a swipe at the Know-Nothings, declaring the Democrats' opposition to political parties who based their "exclusive organization upon religious opinion and accidental birthplaces." Aside from these pronouncements on the pressing contemporary issues, the Democrats also unanimously approved their traditional stances: a tariff for revenue only and strict limits on the use of federal funds for "internal improvements." (Interestingly, according to one resolution, those strict limits did not preclude the building of a trans-continental railroad.) On foreign policy, a heavy majority of the delegates, both north and south, supported the United States's hegemonic position in the western hemisphere, but no resolution actually called for further expansion.[40]

All this, of course, was simply the preliminaries. The next day, the battle began for president, and for all the ballots, Bright held the Indiana delegation firmly in Buchanan's column. Bright's biographer maintains that the Indiana vote had a marked effect upon Ohio and waverers in general, and on the initial ballots this was so, but it was Tennessee's switch to Buchanan on the 15th ballot that prompted Douglas to withdraw. This left Buchanan effectively unopposed, and he was unanimously nominated by roll call on the 17th ballot. (To sectionally balance out the ticket, the convention chose between nine slave state nominees for vice president soon afterwards. Kentuckian John Breckinridge got the spot.) Not so strangely the enthusiasm that greeted Buchanan's victory fell far short of the ardor that Douglas appeared to command at the point of his withdrawal. For some minutes the delegates had prevented William Richardson from reading the

---

40. Hesseltine, "Trimmers," 36-38. Bain, *Convention Decisions,* 57-58, Appendix.

fateful telegram that Douglas had sent him, and after the deed was registered, pro-longed cheers for "Little Dug" eclipsed anything that Buchanan could produce. That the nomination, while readily accepted, did not greatly appeal to the hearts of Democrats, may somewhat be gleaned from the reception the Illinois delegates received at Indiana train stations as they returned from Cincinnati. Determined to be gracious at every stop, the Illinois delegates shouted loudly for Buchanan. To their astonishment, the Hoosiers shouted back, "Damn Buchanan, Hurrah for Douglas."[41]

While most Democrats in Indiana probably preferred Douglas to Buchanan, the nomination was not truly a liability for the state party. Many Douglas Dem-ocrats, while perhaps angered at Bright and the old-liners, did not question Bu-chanan's Democratic credentials or competence and clearly preferred him to any Republican or Know-Nothing. Moreover, his nomination made it certain, unlike in 1852, that the Bright machine would be very active in the canvass, a fact highly necessary to success in this very volatile year. On the national level, the election was to be a three-cornered race when the 'North Americans' essentially fused with the Republicans in mid-June. They had nominated Nathaniel Banks at their own convention, but his refusal to accept the nomination led them to support John C. Fremont, the Republican candidate and Mexican War hero. Because of Fillmore's early nomination by the 'orthodox' Know-Nothings, the Democrats would for-tunately face a divided opposition, but this was the first time they had to face a singular, if sectional, anti-slavery party. And the North comprised more than 60 percent of the electoral vote. In relation to Indiana, the rhetoric of the Republican national platform was rather more radical than the Indiana People's Party, but both were firmly anti-slavery and would offer a test of Indiana sentiment on the pressing question of the day. The real question in Indiana was how many Fillmore voters there were and who they would vote for in the state election. Indiana Dem-ocrats, and Democrats in general, then, were entering a race that was truly new and rather unpredictable.[42]

---

41. Bain, *Convention Decisions*, Appendix. Van der Weele, "Jesse Bright," 176, 178. Hesseltine, *Trimmers*, 52-53. Lynch, "Douglas-Buchanan Contest," 132. Van der Weele, "Jesse Bright," 179.

42. Van der Weele, "Jesse Bright," 183. Whereas the People's Party in Indiana spoke in general terms against the extension of slavery, the National Republican Party quoted the Declaration of Independence and declared slavery itself "barbaric." It also contained no plank for the Know-Nothings. Bain, *Convention Decisions*, 54-55. For a detailed discussion of how the 'North Americans' fused with the Republicans, see Gienapp, *Origins*, 330-334. Thornbrough, *Civil War Era*, 74. Phineas Kent wrote English in early July that while "the union of the two branches of the democracy at Cincinnati is not very cordial, [the factions of the Hoosier opposition] fight each other with an animosity that they formerly fought the great democratic party." P.M. Kent to WHE, July 5, 1856, English Papers.

4.

Whatever the fortunes of the Democracy on the state and national level, in Indiana's Second Congressional District it had apparently regained its command over the fusionists. Only Floyd County remained in opposition hands after the fall county elections in 1855, an election that saw the Democrats poll a 2,700 majority in the whole district. In the municipal voting held the following April, many of the towns that had gone fusionist back in 1854 in the midst of plans to repeal the Missouri Compromise returned to the Democratic fold. In the few that refused to succumb, including New Albany, opposition majorities were cut by half. Because the district had never been a haven for incessant anti-slavery appeals, the local People's Party had depended on a strong Know-Nothing movement to put it over the top, but with the general decline of nativist sentiment by 1856, it was hard-pressed to sustain its triumphs of two years earlier. Continual bickering within the fraying fusion, between those in the district who did support the state party's stress on anti-slavery and the more numerous nativists who didn't, further demoralized the opposition.[43] Yet the Kansas civil war offered them an opportunity to reverse their recent misfortunes. Much could be salvaged if the Democrats were defeated in the state election, and even more if the Second District opposition could defeat the Democrats in the race for congressman.

What initially must have given Milton Gregg and company hope for success was the fact that as early as 1854, hard upon his victory to a second term as congressman, William English had pledged himself uninterested in reelection. A most popular congressman, a third nomination would have been his for the asking, but he had apparently decided to honor the general two-term rule that had prevailed in Indiana in the 1840s and was still regarded as orthodox by traditionalists. Those who supported it believed that it preserved party harmony by allowing for the ambition of deserving party members; it also harmonized with the democratic maxim that any intelligent man could guide the reins of government. Despite the "earnest appeals" and "solicitations from his friends," English remained unmoved throughout 1855. About two weeks before the state convention met in January 1856, the *New Albany Ledger*, expressing "regret that Mr. English is pledged not to be a candidate for reelection to the position which he fills," hoped that "perhaps his services will be required in a more exalted position." But if that was intended as a trial balloon to test English's popularity at the state party convention, it did not get off the ground.[44]

---

43. *New Albany Ledger,* October 12, 13, 1855, April 9, 15, 1856. *New Albany Weekly Tribune,* April 16, May 16, 1856. *Paoli Eagle,* April 17, 1856. For disagreements among the factions of the opposition see the rest of the chapter.

44. *New Albany Ledger,* June 12, 1856. *Ledger,* December 22, 1855.

Despite his privately oft-repeated desire to stand by his pledge, there were those who refused to take him at his word. Foremost among them was Phineas M. Kent, English's longtime political advisor. In February, Kent wrote English that he was "heartily sick of the class of men who are urging their claims for a seat in Congress." Although he allowed that they were "good Democrats," he notified English that if none more qualified "can be induced to make the race, you must not be astonished if we should counsel you again to suffer the use of your name." At the time that Kent wrote this letter, the two most prominent candidates were James A. Cravens of Washington County and Daniel Hufstetter of Orange County. Their backgrounds were remarkably similar. Both men were born in the upper South—Cravens in Virginia and Hufstetter in Kentucky. Both had served in the Indiana House and Senate, had been delegates to Democratic national conventions, were extensive landholders and moderately wealthy farmers, and had been presidents of the Washington and Orange County Agricultural Society. The most important difference between them concerned the military: Cravens had served with distinction as a major in the Second Indiana Regiment during the Mexican War, and since 1853 he had held the honor of brigadier-general in the Indiana militia.[45]

Other possible nominees included Horace Heffren, 1852 co-editor of the *Washington Democrat* and a nephew of former congressman Cyrus Dunham, and William Sherrod, a physician from Orange County who had served in both the Indiana General Assembly and the constitutional convention of 1850-51. Of all the candidates, English favored Cravens. They had been longtime friends, and English made it clear to Cravens that he supported him soon after the Washington County farmer decided to run. Kent's opposition to all the candidates rested primarily on their lack of "ability"; he simply believed them "unqualified." In Cravens's case, however, he may also have had a personal reason for his antipathy, for while he served as sutler to the Second Indiana in Mexico, Kent believed that Cravens cheated him out of proper payment for his services. A keen political manipulator, Kent was not an enemy one desired.[46]

English received earnest appeals to run from others besides Kent, and he was thus obliged to respond publicly. Consequently, on the last day of February 1856, he published a letter in the *New Albany Ledger* addressed to "a distinguished

---

45. P.M. Kent to WHE, February 6, 1856; J. A. Cravens to WHE, January 19, 1856, English Papers. Shepherd, *Biographical Directory*, 84, 196. *Washington (County) Democrat,* March 7, 1856.

46. J.A. Cravens to WHE, January 1, 1856, English Papers. Woollen, *Eminent and Self-Made Men,* District 3, 21; Miller, *Indiana Newspaper Bibliography,* 483. Shepherd, *Biographical Directory,* 352. Riker and Thornbrough, *Indiana Election Returns,* 339. *Paoli Eagle,* July 6, 1855. WHE to Mardulia, May 14, 1856; J.A. Cravens to WHE, January 19, 1856; P.M. Kent to WHE, March 9, 10, 1856, English Papers. *New Albany Tribune,* June 26, July 16, 1856. Besides the letters from Cravens cited above, another mentioned "an agreement" between English and Cravens witnessed by "J.D. Bright." No particulars were mentioned. J.A. Cravens to WHE, June 13, 1856, English Papers.

Democrat of the Second Congressional District." Its significant characteristic was its ambiguity, revealing to any close observer English's sometimes-used ability for political dissimulation. In the body of the letter English noted that he had "repeatedly said, during and since the last canvass, both in public and in private, that I did not expect or desire to be a candidate. I was certainly sincere in making these declarations and intend to maintain the same position to the end." This was not what would be called in coming years a Shermanesque statement of refusal. Moreover, the first sentence read, "I will not be so unjust to the generous men who have stood by me when I asked their assistance, as to peremptorily say that I would not accept renomination under any circumstances." Although the rest of the letter properly maintained that "there are worthy, faithful, and talented gentlemen in our party" who can be nominated, and that the convention "can have no difficulty in selecting a suitable person to succeed me," English had undeniably left the door open, pretty widely, to encourage his most ardent supporters—certainly open enough to satisfy Kent. Ten days later, the redoubtable manipulator wrote his client that he saw no danger in the "resignation letter." Kent noted it was very well written, added to English's strength, and its cautious wording made it unobjectionable to the aspirants for the nomination. Kent's analysis seems to betray an overwillingness to put what we would call today a 'positive spin' on the situation. More characteristically, Kent noted that as English was in Washington, he would be removed from the political infighting, tackling "real issues" at the nation's capital, and could surface at the proper moment as the experienced statesman the Democrats needed to ensure victory.[47]

One can only speculate as to what drove English, however surreptitiously, to once again make himself available. Veiled references in letters to his wife later that year indicated that he had probably promised her in 1854 that he would not again stand for reelection—perhaps she had released him from these promises. Or maybe with Jesse Bright as the Indiana senator from the south of the state, English no doubt saw his advancement to that position blocked for the moment. Perhaps he had grown accustomed to his post and was loath to surrender it. Or it could well be that he had convinced himself that none of the other hopefuls were up to the task in these perilous political times. At any rate, although Kent was the most persistent person working for his renomination, many others, as Kent put it, were "anxious" to see it accomplished. Henry Comingore of the *Paoli Eagle* noted that despite public support for the announced candidates, "quite a number of boys" wished that English would be rechosen. Loyal postmaster Frank Gwin simply wrote English that while there were four or five candidates in the race, "you are preferred." One constituent, J.C. Huckleberry, wrote English that "the precedents in our district are in favor of you continuing in the public service at least another

---

47. *New Albany Ledger*, February 29, 1856. P.M. Kent to WHE, March 10, 1856, English Papers.

term." He noted that John Carr, Thomas Henley, and Cyrus Dunham all served three terms. Even Cravens was aware of the sentiment for English, averring to the congressman (probably incorrectly) that others had put a "very different construction [on his *Ledger* letter] from that you intended it should receive." Predictably, Cravens counseled his friendly rival that he thought that "the policy of a third canvass for any office will not be well sustained."[48]

As the contest moved through the spring toward the date of the district convention on June 10, only Cravens, outside of the unannounced English, showed any real strength across the district. By May, Hufstetter and Sherrod had been primarily relegated to favorite sons of Orange County, and Heffren had completely dropped out. The most prominent alternative to Cravens eventually turned out to be James S. Athon, the physician who had been one of English's Democratic opponents in 1852. Soon after his disappointment in that election, Athon was appointed superintendent of the Indiana Asylum for the Insane (a not inappropriate position from which to enter politics in 1856), and he held that position during the prenomination canvass. A loyal Second District Democrat and a well-respected doctor, Athon had first been "spoken of as a candidate" in mid-February, and by April 17, he was so confident of victory that he wrote one of his friends, saying "if there was no change before the 11th of June next, I shall be nominated for Congress." For his part, Cravens wrote English on May 22 that it was he who would be the nominee "if my friends but do their duty." The next day, Norman wrote English that the contest had definitely boiled down to one between Cravens and Athon.[49]

At this juncture, just three weeks before the district convention was scheduled to meet, Thomas L. Smith of New Albany also agreed to allow his name to be put into nomination. Smith was on the Board of Directors for the Indiana State Bank, acted as the Bank's attorney, and had been most influential in apportioning its original stock to favored subscribers, including Michael Bright and Phineas Kent. He was highly respected at the bar and had served for a brief time on the State Supreme Court. President of the Democratic state convention in 1852, Smith was well trusted in old-line circles, and he had as many friends among Whigs as among Democrats. Cravens saw behind Smith's candidacy a clear attempt of the New Albany urban regency to deny him the nomination. It foreclosed the

---

48. WHE to Mardulia, December 7, 1856; P.M. Kent to WHE, March 9, 1856; Henry Comingore to WHE, March 16, 1856; Frank Gwin to WHE, May 26, 1856: J.C. Huckleberry to WHE, May 3, 1856; J.A. Cravens to WHE, March 18, May 22, 1856, English Papers. One township, Howard, in Cravens's own Washington County, simply and boldly resolved that "we are in favor of Hon. Wm. H. English as our nominee at our next congressional convention to represent us in Congress'." *Washington* (County) *Democrat,* June 6, 1856.

49. Woolen, *Biographical and Historical Sketches,* 479. *New Albany Ledger,* April 28, 1853. *Paoli Eagle,* February 15, 1856. James S. Athon to David W. Dailey, April 17, 1856; J.A. Cravens to WHE, May 22, 1856; J.B. Norman to WHE, May 23, 1856, English Papers.

important county of Floyd to his ranks, and, with Athon apparently in command of Perry and Clark, and Orange committed to its own favorite sons, Cravens's chances appeared to decline. He had counted on at least a part of Floyd's delegation, and his personal problems with Kent led him to write that "Kent is playing the devil, and Smith is the cat's paw."[50]

Between the time of Smith's announcement and the day of the convention, most of the counties met separately to discuss which nominee they favored. Cravens believed himself supported in Washington and Harrison. His home county "cordially recommended" him "as a suitable person to put into nomination," and Harrison, while leaving its delegates uninstructed, took "pleasure in bearing testimony to the gallantry, ability, and Democracy of Gen. James A. Cravens." Clark, as expected, recommended Athon to the convention, and the Floyd delegates were instructed to use "all proper means" to secure the nomination for Smith. Orange, Perry, and Scott refused to commit themselves, but wisdom on the eve of the convention put these counties in Sherrod's, Athon's, and Cravens's columns respectively. Only Crawford, with its meager six votes, appeared completely uncommitted. All this added up to the following pre-convention breakdown:

	Athon	Cravens	Sherrod	Smith	Unknown
Clark	18				
Crawford					6
Floyd				18	
Harrison		13			
Orange			10		
Perry	8				
Scott		7			
Washington		16			
TOTAL	26	36	10	18	6

[51]

50. *New Albany Ledger*, May 26, 1856. *Paoli Eagle*, May 29, 1856. R.E. Banta, *Indiana Authors and Their Books* (Crawfordsville: Haddon Craftsman, Inc., 1949), 362. Esarey, "State Banking," 288-296. *New Albany Tribune*, January 11, 1857. *Indiana State Sentinel*, February 25, 1852. *Ledger*, September 16, 1857. Thomas Smith to WHE, April 3, 1844; Simeon K. Wolfe to WHE, June 4, 1856; J.A. Cravens to WHE, May 23, 1856, English Papers.

51. *New Albany Ledger*, April 14, 1856. *Paoli Eagle*, May 22, 1856. *Ledger*, June 9, 1856. *Eagle*, May 29, 1856. Simeon K. Wolfe to WHE, June 4, 1856; James S. Athon to David W, Daily, April 17, 1856, English Papers. *Eagle*, June 5, 1856.

Besides passing resolutions concerning the vote for congressional nominee, almost every county had glowingly thanked English for his ability and service to the district. Washington County "cordially approve[d] and endorse[d]" his course "during the present session of Congress;" Harrison County, after lauding him for his "unwavering and able advocacy of Democratic measures," applauded the disinterestedness and distinguished patriotism "that characterized his refusal to have his name presented before the convention." Floyd, Clark, Orange, and Crawford similarly praised their congressman. On the eve of the convention, Simeon K. Wolfe, editor of the Corydon *Harrison Democrat*, wrote that "if Bill English had not partly tied his hands by promises, pledges, or something of the kind, there would be no difficulty in his getting the nomination." But English had indeed tied his hands, and he remained in the nation's capital dealing with national affairs while Athon, Cravens, Smith, and Sherrod assiduously campaigned in southern Indiana. (His father, Elisha, however, would personally attend the congressional convention.)[52]

On the evening of June 10, as scheduled, the convention commenced in Salem, Washington County. The program for that session called for the candidates to express their views "upon the great political issues of the day." Each did so, though their remarks unfortunately went unrecorded. After a final speech by the district presidential elector, the meeting broke up at midnight with "three cheers for Buchanan and Breckinridge." The next day at 10 a.m., the convention convened at the courthouse to frame resolutions and organize the rules for balloting. By 2 p.m., this business was completed. Buchanan and Democratic nominee for governor, Ashbel Willard, were warmly advocated, as were "the principles enunciated in the resolutions of the recent Democratic National and State Conventions." And the delegates pledged themselves to "gallantly contend against all the combined forces of abolitionism, Fusionism, Maine Lawism, Black Republicanism, and every other ism." Not insignificantly, but, in truth, predictably, one of the resolutions applauded "the Hon. Wm. H. English" for winning "laurels for himself," and for reflecting "honor upon his District and State by his able and consistent career in Congress."[53]

The stage was now set for balloting. The convention first adjourned to a "grove near town" in order to accommodate the number of delegates, who had swelled to 2,000. After a brief disagreement over apportionment (not wide enough to make much difference to any of the candidates) the balloting commenced. On the first ballot, all of the candidates received their expected support; Crawford,

52. *New Albany Ledger*, April 14, 1856. *Paoli Eagle*, May 22, 1856. *Ledger*, June 9, 1856. *Lexington National Guard*, [1856], in English Scrapbook, 65. *Eagle*, May 29, January 3, 1856. Shepherd, *Biographical Directory*, 426. Simeon K Wolfe to WHE, June 4, 1856, English Papers. *Washington* (County) *Democrat*, June 20, 1856.

53. *Paoli Eagle*, June 19, 1856.

the only uncommitted county, split its vote between Cravens and Athon, making the final tally Cravens 39, Athon, 29, Smith 18, and Sherrod 10. This left Cravens 10 votes short of nomination, and on the next ballot he gained the rest of Crawford, leaving him seven votes short at 42. For the next 33 ballots, except for a brief time when Crawford switched to Athon, Cravens held his position; so did Smith and Sherrod, but Athon suffered a major setback when Perry left him and switched to Smith on ballot 15. From that ballot through number 35, the convention remained stuck at Cravens 42, Smith 26 (Floyd and Perry), Athon 18 (Clark), and Sherrod 10 (Orange). It was then, after the 35th ballot that Athon decided to withdraw. The *New Albany Ledger* later noted that "many of Dr. A's friends regretted this step on his part, as they thought that circumstances might have occurred which would have resulted in his nomination," and his withdrawal gave some substance to an earlier remark by Kent that Athon was "not vigorous enough" in his quest. At any rate, Athon's move left Clark as the key county, for its now released 18 votes could seal the deal for Cravens or muddle things further.[54]

Athon withdrew with the customary speech "kindly thanking his friends" and "pledging himself to heartily support the nominee of the convention." After the delegates gave the required three cheers for his sacrifice, they buckled down to balloting again. In what was certainly a very decisive ballot, Clark decided it could not go for Cravens and instead cast its vote for Sherrod. This was not the only switch, for the Perry delegates, perhaps out of panic, brought out English's name for the first time and gave him their eight votes. The 37th ballot thus read:

	Cravens	Sherrod	Smith	English
Clark		18		
Crawford	6			
Floyd			18	
Harrison	13			
Orange		10		
Perry				8
Scott	7			
Washington	16			
TOTAL	42	28	18	8

54. *Ibid. Washington* (County) *Democrat,* June 20, 1856. *New Albany Ledger,* June 14, 1856. P.M. Kent to WHE, March 10, 1856, English Papers.

Clark's decision to prevent Cravens's nomination perhaps stemmed from the desires of the more cosmopolitan Jeffersonville delegates. While Smith was a lawyer and Sherrod was a physician, Cravens was a Cincinnatus, a soldier-farmer, whose patriotism and Democracy were hardly in question but whose talent may have seemed inferior to his rivals. The 'metropolitans' of Jeffersonville may simply not have had much in common with him (as the denizens of New Albany also did not). As for Perry, it had already shown a willingness to back any candidate in opposition to Cravens. This became crystal clear on the next ballot when, noting that their English gambit struck no response, the Perry delegates went for second-place Sherrod. He was the fourth candidate that Perry had voted for, and none of them was Cravens. Perry's vote for the surgeon on ballots 37 and 38 made the tally Cravens, 42, Sherrod 36, Smith 18.[55]

When Perry brought out English's name, Kent no doubt monitored events keenly. His definite but rather secret desire (very likely along with other of New Albany's prominent men) was to renominate the congressman. That English did not stop Kent from acting on his behalf plainly shows that he would willingly acquiesce if his success could be perceived to have been achieved honorably. Indeed, back in March, Kent had written English plainly that as "these are times of political danger…we must have the ablest men as candidates. [Therefore] I shall use every honorable means to impress upon our friends the importance of your nomination."[66] Kent had not used Perry's injection of English's name on the 36th ballot to make his pitch because it was premature. Now that Clark had shown that it would rather not support Cravens, Kent only had to hold Floyd to Smith (whom he and others no doubt saw as a stalking horse for English) and ensure Orange stuck with Sherrod to keep the process deadlocked until English's name could be served up as the only man around whom the delegates could harmonize.[56]

The extraordinary climax came after the 42nd ballot. Between ballots 37 and 42, Cravens held his ground, but except for Orange County, the opposition to Cravens fused around Smith, so that the result of ballot 42 read Smith 44 (Floyd, Clark, and Perry), Cravens the same 42, and Sherrod 10 (Orange). Clearly Orange, pledged to vote as a unit, was in the catbird seat, and when Sherrod withdrew at the end of this ballot, it appeared obvious that Orange could use its 10 votes to decide the nominee. It was at this point that Cravens's earlier assessment of "Kent as the devil and Smith as the cat's paw" revealed itself to be true. While the Orange delegates huddled together to decide the fate of the convention, Chairman Elijah Newland recognized Kent's desire to speak. In a short speech that Cravens later called "rabble-rousing," but which Kent simply referred to as "a flourish," the New Albany regent withdrew Smith and in his place substituted

55. *Paoli Eagle,* June 19, 1856.

56. P.M. Kent to WHE, March 9, 1856, English Papers.

a name which would at its pronunciation alone, thrill the heart of every man. A name which we could rally around as a band of brothers—a name that led the battle in the heat of the fight during the bloody contest of 1854—that had stood shoulder to shoulder in Congress with the gallant minority, and beat back the combined legions of fanaticism—a name that commanded the attention, respect, and admiration throughout the District, State, and entire Union—the name of the gallant William H. English, of Scott.[57]

According to the minutes of secretaries Luciene G. Matthews and Henry Comingore, Kent's speech was answered by a Bunyanesque "one universal shout, loud and continued applause, and wild excitement. Shout after shout went up until the very forests around echoed and reechoed them." Amid this revelry, the 43rd ballot was taken. When Crawford slipped away from Cravens and Orange cast its vote for English, Kent had accomplished his purpose. The final tally read 60 to 36, and minutes later English's renomination, so unexpected by most, but so well played out by one, was made unanimous. "Our boys were never better pleased," wrote Comingore to English two days later. "I have attended every Congressional Convention in my district for the last eighteen years, and I never witnessed as much enthusiasm and good feeling at the result of a Convention as was manifested at this one."[58]

In general, Comingore's harmonious assessment was accurate, but not all were satisfied. Perhaps most revealing was a letter to English from John L. Menaugh, longtime Washington County Sheriff and Treasurer, and one of the most important politicos in the district. Menaugh, who had loyally backed Cravens, his fellow Washingtonian, believed that English's letter of disavowal had brought many candidates into the field unnecessarily. In a sense, Menaugh accused English of acting irresponsibly, for as Luciene Matthews wrote on the same day, had English "intimated in any way that he desired the nomination no other candidate could have stood a chance." Cravens, of course, was the most keenly disappointed. Two days after he was defeated, he lamented how he had been "most foully used in the Convention." He wanted to know if English would allow himself "to be made the implement in the hands of P. M. Kent to crush me," and he intimated that if English accepted the nomination, he would be repudiating a solemn agreement

---

57. *Paoli Eagle,* June 19, 1856. J.A. Cravens to WHE, June 13, 1856; P.M. Kent to WHE, June 13, 1856, English Papers. *Eagle,* June 19, 1856.

58. *Paoli Eagle,* June 19, 1856. *New Albany Ledger,* June 12, 1856. Henry Comingore to WHE, June 13, 1856, English Papers.

made between the two of them. "My time and money had been given freely," he mourned, "I am crushed, and perhaps forever."[59]

To help heal Cravens's wounds, English quickly wrote him back, and by the end of June Cravens had apologized for his earlier "communication." He refused, however, to excuse Kent, whose actions he still believed had clearly cost him the nomination. According to Cravens, Kent made his speech as soon as he had learned Orange County had decided to put Cravens over the top. Had Kent kept still, Cravens would have been nominated. Comingore later denied to English that Orange County ever decided to go for Cravens, but a correspondent of the *New Albany Tribune* (admittedly likely to make trouble) claimed that he had seen Cravens thanking the Orange delegates and vigorously shaking their hands. The *Tribune* further argued that Kent, who was "'bobbin round' the Orange delegation" and who believed that Cravens "could not come within 2,000 votes of being elected," then decided to make his speech. Whatever the precise truth of events, few could deny that Kent was instrumental in preventing Cravens's nomination. "You have no idea of the feelings raised against him and things now said of his conduct," Cravens wrote of Kent, and Matthews confirmed to English that it was "true that there were some hard feelings against Kent and others for bringing about your nomination." As for Kent himself, he dismissed these denunciations: "The truth is, the more I learn of the man [Cravens] and his standing at home, the better I am satisfied at the action of the Convention. It was a most fortunate escape from weakness to strength."[60]

Kent had once written English that any ill will he might promote toward himself as a result of his actions was not as important as the nomination of an able man. Whether Cravens, Sherrod, Athon, and even Smith were not congressional timber is difficult to discern, but the whole district agreed that English certainly was. The fact was that had Cravens gotten the nomination it would have been over the opposition of Clark and Floyd, the two most populous counties in the district and the two most threatened by Know-Nothingism. As Matthews commented, "any other result would have given dissatisfaction." Throughout the district, ratification meetings praised the work of the delegates, and Cravens himself publicly pledged "gallant English my hearty support." The national Democratic press also chimed in. The *Washington Union* knew "of no representative of the people who more richly merited this flattering evidence of confidence, esteem, and regard

---

59. J.L. Menaugh to WHE, June 23, 1856; L.G. Matthews to WHE, June 23, 1856; J.A. Cravens to WHE, June 13, 1856, English Papers. Two years later, again denied the nomination, Cravens noted at the 1858 congressional convention that "justice was denied me at Salem in the last congressional convention." *Washington* (County) *Democrat*, August 5, 1858.

60. J.A. Cravens to WHE, June 25, 1856, English Papers. A few weeks later English offered Cravens a position in the Nebraska Land Office, but Cravens politely refused him. J.A. Cravens to WHE, July 18, 1856, English Papers.

than Mr. English. His abilities, which are of the first order, are only equaled by his aptitude for, and his application to, public business." The *Washington Star* applauded the Second District's disregard of "the two-term rule, so destructive to the utility of members [of congress]." It remarked that "Mr. English is a man of excellent sense and great industry [and] to displace him under such circumstances for a new man would be an act of extreme folly on the part of any constituency."[61]

All these expressions of praise laid to rest any doubts English had in accepting the nomination. As a secretary of the convention, Luciene Matthews had formally notified English of his selection in a letter dated June 12. For a couple of weeks English delayed responding, "in order to learn," he said later, "whether any portion of our political friends dissented from the action of the convention." In the meantime, the Democratic sheets of the district implored him to accept, one arguing that "the people and only the people have a right to select their public servants, and it is a question of doubt whether, when so selected, a Democrat under ordinary circumstances has the right to decline." In short, as the *Jeffersonville Democrat* maintained, English was compelled to accept the nomination by "duty, patriotism and gratitude." Matthews privately counseled English that to refuse the nomination "would make the next nominee a less honorable one and furnish grist for the enemy's mill," and Cravens himself publicly stated that it was "as much [English's] duty to accept [now] as it was before to decline." Convinced, then, that "no dissatisfaction" existed, English slyly wrote back publicly on July 1 that, despite "my own inclinations and former declarations, in view of this expression of [the district's] will…the path of duty is plain before me." "No patriot can be blind to the dangers which seem to be gathering around us," he continued, and "with that high sense of honor and devotion to principle which should ever characterize true Democrats," he accepted the nomination.[62]

Few politicians have played the game so well. In 1854, English was probably sincere when he expressed his desire to retire two years later, but his equivocal "resignation" letter of February, coupled with his unwillingness to instruct Kent to cease efforts on his behalf, illustrate that, by 1856, he still wished to remain a congressman. Perhaps the congressional battles of that year had made him realize that he could contribute both to the Democratic cause and his own ambition by

---

61. P.M. Kent to WHE, March 9, 1856; L.G. Matthews to WHE, June 23, 1856, English Papers. *New Albany Ledger,* June 17, 18, 30, 1856. J.A. Cravens to *Lexington National Guard,* June 19, 1856, in English Scrapbook, 65. *Washington Union,* reprinted in *Ledger,* June 21, 1856. *Washington Star,* reprinted in *Eagle,* June 26, 1856.

62. Luciene G. Matthews, Secretary of the Convention, to Hon. William H. English, June 12, 1856, English Papers. William H. English to Secretary of the Convention Luciene G. Matthews, July 1, 1856, in *Paoli Eagle,* July 10, 1856. *Washington* (County) *Democrat,* June 20, 1856. *Jeffersonville Democrat,* reprinted in *New Albany Ledger,* June 30, 1856. J.A. Cravens to *Lexington National Guard,* June 19, 1856, English Papers. William H. English to Secretary of the Convention Luciene G. Matthews, July 1, 1856, in *Eagle,* July 10, 1856.

remaining where he was. As he wrote in his acceptance letter, "the black blight of Abolitionism and slavery fanaticism has brought the nation to the very verge of that fearful crisis so much dreaded," and he may well have understandably and genuinely believed that experienced men needed to be at the seat of power. At any rate, to whatever merits of his own he owed his renomination, it was to Phineas Kent that he was most indebted. In the next session of Congress, English assiduously worked to repay that debt, attempting to find Kent a suitable and lucrative position in a foreign mission. But that was not to be, and soon thereafter Kent decided to leave the Second District for good, seeking a different life in newly settled White County. He had already sold his "fine mansion on Main Street" and later in 1857 relocated to the new frontier village of Brookston 180 miles away from New Albany. There he lived for the rest of his days, until his death in 1888, as a gentleman farmer on 1,600 acres of "rich deep black loam soil," disturbing his former congressman principally for the best and latest reports from the United States Department of Agriculture.[63]

5.

Despite Phineas Kent's expressed belief that a Cravens candidacy would have jeopardized Democratic victory in the fall, whomever the Party nominated still had a cultural advantage over the Opposition. Around the rest of the state the ascendency of anti-slavery sentiment in the People's Party platform might perhaps work to the opposition's advantage, but in southern Indiana it was by no means dominant and somewhat of a liability. Within the urban and quasi-urban strongholds of the second district Opposition—New Albany and Jeffersonville, especially—nativism and temperance reigned supreme within the fusion, and more than a few old-line Whigs expressed the desire to sit out the election rather than vote for a congressional candidate of the Fremont stamp. At the same time, there were Republicans in the Second District who would hardly support a candidate pledged to Fillmore. This was the dilemma that faced the fusionists when their congressional convention met in Corydon on July 1. Three candidates presented themselves for nomination: Randall Crawford of Floyd, a Fremont man; David T. Laird of Perry, a Fillmoreite; and John D. Ferguson of Clark, English's opponent of 1852 and an old-line Whig who probably inclined more to Fillmore than Fremont. For over 20 ballots, the tally stood Crawford 42, Ferguson 22, Laird 21. Needing only one more vote to be nominated, Crawford was unable to succeed because the staunch Fillmore men would not vote for him. Evidently, neither

---

63. William H. English to secretary of the Convention Luciene G. Matthews, July 1, 1856, in *Paoli Eagle,* July 10, 1856. For attempts to find Kent a position see WHE to Howell Cobb, March 1857, and M.G. Bright to Kent, March 20, 1857, English Papers. *New Albany Weekly Tribune,* January 16, 1856. *New Albany Ledger,* June 9, 1857. Shepherd, *Biographical Directory,* 219. P.M. Kent to WHE, July 11, 1860, English Papers.

Laird nor Ferguson would withdraw for the other, and the convention adjourned for a time, effectively deadlocked.[64]

By the time the delegates reconvened, the Fillmore men had somehow induced both Ferguson and Laird to withdraw in favor of one John M. Wilson. Wilson was rather an odd choice for a candidate. Born in the East, he had spent most of the 1840s practicing law in Cincinnati. Only as recently as 1853 did he move to Indiana, and he had never held a political position of any note either in Ohio or anywhere else. His primary asset appears to have been his oratorical ability. In the off-year elections of 1855, he lent great service to the Know-Nothings by speaking to crowds throughout the district. Unquestionably, he preferred Fillmore to Fremont, but very pragmatically he downplayed this preference and welcomed the advice and support of Fremonters to the cause. Crawford and Laird, former judges, and Ferguson, a gifted lawyer and an ex-state representative, were all probably more deserving than Wilson. But they destroyed their chances by fratricide, and, when Wilson's name was brought forth, he immediately tallied 49 votes, six more than necessary for nomination.[65]

The Democrats were delighted by the opposition's choice. From Louisville, English's old friend Thomas Ware Gibson wrote that "a better selection *for you* could not have been made." Norman wrote English that Wilson was "one of the most ultra and violent of the Know-Nothings. He has no regard for principles; [he] will make his speech to suit his crowd." Matthews claimed that Wilson had no ability, just a "loud voice;" he was "generally regarded as a rabble-rouser [who] would do anything and tell any lie to gain a vote." Using even what he must have recognized as hyperbole, Matthews called Wilson "perhaps the most unscrupulous man in Indiana." Michael Kerr, the 29-year-old prosecuting attorney of Floyd County and present candidate for the state house, wrote that Wilson was the weakest man the opposition could have nominated. The *New Albany Ledger* agreed, and, privately, Norman wrote that he had "no idea why [the fusionists] would nominate him if they thought there was any chance."[66]

---

64. The *New Albany Ledger* noted on May 6, 1856 that the Know-Nothings were "more powerful here than anywhere else in the State." *New Albany Tribune*, July 3, 1856. *Ledger*, July 3, 1856. Michael C. Kerr to WHE, July 2, 1856, English Papers.

65. L.G. Matthews to WHE, July 17, 1856, English Papers. *New Albany Ledger*, July 2, 1856, September 11, 1855. *New Albany Tribune*, July 3, 1856. M.C. Kerr to WHE, July 2, 1856, English Papers. One correspondent wrote English that "Laird appears to be very disappointed not to have the honor to get beat by you… That Mr. Wilson was preferred to him he thinks the greater an injustice as he considers himself a second Jefferson in judgment and another Clay as orator." Otto Schieffner to WHE, July 19, 1856, English Papers.

66. T. Ware Gibson to WHE, July 4, 1856; J.B. Norman to WHE, July 12, 1856; L.G. Matthews to WHE, July 7, 1856; M.C. Kerr to WHE, July 2, 1856; J.B. Norman to WHE, July 12, 1856, English Papers. Michael Kerr later served eight years in the United States House of Representatives, two of them as speaker. Woolen, *Biographical and Historical Sketches*, 335; *Biographical Directory of U.S. Congress*, 1337; Shepherd, *Biographical Directory*, 220.

The opposition's chances did indeed appear small. Besides the apparent weakness of its candidate, the division between Fillmoreites and Fremonters was never successfully mended. The two most important opposition newspapers outside of the *New Albany Tribune*, the *Corydon Argus* and the *Jeffersonville Republican*, came out for Fremont and Fillmore, respectively. (Beatty had sold his *Cannelton Reporter* to Joseph M. Prior back in February; Prior changed the name of the newspaper twice, adopted strong Republicanism—calling property in slaves "against Natural Rights"—then suspended the paper in September. He finally sold it to John B. Maynard in December who changed it into a Democratic sheet.) Gregg, who, like most Second District oppositionists, was primarily a Fillmoreite, consistently tried to downplay the division. He had argued earlier in the year that both factions denounced the Kansas-Nebraska Act, were opposed to slavery extension, favored a "sound prohibitory liquor law," and supported the policy of suffrage restriction to United States citizens. But Gregg's analysis even then was clearly obsolete, for the American Party no longer truly opposed slavery extension, and the Republicans had distanced themselves considerably from nativism. The tension between the two groups was made manifest at a gathering in New Albany held on July 12, 10 days after Wilson was nominated. Originally billed as a Fillmore rally to appoint delegates to the Know-Nothing state convention, a handful of Republicans showed up in hopes of discouraging any action designed to promote a separate opposition state ticket. Both Wilson and Gregg addressed the crowd, but when Wilson refused to make his preference for president known, "his remarks were very coldly received." And Gregg's inept attempt to chastise the obstinacy of both groups ended in his being drowned out by cries of "Fillmore." When Republican Randall Crawford rose to speak after Gregg, the crowd became so incensed that he gave up without even uttering a word.[67]

Wilson again tried to talk sense to the Fillmoreites of New Albany a week later, but according to one sarcastic English correspondent, the crowd "hooted down" his suggestion that "Sam and Sambo would have to join hands, kiss each other, and unite for the common good against the great enemy." Essentially, Wilson's appeals were made for the sake of the state ticket, which was dominated by Republicans, but he knew that local defections caused by the state candidates would certainly have their effect on the congressional race. Wilson was prescient enough to conclude that the Republican Party, not the American one, was the party upon which the oppositionists should stake their future, though he obviously hoped it would be a Republican Party in league with nativism. Perhaps his usefulness as a candidate was that his credentials as a Know-Nothing might enable him to convince other nativists of this conclusion. But to many of the

---

67. *New Albany Ledger,* July 22, 1856. Miller, *Indiana Newspapers,* 356. *Indiana Reporter,* July 22, 1856. *New Albany Tribune,* July 21, 1856. *New Albany Weekly Tribune,* January 23, 1856. Gienapp, *Origins of Republican Party,* 305-306. *Ledger,* July 14, 1856.

Know-Nothings, the Republicans appeared worse than the Democrats, especially a rather conservative Democrat like Bill English. Throughout July, English received letters from the New Albany regency telling him that he would receive the votes of "many Fillmore men in our county." In Orange, too, Comingore reported that the Know-Nothings would rather support the Democrats than the "abolition ticket." To the conservative Fillmoreites, Sumner was as guilty as Brooks, and the Topeka government was treasonous. As a self-described "old-line Whig" wrote English earlier that year, the fact that the Second District congressman was called a "doughface" was unimportant because that epithet had been "so freely applied by Union-hating hypocrites." No "'52 Whig," he argued, could truly affiliate himself with "black republicanism."[68]

These considerations caused certain complacency in the Democratic camp. "The Democracy here are in good spirits," wrote W.J. Newkirk to English from New Albany. "[T]hey do not think it hardly worthwhile to hold any meetings yet, seeing that the Hindoos are splitting up so bad that the effort to elect our whole ticket in October and November will be so easy that it is hardly worthwhile for us to make an effort." But other more influential Democrats were more cautious. James Cravens, while acknowledging that the opposition was divided at the moment, argued that "common sentiment of hatred to the Democracy has always brought them together," and Michael Kerr noted that the opposition was "organized most thoroughly and getting warmed up." In fact, despite their obvious division, the Republicans and Americans had managed to fuse into one district central committee headed by Gregg, and the Democrats could never be sure that the opposition would not find some way of compromising its differences. In anticipation of this event, the Second District Democracy sent out appeals for funds. As Kerr wrote English, "the Democracy here are not, and have not been for some time, very liberal in their donations. We have therefore generally to confine our calls for money to a zealous few who always give." In essence, English was asked to donate not only to his own campaign but to the Democracy at large. "Please do the best you can for us," Kerr concluded, "we will see that it shall be a good investment."[69]

While English remained in Washington, the Democrats of the Second District began the campaign. That year, they had seven newspapers in the district,

---

68. W.J. Newkirk to WHE, July 19, 1856, English Papers. Both Norman and Newkirk had concluded that Wilson had essentially switched to Fremont by the early part of July. J.B. Norman to WHE, July 16, 1856, English Papers. W.W. Tuley to WHE, July 26, 1856; J.B. Norman to WHE, July 12, 1856; Henry Comingore to WHE, July 13, 1856; Michael Kerr wrote English "your prospects are improving every day here. Several Know-Nothings have openly avowed their determination not only not to vote for Wilson, but to vote for you." M.C. Kerr to WHE, July 19, 1856, English Papers.

69. W.J. Newkirk to WHE, July 19, 1856: J.A. Cravens to WHE, July 18, 1856; M.C. Kerr to WHE, July 19, 1856, English Papers. *New Albany Ledger,* July 18, 1856. M.C. Kerr to WHE, July 19, 1856, English Papers.

one for each county but Crawford. For the first time, this equaled the number the opposition had, and the Democratic central committee decided to supplement these with a weekly campaign sheet freely distributed. The publication of such a sheet was one of the reasons why Kerr solicited donations, but his principal reason was to buy all the "flags, mottoes, transparencies, cannon, etc., etc.," needed to stage "a Grand Rally that would surpass all the demonstrations of our memories—a splendid torchlight procession at night and speakers in the afternoon." "We are well satisfied," he wrote, "that what we want now [is] to stir up the zeal and enthusiasm of our party." Only by excessive complacency, Kerr realized, could the Democracy be beaten.[70]

With the state and presidential campaigns in full swing, English returned to the district on August 21 while Congress met in special session. His ostensible reason for missing the session, called by Pierce to deal with the Army Appropriations Bill, was that his wife had become seriously ill. Yet, soon after he returned, he pitched into the campaign. He appeared with Sherrod and William B. Beach, the Democratic candidate for Clerk of the state Supreme Court, on August 23 in Clark County. On August 29, learning that Wilson had an appointment to speak at New Salisbury in Harrison, English traveled there and made a reply to his opponent's arguments. The *New Albany Ledger* maintained that English's appearance "decompose[d]" Wilson, and whether this was true or not, Wilson now had to contend with the fact that he could no longer canvass the district with his opponent 500 miles away. Indeed, the next day, the candidates conferred and decided upon 33 joint appearances between September 2 and October 13.[71]

Some Democrats had counseled English not to make that joint agreement. Newkirk, for example, argued that because Wilson could not possibly command as much crowd appeal as English, the joint appearances would only assist the enemy. Yet tradition still called for a joint canvass, and English probably considered such advice dishonorable. The *New Albany Tribune* later complained that English had drawn up the appointments in such a manner as to "break down" his opponent. The paper maintained that the distances between the appointments were often 30 to 40 miles, no problem for English who traveled by carriage, but uncomfortable for Wilson who rode to each place upon his horse. Yet an inspection of the list reveals that this charge was unfounded—almost all appointments were no more than 15 miles apart. Gregg's other charge, that English purposefully

70. The seven Democratic newspapers were: *The Jeffersonville Democrat, New Albany Ledger, Harrison County Democrat, Paoli American Eagle, Lexington National Guard, Washington Democrat,* and *Cannelton Reporter* (changed from neutral to Democrat). The Opposition press consisted of the *Jeffersonville Republican, Corydon Western Argus, Paoli Constitutionalist, Lexington Western Casket, Salem American Citizen, The New Albany Tribune.* There was also another newspaper in Perry County. Miller, *Indiana Newspaper Bibliography,* 40, 44, 47, 48, 49, 153, 155, 344, 480, 483. M.C. Kerr to WHE, July 19, 1856.

71. *New Albany Ledger,* August 30, 1856. *New Albany Tribune,* September 2, 1856. *Ledger,* September 3, 1856.

staged the appearances "in small inconvenient houses" to deny Wilson the advantage of his strong voice, may have contained more substance.[72]

Of course, the reports of the canvass reflected the partisan views of the reporters. While to the Democrats Wilson "ranted [and] contrary to the expectation of his friends came out second best," to the opposition English lied incessantly and plied his audience with liquor. Throughout the campaign, the Democrats tried to pressure Wilson into announcing his choice for president, and, when he continued to refuse, they increasingly labeled him a Republican. In early September, Wilson accused the Democratic Party of supporting the extreme laws of the pro-slavery Kansas legislature, but English used this accusation to illustrate to the electorate that his opponent did not stand with the American Party. Reading a resolution that pledged one of the political parties to "the maintenance and enforcement of all laws until said laws shall be repealed," English asked Wilson whether that was the plank to which he referred when he accused the Democratic Party of backing slavery in Kansas. When Wilson nodded, English shot back that what he read was a plank not from the Democratic Party but from the American Party. The *New Albany Tribune* appears to have been more embarrassed by this incident than Wilson, for the candidate apparently had stronger anti-slavery sentiments than did Gregg and the bulk of the Fillmorites.[73]

Wilson was not so foolish as to pursue the Kansas issue throughout the canvass. He no doubt quickly became aware (if he did not know already) that a majority of the voters in the district, including a majority of the opposition, distrusted the Republican approach and favored something like the Toombs Senate bill. In a letter to the *Indianapolis State Journal* editor John Defrees that year, Schuyler Colfax called southern Indiana "that most benighted region…" The opposition candidate for governor, Oliver Morton, refused to appear with Willard in that part of the state for fear, as one southern Indiana Democrat said, "that Willard would expose his [Morton's] niggerism in this region and he would lose a great number of votes." Any attack on the Democrats' Kansas policy was refashioned by the Party as support for abolitionism and disunion. As English put it in his acceptance letter to Matthews:

> The people cannot fail to see that but for violations of the Kansas law that Territory would have been blessed with profound peace, as Nebraska has been, which was organized at the same time under the same law. The responsibility will mainly rest upon those unscrupulous politicians and dangerous fanatics who have thrown obstacles in the way of the execu-

72. W.J. Newkirk to WHE, July 19, 1856, English Papers. *New Albany Tribune*, September 3, August 24, October 9, 1856.

73. *New Albany Ledger*, September 10, 1856. *Jeffersonville Democrat*, reprinted in *Paoli Eagle*, September 18, 1856. *New Albany Tribune*, October 9, 1856. *Ledger*, September 11, 1856. *Tribune*, September 13, 1856.

tion of the Kansas-Nebraska Act—who have violated the letter and spirit of its provisions, and now refuse to support any *practical* measure likely to insure the early and *regular* admission of Kansas as a State, under a constitution to be legally adopted by the actual and undoubted citizens of the Territory, because it would deprive them of a fruitful source of agitation in the approaching canvass. Rather than fail in their mad designs, they would let discord reign supreme.[74]

Again, while there is a great amount of truth to English's assertions, he rather glosses over, as the Democrats generally did, the early electoral corruption caused by the pro-slavery party in Kansas.

While Wilson and Morton recognized the futility of presenting the Republican case to the Second District voters, the Democratic press refused to win its points merely by default. Alongside their charges of abolitionism and disunion were blatant appeals to racism. "There were a great many niggers," the *New Albany Ledger* reported, who marched in a Fremont procession held in Indianapolis in July. These "niggers," Norman wrote, "were regarded with the utmost regard and fraternal affection by their white brethren. It is notorious in that part of the state little or no distinction is made between niggers and white men." Arguing (falsely) that George Julian and other abolitionists had gained control of the People's Party, the *New Albany Ledger* accused them of promoting blacks "to look at *this* land as their home and the home of their children," and of teaching them that "*here*" they will shortly attain those rights which now belong exclusively to the white race." These rights, according to the *Ledger*, included suffrage, and should the opposition succeed, "the moment the slaves were given their liberty [they] will flock hither in considerable numbers" to exercise these rights.[75]

Considering these sentiments, a political fuss was created when the People's Party used a black clergyman to follow Willard around the state. The black minister, William Anderson of Madison, made at least one appearance in the Second District. Anderson's speechmaking led the *New Albany Ledger* to declare that "the Black Republican leaders are lost to all sense of shame." It expressly counseled its readers not to forget that "Judge Morton hired a *nigger* to follow Gov. Willard, and that Black Republicans turned out *en masse* to applaud his speeches." When

---

74. Colfax to Defrees, October 27, 1856, in Smith, *Colfax*, 84. W.J. Newkirk to WHE, July 19, 1856, English Papers. William H. English to secretary of the convention Luciene G. Matthews, July 1, 1856, in *Paoli Eagle*, July 10, 1856. The *New Albany Ledger* noted that "the Democratic Senate had twice passed bills annulling [the Shawnee Mission] laws and providing for a quiet and peaceable election…but the House tabled those bills. The truth is that the Black Republican Party was determined that the laws should be kept on the statute books until after the Presidential election." September 12, 1856.

75. *The New Albany Ledger*, July 18, 16, August 11, 15, 1856. The *Ledger* had also noted in June, "it is supposed that both parties will go for 'Buck' in the ensuing Presidential election—the Democrats for Old Buck of Pennsylvania, and the abolitionists for the first big 'buck' nigger that comes along." June 10, 1856.

English returned to the lame duck session of Congress in December, he brought up the matter in a debate with the defeated oppositionist Will Cumback of the Third District. When Cumback noted that Willard had invited "any speaker" to meet him and then "backed out when a black one came," English responded that Willard had acted properly: "Governor Willard certainly did not shrink from any contest with his political enemies which a gentleman might honorably engage in. If he backed out with an association with a Negro, it was more than many of my colleague's associates would have done."[76] Although he was less shrill in his racism, no quote can more poignantly display that English, like the Second District at large, refused to accord blacks the perquisites of humanity.

Although the Second District Democrats suspected Wilson of abolitionism, these racist appeals were aimed more at Morton than at him, and they were primarily intended to drive Fillmoreites away from the People's Party state ticket. Still, this probably also worked as a way to dissuade the Fillmoreites from voting for Wilson. But despite his willingness to embrace the Republicans among the fusionists and his general belief that the Republican Party was the probable successor to the Whigs in the North, Wilson had solid credentials as a nativist. Indeed, as late as July 1856, Norman labeled him "one of the most ultra and violent of the Know-Nothings." In 1855, Wilson traveled the district in support of the nativist cause, and his speeches followed the Know-Nothing thesis that foreigners needed to be excluded from the American political process because they did not make good republicans. Like slavery, Wilson argued, foreign cultures destroyed the sober, industrious, independent spirit that was believed to be essential to successful republicanism. He may also have preached the more unsavory aspects of nativism—that immigrants were, as he was accused of saying, "vile, filthy, degraded, and idiotic." Democrats claimed that he was one of the leaders behind the New Albany election riots of 1854. Whether that was true or not, a nativist Fillmoreite could identify Wilson as sympathetic to his cause.[77]

While Wilson's strong Know-Nothing credentials made it difficult for the Democrats to associate him with Morton and Fremont, these same credentials were of course used to help keep the foreign vote Democratic. As early as July, English and other Democrats began to become apprehensive about the German immigrants. Because of their evident anti-slavery proclivities, it was correctly feared that many of them might vote Republican. Taking a page from the opposition, Thomas Gibson went so far as to suggest that "if the Dutch do go off to the abolitionists as I fear they will I am for altering our constitution from debarring them from voting at all." (He was aware that such sentiments were not fit for public

---

76. *Louisville Courier*, n.d., quoted in English speech to Congress, *Appendix to the CG, 34-3*, 105. *New Albany Ledger*, June 24, July 16, 1856. *Appendix to the CG, 34-3*, 105.

77. J.B. Norman to WHE, July 12, 1856, English Papers. *Paoli Eagle*, August 24, September 11, 1855. Democratic German handbill reprinted in *New Albany Tribune*, September 22, 1856.

consumption, evident by his disregarded instructions to "burn this letter" made at the bottom of the page.) The People's Party state committee, wishing to take advantage of this German antislavery trend, printed a handbill in German that pointed out that the Know-Nothings were beaten back at the state convention. It further noted that "it is our duty to prevent an extension of slavery in the west for the benefit of those who may follow, so that they may also find a home." The sheet was distributed to all counties with a large German population, including Harrison, Clark, and Perry. Moreover, the People's Party was systematically attempting to purchase every major German newspaper in the state.[78]

The Democrats of the Second District fought back with their own German handbill, which made clear Wilson's nativism, ending with the admonition that "Mr. Wilson is not the only Republican in Indiana who has expressed himself in such a hateful manner against the adopted citizens." Thus to the nativist opposition the Democrats preached the dangers of Fremont and to the Germans, the dangers of Fillmore. John S. Simonson, English's veteran political friend, was wise enough to divide the Germans into two political camps. It was not the pre-1848 immigrants who were defecting, he argued, but "a portion of the Germans—the transcendental socialists—infidels of the Goddess of Liberty School, who assert that our government is not Democratic and that our people are not sufficiently republican in their proclivities and tendencies." This analysis was supported by the division between the two foremost German newspapers in the state, the *Indiana Volksblatt* and the *Freie Presse*. The *Volksblatt*, founded in 1847, supported Buchanan; the *Freie Presse*, founded in 1854, supported Fremont. The Opposition's decreasing emphasis on temperance, diffused when the Indiana Supreme Court declared the 1855 prohibitory law unconstitutional, also aided the People's Party in its quest for German votes.[79]

Actually, because of the continued strength of nativism in the Second District, German defections were kept to a minimum. Democrats from Perry County wrote English that they feared few crossovers, and Comingore asserted that the Germans were remaining loyal. This was good news if only because the Irish, too, worried the Democrats. Long considered traditionally Democratic and generally untainted by anti-slavery, the Irish should have presented no problem, but a relatively minor incident caused them to threaten voting against English. The genesis of all this was the murder of an Irish waiter at Willard's Hotel in Washington, D.C. by Congressman P.T. Herbert, a California Democrat. A week after the murder, the House considered a motion to investigate the matter, but English and

---

78. M.C. Kerr to WHE, July 2, July 12, 1856; T. Ware Gibson to WHE, July 4, 1856, English Papers. *New Albany Ledger,* July 12, 16, 1856.

79. *New Albany Tribune,* September 22, 1856. John S. Simonson to WHE, June 30, 1856, English Papers. Van Bolt, "Fusion out of Confusion," 360. The prohibitory liquor law was overturned late in 1855. Goodwin, "Tussle with the Traffic," 17-19.

all but two Democrats present voted to table it. On June 12, Norman wrote English that while he heard no complaints on the manner in which English received a third nomination, "one or two Irishmen are complaining about your vote on the Herbert matter." And at the end of July, Ballard Smith, the builder and proprietor of the Cannelton Cotton Mills, and one of English's Perry County confidantes, wrote that Irish anger toward English had increased.[80]

English eventually defended his vote by noting that Herbert was already in police custody when the House moved the resolution. But at the end of July, Herbert was predictably acquitted, and English's only recourse was to state that "perhaps" his vote had been in error. The *New Albany Tribune*, of course, would not let the matter rest, and Gregg wrote that "every Irishman who has any self-respect will hold Wm. H. English responsible for being an accessory after the fact." For its part, the *New Albany Ledger* could not ignore the irony of a Know-Nothing editor advising the Irish, and Norman felt confident that "Irish citizens [would] not be deluded by such miserable hypocritical pretenses." A letter from 17 Irishmen to the *Washington Star*, reprinted in the *Ledger*, stated that they did not hold the Democratic Party responsible for Herbert's freedom. The improper conduct, they asserted, was committed by the jurors, 11 of whom were Know-Nothings, "as hostile to the Democratic party as to the Irish." It is reasonable to assume that English may have lost some Irish votes over the affair, but with so unsympathetic opponent as Wilson, the Irish in the main had nowhere else to go.[81]

While the issue of slavery, nativism, and race played significant roles in the campaign, what really spiced up the contest was the character issue. In 1852 and 1854, however much they disagreed with them, Democrats respected the opposition's candidates. Ferguson was considered intelligent and honorable, and Slaughter was an esteemed Whig editor and lawyer. But Wilson, though not considered untalented, was regarded as generally unseemly. Soon after his nomination, Kerr called him "a corrupt and unscrupulous demagogue, an unprincipled man."[82] He offered no particulars, but one can only surmise that Wilson's activities on behalf of Know-Nothingism had crossed the boundaries of propriety and that the Democrats considered this newcomer excessively ambitious and not too keen on how he achieved his popularity. In the early part of the canvass, these sentiments were

---

80. Otto Schieffer to WHE, July 19, 1856; Ballard Smith to WHE, July 10, 1856, Henry Comingore to WHE, July 13, 1856, English Papers. Joanne Freeman maintains Herbert shot the waiter because he refused "to serve him breakfast past the appointed hour." Dishes and chairs had been tossed around just before the shooting. *Field of Blood*, 223. *CG, 34-1*, 1228-1229. J.B. Norman to WHE, June 12, 1856; Ballard Smith to WHE, July 25, July 30, English Papers.

81. *New Albany Tribune*, September 11, 1856. *New Albany Ledger*, August 1, 1856. *Tribune*, September 24, 8, 1856. *Ledger*, September 4, 2, 1856. The *Tribune* must not have had too much confidence in the Irish switching their votes, as Gregg counseled his partisans to be on the lookout for Democratic importation of illegal Irish voters on election day. *Tribune*, October 14, 1856.

82. M.C. Kerr to WHE, July 19, 1856.

expressed only privately, and, indeed, as far as the character issue went, in August and September, the Democratic press spent much of its time defending William English from charges made against him by the *New Albany Tribune.*

Early in the campaign, repeating charges made in Horace Greeley's *New York Tribune,* Gregg accused English of switching his vote on a bill that was designed to increase the salary of House members from $8 per day to $2,000 per year. This was indeed a significant increase, and Greeley and Gregg maintained that on all procedural votes English voted "yea," but when the bill came to a final vote, assured of passage, English voted "no." Gregg argued that this illustrated cowardice at best and duplicity at worst: "So it would appear from this that the Hon. Wm. H. English concluded to change his vote in the negative, after ascertaining that he could pocket the money just as well without his vote as with it." At first, the *New Albany Ledger* ignored these charges, preferring only to comment that it believed congressmen received "ample compensation" under the old system and that it was "gratified to see that our representative opposed the measure." But the congressman himself, knowing the accusations were false, refused to ignore them. He wrote a short, dignified letter to the *New York Tribune* correcting Greeley, and the venerable editor honorably acknowledged his mistake, noting that English opposed the measure throughout. Gregg, caught in a lie not of his own making, was not so honorable. He not only refused to retract the charges, but claimed that his source was a "disinterested" and reliable one. It was up to the *Ledger* to print Greeley's apology, and it was up to the *Paoli Eagle* to harass Gregg for refusing to follow the example of his more illustrious colleague.[83]

More potentially damaging to English were Gregg's insistent charges that the congressman had avoided his sworn duty by leaving Washington a few days before the end of Congress's regular session. What's more, he remained away for the entire week of the special session called by Pierce. In this instance, Gregg's facts were solid. English had indeed gone west as early as August 16, but not before he paired himself with George Robbins, a Republican from New Jersey. Informed that Pierce was to call a special session, English sent word to Colfax and Smith Miller to continue his pair with Robbins, but, when Robbins returned for the new session, Miller took the liberty of arranging a new pair with Killean Miller of New York. "Although your presence is needed here," the Indiana Miller wrote English,

> I would advise you to consult your own interest about returning in case the session continues. While Southern representatives are within 100 miles of the Capitol, and do not think it worthwhile to return, I do not

---

83. *New York Tribune,* August 18, 1856. *New Albany Tribune,* August 22, 1856. The provisions of the bill and the final vote on it are contained in CG, 34-1, 2160-2161. *New Albany Ledger,* August 21, 1856. *New York Tribune,* August 25, 1856. *New Albany Tribune,* August 30, 1856. *Ledger,* August 28, 1856. *Paoli Eagle,* September 4, 1856.

think it very incumbent upon northern members to jeopardize their interest in a warm canvass by returning to the battleground. [Smith Miller himself was not running for a third term.]

On August 26, Gregg discovered that English was already in the district, and, the next day, the *New Albany Tribune* announced that his "absence from Washington City at the present time is more evidence of his prominent characteristic, to wit: a very decided interest in his individual welfare." In case his readers did not perceive Gregg's allusion, he then made clear that English had avoided his duty in order to come home to look after his "political interests."[84]

In response, the *New Albany Ledger* maintained that in the past eight and a half months in Washington, English "did more than any man in Congress. Not only has he labored faithfully for his own immediate constituents, but he has transacted nearly all the business of Indiana at Washington, for all parties, because he was the most influential man there with the Administration and with all the heads of the Departments." But it was not primarily by this assessment that the *Ledger* defended English's early departure, for that was caused, it stated, by the fact that "his wife has been, and is yet, at the point of death." Gregg, Norman noted, apprised of these facts, still callously charged English with dereliction of duty. It was indeed true that in Congress Smith Miller stated to his colleagues that English was "detained at home by reason of severe sickness in his family," but, in the letter earlier quoted, he made no mention of this, an unlikely omission if indeed Mardulia was at death's door. Moreover, the *New Albany Tribune* noted that considering the gravity of his wife's illness it was strange that her husband had gone out so soon on the stump and had "made appointments with his opponent every day up to the election [taking him] away from home almost every day up to that time." The *New Albany Ledger* countered that what really annoyed the *Tribune* was that English's return spoiled the opposition's strategy of having "Wilson go through the district retelling the slander against English and the Democratic Party before Mr. E. should be able to meet and refute his statements." Be that as it may, the evidence appears to confirm that English returned more for political reasons than for family ones. Significantly, he was out campaigning almost immediately after he returned, despite the *Ledger's* claim that he refused to leave Mardulia's bedside "even after she was considered beyond danger." As Riff Randall later said of her parakeet that was found alive after being reported dead: "must have got better."[85]

---

84. *CG, 34-1*, 2189. Smith Miller to WHE, August 19, 1856, English Papers. *CG, 34-2*. 2-3. Smith Miller to WHE, August 28, 1856. *New Albany Tribune*, August 26, 27, 1856.

85. *New Albany Ledger*, August 27, 1856. *CG, 34-2*, 67. For English's early appointments on the stump see text to footnote 82. *New Albany Tribune*, September 2, 1856. *New Albany Ledger*, September 1, 1856. Riff Randall, played by P.J. Soles, was a character in the 1979 film *Rock and Roll High School*.

Actually, the reason English left Washington so early did have much to do with his campaign for reelection, but it was not simply to reach the district before Wilson gained too much of a head start. On or about July 12, English received a letter from Phineas Kent that went beyond the vague allusions to Wilson's lack of character. Kent, agreeing with other Democrats that Wilson was "totally destitute of moral or even political principle," informed English that he had heard rumors pertaining to Wilson's conduct while living in Cincinnati. Kent believed that they were serious enough to be "inquired into, and if [Wilson's behavior] was as bad as his Know-Nothing friends say it was, the public should know it." Exactly what these rumors were, Kent did not say, though perhaps he detailed them in another letter that has not remained available. At any rate, English clearly decided that as soon as he could, he would leave Washington for Cincinnati. On House votes contemplating an adjournment date, English consistently voted to adjourn early, and, when he finally did leave Washington, it was not directly to go home to Lexington but to make a stopover in the Queen City. Considering that he could well predict Gregg's attack on him for leaving Congress before the session ended, only the hope of retrieving some very damaging evidence on Wilson could have compelled him to exit Washington when he did.[86]

From hotel records and eyewitness accounts, it later became clear to all that English did indeed go to Cincinnati before he returned home. While there, he investigated the rumors of which Kent wrote and returned to the Second District carrying a series of court-sworn depositions in his pocket. For a month, the whole trip to Cincinnati, including the depositions, was kept secret, but, on September 25, three weeks before the election, a Democratic weekly published in Clark County broke forth with allegations that rocked the campaign the rest of the way. Printing in full the statements of Irid Brickett and attorney Charles S. Bryant taken in Cincinnati on August 19, the *Jeffersonville Democrat* accused Wilson of real estate fraud, seduction upon promise to marry, performance of an abortion, and manslaughter. Both deponents told a story of a man who, after attempts to cheat a couple out of their land, seduced the couple's daughter, impregnated her, and effectively murdered her by carelessly aborting the pregnancy. Brickett was a simple businessman, but Bryant was a long-time resident of Cincinnati, a respected Whig lawyer who had decided to vote for Fremont in the presidential election. In the ensuing weeks, the *Democrat* printed supporting depositions from other citizens of Cincinnati impugning Wilson's character and labeling him in almost all instances "a bad and immoral man."[87]

---

86. P.M. Kent to WHE, July 9, 1856, English Papers. *CG, 34-1,* 1710.

87. Milton Gregg later went to Cincinnati to prove that English had stopped there before going home. English registered at the Burnet House in the city from August 18 to August 21. Gregg also showed that the congressman accompanied two men to a Notary for depositions. *New Albany Tribune,* October 7, 1856. English acknowledged going to Cincinnati while on the stump at Springtown on October 6. *Tribune,* Oc-

How many leading Democrats of the district knew of these depositions before they were printed is difficult to say, but, once the *Jeffersonville Democrat* published them, the *New Albany Ledger* and the *Paoli Eagle* quickly proclaimed their veracity. Within a week, both newspapers fully reprinted them. The burden of defending Wilson rested upon Milton Gregg. He attacked the task energetically. "A dirty, unscrupulous locofoco sheet at Jeffersonville has hatched up some most horrible stories in regard to Mr. John M. Wilson," the *New Albany Tribune* recorded on September 27; later, it labeled Bryant "a police lawyer" and Brickett "a perjured knave." Within a few days, Gregg published counter statements made by other citizens of Cincinnati, including four doctors who certified that "there is no evidence that Elizabeth Binnegar died from an abortion, or any attempt to produce an abortion." Gregg was even able to procure a certified statement, dated September 29, 1856, from Elizabeth's parents, relieving Wilson of any "dishonorable conduct" towards their daughter and calling the charges against him "grossly slanderous and malicious." (Of course, if the parents admitted that the charges were true, their daughter's reputation would have been quite sullied.) Taking the offensive, Gregg threatened to publish documents from a Kentucky court that would show it was William English who truly possessed the immoral character assigned to Wilson. The *Ledger* challenged Gregg to make good his threat, but the *New Albany* editor, proclaiming the high road, declined to do so.[88]

On October 4, the Opposition came out with a pamphlet, distributed throughout the district, entitled "Vindication of John M. Wilson." But by that time new accusations had been made against the fusion nominee. These came from one Eliza Mason, a widow, who produced a letter Wilson had written her, which appeared to confirm that he had fathered her daughter out of wedlock and thereafter refused to support her. Evidently, Mrs. Mason, who was well connected to some powerful persons in Cincinnati, actually had tried to gain revenge by shooting at Wilson; soon thereafter he left for Indiana. The editor of the *Jeffersonville Democrat* not only printed Mrs. Mason's story but brought her and her daughter to the Second District where she boldly attended one of the last appearances Wilson made in the campaign. The *New Albany Tribune* refused to believe any of these charges and sarcastically queried "who will believe a *widow*, one who had been a play actress, who had practiced medicine (including obstetrics and dissections), who was a strong-minded woman, *could* be seduced by a young man, one whose years numbered less than her own?" A weary defense at best, and Mrs.

---

tober 8, 1856. The *Paoli Eagle*, reprinting from the *Jeffersonville Democrat* on October 2, 1856, contains the Brickett and Bryant depositions. Supporting depositions can also be located in the *Eagle*, October 9, 1856.

88. *New Albany Ledger*, September 26, 29, 1856. *Paoli Eagle*, October 2, 1856. *New Albany Tribune*, September 27, 28, October 1, 6, 1856. *Ledger*, October 6, 7, 1856.

Mason's appearances in New Albany with her child probably spoke far more eloquently than Gregg's typeface.[89]

For his own part, Wilson appears to have acted dignified during the whole affair. On the stump he limited himself merely to a refutation of the charges, and, quite possibly, it was he who counseled Gregg not to publish the court records pertaining to English from Kentucky. His major thrust against the accusations came in the form of threats to file a slander suit against English and libel suits against the *New Albany Ledger,* the *Jeffersonville Democrat,* the *Paoli Eagle,* the *Salem Democrat,* and the *Indiana State Sentinel.* Evidence indicates that English was more willing than the editors to go to trial, probably because, as a lawyer, he knew how difficult it would have been for Wilson to prove his case—or simply because the congressman had loads of money. Yet the editors were not so frightened as to cease their accusations. Four days before the vote, the *Ledger* remarked that the defeat of Wilson would "deter youthful aspirants from embarking on a career of debauchery and licentiousness,

> and will prevent political parties from bringing into the field for responsible positions men upon whose character the dark stain of reproach rests…All men who love virtue better than vice, all men who wish to see our aspiring youth become examples of moral purity and elevated character to their fellow citizens, all men who want to see honors and offers become the reward of an upright and meritorious life, should vote against such men as John M. Wilson.[90]

On the last weekend of the canvass, the campaign was elevated when Howell Cobb of Georgia, the noted southern Unionist, came to the district. There were few counties north of the Ohio River where any southerner would be as welcome as he apparently was in Floyd and Clark. The mere fact that he made an appearance there illustrates that English's district was exceptionally conservative on the slavery issue. He was probably brought to the district by Jesse Bright, who may have used him to counter the belief promoted in the *New Albany Tribune* that the exceedingly pro-slavery *Charleston Mercury* spoke for the southern Democracy. Whether or not Cobb had any effect, two days after he left, the district's voters went to the polls and gave English a smashing victory and the state ticket a healthy majority. As a whole, the district gave the Democratic state ticket over 57

89. *New Albany Ledger,* October 2, 6, 1856. Eliza Mason's letter is printed in the *Paoli Eagle,* October 2, 1856. Mrs. Mason was the widow and sister of two professors. *Ledger,* October 14, 1856. *New Albany Tribune,* October 3, 1856.

90. The *New Albany Tribune* and *New Albany Ledger* of October 9, 1856 both contain reports of Wilson's forbearance on the stump. The *Tribune* listed the possible libel defendants in its issue of October 8, 1856. J.B. Norman to WHE, November 26, 1856, English Papers. *Ledger,* October 10, 1856.

percent of its vote, and in no county did the percentage fall below 53. The conservative Democratic nature of southeast Indiana becomes especially clear when it is compared to the rest of the state, for outside of the district, Willard polled less than 51 percent of the vote. Only in "the pocket," Indiana's First Congressional District in the southwest, did he equal the showing he made in the Second. As for English, he actually outpolled Willard by 38 votes, while Morton and Wilson were separated by only a single tally. The official congressional vote, 10,577 to 7,927, was the largest congressional margin the district had ever witnessed. The returns from Jeffersonville and New Albany, the two major cities and opposition centers, illustrate the extent of English's victory. Whereas in 1854 Slaughter defeated English in these two cities by a combined total of 848 votes, in 1856, that margin was reduced to 173.[91]

One month later, the Democratic state victory in Indiana was followed, in truth, by Buchanan's more impressive triumph in the state in the presidential election. In a three-cornered race, Buchanan actually polled a majority of the state's vote, 50.3 percent to Fremont's 40 percent and Fillmore's 9.7 percent. In the Second District, Buchanan did even better than either Willard or English, gaining 10,877 votes and a 57.8 percentage. Whereas Fremont and Fillmore together polled only 12 votes more than Wilson, Buchanan tallied as many as 300 votes more than English. It was perhaps the behavior of some old-line Whigs that produced this result. Unable to vote for Wilson because of his character (or nod to the Republicans) or for English because of his rather obnoxious dyed-in-the-wool Democracy, these Whigs may have simply decided to boycott the congressional election. On the state level, the People's Party's clear anti-slavery stance probably deterred them there. But Buchanan's equally clear conservatism and the fact that only he, not Fillmore, could prevent the state from going for Fremont most likely promoted these Whigs to vote Democratic in the presidential contest. Such, anyway, was the reasoning of Henry Clay's son in Kentucky and Rufus Choate in Massachusetts, the latter writing publicly that it was his duty as a Whig "to unite with some organization of our countrymen to defeat and dissolve the new geographical party calling itself Republican."[92]

Postmortems on the election again illustrated the conservative nature of the Second District. In the presidential vote, Fillmore outpolled Fremont 6,071 to 1,401. Counting Buchanan's vote, Fremont received a paltry 7.6 percent of presidential votes cast in the District, approximately 32 percent lower than he received

---

91. *New Albany Ledger,* October 12. 1856. Voting results by county can be found in the *Ledger,* October 29, 1856. Gubernatorial returns may be found in Pitchell, *Indiana Votes,* 8-9, and for the district in detail in English Scrapbook, 69, 70. Floyd County's vote is also listed in the *New Albany Tribune,* October 15, 1856.

92. Burnham, *Presidential Ballots,* 410. *New Albany Ledger,* October 29, 1856. Nevins, *Ordeal, vol. 2,* 492. Horace Greeley predicted to George Julian that Buchanan would not get 21,000 votes between Indiana's first two districts. He got 24,000. Greeley to Julian, August 2, 1856, in Clarke, *Julian,* 177-178.

statewide. Gregg and others had constantly urged fusion of the Fillmore and Fremont electoral tickets, but having failed to accomplish that, they knew that Buchanan would win. The Democrats, naturally, viewed the results as a "rebuke to the Wooley party." One Democrat wrote that this election "will long be remembered as the day of finality to abolitionism in Indiana." (As with other finality resolutions, this one was wrong.) In general, the Indiana Democracy made a political comeback in 1856. It won six of 11 congressional seats, received a majority of state legislators on joint ballot (no small matter with a still-vacant United States Senate seat), and helped destroy the challenge of the Know-Nothings that had appeared so formidable two years earlier. As one Democrat put it, "gloriously have we triumphed over the most desperate coalition of isms that has ever disgraced our country."[93]

While the Democrats of Indiana rejoiced, a keen Republican observer could point to the fact that Buchanan's victory nationwide was predicated on a division of the opposition. In the North, only in Indiana and Pennsylvania (Buchanan's home) did he, in fact, poll a clear majority. Sober Democratic politicos quickly observed that a re-fusion of anti-Democrats could spell future defeat, and the likelihood of new troubles in Kansas might give the opposition that opportunity, even in Indiana. For the moment, however, Democrats, especially Hoosier Democrats, basked in victory. When he came to New Albany after his triumph, English was feted and "warmly congratulated by the Democracy." This may have produced in him a sense of déjà vu, for he had been victorious now for over a decade in the political arena. But 1856 also had its unique aspects. His election that year followed his experiences, for the first time, as a minority legislator. Through it all he had apparently increased his influence in party circles. As the *Washington Union* put it, he was "one of a noble band of northern Democrats who stood firm on every trial, and defied the assaults of agitators and fanatics."[94] Now he would return to Washington with a clear mandate to continue his struggle, in tandem with the Democratic Party, to prevent an anti-slavery revolution in American politics. Perhaps confident he could do so after his second reelection, future pitfalls, which in some measure he helped to foment, were to make that a difficult task indeed.

---

93. *Tribune Almanac and Political Register for 1857 (New York: Greeley and McGrath, 1857), 58-59.* Among the opposition in 1856 there were two plans to achieve a united presidential ticket. The Fillmore men wanted the Republicans to drop five of their electors and substitute five Fillmoreites. This the Republican Party refused to do. On the other hand, the Republicans proposed that if the American Party withdrew its ticket in Indiana, the Republicans would withdraw its ticket in Kentucky. Considering that Fremont had no chance at all in Kentucky anyway, the Fillmoreites would not bite. Schuyler Colfax to John Defrees, October 27, 1856, in Van Bolt, "Rise of the Republican Party," 215. Schuyler Colfax to Horace Greeley, October 27, 1856, in Smith, *Colfax,* 84. L.L. Stewart to WHE, November 20, 1856; John [Simler] to WHE, January 2, 1857, English Papers.

94. Burnham, *Presidential Ballots,* 410. *New Albany Ledger,* October 30, 1856. *Washington Union,* reprinted in *Paoli Eagle,* April 10, 1856.

CHAPTER SIX

Lecompton

Reelected for the second time by a great majority, William English was bound to hold a prominent position in forthcoming Democratic Party councils. Rumors quickly began to circulate predicting his bright future. Some suggested that he was due a shot at the speakership; others promoted him, young as he was, for Buchanan's cabinet. His close relationship with senator Bright only enhanced his prospects. As one of the principal planners of Buchanan's nomination and election, Bright was rewarded with control of all major patronage appointments in the Northwest, and as one of Bright's primary lieutenants, English was given free rein over the federal patronage of his own district. He used it, of course, to reward his friends and ease the disappointment of his erstwhile Democratic rivals. He offered James Cravens a position in the lucrative Nebraska Land Office, but he turned it down. William Sherrod, however, accepted one as a clerk in the Federal Pension Office. Samuel Crowe, longtime confidant from Scott County, whom English had already made postmaster of Lexington in 1853, was promoted to a $1,400 clerkship in the General Land Office. Likewise given federal employment were Lewis Jordan, Harrison County's leading Democrat, and Hamilton Smith, the founder of the district's most prosperous manufacturing concern. In sum, Democrats of the Second District were well cared for by their increasingly powerful patron.[1]

The results of the 1856 election were indeed welcome, but one unresolved problem existed. In early November, English received a letter from Luciene Matthews informing him that John M. Wilson had made good on his threat to sue certain Democrats for libel. Matthews wrote that both English and the editors of the *New Albany Ledger* were compelled to appear before judge Alexander An-

---

1. J.B.A. Archer to WHE, July 6, 1856; L.M. Smith to WHE, January 8, 1857; S.S. Crowe to WHE, February 5, 1857, English Papers. Van der Weele, "Jesse Bright," 191. Nichols, *Disruption*, 99. James Cravens to WHE, July 18, 1856. *New Albany Ledger*, January 21, 1858, *New Albany Tribune,* January 28, 1858. Woolen, *Eminent and Self-Made Men*, District 1, 53.

derson of New Albany's Court of Conciliation on January 23. Wilson was suing the alleged libellants for a total of $10,000. Fortunately, judge Anderson was a friend of English's, but this did not calm the fears of John B. Norman, who was primarily concerned with the financial cost of a drawn-out legal battle. He consequently made a deal with Wilson whereby the *Ledger* would print a retraction of its charges if Wilson could produce testimony casting doubt upon their veracity. This Wilson did, and on November 24 the *Ledger* printed the following:

> During the pendency of the late canvass for Congress in the Second Congressional District, some pretty severe things were said by the party press on both sides in reference to the candidates for Congress. It will be remembered that during the canvass we copied into the Ledger certain statements made by Messrs. Bryant, and Brickett of Cincinnati, in relation to the antecedents of John M. Wilson. At that time we had seen no rebutting evidence, leading to show Mr. Wilson innocent of the charges so made. We deem it but justice, however, to say that a friend of Mr. Wilson has shown us certain affidavits and depositions in his defense which seem to indicate that so far as the aforesaid publication was concerned, injustice was done him. Wishing to deal fairly and frankly with all parties, we cheerfully make this statement, and would publish Mr. Wilson's evidence but for its great length.[2]

English had advised Norman not to print this statement; at least a letter from the congressman to the *Ledger* on November 26 implies as much. Norman wrote English that he "did not attribute the same importance to the [retraction] as you seem to do," and added that his own opinion was "that we had better let the matter drop quietly and say no more about it except on great provocation." Why English was so opposed to the policy is unclear especially in light of the fact that he had received information as early as October 3 that appears to have cast great doubt on the charges leveled at his opponent. One T.S.D. Miller had written English that his informant in Cincinnati could "obtain no clue or evidence of the truth of the report against Wilson referred to in your letter." Perhaps Miller's information referred to different charges than the ones made in the campaign, but another letter, this one written by English himself to his wife the next January, indicates that at least some of the allegations made against Wilson were highly suspect. Writing from Washington, D.C., English told Mardulia that he "was likely to have great trouble with Mrs. Mason as you will see from the enclosed letter [not extant]…It is a direct attempt at extortion. I am sorry to say that I have

---

2. L.G. Matthews to WHE, November 9, 1856; Alex Anderson to WHE, February 5, 1855; J.B. Norman to WHE, November 24, 1856, English Papers. *New Albany Ledger*, November 24, 1856.

entirely changed my opinion of the woman and it is a source of gratification to me that I avoided being in her company as much as possible." While such letters do not prove that the allegations against Wilson were false, they do indicate that Norman's decision to print his retraction was politically prudent.[3]

But Norman's retraction was merely a sideshow to interregnum politics in Indiana. The main spotlight was on Indianapolis, where the legislature was scheduled to select two United States senators. Ever since the previous summer, Jesse Bright had been actively engaged in promoting his own reelection and that of a friendly co-senator, but two stumbling blocks appeared in the way of his success. First of all, although the Democrats had a small but comfortable majority on joint legislative ballot, the opposition now controlled the state Senate. In imitation of the 1855 Democracy, it planned to use its control to refuse to vote the Senate into joint session, thereby preventing, as in 1855, any election for United States senators. The second stumbling block concerned who the Democratic caucus would choose to accompany Bright to Washington. It was generally conceded that the Party would nominate Bright to succeed himself, but the senator feared that the Democratic legislators were also intent upon the nomination of his hated rival, Joseph Wright, to fill the vacant short-term seat. This Bright could not allow, and in opposition to Wright he again supported Dr. Graham Fitch, the former free soil congressman who since attaching himself to Bright in 1854 had become enlightened to the rewards of doughface politics.[4]

Ex-senator John Pettit also declared his candidacy, but he was generally unfavored by the Democratic masses. Indeed, much to Bright's consternation, so it seemed was Dr. Fitch. Norman remarked in late January that the "private sentiment" of the Party overwhelmingly favored Bright and Wright for the two positions, but the ever-insightful Phineas Kent understood that Wright could not be nominated. "It is hardly possible for J.A. Wright to succeed," he wrote, "[for] there is hardly a prominent democrat in this state but is opposed to his election, and this he knows and feels keenly." Kent's analysis shows that the same breakdown illustrated at the 1856 state convention still persisted: Bright was strong with the leadership and Wright with the rank and file. If Hoosier Democrats en masse could have voted for their senators, Wright would have easily won a seat; but state legislators were too often amenable to Jesse Bright's persuasion, and among them Wright was not so popular. By the time the date of the Democratic caucus

---

3. J.B. Norman to WHE, November 26, 1856; T.S.D. Miller to WHE, October 3, 1856; WHE to Mardulia, January 18, 1857, English Papers. It is perhaps noteworthy that the opposition had already charged that Eliza Mason had been paid to besmirch Wilson's character.

4. Shepherd, Biographical Directory, 513-515. Van der Weele, "Jesse Bright," 193, 197. In Fitch's first incarnation as a Bright selection for senator back in 1855, he attempted to explain away his pro-Wilmot comments made in 1849 as not "his honest convictions, but rather ones that were written by him to save the Democratic party from the insane spirit that pervaded the country at the time." New Albany Tribune, September 28, 1854.

approached, Wright could see that Bright had bested him again. At the meeting itself on January 30, Wright declined to have his name put in nomination. "Fitch would have beaten him badly," Sherrod wrote English from Indianapolis. After Wright (and Pettit) withdrew, Bright and Fitch were selected by acclamation.[5]

Although Wright could not have beaten Fitch, his mere attempt could have further divided the Party. Because most Democrats probably wished to avoid such a display of disunity, Wright was able to gain something for his withdrawal. Shortly before the caucus, Wright allowed congressman John G. Davis to approach congressman-elect James Hughes, a Bright confederate. According to Hughes, "Governor Wright wished Davis and myself to confer together with a view to making some political arrangement by which a contest in caucus between Dr. Fitch and Gov. Wright should be avoided." Hughes maintained that at that interview nothing was accomplished because he could not guarantee Wright a position in Buchanan's cabinet if he withdrew. But soon after, new Indiana lieutenant governor Abram Hammond stepped in and negotiated an agreement whereby Bright would personally lead a movement to petition Buchanan to place Wright in his cabinet if the governor withdrew from the Senate race. Before this agreement was finalized, Bright protested that an outright petition for a cabinet post would be "indelicate towards Mr. Buchanan," so it was agreed to amend the resolution to read "a first-class appointment." Wright apparently approved the new formula, and the caucus so resolved. Wright partisans claimed that the substitution of "first-class" for "cabinet" was merely a polite formality, and that Bright was clearly under an obligation to promote his rival for a cabinet post. But Bright partisans maintained that the final resolution was manifestly intended to free the senator from any such obligation and that Wright might have to settle for an important foreign mission.[6]

---

5. *New Albany Ledger*, November 29, 1856. Pettit had written R.M.T. Hunter, the powerful Virginia United States senator, in November, asking him to "write Mr. B[right] *at once*, urging him to write his friends in the matter for our mutual election." Pettit to Hunter, in Ambler, *Correspondence of Hunter*, 200. *Ledger,* January 23, 1857. Crane, "Joseph Wright," 234. P.M. Kent to WHE, January 23, 1857; Wm. F. Sherrod to WHE, January 30, 1857, English Papers. Wright himself, not the bare-knuckled fighter that Bright was, explained his withdrawal to a friend this way: "The controversy [in caucus] was to be voting viva voce or by ballot, my friends insisting on the viva voce vote. It is humiliating to think that I should have succeeded if the voting had been viva voce, otherwise if by ballot. Such is the corruption of the times. Now there was a great number of members, in spite of all that I could do, would have left the caucus, broken the same up, and my enemies would have called me a disorganizer." Joseph Wright to [unintelligible], February 2, 1857, Wright Papers, Indiana Historical Society, Indianapolis, Indiana. One might question Wright's reasoning on the grounds first, that a silent ballot, where some members could resist Bright's arm twisting, should have favored him, and secondly (as the next paragraph illustrates) he knew he would be beaten for the party's Senate selection, and he may well have used the fear of Democratic disorganization to accept a deal from the Bright forces *before* the Democratic caucus convened.

6. *New Albany Ledger*, February 2, 9, 18, 1857. Crane, "Joseph Wright," 235-236. Pettit, too, was provided for. It was understood that some judicial position would be offered him by the incoming administration, either in the territories or in the new federal district expected to be created in Indiana. *Ledger*, February 2, 1857. *New*

Anyone could foresee that this discrepancy would cause future problems if Wright were not tendered a cabinet appointment. This was especially the case because Indiana was all but promised a place in the cabinet for its effective support of Buchanan both at the Democratic National Convention and in the November election. Actually, it was Jesse Bright who was most often mentioned for that position. As early as November 1, 1856, before Buchanan was even elected, the *New York Herald* had Bright slated to head the Interior Department, and it was widely believed that winter in and out of Washington that he would be tendered a place. Historian Roy Nichols maintained that Buchanan seriously considered Bright for a post, even at the expense of angering Douglas, but it was understood that the position would only be offered if Bright failed to secure his reelection to the Senate. Here lies, perhaps, part of the reason for Bright's unwillingness to fully accommodate Wright. No doubt Bright did not want to see his archrival at the center of power anyway, but he must have been doubly concerned lest the refusal of the Indiana state Senate to go into joint session deny him his reelection. In that case, he may well have had to claim the cabinet post as his own. As it turned out, the Democratic Indiana state senators alone met with the Indiana House and held a somewhat suspect election that easily selected Bright and Fitch. Quite correctly the Opposition press denounced this irregular procedure, but the Democratic press, including the *New Albany Ledger*, defended it on the ground that the legislature composed a quorum. For good measure Norman also wrote that "there can be little doubt of the fact that the refusal of the Black Republican members of our legislature to consent to go into the election of U.S. Senators was the result of interference of persons outside the State, and was planned by the great abolition leaders of the North and East." But the Opposition did not need outside interference merely to copy the Democratic politics of 1855.[7]

Bright's election, though certain to be challenged in the United States Senate, left Wright as the leading candidate for Indiana's place in the cabinet. Yet, other Hoosier names had also appeared in the national press. Throughout December, the *New York Herald* correspondent, believing that Bright would indeed choose to go back to the Senate, brought out the name of William H. English as a fit substitute. This correspondent had correctly placed Lewis Cass in State and Howell Cobb in the Treasury, and he "looked carefully through [his] horoscope," and rightly predicted Isaac Toucey and Aaron Brown among the appointees (although

---

Albany Weekly Tribune, February 4, 1857. English may also have been in on this deal-making as well, because he wrote Wright in mid-November asking the governor if he were "likely to be at home about the 27th or 28th Inst." English went on to say, "I enquire because I should like to see you for a few moments before going to Washington and will take Indianapolis on my route if you are likely to be at home." WHE to Joseph Wright, November 19, 1856, Wright Papers, Indiana State Library.

7. Van Der Weele, "Jesse Bright," 192. *New York Herald* quoted in *New Albany Weekly Tribune*, November 19, 1856. Nichols, *Disruption*, 70. Van Der Weele, *"Jesse Bright,"* 193-200. *Paoli Eagle*, February 12, 1857. *Weekly Tribune*, February 18, 1857. *New Albany Ledger*, February 10, 16, 1857.

he had them in the wrong positions). English, who by this time was in Washington awaiting the start of Congress, wrote his wife hopeful that "no definite idea can be formed yet about the Cabinet or anything else, and *I am just in the condition not to be surprised at anything which may happen.*" The *New Albany Ledger*, having noticed the *Herald's* prediction, appeared somewhat stunned, stating that English was "yet a very young man, and such positions are usually conferred only on the middle-age and old." Yet Norman was quick to add that English was "energetic, firm, industrious," qualities appropriate for a cabinet member. This contrasted sharply with the *Indianapolis Journal's* assessment. Mr. English, the Republican *Journal* opined, "has never shown himself to possess the least capacity for discharging administrative duties," a pretty tepid criticism. The *Journal* completed its comments by ignoring any fair-minded assessment of English's abilities and instead focused on the congressman's new beard and signature capability, maintaining that "the only distinguishing qualities manifested by him is a capacity for making money and for giving a happy turn to his hair whiskers."[8]

Actually, despite the *Herald's* promotion, it appears that English was never seriously considered for a position in Buchanan's administration. Nowhere in Roy Nichols's discussion of the president's cabinet-making is he mentioned, and after the Wright-Bright agreement of January 30 it would have been especially treacherous if senator Bright had allowed another Hoosier into the cabinet before Wright. In early February, Samuel Crowe wrote English that for the sake of "the Young Democracy of the State," he should press his claims for a post. "This is not alone my opinion, but the opinion of numbers of your warm political and personal friends." But considering Bright's delicate position in relation to the Wright agreement, English was not likely to embarrass his mentor. Moreover, he would write his wife in January that "I want nothing from his [Buchanan's] administration and *should ask nothing*—I have had much more already than falls to the lot of most men, and especially that of my own age." At any rate, in the end, much to Indiana's chagrin, neither Bright, nor Wright, nor any other Hoosier was invited into Buchanan's cabinet. By February 21, the Interior Department had been filled by Jacob Thompson of Pennsylvania, and by Buchanan's inauguration only the positions of navy secretary and attorney general remained open. On March 6, those two were filled—one by a New Englander and the other by Buchanan's close friend, Jeremiah S. Black.[9]

On March 10, it was left to the *New Albany Ledger* to sum up Indiana's disappointment and the reasons therefor:

---

8. William French to WHE, December 2, 1856, English Papers. *New York Herald*, in *English Scrapbook*, 74. WHE to Mardulia, December 7, 1856, English Papers. *New Albany Ledger*, December 9, 1856. *Indianapolis Journal*, in *Ledger*, December 9, 1856.

9. Nichols, *Disruption*, 65-84. S.S. Crowe to WHE, February 5, 1857; WHE to Mardulia, January 25, 1857, English Papers. Nichols, *Disruption*, 79, 84.

> Within a month after the presidential election if anyone had said that
> Mr. Buchanan would not have conferred a Cabinet appointment upon
> Indiana, the unlucky individual would have been set down as demented
> or Mr. Buchanan set down as a very ungrateful man. [But] we have our-
> selves only to blame. Local feuds and jealousies and rivalries have pre-
> vented our state from receiving the reward to which her great service and
> proud position justly entitle her.

Party division indeed was the underlying factor in Indiana's lost opportunity, and
it is indeed a fact that Bright never pressed the claims of any Hoosier but himself,
and *that* for a short time at best. Soon after he was 'reelected' to the Senate, Bright
visited Buchanan at his homestead in Wheatland directly on the heels of a visit
by John G. Davis. Davis had gone to present governor Wright's claims personally
to the president-elect; Bright's visit, besides informing Buchanan of his decision
to retain his Senate seat, was used to counter Davis's arguments. When Wright's
son-in-law, Austin M. Puett, traveled to Wheatland immediately after Bright to
head off any damage, Buchanan informed him that "a designation from Indiana"
had already stated that the caucus agreement did not mean the cabinet. A few
days later, the *Washington Union*, essentially the organ of the new administration,
wrote that the phrase "first-class appointment" was "clearly intended to be some
appointment outside the Capital."[10]

About a month after Buchanan's inauguration, Bright wrote English that he
had never "urged any particular man for a cabinet position from Indiana after Mr.
Buchanan reached Washington." Thus Wright was not recommended for the still
open spots in the Justice and Navy departments. Cryptically, Bright added that
he "was asked to do so and declined for reasons entirely satisfying to myself." All
this evidence seems to prove that the senator never intended to present Wright's
appointment, despite pressure from some members of the Hoosier Democracy.

---

10. *New Albany Ledger*, March 10, 1857. Crane, "Joseph Wright," 237. Nichols, *Disruption*, 78. Van Der Weele,
   "Jesse Bright," 204-205. Crane, "Joseph Wright," 237-238. John G. Davis had visited Buchanan pressing
   Wright's claims partly because he received a plethora of letters from those in the February Democratic caucus expressing the fact that although it was true that it was then deemed "indelicate" to demand Buchanan
   give Wright a Cabinet position, that was the post that many Democrats had in mind when designating a
   "first-class appointment." See Aquilla Jones [state treasurer] to Davis, February 20, 1857; Michael Branson
   to Davis, February 20, 1857; Abram Hammond to Davis, February 21, 1857; A.M. Puett to Davis, February 25, 1857, John G. Davis Papers, Indiana Historical Society, Indianapolis, Indiana. Leroy Woods, a
   representative from Clark County and a member of the caucus, plainly maintained about the "arrangement"
   that he had "no hesitation in saying that…*clearly* and *honestly*…we were recommending him to a Cabinet
   office…and a large majority of the caucus members understand the same." Leroy Woods to Davis, March
   4, 1857, Davis Papers. Interestingly, back in November, 1856, Wright had written that the "news of the
   day" that northwesterner Lewis Cass was to be in the Cabinet as secretary of state led him to believe that
   Buchanan "will not likely take one from Indiana." Joseph Wright to Henry Wise [governor of Virginia],
   November 2, 1856, Wright Papers, Indiana Historical Society.

He may have protested to Thomas Hendricks that "I have tried in good faith in all that I have done," but that was not the way the Wright forces saw it. As the year passed into June and Wright still had not been tendered any appointment at all, Democratic newspapers from northern Indiana began to abuse Bright mercilessly. Even the *New Albany Ledger* later admitted it had doubts whether Bright would honor his bargain. *Paoli Eagle* editor Henry Comingore, more servile to Bright than was Norman, denounced the senator's abusers as "organs of a faction [and] hardly dry behind the ears," but the cries of treachery would not be silenced.[11]

Finally, on June 3, the news reached Indiana that Wright had been offered appointment as ambassador to Prussia. Although this may have been reasonably considered a "first-class appointment," the partisans of governor Wright were not to be satisfied so easily. The *Vincennes Sun* noted that "but for the successful efforts of a few scheming demagogues he [Wright] would have been where the true Democracy of Indiana wish that he should be—in the U.S. Senate or in Mr. Buchanan's cabinet." Some of Wright's supporters even went so far as to advise him to decline the appointment, but on June 19 the *Indiana State Sentinel* carried the news that Wright had decided to accept. This did not end the controversy. For the next several months, backers of the ambassador-designate, including principally congressman Davis, son-in-law Puett, and Indiana Supreme Court reporter Gordon Tanner, launched a blistering campaign of abuse aimed at Bright. In an open letter to Bright published in many Democratic newspapers, Tanner boldly accused the senator of using "scribbling parasites" of the party press to do his bidding: "They have no praise but for you, and your inferior associates. They have nothing but gibes and sneers for the Democrat who does not bow down with them and worship you. Service to the party, and sacrifices for its success command no recognition from them, unless homage to your sublime inferiority is added as a crowning grace." Astonishingly, the Tanner letter was justified by a large part of the Democratic press. Even the *Sentinel* took note of it. Comingore, contrary to his earlier advice that newspaper editors should steer clear of controversy calculated to "result in the injury of the Democratic cause," labeled Tanner a

---

11. Jesse Bright to WHE, April 16, 1857, English Papers. Jesse Bright to Thomas Hendricks, February 23, 1857, Bright Papers. *Paoli Eagle*, June 4, 1857. *New Albany Ledger*, June 8, 1857. *Eagle*, June 4, 1857. Wright himself greatly distrusted Bright to carry out any agreement, as he understood that despite the deal, "[i]f, however, my enemies in Indiana are privately at work to defeat me, all I ask of the President is to know the same." Joseph Wright to [unintelligible], February 2, 1857, Wright Papers, Indiana Historical Society. A few months earlier he took the measure of Bright as a politician by noting that "despite his [h]aving been a Senator for twelve years, he has never made a speech [not actually true, but close], written a report, nor as far as I know taken a part in any public measure (except Texas stock)." He also made clear Bright's doughface credentials by noting the senator's votes "against the Wilmot Proviso and for the Fugitive Slave Law." Joseph Wright to Henry Wise, November 25, 1856, Wright Papers, Indiana Historical Society. Thomas Clark, state representative from Madison County, colorfully wrote that he "had no more confidence in Jesse D. Bright's declarations of his adherence to the compromise effected that night [in caucus] than I had in the Devil." Thos. G. Clark to John G. Davis, February 20, 1857, Davis Papers.

"disappointed fool." But the *Paoli Eagle* was already considered a scribbling minion of Jesse Bright's, and the Wright editors had already attributed Comingore's opinions to the fact that Tanner and associates had attacked "one of his masters."[12]

Interestingly, Bright's reaction to all of this was rather mild. In late August, while English was in Kansas locating land warrants, Bright wrote him that "everything looks well for our party in this State. A few traitors have been trying to raise some excitement, but their efforts have proven a dead failure. In short, the Wright and Co. concern have failed." Bright predicted that with their "cowardly leader" overseas, "the other partners [would] have [to go] into liquidation." Subsequent events would prove this assessment to be extremely optimistic. The Wright clique, unlike the Bright one, was not top-heavy; it rested on the broader base of rural Democrats who recognized that Wright had "done more for the agricultural interest of Indiana than any man who trod her soil."[13] And it was not composed of doughfaces. Quite contrary to Bright's triumphant tone, these Democrats were not about to surrender, and the persistent factionalism that had divided the antebellum Indiana Democracy was about to produce its rather unexpected denouement.

2.

While the Indiana Democrats squabbled over senatorial politics, the lame duck session of the 34th Congress met in Washington. As did many sessions during an interregnum, this one concentrated on politics. One of the issues to arise within this context concerned an examination of the meaning of popular sovereignty, and the way in which it was used in the recent campaign and in Kansas itself. In the 1856 elections, northern Democrats had continued to maintain that free soil was well served by the doctrine. They generally argued that no matter what events preceded statehood, when Kansas and other territories were ready to come into the Union, the preponderance of northern emigrants would ensure that they came in as free states. Congressman John Sherman of Ohio and other Republicans noted that such statements rather ignored the strength of the pro-slavery partisans in Kansas. In essence, Republicans charged, the northern Democrats had argued during the campaign that popular sovereignty would save the ter-

---

12. *New Albany Ledger,* June 4, 1857. *Vincennes Sun* in *Paoli Eagle,* June 11, 1857. *Ledger,* June 8, 1857. *Indiana State Sentinel,* June 19, 1857. Crane, "Joseph Wright," 241. Gordon Tanner to Jesse Bright, July 2, 1857, Bright Papers. J.B. Norman to David McClure, July 8, 1857, English Papers. *Eagle,* July 30, 1857. Comingore probably called Tanner a disappointed fool because Tanner was angry with Bright for having allowed his campaign sheet to fall in arrears. *Ledger,* July 1, 1857; *Eagle,* June 11, 1857.

13. J.M. Whitfield to WHE, May 9, 1857; Jesse Bright to WHE, April 16, 1857; WHE to Mardulia, January 18, 1857; Jesse Bright to WHE, August 19, 1857, English Papers. *Vincennes Sun* in *Paoli Eagle,* June 11, 1857.

ritories for freedom when they clearly knew that their southern colleagues were assiduously working to make Kansas a slave state. Because of the Democratic support for territorial sovereignty, Republicans argued, should the 'slavocracy' prevail and somehow send a Kansas constitution to Congress that sanctioned slavery, the northern Democrats, despite their repeated assurances to their constituents that Kansas would become a free state, would be forced to approve it.[14]

Essentially, the Republicans pursued this argument for two reasons. First of all, they wished to show the Northern voter that popular sovereignty and the Democratic Party could not be trusted to keep the West free. But secondly, they wished to exacerbate the differences between the northern and southern wings of the Democratic Party itself. Ever since the passage of the Kansas-Nebraska Act it was well known among those who cared to examine it that northern and southern Democrats disagreed upon the fundamental question of when popular sovereignty allowed territorial citizens to abolish slavery. The typical northern Democrat, besides often claiming that the territories were "naturally" free (so that only a positive law could fashion slavery upon them), argued that the territorial legislature could at any time pass laws abolishing or legalizing slavery. On the other hand, southern Democrats argued that the territories were "naturally" open to slaves or any other property, and slavery could not be abolished by a territorial legislature. Only when the territorial citizens framed their state constitution, they declared, could they abolish slavery. Because the pro-slavery party had been in control of the regular Kansas legislature since its inception, these differences had not yet come into practical conflict. But the Republicans hoped that by repeating the charge that the northern Democracy was hypocritical in its assurances that Kansas would become a free state, they might be able to bait one of the northern Democratic congressmen to defend their position thereby giving the Republicans a chance to illustrate the Democracy's inconsistencies.[15]

Few northern Democrats had either the ability or inclination to so engage the opposition; most probably felt that little was to be gained by the attempt. But William English apparently believed that to allow the Republican arguments to go unchallenged not only enhanced their veracity but greatly threatened to

---

14. *CG, 34-3*, 55, 100, 138. *Appendix to the CG, 34-3*, 92.

15. For the typical northern Democratic position see English's speech of March 31, 1854, described in Chapter 3, pp.122-127 For a good explication of the southern position, note R. M. T. Hunter's letter to Shelton F. Leake in October, 1857: "Most of the southern men (of whom I was one) believed that property in slaves was as much entitled to the protection of law in the Territories as property in anything else; but whilst the northern friends of the Kansas act would not concede this, they agreed to unite in repealing the Mo. restriction so as to remove the ban under which the domestic institutions of the south had been placed by federal legislation. Accordingly, a bill was passed upon the principle of non-intervention, in regard to slavery, so far as the general government was concerned, and which left the whole subject within control of the people of these territories, *when they should apply for admission as state* [emphasis added]." October 16, 1867, in Ambler, *Correspondence of Hunter*, 238.

destroy the harmony of the Democratic Party by default. English understood that a debate raged within the southern Democracy between those who believed that "popular sovereignty was as bad as Sewardism," and those who reasoned that the rights of slaveholders could be best protected by supporting northern conservative Democrats in their battle with Republicans. On the one side were the so-called 'fire eaters,' essentially heirs to Calhoun, who viewed all northerners as unfriendly to the South and unreliable on the slavery issue; on the other side were the moderates who hoped that conservative sentiment was just strong enough in the North to defeat what they considered extremism and allow the Democratic Party to control the national government. The moderates had won a victory, slim as it was, with Buchanan's triumph in 1856, and in order for the Democratic Party to remain harmoniously conservative, English believed that he had to deny Republican allegations that the northern Democracy was unalterably free soil. While this might run the risk of further labeling northern Democrats as insufficiently anti-slavery up North, English apparently believed that this was the price to pay for a united Democratic Party. Without that, the Union itself was endangered.[16]

These were the stakes of conservatism, and on December 17 English rose to their defense. His basic plan was to illustrate that great divergences in policy existed not primarily between Democrats, but between Democrats and Republicans. Using Indiana as an example, he first noted that the opposition state platform "utterly repudiated" the Kansas-Nebraska Act, while the Hoosier Democracy effectively resolved to stand by its promise to allow future slave states into the Union if their citizens so demanded. There was no hypocrisy here, English argued, for although "I may prefer, and do prefer, that Kansas shall be a free state," the Indiana Democracy approved of popular sovereignty and congressional non-interference in contradistinction to the Republican principle of congressional restriction. And it did so with the full realization that such reliance on the will of the territorial citizens might work to produce a slave state in the future. Abstractly, English's argument was sound, but in practice both he and many other Democrats had assured their constituents that the profitability of slavery in the newly organized part of the Louisiana Purchase, as well as those of the Mexican Cession, was climatically impossible, and by supporting the policy of popular sovereignty, they could accomplish the same ends as congressional restriction without the rancor

---

16. English's proclivity toward Democratic harmony may be gleaned from his speech in March, 1856 in the 34th Congress's first session (see pp.192-195). The Sewardism quote is from William B. Hesseltine, ed., *Three against Lincoln: Murat Halstead Reports the Caucuses of 1860* (Baton Rouge: Louisiana State University Press, 1960), 6. Seward, of course, was the considered radical anti-slavery senator from New York. South Carolina Congressman James Orr was a good example of what English, for the moment, would consider a southern moderate. Roger P. Leemhuis, *James L. Orr and the Sectional Conflict* (Washington, D.C.: University Press of America, 1979), 30, 31, 63. Joel L. Silbey, "The Southern National Democrats, 1849-1861," *Mid-America*, 47, no. 3 (July 1965), 181-182.

of Republicanism. That the Indiana Democracy had rather purged their Wilmot element then, as English further averred, was helpful but superfluous.[17]

The opposition was quite willing to illustrate that English's conclusions were specious. Humphrey Marshall, Know-Noting congressman from the Louisville area of Kentucky who had tangled with English before on federal transportation bills affecting their mutual region (and had in 1850 interestingly succeeded John W. Davis as commissioner to China), was the first to respond. Attempting to destroy English's claims of a united Democracy, Marshall asked him an obvious question: "When the gentleman of Indiana speaks of the freedom of the people of a territory [to legislate upon slavery] does he mean that the people when in a territorial condition have that freedom?" In other words: does a territory have the right to legislate against slavery before it frames its state constitution? English, of course, held that it could, but in anticipation of Marshall's rejoinder, he acknowledged that many southerners held that slavery may only be restricted "when the people meet for the purpose of framing a state constitution." He still tried to maintain, however, that "a portion of [southerners] hold as I do that the right of the people begins at an earlier period." Marshall quickly responded that "there are very few who believe that," and English was forced to admit that he was "sorry there were not more." In fact, it would have been difficult to find even one southern Democrat who at least publicly would admit to English's construction. In an interesting addendum, English attempted to logically show why his interpretation was the correct one:

> Unless the people of a territory had the right under their territorial government, to decide this question for themselves, I could not conceive the necessity for the repeal of the Missouri restriction. The people, under that law, could establish or prohibit slavery, when they came to be admitted as a State, just as well as under [the southern] construction of the Kansas bill. Then what was gained?[18]

This was rather an attempt to win Southerners over to his position, but it was analytically flawed. Under the Missouri Compromise no slaves could enter the Louisiana Purchase territory north of latitude 36 degrees 30 minutes, which included the eventual boundaries of Kansas and Nebraska. This made it impossible that any slaveholders would enter that territory (at least with their slaves) and therefore highly unlikely that the ensuing state constitutional convention would sanction slavery. The obvious "gain" of the Kansas-Nebraska Act, certainly from

---

17. *Appendix to the CG, 34-3,* 106, 107.

18. Dubin, *U.S. Congressional Elections,* 172; Parsons, *U.S. Congressional Districts,* 58-59. http://history.state. gov/departmenthistory/people/chiefsofmission/china. *Appendix to the CG,* 107.

many southerners' viewpoint, was the permission granted to slaveholders to take their chattel into previously restricted territory. This change not only treated their peculiar institution equally, a point of honor, but materially offered the possibility of extensive southern migration and the later real possibility of a new slave state. That English ignored this point either illustrates his disrespect for southern analytical powers or that he lacked some of his own.

English's addendum allowed Ohio Republican John Sherman to insightfully propose a question that forced English to acknowledge a fundamental disagreement among Democrats. "Prior to the prohibition of slavery in a Territory by a territorial government," he asked, "have the citizens of the South the right to take their slaves there and hold them as such?" In other words, are, or are not, the territories "naturally" free? This spoke to such an elemental disagreement between northern and southern Democrats, that English naturally had difficulty giving a definitive answer. "My individual judgement," he initially responded, "is that slavery is not carried into the Territory of the U.S. under the operation of the Constitution." But he added that his own interpretation of constitutional law might not be correct, and in anticipation of the much discussed possibility that the United States Supreme Court might decide the question in the case of *Dred Scott v. Sandford*, he stated that he was "willing to acquiesce in that decision, whatever it may be." Pressed by Sherman to admit that his interpretation of the constitution differed from that of the southern Democracy's, English admitted that it did "with a portion of it." Consequently he was once again forced to take refuge in the fact that "the question is a constitutional one, and the Democratic party, North and South, will acquiesce in whatever may be the decision of the court."[19]

Having taken refuge under the justices' robes, English was further forced into evasion by Hoosier lame-duck congressman Harvey Scott. Asked three times by Scott "whether he and his party in Indiana hold that slavery is lawfully in Kansas at this time," English essentially refused to answer. Replying disingenuously that he had "never sufficiently examined [the laws of Kansas] in reference to that question," he went on to hypothetically note that "if slavery be there legally, and by the will of the people, I shall not interfere with it."[20] There was a cleverness to these words but a greater dishonesty. "If" was the key word because it essentially referred to whether the election to the Shawnee Mission Kansas legislature was proper or fraudulent. But of course the Pierce administration, and the Democratic Party in general, had already refused to admit any fraud in the legislature's election, considering it the legitimate lawmaking body of Kansas and considering its proslavery laws legal. Although Democrats were willing to support the Toombs Bill 'compromise', until and unless that bill was passed, and depending

---

19. *Ibid.,* 107-108.

20. *Ibid.,* 108.

on the results of its suggested investigation, the Shawnee Mission government remained legitimate. In a real sense, that legislature, the Democrats maintained, represented popular sovereignty realized in Kansas. All politicians were aware of the pro-slavery legislation it had passed, and, as Scott knew, consistency dictated that English thereupon acknowledge that, at least for the moment, slavery existed in Kansas. But he could not acknowledge that slavery existed in Kansas without contravening all the promises of freedom he had made to his constituents. And he could not admit that slavery was *not* legal in Kansas without contradicting his willingness to uphold popular sovereignty even if it led to condoning the spread of slavery. He no doubt suspected, of course, that the Shawnee Mission legislature had been fraudulently elected, but he had always voted contrary to that suspicion, and had thereby hoisted himself on the horns of his present dilemma. Indeed, in his zeal to present a harmonious party, he could choose neither horn.

Ultimately, the actual way he could harmonize the Party and attempt to distinguish the northern Democracy from the free soil proclivities of the Republicans was to use a racial frame of reference. Near the end of his speech he played this card. "The lowest and most Godforsaken nigger-stealing Abolitionists," he noted, "were found [in Indiana] doing battle against the national Democracy, side by side with my colleague [Republican Will Cumback] and the leaders of the Black Republican Party." At this point English brought out the story of William Anderson (see p.257–258), maintaining that no honorable gentleman—certainly no Democrat—would ever associate themselves on the stump "with a Negro."[21] This argument was one that southern moderates could use to their advantage. It suggested a common alliance of all Democrats, North and South, not only against abolitionism, but more importantly against the Republican tendency to treat the African-American as at least civilly equal. It suggested a tack, considering the deep racism in much of the North, on which the Democratic Party could unite to prevent the success of Republicanism. For all the constitutional arguments so often expressed, it was probably true that a key difference between Republicans and Democrats concerned to what lengths a 'superior' race was willing to go in legislating restraints on an 'inferior' one. It was not that most Republicans disagreed with Democrats on whether blacks were inferior to whites, it was rather the degree to which they stressed that point and the societal actions they were willing to allow in recognition of it. When Abraham Lincoln later turned his debates with Stephen Douglas into one over ethics, not constitutional differences, he clearly

---

21. *Ibid.* The virulence by which some Democrats expressed the idea of the inferiority of the black race can be evidenced by this comment of Henry Comingore's in his *Paoli Eagle:* "There are some who assert that the nigger is, by nature, equal in intellect with the Anglo-Saxon; and that, had he the same advantages, he would raise himself to as high a notch on the scale of humanity. We shouldn't wonder if they can prove it, just as easy as I could prove that my little terrier-dog knows more than I do. He can 'smell a rat' any time o'night—and that passeth my comprehension." *Eagle,* February 12, 1857.

stated the essential difference between the two parties. And William English, at least subconsciously, appeared to recognize this; as time went on, he would increasingly return to this theme until by 1860 it dominated his arguments.

Unable to make congruent the irreconcilable constitutional and logical positions of the northern and southern Democracy, it is no wonder English turned to this emotionally cultural unifier. In the peroration of his effort, he retreated into the platitudes of conservatism. "We want a firm, conservative, national administration," he exhorted, "which I have the confidence we shall have—one looking to the confidence of the *whole* people and the perpetuation of the Union under the Constitution as paramount objects—conciliatory in its character—respecting the rights of all and just to all, but firm and decided in rebuking sectionalism and fanaticism, no matter from what quarter it may come."[22] These were admirable sentiments, but Buchanan would prove to be neither firm nor impartial, and English would soon have to make a number of unpleasant choices that he had so long avoided. Whether he suspected that or not is difficult to say.

Remarkably, yet predictably, the Democratic press lavished praise on its young champion. Perhaps because they were simply awed by the courage the northern Democrat displayed in attempting such a thankless task, editors from New Hampshire to Texas applauded the effort. One newspaper claimed that English's speech "was a decided hit, and seemed to take the House and all who heard it by storm," and the New York *Banner of Liberty*, confusing him with his uncle, wrote that "Col. English is a representative of whom his constituents may be proud." At least as proud were *the New Albany Ledger* and the *Paoli Eagle*, as not only did they print his effort in full, but they both also consistently published favorable notices whenever they located them. Most Democratic sheets believed that English outshone his "inquisitors," as one put it, "like Gulliver among the Lilliputians." The *Louisville Times* called him "evidently one of the very best intellects on the floor of Congress," and wrote that "he has proven himself a full match for the most powerful minds of the opposition." The editor claimed that "Marshall, Sherman, Scott, and Cumback could not overturn his invincible positions...Every issue they raised was fairly met and recoiled upon them." From New York the *Daily News*'s Washington correspondent declared that English thwarted the opposition: "[He] boldly maintained himself in debate, and vindicated the nationality of the Democracy of the North." If nothing else, the effort made him a congressman to watch. "English is a growing man in public favor," one Kentucky editor wrote, "and has a brilliant career before him. There is no station which he is not equal, and none within the gift of his state or Union that we would not be proud to see him fill." From as far away as Texas another editor predicted for English "a high destiny," and the *Fort Wayne Jeffersonian* hyperbolically summed it all up by

---

22. *CG, 34-3*, 108.

noting that despite his youth, "Mr. English's name is known from one end of the nation to the other."[23]

To his considerable credit, from the time he entered Congress English had refused to duck the slavery issue. As a reward he had steadily gained prestige within the national party, yet any objective observer could not have failed to see that his latest effort essentially miscarried. Not only had he failed to illustrate the consistency of the Party on the issue of popular sovereignty, he also failed to convince even the southern moderates that northern Democrats were not essentially anti-slavery and a minor species of free soil. Of all the plaudits of English's speech, only one came from a Deep South newspaper, the *Austin State Gazette,* and even this one was conditional and incomplete. The *Gazette's* editor, John Marshall, primarily had his own self-interest in mind. In a private letter to English he offered to promote the young Hoosier's political career by helping to place him "on the rising ground with the Southern Democracy." Although admitting that "sectionally we have our peculiar likes and dislikes," Marshall specifically offered to procure for English profuse letters of introduction to southern representatives and senators—but only if the congressman worked to help make Marshall agent to examine the U.S. Depositories. Marshall naturally saw this bargain as "mutually advantageous," and he was clever enough to sweeten the bait by stating he would use his new position to strengthen the harmony between the northern and southern Democracy. The letter was marked "private"; one gets the impression that the Indiana congressman was not the only representative Marshall solicited. While one editor maintained that some southern representatives had sent copies of English's speech to their constituents, neither the *New Albany Ledger* nor the *Paoli Eagle* ever reprinted encomiums from any other deep southern newspaper but the *Gazette.*[24]

In an attempt to claim that English's effort did produce acceptance in the Deep South, the Washington correspondent of the *New York Daily News* remarked that none other than Preston Brooks declared his concurrence with English "in all his views except those as to popular sovereignty." A 20th century analogy of this endorsement might be that Ralph Nader concurred with all the views of the president of General Motors, except those as to car safety. The *Daily News* correspondent must have realized the nonsense of his statement, for he quickly added that the differences between English and Brooks were of little consequence

---

23. English Scrapbook, 72-73. *New York Banner of Liberty,* December 17, 1856, in *New Albany Ledger,* January 19, 1857. *Louisville Times,* in *Paoli Eagle,* February 26, 1857. *New York Daily News,* in *Ledger,* December 26, 1856. *Austin State Gazette,* in English Scrapbook, *73.* *Fort Wayne Jeffersonian,* in English Scrapbook, 72.

24. John Marshall to WHE, February 9, 1857, English Papers. English Scrapbook, 72. The *Maryland Republican* applauded English's speech, but only to heap abuse on Humphrey Marshall; Know-Nothingism was strong in Maryland, and Republicans there were battling Know-Nothings for control of their fusion. *New Albany Ledger,* January 19, 1857.

because their views could be "easily reconciled by the judiciary." Again the refuge was to the *Dred Scott* case, one on which each section of the Democratic Party had increasingly come to look upon to sustain its views. President-elect Buchanan himself had high hopes that the Supreme Court would resolve the issue. As has been well documented, he lobbied with at least two justices to get the Court first to decide the case before his inaugural, and, second, to resolve it in line with the southern position when it became apparent that a so disposed seven man majority might be fashioned. Although the Court was unable to announce its decision before March 4, Buchanan, in full knowledge of its main holding, disingenuously announced that he would abide by whatever the justices determined. Two days later, on March 6, the decision was publically rendered.[25]

The background and holding of *Dred Scott v. Sandford* are well discussed in many historical works. Suffice it to say that the slave Scott, with the aid of numerous abolitionists, was suing for his freedom on the ground that in the 1830s he had once resided with his master in the free state of Illinois for two years and the free territory of Wisconsin for some time thereafter. He argued that by residing in these areas that prohibited slavery, he had inferentially and legally become free. Through numerous appeals and the transference of the case from state to federal courts, the United States Supreme Court first heard the argument in 1856. Initially the Court was prepared to dodge the substantive questions involved by merely procedurally denying Scott's right as a slave to sue in federal court. But two of the northern justices on the Court were determined to file opinions based upon the Republican proposition that Congress had full power to legislate on the question of slavery in the territories and that, therefore, the congressional act of the Missouri Compromise (extant during Scott's sojourn) worked to grant Scott his freedom from his residence in Wisconsin territory. So challenged, the Court's southern majority decided to counter the concept of plenary congressional power and wound up declaring that the Missouri Compromise, which had been on the books for 34 years before repealed by the Kansas-Nebraska Act, was, after all, unconstitutional on the ground that it deprived slaveholders of their equal right to take their property into the federal territories. That is, it was contrary to the Fifth Amendment's stipulation that "no person shall…be deprived of life, liberty, or property without due process of law." As Chief Justice Roger Taney put it, "an act of Congress which deprives a citizen of the United States of his liberty or property merely because he came himself or brought his property into a particular territory

---

25. *Daily News* quoted in *New Albany Ledger,* December 2, 1856. As to Buchanan's machinations, see his correspondence with Justices Catron and Grier in John B. Moore, ed., *The Works of James Buchanan: Comprising his Speeches, State Papers, and Private Correspondence, vol. 10* (1911; repr., New York: Antiquarian Press Ltd., 1960), fn. 1, 106-108.

of the United States, and who had committed no offense against the laws, could hardly be dignified with the name of due process of law."[26]

By declaring that Congress had no power to restrict slavery in the territories, the Court had of course denied the constitutionality of the essential part of the Republican Party's platform. But it also implied that the Northern Democratic reading of popular sovereignty was also unconstitutional, for, as Taney wrote, "if Congress itself cannot [exclude slavery]—if it is beyond the powers conferred on the federal government—it will be admitted, we presume, that it could not authorize a territorial government to do so." In other words: a territorial legislature, the mere creation of Congress, could not do what Congress could not do. Other justices in their concurring opinions were not so sure, but Taney's opinion was generally held to be the Opinion of the Court (though Republicans believed much of the holding was *obiter dicta*.)[27] Logically, then, the *Dred Scott* decision completely supported the southern Democratic understanding of popular sovereignty. In the first place, the territories were 'naturally' open to slavery; in the second, territorial governments could not prohibit slavery from their boundaries, and, therefore, the first time that slavery may be so restricted was at the point the territorial citizens adopted their state constitution. In English's speech he had vowed to abide by the Court's resolution of these vexing questions, and at least he now had to admit that his understanding of the Kansas-Nebraska Act was constitutionally specious, and, indeed, that his insistence in 1854 that Douglas explicitly include the right of popular sovereignty in the bill was remarkably superfluous.

Aside from its constitutional implications, the *Dred Scott* decision seemed destined to have a direct effect on the settlement of Nebraska and the Mexican Cession territories. But as it pertained to Kansas, events there had proceeded at such a rapid pace that the decision appeared to come too late to have any practical results. That is, in the same month as the decision was handed down the pro-slavery territorial legislature, now meeting in Lecompton, had arranged to hold an election in June for delegates to a state constitutional convention. No longer germane was whether slavery already existed in Kansas or whether the territorial legislature could outlaw it there, for apparently the territory would soon be at the stage when it passed into statehood. For the next four years *Dred Scott* would continue to embarrass the northern Democrats, and they would be forced to adopt specious solutions, like Douglas's so-called Freeport Doctrine (see p.297), to ac-

---

26. The Dred Scott case is discussed in myriad secondary works, but the two I found most illuminating were Stanley I. Kutler, ed., *The Dred Scott Decision: Law or Politics?* (Boston: Houghton, Mifflin Co., 1967) and, cited earlier on the territorial question, especially and exhaustively, Fehrenbacher, *The Dred Scott Decision.* Chief Justice Taney's opinion may be found online at http://www.loc.gov/resource/llst.022. Accessed March 20, 2019.

27. Ibid. On the point that other justices were "not so sure" of Taney's limitations on a territorial legislature, see Fehrenbacher, *Dred Scott,* 400, 404.

commodate it. But in the spring and summer of 1857, all eyes focused narrowly on Lecompton, which was not only the new capital of Kansas but also the designated site of the upcoming constitutional convention. Here, it appeared, the nation would discover whether or not English (and other northern Democrats) had indeed miscalculated when they promised their constituents that Kansas would not become a slave state. If so, English might be forced to uphold his other pledge made in his recent speech, that if the people of Kansas "decide that it shall be a slave state, I shall vote to admit her if I occupy a seat on this floor."[28]

3.

It was events in Kansas during Pierce's last few months in office that led the pro-slavery legislators to make plans for premature statehood. They acted swiftly, primarily because they understood that time was against them. Already most observers, including the third governor of Kansas, John Geary of Pennsylvania, believed that the territory possessed a clear free-state majority, and the upcoming spring migration was destined only to increase it. The proslavery forces could continue to pursue a policy of wholesale electoral fraud, but soon they would be so outnumbered that such machinations would no longer be viable. The time had come to bring Kansas into the Union as a slave state. As always, southerners saw the stakes as enormous. Back in 1855 David Atchison had predicted "if we win we carry slavery to the Pacific Ocean—if we fail we lose Missouri, Arkansas, and Texas, and all the territories." He warned that "the game must be played boldly." Almost two years later Thomas W. Thomas wrote Alexander Stephens, "Kansas must come in as a slave state or the cause of southern rights is dead."[29] The pro-slavery Kansas legislature understood its duty.

Meeting in January and February of 1857, the territorial legislature passed a law over governor Geary's veto authorizing registration of voters in March and a constitutional convention election in June. The early registration was obviously intended to exclude new migrants, and for good measure, the control of the whole

---

28. Nichols, *Disruption*, 113; Potter, *Impending Crisis*, 302; Allan Nevins, *The Emergence of Lincoln, vol. 1*, (1947; repr., New York and London: Charles Scribner's Sons, 1975), 137; Etcheson, *Bleeding Kansas*, 140, 141. *Appendix to the CG, 34-3*, 106-107.

29. By late summer, Howell Cobb confirmed the demographic fears of the pro-slavery party in Kansas by noting that "a large majority [in the territory] are against slavery," Cobb to Alexander Stephens, September 12, 1857, in Phillips, *Correspondence of Toombs, Stephens, Cobb*, 422. This particular legislature was actually the second official one elected in Kansas Territory, in October 1856. It was elected without free-state settler participation, as 'their' government was essentially in Topeka. Nevins, *Emergence of Lincoln, vol. 1*, 133-139; Potter, *Impending Crisis*, 300; Kenneth Stampp, *America in 1857: A Nation on the Brink* (New York and Oxford: Oxford University Press, 1990), 156. David Atchison to R.M.T. Hunter, April 4, 1855, in Ambler, ed., *Correspondence of Hunter*, 161. Thomas W. Thomas to Alexander Stephens, January 12, 1857, in Phillips, ed., *Correspondence of Toombs, Stephens, and Cobb*, 392.

electoral process was put in the hands of the legislatively appointed pro-slavery partisans. These conditions were clearly unacceptable to the free-staters, still 'organized' under the Topeka government, and it was unlikely that they would participate in the election. Also unsettling was the fact that the election law made no stipulation for submission of the constitution to the people of Kansas for ratification. The distinct possibility existed that an unrepresentative convention, once writing a constitution favorable to slavery, would bypass the electorate and send the document directly to a Congress dominated by southern Democrats and their northern allies.[30]

This was the situation on March 4 when Buchanan took over the presidency from Pierce. If at this juncture he had any policy for Kansas it was simply to bring it into the Union as a Democratic state in time for the election of 1860. Whether it came in as a free state or slave state was not as significant to him as its party affiliation, but certain actions soon after his inaugural showed that he initially believed it was at least important that Kansans as a whole have a fair chance to ratify its convention's product. In the first place, Buchanan assiduously sought the services of Robert J. Walker, James K. Polk's secretary of the treasury, as Kansas governor. Originally the President had considered Walker for Secretary of State, but a peculiar set of interests had forced him to choose Lewis Cass instead. Born in Pennsylvania, but since 1826 a citizen of Mississippi, Walker could most fairly be classified as a moderate among southern slave-owners. In many ways he resembled midwestern Jacksonian Democrats, including English. An ardent expansionist, heavily invested in railroad promotion and land schemes, he typified the Young America approach to politics. On the slavery issue he supported the basic essence of popular sovereignty as it applied to constitution-making. In a letter to Buchanan delineating his terms of acceptance, he wrote that "I understand that you and all your cabinet cordially concur in the opinion expressed by me, that the actual bona fide residents of the territory of Kansas, by a fair and regular vote, unaffected by fraud or violence, must be permitted in adopting their state constitution, to decide for themselves what shall be their social institutions." Buchanan appointed Walker with this express understanding. As late as July 12, Buchanan wrote the new governor that "on the question of submitting the constitution to the bona fide residents of Kansas, I am willing to stand or fall. It is the principle of the Kansas-Nebraska bill, the principle of popular sovereignty, and the principle at the foundation of all popular government." Such a forthright statement com-

---

30. Stampp, *1857*, 156; Nevins, *Emergence of Lincoln, vol. 1*, 137-138; Potter, *Impending Crisis*, 300. The so-called 'revisionist' historians of the 1930s and 1940s never mentioned that the machinery of the delegate election was to be controlled by the pro-slavery forces, implicitly criticizing the free-state boycott. See, for example Avery Craven, *The Coming of the Civil War*, 2nd ed. (Chicago and London: The University of Chicago Press, 1957; 1st ed., 1942.), 387-388, and George Fort Milton, *The Eve of Conflict: Stephen A. Douglas and the Needless War* (Boston and New York: Houghton-Mifflin, 1934), 265-266.

ported well with English's own earlier assessment of the president, made to his wife, that he had "great confidence in Mr. Buchanan as a man and a statesman." He did add that he "sincerely hope[d] my expectations may be realized."[31]

The choice of Walker for governor pleased neither the radical free-soilers of the North nor the more extreme pro-slaveryites of the South. But it did seem to satisfy the less extreme elements of both sections. At this point, then, Buchanan appeared to be following the moderate part of his Party supported by Democrats like William English, who desired foremost that majority rule on the slavery question be allowed to prevail in Kansas. Indeed, Walker's appointment was fully applauded by Stephen Douglas, who had strongly urged the Mississippian to accept. Buchanan himself had so decidedly desired Walker for the post that he agreed to allow him to choose his own secretary (Frederick P. Stanton of Tennessee), and to be backed by 1,500 troops under the command of William S. Harney. Through it all, Walker had a grand scheme to bring to Kansas continued peace and the reign of the Democratic Party. In essence, he planned to wed popular sovereignty to the acquisitive tendencies of Young America. Basic to this program was the inclusion of a gigantic grant of federal land, twice the size usually allotted to a new state, in Kansas's constitution. Such a grant, Walker reasoned, might salve the losers in the contest of whether Kansas became a free or slave state. It could be used to enrich many citizens, who, in anticipation of state land sales, would vote for the constitution despite their disagreement with the provisions affecting slavery. A fair vote on the constitution was essential to this scheme, but no better example could be noted for the primarily amoral approach to the slavery issue possessed by the moderate Democratic group.[32]

Needing to complete some business transactions back East, Walker did not leave for Kansas until May 1857, but Stanton set out immediately, and by mid-April he had taken up residence in Lecompton. Too late to influence a fair census and registration, Stanton could not convince the free-staters to participate in the June election for constitutional delegates. He did, however, attempt to keep their confidence by proclaiming that the convention ought to "in some form provide

---

31. Robert Toombs appears to have understood that at this point Buchanan's concern for the Democratic Party's success in Kansas superseded slavery's success when he noted months later that Buchanan's failure to fire governor Walker in the summer of 1857 was proof that "the rights of the south had been deliberately betrayed to build up the Democratic Party at the North." Toombs to Alexander Stephens, February 7, 1858, in Phillips, *Correspondence of Toombs, Stephens, and Cobb,* 430. Nichols, *Disruption,* 106-108, 69; Nevins, *Emergence of Lincoln, vol. 1,* 144-145; Stampp, *1857,* 159-160. Walker's letter to Buchanan, dated March 26, 1857, is in Nichols, *Disruption,* 107. Buchanan's July 12 reply is in Stampp, *1857,* 175. WHE to Mardulia, January 25, 1857, English Papers. Although Walker was probably Buchanan's first choice for secretary of state, the lukewarm attitude of some southerners, Howell Cobb's refusal to serve 'below' someone not clearly his senior, and the need to somehow reward a northerner amenable to both Douglas and Bright, persuaded the president-elect to choose Cass instead. Nichols, *Disruption,* 69-70, 75; Nevins, *Emergence of Lincoln, vol. 1,* 145.

32. Nevins, *Emergence, vol. 1,* 144-146. Stampp, *1857,* 160. Nichols, *Disruption,* 107, 112.

for submitting the great distracting question regarding their social institution, which has long agitated the people of Kansas, to a fair vote of all the actual *bona fide* residents of the territory." Though subsequent events may lend some ambiguity to Stanton's remarks, one month later, governor Walker arrived and made explicit his wishes, approved by Buchanan, in his inaugural address. "In no contingency," he said, "will Congress admit Kansas as a slave state or a free state unless a majority of the people shall first have fairly and freely decided this question for themselves by a direct vote on the adoption of the Constitution, excluding all fraud and violence."[33]

Although most free-soilers in Kansas still planned to boycott the June delegate election, Walker's pronouncement appeared to reassure them that future elections might be more impartial. It led them to concentrate their energies on the upcoming October territorial legislative election and the ratification vote on the yet to be written constitution that would probably take place soon thereafter. On the other hand, the pro-slavery partisans were incensed by Walker's inaugural speech. Not only had he attempted to dictate procedure to the upcoming convention, he had made some oblique remarks concerning an "isothermal line" above which slavery could not profitably exist, and he implied that Kansas was above this line. He was also considered far too chummy with the free-staters in general and the leaders of the Topeka 'government' in particular. Southerners within and without the territory began to abuse the governor. From their vantage point he was unconstitutionally intervening into the legal process and clearly choosing sides. Any credibility he might have had with this group was destroyed by his inaugural, and his hope for functioning as an impartial mediator was no longer possible. Indeed, his function now would change to becoming a watchdog over the pretensions of the pro-slavery partisans. Some southerners accused him of treason to his section, but John Quitman, viewing Walker as more Pennsylvanian than Mississippian, saw the situation clearly: "Like most Northern politicians, he desired Kansas to come in as a "free state". They esteem the ascendency of the party of more importance than the rights of the South and believe the former would be best served by Kansas coming in as a free state."[34]

---

33. Nichols, *Disruption*, 107. Nevins, *Emergence of Lincoln, vol. 1*, 149-150. *New Albany Ledger*, May 1, 1857. Nichols, *Disruption*, 114, 117-118. Stampp, *1857*, 165.

34. Robert Toombs succinctly summed up the general anger toward Walker when, in relation to the governor's call for the Lecompton constitutional delegates to submit their work to Kansas voters at large for ratification, the Senator noted "[i]t is none of his business whether they do or do not…Now the Convention ought never under any circumstances comply with his demand." Toombs further went on to note that Walker's "'isothermal' and 'thermometrical' arguments and follies…is a direct government interference…and it is this which so much aroused the South. The condemnation of him is universal." Toombs to W.W. Burwell, July 17, 1857, in Phillips, *Correspondence of Toombs, Stephens, and Cobb*. One correspondent of Alexander Stephens's also noted Walker "puts himself in thought, feeling, and hope with our enemies." And in noting that "[o]ur victory [the 1856 election] is turned to ashes on our lips," he indicts the president as well,

Amidst these attitudes, the election for convention delegates occurred on June 16. No free-soilers were even entered as candidates, so it is not surprising that all 60 delegates-elect were pro-slavery. The *New Albany Ledger* blamed the free-state boycott on "abolitionist" leaders and Republicans who counseled such a course in order to "let the Kansas election go by default to permit a proslavery constitution to be framed and adopted, and then to renew the strife in the halls of Congress." Norman's analysis was consistent with the narrow conservative and moderate northern Democratic approach to Kansas politics. Northern Democrats generally refused to look behind the actual election to the unfair machinery influencing its outcome. Stephen Douglas, for example, thought that the free-staters brought unnecessary defeat upon themselves. In any event, the delegates chosen in this election were certainly unrepresentative of all of Kansas. There was no doubt that they would write a pro-slavery document; the only question was as to its submission to the people for ratification. A hard line group of delegates counseled no submission whatever, while a more moderate group, in Stanton's terms, promoted "some form...for submitting the great distracting question to the people of Kansas." The delegates first convened on September 7– but for only four days of organization. They then adjourned to await the outcome of the regular territorial legislative election scheduled for early October. After that, they would compose their work and decide on how and whether to submit that work to the voters.[35]

Urged on by eastern Republicans and Douglas Democrats and reassured again by Walker that under federal law administered by him the vote would be fair, the free-staters eventually agreed to participate in the October election for territorial legislators. After the two days of balloting, on the 5th and the 6th, the unofficial vote count elected the Republican candidate for territorial delegate; yet, strangely, the pro-slavery forces appeared to capture the legislature. Soon thereafter, however, an inspection of the discrepancy revealed that well over a thousand votes in each of two counties, votes necessary to elect a pro-slavery legislative majority, were quite obviously fraudulent. Governor Walker, more clear in his own

---

maintaining that by his appointment and failure to recall Walker, "Buchanan has turned traitor...We are betrayed." Thomas W. Thomas to Stephens, June 15, 1857, in Phillips, 400-401. Stampp, *1857*, 166-167, 169-170; Nevins, *Emergence of Lincoln*, vol. *1*, 153-155, 162-163, 165-166. Leemhuis, *James L. Orr*, 54-55. Michael A. Morrison, *Slavery and the American West* (Chapel Hill and London: The University of North Carolina Press, 1997), 198. Quitman quote is in a letter to Lawrence Keitt, July 23, 1857, quoted in Nevins, *Emergence of Lincoln, vol. 1*, 163.

35. The deputies appointed to take the census for registration failed to do so in nineteen of Kansas's 38 counties, so none of those could be apportioned. In 15 counties no registry of voters was attempted. No voting place was recognized in Lawrence, and registration in Leavenworth was incomplete. In the election, of the 9,251 registered voters, only 2,000 actually cast ballots. *House Report no, 377, 35-1.* Stampp, *1857*, 167-168. *New Albany Ledger,* April 1, July 3, 1857. Nevins, *Emergence, vol. 1*, 150, 132. Nichols, *Disruption, 125.* Stampp, *1857,* 266-267.

policy than other Kansas governors, threw out these tainted ballots. Considering his promises for a fair election and the transparency of the fraud, no other course was open to him. He was lauded for his action by much of Northern opinion, but predictably and mercilessly the pro-slavery forces generally unleashed a furious attack against him both in the press and in Washington. Difficult to deny the frauds, they generally accused Walker of illegally going behind the returns, a task they maintained was reserved for the courts or the legislature. Buchanan, himself, shaken by the southern reaction, remained rather silent, refusing to condone Walker's course of action.[36]

Meanwhile, the Kansas constitutional convention reconvened in Lecompton. In most respects, but not all, the document they then drafted was similar to other state constitutions, phrases often lifted word for word. There were, however, some mildly controversial clauses, such as the procedure by which judges were selected, location of the state capital, qualifications for voting and office-holding, and banking requirements, that by themselves would rather demand full submission to the people for approval. But it was the article concerning slavery that most obviously demanded popular ratification. It not only legalized slavery in the proposed state of Kansas, but also enacted a slave code and declared that the right of property, in slaves as well as other forms, "is before and higher than any constitutional sanctions." Clearly aware from the recent election returns that any submission of a pro-slavery document to the people of Kansas would be rejected, most of the delegates at first were of the opinion that it should not be submitted at all. Indeed, in the past (though not for 20 years) some state constitutions went into effect without submittal. However, so naked a disregard of recent democratic procedure and the Buchanan administration's promise to Walker that any constitution must be submitted, made no popular ratification not only politically impossible but destructive of any real sense of the Democratic ideal of popular sovereignty. Certainly it would cause the future political defeat of the national Democratic Party by destroying it in the North, and Buchanan sent an agent to Lecompton to help work out some compromise.[37]

The eventual formula was curious. The delegates decided that the whole constitution would not be submitted for ratification, but the citizens would be allowed to choose between two clauses affecting slavery. One of them (labeled "Constitution with Slavery") essentially ratified the slavery provisions in Arti-

---

36. Inspection of the votes in one county revealed that the names of 1,500 registered voters who 'cast' ballots had been copied out of the Cincinnati directory of citizens. In one precinct the number of votes well exceeded the male population of the whole county surrounding that precinct. In another county, where only about 100 men lived, three of that county's precincts 'cast' 1,200 votes. These two counties also had these fraudulent votes recorded in the same hand. Stampp, *1857*, 261-264; Etcheson, *Bleeding Kansas*, 153.

37. The Lecompton Constitution may be found at https://www.kansasmemory.org/item/90818. The quote on property is on p. 183, section 1 of Article VII. Stampp, *1857*, 272-273. Nevins, *Emergence of Lincoln, vol. 1*, 234.

cle VII of the Constitution. The other (labeled "Constitution with no Slavery") amended the slavery article (Article VII) by forbidding any future importation of slaves into Kansas, but it protected the continued right to own about the 200 or so that already existed there. It also specifically noted that the property in these slaves would "in no manner be interfered with," perhaps allowing that the descendants of these 200 could also become slaves. Moreover, no matter which clause was chosen, the Constitution could not be amended until 1864, thereby preventing, at least until then and perhaps forever, full abolition. Finally, to insure that neither Walker nor the newly elected free soil legislature could foil their plans, the delegates gave full power to administer this "clause" election to the Convention's president. That referendum was scheduled for December 21.[38]

Predictably (and understandably) Republican editors inside and out of Kansas denounced the Lecompton constitution and the scheme to effectuate it. More significantly, so did many northern Democrats. They took their lead from the *Chicago Times*, the organ of Stephen Douglas. Soon after the Lecompton convention adjourned, the *Times* pronounced the delegates' work unacceptable, as their refusal to submit the complete constitution had violated the essence of popular sovereignty.[39] Douglas had always argued that slavery was only one domestic institution among many; in fact, the partial intent of the popular sovereignty doctrine was to diffuse the emotion surrounding the slavery issue by reducing its status to equal to that of banking, immigration, taxation, education, and any other political matter. But the Lecompton scheme of submittal reintroduced the notion that the slavery issue deserved preferential treatment, a notion actually promoted by fire-eating southerners on one side and abolitionists on the other.

In southeastern Indiana the *New Albany Ledger* echoed the anti-Lecompton sentiments. Even before he vented his anger over non-submittal, Norman began to criticize the pro-slavery forces in Kansas for the fraud they committed in the territorial elections in October. The *Ledger* labeled the South's criticism of Walker "hardly an honorable course considering the circumstances." It could not believe that Southerners wished "to see pro-slavery rule perpetuated in the Territory by such gross and infamous means" and expressed the hope that the bulk of southerners did not reflect the attitude of their editors. Norman defended Walker's disqualifications as authorized by the Kansas-Nebraska act and believed them to be the only possible course considering the clarity of the fraud. Indeed, the electoral chicanery had created an atmosphere of suspicion toward southern motives, and the news of non-submission, coming hard upon the heels of the fraud, effectively

---

38. The procedure for the election concerning the slavery clause is in the "schedule" of the Constitution, section 7. https://www.kansasmemory.org/item/90818, 189. See also Stampp, *1857,* 274-275; Nichols, *Disruption,* 130-131; Nevins, *Emergence, vol. 1,* 235.

39. Nevins, *Emergence, vol. 1,* 237. Johannsen, *Stephen Douglas,* 585. See also Stampp, *1857,* 277-279 for Republican and northern Democratic reaction.

confirmed those suspicions. On December 9 the *Ledger* noted that the submission of a "single clause…does not come up to our notion of popular sovereignty." This was especially true because the delegates did not represent the citizenry of Kansas: "No miserable minority," Norman wrote, "such as the vote by which the Lecompton Convention was chosen, could be justly regarded by Congress as evidence of the wishes of the people."[40]

Although it was the most influential Democratic sheet in southern Indiana (and certainly in the Second District), the *New Albany Ledger*'s opinion did not go unopposed. Before the Lecompton convention met, Henry Comingore's *Paoli Eagle* foreshadowed the position it would hold throughout the controversy. Always more willing to take the southern view of things than Norman, Comingore had written as early as July that "the Convention had ample authority to determine, of itself, whether it will adopt a constitution with or without slavery [and] whether that constitution shall be submitted for ratification." This was written in response to Walker's "intervention" in the matter when he counseled full submittal. The *Eagle*, which remained curiously silent on the October electoral frauds, well predicted the southern line. For example, writing to a political supporter in Virginia, Senator R.M.T. Hunter explained that "the question of submitting [the Lecompton convention's] work to the people for ratification was one to which that body had jurisdiction alone, unless indeed the act which called them into being had required final ratification by the people." This position, of course, was strictly legalistic, but, naturally, it avoided the question of *why* the legislature had neglected to require submittal and how ethical such defense of the convention's actions were. Some prescient moderate southerners, even in the Democratic Party, reflected upon how support for non-submittal could destroy the Democracy's chances in upcoming national elections. Yet, when all was said and done, Hunter's and the *Eagle*'s position appeared to be the one generally favored in the South.[41]

In the same Hunter letter just quoted, the senator added that, concerning the question of submission, "the practice of states applying for admission has been in both ways, [and] the power of the convention to determine for itself has never been controverted heretofore, so far as I am informed." In response to this argument, the *New Albany Ledger* noted that the practice of non-submittal had lapsed for two decades. Since Michigan's application in 1837, all six conventions had submitted their constitutions for approval. Indeed, when Wisconsin attempted to enter the Union in 1846 without popular ratification of their convention's product, Congress refused to admit it until the constitution was submitted. To the *Ledger* and all Democrats who supported the Douglas position, popular sover-

---

40. *New Albany Ledger,* December 9, November 7, 14, 1857.

41. *Paoli Eagle,* July 30, 1857. R. M. T. Hunter to Shelton F. Leake, October 16, 1857, printed in Ambler. *Correspondence of Hunter,* 239. See also Hunter to citizens of Virginia, October 26, 1857, in Ambler, *Correspondence,* 247-248. Stampp, *1857,* 279-81. Potter, *Impending Crisis,* 313.

eignty reigned as the accepted party ideology, and at the very least it meant majority approval of the state's organic document. The narrow, legalistic position of the South was outdated, and, like the Republican theory of congressional restriction of slavery, it had been replaced by Douglas's new principle.[42]

In a real sense, much of the northern Democracy had grown tired of the South's persistent attempts to expand slavery even at the risk of a foreign or civil war. Even before Lecompton and the electoral frauds of 1857, northern Democrats had become angered at new talk of reviving the African slave trade (illegalized since 1808) and especially at the support southerners gave to individual southern attempts to seize land for the United States in the Caribbean or Central America—so called "filibustering." David Potter states that one such filibusterer, the Tennessee-born "grey eyed man of destiny," William Walker, was "something of a hero to the American public, northern as well as southern," but, in the summer of 1857, both the *New Albany Ledger* and the *Paoli Eagle* believed otherwise. Norman wrote of Walker "that anybody should have for him any admiration or respect, or should view him in any other light than that of a poor creature, as destitute of ability as he is of honesty, or humanity, we cannot very well understand." And Comingore argued that "Walker's whole conduct in his filibustering career has been marred with the most cold-blooded murders and ingratitude that a man could be guilty of." So, too, concerning the African slave trade. When Southerners circumspectly began to talk of reviving the practice, a congressional resolution was introduced and passed denouncing its revival in moral terms. Forty-four southern Democrats voted against the resolution while English and all northern Democrats but three supported it. To many northerners, then, Lecompton represented just the latest example of the underhanded and immoral "slavocracy." And, because it challenged the sacred doctrine of popular sovereignty, it was clearly the most dangerous.[43]

The rift between the northern and southern Democracy put the Buchanan administration in a most awkward position. As late as mid-July, the administration, through the *Washington Union*, had fully sustained the principle of submission of the Constitution; but, during the next few months, the president became persuaded that resistance to the plans of the southerners would destroy the Union itself. Consequently, on November 17, the *Union* reversed itself and completely endorsed the Lecompton scheme. Certainly most suspected the *Union's* editorials

42. Hunter to Leake, October 16, 1857, in Ambler, *Correspondence of Hunter*, 239. *New Albany Ledger*, December 1, 14, 1857. Alexander Stephens, in a speech to his constituents, added to the legalistic arguments of the South the notion that, if Lecompton were sent to congress for approval, the only appropriate constitutional question for Congress was whether "the new state . . . is republican in form." Speech of August 14, 1857, in Phillips, *Correspondence of Toombs, Stephens, Cobb*, 417.

43. Potter, *Impending Crisis*, 194-195. *New Albany Ledger*, June 3, 1857. *Paoli Eagle*, July 2, 1857. *CG*, 34-3, 124.

merely reflected the position of southerners in Buchanan's cabinet; the president removed all doubt whether it was his policy as well in his annual message to Congress on December 8. Claiming that his earlier instructions to governor Walker concerning "full and fair submittal" were meant only in reference to the slavery question (though, interestingly, the partial submittal was not even fully that), the president urged all Kansans to participate in the December 21 vote called by the convention. In one of the most tortured interpretations of the Kansas-Nebraska Act ever attempted, he declared that the phrase "domestic institutions" was limited to family relationships, and that such relationships included that between master and slave but none other in the Lecompton document. As to whether Congress should admit Kansas upon the results of the December 21 vote, Buchanan was not explicit, but the message, fully read, implied as much. Waiting only one day, Stephen Douglas, on December 9, rose in the Senate to denounce Buchanan's remarks. The fight would ensue in earnest.[44]

4.

Buchanan's message and Douglas's response were the first major declarations made on Kansas politics in the first session of the 35th Congress. Elected, for the most part, a year earlier, both houses of this Congress displayed Democratic majorities. In the House of Representatives, the Democrats claimed 128 seats to the Republicans' 92, and the all-southern American Party's 14. Divided sectionally, 53 Democrats came from the free states and 75 from the slave states so that most observers conceded the speakership to a southerner. The earliest, most prominent, candidate was James L. Orr of South Carolina. Orr had served in the House since 1849, and was the leader of the moderate wing (still existent) of the South Carolina Democrats. While the Palmetto fire-eaters, such as Lawrence Keitt and Preston Brooks, completely distrusted northerners, remained aloof from the national Party, and essentially believed secession inevitable, the moderates held that South Carolina could best protect its own interests by making political alliances with northern Democratic conservatives. These were exactly the type of men that English wished to bolster in his speech a year earlier. To English, Orr, and others

---

44. Washington dispatch of July 7, 1857 in the *New Albany Ledger*, July 8, 1857. Nevins, *Emergence, vol. 1*, 241-249. Nichols, *Disruption*, 159. Both Alexander Stephens and his brother, Linton, were somewhat surprised and certainly disappointed at Douglas's position. Little Alec, after two meetings with Douglas taken before the Little Giant's speech that he intended to oppose Lecompton, wrote to his brother that Douglas's "course . . . will do us damage." Alexander Stephens to Linton Stephens, December 4, 1857, Stephens Papers, Manhattanville. Linton believed that Douglas had not before made full submittal of a territorial constitution a requirement of popular sovereignty. Linton Stephens to Alexander Stephens, December 10, 1857, Stephens Papers, Manhattanville.

of similar ilk, the extreme southerners were believed nearly as dangerous as the Republicans—indeed, they gave each other life-sustaining force.[45]

Although certainly a moderate in South Carolina, Orr's positions were still essentially southern. For example, he called for an aggressive foreign policy with its eye especially on obtaining Cuba, and, in 1856, he served as Preston Brooks's most effective spokesman during the expulsion proceedings that summer. On the question of popular sovereignty, Orr firstly supported the position, since upheld by at least four justices of the Supreme Court in *Dred Scott*, that a territorial legislature could not bar slavery. That Court holding certainly appeared to limit territorial popular sovereignty where slavery was concerned, and it had put Stephen Douglas in a bind, one that, as early as the summer of 1857, he would try to get out of by arguing that a territorial legislature, by refusing to adopt necessary legislation needed to protect slavery (e.g., fugitive slave laws, slave patrol conscription, forced illiteracy of slaves, i.e., slave codes in general), could still, thus, exercise its control over the institution. (This position would eventually become best known in 1858 through the so-called "Freeport Doctrine" of the Lincoln-Douglas debates. It is sometimes referred to as "residual popular sovereignty.") Interestingly, because of Orr's strong belief in the concept of non-intervention by the federal government into the affairs of a territory, the South Carolina congressman did not dispute Douglas's contention. He also, for similar reasons, rejected the extreme southern demand that the federal government enact a territorial slave code to counter Douglas's assertion and fully effectuate *Dred Scott*. These positions, coupled with Orr's apparent friendliness to certain speculative schemes, made him suspicious among the fire-eaters.[46]

Consequently, a month before Congress was scheduled to convene, some southerners looked for another candidate. At first they tried to enlist Alexander Stephens. Stephens was not, to be sure, an extremist, but he was more charismatic and clever than Orr, and more keen to the defense of slavery. He was also highly respected by the Party in general. But Stephens did not want the job, and he recommended John Letcher of Virginia in his stead. "One or the other might be

---

45. *CG-35-1*, 1. There were eight Pennsylvania congressmen who were elected in a Republican-American fusion. Dubin, *Congressional Elections*, 178, 180. Nichols, 156-157. The *New Albany Ledger* mentioned Orr as early as May 29, 1857. *Biographical Directory of American Congress*, 1494. Leemhuis, *Orr*, 30-31, 63.

46. Leemhuis, *Orr*, 44, 52, 61-63, 29, 33. For Douglas's earliest iteration of what later became the Freeport Doctrine, see Fehrenbacher, *Dred Scott*, 456, and Johannsen, *Stephen Douglas*, 569. Orr was rather well regarded enough by even some conservative Republicans and old-line Whigs. Orville Browning recalled that Justice John McLean, a dissenter in *Dred Scott* and sometime Whig and Republican seeker of the presidency, maintained that Orr "is the best and most conservative Southern Democrat he knows. That *sub rosa* he is in favor of making Kansas a free state . . . " While that analysis may have been rather too optimistic on McLean's part, it certainly illustrates why Orr might be distrusted by the fire-eaters. Theodore Calvin Pease, ed., *The Diary of Orville Hickman Browning, vol. 1*, (Chicago: Blakely Printing Co., 1927), 295, diary entry on 7/17/57.

elected," Robert Toombs wrote the editor of the *Baltimore Patriot*, "and I wish you would press that view before the public in some suitable form." One correspondent of R.M.T. Hunter's wrote that "if the Southern Rights men will go into caucus they can control [the] nominee," and he suggested another Virginian, Thomas Bocock, as a suitable candidate. Bocock was similar to Stephens in that he positioned himself somewhere between the moderates and the extremists. Yet, when the Democrats north and south caucused on December 5, Orr prevailed, and, in the election for speaker in the House two days later, no Democrat voted against him. Picking up another three ballots from the Know-Nothings, Orr easily defeated Republican Galusha Grow by 44 votes.[47]

What probably blunted any fire-eater challenge in caucus was the eventual realization that they could not win with a southerner of their ilk. Orr was a southern candidate fully supported by Buchanan, Douglas, and the northern Democrats in general, and it would have been too destabilizing for Democrats and too felicitous to the Republicans to cause a fight within the Party. The momentary strength of the Party's moderate northern-southern alliance may also be recognized by the election of James C. Allen, a Douglas Democrat, as clerk. An interesting sidelight to the clerk election was that Allen was opposed by Bright lieutenant and Indiana United States marshal John L. Robinson. Robinson had sought the post as early as the previous May, and, in some sense, the contest between Allen and Robinson boiled down to one between Douglas and Bright. The Indiana Democracy itself appeared to be divided, for Wright and his cohorts were said to be in Allen's camp. In a letter to English in October, Robinson wrote that he "rel[ied] a good deal on the Seven[?] Indiana Democratic members." Unfortunately, there is no evidence to suggest how most of these congressmen voted. Certainly, John G. Davis, a strong Wright man, must have voted for Allen, and English probably supported Robinson. The *New Albany Ledger*, noting that "there is no more noble champion of Democracy in the West, and none more deserving of high honors than Mr. R.," eventually offered the Marshal its condolences. But the Wright faction had to be pleased.[48]

A few days after the elections in the House, Orr was reported "closeted with political friends" in a discussion over the standing committees. Quite possibly, English took part in those parleys. Of the six Democrats elected from Indiana,

---

47. Nichols, *Disruption*, 157. Toombs to W.W. Burwell, November 20, 1857, in Phillips, *Correspondence of Toombs, Stephens, Cobb*, 426-427. D.H. Wood to R.M.T. Hunter, November 11, 1857, in Ambler, *Correspondence of Hunter*, 253. *New Albany Ledger*, November 11, 1857. *CG, 35-1*, 2.

48. Roy Nichols claimed that Orr was the administration candidate for speaker and Allen the Douglas man for clerk, but Robert Johannsen states that both were supported by Douglas. Nichols, *Disruption*, 157; Johannsen, *Stephen Douglas*, 589. *Washington Star*, in *New Albany Ledger*, May 29, 1857. F.P. [Raudad] to WHE, October 20, 1857, English Papers. *Cincinnati Enquirer*, in *Ledger*, November 18, 1857. J.L. Robinson to WHE, October 24, 1857, English Papers. *Ledger*, December 9, 1857. There were six, not seven, Democratic congressmen from Indiana.

he had served the most consecutive terms of any of them. Having already served with considerable distinction, and having achieved a fine reputation in Party circles both North and South, he would at least be in line for a respectable chairmanship. In early 1857, he had been mentioned for both a Cabinet post, and, in the event that Bright received one instead, elevation to the Senate. One Hoosier employed in Washington had also pressed English "to present your claims to the next congress for Speakership." This correspondent remarked that "your ability, experience, and successful canvass in your district entitle you that place." That prospect was obviously closed, but Orr may well have shared the opinion of one of English's most influential constituents who gushed of his congressman that "no man in the State has more friends—no man occupies a more favorable position. You are unquestionably the rising man of the State." (In confirmation of this assessment, the town of Hartford, in Crawford County, changed its name to "English" in honor of his re-election.)⁴⁹

Whether or not English actually had a hand in shaping the committees, he fairly received his due. When the positions were revealed, his name stood as chairman of the committee on post office and post roads, a very respectable appointment. Moreover, he retained his position as a regent of the Smithsonian. The *New Albany Ledger* proudly announced that such appointments confirmed the belief that English had won an "enviable place" in Congress. The only other Hoosier Democrat receiving a significant placement was James Hughes, put on the Committee on Territories because he was understood to be favorable toward the Lecompton Constitution. Smith Miller, congratulating English for receiving the "position what you were entitled to," wondered why his own successor, William Niblack, "was entirely lost site of." Niblack had been given the not-even-dubious honor of a seat on the Mileage Committee.⁵⁰ There could have been little doubt that English was the recognized leader of the delegation, and he was to be an even greater force in this session than any other.

For its first five months, from December 1857 through April 1858, the 35th Congress was essentially preoccupied with Lecompton, and Douglas's speech to the Senate was the touchstone for many northern Democrats. Douglas, first of all, declared that popular sovereignty demanded full submission of a Kansas constitution; secondly, that Congress should make new provisions for fair elections in Kansas. (The second point ran contrary to the non-interventionist policy of the

---

49. Dispatch from Washington, in *New Albany Ledger,* December 14, 1857. William Sherrod had written English that "if Bright goes into the cabinet, I think we would not have much difficulty in making you his successor." January 30, 1857, English Papers. See also S.S. Crowe to WHE, February 5, 1857; L.M. Smith to WHE, January 6, 1857; J.B. Archer to WHE, July 6, 1856, English Papers. Pleasant, *History of Crawford County,* 150.

50. Nichols, *Disruption,* 158. *CG, 35-1,* 31. *New Albany Ledger,* December 23, 1857. Smith Miller to WHE, December 28, 1857, English Papers.

Party; it suggested that Douglas had become sensitive to the fraudulency of elections.) This speech brought on a long-delayed break in the Democratic Party. A
slim majority of northern Democrats in the Senate, following Buchanan's administration, joined the southerners in supporting Lecompton and its partial submission scheme. These included Bright and Fitch, who, if for no other reason, needed
the Administration's support against the Republican legal challenge to their seats.
In the House, most of the six Indiana congressmen were loath to take sides. "A
majority of the delegation," wrote an Indiana Democrat working in Washington,
"will not define their position until it is necessary." A rumor that "the Democratic
delegation from Indiana could not support the Lecompton Constitution," spread
by the *New York Times*, was immediately squelched by English. The reporter had
maintained that the Indiana congressmen had expressed their solidarity with
Douglas "in a long interview with the President." In the *Washington Union*, English replied that he "was present at the interview alluded to," and the delegation
made no such declaration. "The visit was not one of a political character at all"
English maintained, "but merely a social call, to pay our respects to the Chief
Magistrate of the Nation."[51]

Despite English's disclaimer, it is difficult to believe, at this point, that Kansas politics would not enter such a discussion between the president and a state's
congressional delegation. Alexander Stephens claimed a few weeks later that three
of the six Hoosier Democrats were "with us . . . on the Kansas issue," and, as
it turned out, that was a rather accurate assessment. John G. Davis, a staunch
Douglasite from the west central part of the state, was certainly against Lecompton; James Hughes, a little southeast of Davis, was just as certainly for it. William
Niblack, representing the southwest "pocket" appeared to be leaning toward the
administration: having been chosen to replace congressman-elect James Lockhart
who had died a few months before Congress convened, he owed his election to
the pro-Lecompton party leadership in his district. Not much yet was known
about the views of James H. Gregg and James B. Foley. Gregg was a longtime
lawyer; Foley, on the other hand, was, in English's words, "a plain, unsophisticated
farmer," though cosmopolitan enough to be called "clever" by another Hoosier
employed in Washington. All the northern districts of Indiana were represented
by Republicans and, thus, were, of course, anti-Lecompton. As for English, he
publicly stated he would define his position when presented with "all the facts,"
and only when "the question comes up immediately for action."[52] Congressmen
were in the realm of Nebraska 2.0.

51. *CG, 35-1*, 14-18. Nevins, *Emergence of Lincoln, vol. 1*, 258. Lewis Jordan to Samuel Douglass, December
    18, 1857, English Papers. *Washington Union*, December 14, 1857.

52. Alexander Stephens to Linton Stephens, January 3, 1858, quoted in Johnston, *Life of Stephens*, 328. Smith
    Miller to WHE, December 28, 1857, English Papers. *Biographical Directory of American Congress*, 1032. En-
    glish's remarks on Foley are in *34-3, Appendix to the CG*, 105. Lewis Jordan to Samuel Douglass, December

Many northern Democrats were in general caught between their desire to support the Democratic Party as represented by the Administration and their wish to stick to the principle of popular sovereignty as understood by their constituents. This, of course, was not dissimilar to the Nebraska conundrum of party loyalty versus the Missouri Compromise. But English was in an even more sensitive position than most. As chairman of a major committee, he was probably expected to toe the Party line. After many years as a loyal, hardworking Democrat, he had finally achieved entrance into the innermost circles of national political power. Both loyalty and ambition, therefore, almost compelled him to stand with the administration. Rather unnecessary to add, his attachment to Senator Bright also drove him in this direction. If Foley, Gregg, Davis, and even Niblack bolted the Administration, the repercussions for them would not nearly be as damaging as if English did. On the other hand, English had publicly staked out a position on popular sovereignty that left him in principle fairly opposed to Lecompton. In his lame-duck session speech a year earlier, he had told the House that, "whenever the people of a Territory come to form a State government, the will of the people, *clearly expressed*, shall be the paramount law." In the same speech, when he said that he would be willing to admit Kansas as a slave state, the key condition he gave was that "the will of the people" had to be "*fairly and fully expressed*" on the question.[53] Whether English held that *full* submission of the constitution was necessary does not seem to have been as important to him as whether there was a truly democratic decision on the issue of slavery. The only way he could reconcile principle with party loyalty was to somehow discover fairness in either the election to the Lecompton convention or the forthcoming election on the submitted clause concerning slavery.

In such a delicate balance, the opinion of his constituents could prove to be decisive. By all appearances, most Second District Democrats favored the position of Stephen Douglas. Norman, while declaring that "the politicians dislike the idea of breaking with the Administration," also reported that it was "unquestionably the general feeling [of the District] that the whole constitution should be submitted to the vote of the People." Most of the Democratic county conventions called to select delegates to the upcoming State Convention passed resolutions to that effect. Floyd County labeled the Lecompton scheme "anti-democratic and despotic," and recommended that Congress reject Kansas's admission under it. Washington County resolved that the principle of popular sovereignty demanded that new states be admitted only when Congress was "satisfied" that their constitutions were "approved by a majority of the people who are to live under and be

---

18, 1857, English Papers. Parsons, *Congressional Districts*, 55-56; Dubin, *Congressional Elections*, 176. Letter to *Washington Union*, reprinted in the *New Albany Ledger,* December 21, 1857.

53. *CG, 34-3*, 106.

governed by it." Yet both counties, preferring to believe that the president would eventually see the light, expressed "undiminished confidence" in Buchanan. "The Administration was too quick in committing itself," lamented Norman. "As matters now stand, we know not what to say or do—at least that is my fix."[54]

There were Democrats in the district, of course, who leaned away from Douglas and toward the Administration. Prominent among them was Henry Comingore, but, until January, English could only infer the editor's position from the *Paoli Eagle's* refusal to take any notice of the Party's diversity on Lecompton. Lewis Jordan, a federal appointee from Harrison County, argued that "it would have been better for the North if the [Lecompton] convention had submitted the whole constitution to the people," but, as it stood now, it would "be best for Congress to receive the State into the Union under Lecompton and close the matter." Jordan believed that quick admission would allay excitement that otherwise would continue for several years. This was a much too optimistic assessment, for it completely ignored the probability of future Republican efforts to amend, resubmit, or overturn the Kansas Constitution, all attendant with the required propaganda. More to the point, it ignored the devastating political effect admission under Lecompton would have on the northern Democracy. As Norman queried, "ought we to run the risk of another agitation next year, resulting in driving off another battalion of Democrats in the hopes of recruiting our ranks from the old Whigs and Know-Nothings?" English was quickly made to understand that a victory for the Administration in this matter might mean Republican rule in Indiana for the next decade.[55]

As English anxiously ruminated upon these conflicting considerations, one of his less cautious colleagues stormed ahead. On December 16, the House resolved itself into the Committee of the Whole to discuss Buchanan's opening message. Samuel S. Cox, a Douglas Democrat from Ohio, announced that he intended to introduce a bill enabling Kansans to write a new constitution, providing that "said constitution shall be submitted to the people for acceptance or rejection." Quickly, Indianan James Hughes was on his feet, ridiculing Cox for his impatience in the matter. "He proposes not to stand by the President," Hughes said of Cox. "If such was my conviction I should hold it back to the last moment. If I felt myself compelled to separate from the Democratic party and from the administration, I should go reluctantly; I would not be the first to yield ship." Cox refused the implication that he was acting against his Party. He replied that his principles came directly from "the Cincinnati platform [and] the pledges of Mr. Buchanan to the instructions given to Gov. Walker." Relying upon those expressions of

---

54. J.B. Norman to WHE, December 30, 1857, English Papers. *New Albany Ledger,* December 28, 1857. J.B. Norman to WHE, December 21, 1857, English Papers.

55. The *Paoli Eagle's* silence on Lecompton lasted through February 11, 1858. Lewis Jordan to Samuel Douglass, December 18, 1857; J.B. Norman to WHE, December 21, 1857, English Papers.

popular sovereignty, Cox added, he could not be driven "out of the Democratic party by any little scornful indignation from Indiana." The *Congressional Globe* reported that laughter followed Cox's last remark, but Hughes doggedly pressed on. Correct in his assumption that the majority of Democratic congressmen and senators would follow the Administration, Hughes queried whether Cox would "go to those men and to that party who are attempting to force upon the people of Kansas the Topeka Constitution." Cox naturally replied that he would become no Republican, whereupon Hughes commented that perhaps Cox's "idea" was to "form his own party." Hughes then sneered sarcastically, "it is to be regretted that some gentlemen are not either of sufficient importance in the country to build up a new party, or sufficiently humble to follow faithfully in the ranks of one already arranged."[56]

Hughes's harassment of Cox illustrated the heavy hand the Administration was going to take with recalcitrant northern Democrats. It reflected Buchanan's famous remark to Douglas in early December, when the president, apprised that Douglas would oppose him on Lecompton, reminded the senator of the fate of Tallmadge and Rives for their apostasy during Jackson's presidency. Essentially, the Administration was determined to make Lecompton a party test, and was threatening to read out of the Party any Democrat who failed it. The selection of Hughes as northern Democratic point man was curious but instructive. As a judge, Hughes was reputed to have been competent, but also "combative" and "arbitrary." According to one source, he had a "natural tyrannical and overbearing disposition." The Administration's choice of Hughes certainly appeared to reflect its view of the matter. It was not set to appeal to reason (perhaps because it felt that reason was against it) but by intimidation. Throughout the early debate on Lecompton, Hughes would often suddenly rise to remind his northern Democratic brethren of their treachery. Two days after the Cox fracas, Lewis Jordan wrote home that the feisty Hoosier was somewhat of an embarrassment to his own cause: "Hughes has ruined himself already in the estimation of the House. He has been decided out of order no less than four times."[57]

Hughes was not the only Hoosier to publicly side so early with the Administration. In the Senate, there was Graham Fitch. He was one of a trio of Demo-

---

56. *CG, 35-1,* 57-58.

57. Perhaps every work dealing with the coming of the Civil War contains Buchanan's remarks to Douglas and Douglas's response: "Mr. President, I wish you to remember General Jackson is dead." The exchange appears to have first been revealed by Douglas in a speech he made in Milwaukee on October 20, 1860, reported by The New York Times on October 22, 1860. See www.nytimes.com/1860/10/22/archives/the-lecompton-constitution-was=mr-douglas-its-author-his-speech--at.html. Accessed, March 19, 2019. H.L. Duncan, "James Hughes," *Indiana Magazine of History* 5, no. 3 (September 1909), 89, 87. Lewis Jordan to Samuel Douglass, December 18, 1857, English Papers. One letter written from Louisville told English that Hughes perhaps had designs on "superseding you in the Indiana delegation." S. Green to WHE, November 25, 1856, English Papers.

crats who attempted to answer Douglas's speech earlier that month. Afraid that the Indiana Republicans would successfully challenge his seat, Fitch early aligned himself with the Administration to ensure its support when needed. His remarks combined attacks on both the Topeka Republicans and Douglas himself, intended obviously to link the two in the public mind. And he echoed Buchanan's admonition to party traitors, dredging up the fate of Aaron Burr and Martin van Buren. He denounced Douglas bitterly, accusing him of excessive ambition. From Indiana, the collective response was one of embarrassment. Many Democratic newspapers, including the *New Albany Ledger*, had reprinted Douglas's December 9th speech. Fitch's position, correctly perceived to mirror that of Jesse Bright's, seemed to spell real trouble for the state Democracy. Norman wrote English, almost apologetically, that he published Douglas's speech only because he "had been requested to do so by a large number of our subscribers." He added that this was "not intended, of course, as an indication of preference for the Little Giant over any distinguished Indianan, or as an unequivocal endorsement of Douglas's views. I presume Gov. Bright is perfectly aware of the warm friendship I entertain for him personally and politically, and hope to be able to give evidence of it when occasion shall arise." Such was Bright's influence that he did not even need to utter a word of his position to thoroughly frighten wayward Democrats, especially those who lived partly off the federal trough.[58]

"As matters now stand," the *New Albany Ledger* candidly announced on December 22, "Kansas affairs are so complicated that the patriot scarcely knows what is his duty to his country." The Lecompton election on the slavery clauses had taken place a day earlier, but the results were not yet known, and other events in Kansas since the adjournment of the Lecompton convention were the source of the *Ledger's* great anxiety. Angered not only by the convention's refusal of full submission, but also by its stated dictatorial takeover of the pre-state government effective on December 1, anti-slavery Kansans demanded that acting-governor Stanton respond by early convening the recently elected territorial legislature. On December 7, Stanton complied, and the legislature a few days later passed a law submitting the full Lecompton Constitution to a popular vote on January 4th. Thus, when the *Ledger* expressed its confusion, the "clause" election of December 21 was to be followed by a full submittal election two weeks later. Both elections, of course, were deemed irregular; the first by the free-staters and the latter by the pro-slavery forces. Further complicating these arrangements was the Administra-

---

58. Nevins, *Emergence of Lincoln, vol. 1,* 290. *CG, 35-1,* 137-139. *New Albany Ledger,* December 21, 1857. Washington Dispatches in *Ledger,* December 28, 1857. J.B. Norman to WHE, December 21, 1857, English Papers. In April 1857, the *Ledger* fulfilled its contract with the 34th Congress to print the federal laws, and, in the 35th Congress, English had secured the Administration's agreement to grant the *Ledger* the Post Office printing. *Ledger,* December 21, 1857. On January 7, 1858, the *Ledger* admitted that "it is thought by many that the views of Senator Fitch are endorsed by Senator Bright." Norman pathetically added, "we are satisfied this opinion is erroneous except in a qualified sense."

tion's petulant removal of Stanton on December 10, immediately after it received word of his actions. Yet, probably to prevent bloodshed, Buchanan instructed his newly appointed governor, James W. Denver, to enforce the law of the legislature and allow for a full submission election on January 4.[59] As the year turned from 1857 to 1858, the whole country seemed to hold its breath.

5.

The jumble of elections and the somewhat inconsistent attitude of the Administration allowed the *New Albany Ledger* to continue to hope for some accommodation. On December 26, it announced that the January 4 vote was the true test. This especially became the case when, a couple of days later, the results of the December 21 election showed that "the Constitution with Slavery" was adopted because of a free-state boycott. The *Ledger* declared, rather improperly, that the boycott was caused by the knowledge that an election was to occur two weeks later "at which the whole instrument is to be submitted." It argued that the results of that election would be "just as valid" as the results of the earlier one. In truth, the free-staters had long decided not to take part in the "clause" election essentially because it did not allow for a vote on full abolition and the machinery of the registering and balloting was completely in the hands of the pro-slavery forces. In a less certain tone, Norman privately asked English, "What is the administration to do with the election on the 4th?" Norman lamented the fate of the Party if it were to be forced to ignore an anti-slavery victory in that instance: "If the party takes that ground inevitable defeat awaits us. We cannot carry more than two Districts in Indiana and will lose the legislature and the Senate . . ." Greatly frustrated, evoking a conspiracy theory adhered to by Stephen Douglas, Norman added that "the entire Northern Democratic party ought not to be needlessly sacrificed to gratify Jeff Davis and other fire eaters who are anxious to get out of the Union, and want some excuse for doing so."[60]

Amidst these premonitions of disaster, the Democratic State Convention met in Indianapolis on the traditional date of January 8. Relations between the Party leadership (Bright and his lieutenants) and the rest of the Indiana Democracy were so bad that some had suggested the meeting be postponed. English was one of them, for Norman wrote him in late December that "I fully concur with you in the opinion that our State Convention ought to be postponed till Spring. The Kansas question is a very ugly one to take a position on now." But such desires

59. *New Albany Ledger,* December 22, 1857. Nevins, *Emergence of Lincoln, vol. I,* 265-268. Washington Dispatch, December 23, 1857, in *Ledger,* December 24, 1857.

60. *New Albany Ledger,* December 26, 29, 1857. Nevins, *Emergence of Lincoln, vol. 1,* 137-138; Potter, *Impending Crisis,* 300. J.B. Norman to WHE, December 30, 1857, English Papers.

went unheeded. On the eve of the convention, Democrats, as usual, gathered at Indianapolis in the hall of the House of Representatives to listen to addresses by Party notables. The division among the speakers mirrored the division within the party. Ex-senator Pettit, congressman Hughes, and governor Willard all spoke for the Administration—the latter perhaps in more moderation. Robert Lowry, Lew Wallace, and Henry Secrest, three young Democrats with their best political days ahead of them, generally supported Douglas. The pro-administration *Indiana State Sentinel* lavishly reported that Hughes's argument was "telling [and] statesmanlike," and ended "amid hearty and universal cheers." On the other hand, William W. Tuley, city commissioner and sometime chief clerk of New Albany, wrote English that "James Hughes made an ass of himself and better staid in Washington."[61]

Once the convention got down to business, it was clear that a majority of the delegates, unreflective of the rank and file of the Party, were friends of the Administration. Tuley wrote English that "the unmistakable feeling of the Democracy is against the course of the President and Messrs. Bright and Fitch"; yet many delegates were, in the words of one Douglasite, "postmasters and other minions of patronage" loyal to the Bright machine. English wisely had decided not to attend. As chairman of a major congressional committee, it would have been difficult for him to leave Washington anyway, but his decision was most likely caused by the desire to keep his options open. As one Democrat wrote to him from Indianapolis, "you are claimed on both sides of the question." Hughes was there, as aforementioned, but so was congressman John G. Davis to balance him out. (In fact, on the night before the convention, the two exchanged public unpleasantries.) Jesse Bright, wishing at all costs to avoid an anti-Lecompton resolution, did not feel safe enough to leave the convention to the guidance of his lieutenants. He took no chances and attended the gathering personally.[62]

An early test came on the vote for permanent chairman. The Bright forces nominated governor Willard, and pressed his selection in the name of "harmony." This led the other candidate, anti-Lecomptonite William Holman (former state legislator and future congressman), to let it be "understood" that he was not "antagonistic to Gov. Willard or any other National Democrat," but he came to the

61. *New Albany Ledger,* January 5, 1858. J.B. Norman to WHE, December 30, 1857, English Papers. *Indiana State Sentinel,* January 9, 1858. W.W. Tuley to WHE, January, 1858, English Papers.

62. Peek, "The True and Everlasting Principle," 382, 389. *New Albany Ledger,* January 12, 1858. W.W. Tuley to WHE, January 1858, English Papers. Besides Tuley, Kent (still in New Albany), Norman, and Frank Gwin were delegates from Floyd County. Jesse Bright had moved himself into English's district, and was a delegate from Clark County along with Amos Lovering. Heffren, Cravens and William Williams were there from Washington County. *Indiana Weekly Sentinel,* January 13, 1858. Dick Ryan to *New Albany Tribune,* January 26, 1858. Winston S. Pierce to WHE, January 8, 1858, English Papers. *Indiana State Sentinel,* January 9, 1858. Winston S. Pierce to WHE, January 8, 1858, English Papers. Van Der Weele, "Jesse Bright," 226-227. *Indiana State Sentinel,* in *Ledger,* January 11, 1858.

convention "representing principles." In a revealingly close vote, Willard defeated Holman 278 to 233. Although delegates chose between the nominees for other reasons besides Lecompton, the vote illustrated that Bright's hold was tenuous. Indeed, had Willard not been the Party's titular head, the "minions of patronage" might have been won over to the popular Holman. Willard took the chair dutifully preaching harmony: "Let us go to work for the advancement of democracy and civil liberty. Let us do this, and when we pass from this hall there will be but one weeping and wailing, and that will be in the Black Republican camp." He then appointed five secretaries regardless of their position on Lecompton, including John B. Norman of New Albany.[63]

But Willard had trouble forcing togetherness on a very divided party. Soon after he took command, a debate ensued over the traditional power of the chair to appoint the Committee on Resolutions. Anti-Lecomptonites, including Lew Wallace (state senator from Montgomery County) and Henry Secrest (probable successor to congressman John G. Davis) pressed for a new rule designating that the delegates from each district choose their own representatives on the committee. Opposing that position was Joseph W. Chapman (Bright's law partner), ex-senator Pettit, and Hughes. On the motion of John L. Robinson, the convention bowed to the collective weight of the party elders and tabled the anti-Lecomptonite approach. Eventually, the Bright forces allowed for a compromise whereby two delegates from each district, one presumably pro-Lecompton and the other anti-Lecompton, appointed by the chairman, would serve on the committee. From the Second District, such was indeed the case, for Norman served with Horace Heffren, a Washington County protégé of Henry Comingore. A perusal of the other members, however, illustrates that Willard 'cheated' a bit. For example, in the Third District, Chapman was appointed alongside Cyrus Dunham, both Lecomptonites.[64]

After recessing two hours for lunch, the delegates returned to nominate state officers without much altercation. Anti-Lecomptonites and Administration men appeared to share the places on the ticket. The real fight was expected over the resolution on Kansas, but, before the Resolutions Committee returned with its report, senator Bright was invited to address the convention. Eschewing generalities and limp appeals to harmony, the party boss defended Buchanan's course on Lecompton and attempted to show how it aligned with the Cincinnati platform. As he was about to enter into a "thorough discussion of the questions arising

63. *Indiana State Sentinel*, in *New Albany Ledger*, January 11, 1858. The Second District delegates voted 44 to 10 for Willard; three of the votes for Holman, interestingly, coming from Scott County, and the other seven from the county of Washington. *Indiana Weekly Sentinel*, January 13, 1858.

64. *Ibid*. Shephard, *Biographical Directory*, 406 for Wallace, 62 for Chapman. Secrest's political position is noted in *The New Albany Ledger*, July 12, 1858. Dunham's position is stated in J.B. Norman to WHE, March 31, 1858, English Papers.

with respect to Kansas," however, the Resolutions Committee returned and the attention of the delegates shifted to its report. Realizing the importance of the moment (and thoroughly confident the committee would vindicate his position), the senator sat down and allowed the report to be read.[65]

Committee chairman Daniel Vorhees prefaced the report by noting that it received the concurrence of all the committeemen. Specific resolutions endorsed *Dred Scott* (emphasizing that opponents to it were animated by the "loathsome doctrine of 'negro equality'"), upheld the legality of the elections of Bright and Fitch, arraigned on seven counts the Indiana State Republican Party and its legislators, and approved the gubernatorial course of governor Willard. Concerning Kansas, the committee expressed in general terms its undiminished confidence in James Buchanan and endorsed his Administration. No resolution spoke specifically to Lecompton, but the following two were obviously intended to fashion a platform upon which both sides could stand:

> That the right of the people of any State in this Union to mold their laws and institutions to suit themselves, and not others, being an unquestioned right, it follows the manner in which this high duty to themselves is discharged is not a proper subject for the dictation of any sister State or of all the States in the confederacy in Congress assembled, save only that the Constitution and the U.S. laws shall not be violated. That we endorse and reaffirm the platform laid down by the National democratic Convention of 1856, as embodying the spirit and the letter of the law of our political gravitation, which constitutes the Union as it is, holds each State in its own particular sphere, and reduces the theory of self-government to a practical reality.[66]

Notably, these two resolutions, most especially the first, concentrated on a state's independence but did not essentially address the question of the independence of a territorial government or constitutional convention. These resolutions were clearly a remarkable attempt to sidestep the major political issue at hand. One hundred and eighty-six delegates refused to endorse this platform, but they were not nearly enough to defeat it. Despite the dissatisfaction of so large a minority, the Bright forces pressed for adjournment *sine die*, and they might have gotten it were it not for a letter read from Aquilla Jones, the Democratic state treasurer elected in 1856 and renominated this year. A longtime leading Democrat from Bartholomew County, Jones informed the convention that he could not in good conscience "accept the honor you have offered me upon the Platform you have

---

65. *Indiana State Sentinel,* in *New Albany Ledger,* January 11, 1858.

66. *Ibid.*

this day adopted." He was "impelled to this conclusion, not so much by anything you assert in your resolutions, as by the fact that in my humble judgment, some of the favorite measures, and at least one vital principle of the Democratic party, have either been omitted or asserted in such a manner as to be susceptible to an equivocal construction." Indeed, the "favorite measure" of the Kansas-Nebraska Act and the "vital principle" of popular sovereignty were never mentioned in the resolutions. Jones's rather courageous move stimulated the anti-Lecomptonites. While balloting proceeded on the selection of a new nominee for state treasurer, Lew Wallace perfected an additional resolution to the platform:

> That we are still in favor of the great principle of the Kansas-Nebraska bill and that by a practical application of that doctrine, the people of a State or of a Territory should be as they are inalienable invested with the right of ratifying or rejecting, at the ballot box, any constitution that may be framed for their government; and that now and hereafter no Territory should be admitted into the Union, as a State, without a fair expression of the will of the people being first had upon the constitution accompanying the application for admission.[67]

When the new nominee for state treasurer was finally selected, Wallace presented his work and had it referred to the Resolutions Committee. Forced to deal directly with the issue of submitting Lecompton to the people of Kansas, the committee split for the first time. The majority report submitted a substitute resolution that allowed the people of a territory "to reserve for themselves" the right of submittal, in effect implying that, since this was not expressly done by Kansans before the Lecompton convention, non-submission was legal. It also excluded the "now" in Wallace's resolution and simply stated that "hereafter it would be better for the purpose of avoiding doubt and difficulty" that territorial constitutions be submitted to the people. The minority report, on the other hand, more closely followed Wallace's own resolution. After a bit of maneuvering, both reports were dropped in favor or Wallace's own substitute for his original resolution:

> That we are still in favor of the great doctrine of the Kansas-Nebraska bill, and that by a practical application of that doctrine the people of a State or of a Territory are invested with the right of ratifying or rejecting at the ballot box any constitution that may be formed for their government, and that hereafter no Territory should be admitted into the Union as a

---

67. *Ibid.* Woolen, *Eminent and Self-Made Men*, District 7, 108-109. *Indiana State Sentinel*, in *New Albany Ledger*, January 11, 1858.

State without a fair expression of the will of the people being first had upon the constitution accompanying the application for admission.

Comparisons between Wallace's original suggested resolution and his substitute show only minor changes, mostly of style, though substantively the omission of "now" would soon cause problems. Believing either that they could not defeat the resolution, or that they could somehow later circumvent it, the Bright forces refused to break up the convention over it. They let it pass, 278 to 114, and the delegates adjourned for good.[68]

"It would not be the truth to say that the proceedings of the Convention were conducted in harmony and good feeling," the *New Albany Ledger* reported a few days later; and in a letter to English, ex-congressman William Watson Wick added, "it was a mistake to attempt to conduct affairs at our 8th Jan. Convention with a strong hand as was done." From New Albany, Michael Kerr agreed, lamenting that Bright had "attempted [and] partially succeeded in dictating opinions and platforms to the Democracy of Indiana." But, in the same issue where Norman lamented division, he also noted that the adoption of Wallace's resolution "seemed to calm the angry elements and restore a portion of good feeling and harmony." Wick cautiously agreed: "Wallace's resolution . . . will restore a feeling of compact, though it may be that the actions of the convention, taken as a whole, had deepened fears and prejudices."[69]

A few days later, all pretense of harmony was destroyed when disagreement developed over exactly what Wallace's accepted resolution meant. First of all, on January 12, the *Washington Union* carried an article that said that the resolution did not represent "the true sentiments of the Convention." It claimed that "the malcontents" took advantage of the poor attendance at that late hour and "reversed the action of the full convention." The *New Albany Ledger's* editor scoffed at such a suggestion. "Everyone who was there knows it to be untrue," Norman wrote English privately. "*There can be no question of this,*" he emphasized. Then, Graham Fitch, speaking before the United States Senate, explained that the resolution did not include Kansas anyway. "[It was] amended in such a manner as to make it sustain the Administration," he declared. Essentially, Fitch argued that the omission of the word "now" from the "now and hereafter" of the original was explicitly accepted because it meant that Kansas was excluded from the principle of submission. Only future territorial conventions were compelled to submit their work for ratification. Though not unreasonable as to its syntactical interpretation,

---

68. *Indiana State Sentinel,* in *New Albany Ledger,* January 11, 1858. The Lecomptonites believed, probably because of the omission of the "now," that the convention had "secured a reliable victory for our friends." Ashbel Willard to James Buchanan, January 9, 1858, English Papers.

69. *New Albany Ledger,* January 12, 1858. W.W. Wick to WHE, January 26, 1858; M.C. Kerr to WHE, January 23, 1858, English Papers. *Ledger,* January 12, 1858. W.W. Wick to WHE, January 12, 1858, English Papers.

the *Ledger* sarcastically noted that Fitch's interpretation "will be news to most of the members of the Democratic State Convention." Norman later privately labeled Fitch's explanation "preposterous." And Lewis Jordan wrote that "no man of common sense would ever try to torture the resolution into a meaning so utterly inconsistent with its language."[70]

Because Bright fully agreed with Fitch's interpretation, anti-Lecompton Democrats of Indiana looked to Stephen Douglas to set matters right in the Senate. The Little Giant pointed out that "hereafter" referred to Congress's duty, not a territory's. Wallace's resolution antedated congressional action on Lecompton, he noted, and when it mandated that "hereafter no Territory should be admitted into the Union as a State without fair expression of the will of the people being first had upon the constitution accompanying the application for admission," it meant that *Congress* should reject any such application it had not yet acted upon. In a sense, Douglas's cleverness saved the day. Even major Administration sheets in Indiana began to admit that the resolution was truly intended to apply to Kansas, and Wallace himself came forward to endorse Douglas's explanation. "I was sorry to see Fitch make such a Jack of himself," Lewis Jordan sighed to Samuel Douglass.[71]

Incensed by senator Fitch's attempt to snatch their victory away from them, the Indiana anti-Lecomptonites struck back. First of all, the venerable editor of the *Indiana Volksblatt* addressed letters to the Democratic state nominees asking them to state their understanding of Wallace's resolution. All of them agreed the resolution demanded submittal of the Constitution in all cases, including Kansas. Still not done, the anti-Lecomptonites promoted a second Democratic convention and scheduled it to meet on George Washington's birthday. It was to formally clarify the Party's stand against Lecompton. As the *New Albany Tribune* noticed, the call was endorsed by "rather prominent Democrats, but very few officeholders." Yet, among them was English's political friend William Wick, who at that moment held (albeit very tenuously) the important position of postmaster for the city of Indianapolis. Other promoters included ex-*Sentinel* publisher Austin Brown, Grafton Cookersly (leading Vigo County politician and a member of the 1850–1851 constitutional convention), and Royal S. Hicks (Spencer County's foremost anti-Lecomptonite and publisher of the *Franklin Democrat*). Both Nor-

---

70. *Washington Union*, January 12, 1858. *New Albany Ledger*, January 19, 1858. J.B. Norman to WHE, January 15, 1858, English Papers. *CG, 35-1*, 272, 271. *Ledger*, January 19, 1858. J.B. Norman to WHE, January 21, 1858; Lewis Jordan to Samuel Douglass, January 21, 1858, English Papers.

71. *CG, 35-1*, 271-272. *New Albany Ledger*, January 26, 1858. Norman claimed that the *Indiana State Sentinel*, *Lafayette Argus*, and *Rushville Democrat*, all presented true versions of the Wallace Resolution. J.B. Norman to WHE, January 27, 1858, English Papers. Wallace wrote the *Sentinel* a letter, published in the *Ledger*, January 20, 1858. Lewis Jordan to Samuel Douglass, January 21, 1858, English Papers.

man and Lewis Jordan blamed the call on Fitch. Jordan added, "I cannot see how the party is going to escape a great rout next fall if this gaming does not cease."[72]

The *New Albany Ledger's* reaction to the call for another convention is instructive, if only to illustrate how difficult it was becoming for anyone to hold some middle ground between what now might be termed the Douglas wing and the Bright wing of the Indiana Democratic Party. Although, as an editor, Norman was naturally more outspoken than so cautious a politician as English, both were equally passionate on the issue of party schisms. To both, the Democratic Party offered the best hope to the nation on a variety of issues. Thus, it was that Norman wrote his congressional friend that he would "endeavor to throw cold water on the [February 22] movement." In the *Ledger,* he termed the call disharmonious and begged the promoters to be satisfied with a resolution that almost all Democrats believed was anti-Lecompton. Norman's newspaper declared that it did not wish to sacrifice principle, but, under the circumstances, "the platform adopted was all that could be reasonably expected if the party was to remain united." It refused to print the names of the new convention's promoters. The moderate tone of the *Ledger* may be fairly contrasted with the combative one taken by Henry Comingore's *Paoli Eagle.* Comingore, whom Norman later termed "a furious Lecomptonite," took the line that the promoters of a new convention were simply factious. Privately, he wrote English that "a few damned old broken bloats in our party" were using the call "to get up a Douglas party in Indiana." He had already misasserted that the delegates to the January convention "fairly represented their constituents," and the proceedings there "were conducted honorably and fairly." About a year earlier, the *Madison Courier* noted that the *Ledger*, unlike the *Eagle*, "lied 'sorter between the genuine Democrats of the pocket and the 'cent and shilling Democrats' of Northern Indiana," but this was an increasingly difficult place to remain.[73]

On January 4, Kansans, primarily of the free-state persuasion, went to the polls and cast 10,221 votes to reject Lecompton; only about 200 voted to ratify. Anticipating such a vote English had privately asked his leading constituents if the Party could "possibly sustain [itself] before the people of Indiana if we vote to bring Kansas into the Union with a slavery constitution which her people have expressly repudiated?" Corydon editor Simeon K. Wolfe was incredulous: "You intimate it is possible that Southern influence is so strong in Washington that the

---

72. *Paoli Eagle,* January 18, February 4, 11, 1858. *New Albany Ledger,* February 1, 1858. J.B. Norman to WHE, January 27, 1858, English Papers. *New Albany Tribune,* January 21, 27, 1858. Elbert, "Southern Indiana Politics," 54, n. 41. J.B. Norman to WHE, January 24, 1858; Lewis Jordan to Samuel Douglass, January 24, 1858, English Papers.

73. J.B. Norman to WHE, January 24, 1858, English Papers. *New Albany Ledger,* January 20, 27, 1858. J.B. Norman to WHE, March 31, 1858. Henry Comingore to WHE, [1858], English Papers. *Paoli Eagle,* January 28, 14, 1858. *Madison Courier,* in *Ledger,* January 7, 1857.

President may recommend such a course! Surely the South is not so blind as to ask such a thing, nor the President so weak as to grant it." Things looked different on the Potomac. No matter how consistently English was told by his Indiana confidantes that "the Democracy here sustain the position of Judge Douglas to a man almost," or that "four-fifths of the district are Anti-Lecompton," or that "our two Senators would be beat in a popular vote by 20,000," the pressure in Washington by the Administration to support Lecompton was intense. English might have wished that Comingore and the Orange County boys, who called Douglas's position "damned stuff" and questioned his sincerity, reflected the district's majority position. But such was not the case. Norman answered English's query by simply stating that the Party would indeed not be able to "sustain" itself in October if Lecompton went through. Even Phineas Kent, whom Norman described as "a devoted friend of Bright and Fitch," acknowledged that "deference was necessary to the popular sovereignty sentiment." English's representative duty was clear, but could he safely abandon his powerful allies in Washington; and if he did, would the country and the whole Democracy be better off for it?[74]

6.

On February 2, 1858, ignoring the January 4 vote, James Buchanan formally submitted the Lecompton Constitution to Congress and recommended that Kansas be admitted to the Union under it. He explained that his instructions to governor Walker requiring popular ratification "had no object in view except the all-absorbing question of slavery." This, according to the president, had been done by the Kansas constitutional convention in the clause election of December 21. Moreover, popular sovereignty in general had not been violated because Kansas, through their legislators in early 1857, had not required the convention to submit the constitution for approval. Should the people of Kansas now wish to register their disapproval of any part of the constitution, they could always amend it even if they had to wait until 1864 as so stipulated in Lecompton itself. "The small difference in time," Buchanan argued, "is of not the least importance, when contrasted with the evils which must necessarily result to the whole country from a revival of the slavery agitation." On the other hand, speedy admission would promote "domestic peace."[75]

74. Stampp, *1857*, 321. S.K. Wolfe to WHE, January 12, 1858; J.A. Cravens to WHE, January 29, 1858; M.C. Kerr to WHE, January 23, 1858; W.W. Tuley to WHE [Jan., 1858]; Henry Comingore to WHE [1858]; J. B. Norman to WHE, January 21, 27, 1858, English Papers.

75. *CG, 35-1,* 533-535. Buchanan had shown one of his drafts to Alexander Stephens, who, as chair of the Committee on Territories, was to shepherd Lecompton and Kansas admission through the House of Representatives. Stephens made several suggestions that Buchanan incorporated. Alexander Stephens to Linton Stephens, February 3, 1858.

There was nothing new or surprising in this message; its contents were well anticipated. By the time the House received it, most congressmen had already split into six distinct groups aligned along two positions. Supporting Lecompton and the admission of Kansas under it were all the southern Democrats, about 35 of their northern brethren, and more than half of the Know-Nothing southern Americans. Against admission were all the Republicans, perhaps six southern Americans (there were no actual northern Americans), five of whom were from Kentucky and Maryland (two hearty Know-Nothing states), and about 20 northern Democrats known as "anti-Lecomptonites." Without these rebellious Democrats, Congress would have been certain to approve Lecompton. Even with them, Buchanan still believed he could drive Lecompton "naked" through the legislature. But, since mid-January, the anti-Lecompton Democrats had regularly caucused together to prevent just that, and, in consultation with Republicans (who gladly took a back seat), they had come up with a plan. As soon as they could, after Buchanan's message was read, they would try to move consideration of the message away from Alexander Stephens's Territorial Committee and into a select committee instructed to thoroughly investigate electoral politics in Kansas. At the least, this move would indefinitely postpone consideration of any bill to admit Kansas. And once fraud and chicanery were unalterably proven, they would then demand a new congressional act enabling Kansans (now under a free-state legislature) to frame a new submittable constitution.[76]

In anticipation of this move, the Administration authorized James Hughes to follow Stephens's orthodox motion (to refer the president's message to his Territorial Committee) with one of his own moving the president's message to consideration by a select committee *without* instructions to investigate. Buchanan hoped that such a motion might divide the anti-Lecomptonites and ensure success. Consequently, as soon as the president's message was completely read, the actors readied to play their appointed roles. When Stephens finished making his own motion, Orr recognized Hughes, but before the Hoosier could utter a word, Thomas L. Harris, Douglas Democrat from Illinois, was on his feet asking the doughface to yield for a substitute motion. The following short colloquy rather illustrates the tension of the moment and, in truth, the contempt the anti-Lecomptonites had for the northern Lecompton Democrats:

Hughes:	Will the gentleman inform me what [the motion] is?
Harris:	That's my business.
Hughes:	The gentleman asks for my courtesy and declines to return it.

76. Nichols, *Disruption*, 162-163, 164. Thomas Schott, Alexander H. *Stephens of Georgia: A Biography* (Baton Rouge and London: Louisiana University Press, 1988), 244.

Harris: I ask no courtesy.

Hughes: And I ask none of you. I will not be unparliamentary.

Excitement reigned on the heels of Hughes's final riposte and Orr had to gavel congressmen into their seats. After some time, this first of many vociferous altercations finally subsided.[77]

Stephens, fearful and uncertain of the strength of the anti-administration forces, instructed Robert Letcher of Virginia to move for an adjournment before anything further ensued. Letcher's motion brought on the initial actual test vote on the Lecompton issue. When the roll call was completed, the anti-Lecomptonites celebrated their first triumph. Twenty-two Democrats abandoned the Administration, and along with 83 Republicans and two Americans they defeated the motion to adjourn 109 to 105. "Three southern men were out of their seats," Stephens lamented to his brother. "Had all of them been in their seats the Speaker would have brought it to a tie." (Though that would still have not passed the motion to adjourn.) About a month earlier, Stephens had hoped that 33 northern Democrats would stick with the Administration; only 24 actually did. The anti-Lecompton Democrats came predominantly from the West. They included all five congressmen from Douglas's Illinois, six out of eight from Ohio, six from Pennsylvania's trans-Appalachian region, and half the delegation from Indiana. Among the latter was William English.[78]

Had it been up to English himself to decide when to formally cast his lot with one side or the other, he would have certainly delayed it further in hopes of a compromise. "It is proper for you to stand by the President as long as you can do so and not violate any great principle," Cravens had written him a week earlier. Winston Pierce had suggested that, because "Mr. Buchanan did not indicate his views since called upon to do so, I think you are right in declining to say how you will go until called upon." He had now been called upon. "We are satisfied," the *New Albany Ledger* stoutly stated in January, "that he [English] will carry out the wishes of his constituents, and that he will make no exception in favor of the Lecompton Constitution—sacrifice no principle to gain favor with a Northern or Southern clique, but will firmly adhere to and support the Cincinnati platform." The *Ledger* got it right.[79] Fundamentally a western man, wedded to popular sovereignty as Douglas and he understood it from practically his first month as a congressman, English stood with that principle and against most of those with

---

77. *CG, 35-1*, 533-536. *New Albany Ledger*, February 3, 1858.

78. *CG, 35-1*, 536. Alexander Stephens to Linton Stephens, February 3, 1858, in Johnston, *Life of Stephens*, 328. *CG, 35-1*, 536.

79. J.A. Cravens to WHE, January 24, 1858; Winston S. Pierce to WHE, January 8, 1858, English Papers. *New Albany Ledger*, January 8, 1858. *CG, 35-1*, 536.

whom he had allied for over four years. In doing so, he also split from fellow southern Hoosier William Niblack of the First District, and instead joined with James Foley and ultra-Wright man John G. Davis. His vote clearly appeared to be an act of forthright political independence.

Yet such was the paranoia and distrust of the anti-administration forces that, despite the fact that English had often caucused with the anti-Lecomptonites, he was essentially considered an unsteady ally. In truth, such fears were not completely unfounded, for, in his desire for party harmony, some of his actions did indeed cause concern. For example, English continued to caucus with the regular Democrats as well as the renegades; and while other anti-Lecompton Democrats also considered this a prerogative, English went so far as to accept caucus appointment to a committee designed to promote party discipline. There is every reason to believe that although he had voted with the anti-Lecompton Democrats on the adjournment issue, he was taken by surprise at such an early vote and refused to completely close his options—and the anti-administration forces knew it.[80]

In any event, soon after the adjournment vote failed, Hughes regained the floor and formally moved to refer the president's message to a select committee without investigatory powers. After Hughes made a rather obnoxious pro-Lecompton speech, interrupted by questions, calls for order, and failed motions of adjournment, Harris ended the session with his own motion to amend Hughes's motion by instructing the select committee "to inquire into all the facts connected with the formation of said Constitution and the laws, if any, under which it was originated"—in other words, a thorough investigation of Kansas politics surrounding Lecompton. Because both sides were uncertain of victory, as well as the fact that most members were worn out, the House adjourned, and voting on the various motions was thus postponed. During the next couple of days, both anti-Lecompton Democrats and House Democrats as a whole held caucuses, but, on Friday, February 5, Harris unexpectedly moved for a vote on his proposal. Stephens, again fearing that the Administration would be defeated, began delaying tactics that lasted throughout the night. Several motions were made to adjourn, and a roll call was taken for each. That in itself consumed about four hours. When southern Democrats absented themselves to prevent a quorum, the anti-Lecompton Democrats and Republicans forced the sergeant-at-arms to fetch them. At 2 a.m., these parliamentary maneuvers degenerated into a congressional fracas when Republican Galusha Grow and fire-eater Lawrence Keitt turned a shouting match into fisticuffs. Before long, a dozen House members were flailing away at one another. The melee ended in laughter when William Barksdale of Mississippi, having had his toupee knocked off, put it back on his head inside out. It was about an hour before the House finally got back to business, but the

---

80. Nichols, *Disruption*, 171.

delaying tactics continued. Finally, exhausted, the members agreed to adjourn until Monday morning.[81]

The weekend was filled with caucuses and counter-caucuses all intended to bring out the maximum vote for each side. When the House took up the matter on February 8, Harris moved that a vote be taken on his motion for full investigation. Stephens objected, but Harris's motion had precedence. Orr ruled that the first vote would be taken on Stephens's original resolution that the president's message be referred to his Committee on Territories, and, if defeated, it would be followed by Harris's substitute amendment to Hughes's resolution for a select committee. Using all his powers as majority leader and whip, Stephens almost succeeded in getting his resolution passed, but the final tally read 114 to 113 against him. Burns of Ohio had slipped away from the anti-Lecomptonites, but he was replaced by his fellow Buckeye, George H. Pendleton. One anti-Lecomptonite, William Reilly of Pennsylvania, did not vote; he would soon desert to the Lecomptonites. English, Foley, and Davis held fast, but, had it not been for an absent Milledge Bonham of South Carolina, the Lecomptonites might have won. The anti-Lecomptonites quickly demanded a vote on Harris's amendment. Perhaps delaying for the appearance of Bonham, John Cochrane of New York asked the clerk to re-read Harris's substitute resolution. English, uncharacteristically impatient with these tactics, objected that "it has been read half a dozen times already," but Cochrane had his way. When the vote was finally taken the anti-Lecomptonites succeeded again. Pendleton retreated back to the Administration, but Niblack joined the anti-Lecomptonites, and the final margin was three votes, 114 to 111. The substitute having passed, Hughes's now amended resolution to send to the select committee with investigating powers also passed 115 to 111.[82]

The anti-Lecomptonites had won a significant victory; the only question now was the composition of the select committee. Speaker Orr promised to put an anti-Lecompton majority on it, but many suspected he would act otherwise. On February 11, these suspicions were borne out. The speaker now contended that, because the issue was actually the president's message, the Administration de-

---

81. *CG, 35-1,* 536-541. *New Albany Ledger,* February 4, 10, 1858. *Cincinnati Enquirer,* in *Ledger,* February 12, 1858. Nichols, *Disruption,* 164-165. Freeman. *Field of Blood,* 236-243, has a good account of Keitt/Grow and nicely stresses its passionate manliness, that is, the physical pride the northerners showed in their physical defiance of southern arrogance. The *Enquirer* correspondent reported "three black eyes (bad) . . . two black eyes (slight) . . . three severe contusions . . . two slight contusions." For another account of the fracas, see Hunt, *Israel, Elihu, and Cadwalder Washburn,* 190. Also: Robert Isilivech, *Galusha A. Grow: The People's Candidate* (Pittsburgh: University of Pittsburgh Press, 1988), 164; Schott, *Stephens,* 245-246. Stephens commented in a letter to his brother detailing the fracas: "[B]ad feeling was produced by it. It was the first sectional fight here on the floor—and if any weapons had been present it would probably have been a bloody one." Alexander Stephens to Linton Stephens, February 5, 1858, Stephens Papers, Manhattanville.

82. *New Albany Ledger,* February 10, 1858. *CG, 35-1,* 621-623. Caruthers of Missouri was also absent ill. Nichols, *Disruption,* 165.

served a majority on the committee. Though he officially designated Harris as chairman, the full membership included eight Lecomptonites and seven anti-Lecomptonites. So constructed, the committee's purpose was aborted throughout its proceedings, for whenever the Republicans or Douglas Democrats called for specific documents to investigate, the majority voted against them. Such documents included Walker's letter of acceptance, a record of the January 4 election, statements by numerous Kansans, authenticated records of the territorial legislature, and various election returns and census reports. The committee met for three weeks, and, as the *New Albany Ledger* reported, the members voted down "all propositions to proceed to discharge of the duty for which they were appointed." Orr's trickery had served its purpose: the committee's final report, written by Stephens, predictably upheld the legality of the Lecompton Constitution and criticized the position and deeds of Douglas, Walker, and Stanton. All amending motions to this report were defeated. Harris, thus, filed a minority report that essentially stated that the committee had not done its job. It recommended, therefore, that Kansas could not yet be admitted.[83]

During the time the select committee met, the Administration began to remove from federal office Democrats who had acted with the anti-Lecomptonites. In Indiana, that included William Wick. On March 8, Wick wrote English that he had been "superseded in the P.O.," a reference to his dismissal as postmaster of Indianapolis. His reappointment had long been held up, and he was replaced soon after he joined the February 22 convention. Two months later, he wrote that it was the first time in his life that he had been "constrained to feel a consciousness of exceeding wrong, neglect, injustice, accomplished by fraud and dishonor. It came upon me unexpectedly," he wrote, "and it hurt badly." Other postmasters also lost their jobs, and the United States district attorney for Indiana's First District, Alvin F. Hovey, was removed without the knowledge of congressman Niblack and despite the representative's subsequent protestations. In New Albany, Norman also felt the heat. For some time now, the contract the House had given the *New Albany Ledger* to publish the United States laws had been held up in the Senate by Fitch's refusal to support it. (In fact, a couple of months later, the *Ledger* lost the contract to Comingore's *Paoli Eagle*.) In later February, Fitch even threatened to have Norman removed as surveyor of the port. "A slave to those above him," Norman wrote of the junior senator, "he would have all what he considers

---

83. *CG, 35-1,* 679. Nichols, *Disruption,* 167. The anti-Lecomptonites of the Committee were composed of five Republicans and two Democrats. At one point, Harris and the anti-Lecomptonites had decided to appeal Orr's committee selection and take the appointment from him, but they eventually changed their minds for fear of failure. *New York Tribune,* in *New Albany Ledger,* February 11, 1858. *Ledger,* February 17, 18, 24, March 1, 5, 1858. Final majority and minority reports in *House Report 377, 35th Congress, 1st session,* May 11, 1858.

beneath him slaves to himself." Throughout Indiana the Administration continually threatened anti-Lecompton editors with loss of patronage.[84]

Such actions were not merely intended to punish rebel Democrats at large but to pressure congressmen to think twice before abandoning the Administration. In 1854, the Democratic leadership had been confronted with a similar rebellion over the Kansas-Nebraska Bill, and it had used similar tactics to overturn the votes of numbers of northern Democrats. It was confident it could do so again. On February 8, the *Washington Union* formally read Thomas L. Harris out of the Party, and it labeled as "a little corporal's guard of renegades" all Democrats who acted with him. Technically, this included English, and, indeed, Luciene Matthews wrote him from New Albany that "the *Union* has commenced reading you out of the party." If the administration forces had wanted, they could have threatened to remove English as chairman of the Post Office Committee, remove the effective and loyal Frank Gwin as New Albany's postmaster, or follow through with removing Norman as surveyor of the New Albany port. But it did not so pressure the Second District congressman. Partly, this may be explained by English's previous yeoman service to the Party, in part by his relationship with Jesse Bright and also by the respect his character commanded. But, principally, the Administration recognized that English was not above compromise, that, although he would probably never suborn his principles in this matter, he might be useful in preventing full-scale disaster. His willingness to harmonize was one of his most salient characteristics, and the Administration hoped to use him in this capacity. Subsequent events, at least, support this interpretation.[85]

Not so James Foley. A first-term congressman-farmer, Foley had neither the respect nor utility accorded to English. In the *Rushville Jacksonian*, John L. Robinson abused him almost daily. Alluding to an earlier congressman of the Fourth District, Robinson wrote that Foley was "treading but too certainly the path of his illustrious predecessor . . . *Jim Lane*. It is unnecessary," Robinson warned, "to say where that path leads, and that the tracks of those who take it, so far as Democrats are concerned, all leads like animals into the den, *one way. They never return.*"

---

84. W.W. Wick to WHE, March 6, May 8, 1858, English Papers. Elbert, "Southern Indiana Politics," 34. *New Albany Ledger,* March 29, April 9, 1858. *Madison Courier,* March 5, 1858. J.B. Norman to WHE, March 5, 1858, January 17, 1858, English Papers. Wick wrote English in early May that, in Indiana and elsewhere, the anti-Lecomptonites "were treated and scorned as Black Republicans." Wick to WHE, May 8, 1858, English Papers. Wick made a retreat back to orthodoxy by 1860. See Wick to R.M.T. Hunter, May 6, 1860, in Ambler, *Correspondence of Hunter,* 325. One historian argues that, while patronage and other tactics were similarly used by the Pierce administration during the Kansas-Nebraska Act, during the Lecompton battle, "never had the President used the patronage power so flagrantly." Summers, *The Plundering Generation,* 252. The later so-called congressional "Covode Report" of the next Congress makes this abundantly clear as well (see chapter 9 for context of Covode Report).

85. *New Albany Ledger,* February 10, 1858. Luciene Matthews to WHE, February 11, 1858, English Papers. For the Administration's use of English see Chapter 7.

For their part, Bright and Fitch threatened to have removed certain officeholders whom Foley had gotten appointed in his district. According to one source, Foley met the two senators "at their rooms one day" and denied their right to take such action. "Suddenly removing his coat, [Foley] offered to settle the matter on the spot by recourse to the 'manly art.'" Bright and Fitch declined the invitation, but the congressman "heard no more of their threatened interference."[86] As for John G. Davis, the third steady Hoosier anti-Lecomptonite, he had long been opposed to the Administration as a loyal Wright and Douglas man. Direct pressure on him would have been useless.

In this period, stormy meetings of the House Democratic caucus were the rule. During one gathering, a heated discussion over Lecompton led William Barksdale to label the Douglas Democrats no better than Republicans. After much noise and confusion, Samuel Marshall of Illinois warned the leadership not to make support for Lecompton a test of one's Democracy: "Suppose it should turn out that a majority of the Democratic party were opposed to Lecompton? Who then would be read out of the party?" He reminded many of the Lecomptonites that he had been a Democrat for many more years than most of them, and his Democracy was well defined. As Norman wrote English in early March, "it has come to a pretty state of things when a few officeholders, and cringing sycophants who want office, are to read out of the Democratic Party all who refuse to bow to their behests." English apparently agreed, for Norman was responding to English's own concerns over the "tyranny and despotism of the Lecomptonites at Washington."[87]

Norman's labeled "sycophants" were well represented in the Indiana Democratic Club of Washington, D.C. Composed of Hoosier federal officeholders, the club passed resolutions supporting Lecompton. Its principal officers, president Finley Bigger and secretary Robert S. Sproule, were longtime confederates of Jesse Bright. Others included Thomas Hendricks (United States land commissioner and future governor and vice-presidential nominee) and William Sherrod (an English patronage "appointee" as pension agent). In all, there were about 45 of them. Lewis Jordan, now a mild anti-Lecomptonite, noted that those of his persuasion, "staid away from the meeting when [the resolutions] were to be passed." He singled out Sherrod as one of the measures' sponsors. The resolutions stated that the doctrine of submission was new and unnecessary to admission as a state: "It would be an unwarrantable assumption of power on the part of Congress, and a violation of the Kansas-Nebraska Act, to deny admission to the state of Kansas on this ground." The *New Albany Ledger* noted that such a position was

---

86. *Rushville Jacksonian,* February 12, 1858. Lane of course had completely abandoned the Democrats and became one of the leading Republicans in the Kansas, Topeka, movement. On Foley's challenge to Bright and Fitch, see Woolen, *Eminent and Self-Made Men,* District 4, 24.

87. *New York Herald,* February 14, 1858. J.B. Norman to WHE, March 6, 1858, English Papers.

in direct conflict with the Lew Wallace resolution passed at the Democratic State Convention. Norman attributed that to the fact that most members of the Club had "not spent one day in Indiana since the Lecompton question was started." Notably, Norman wondered whether the group could be trusted to act "in good faith toward the State ticket."[88]

7.

Amid these pressures and resentments, English dutifully attended Congress and listened to scores of speeches on Lecompton. Only after three full weeks of apprising "all the facts and arguments presented," and only two days before the Stephens majority report finally reached the House floor, did English rise to make his own lengthy contribution. "I have thus far in the session carefully abstained from taking any part in the discussion of the vexed question," he began, "deeming the premature introduction of the subject into the debates of Congress exceedingly unfortunate, because calculated to lead to bad feeling in the Democratic party and the country." But, "The time for action, however, has arrived." Still considered by the anti-Lecompton forces an uncertain ally, his remarks were no doubt accorded special attention. Five days earlier, Hughes had made a forceful pro-Lecompton speech at a Tammany Hall meeting in New York City, and only that morning Bright had written English asking him "to conform as near as you can to the views of the great democratic party, which is now assailed fiercely enough, God knows, by its ancient enemies." No one knew for sure how much English would succumb to these pressures. As a British clergyman traveling in Indiana a few months earlier said of the Hoosier Democrats, "unflinching adherence to party is principle with them, and to forsake a party is regarded as an act of the greatest dishonor."[89]

The greatest portion of English's speech made clear that he remained a staunch anti-Lecomptonite. One by one he addressed the arguments in favor of Lecompton, and one by one he disposed of them. William T. Spicely, formerly of Orange County but more recently a Kansas member of the Lecompton Convention, had written English that the delegate election had been "conducted fairly." He blamed Kansas's slave status squarely upon the boycotting voters. Comingore, though admitting that "fraudulent voting cannot be prevented in the territories" wondered why "the Free State men [did] not act the part of good citizens and aid in preventing frauds?" English answered these assertions by noting that this particular fraud was of the most intrinsic kind: no census taken in 19 of 34 counties; no registry of

---

88. *New Albany Ledger,* March 6, 1858. Lewis Jordan to Samuel Douglass, February 20, 1858, English Papers. *Ledger,* March 6, May 14, 1858.

89. *CG, 35-1,* 1013. *New Albany Ledger,* March 8, 1858. Jesse Bright to WHE, March 9, 1858, English Papers. Fred S. Johnson, "Americans and American Methodism," quoted in Van Bolt, "Rise of the Republican Party," 219.

voters in 15 counties; all election officials pro-slavery. He even noted that, when citizens of the aforementioned counties attempted to complete their own census and registration, the convention still refused their delegates. Such extensive fraud justified a free–state boycott, for no election under these conditions could have fairly registered their will.[90]

By examining the corruption attendant to the election of the Lecompton delegates, English implied that congressmen should take this factor into account when deciding the pending question, and that the massive incompetence and fraud invalidated the whole process. Southerners and Administration men dis-agreed on the ground that such inspection amounted to federal interference in territorial affairs, contravening the supposed "non-interference" policy of the Kansas-Nebraska Act. Indeed, according to some southerners, Kansas at this stage existed as an "inchoate" state. To them, a territory's rights as a state existed just prior to the formation of its constitution, and whether Congress wished to admit Kansas or not should have nothing to do with the manner in which its organic law was formed. Once again, the proper interpretation of federal authority under the Kansas-Nebraska Act was in dispute. Consequently, while not conceding the point, but like a good lawyer, English moved to the question of whether the con-vention was obliged to submit Lecompton for popular ratification. Again, south-erners said this was not required—that a constitutional convention was sovereign, an extension of the people themselves. The *Paoli Eagle* agreed: "This doctrine [of full submittal] was never advocated by any portion of the democratic party, until Douglas brought it up . . . The Democratic doctrine is for the territories to adopt their constitution in their own way—if they require their delegates to submit a constitution to a vote of the people, all right—if they are willing to take it without its being submitted to them, outsiders have no right to object." Even an anti-Le-comptonite friend of English's, Winston Pierce, admitted that "there is no *legal* responsibility resting on [the convention] to submit any part of it," and Lewis Jordan noted that the absence of the doctrine in Kansas's enabling act allowed Kansas to follow "the old established precedents."[91]

English met these strictly procedurally legal interpretations not initially, as many of his colleagues had, with demands for equity but with a new constitu-tional wrinkle. He asserted that the sovereignty of a constitutional convention was "not to be exercised upon a mere implication; and if it [such sovereignty] is not expressly granted it is a power *reserved* to the people." His touchstone for

90. Spicely's antecedents are noted in the *New Albany Ledger*, June 23, 1853, July 6, 1857. W.T. Spicely to WHE, February 16, 1858, English Papers. *Paoli Eagle*, March 19, 1858. *CG, 35-1*, 1014. By quoting these facts, English must have had access to Harris's minority report.

91. R.M.T. Hunter to Virginia Democrats, October 28, 1857, in Ambler, *Correspondence of Hunter*, 247. John Millson in *CG, 35-1*, 1889. *CG, 35-1*, 1014. *Paoli Eagle*, February 25, 1858. Winston S. Pierce to WHE, January 8, 1858; Lewis Jordan to Samuel Douglass, January 12, 1858, English Papers.

such an argument was that in the United States's system, "powers not expressly delegated, are reserved to the people." Although this appears to be a particularly modern interpretation of the Tenth Amendment (the 19th-century formula having been "powers not expressly delegated to the *federal* government are reserved to the *states*"), it had the proper ring of liberty to it and served English's purpose well. He then showed that no such sovereignty had indeed even been expressly granted to the Lecompton convention—not in the congressional enabling act, not in Buchanan's instructions to Walker (which appeared, indeed, to state just the opposite), and not in Walker's own "repeated declarations." Moreover, he presented a letter from the Douglas County Democratic candidates to the Lecompton convention pledging their support for submittal. As for those cases where state constitutions had been declared final when no express power of sovereignty was granted to the constitutional convention, English answered that these instances occurred in earlier times, "when restrictions on the expression of the will of the people, in the shape of provisos and Missouri Compromises, were much more in vogue than they are in this day of light and knowledge." (His clever implicated indictment of the anti-slavery Wilmot "proviso" and the perceived anti-slavery Missouri Compromise was clearly intended to appeal to the South.) He directly argued that his constitutional interpretation aligned with "the beginning of a new era," initiated with the 1850 Compromise and confirmed by the principle of popular sovereignty.[92]

As for Buchanan's argument that the mere submission of the slavery clause complied with the requirements of popular sovereignty, English simply countered that "Negro slavery is not the only domestic institution, or the one, in my judgment, most sacred." The claim of popular sovereignty was that it professed to treat slavery like all other domestic institutions. Partial submittal was inconsistent with this claim, however tendentious that claim was. Moreover, clearly, the actual form of this present partial submittal, where even a vote for "the Constitution without Slavery" allowed continuation of slavery in Kansas, made Buchanan's argument even more spurious. To those who argued that Kansans could amend that clause in seven years, when, no doubt, the state will have a large anti-slavery majority, English replied that "the whole history of Kansas leads me to distrust that abstract assertion."[93]

The last argument that English addressed was the one rather akin to that used in connection to the Kansas-Nebraska Act: that, in this case, passing Lecompton and thus getting rid of the issue quickly would diffuse, if not end, the slavery controversy. During Kansas-Nebraska it was argued that 'localizing the issue' would diffuse it by removing it from the halls of Congress, a point acquiesced in at the

92. *CG, 35-1*, 1014-1015.

93. *Ibid.*, 1015, 1016.

time by English himself. The argument now was just 'move on'. Wryly, and perhaps self-consciously, he noted that "this is not the first time I have heard there was to be an end to the slavery agitation." Most politicians from southeastern Indiana doubted such a happy result would follow Lecompton's approval. Thomas L. Smith, erstwhile English stalking horse and the rather shady but competent lawyer for the Jeffersonville Branch of the Indiana State Bank, who supported Lecompton, admitted that "revolution" would meet "its return to the territory with the approbation of Congress." Michael Kerr also doubted that approval of Lecompton would "allay or localize excitement in Kansas." He predicted that should Lecompton be approved, the free-staters, "if necessary, [would] by bloodshed, organize a state government under the Topeka Constitution . . . and then send their federal representatives to Washington. Will not the South," he asked, "raise a howl against admitting to seats or recognizing as agents, the representatives of revolution?" English saw the same scenario. The admittance of Kansas under Lecompton, he said, would "be the signal for such agitation as the country has never known, and instead of withdrawing troops from Kansas for service in Utah, still more troops [would] be required to aid the 2,000 pro-slavery men in Kansas to force the institution down the throats of the 15,000 free-state men in that Territory." This was not the way, he later noted, to build up the Democratic Party in Kansas.[94]

The solution English offered to all of this was pure Douglas: "I think we should regard the Lecompton Constitution as 'unmade', repudiated, rendered null and void; and adopt legislation [mandating that] before Kansas is admitted, her people ought to ratify, or at least have a fair opportunity to vote upon, the constitution under which it is proposed to admit her." In other words, Congress should pass a new enabling act stipulating submittal. As it stood, English reasoned, "the technicalities of the law" may be on the side of the Lecomptonites, but equity and justice opposed them: "The great fact which stares the whole country in the face, and which no man can deny, is that the Lecompton constitution does not embody the will of the people of Kansas, and that they do not wish it imposed and fastened upon them as their organic law."[95]

Fifteen months earlier, English had appealed to southern moderates not to forsake the northern Democracy, nor to believe that popular sovereignty was just as anti-slavery a procedure as congressional restriction. But now 22 northern Democrats were allied with the Republican Party to prevent slavery from claiming Kansas, and few southerners, whether moderate or otherwise, saw much efficacy in a doctrine and procedure so construed to cheat them out of what they consid-

---

94. *Ibid.,* 1016. Esarey, *State Banking,* 288-296. Smith's and Kerr's opinions are both expressed in M.C. Kerr to WHE, February 19, 1858, English Papers. *CG, 35-1,* 1016.

95. *CG, 35-1,* 1015, 1017, 1014.

ered was their fair inheritance. "All knew," Alexander Stephens said two years later, "that [Lecompton] was procured by stratagem. I supported it not in consideration of any matters connected with its formation, except that it was framed in strict and technical conformity with the enabling act. I thought it ought to be adopted, and think so yet, because it gave us only what we were entitled to under the Kansas-Nebraska Act."[96] It took less than four years for the abstract differences over Kansas-Nebraska to blossom into practical opposition. Southern Democrats had always stressed the non-interference aspect of the Act, Northerners its principle of local majority rule. Both sides had expected their interpretation to gain them Kansas. Both could not be served.

Yet some Democrats refused to admit that the Party could not survive intact despite these differences, and, for two more years, they tried to keep it together—to harmonize against the inveterate foe. English was one of them. During his speech he noted, "I plead guilty to being devoted to the Democratic party:

> I have clung to it with unwavering fidelity, under all circumstances. I do not mean to say that the Democratic party is always right, upon all subjects, but I have thought, and still think, it is more nearly so than any other political organization; and that, even if wrong on an isolated measure I could do more good by staying in that party, and laboring to get it right, than in any other position.[97]

"Laboring to get it right"—that is exactly what he was trying to do. Most of his speech was devoted to argumentation concerning both the political, practical, and even constitutional aspects of the debate over Lecompton, but here and in spots elsewhere he spoke as a party man directly to the Southern Democrats. Refusing to forsake the majoritarian aspect of popular sovereignty, he told his southern brethren that it "is the very cornerstone upon which our political institutions are built, the right of the people to govern and of the majority to rule." This was thoroughly Democratic doctrine, he asserted (albeit insensitive to Tocqueville's possible tyranny of the majority), and in all events it must be respected by the whole party. When the Administration and the South supported Lecompton, they supported, in his alter-ego's words, a "plain and palpable violation of the Democratic creed." It could not be tolerated.[98]

---

96. Alexander Stephens [May 1860], in conversation with Richard H. Johnston, in Johnston, *Life of Stephens*, 356.

97. *CG, 35-1*, 1015.

98. *CG, 35-1*, 1013. J.B. Norman to WHE, March 5, 1858, English Papers. English was not unaware that the majority of congressmen opposed to Lecompton were Republicans who preferably opposed popular sovereignty in favor of congressional restriction of slavery. But, being in a congressional minority, the Republicans had no choice but to ally with the northern Democratic anti-Lecomptonites and their support

But English refused to stand on principles alone, for he tried to convince the southern Democrats that their respect for this principle would reward them in the end. Should Lecompton pass, a measure that "nine-tenths of the people of the free states hold to be a fraud and at war with the plainest principles of justice and republican government," the northern Democracy would be destroyed at the next election. When that happened, who would protect the South when its "peculiar institutions are assailed [by] this fearful army of fanatics, this great army of Abolitionists, Know-Nothings, and Republicans?" What would happen when "Cuba and the countries south of our present limits get ready to come to us?" The South needed the northern Democracy, English reasoned, for northern Democrats had always stood up for the South's just rights. In 1854,

> we northern supporters of the [Kansas-Nebraska] measure went home to encounter the fierce and vindictive character of which our southern brethren have scarcely a conception; and which, I am sorry to be compelled to add, I fear they did not fully appreciate, or have too soon forgotten. We were denounced as dough-faces and traitors; we were hung in effigy, and every indignity that the ingenuity and malignity of fanaticism could devise was heaped upon us . . . You gentlemen of the South were at home at your ease, because you had not run counter to the sympathies and popular sentiments of *your* people: *you* went with the current—*we* against it. *We risked* everything—*you* comparatively nothing. And the results of the election speak for themselves.

Was more now needed to demonstrate the northern democracy's sensitivity to southern equality? Southern Democrats should think twice before proscribing their northern counterparts, a policy destined to leave them at the mercy of an angry and extremist North.[99]

As earnest and principled as this attempt to harmonize the Party was, it was destined to fail because it misread the southern mind of 1858. To English and the northern Democrats, the Party was almost an end in itself, staving off Whig and now Republican attempts to foist aristocracy on the common folk. Such was the essence of the Jacksonian Party. But, to southern Democrats, and this was essentially a moderate argument, the national party had become useful for one purpose: to allow the South to nurture and expand its peculiar institution, and inferentially to hold in check those forces which would treat southern ways as

---

of popular sovereignty if they were to prevent Kansas from becoming a slave state. Nevins, *Emergence of Lincoln, vol. 1,* 296; Johannsen, *Stephen Douglas,* 601. English himself recognized this when he defended the northern Democrats who allied with Republicans by rhetorically asking whether "Democrats are to forsake a Democratic principle just as soon as the Republicans come to its aid?" *CG, 35-1,* 1016.

99. *CG, 35-1,* 1013.

inferior and uncivilized. As Linton Stephens wrote to his brother, "the true issue is, and Congress ought to be held to it, whether a state with slavery is fit to be admitted into the Union." Believing honestly that Lecompton was legal, and that the Kansas free-staters' boycott was unnecessary, they deprecated northern Democratic efforts to change the rules to suit themselves. "[The Southerners] persist in their made Kansas phantom," wrote one Democrat to English; but the South was earnest in its conviction. And a Democratic Party that refused to tolerate the defendably legal expansion of slavery was not a party fit to survive.[100]

As for English's assertions that the South needed the northern Democracy to protect its just rights, many southerners were becoming convinced that the same northern Democracy was actually hostile to their prerogatives. So reasonable a southern Democrat as Alexander Stephens noted with anger that Buchanan's hostility toward William Walker's filibustering was governed, not by international law, but by his hostility to slavery. "[T]he object of this government, " Stephens wrote, "[is] to prevent any colony or state arising in Central America on the basis or status of the Southern states." For many southerners, Lecompton was a test of northern Democratic fidelity; and not just an abstract one like support for the Kansas-Nebraska Act. "Should the Constitution be rejected," John A. Quitman wrote, "the South must regard the plighted faith of the Northern Democracy violated. It will assure us that no more reliance can be placed on them to aid us in protecting our rights; that National Democracy is worthless."[101] Essentially, English's principles were not Southern principles. Ever conscious of their minority status, southerners put only as much faith into popular sovereignty as to nullify the Missouri Compromise. Majority rule meant little to an embattled minority.

Historians have made much over the concept of "honor," affecting both sections, but especially representative of the Southern attitude. In essence, many southerners believed that they were treated unequally, as their peculiar domestic institution was not accorded the equal respect of other state institutions. Refusing at least publicly to face the fact that slavery *was* qualitatively different from other institutions (a refusal actually abetted by Douglas's Kansas-Nebraska Act), they bristled when it was criticized, and maintained that such criticism treated their society in an inferior manner. In truth, relatively few southerners believed that slavery would exist in Kansas for long, even if Congress admitted the state under Lecompton, as they understood that free-soilers would most likely so outnumber pro-slavery Kansans at least by 1864 that the Constitution would be amended to

---

100. Linton Stephens quoted in Nevins, *Emergence of Lincoln, vol. 1,* 282. Joseph Low to WHE, March 10, 1858, English Papers.

101. Alexander Stephens to Linton Stephens, January 20, 1858, in Johnston, *Life of Stephens,* 329. Quitman to [unsaid], February 1, 1858, quoted in *Emergence of Lincoln, vol. 1,* 284-285.

abolish it. As Thomas Ritchie's *Richmond Enquirer* noted, slavery was not likely to remain for long in Kansas: "It is therefore the great principle of equality for which we are contenting." If northern Democrats would not permit slavery, even temporarily, in Kansas, it was indicative that it would be permitted nowhere.[102]

Ever hopeful of compromise, English either misunderstood or had not yet realized the depth of southern pride and fear. Like many northern Democrats, he considered popular sovereignty so fair-minded, so American, that he was hard-pressed to abandon its lure. Almost completely, despite the warnings of his correspondents, he disregarded the growing sentiment toward disunion among his southern colleagues. Believing that the Democratic Party was "a healthy organization [where] people breathe freer and deeper because it respects the rights of all," he was loath to believe that it could not solve the problem of slavery among mutually agreeable lines. All he asked, as if this was only a minor request, was that majority rule be respected, never truly understanding that the South saw restricting slavery as tyranny toward the natural rights of property. As he noted in his speech, he still hoped for some sort of reasonable compromise on the issue at hand:

> I am not so wedded to any particular plan that I may not, for the sake of harmony and as a choice of evils, make reasonable concessions, *provided that the substance would be secured*; which is the making of the constitution, at an early day, conform to the public will, or at least that the privilege and opportunity of so making it be secured to the people beyond question.

Here, he stood; this was as far as he would go. "If for these honest convictions I am to lose the favor of southern gentlemen, or of the Administration," he continued, "so be it. I shall do my duty here as well as I know how, and return to the bosom of my generous constituents with a clear conscience."[103]

---

102. Morrison, *Slavery and the American West*, 200-203. *Enquirer* quote from January 30, 1858.

103. *CG, 35-1*, 1016, 1017. Both James Morrison and Michael Kerr mentioned the subject of disunion in letters to English. Kerr believed that southern secessionists saw the admission of Lecompton as especially fruitful because it would put into Republican hands a "whip of scorpions" to promote northern anti-southernism. This would work to "accelerate the consummation of the real purpose of the South, the dissolution of the Union." Kerr to WHE, February 19, 1858, English Papers. Morrison saw "one of two reasons of sufficient weight to cause all this hubbub. They are covert reasons and will remain so until the public mind is sufficiently inflamed to receive and endorse them. That day no true patriot would wish to see." Fearing that his prediction might stay English's course, Morrison ended with the advice that his congressman not swerve from his duty, for in that manner he was likely to hasten dissolution. "Do right now," he concluded, "and let the future take care of itself." Morrison to WHE, February 16, 1858, English Papers. English made no allusion to such thoughts in his speech.

All in all, considering English's ambition, his closeness to Bright and the southern leaders in the Party, his desire to be faithful to the Administration, and the lack of any need to appease a constituency from whom he most likely would not ask for a fourth term, his stand was rather both courageous and principled. Only the most suspicious skeptics could doubt his fidelity to anti-Lecomptonism. They hoped it would not weaken.

CHAPTER SEVEN

The English Bill

A side from the predictable sniping of the *New Albany Tribune*, both Republicans and Democrats in southeastern Indiana were generally well satisfied with English's anti-Lecompton speech of March 9. "I have always despised this truckling on the part of the Democracy to the slave power, and want of independence exhibited by democrats generally on the subject," Luciene Matthews wrote English directly. "Your speech has completely vindicated our party and set us right." The *New Albany Ledger* dubbed the speech "a most excellent one," and even the *Paoli Eagle* grudgingly admitted that "Mr. English made about the best speech that has been made against the Lecompton Constitution." And Phineas Kent, who was not averse to Lecompton, judged English's effort "the best speech you ever delivered," primarily for its typically fair tone: "If all our democratic friends who unfortunately differ on this vexed question, would manifest the same good temper less bad feeling would exist." The Republican *Madison Courier* called his effort a "manly, bold" one, especially for a congressman who "throughout his congressional career [has] shown so much fidelity to the interests of the South." And the Republican *Corydon Argus* praised him for his "manly course in opposition to this iniquitous proceeding." It wryly added that "it doesn't matter for the honor and safety of the nation whether or not Mr. E. feels that a vote in favor of Lecompton would be signing his political death warrant." Republicans could only be so gracious.[1]

From around the state the Anti-Lecompton Democracy applauded him. A correspondent of John G. Davis and former state representative maintained he

---

1. L.G. Matthews to WHE, (1858), English Papers. *New Albany Ledger,* March 16, 1858. *Paoli Eagle,* April 15, 1858. P.M. Kent to WHE, March 22, 1858, English Papers. *Madison Courier* and *Corydon Argus* from English Scrapbook, 78. The *New Albany Tribune* sarcastically commented, "[h]ere is a specimen of Hoosier eloquence that must have made those southern Democrats to whom Mr. English appealed quake in their boots. Like everything emanating from this great man, it must have produced a decided sensation, and soothed troubled waters of the Democratic quagmire. It is presumed when they heard his sayings they all went out and took a drink together." *Tribune,* March 13, 1858.

was "very glad" to receive it in the mail. The *Decatur Democrat* praised the speech generally, and the *Terre Haute Journal* called it "one of the ablest, clearest, and most concise speeches that has ever yet been made against [Lecompton]." The *Journal* also noticed that "the hired letter writers and the tools of power" had already begun to "heap upon [English] their party slang and unmeasured abuse." But the Second District congressman, the *Journal* continued, should "heed them not, for his constituents will take care of him and the Democracy all over the State will honor him for his devotion to the principles of the Democratic party." Accordingly, Michael Kerr simply noted that English's "Anti-Lecompton speech [has been] highly spoken of by all your constituents here whom I have heard express their opinion." There were, of course, some Indiana Democrats opposed to Lecompton, who were not quite so enamored of English's speech. Amos Lovering, a fierce anti-Lecomptonite, for example, spoke for some who "complained that the last of your speech is for compromising and [we] fear that you will support some measure evading the principle in the contest." There were some, in other words, who could not believe, understandably, that a close Bright ally would not in the end squirm his way back toward the Administration.[2]

In point of fact, Jesse Bright excused his young friend for his anti-Lecomptonism, and he graciously let English know he understood that he had "not sought by anything you have said or done to embarrass or strike at me." Bright "regretted" that he and his protégé "could not have harmonized on this question," but he "sincerely hope[d] that we yet will be able to do so." English, too, hoped that he could be saved from the disagreeable task of voting with 90 Republicans to defeat the Democratic administration. As long as "the will of the people of Kansas" was upheld, he had admitted (as Lovering noted) he "might be induced to go for" another solution besides simply a new enabling act. This much, he believed, he owed to Bright and Buchanan. Consequently, from the day of his speech until the end of the controversy English toiled to reconcile the duty he owed to popular sovereignty with the loyalty he owed to the "national Democracy."[3]

English's part in the congressional proceedings of March 11 and 12 illustrates his persistent attempt to find middle ground. As noted in the last chapter, a select committee was given investigatory powers to decide whether Lecompton was fairly enacted. But, because speaker Orr had so constituted the committee, improperly, with a pro-Lecompton majority, little actual testimony was taken, and little real investigation was done. This produced a majority report that ignored the shady manner by which Lecompton was pushed through. Since early in March, the majority on the committee had adjourned its proceedings, and Alex-

---

2. Samuel Clark to John G. Davis, March 15, 1857, Davis Papers. *Journal* and *Democrat* from English Scrapbook, 78, 81. M.C. Kerr to WHE, March 27, 1858; Amos Lovering to WHE, March 21, 1858, English Papers.

3. Jesse Bright to WHE, March 9, 1858, English Papers. *CG, 35-1,* 1016-1017.

ander Stephens had been ready to present this report. But, because the minority was not ready with its own report, Stephens agreed to wait a week. On March 10, one week having expired, he formally tried to present his report, but, at that point, opponents of Lecompton objected to its presentation on the grounds that it was out of order during regular business. Acting honorably, the speaker agreed, but this anti-Lecompton tactic was only a delaying action. At the moment, the opponents of Lecompton did not have a thought-out long-term strategy. They agreed, of course, that the select committee had shirked its responsibility, and some of them wanted to directly challenge the speaker's power of appointment by revamping the committee's membership on a full vote of the House. But, apparently, most anti-Lecomptonites felt this was too risky a course that might infuriate some of the Democrats in the coalition, so it was finally decided that Thomas Harris, nominal chairman of the select committee, should attempt to reopen the committee by reading its journal to the House to prove it had not yet fulfilled its duty. Once that was achieved, Kentucky American congressman (and inveterate anti-Democrat) Humphrey Marshall agreed to offer a resolution that would empower only seven of the committee's 15 members to call for any information or witnesses they thought necessary.[4]

On March 11, they sprang into action. Harris gained the floor and raised what he called a matter of privilege. Claiming that the select committee had adjourned before executing its responsibilities, he proposed to read the minutes from the committee to prove this charge. But the speaker was not to be manhandled so easily. Orr responded that Harris's request was not a matter of privilege, and the only way the House could decide whether or not the committee had fulfilled its responsibilities was to have it submit its report. Refusing to concede defeat, Harris appealed the speaker's ruling. Stephens moved to lay the appeal on the table, but, largely because a score of Lecomptonites were absent, the House easily defeated his motion. Three Anti-Lecomptonites from Indiana—English, Davis, and Foley—held firm and voted against Stephens's motion, but Niblack, perhaps chastened by the Hovey incident, went back to the Lecomptonites and voted to table. Bargaining and parliamentary maneuvers delayed further consideration of the appeal matter for one day, and the House adjourned with the question of appeal still pending.[5]

The next morning, the debate ensued. The speaker began by offering precedents to prove that "it is not competent to refer in the debate in the House to what transpires in the Committee." Harris, naturally, refused to support these precedents, arguing that it was a matter of privilege in cases when the "conduct

---

4. Alexander Stephens to Linton Stephens, March 11, 1858, in Johnston, *Life of Stephens*, 330. *CG, 35-1*, 1037. Schott, *Stephens*, 247. *Cincinnati Gazette*, March 8, 1858, in *New Albany Ledger*, March 10, 1858.

5. *CG, 35-1*, 1075-1077. Alexander Stephens to Linton Stephens, March 11, 1858, in Johnston, *Life of Stephens*, 330-331.

[of representatives] is not in accordance with the order of the House." But it was Galusha Grow, Republican floor leader, who made the essential point. He noted that "it may be difficult to find in the books an exact precedent which shall apply to this case precisely for the reason that the parliamentary law requires that when a legislative body orders a thing to be done through the medium of a committee, the presiding officer shall appoint a majority of that committee from those who are in favor of carrying out the order." This was manifestly not done by Orr, and, as Grow stated, "being a violation of parliamentary law, we should be at a loss to find a precedent to apply to such a case." Grow was obviously impatient with the strategy of the anti-Lecompton Democrats and he cut straight to the heart of the matter. Stephens kept trying to call him to order, claiming that his remarks were wider than the question allowed, but Grow refused to be silent and the debate grew contentious.[6]

At this point, when fisticuffs might have been soon in coming, English entered the fray. He agreed with Grow "that parliamentary law and practice required that this committee should have been so constituted . . . that a majority of it should have reflected the opinions of a majority of the House." But, whether or not the committee was properly composed, he continued, the essential question was whether it had carried out its obligations. To determine the answer to that question, English suggested that Harris withdraw his appeal on the question of privilege concerning the direct reading of the Committee's journal before the House and simply submit his minority report along with Stephens's majority report. Within Harris's report he could include the committee's minutes along with his own interpretation, "so that all facts may be brought before the House." The consideration of the reports may then be postponed "to some future day in order that gentlemen may examine the records to see whether the Committee has executed the order of the House."[7]

At other times, in other circumstances, such a suggestion would have been easily adopted. But the distrust the anti-Lecomptonites held for their adversaries doomed so reasonable a compromise. When Stephens disingenuously noted that English's plan "was exactly what I have been desiring all the time," he foolishly helped destroy it. The Republicans were constantly wary of the wily Georgian, and they reasoned that anything he approved must be contrary to their own interests. William Montgomery, anti-Lecompton Democrat from western Pennsylvania, worried that as soon as both reports came in Stephens would immediately move for a vote on them. English responded that, "if they have a majority, let the will of the majority prevail," but he also noted that "the majority will be the other way." Stephens himself replied to Montgomery that he would allow three

---

6. *CG, 35-1,* 1103-1107.

7. *Ibid.,* 1107.

days for discussion; such "ample time," as Stephens put it, conformed to English's plan. Montgomery, unconvinced, countered that Stephens could only speak for himself, implying that other members may not be so generous. Israel Washburn, Republican from Maine, feared that Stephens might even seek to substitute a Joint Resolution for the Admission of Kansas to his majority report. Stephens promised not to do so; but when Washburn demanded he demonstrate his good intentions by allowing the majority report to come before the House as part of the minutes of the committee, Stephens declined: "I stand by the rights of that committee," he replied.[8]

To mollify Montgomery and Washburn, English agreed to amend his proposal to explicitly state that the two "reports shall not be accompanied by any bill or joint resolution," but Washburn and some other Republicans were not satisfied. Washburn would, however, not object if English amended his plan to read that "no action of the House [on the reports] shall be construed as an admission of Kansas." English was stupefied by this paranoia, and he no doubt sensed objections would keep coming. Unlike the Republicans and a portion of the anti-Lecompton Democrats, he trusted the administration forces to play fair. Indeed, he had the highest regard for Stephens and the Democratic leadership. But that was exactly why he could not be trusted. Although the chance was minute that his plan would lead the House to the admission of Kansas, Orr's unscrupulous appointment of the select committee made even the merest hint of compromise unacceptable to most opponents of Lecompton. They could no longer appreciate a gentlemanly willingness to contest the issue fairly, and English's approach continued to mark him, quite correctly, as an anti-Lecomptonite to be watched. Consequently, soon after his colloquy with Washburn, a plethora of objections killed his proposal.[9]

English's plan was actually more than just a reasonable proposal. Some anti-Lecompton Democrats, probably a minority, believed that Orr's ruling on Harris's privilege motion was indeed parliamentarily correct. They were, consequently, loath to vote against the speaker, though they supported Harris's ultimate aims. English's suggestion was therefore designed to prevent them from a difficult vote, and it only failed because Republicans suffered under no such difficulty. His plan's defeat led the House back to this question of Harris's appeal, and, predictably, Stephens once again moved that it be tabled. During the roll call, when the clerk reached English's name, the embittered Hoosier, while continuing to vote with his anti-Lecompton allies against tabling, maintained he did so "without intending to commit myself against the [actual] decision of the Chair." Lawrence Hall of Ohio, another anti-Lecompton Democrat, made substantially the same remark.

---

8. *Ibid.*, 1107-1108.

9. *Ibid.*, 1108-1109.

The final tally showed that the opponents of Lecompton were again victorious, but this time by the mere margin of two votes—111 to 109. Uncertain of both English and Hall on a straight test of the speaker's ruling, the anti-Lecompton leadership decided to leave it at that for the day. Having prevented the majority report from coming into the House, and again demonstrating that they held a majority, Harris withdrew his appeal rather than suffer a demoralizing defeat. English may have failed in his primary objective, but his bold declaration saved him and other Democrats from a difficult vote. The House then adjourned over the weekend until Monday.[10]

A few days after these proceedings, William Montgomery introduced into the House the anti-Lecompton counter-formula to Kansas's immediate admission. It provided that an extra session of the Kansas legislature apportion districts from which delegates would be selected to approve or amend the Lecompton Constitution. Once considered by the delegates, the Constitution would then be submitted to Kansans for ratification, and, if accepted, the president could proclaim Kansas a state immediately. One week later the Senate voted down a similar substitute submitted by John J. Crittenden of Kentucky, and passed a bill simply admitting Kansas under Lecompton. The only substantial change made by the Senate was to greatly reduce an exorbitant federal land grant attached to the Constitution. On March 28, two days after the Senate vote, majority and minority reports of the select committee having become superfluous, Stephens announced his intention to take up the Senate bill (S 161) in the House on April 1. If the administration was to win back any wavering anti-Lecompton Democrats they had about a week to do so.[11]

On March 26 and 27, two very different attempts were made on the floor of the House to pressure anti-Lecompton Democrats to come back to the fold. The first, by "Extra Billy" Smith of Virginia, illustrated that no Democrat was above proscription, for Smith severely criticized Virginia governor Henry A. Wise for an anti-Lecompton speech he made in New York on January 8. Perhaps playfully, yet also pointedly, English rose to ask Smith whether the chief executive of Vir-

---

10. *New Albany Ledger*, March 18, 1858. *CG, 35-1*, 1109-1110. Alexander Stephens to Linton Stephens, March 12, 1858, in Johnston, *Life of Stephens*, 331. In the same letter, Stephens complained to his brother, "as usual we lost the question [on the tabling motion] by the absence of two Southerners, Caruthers of Missouri and Branch of North Carolina." Stephens Papers, Manhattanville. Throughout the long struggle, Stephens lamented the unfortunate absence of southern congressmen.

11. *CG, 35-1*, 1150. *New Albany Ledger*, April 2, 1858. Nichols, *Disruption*, 169-170. *CG, 35-1*, 1343. Stephens viewed Montgomery's proposal with great apprehension. He summed up his fears, one day after the Pennsylvanian's proposition, to his brother with this terse phrase: "So you see, the chances for Lecompton at this time are bad enough." Alexander Stephens to Linton Stephens, March 17, 1858, Stephens Papers, Manhattanville. It is interesting that Stephens did not seem to mind that some northern Democrats voted anti-Lecompton; it was the six southern Americans that brought forth his ire, for, in his mind, they unpardonably abandoned the South. Stephens to Linton, March 9, 1858, April 2, 1858, Stephens Papers, Manhattanville.

ginia was in or out of the Democratic Party. Taking the bait, Smith replied that he was out: "All gentlemen who refuse to cooperate with the Democratic party in the great measures of the party, are necessarily outside of that party." Ignoring the obvious reference to himself, English wondered if Extra-Billy too was not out of the Party because he had supported Wise for governor. Smith replied he supported principles, not men, but John G. Davis, picking up on English's line of argument, noted that this was exactly what the anti-Lecomptonites were doing. If the governor of Virginia could act contrary to Democratic principles, so could the president. And, if the president could read other Democrats out of the Party, why couldn't the governor do the same?[12]

A more intelligent way to enforce orthodoxy was made the next day by Joseph Lane. The former Hoosier war hero and now delegate from the Oregon Territory, Lane questioned the sincerity of anti-Lecompton Democrats when they declared their willingness to vote for the admission of a new slave state. "Everybody knows that Kansas will not long be a slave state," he asserted. "Slavery will not long exist there, but the principle, nevertheless does exist: and that is whether another slave state shall ever be admitted into the Union." Often the defender of the northern Democracy, English protested the charge of insincerity, asking Lane whether he actually "knows of any northern Democrat who takes the ground that no slave state shall hereafter be admitted to the Union?" Lane replied that "an [anti-Lecomptonite] may say he is willing to vote for the admission of a slave state, but when it comes to the point, he will not do it. How are we to know that he will do it?" As Lane had clearly struck a nerve, English made it more personal and closely related to principle, asking Lane if he specifically "means to say that I would not vote to admit a slave state into the Union if it were the will of the people of a State to recognize slavery?" Lane retreated into accusing the anti-Lecomptonites with acting with a party (the Republicans) that "would not vote for the admission of Kansas with slavery, if every man, woman, and child, in the Territory, should ask it."[13] Such an argument revealing the Republican position was indeed true, but it was beside the point. The real problem for southerners was that mere northern Democratic abstract declarations of solidarity were no longer good enough for the "national" southern-dominated Democracy, just as "squatter" sovereignty wasn't. Threatened by abolitionist enemies and the Republican Party, a true Democrat had to follow the policy of rather complete non-interference into territorial affairs and the inviolability of territorial slave property in preference to majority rule. Only then would the sections be equal.

---

12. *CG, 35-1,* 1372. William Smith of Virginia was known as "Extra Billy" Smith because another William Smith, from Alabama, William Russel Smith, served with him in the 33rd and 34th Congresses and had preceded "Extra Billy" in the 32nd Congress. *Biographical Directory of U.S. Congress,* 1940, 1942.

13. *Ibid.,* 1396.

Bullying on the floor of Congress, or using patronage and other threats, was not the only way the Administration tried to turn the anti-Lecomptonites. If the Administration was to avoid humiliating defeat it began to realize that some sort of compromise that reconciled competing forms of "principle" would have to be achieved to win over at least five of the recalcitrant Democrats. Consequently, the Party called for a Democratic House caucus to meet on the night of March 27. The Administration's plan was to have the caucus select a committee composed of equal numbers of Lecompton and anti-Lecompton Democrats to thrash out an acceptable eleventh hour settlement. A long shot, indeed, but the Administration believed it was worth the effort.[14]

When the caucus convened at around 7:30 p.m., about 70 of the 91 Democrats attended, including most of the anti-Lecomptonites. Alexander Stephens began the meeting by stating that the object of the caucus was for Democratic Lecomptonites and anti-Lecomptonites to "confer together and see if by some arrangement the discordant elements could be made to unite." As soon as he finished, William English gained the floor and offered the caucus the following resolution:

> That a committee be appointed by the chair to consist of ten Lecompton and ten Anti-Lecompton Democrats, whose duty it shall be to confer together, and ascertain whether anything can be done to secure harmony and concert of action in reference to the question of admitting Kansas into the Union, and that said committee report the result of their deliberations, to this caucus, for its consideration on Tuesday evening [March 30] at 8:00, to which time the caucus will adjourn.

Before he sat down, he made a little speech in support of this plan. The great "calamity" that must be avoided, he asserted, was "the division and overthrow of the democratic party and the elevation to its place of one purely sectional." This was the immediate threat, and it was likely to come to place if the two opposing Democratic groups could not unite. Whatever differences existed between Democrats on Lecompton, there must occur a concerted attempt to reconcile them. The issue now "was not so much what ought to have been done with this question originally, as what could be done with it in the position to which it has drifted."[15]

Obviously, English's part in this caucus may not be attributed to mere spontaneity. Evidence exists to suggest that he was acting with the full knowledge of the Administration and its congressional supporters. On March 22, president Buchanan had penned a note to the young Hoosier suggesting "some ideas which

---

14. *New York Herald* dispatch, March 27, 1858, in *New Albany Ledger*, April 1, 1858.

15. *Ibid.*

may prove valuable to yourself." Unfortunately, the part of the communication containing the ideas themselves has been lost, but they no doubt referred to the substance of the aforementioned resolution as well as plans of action once the compromise committee was formed. How long English had been conferring with the Administration is unclear, but he probably exchanged views with Buchanan a few times previous to this; and his prominence in caucuses in general appears to confirm that he was privy to the desires of the Lecompton forces. Whether he used his feet in both camps to relay privileged information between them cannot be known for sure, and it would be uncharitable to label him a spy. But it is again clear why the anti-Lecomptonites distrusted him. Buchanan had ended his note by writing English that "the present occasion [is] the most fortunate of your life. It will be your fate to end the dangerous agitation, to confer lasting benefits on your country and to render your character historical."[16]

Buchanan's attempt at flattery was unnecessary. English had long staked out his position on Lecompton, and was certainly willing to compromise along principled lines. Moreover, whatever historical and political benefits he might attain were clearly to be weighed against the calumny that would follow, should he be judged a traitor to the anti-Lecompton cause. He was willing to gamble with his political future, that is, to risk alienating his anti-Lecompton constituency, not for any selfish historical fame, but simply to allay the danger the Lecompton issue posed to the Democratic Party. One of his political advisors, Winston Pierce, had written English a few weeks earlier that "Old Buck, Cobb [secretary of treasury from Georgia], Floyd [secretary of war from Virginia], Slidell [Louisiana senator], and Bright cannot destroy *Douglas* but *can* make themselves fame for having destroyed the Democracy faster than any of the same number have done before," and it was to prevent this that English acted as he did. "You must look out," his uncle warned him from Kentucky, "there are more eyes upon you at this time than any other man in the United States." And William Wick warned him against "ministering to the ambitious plans of others."[17] But English was clear as to his goals, and, whatever one might think of the merits of saving the Democratic Party, it was this, and not his own place in history, he primarily wished to promote.

English's caucus resolution was unanimously adopted. It was now up to John Cochrane of New York, caucus president, to appoint the 20 committeemen. As

---

16. James Buchanan to WHE, March 22, 1858, English Papers. Buchanan wrote in this letter that "I *repeat* that I consider the present occasion the most fortunate of your life." [Emphasis added.] Since that was the first mention of this sentiment in the letter it stands to reason that the two had conferred earlier.

17. Winston Pierce to WHE, March 10, 1858; S.S. English to WHE, March 26, 1858; W.W. Wick to WHE, February 21, 1858, English Papers. Some historians have called Buchanan and his southern advisors, like those mentioned in Pierce's letter, the "Directory," an obvious reference to the executives in France from 1795-1799 during the French Revolution. The term is indicative of the fact that historians have believed Buchanan acted under the sway of self-interested and none too punctilious southerners.

the resolution's sponsor, English was designated chairman, and he was included as one of the 10 anti-Lecomptonites. Of the other nine appointed opposed to the Administration, two appeared somewhat uncertain of their position (Owen Jones and William Dewart of Pennsylvania), one other had cast only one vote against Lecompton (Pendleton of Ohio), and a fourth had yet to vote with the anti-Lecomptonites at all (Horace Clark of New York). Although the *New York Tribune* exaggerated when it stated that "every single Anti-Lecompton Democrat who has been reported open to conviction" was on the list, it was correct in noting that not "a one of those who are known to be inflexible" were chosen. But it is quite possible that none of the adamant anti-Lecomptonites had attended the caucus, so that they could not be put on the committee. On the other hand, of the 10 Lecomptonites, eight came from the South, and one of the northerners was none other than Buchanan's close friend, J. Clancy Jones. In truth, Greely had reason to complain.[18]

"In selecting Mr. English as the agent of this experiment," the *New York Tribune* continued, "[the administration forces] knew their man. His position has never really been fixed, and although a recent speech gave every assurance of decision, he had faltered since then, and is now counted with the South and its allies." Greeley's penchant to see the issue from the Republican perspective did not allow him to appreciate English's position. But, even so, his analysis correctly implied that English's prominence on the caucus committee served as a smokescreen for the Administration. In Cochrane's formal notification to English of his appointment, he requested that the 35-year-old chairman consult with the more experienced Alexander Stephens before the committee met. Stephens was put on

---

18. *New York Herald* dispatch, March 27, 1858, in *New Albany Ledger*, April 1, 1858. Cochrane's original list was amended to substitute Lawrence Branch of North Carolina for John Sandidge of Louisiana. Constancy of anti-Lecomptonism garnered from *CG, 35-1* votes, 536, 598, 622, 692-693, 1075, 1109. *New York Tribune*, March 30, 1858. Following is the full committee, gained from J. Cochrane to WHE, March 28, 1858, English Papers.

Lecomptonites	Anti-Lecomptonites
Stephens (GA)	English (IA)
Keitt (SC)	Foley (IA)
Branch (NC)	Groesbeck (OH)
Quitman (MP)	Cockerill (OH)
Houston (AL)	Pendleton (OH)
Bocock (VA)	Hall (OH)
Craig (MO)	O. Jones (PA)
Stevenson (KY)	Dewart (PA)
J.C. Jones (PA)	Clark (NY)
Corning (NY)	McKibben (CA)

the committee as well, and clearly the White House expected *him* to pull the strings on his Hoosier marionette. Indeed, throughout the congressional session, Stephens had been in charge of Lecompton, and he no doubt recognized English's usefulness. Henceforth, from this point until the end of April, English and Stephens may be seen working in concert, despite the fact that neither abandoned their competing principles.[19]

The Georgian dyspeptic and the Indiana trimmer had already recognized what would be their main line of attack. As early as mid-February, English had asked his leading constituents how they felt about a compromise that admitted Kansas under Lecompton with the express proviso, despite its own clause, that the citizens of the new state be allowed to amend their constitution before 1864. The answers he received varied. Simeon Wolfe, probably the least committed anti-Lecomptonite among his advisors, believed such a solution was acceptable. It would at least dispose of the matter well before the October elections. Michael Kerr was somewhat less optimistic. He allowed that English should be "governed in this matter by circumstances at the time," but it appeared to him "that the only safe position is upon the just and true principles of popular sovereignty." Luciene Matthews was more direct: "I cannot refrain from telling you not [to] sacrifice the *principle* for the sake of the unity of the party . . . for I tell you honestly that the people of the Southern district will not now wink at a compromise if the vital part is not there." He added that "giving the right of the people to alter their form of government *will not satisfy*. Nothing less than the submission of the Constitution to a vote of the people, *fairly* and *squarely*," would be acceptable back home.[20]

Even more adamant was the reply of James M. Morrison; it deserves to be repeated in full:

> I answer *no*. There are a few here [New Albany], and a few more throughout the District, that hold such a horror of breaking up the party that they are ready to consent to any arrangement that promises to withdraw the question from the National arena, and localize it, but the great mass of the unassuming, non office seeking democrats in the district (in my opinion) wish to see the matter settled without any sacrifices to principle. In a personal point of view (as far as you are concerned) it would be looked upon as a backing down to admit Kansas under the Lecompton Constitution, even if Congress should couple such admission with a solemn declaration that the people have a right to change it, at any time previous to 1864. The South would declare such declaration of non-ef-

19. *New York Tribune,* March 30, 1858. J. Cochrane to WHE, March 28, 1858, English Papers. For the collaboration between Stephens and English see this chapter, section 2.

20. S.K. Wolfe to WHE, March 26, 1858; M.C. Kerr to WHE, February 19, 1858; L.G. Matthews to WHE, February 16, 1858, English Papers.

fect and stigmatize it as interference. It would only tend to complicate the affair still more, and unsettle that which (when done) ought to be stable, permanent.

Morrison also went deeper. He understood that such a compromise implied that Lecompton did not reflect the popular will, but it admitted such implication in such a surreptitious way that it was almost dishonorable.

> If the Lecompton Convention represented the *people* of Kansas, and the Constitution thus formed expressed fairly *their will*, that clause providing for alteration or amendments after a specified time is just as valid as any other clause in the instrument, and just as proper, for a new State wants quiet and rest to allow things to settle. The best way is the straight-forward way. Get a Constitution embodying the will of the majority, and if they will that it shall not be changed for six or ten years, they have a perfect right to put it in the law, and the courts, it seems to me, would enforce that will regardless of Congress or newcomers.[21]

Publicly, in the pages of the *New Albany Ledger,* Norman wrote that "we have no objection to all compromise, providing the great Democratic principle of popular sovereignty—the right of the people to frame their own institutions—is recognized." This was essentially English's position as well, and the heart of the matter concerned whether or not, despite Morrison's objections, the compromise surrounding the amending process could be considered congruent with popular sovereignty. Apparently English thought so, for, on the morning of March 29, at the first (and only) meeting of the caucus committee, he offered the following resolution as a prospective amendment to S 161:

> Be it further enacted that the State of Kansas be admitted into the Union upon the express fundamental condition that the legislature of such state . . . have the right at any time, to submit the question to the vote of the people of said State, whether they will or will not have a convention to change, alter, or modify their constitution, and the right to adopt all necessary means for giving effect to the popular will in relation thereto.

Quite obviously, the unstated supposition of this resolution was that the now free-soil dominated territorial legislature could immediately begin a process to amend the Lecompton Constitution to prohibit slavery in the state. If that was indeed

---

21. J.M. Morrison to WHE, February 16, 1858. Morrison's understanding of the extreme southern position on the matter was gleaned from various southerners who had already expressed themselves in just this way.

the underlying intention of the resolution it ignored some basic facts. According to Lecompton, in order to amend the constitution the legislature had to pass a bill, by two-thirds vote of each house, authorizing an election of the Kansas voters to ratify the call for a convention by majority vote. Although the free-soilers now controlled the legislature, they did not do so by a two-thirds majority in the territorial House of Representatives, so that a call to amend the constitution would not succeed.[22] Indeed, two-thirds was such a high margin that it is problematic when, if ever, such a call could be made if abolition was the goal. Moreover, the Lecompton Constitution maintained that no amendment could "be made to affect the rights of property in slaves." There was nothing in this resolution that changed any of those procedures and restrictions. Unless the intention of the resolution was to fully substitute it for the amending clause in Lecompton (and there is nothing in it that maintains that intention) it would hardly be satisfactory to any committed popular sovereignty anti-Lecomptonite. It certainly did not truly honor English's own professed principles.

Ironically, however, the first objections came from four southerners on the committee. As predicted by James Morrison, these four—Keitt, Quitman, Branch of North Carolina, and Bocock of Virginia—reasoned that such a resolution denied the sovereignty of the Lecompton convention and was an unwarranted intervention by the federal government. Despite support for the resolution by Stephens and the three other southerners, the opposing four would have none of it. As the *New York Tribune* reported, "the conference consequently broke up in a row, leaving the anti-Lecomptonites more hostile than ever to Lecompton.[23]

After the failure of the caucus committee, no further effort was made to reconcile the factions. A full House Democratic caucus once again convened on March 30, but only to hear of the committee's inability to agree on anything and to recommend the Party's course in the House on the vote on Lecompton scheduled for April 1. As the committee's chairman, it was English who relayed the depressing news of the deadlock to the full caucus. Then, before the Democrats could proceed to a resolution concerning the April 1 vote (a resolution certain to recommend approval of Lecompton), two anti-Lecomptonites, Horace Clark of New York and Samuel Marshall of Illinois left the meeting, stating that they obviously belonged elsewhere. They were followed by nearly all the anti-Lecomptonites in attendance. Whether English joined them is difficult to determine, but

22. *New Albany Ledger,* March 25, 1858. A few days later the *Ledger* noted that it was wary of the Committee of Twenty. *Ledger,* March 30, 1858. Lecompton's amendment process is in the "Schedule" portion of the Constitution, section 14. https://www.kansasmemory.org/item/207409/text. The new legislature had nine free-staters to four proslavery members in the Council (upper House) and a 24-14 majority in the House of Representatives. Alice Nichols, *Bleeding Kansas* (New York: Oxford University Press, 1954), 119.

23. *New Albany Ledger,* April 15, 3, 1858. Lewis Jordan to Samuel Douglass, February 20, 1858, English Papers. *New York Tribune* dispatch, March 30, 1858, in *Ledger,* April 2, 1858.

at any rate an anti-Lecompton caucus held earlier in the day had absolved him of any wrongdoing in his attempt at compromise, and English himself vowed to stand by the Montgomery substitute. With most of the anti-Lecomptonites having absented themselves, the regular Democratic House caucus resolved "to vote on the bill as it came from the Senate."[24]

"After the contemptuous rejection of all efforts of compromise by the Lecomptonites," the *New Albany Ledger* stated, "the responsibility of disorganization, if such a result should unfortunately follow, does not rest with the anti-Lecomptonites of the Democratic party." Privately, Norman wrote English that the Montgomery substitute "ought to be adopted." Not only was it "fair," but it "would save the Democratic party of the North." Having already committed himself to vote for it, English naturally agreed, but he was not as quick as Norman to give up on the nationality of the Party. A letter English wrote to Buchanan one day before the House was scheduled to vote on Lecompton illustrates both his cleverness and how fine a line he continued to walk between the Party's two factions. It is illustrative of English's uncommon political ability to balance personal conviction with party necessity, and evidently he dropped off the letter at the Executive Mansion and left without even asking to see the president. "Permit me to give you my present impressions in reference to the bill admitting Kansas," he began. Everyone knew that while the Republicans wished to reject S 161 outright, the anti-Lecomptonites simply wanted to tack on the Montgomery amendment. English advised Buchanan to allow the anti-Lecompton Democrats to succeed, and not accede to those Lecomptonites who wished to get a straight vote on S 161. "In my judgement [the extremist Lecomptonite] course would be unwise. It hazards everything. If...the House should be brought to a vote on the naked Senate bill *it will be lost...The result could not be avoided.*" It would, as well, play into the Republicans' hands, for outright defeat of S 161 would not allow for the possibility of a conference committee to try for one last compromise. Or as English put it, "[o]n the other hand, if [the bill is] left open it *will pass with [Montgomery's] Amendment*...[T]he chance [then] of a favorable adjustment would still be open through the medium of a Committee of Conference, and not without reason for hoping a successful ultimate result." He ended noting that he was sincerely desirous of doing all that I can honorably do under the circumstances which surround me to carry out your wishes."[25]

---

24. Washington D.C. dispatch of March 30, 1858, in *New Albany Ledger*, March 31, 1858. *Madison Courier*, March 31, 1858.

25. *New Albany Ledger*, April 6, 1858. J.B. Norman to WHE, March 31, 1858, English Papers. Upon receiving English's letter, Buchanan wrote "[t]he enclosed note was brought to me by W. English, but he left it without asking to see me." James Buchanan to Howell Cobb, March 31, 1858, Buchanan Papers, University of Pennsylvania. WHE to James Buchanan, March 31, 1858, English Papers.

Whatever "wishes" English desired to execute, they did not include granting Kansas statehood "naked" under Lecompton. *That* he could not "honorably do under the circumstances," and Buchanan was no longer under the illusion that that was possible. But English's loyalty to the Party, and his belief in its importance, could yet be used to delay a complete and final defeat for the Administration. The only course left was to keep S 161 alive and hope that it could be readjusted to include just enough of the principle of popular sovereignty to win over enough dissenting Democrats without losing the support of the more extreme southerners. That had been English's mission as caucus committee chairman, and that continued to be his mission afterward. Most historians, citing Roy Nichols, have concluded that the suggestions outlined in English's letter originated in the mind of Alexander Stephens. Quite possibly that was the case, but Stephens could have written directly to Buchanan privately himself, which he appears not to have done. As long as Stephens's role wasn't public, where was the harm it might do? It is just as possible that English came himself to the natural conclusion that a conference committee of the Senate and the House was the only way still open by which the damage to the Party might yet be repaired. As always, he was quite willing to work toward that end.[26]

Buchanan forwarded English's note to Howell Cobb, asking the treasury secretary to keep its contents "*perfectly confidential*," and instructing him that "W. English's name must not be used or communicated to anyone."[27] Since mid-March the Administration had hoped the Indiana congressman would deliver it from certain humiliation, and so delicate a plan as he now proposed must be executed with utmost discretion. Buchanan was aware that English's credibility as an anti-Lecomptonite was essential to success—that only if the anti-Lecompton Democrats continued to believe he would not traduce the principle of popular sovereignty would they trust his appearance on a conference committee. Buchanan had no choice but to hope that English's plan could succeed, and that a politician decidedly the president's junior in age, experience, and position could pull him through.

2.

In the early afternoon of April 1, spectators crammed into the House gallery to witness the vote on Lecompton. As promised, Stephens brought S 161 onto the

---

26. Roy Nichols wrote, "Stephens and his collaborators now adroitly led English to 'invent' this strategy. The Hoosier congressman reported it to Buchanan as something new, writing him how it could be done." Nichols, *Disruption*, 173. The footnote to the paragraph containing Nichols's information contains no citation supporting it. Yet Nevins, *Emergence of Lincoln, vol. 1,* 297, Johannsen, *Douglas,* 609, and Potter, *Impending Crisis,* 323, all repeat the assertion.

27. James Buchanan to Howell Cobb, March 31, 1858, Cobb Papers, University of Georgia Library.

House floor and had it read by its title. As English suspected, the Republicans objected to a vote upon it, so that the original question before the House became not whether to pass the bill but whether to reject it. Should that succeed, and the House not pass even an altered S 161, parliamentarily there could be no recourse to a conference committee. Only three Democrats voted with the Republicans to kill the bill; all other Democrats, including 20 of the anti-Lecomptonites, voted against rejection of the bill so that they could then vote for the Montgomery amendment/substitute. The result was the bill was kept alive, 137 to 95. Immediately thereupon Montgomery offered his Amendment to allow the new Kansas territorial legislature to send Lecompton whole to the people for ratification or rejection. Every House member voted except Caruthers of Missouri. One hundred and four Democrats (31 northerners and 73 southerners) and eight southern Know-Nothing 'Americans' voted against Montgomery. But a coalition of 92 Republicans, six southern Know-Nothings (to embarrass the Democratic administration) and 22 anti-Lecompton Democrats, including English, carried Montgomery's substitute amendment through. The final tally read 120 to 112, and upon its announcement opponents of Lecompton rejoiced, and the gallery burst into "considerable applause." Upset by the spectators' reaction, Lawrence Keitt insisted that they be removed. But his nemesis, Galusha Grow, always angered by what he considered southern arrogance, pointedly noted that "there was no objection when the applause was on the other side." The spectators remained.[28]

Once the Montgomery amendment was substituted for the Senate bill, the House passed the revamped measure by an identical 120 to 112 vote. English, Foley, and Davis held firm to the end. Greatly gratified, the *New Albany Ledger* chided those who doubted English's constancy. "The Washington correspondents of the New York Republican papers have had a good deal to say recently about the position of Hon. W. H. English," edited Norman. "They have had it that he intended to abandon the position assumed in his speech and vote for Lecompton, just as it came from the Senate." Obviously, Norman noted, they were wrong. As long as the bill refused to acknowledge effective popular sovereignty, English would not support it. But his fidelity to Montgomery's solution was never as great as his opposition to Lecompton 'naked'. "He voted with the anti-Lecomptonites today," Schuyler Colfax wrote of English, "but it will be no injustice to him to

---

28. *CG, 35-1*, 1435-1437. In a letter to Charles Heaton, Schuyler Colfax remarked that southern congressmen, "with rare and honorable exceptions," were given to demanding rather than reasoning. Colfax to Heaton, December 25, 1855, in Smith, *Schuyler Colfax*, 70. It of course must be stated that the 22 Democrats were essential to Montgomery's success, but it is often unstated that in equal measure so were the six southern Know-Nothings. If four of them had voted against Montgomery it would have failed. Alexander Stephens might have been "mystified" why these southern Americans would vote essentially against the South (see letter to his brother the day after the vote, April 2, 1858, Stephens Papers, Manhattanville), but at least five of them wanted to illustrate to their state constituents that the national Democratic Party was not necessarily the savior of slavery. Overdyke, *Know-Nothings in the South*, 285; Cooper, *Liberty and Slavery*, 258, 262.

say that his repeated efforts to bridge the gulf between the two wings of the Democracy indicate that he is less decided and unyielding than the rest of them."[29]

Of course Colfax was right. English's letter to Buchanan expressly predicted a "favorable adjustment" if the House and Senate could approve the formation of a conference committee. The day after the House vote, on April 2, the senators rejected the Montgomery substitute; on April 8 they sent it back to the House. Rumors had been circulating that a number of anti-Lecomptonites had defected (including English), and the Senate hoped that a new vote there would prove different. But as late as April 7 the Republicans remained confident. "All indications for the struggle remain satisfactory," the *New York Tribune* announced, "no signs of weaknesses are discovered." The next day Montgomery moved that the House refuse to yield, and that it adhere to its own formula. Immediately, English was on his feet, asking Montgomery to withdraw his motion, so that he could make one of his own. Suspecting that English wished to move the bill to conference, Montgomery refused. The House then adhered to its own bill. No votes changed, but English (and Lawrence Hall of Ohio) voted after the roll call was completed, and after they knew that the House had adhered without them.[30]

Once the House held firm, the only course open to the Senate was to sue for peace. On April 13, although the senators again rejected Montgomery's substitute, they also called for a conference with the House. One day later Montgomery moved that the House adhere to his bill again and refuse the Senate's plea, but he could not have been as confident of success as he was a few days earlier. A caucus of anti-Lecompton Democrats meeting that morning had divided on the question of ratifying a conference. According to one source, almost half of them were willing to accede to the Senate's wishes, "because it was understood that the Speaker would give them a Committee favorable to their side of the question." Under these conditions, out of respect to the Senate, they could afford a conference. William English, no doubt, was instrumental in promoting this argument. At the same time some anti-Lecomptonites were also receiving strong Administration promises of patronage for their constituents. Ohio was promised two military commissions in anticipation of the Army's drive into Utah to suppress

29. *CG, 35, 1,* 1437-1438. *New Albany Ledger,* April 2, 1858. Schuyler Colfax to anonymous, April 1, 1858, in Moore, *Life of Schuyler Colfax,* 107-108. It is always possible, of course, had the Montgomery vote been closer, English may have switched sides. But no evidence supports this conclusion. Leonard Richards claims English really "supported the Lecompton Constitution," with no evidence to support that claim. *The Slave Power,* 207.

30. *CG, 35-1,* 1445. *New York Tribune,* April 5, 1858, in *New Albany Ledger,* April 8, 1858. *New York Times,* in *Ledger,* April 8, 1858. *New York Herald,* April 7, 1858, in *Ledger,* April 10, 1858. *New York Tribune,* April 7, 1858, in *Ledger,* April 12, 1858. *CG, 35-1,* 1544-1545. *New York Tribune,* April 8, 1858, in *Ledger,* April 13, 1858. *Madison Courier,* April 8, 1858, in *Ledger,* April 21, 1858.

the Mormons, and New York was promised six important federal appointees.[31] Montgomery and the staunch anti-Lecomptonites had to be worried.

Immediately after Montgomery made his motion to adhere, English rose and was recognized by Orr. "I rise for the purpose of propounding to the Chair what I consider to be a pertinent question," he began. He wanted Orr to affirm that should Montgomery's adherence be voted down the speaker would appoint to the conference committee a majority of House opponents of Lecompton. Orr had of course foiled the anti-Lecomptonites earlier in the session by his composition of the Harris committee, and English knew that the only way enough Democrats would refuse adherence and vote for a conference would be if the Speaker assured them that he would not again act so improperly. But the Republicans knew what English was up to, and considering that the question at hand was adherence, not a conference, they objected to his interrogatory as impertinent. Orr could not do otherwise but instruct English to be seated. But before the feisty Hoosier complied, he let the House know he had "confidence in the Presiding Officer" to apply "parliamentary law as I have indicated." And he let the members know that should Montgomery's adherence motion be defeated he would "move to accede to the Senate's request for a Committee of Conference." Paroxysmal cries of "Order!" accompanied his conclusion.[32]

After English finished, the House voted on the motion to adhere to Montgomery. With 16 members paired, should the vote have mirrored the earlier adhesion, 112 members would have voted to adhere and 104 would have voted against. But when the tally was completed, the anti-administration adherers appeared to prevail by a single vote, 108 to 107. The *Congressional Globe* did not record how the members voted, but subsequent events make clear that English was joined by Pendleton and Hall from Ohio and Owen Jones of Pennsylvania in deserting the anti-Lecomptonites. The one vote anti-administration majority, however, did not last long. Exercising his option to vote in order to decide a question, the speaker voted against adherence, and thus it failed to pass, 108 to 108. By this very skin of its teeth, the Administration prevented the House from blocking a conference vote.[33]

Quickly, English was again on his feet. "I do not want my action on this occasion to be misunderstood," he explained. He was still "decidedly opposed to the Senate bill in its present shape," yet he was "not prepared to say to a coordinate branch of the national legislature that I am unwilling to confer with them upon a

---

31. *CG, 35-1*, 1559, 1589. *New Albany Ledger*, April 15, 1858. Nichols, *Disruption*, 174. That the Senate adhered to its own bill and also called for a conference was very strange procedure. Usually an adherence vote is tantamount to complete rejection of the other house's point of view. *Ledger*, April 14, 1858. *New York Times*, in *Ledger*, April 8, 1858.

32. *CG, 35-1*, 1589.

33. *Ibid.*

subject of great public interest." Such was due the Senate "as a matter of courtesy and invariable parliamentary usage." All that may have been true, but English's real reason had less to do with legislative precedent and civility than with the harmony and continued dominance of the Democratic Party. He believed it essential that the Party shed its image of pro-Lecomptonism and revitalize the proper one of popular sovereignty. Some formula may yet be found, and the conference was the last chance. "I therefore move that the House agree to the conference proposed by the Senate," he concluded, "and that three managers be appointed to manage the conference on the part of the House of Representatives."[34]

Desperately did the Republicans attempt to thwart the Administration's plans. Israel Washburn rose to point out that the House had not yet actually receded from Montgomery's bill; it had only failed to adhere to it. In such a case, he argued, it was not yet proper for the House to entertain a motion on conference. Orr, evidently prepared for such an argument, overruled Washburn's point of order and cited an 1834 precedent. He also told the Maine congressman that he could "find perhaps fifteen or twenty precedents exactly similar." But Washburn was unconvinced, and he wished to state the reasons why this case was unique. Thomas Clingman of North Carolina objected to Washburn's continuing, and members from all sides entered the debate. After a few minutes of grand confusion, Orr eventually and disingenuously ruled that English's motion technically became an amendment to Montgomery's motion to adhere.[35] For a couple of reasons the Republicans were chary to appeal the speaker's decisions: one, because they might lose, but, more importantly, if the vote to go into conference was the same as that to adhere to Montgomery, the anti-Lecompton forces would win. A 108 to 107 majority in this case would not allow the speaker to vote, as this was a positive vote on conference and a tie would not pass it, i.e., would not change the decision. So, an appeal of Orr's ruling could well be less decisive than a straight vote to agree to a conference.

Fortunately for the Administration, however, an absent Lecomptonite on the previous vote returned in time. The result after roll call thus read 108 to 108, and Orr duly broke the tie to gain a conference by one vote. (Some anti-Lecompton Democrats maintained that their vote to confer with the upper house was simply "an act of courtesy to the Senate.") Upon the announcement of the final result there was some applause from the gallery, but the demonstration was less vociferous than that which had welcomed the anti-Lecompton victory of April 1. The House, then, by an identical vote, passed Montgomery's motion to adhere with English's conference amendment tacked on, thereby rather imitating the strange procedure in the Senate. These were the first House votes actually won by the

---

34. *Ibid.,* 1589, 1590.

35. *Ibid.,* 1589-1590

Administration, and some evidence suggests that other anti-Lecompton Democrats may have been willing to go for a conference had their votes been needed. Surprisingly, in the main, the Republican press was not overly distressed by the result. "The Anti-Lecompton side of the House is still confident that all will come out right at last," the *New York Tribune* declared. It took at face value English's statement that he and other trimmers had only voted for a conference out of parliamentary courtesy. One Republican sheet noted that English and the other anti-Lecompton Democrats who voted for a conference "have not swerved, and cannot be induced to swerve, from the fundamental principle that the people of Kansas shall be allowed a full and fair opportunity to adopt or reject their own constitution." It concluded that "no instrument which has not been thus submitted can be carried by their votes."[36]

Yet although they attempted to display continued optimism, Republicans were not without their suspicions. Most of these, once again, centered around the constancy of a particular Hoosier congressman. While Greeley allowed that English's motives were honorable, he also wrote that "English is now in a position where he will be compelled to take the responsibility of defection, if designed." Another editor, wary lest some compromise be effected to allow "members of *easy virtue* to walk over to the administration's side," was somewhat more direct: "Mr. English has surprised us for the third time. We will never be again, no matter what he may do." From Indiana, one correspondent of John G. Davis, responding to a letter from the congressman that said that English's course is "straining," noted that "the masses distrust him and speak of his vassulating course.": "I do hope he would do right in the Lecompton fight, but I have my doubts." The *New Albany Ledger*, of course, defended its congressman. "If the Lecomptonites have for a moment supposed that the vote of Mr. English in favor of the conference indicated any wavering or hesitation on his part in his hostility to the Senate bill," Norman wrote, "they do not know their man." Almost as wedded to the harmony of the Democracy as English was, Norman agreed that there was no harm in trying to compromise the differences. And William Williams's anti-Lecompton *Washington Democrat*, while believing it had "little faith" that the Conference Committee would be able to "accomplish anything," still thought "there is no harm in *trying* to bring about an arrangement which shall put an end to the Kansas imbroglio and reunite the different segments of the Democratic Party." On the other hand, William Wick warned the young congressman that his "last movement and attitude [was] subjecting [him] to criticism and doubt." He wrote that from his own vantage point it might have been better to have let the bill die: "All the *political* or party damage which can possibly be done by K[ansas] and its affairs has been

---

36. *Ibid.*, 1590. *Brookville American* (Franklin County, Indiana), April 23, 1858. *Daily Pennsylvanian,* in English Scrapbook, 87. The *New York Tribune* on April 14, 1858, noted that Foley would have voted with the Administration if needed. *Madison Courier,* April 19, 1858.

done. The *hoary* question, if left alone, will become lighter and lighter, and attract less attention." But Wick did allow that had he been at Washington, where matters "rest heavy on our head, I expect I would have voted for the conference myself." For the moment, most other critics held their speech.[37]

The next major move concerned exactly who would be put upon the conference committee from the House. Orr had privately assured English and others that the Lecomptonites would not have a majority, and it was generally assumed that one Lecomptonite, one Republican, and one anti-Lecompton Democrat would serve. The great question was which anti-Lecompton Democrat the speaker would choose. The Republicans, who understandably distrusted English, believed that Montgomery was entitled to be chairman because he had made the original motion to adhere to the House bill. After all, Orr himself maintained that English's motion to confer was simply an amendment to Montgomery's own suggestion. Republican congressmen even showed Orr a precedent to support their case. But Orr ruled that the precedent was not controlling because in that instance the motion and the amendment were not antagonistic. For his part, completely disingenuously, English claimed he had no wish to serve as a manager, and would "cheerfully" waive his right in favor of Montgomery. Had English actually believed what he stated, his whole plan would have gone awry, for it would be hard for Montgomery to agree to anything that would also appeal to the Administration. A full day after the conference resolution passed, the speaker had still not made his final decision, and many expected that Montgomery after all would be appointed.[38]

But on April 16, as he originally indicated, Orr indeed selected English as the representative of the anti-Lecompton Democrats. Stephens and William A. Howard, Republican from Michigan, were selected to join him. Some anti-Lecompton Democrats were clearly disappointed. The *Ohio State Journal* declared that it never had "confidence in the strength and durability of [English's] spinal cord. He has all along been one of the most unreliable of Douglas Democrats." Subsequent events later led the Republicans to speculate that "Mr. Orr understood Mr. English's position, and was in secret with his plans and machinations,"[39] and it is indeed quite probable that Orr was consulted by the Administration. Yet no covert conspiracy was necessary for the speaker to choose English over Montgomery. All knew that English greatly desired an honorable compromise, while

---

37. *New York Tribune* dispatch, April 15, 1858, in *Madison Courier,* April 19, 1858. English Scrapbook, 87. A. May to John G. Davis, April 21, 1858, Davis Papers. *New Albany Ledger* April 15, 1858. *Washington (County) Democrat, April 22, 1858.* W.W. Wick to WHE, April 17, 1858, English Papers.

38. *New York Tribune,* April 14, May 5, 1858. *New York Tribune* dispatch, April 15, 1858, in *Madison Courier,* April 19, 1858.

39. *CG, 35-1,* 1627. *Ohio State Journal,* April 16, 1858, in English Scrapbook, 89. *New York Tribune,* May 5, 1858.

Montgomery was one of the staunchest critics of Buchanan and Lecompton. Had Orr done otherwise he would have strangely acted against his own interests and have doomed any possible settlement.

By the rules of Congress, English became the committee's chairman. From the Senate side came Lecomptonites R.M.T. Hunter of Virginia and James S. Green of Missouri, accompanied by leading Republican William Seward from New York. English was the only northern Democrat on the committee, and as the swing vote from the House it was clear that any real compromise would have to gain his approval. "The report and doings of this committee will depend upon the opinion of Mr. English," the *Evansville Daily Journal* stated bluntly. Having supported compromise and party harmony for most of his political life, he would now get a chance to apply these principles within the context of popular sovereignty. "William H. English occupies a high position before the country," wrote the Washington correspondent of the *New Albany Ledger* about a month earlier; "he stands between the two extremes of North and South."[40] It was time to see if that position could still accomplish anything effective.

The committee convened the same day the House conferees were appointed, April 16, only to adjourn because Stephens reportedly was too sick to attend. Stephens must have recovered by the following day, for he attended the House "interrupted every minute by inquiries as to what is the prospect." But that was Saturday, and, whether for that reason or some other, the committee of conference held no session. In the meantime, English received suggestions from all quarters. John Gilmer, Know-Nothing anti-Lecompton congressman from North Carolina, suggested that the committee draw up a bill admitting Kansas as a state with the "proviso that nothing in this act should be so construed as to approve, reject, or give construction to any state constitution." An unorthodox approach to be sure, admitting a state without approving its organic law. Phineas Kent believed that the Republicans (at least in Indiana) would approve English's caucus committee formula of March concerning Lecompton's amending process. Such a solution would at least help in the upcoming canvass, though Kent was blind to its certain defeat in the Senate and probably did not know the actual provisions of Lecompton's amending clause. The Washington correspondent of the *New Albany Ledger* simply counseled that Kansas should be made to wait "until she arrives at a population sufficient to entitle her to one representative in the House of Representatives."[41] As it turned out, this anonymous journalist was on the right track.

---

40. Nichols, *Disruption,* 175. *Evansville Daily Journal,* April 17, 1858, in English Scrapbook, 89. *New Albany Ledger,* April 19, March 25, 1858.

41. Nichols, *Disruption,* 175. Alexander Stephens to Richard M. Johnston, April 17, 1858, in Johnston, *Life of Stephens,* 332. John Gilmer to WHE, April 17, 1858; P.M. Kent to WHE, April 11, 1858, English Papers. *New Albany Ledger,* April 14, 1858.

"It is amazing to see how Mr. English is courted and flattered by the administration and its followers," a correspondent of the Republican *Philadelphia Inquirer* reported. "I have not the least doubt that he could demand and receive the French or English mission, and have his credentials in his pocket in twenty-four hours, if he would pledge himself to join his Lecompton colleagues in the Conference Committee." More than likely the reporter was correct, but it was not for office that English toiled. Greatly troubled by the fact that he had been directly giving aid and comfort to the Republicans by his opposition to Lecompton, the young congressman was certainly open to working closely with the Administration and its friends to an honorable compromise. Evidently, while the committee still waited to meet formally, English conferred with party leaders, including Bright, in framing a bill. "The suggestion of Mr. English to which you referred last night," Robert Toombs wrote Buchanan on Sunday, April 18, "meets with a good deal of favor among our friends. And if it meets your approbation," he continued, "I think it will pass." Possibly this referred to at least a kernel of what would become the final bill. On the same day as Toombs's letter, the Democratic conferees met together in Stephens's rooms; there they worked their bill into shape and compared notes on its chances for success.[42]

The first full meeting of all the conferees occurred on the morning of Monday, April 19. Democratic senator Green offered two propositions. One was similar to Gilmer's solution: admit Kansas without a constitution and let the Kansans decide that later; the other was similar to English's caucus resolution: insert in Lecompton's preamble the right of Kansans to change their constitution at will. Neither was accepted, either because the House conferees had another plan, or because these propositions had already been discussed and disapproved in one house of Congress or the other. Upon their rejection, English announced he would submit a measure the next day. He gave no details, but the national Press was able to discover the general outlines of his bill by late that afternoon.[43]

Evidently, the Senate bill was to be ingeniously amended. As earlier noted, the Lecompton delegates had accompanied their constitution with a request of federal land that was about six times the normal land grant to a new state. S 161, the failed Crittenden amendment in the Senate, and the Montgomery substitute in the House had all reduced that grant to its traditional size. English's conference proposal also reduced it, but instead of simply denying the extra acreage, his proposal allowed Kansans either to accept or reject this reduction. English and Stephens contended that although the land grant was not strictly part of the

---

42. *Philadelphia Enquirer,* n.d., in English Scrapbook, 88. *New York Evening Post,* April 29, 1858, in *New Albany Tribune,* May 2, 1858. Toombs to Buchanan, April 18, 1858, in Phillips, *Toombs, Stephens, Cobb,* 433. Nichols, *Disruption,* 175-176.

43. *Daily Pennsylvanian,* April 20, 1858, in English Scrapbook, 89. Washington dispatches in *New Albany Ledger,* April 20, 1858. *Ledger,* April 23, 1858. *New Albany Tribune,* April 21, 1858.

constitution, it had accompanied Lecompton to Congress, and that any change made to it required the permission of Kansans. This was a novel approach. Most amended grants were merely mandated by Congress. (After all, it was the federal government's land.) But this situation called for creative unorthodoxy. Specifically, a territorial election would be held, under the supervision of the territorial governor, territorial secretary, the two presiding officers of the territorial legislature, and the territory's United States district attorney, to accept or reject the congressionally amended ordinance. Ballots would be labeled "For the proposition of Congress and admission," and "Against the proposition of Congress and admission." This meant that if the proposition of Congress to amend/reduce the land grant was accepted by Kansas voters ("for the proposition"), Kansas would become a state immediately with the Lecompton Constitution as its organic law. On the other hand, if the proposition of Congress to amend/reduce the land grant was denied by Kansas voters ("against the proposition"), Kansas would not be allowed to apply for admission to the Union until its population, "ascertained by a census duly and legally taken," equaled "the ratio of population required for a member of the House of Representatives of the United States." In this manner Lecompton would be indirectly submitted to the people of Kansas: a vote for the congressional proposition was a vote for Lecompton; a vote against the proposition was a vote against it. Whether that would please southerners, as well as enough anti-Lecomptonites, remained to be seen.[44]

The next morning, April 20, English formally submitted his proposal to the Conference Committee. Without debate it was immediately accepted by the three Democratic Lecomptonites, Stephens, Hunter, and Green. Congressman Howard, on the other hand, proposed to amend it so as to allow the citizens of Kansas to vote on a recently framed free-state constitution at the same election; thereby countering the population penalty English's proposal contained if Congress's proposition should be denied. Predictably, Howard's proposition "received no favor from the Committee." Seward was, however, able to get the Democrats to agree to postpone the final committee vote for two hours while he and Howard conferred with their side. During that postponement, reports began to circulate that the anti-Lecompton Democrats were greatly dissatisfied with this new proposal. The *New York Tribune* reported that "not a single true anti-Lecomptonite has wavered. There is most intense indignation at English's conduct." By 2 pm, when the committee was to reconvene, the *Tribune* continued to predict that it

---

44. *Daily Pennsylvanian*, April 20, 1858, in English Scrapbook, 89. Washington dispatches in *New Albany Ledger*, April 20, 1858. *Ledger*, April 23, 1858. *New Albany Tribune*, April 23, 1858. The actual text of the conference bill may be found in the appendix of this book, which was copied from *CG, 35-1*, 1765-1766. Although it was avoided in the coming debate, it is interesting to note that should the congressional proposition be rejected, any later territorial law enabling a new constitution to be written could decide "as to the mode and manner of its approval or ratification by the people of the proposed state…" Even in that phrase there is some room to deny a full popular vote in the future.

was "almost certain Mr. English's proposition will be defeated." But it was not really the anti-Lecompton Democrats who appeared to be the greater opponents of English's formula. When Seward and Howard punctually appeared back at the committee room they found no one to greet them. After waiting for an hour Seward finally located Green who told him that radical southern opposition had waylaid the plan. Although well satisfied that the proposal, because of its population clause, would at least keep Kansas out of the Union for a couple of years, these southerners refused to vote for what they considered effective resubmittal of Lecompton. By that evening, all the proposal had accomplished was to anger both the anti-Lecomptonites and a significant portion of the southern Democrats.[45]

It took two days for the Administration to quell the southern rebellion in its ranks. Interior secretary Jacob Thompson of North Carolina suggested to English that the Kansas ballots merely read "Proposition Accepted" and "Proposition Rejected," thereby avoiding the longer language that more clearly implied complete resubmittal. English accepted this suggestion and inserted it into the proposed bill. Stephens then made the rounds of "all the leading men from the South," and he got enough approval to lead him to believe that this 'English Bill' would pass. Apparently, both English and Stephens counted on enough anti-Lecompton Democratic defection as well. Consequently, on April 22 the conferees voted the proposal out of the committee, 4 to 2. Later that day, in Congress, English notified his colleagues that he would introduce his plan to the full House on April 23 at 1 pm.[46]

For helping the Administration out of its great difficulty, English was mercilessly castigated by the Republican press. The line most often heard was that he had earlier associated with the anti-Lecomptonites to gain their confidence so that he could better betray them in the end. "English had been playing a deceptive part from first to last," Greeley wrote earlier, "acting under the direction of Bright and his employers in the administration. He effected sympathy with the honest anti-Lecompton Democrats only that he might the more betray them; and through his agency, it is believed, all their private proceedings obtained publicity." Republicans generally held, as the *Louisville Journal* put it, that "he was appointed [to the conference committee] with the express view and intent that he should act the traitor, and he had, beyond all question, either promised positively or intimated unmistakably that he would act that part." And the *New York Evening Post*, which

---

45. *Daily Pennsylvanian*, April 20, 1858, in English Scrapbook, 89. Washington dispatch, April 10, 1858, in *New Albany Ledger*, April 21, 1858. *Ledger, April* 23, 1858. *New York Tribune*, in *New Albany Tribune*, April 25, 1858. Nichols, *Disruption*, 176.

46. Nichols, *Disruption*, 176-177. Jacob Thompson to WHE, n.d., in Elbert, "Southern Indiana Politics," 41, fn. 20. Alexander Stephens to Linton Stephens, May 1, 1858, in Johnston, *Life of Stephens*, 333. Washington dispatch, April 21, 1858, in *New Albany Ledger*, April 23, 1858. *CG, 35-1*, 1743. The *Ledger* reported that by April 22 the rather radical "South Carolina and Mississippi delegations had voted to support the bill." *Ledger*, April 27, 1858.

had often wondered why Jesse Bright's great protégé had become an anti-Lecomptonite, exclaimed, "now all is explained. He was in the opposition camp as a spy, and was acting under the direction of Bright."[47]

The political wags, of course, had a great time with all of this. "Mr. English's bill, though neither fish nor fowl," one very bad punster noted, "is unquestionably foul." More commonly one read something such as, "the Buchanan Administration seems likely to become notorious for 'its use of bad English'"; or, "[we] have often heard of people abusing the King's English. We think that President Buchanan's 'English' cannot be too roundly abused, for our President has really got the meanest and basest 'English' that any President ever had." More original was one commentator who declared "English is Bright's *reclaimed* fugitive slave [who] after his short escape from 'service and labor' was caught" and returned to the fold." The pro-Administration *Washington Union*, noting both the more humorous and more serious attacks on English, hoped that "this may be a lesson to him, and those like him, who had consorted for a time with the sectional opposition to democratic principles and the inveterate foes of the democratic party." The *Paoli Eagle* simply remarked that it thought "friend English begins to see the folly of his course—and we hope it will have the effect of making a wiser man out of him." Of all the Republican comments, Michael Garber's *Madison Courier* best, though not quite fairly, caught the gist of English's actions: "Mr. English certainly acted in bad faith to the 92 Republicans, 6 South Americans, and 12 [?] Douglas Democrats. He joined them for a purpose foreign to the wrangling over Lecompton. His object, now avowed, was to reconcile the differences in the ranks of the Administration party, no matter what the sacrifice." It was Garber's last clause that is especially problematic. To be sure, English sacrificed the Republicans, but whether or not he sacrificed the anti-Lecompton principle of popular sovereignty was less certain.[48]

Some Indiana attacks were personal. The *Brookville American* baldly stated that no one who "has known 'Bill English' and his political history believed for

---

47. *New York Tribune*, April 1, 1858, in *New Albany Tribune*, April 25, 1858. In connection to the substance of English's conference measure, though calling it a "vicious blunderbuss," Greeley actually did not fear the consequences of its possible passage. He wrote Schuyler Colfax "[I]f it is passed, I shall not shed a tear. The Kansans will dispose of it." O.J. Hollister, *Life of Schuyler Colfax* (New York: Funk and Wagnalls, 1886), 121, fn. 1. Louisville *Journal*, in *New Albany Tribune*, April 26, 1858. *New York Evening Post*, April 29, 1858, in *New Albany Tribune*, May 2, 1858.

48. *Louisville Journal*, in *English Scrapbook*, 117. *English Scrapbook*, 114. *Washington Union*, in *English Scrapbook*, 105. *Paoli Eagle*, April 29, 1858. *Madison Courier*, May 7, 1858, in *English Scrapbook*, 117. A month later the *New Albany Tribune* also noted "with a prophetic eye that was truly marvelous, Mr. English saw how this question of sovereignty in Kansas could be settled, to at least the harmony of his party. Will anyone blame him for this prudent sagacity? Are not party interests 'above any earthly consideration'? [The Conference bill] was intended to relieve Kansas, but more especially the party to which he belongs." *Tribune*, June 3, 1858.

a moment that he was designated for this important part for other than corrupt purposes." A correspondent of John Davis's declared that

> from the first time he [English] was a candidate for Assistant Clerk or our legislature [he was] not reliable. But as he had taken his stand and published to the world his speech defining his position I thought he would adhere to it from his motive of interest, for he, like yourself, was in a position to break down Bright and might go on to take his place. But it seems he prefers to play 'second fiddle'.

Another Davis correspondent claimed not only that the Conference measure was *"universally condemned,"* but that "English will now enjoy the most unenviable reputation of any man in the State."[49]

Of all the serious disagreements with the bill, there were three basic criticisms of it from the partisans of unalloyed popular sovereignty. The most often repeated was that this English Bill offered a bribe to the people of Kansas in the form of a land grant if they accepted the proposition, and, in effect, voted for admittance under Lecompton. If they didn't accept the terms of the bill, the critics argued, "three million acres of 'choicest land' will be forfeited." The gist of this argument was not, as historians and contemporary defenders of the bill sometimes have presented it, that Kansans were being bribed with an exorbitant amount of land, for, in fact, immediate admission would only get Kansans a traditional and regular amount of federal land. Rather, the critics' argument was that while the conference bill guaranteed Kansans *some* federal land if they voted to enter the Union immediately under Lecompton, should they refuse the proposition they could never be certain that those lands would be offered again. When a partisan of the bill noted that "so far from being a bribe, [the English bill] in fact strikes out sixty million acres [that were in] the original bill," (actually 21 million) and therefore Kansans, by having their land grant reduced, are not truly bribed to support Lecompton, he was right, but he was not speaking to the actual objection. Historian Frank Hodder's rather famous article proving, too, that the English Bill only offered the normal size land grant, though true, similarly misses the point. When the *New Albany Ledger* noted, in defense of the bill, that the Crittenden substitute offered precisely the same grant as English's measure, the *New Albany Tribune* wisely countered with the point that the superiority of the Crittenden amendment was that under it Kansas was guaranteed to "receive the same amount of lands whether [it] came in as a slave state or a free state." This, not the actual amount of land granted, was why the critics called the English Bill a "bribe to

49. *Brookville American*, April 30, 1858. [Unintelligible] to John G. Davis, May 7, 1858; Ezra Read to Davis, May 2, 1858, Davis Papers.

the people of Kansas," and this is why it was not considered a fair use of popular sovereignty.[50]

To be sure, this argument of the opponents revealed a great sense of distrust. As the *Louisville Journal* tried to point out to these critics, Kansans "are very sure to obtain [the proper land grant] whenever they are entitled to admission under the proposed bill." But it must be remembered that the anti-slavery forces had been rather despotically thwarted at almost every point of the Lecompton debate, and they were scarcely in a mood to trust the future of free soil to an Administration-backed plan. Moreover, the *Journal's* defense contained within it an allusion to the second major criticism of the conference bill, the provision stipulating that the rejection of the bill's proposition required that it had to wait until it contained a population of approximately 93,000 to apply again for admission. "This is the penalty to be imposed upon recusancy in refusing to bow submissively to the will of President Buchanan," the *New Albany Tribune* wrote soon after it learned of the bill, "and in this way it is proposed to force a slave constitution upon an unwilling people." Alluding to the fact that Kansas contained only about 40,000 citizens in April of 1858, Lew Wallace noted that "the English Bill establishes that, in Congressional eyes, two northern men, like Mr. English, lack a fraction of being equal politically to one Mr. Stephens of Georgia." Defenders of this provision noted, quite correctly, its virtue as a general rule. "*No State* should ever be admitted until her population entitles her to at least one Representative in Congress," the *New York Times* opined. Such was to be the case for Minnesota. But the facts remained that, one, other states had been admitted with an unrequisite population, and, two, Kansas could still so be admitted if it voted 'for the proposition.' Indeed, even Howell Cobb somewhat correctly noted to Stephens that "the only feature in the English bill which made it acceptable to the South [was] the representative population provision."[51] Again, strict popular sovereignty advocates could claim that the scales were not equally balanced.

---

50. Unknown newspaper, April 22, 1858, in English Scrapbook, 93. Examples of historians reworking the opposition argument include Johannsen, *Douglas,* 611, and Nevins, *Emergence of Lincoln, vol. 1,* 298—not to mention a plethora of 19th Century historians after the war. Unknown newspaper, April 27, 1858 in English Scrapbook, 90. See Frank H. Hodder, "Some Aspects of the English Bill for the Admission of Kansas," *Annual Report of the AHA for the Year 1905, vol. 1* (Washington, D.C.: Government Printing Office, 1908), *passim. New Albany Ledger,* May 4, 1858. *New Albany Tribune,* May 1, 1858. *Germantown Telegraph,* in English Scrapbook, 99. In truth, some Republican sheets did argue that the land was simply a large bribe. See, for example, the *Madison Courier,* April 24, 1858, where the editor calls the grant "an immense number of acres."

51. *Louisville Daily Journal,* April 28, 1858, in English Scrapbook, 97. *New Albany Tribune,* April 22, May 14, 1858. *New York Times,* n.d., in English Scrapbook, 97. Howell Cobb to Alexander Stephens, September 8, 1858, in Phillips, *Toombs, Stephens, Cobb,* 443. The 1850 census had revealed that the average constituents per representative was 93,200. https://en.wikipedia.org/wiki/United_States_congressional_apportionment. Accessed, 12/20/2018.

The final major popular sovereignty argument against the bill was that it actually never sought to submit Lecompton directly to the people. Indirectly, perhaps, it was submitted, but directly the citizens of Kansas only got to vote on the land ordinance. Yet to some very important popular sovereignty advocates, such as Robert Walker and Frederick Stanton, this discrepancy was unimportant: effectively Lecompton was submitted. Moreover, Stephen Douglas himself was almost inclined to agree. "If the English Bill passes with the support of your friends," Douglas was told, "it will be regarded by the country as a magnificent triumph of the principles you have advocated." Despite these assurances, what probably gave the opposition's argument some credence was that most Southerners adamantly held that English's formula did *not* amount to submittal, and that Congress had set no new precedent mandating that the people must ratify a constitution. Thus, the South's legal/constitutional point was upheld and might again be used in the future.[52] Actually, this last point of contention reflected what may be considered the beauty of the English Bill: its ambiguity. It allowed both southerners and anti-Lecompton Democrats ("of easy virtue"?) to claim victory. In the *New Albany Ledger's* words, it allowed "the Lecomptonites in Congress a hole through which they may crawl out of their dilemma." On the other hand, the virulently anti-Lecompton *Clark County Democrat* angrily replied that the spineless among the anti-Lecompton Democrats were the ones crawling "through an exceedingly small hole." Whatever one may think of the bill's attachment to principle, it could not be denied (as Garber had realized) that it was the first viable attempt to patch up the Democracy. From the Republicans' viewpoint, the *Ledger* noted, "Mr. E. has committed the unpardonable sin: He has introduced a measure which has massed Congress and reunited the Democratic party."[53] Whether it had united the party enough, in theoretical terms, was questionable. Whether it had even united it enough to pass it in Congress was also not certain. In no sense was victory truly yet secured.

3.

Punctually, as promised, English reported the conference bill to an expectant House at 1 pm on April 23. He accompanied the report with a short speech. Scarcely exaggerating, he began by declaring that "a great question—perhaps the

---

52. Johannsen, *Stephen Douglas*, 611. Nevins, *Emergence of Lincoln, vol. 1*, 299. Nichols, *Disruption*, 177, 179. *New Albany Ledger*, May 3 1858. J. Spence to Stephen Douglas, April 23, 1858, in Johannsen, *Stephen Douglas*, 611. See section 3 of this chapter for southern position on submittal. *Louisville Democrat*, in *Ledger*, May 3, 1858.

53. *New Albany Ledger*, April 26, 1858. *Clark County Democrat*, May 1, 1858, in English Scrapbook, 107. *New Albany Weekly Ledger*, in English Scrapbook, 105. Washington dispatch, April 23, 1858, in the *New Albany Ledger*, April 23, 1858.

greatest of the age—one which has agitated and engrossed the public mind for the past four years—has at last come to a crisis." It was in the power of this Congress, he continued, to alleviate this crisis and vote for a bill that was the "very best [solution] in view of the embarrassing circumstances surrounding the question." He limited his answers to the criticisms of the bill to the most easily countered charge that the land grant was a bribe. He correctly noted that both Senate Bill S 161 and the Montgomery substitute had already altered the land grant. On the grant itself he adequately showed that Kansas's original request was "peculiar," and that the conference bill conformed to the traditional allotment given to other states: "Under the amendment Kansas would receive 20 million acres of land less than she would receive under her original requested ordinance, making a difference in favor of the United States of [approximately] $25,000,000."[54]

Tellingly, English refused to touch upon the question of submittal or even directly upon the population provision. Instead, in measured hyperbole, he concluded his brief remarks with an appeal to patriotism and practicality. Passage of the bill, he averred, would decrease the danger to the "peace and prosperity of the country," while its defeat would tend "to scatter terror and alarm, paralyze business, injuriously affect the value of private property, convulse the Union, and endanger its very existence." Pass the measure and "the Kansas question departs at once from the halls of Congress, perhaps never to return." And even if it should return, "it will be at some future period, and deprived of all the power of doing evil."[55] Although he could not express his firm belief that, as reflected by the composition of Kansas's new territorial legislature, the territory's free-state majority would end the crisis. He could not make such conviction aloud, but he hoped that all northern Democrats could infer its truth from his general tone.

Believing they had a current majority in the House, English and Stephens planned to lead the members into consideration of the conference bill the very next day. They hoped to avoid debate on the bill until then, and at the end of his short presentation English moved to postpone debate on its merits until April 24 at 1 pm. But Howard wanted five minutes to reply to English's remarks, and his attempt to speak to English's presentation set off a general battle on the floor. Orr, supported by Stephens, continually ruled that Howard could not speak to the merits of the bill while English's motion controlled debate; he could only address the particular point of postponement. Howard thus propounded an amendment to English's motion, proposing that such postponement of debate be extended five days to April 29, whereupon Montgomery chimed in (to Republican cries of "That is right!") that Howard extend his amendment three weeks so "we can have the voice of the country on this question." After an adjournment for the

---

54. *CG, 35-1,* 1766.

55. Ibid.

day, and continuation of proposals and counter-proposals on Saturday, the 24th, and Monday, the 26th, concerning when debate should begin on the conference bill, the House eventually agreed, 104 to 101, that it would begin consideration of it on Wednesday, April 28. Considering that the bill's northern opponents had eventually bonded around a May 10 consideration, April 28 was a victory for the proponents of the bill, especially as it was understood that debate would last for two or three days before a vote was taken. The anti-Lecompton Democrats voted 11 to 7 for the April 28 date, confirming, perhaps, the future success of the bill. But there were still several southerners in the House who refused to support the conference measure.[56]

About one hour after the vote on when to begin debate, Republican congressman Francis Spinner of New York, hoping to defeat the bill when it came up for vote, attempted to introduce a resolution that was eventually intended to reflect adversely on English's character. He began his attack by casting aspersions on Jesse Bright with the eventual intention of associating English with Bright's and other Hoosiers' malfeasances. Reporting a story carried by an Iowa newspaper, the *Burlington Hawkeye,* he read to the House certain facts in the article as part of the preamble to his resolution:

During the second week, after the [Land] office [at Council Bluffs] had opened, an order was received from Mr. Commissioner Hendricks, at Washington, to locate six thousand acres in the name of Hon. Jesse D. Bright of Indiana. Of course the order was complied with, out of the regular office hours, and thus the honorable senator got a nice slice of the public land at a single haul, while the rest of us had to take at the mill as the wheel rolled round. Wonder if the peculiar position of Senator Bright occupies toward the Administration had anything to do with this piece of party favoritism? Was it any part of the price paid for his support of the Lecompton Constitution?

56. *CG, 35-1,* 1767-1770, 1779-1781, 1806-1810. Nichols, *Disruption,* 177. James Hughes's numerous attempts to bring Howard to order occasioned laughter and derision on the part of the House. Orr finally silenced the unrespected Hoosier, and he was heard from no more on the matter. *CG, 35-1,* 1767-1768. The few pro-Lecompton southerners who were opposed to the conference bill were Quitman of Mississippi, Bonham of South Carolina, James Stallworth and Eli Shorter of Alabama, and Robert F. Trippe of Georgia. *CG, 35-1,* 1768. Washington dispatch in *Madison Courier,* April 24, 1858. *New York Herald,* April 24, 1858. For a while, buoyed by their delaying tactics, the Republicans allowed themselves to hope that the conference bill might indeed be defeated. Overhearing remarks to that effect, English, apparently annoyed, offered to wager $5,000 with any Republican within earshot who actually believed they could defeat the bill. He boasted that such was the same amount he had won betting on the last presidential election. Evidently bemused, congressman John Sherman of Ohio, sitting nearby, turned in his seat and wryly exclaimed, "English you appear to have more money than any of us." According to the report of the incident, "the member from Indiana retired." *Cincinnati Gazette,* n.d., in English Scrapbook, 107, 112.

Before Spinner could proceed any further, Orr ruled that he was out of order. The Republicans loudly complained that inasmuch as the resolution was not completed the speaker's decision was premature. Ever eager to illustrate his fidelity to Bright, James Hughes began a rather ineffective defense of the senator; but he too was ruled out of order because Garnett Adrian of New Jersey was ruled to have moved to adjourn right before him. At this point English gained the floor, asking congressman Adrian to withdraw his motion "for one moment," which he did, and began a "personal explanation." He stated that he knew well of the transaction to which Spinner referred and asserted that there was nothing at all discreditable in it. Employing a tactic often used by politicians, he labeled Bright's detractors unprincipled and bid them defiance. "This insinuation proceeds from mere party malice," he declared, "and as one of the friends of the Senator I am perfectly willing to have the matter investigated." Here he was cut off by Republican cries of "order," and forthwith the House adjourned.[57]

Although Spinner had been unable to finish the reading of his resolution, it was printed in full in the New York press. The complete resolution reveals his true intent, for a second part of the preamble proclaimed that Bright's purchase was not merely for his own benefit but for the benefit of William H. English and James Foley. Apparently all three names were entered on the registry. Bright received 2,400 acres, English 2,280, and Foley 1,440. The implication of a bribe was obvious. The next day, one day before the House was to consider the English bill in full, the Indiana Democracy formally retaliated. Hughes began by introducing a resolution calling for Spinner's censure on the ground that he had attempted to besmirch the integrity of two House members. In order to uphold its dignity, Hughes averred, the House should "set a seal of condemnation" upon those members who abuse their privileges when they embody "in the form of official proceedings scandalous and false matter, thus giving it an importance it intrinsically does not possess." Hughes essentially argued that the House was compromised, for Spinner never intended to get a vote on his resolution but only intended to gain publicity. If this was Spinner's motive, he had certainly accomplished it. On April 28 the *Louisville Journal* picked up the story and derived from it, "another illustration of the truth that where a traitor is wanting and the power to reward treachery is sufficiently great, the traitor will generally be forthcoming." And as the Republican *New York Evening Post* put it, "[u]pon the whole there is little doubt that this extraordinary privilege was accorded to those men as a bribe. Whether Foley or English would have been converted to Lecomptonism without the bribe is a question they may discuss with their constituents."[58]

---

57. CG, 33-1, 1812-1813..

58. *Ibid.*, 1829-1830. *Louisville Journal*, in *Madison Courier*, April 28, 1858. *New York Evening Post*, in *New Albany Tribune*, May 5, 1858.

When Hughes finished speaking, English was accorded the floor. In the five years he had been a member of the House, he began, "I never have uttered a sentence reflecting upon the personal character of any of my associates on this floor; and never before have I had occasion to notice or to refer to any charges of a personal character against myself; nor do I seem it necessary than to say more now to make a plain, unvarnished statement of the facts in this case." He tried to hold his temper, proceeding at first in lawyerlike fashion to illustrate that the land transaction was in complete conformity with the law. Moreover, he noted that because the registry occurred in February, and he had voted against Lecompton continually through to Montgomery's substitute in early April, the connotations of any bribe were blatantly false. But he could not hold his anger by the end of his comments. "If the gentlemen from New York," he concluded, "or any other gentleman inside or outside this House, makes that charge, or insinuates my course in relation to the Kansas question has been influenced by any other than worthy, proper, and patriotic motives, I denounce him and send him forth branded as a liar, a poltroon, and a coward." The *Congressional Globe* reported that cries of "Good!" were heard emphatically in support of English's peroration. For his part, Spinner, only slightly chastened, rose to defend his attempt to gain an investigation. In the end, the whole matter was tabled. It may be interpreted that this Republican attempt to sully the character of the reputed author of the conference proposal illustrated insecurity as to the final outcome of the vote on the bill. Despite the *New York Tribune's* assertion on the same day that the bill would not pass the House, Spinner's tactics appeared to be that of a desperate party. For English, it could only confirm his natural inclination to cleave to the Democracy, his dalliance among the Republicans becoming daily more distasteful. Whether Spinner's ploy would drive wavering anti-Lecomptonites away from the conference bill was problematic.[59]

As prearranged, on April 28 at 1 pm, the House took up discussion of the English Bill. The reasons for being for or against the compromise have already generally been stated, but it is instructive to see how a Republican, a few Anti-Lecompton Democrats, southerners, and an anti-Lecompton Know-Nothing expressed themselves on the matter. Because English had already made a short speech in favor of the bill upon its introduction, the two sides agreed to allow William Howard, Republican House member on the conference committee, to open up the debate. The Michigan congressman naturally touched on all the orthodox anti-Lecompton objections to the conference report. Although he agreed that the land offered Kansas should they vote for the congressional proposition was equal to that of Crittenden-Montgomery, he noted that the bill "does not intimate that [Kansas] can have any land at all unless she will take it with this constitution." The

---

59. *CG, 35-1,* 1831. *New York Tribune,* April 27, 1858, in *New Albany Ledger,* April 30, 1858.

population provision that delays Kansas's entrance into the Union if Kansans vote against the congressional proposition, he announced, "fastens upon the North the badge of inferiority"; it was an "insult" to the free states. And, despite the fact that he admitted that the bill effectively submitted Lecompton to Kansans, he deplored the committee's unwillingness to face its principles squarely. "In my judgment," he offered, "instead of meeting this issue fairly, and grappling with it like men, we have neither the position of one or the other maintained." The English scheme did not "rise to the dignity of a compromise, but [was] a species of a dodge." Lastly, he questioned the impartiality of the commission composed to review the propositional election, as three of the five commissioners (territorial governor and secretary, and United States attorney) were appointees of the administration.[60]

Countering Howard, though not on the same day, was Samul S. Cox of Ohio. Cox had been a pretty steady Anti-Lecompton Democrat rather down to the day of this speech, but he had begun to waver possibly under intense patronage pressure. No doubt he needed to explain his apostasy to his constituents, for he had won election in 1856 with less than a majority of the vote by 2 percent over his Republican opponent with 4 percent going for a Know-Nothing American. This he did on April 29, and his arguments reflected the position of all other Anti-Lecompton Democrats who decided to vote for the conference bill. On the issue of the land grant, he simply noted that Kansas will "in the end, by the process of legislation, as every gentleman here knows, get the same lands whether they vote one way or the other." As for the population provision, although perhaps applied unfairly in this case, it was a "salutary" rule that states should not be admitted before a minimum population. (Of course, Cox did not care to emphasize that fact that if Kansans voted *for* the congressional proposition, the territory could come into the Union unsalutarily early.) More pragmatically, he declared that the whole process will not work to delay Kansas's admission for long. He believed that the territory already had the requisite population or at least would have by autumn, and the census called for in the bill did not stipulate it to be a federal one but one that was "duly and legally taken." Most importantly, he noted, even Howard, a Republican, did not deny that the Lecompton Constitution was "*substantially* submitted." And as for the election commission, all who knew governor Denver believed him to be an eminently fair man. Owing to the Democracy "all that I am and still I hope to be," Cox concluded, he came forward "in the spirit of harmony that we may carry on the business of the nation with dispatch and with reference to its higher interests."[61]

---

60. *CG, 36-1*, 1857-1858.

61. Cox may have crumbled under pressure from Ohioans who hoped to gain officer commissions when Buchanan dangled using two Ohio regiments for the Utah expedition against the Mormons. Nichols, *Disruption*, 174. Dubin, *Congressional Elections*, 177. For a good sample of Cox's past anti-Lecompton and

The loyalty to party interests and the implication that such loyalty, at least now, was congruent with high patriotism was echoed by another anti-Lecompton Ohio congressman who declared for the English Bill. Repeating one of Cox's own arguments, William Lawrence said of the Democracy: "in that party I was born; in it I had spent my better days; in it I expect to die; and if political death should be my fate for this vote, my only request is that I may die in the Democratic party, and have the ample folds of her patriotic banner my winding-sheet." Even English might have gagged at so maudlin a paean to his beloved birthright. John B. Haskin, an anti-Lecompton Democrat from New York who would vote to oppose the English Bill, could not allow such sentiments to go unanswered. He grandiloquently likened Cox and Lawrence to Judas Iscariot and intimated that they changed their votes for the 30 pieces of silver in the form of some other pecuniary or personal advantage. Lawrence remained silent, but Cox defended himself by stating that he switched his stance only when convinced by Robert Walker of the bill's merits. When Cox then asked Haskin if the New Yorker doubted his integrity, Haskin replied: "I leave that for the voters to determine." Angered, Cox began to swear at Haskin and was restrained only by the speaker's gavel. When tempers cooled, Haskin noted to the apostates that their stance would cause not only their own political deaths, but the severe desolation of the northern Democratic Party as a whole. He knew not what kind of patriotism that delivered.[62]

These arguments were from Northerners, whether Republicans or various types of anti-Lecompton Democrats. They occurred over parts of three days of wrangling that also saw differences among southerners as well. Strangely enough, it was Lawrence Keitt who made what was the first speech on the moderate southern side. He admitted that the conference bill was "obnoxious" and the "South had no reason to rejoice in [its] passage." But he also claimed it sacrificed no principle on the part of the South and that, "under the circumstances," it should pass. The conference bill did not submit the Lecompton Constitution to Kansans as some had maintained: rather, Lecompton is accepted as a "fixed fact." Had the Lecompton delegates submitted no land proposition, he maintained, "there would be nothing submitted to the vote of the people of Kansas; and so, upon granting the land we have granted, Kansas would now be admitted by the bill as a

---

anti-Conference votes see *CG, 35-1,* 598, 600, 1426, 1437 (2), 1768, 1769, 1770 (2). This particular speech can be found at *CG, 35-1,* 1880-1881.

62. *CG, 35-1,* 1881, 1904-1905. It turns out while Lawrence declined renomination in 1858, Cox went on to serve three more consecutive terms in the House. In all, Cox would serve another seven terms as a representative of New York. *Biographical Directory of the U.S. Congress,* 1426, 884. Cox later wrote that Walker had persuaded both he and Douglas to vote for the English Bill. (Douglas, though, did not remain so persuaded.) According to Cox, the former Kansas governor claimed that "the people of Kansas would kill [the proposition] ten to one." Samuel S. Cox, *Three Decades of Federal Legislation, 1855-1885* (Providence, R.I.: J.A. and R.A. Reid, 1885), 58.

State into the Union."[63] But his reasoning was disingenuous at best and just plain wrong at worst. Though Keitt was technically right that the constitution itself was not being directly submitted, the conference committee only focused on the land grant as a means of compromise because it offered a way to *indirectly* submit Lecompton. If the delegates had not requested any land, a hypothetical that Keitt makes central to his argument, the conferees would have certainly tried to look for another formula to achieve the same purpose.

A more candid southern supporter of the bill, John Millson of Virginia, refused to resort to such sophistry. "It is simply a question," he said, "of the degree to which the North is to be benefitted; it is simply a question of the degree the South is to be injured. [All of these bills] leave us free to do little more than select the mode of our execution. All that we have attempted [in the English Bill] is to choose the easiest death." As long as Kansas remains a territory, he continued, "she must by unchangeable law [*Dred Scott*] remain a slave territory; and slavery can never be excluded until we confer upon her, as a State, the capacity to exclude it." In other words, considering the great majority of free staters there, it benefitted the South to keep Kansas in a "territorial condition." John Quitman followed Millson in debate, and he predictably agreed with the pro-English northern Democrats that Lecompton was effectively submitted by the bill. And he was thus impelled to vote against the measure. It was not that he essentially disagreed with Millson's analysis, but rather that he refused to choose any degree to which the South would be injured.[64]

On the third day of the debate, April 30, Eli Shorter of Alabama, one of the few southern Democrats who had been voting with Quitman against the conference bill on the earlier procedural ballots, significantly switched his position. Although he found the conference measure objectionable and much preferred the Senate bill, he was inclined to vote for it partly because it was so virulently attacked by the Republicans. He was not completely convinced that Lecompton remained unsubmitted, but he took the word of "the gentleman from Georgia [Alexander Stephens] that it was not his intention, in agreeing to the conference report, to refer the constitution back to the people." Shorter essentially suggested that the South defy the Republicans and stand as a unit: "Whatever doubt may exist upon my mind as to its propriety, I intend to sacrifice [that doubt] to the [almost] *perfect unanimity among the Representatives of my section*."[65] (This was indeed the case with the Democratic southerners but not so with the Know-Noth-

---

63. *CG, 35-1*, 1863.

64. *Ibid.*, 1888, 1890. Quitman correctly predicted that the Republicans would soon hold power in Washington, making the whole debate on the English Bill rather superfluous, and, in truth, compelling the South to secede from the Union. The sometime fire-eater would be dead before the summer was out. Robert E. May, *John A. Quitman: Old South Crusader* (Baton Rouge and London: Louisiana State Press, 1985), 347, 349.

65. *CG, 35-1*, 1901.

ing Americans.) Such sentiments illustrated that the Democracy could achieve a certain sort of harmony, but it was not a harmony based upon a common set of ideals North and South. Instead, the united front of the Democracy was achieved through the force of a common enemy, a fact that English touched upon in his speech of 1856 and would increasingly rely upon in the coming years.

This continued division on principle among the Democrats was deftly exploited by American Know-Nothing Humphrey Marshall of Kentucky. Marshall naturally pointed out that the supporters of the conference bill were obviously divided over whether it actually submitted Lecompton or not. Within this division of opinion he included the bill's managers, Stephens claiming it was not submitted, and English claiming otherwise. Upon this declaration, English rose to ask the Kentuckian "what part of my speech" allowed Marshall to make such a statement. Marshall replied that perhaps he was wrong, and, if so, perhaps English might illustrate this. Refusing to be so baited, English retorted, "that is not the question. The gentleman of Kentucky makes a statement in regard to my position. I call upon him to point to the time and place where I have taken any such position on this point." Refusing to be put off by this dodge, Marshall asked English to *now* define "whether he under[stood] the bill as the gentleman from Georgia understands it, or does he understand it just the other way?" To the merriment of the House, English replied that "this bill is drawn in tolerably good English," and he added that all who understood "that language [were] competent to judge" its meaning. But it was Marshall who had the last word:

> If that is all the answer the gentleman has to give, it may go to the country with my mark upon it; that the author here, when the meaning of his act is challenged, declines to tell us what he meant by it in the face of the declaration on the part of his [southern] colleagues that just the opposite is meant by it to what all [the former Democratic Anti-Lecomptonites] pretend to understand.[66]

Marshall was not the only opposition member who tried to embarrass the Democracy by pointing out its inconsistency. Lewis Campbell, now a full Republican of Ohio, interrogated four of the declared anti-Lecompton supporters of the English bill on the same point. Three of them admitted that, "in effect," Lecompton was submitted, thereby disagreeing with Stephens and most of the South. When Campbell inevitably turned his guns upon English, Orr saved the Hoosier from having to reply by declaring that Campbell's continued interrogations were out of order. Campbell haughtily rejoined, "then, Mr. Speaker, we shall meet at Philippi, and discuss this question where the rules of the House do not

---

66. *Ibid.*, 1882.

prevail," an obvious reference to the upcoming congressional elections. Should the bill pass, the Republicans reasoned, much like Haskin did, final victory might yet be theirs in the fall.[67]

Amid all this political maneuvering, the self-deception of it all could be found in a long passage from abolitionist Republican John Bingham in the early stages of the debate. It avoids the cleverness and perhaps even patriotism of the English Bill and frighteningly looks plainly into the future:

> I say to gentlemen on the other side, who compose the majority of this House, you may pass this bill into law; you may induce the majority to accept its proffered bribe; you may thereby impose on this young Territory the shame and crime and curse of this brutal atrocity; you may thereby shake down the pillars of this beautiful free government, and drench this land in fraternal blood, but you can never give permanence to such an act of perfidy, to such a system of wrong. It is too late for that; it is the high noon of the nineteenth century. The whole heavens are filled with the light of a new and better day. Kings hold their power with a tremulous and unsteady hand. The bastilles and dungeons of tyrants, those graves of human liberty, are giving up their dead...Let gentlemen beware of how they attempt, under the power and shelter of a greet central Government, more than imperial in its resources, to crush out the heart and experience of the people. GOD IS IN HISTORY.[68]

The House, exhausted after all this bickering, allowed the managers of the bill to bring it to a vote on the third day of debate, the last day in April. Stephens had previously noted that "[s]ince the report of the conference committee there have been several periods when we could have carried [the measure] if we could have got to a vote, by a majority of eight." But inconsistent attendance stayed the managers' hands, and the diminutive Georgian at one point became worried that despite his majority, he "should not be surprised if we should finally lose." One day earlier, fearing a vote was imminent and his forces not in place, Stephens had to move an adjournment that barely passed, 107 to 105. But in the final analysis, enough anti-Lecompton Democrats, combining hatred for the other party, fidelity to their own, and enough 'submittal' in the bill, pushed the compromise through. Although 13 anti-Lecompton Democrats voted against the measure, nine saw their way to its passage. Six of these supporters were from Ohio and two (English and Foley) from Indiana. Their willingness to vote for the bill allowed it to pass relatively easily, 112 to 103. If Douglas had in the end decided to support

---

67. *Ibid.,* 1902-1903.

68. *Ibid.,* 1866.

the bill, five more congressman from Illinois may have joined them. English and Stephens had accomplished a great victory. As soon as the Senate voted to concur, news of the bill's passage spread quickly, and salutes in its honor "were fired near the Capitol [and] in the vicinity of the White House." The current parliamentary ordeal had ended.[69]

It was with great relief that the Administration avoided a full embarrassing defeat. The so-called 'Directory' and its southern allies well knew this was no victory, but a scene whereby a slave constitution would have been defeated in Congress would have been much worse. Linton Stephens expressed the predictable southern reaction to that potential occurrence when he noted to his brother that "he was sick and tired of the manner in which the subject of slavery is treated by Northern men, Democrats and all. It ought to be so proclaimed to Douglass and his Black Republican backers that if it is decided a state with slavery is not fit to enter the Union, than the slave states should walk out of the Union." But, again, the English Bill had prevented such a scene. The vote on the congressional proposition was months away and the free state of Kansas further than that. If the English Bill had done anything it had given the nation a possible breathing space to come to grips with its great dilemma. On Saturday evening, one night after the passage of the bill, Democratic revelers gathered outside the president's residence to celebrate the aversion of disaster. President Buchanan, senators Toombs of Georgia and Gwin of California, congressman Letcher of Virginia, and, for Union purposes, Henry Clay's son all made brief remarks. But the most telling effort was made by William H. English. After asserting that peace and harmony had been restored to both the nation and the Party, he spent most of his speech castigating those "bad men, who for evil purposes will oppose the wisest and best measures to accomplish their desires." These "Black Republicans," he went on, had supposed that English "had some affinity with them" because of his stand against Lecompton, "but never were they more mistaken." The Republican Party, he argued, thrived on agitation, hatred, and discord, and a victory for it in 1860 would absolutely imperil the Union. While he allowed that some Republicans might be men of honest conviction, the party as a whole reeked of hypocrisy. Its support of the Montgomery bill was not actuated by high principle (for the measure was a popular sovereignty one, not one of congressional exclusion), but by a low desire to break up the Democratic Party. Little trust could be placed in such an organization.[70] In his victory hour, such as it was, English's uncharita-

---

69. Alexander Stephens to Richard M. Johnston, April 29, 1858, in Johnston, *Life of Stephens*, 333. *CG, 35-1.*, 1867. *New York Tribune,* April 30 1858. *CG, 35-1,* 1865, 1905-1906. Washington dispatch in *New Albany Ledger,* May 1, 1858.

70. Linton Stephens to Alexander Stephens, February 5, 1858, Stephens Papers, Manhattanville. It is interesting and also predictable that Alexander, never truly a fire-eater, told his brother that he, himself, did not know what should be done "in case Kansas is refused admission under the Lecompton Constitution." He

ble chastisement of the Republicans exemplified one possible way to prevent the Democratic Party from imploding. The other way would turn out to be increasingly overt racism.

4.

The *New Albany Tribune*, noting that English's White House speech had been widely circulated in the district, sarcastically predicted that "[e]re long it will be translated into the Chinese and Choctaw languages, where it could be still more widely read." What also piqued Gregg was English's appearance on the cover of the well-respected Democratic weekly, *Harper's* magazine. Captured in full 19th century style, hand tucked into the breast of his jacket, English looked the part of the young, sagacious statesman that the editors wished to convey. "We this week present an admirable portrait," the magazine began, "of one who, like Byron, the day after the publication of Childe Harold, awoke and found himself famous, for few public men have been so suddenly called into celebrity as the author of the Kansas Resolutions for solving the Gordian knot of the Lecompton tangle." The article inside very briefly traced English's life in a most favorable light. "His style of oratory is very pleasing, and his manners are particularly winning," the writer concluded. And the editors had "no doubt he will retain the prominent position he has so suddenly acquired."[71] Whatever Gregg, the Republicans, or the northern die-hard anti-Lecompton Democrats might think of English, his stock clearly appeared to be on the rise.

Yet, in the midst a great amount of adulation, English's detractors were not absent from the fray. It seems that before the House had passed the conference bill, English had supplied senator Green with a formal copy of it without properly going through the clerk of the Senate. Noting that Green had procured the bill thusly, David Broderick, anti-Administration Democratic senator from California, denounced the Missouri senator strongly. Coming to Green's defense, English

had not commented on Linton's fiery words because he "was not satisfied what ought to be done in that contingency." He still simply hoped for success from a conference measure. Alexander Stephens to Linton Stephens, April 3, 1858, Stephens Papers, Manhattanville. The events outside the Executive Mansion can be gleaned from the *Washington Union*, May 2, 1858. It might be noteworthy that Alexander Stephens was not at the revelry. Either he was sick, or he knew the victory was hollow. Maybe he was heartsick, for later he confided to his friend Dick Johnston that "we all [knew] that the Lecompton Constitution was procured by fraud…The fraud was glaring. I feel when looking back at it, like the sons of Noah when they saw their father naked—I wished it might be covered up from the world." Quoted in Richard Malcolm Johnston, *Autobiography of Col. Richard Malcolm Johnston* (Washington, D.C: The Neale Co., 1901), 111; requoted in Schott, *Alexander H. Stephens*, 251.

71. *New Albany Tribune*, May 22, 1858. *Harper's Weekly*, volume 2, no. 73 (May 22, 1858), 321-322. One opposition newspaper noted that "William H. English has made his apostasy pay in more ways than one. Not only has he obtained over 2,000 acres of land in Iowa, but what to a man of his foppish nature is more valuable—his picture is in 'Harper's Weekly'." English Scrapbook, n.d., 114.

requested that Broderick apologize. The burly Californian allegedly turned upon the decidedly smaller Hoosier and cried, "Get out of my way, you puppy!" According to Republican reports, English "spaniel-like obeyed the command without a whine." Soon thereafter, the *Washington Union* published a card from English stating that "no such language was ever addressed to me by Senator Broderick, and as far as I know the relations existing between that gentleman and myself are of a friendly character." Be that as it may, no card ever appeared over Broderick's signature. The Democratic *Cincinnati Enquirer* called the story "doubtless untrue…but if it be true, it would certainly convict Mr. Broderick of being a gross, unmannered boor and blackguard." To this, the *Louisville Journal* replied, "Well, some may think it is as discreditable to kick as to be kicked, but we guess it isn't half as uncomfortable."[72]

A more serious threat to English's new political stature concerned the stories circulating that he was actually not the conference bill's author. As one editor put it, "the rascally ingenuity of ingenious rascality of this project is quite above the range of English's capacity." He believed that Stephens was the bill's originator, although he did allow that others made suggestions. Most historians have accepted this version; Roy Nichols called the conference report "Stephens's formula." Stephens himself wrote a confidante one day after the conference committee was appointed that the "whole labor has been on myself," but this probably referred to the Lecompton fight in general. (Even then, it was not true.) On May 14, however, Stephens wrote more explicitly to his brother that "whether the conference bill be right or wrong, I am responsible for it." On the other hand, the *New Albany Ledger,* countering Republican reports of tainted authorship, replied that "the statement that Mr. Stephens is the author of the English Bill, we have very good reason to believe, is not true. The bill is the work of Mr. English." No doubt Norman wished to intimate that he received this information from English himself. Exactly who originated the idea of directly submitting the land ordinance instead of the constitution itself has yet to be made clear, but even Nichols maintained that it was English who "perfected the plan" on April 19. Most likely the bill was shaped in concert—a little from the Cabinet, a little from Toombs and Stephens, and some by English.[73] In the end, the authorship of the bill was less significant than English's positioning and timing; it was for these acts of political acumen, not for any skill in legislative drafting, for which he was pilloried by the

---

72. *New York Evening Post,* in *New Albany Tribune,* May 2, 1858. *Washington Union,* n.d., *Cincinnati Enquirer,* n.d., and *Louisville Journal,* n.d., in English Scrapbook, 113.

73. English Scrapbook, 93. Nichols, *Disruption,* 175. Alexander Stephens to Richard M. Johnston, April 17, 1858; Alexander Stephens to Linton Stephens, May 14, 1858, in Johnston, *Life of Stephens,* 332, 335. *New Albany Ledger,* May 7, 1858. Nichols, *Disruption,* 176. One biographer of Stephens's wrote that "between them [Stephens and English] they concocted the compromise known as the English bill." Von Abele, *Stephens,* 162.

Republicans and others and admired by many as well. And it was also for these skills that the conference report will forever be known as the English Bill.

While official Washington mulled over the passage of the conference bill, Democratic opinion in English's own state and locality was curiously ambivalent. Norman wrote his congressman that in the Second District the bill met "the approbation of the Democracy almost to a man," but he added what he actually meant was that it "will be acquiesced in." William Wick also said that the Democracy "acquiesced" at Indianapolis. It appears that neither Lecomptonites nor anti-Lecomptonites were overjoyed at the bill's particulars, but most of them approved it principally because it promoted party "pacification." Some county and district Democratic conventions passed resolutions supporting the bill; others ignored it, but no official party gathering openly denounced it. Many conventions pointedly coupled their support with fresh denunciations of Lecompton or reaffirmations of fidelity to popular sovereignty. As one anti-Lecomptonite put it earlier, he "intended to be firm [but] not factious." As for the Democratic perception of English's character, it profited from the scathing criticism heaped upon him by the Republicans. Noting the "disposition" of the opposition press "to cast odium upon English's course," the *Cannelton Reporter* responded that "Mr. English has acted in this matter with commendable courtesy, for which he deserves the highest credit." To be sure, the most rabid anti-Bright Democrats in Indiana did indeed denounce the Second District congressman. Amos Lovering, formerly a close associate of English's from Clark County, wondered if he was bribed by more than Iowa land. Writing to John G. Davis, Lovering labeled English "a false hearted *political* traitor, an Arnold, a Bum, a Judas." But such opinions were far from orthodox. When the *Lafayette Argus,* in north central Indiana, maintained that the "political atmosphere is already sensibly cooler" after the conference measure passed, it rather summed up for Democrats both relief and appreciation. And the *Evansville Democrat,* admittedly in the 'pocket', saw "no good reasons for the severe condemnation of Mr. English."[74]

Even well before the formulation of the English Bill, and even before the vote on the Montgomery substitute, leading Second District Democrats wondered whether English would seek another renomination to Congress. As early as January 21, John Norman pledged his support (perhaps to re-ensure his patronage), but he advised English that this time the Democratic incumbent would have to

---

74. J.B. Norman to WHE, March 21, 1858; W.W. Wick to WHE, August 3, 1858, English Papers. *New Albany Ledger,* June 21, 25, 1858. Ebert "Southern Indiana Politics," 86, fn. 59. J.H. Harrison to WHE, February 3, 1858, English Papers. *Cannelton Reporter,* n.d., in English Scrapbook, 96. Amos Lovering to J.G. Davis, May 2, 1858, in Ebert, "Southern Indiana Politics," 44, 42. All the Democratic newspapers in the Second District supported the bill. *Corydon Democrat* in *Paoli Eagle,* July 8, 1858. The *Madison Courier* argued that Norman and the *Ledger* "caved-in like Gen. Foley [hoping] to be 're-instated in full fellership in the democratic party', John L. Robinson consenting." English Scrapbook, 102. *Lafayette Argus,* May 27, 1858, *Evansville Daily Democrat,* April 28, 1858.

actively and openly seek the nomination. In March, English was further pressed to declare his intentions by other party stalwarts, including Phineas Kent who no longer even resided in the district. Perhaps because of the continued unpredictability of the Kansas question, English declined to formally reply to these solicitations, thereby allowing rumors to circulate (not completely unfounded) that he instead intended to shore up his resources for a run at the governorship in 1860. There is no doubt that he had originally intended his present term in Congress to be his last. In December, 1856, he had promised his wife that he would "*never be a candidate for congress again.*" He allowed that "if a higher position should ever come to my lot I should no doubt gladly receive it," but at least for some time between 1859 and 1860 Mardulia could rest assured that he would "be in the bosom of my family." (That family was now at four: a son, Will, was born in 1850, and a daughter, Rosalind, was born five years later on September 11, 1855.) Even as late as December 1857, English had remarked to one editor that he would not be a candidate for reelection "*under any circumstances.*"[75] But he had changed his mind before, and it was not out of the question he would do so again.

One argument his supporters made to persuade him to run, used effectively in 1856, was that the other aspirants for the congressional nomination were not nearly as electable as he was. One correspondent, writing a week after Lecompton's defeat in the House and five days before the vote was cast to go to conference, gushed that English could "unite both sides of the Kansas question [more] than any other person." He maintained that English's leadership of the Caucus Committee of Twenty "was evidence sufficient to both sides of your desire to prevent all causes of disaffection." The writer, J.B. Merriwether, went on to declare that "you could be nominated with but little exertion on the part of your friends or yourself."[76] The promotion and success of the English Bill placed him in an even more moderate position, able now at least to claim the support of both Lecomptonites and anti-Lecomptonites. But considering his pledges to his wife,

75. J.B. Norman to WHE, January 21, 1858; P.M. Kent to WHE, March 30, 1858; J.B. Merriwether to WHE, March 20, 1858; Horace Heffren to WHE, January 30, 1858; W.C. DePauw to WHE, April 8, 1858; WHE to Mardulia, December 7, 1856, English Papers. For William Eastin English's birth see Shepherd, *Biographical Directory,* 119; Rosalind's birthdate is noted in an article on her husband in https://www.myheritage,com/names/willoughby_walling. Accessed, March 9, 2019. William French to WHE, April 7, 1858, English Papers. English could be a romantic correspondent with his wife when he put forth the effort. During this period he guaranteed her that home and hearth were more important than perpetual congressional tenure. In one letter, noting he had had too much to drink at Jesse Bright's residence in Washington, he assured her that "I shall certainly never be a drunkard, but trust that I ever shall be a kind and affectionate husband." And a month later he "close[d]" his letter to Mardulia with "assurances with love and respect to all the household and especially to you, *my own sweet precious wife.*" His letters to Mardy were always signed "William." WHE to Mardulia, December 7, 1856, January 25, 1857, English Papers.

76. Joshua Huckelberry to WHE, February 22, 1858; P.M. Kent to WHE, April 22, 1858; J.B. Merriwether to WHE, April 9, 1858, English Papers.

he probably could not have been persuaded to run simply because he offered the Democracy the best chance of success. Something greater had to be at stake.

Down through most of May, English kept the district guessing. Meanwhile, three other Democrats were seriously angling for the nomination. One of them, Simeon K. Wolfe, the editor of the *Corydon* (Harrison County) *Democrat* and a graduate of the Indiana Law School, was a rather recent Whig convert to the Party. As with many converts, he exhibited an unquestioned zeal in furtherance of his new party's aims, and had by 1858 become one of English's rather regular correspondents. His stance on Lecompton lacked any real attachment to principle; he was convinced popular sovereignty was correct ideologically, but he never counseled voting against Lecompton. The other two candidates were more forthright. First there was James A. Cravens, the frustrated also-ran of 1856. Cravens was a straightforward Douglasite, and he rather believed he deserved the nomination this time around. Once again English's indecision haunted him, and once again Cravens tried to discourage his congressman from seeking re-election. In March he advised English to concentrate his efforts on higher office, predicting that if he did he could gain a Senate seat on the first vacancy available. The third candidate was Dr. William Sherrod, a temporary candidate last time and subsequently a beneficiary of English patronage. Opposite from Cravens, Sherrod was a staunch Lecomptonite who had the full support of the Democratic leadership of Orange County. On this question he represented a minority of the Democracy in the whole district. Although the Democrats tried not to make the Lecompton issue decisive for the nomination, some prominent anti-Lecomptonites feared Sherrod's victory.[77]

As May entered its last week, English finally made his intentions known. A few days earlier, Norman had once again beseeched him to declare his candidacy. Omitting tired appeals to save the local Democrats from an inferior choice, the New Albany editor framed the issue more significantly. "If you are not nominated," he argued, "it will be said that the author of the English bill could not get the nomination of his own party in a district that gave Buck a 1,000 majority, and thus injure the party throughout the State and country." In other words, English's failure to receive the nomination would be used by the Opposition to declare that rank and file Democrats disavowed both the English Bill and the national administration. It would thus greatly embarrass the Democratic Party and almost wholly undo what English had done in conference. Whether Norman's argument was alarmist or not, subsequent events illustrate that it was the primary reason why English decided to renege his pledges to both his wife and others. A little earlier, Kent had counseled him to tell the district that he will not *seek* the nomination

---

77. *New Albany Ledger,* May 27, 1858. Shepherd, ed., *Biographical Directory,* 426. *New Albany Tribune,* December 10, 1857. S.K. Wolfe to WHE, April 25, 1858; J.A. Cravens to WHE, March 21, 1858; J.B. Norman to WHE, January 21, 1858, English Papers.

but still *accept* it if tendered. On May 25, English took this advice, and in a letter to the district's Democratic press he wrote the following:

> Gentlemen. I have received many letters from constituents enquiring whether I am a candidate for reelection to Congress, and if not whether I would consent to become a candidate if the Democratic nomination should be tendered to me. As my time is too much engaged by official duties to answer these letters in detail, I desire to say, through the Democratic press of the District, that my personal preference would be to retire from my present position, and that I am not a candidate for reelection; but if the Democracy, in their wisdom, should declare it to be their personal wish that I should make the race I feel that my personal wishes ought not to stand in the way of a performance of public duty, and to discharge, as far as in my power, a debt of gratitude which I owe my constituents for past favors…
>
> I should more willingly respond to such a call from my Democratic constituents for the reason that I should regard it as evidence of a desire on their part to show to the nation at large, in the most expressive manner, that they approve and endorse the course of *their representative* upon the great measure of pacification which has recently passed the Congress of the United States.[78]

Because English had already been nominated for Congress three times and because he had rather pulled this same stunt in 1856, his letter did not receive the widespread respect that was accorded the similar effort two years earlier. One Democratic editor even had the temerity to exclaim "when a man wishes to be a candidate for office, why not say so, and not resort to the contemptible subterfuge of first intimating a wish to retire, and almost in the same breath *begging* for office again." The fact was that by 1858 there were disaffected Democrats in English's district. On the one hand there were the Lecomptonites, led by Henry Comingore of the *Paoli Eagle*, who remained unreconciled to the English Bill. "We know Mr. English claims *great* credit for what *he* done in effecting a compromise over the Kansas question," Comingore wrote, "but we think he went to a great deal of trouble in assisting to get up the difficulty among democrats, in order to make it necessary to bring about a compromise, that he might be considered the savior of the party." English's nomination letter more firmly placed these Democrats in Sherrod's camp. Secondly, over six years there were a number of disappointed office seekers like William Woolls of the *Clark County National Democrat*. Wools

---

78. J.B. Norman to WHE, May 21, 1858; P.M. Kent to WHE, April 22, 1858, English Papers. WHE to constituents, May 25, 1858, in the *New Albany Ledger*, June 1, 1858 and *Paoli Eagle*, June 10, 1858.

joined forces with Comingore partly because English denied him the chance to become the Charlestown postmaster, but it was true he was also pro-Lecompton. Thirdly, there were the supporters of James Cravens who, derailed in 1856 by the same tactics, were unwilling to suffer such again.[79]

To prevent losing the nomination English needed to hurry home. As Committee Chairman and really part of the Democratic leadership he couldn't leave Washington too early, though he did continuously vote for the earliest possible adjournment dates. Finally, on June 15, he left town. Just four days later he arrived back in Lexington. For a month Sherrod had been travelling the district attacking him, and Cravens had been tirelessly promoting himself. A few days after he arrived home, English received a frantic letter from Michael Kerr imploring him to come to New Albany to shore up support in Floyd County. The next day, Cravens wrote him to try to illustrate to English that the Lecomptonites were so staunchly against him he could not be nominated. Cravens naturally counseled English to support him instead, as he was closer to English politically and he believed he could, without English's baggage, beat Sherrod. For good measure, Cravens threw in that English's defeat in convention would tarnish his chances for higher office and noted that with the perennial also-ran in congress English "would have a true and faithful friend…who will always have your best interest at heart."[80]

Cravens was right about Comingore and Sherrod. Although the Lecompton Democrats were most certainly a minority in the district, English's compromise bill managed to temper the ardor of the anti-Lecomptonites while hardly pleasing die-hard supporters of Lecompton. Comingore, specifically, wanted English punished for his course in Congress. For eight weeks, the *Paoli Eagle* kept up a barrage of attacks on the congressman. Much of the time it argued that English's divagations in Congress had made him a weak candidate, one who was positioned neither to strongly unite the district Democracy nor appeal to the Opposition party that rightly felt betrayed by him. Comingore put it thusly:

> In this district we have had anti-Lecompton and Lecompton men, fighting against making the Kansas question an issue in the coming elections. But very unexpectedly to us, Mr. English comes out in his letter expressing a willingness to accept the nomination for Congress at the coming

79. *Clark County Democrat*, in English Scrapbook, 120. *Paoli Eagle*, June 24, 1858. Other leading Lecomptonites in the district included ex-congressman Cyrus Dunham, ex-state treasurer Elijah Newland, New Albany city councilman and ex-state senator John B. Winstandly, and New Albany mayor Alexander Burnett. J.B. Norman to WHE, February 7, March 31, 1858. English Papers. J.A. Cravens to WHE, March 21, 1858; W.T. Spicely to WHE, June 5, 1860, English Papers. Miller, *Indiana Newspapers, 48.* English Scrapbook, 119.

80. *CG, 35-1,* 2682. *New Albany Ledger,* June 22, 1858. *New Albany Tribune,* June 4, 1858. Rudolphus Schoonover to WHE, June 20, 1858; Frank Gwin to WHE, June 28, 1858; J.L. Menaugh to WHE, June 30, 1858; M.C. Kerr to WHE, June 24, 1858; J.A. Cravens to WHE, June 25, 1858, English Papers.

Convention, upon the ground it would be an *endorsement* of his course upon the Kansas Question. This is at once making the question an issue, and *will result* in creating a *division* in our party in the District…We will not support any person for Congress or anything else, that runs as a Lecompton or Anti-Lecompton man, making that the issue. If such an issue suffers to be made, *defeat awaits us*. The only issue we want is an old-fashioned democratic one, against the enemies of democracy.

Yet, two weeks after this editorial, in his overwhelming desire to defeat English, Comingore disregarded his own advice and baldly brought up English's course in Congress in a most unfavorable, misleading, and dark light:

Mr. English did not only vote with [the Republicans], but he was made their *leader*, and received the encomiums of all the '*Free Nigger*' organs from one end of the Union to the other. His speech against the administration was franked by himself to many of the Black Republican papers in Indiana, and published in many of them and applauded by all of them. Yet in the face of those facts *he asks* the Democracy of the District to *endorse his course* in Congress.[81]

In real jeopardy of losing the nomination, English decided to abandon his passive approach stated in his May 25th letter to the Democratic Press. He therefore changed his strategy and announced he would canvass the district before the congressional convention met to explain his course in Congress. Boldly, he chose Paoli and Orleans, both in Orange County, as his first stops, and he welcomed other candidates to speak along with him. There is some evidence to support the conclusion that his goal was as much to stop Sherrod as it was to nominate himself. John L. Menaugh noted, in passing, that English had told him he would withdraw if Cravens "could get the nomination," but fearing that Sherrod would beat Cravens, English had to compete. Whether that was true or not, by 1858 English had become well disenchanted with the doctor. As a prominent member of the Washington, D.C. Indiana Club, Sherrod had been the prime mover of its pro-Lecompton resolution passed in February. Doubtless English believed this was no way for Sherrod to pay back a congressman who had gotten him his federal appointment in the first place. Moreover, Sherrod had earlier embarrassed English in the previous Congress by leaving his post without resigning or pursuing a leave of absence. Now, to top it all, the Orange County physician had been recklessly informing district Democrats that English had often told him he would

---

81. *Paoli Eagle,* June 10, 24, 1858.

neither seek nor accept a third renomination. English, thus, had both personal as well as political reasons to derail Sherrod.[82]

Against this background English and Sherrod shared the platform at Paoli on July 10. The doctor began by extolling the virtues of the principle of rotation in office. He also repeated his charges that English had promised "not to be in his way in the present canvass." In his reply, English "pitched into Sherrod warmly." He accused him of neglecting his duties in Washington and even farming out the position that English had procured for him. He also labeled Sherrod an inveterate office-seeker, who, if he could not get to Congress or the Indiana legislature, "would go to Washington and try to get an appointment, and if still unsuccessful he would ask Buchanan for some of his old clothes." Admittedly, the source for that last comment was the *New Albany Tribune*. Nevertheless, it is clear that English, fed up with Sherrod and believing him a poor representative of the Second District Democracy, apparently made the audacious conscious decision to personally attack him in his home county. Significantly, no reports of the encounter mention any discussion of Kansas, the ostensible reason that English went to Orange County in the first place.[83]

There is good reason to believe that English's foray into enemy territory did not go nearly as well as he had hoped. On July 12, two days after the Paoli appearance, he penned the following letter to Comingore, which sounds very much like an offer of truce:

> I regret to hear that an impression prevails upon the part of yourself and some others, that there is an effort being made to nominate me as an exclusively anti-Lecompton candidate for Congress. I desire to say to you, in a spirit of kindness, that I think the impression is without sufficient foundation, and at all events, if an effort is being made to nominate me as an exclusively anti-Lecompton candidate, it is without my approval. My own opinion is that all cause of difference between different members of the democratic family was buried when the English compromise bill passed, and ought not to be revived. I expressly disclaim now, as I have always done, the making of Lecompton or anti-Lecompton a test in our conventions, or at the polls. There is no necessity of going back further than the passage of the compromise bill. I stand upon that bill, and it was to that, and not to Lecompton or anti-Lecompton, that I referred to in my public letter to my Constituents.

Comingore responded by printing this letter in his newspaper with his own reply. "I am glad that you expressly disclaim being an Anti-Lecompton candidate for

---

82. *New Albany Tribune*, July 9, 1858. *Paoli Eagle*, July 8, 1858. J.L. Menaugh to WHE, July 17, 1858; J.B. Norman to WHE, May 21, 1858, English Papers. *Clark County Democrat*, June 1858, in English Scrapbook, 120. (The *Clark County Democrat* and the *Clark County National Democrat* were two different newspapers.)

83. English Scrapbook, 190. *New Albany Tribune*, July 20, 1858.

Congress, " he began, "and that you oppose making the Lecompton question an issue in the next canvass." Comingore went on to say that he had understood English to desire his "*whole course* upon the *Kansas question* to be endorsed," something the editor could not do. In the end, Comingore admitted that he now felt "at liberty" to support English if he was nominated, but at no time did he abandon Sherrod. Indeed, a week later at the Orange County Convention, he led the movement to instruct the delegates to vote for Sherrod and "use all honorable means to secure his nomination."[84]

Comingore and his district allies had the advantage of having only one candidate who supported their pro-Lecompton position. They thereby, despite that minority viewpoint, were able to organize and coalesce around one man. They could not thus command a majority, but they might steamroll the convention with their heavy early lead. According to the minutes of the various county conventions during June, and information from political insiders, here is how the convention broke down well before it was to meet on July 29.

	Sherrod	English	Wolfe	Cravens	Uncommitted
Clark	20				
Crawford		7			
Floyd					18
Harrison		17			
Orange	12				
Perry	11				
Scott		7			
Washington				18	
	43	14	17	18	18

[85]

---

84. WHE to H. Comingore, July 12, 1858, English Papers. *Paoli Eagle,* July 15, 1858. *New Albany Ledger,* July 20, 1858. The *New Albany Tribune*, commenting on English's disavowal of being an exclusively anti-Lecompton candidate, retorted, "that is certainly the richest joke of the season. We venture to say there is not a sane man in the District who has entertained such a thought." *Tribune,* July 19, 1858. The *Washington* (County) *Democrat*, a newspaper committed to Democratic Party harmony, lamented how things were "growing warm pretty fast"; it counseled Democratic editors (read: Comingore, and perhaps Woolls of the *National Democrat*) to "go slow," and not let "personal zeal" carry them away. *Democrat,* August 22, 1858.

85. *New Albany Ledger,* June 10, 13, 1858. *Paoli Eagle,* June 17, 25, 1858. *New Albany Tribune,* July 20, 1858. J. L. Menaugh to WHE, July 17, 1858; Lewis Jordan to WHE, July 2, 1858, English Papers.

Aware of these figures, and truly alarmed, English worked hard to convince the Cravens and Wolfe supporters that they could not gain votes outside their home counties and only he could stop Sherrod. While these appeals had some effect, in his dire straits English early felt he needed to beseech a very powerful ally to help him stop Sherrod's momentum. And so, a month before the convention convened at Paoli, English called in the markers that the Administration owed him and enlisted the written help of president Buchanan himself. He boldly beseeched the chief executive to help by allowing English to make public some of their friendly correspondence. The president responded by permitting English to show some letters to "a few discreet friends." Buchanan warned against having this correspondence "published in the newspapers," as "at the present moment [it would] neither benefit you nor myself." The correspondence to which Buchanan refers most likely was one or more of the letters illustrating Buchanan's approval of English's attempts to find a suitable compromise to the Lecompton mess. But Buchanan's response went further:

> I omit no opportunity of expressing my opinion of how much the country owes you for the English amendment. Having lost the bill of the Senate, which I preferred, the country would have been in a sad condition had it not been relieved by your measure. It is painful even to think what would have been the alarming condition of the Union had Congress adjourned without passing your amendment. I trust you would have no difficulty in being re-nominated and re-elected. If I had a thousand votes you should have them all with a hearty good will.

Buchanan's note had the simultaneous effects of undercutting Sherrod, eliminating any undue attention to lack of rotation in office, and generally enhancing English's stature. As one English correspondent wrote, soon after Buchanan's feelings had begun to be made known, "[t]alk about rotation in office will not do when you saved the democratic party from ruin."[86]

When the convention met it selected English-friendly men for Chair and seats on the Resolutions Committee. Soon after, the full strength of the Buchanan endorsement began to make itself patently clear. Before the balloting even began, Cravens cryptically withdrew "solely from a sincere desire to promote in some degree [the] harmony and good feeling of the party." Stunned, the *New Albany Tribune* could only report that Cravens was "induced to withdraw by some secret hocus pocus." Then the Resolutions Committee brought back a resolution endorsing the "House Conference measure as a measure of pacification." And then,

---

86. Lewis Jordan to WHE, July 2, 1858; J.L. Menaugh to WHE, July 17, 1858; James Buchanan to WHE, July 2, 1858; Lewis Jordan to WHE, July 6, 1858, English Papers.

after a brief recess before balloting was to begin, the coup de grace was struck. As the minutes to the convention put it, "W. F. Sherrod announced that he was not a candidate before the convention, and expressed the hope that his friends would concur in the nominee as he should himself." The *Tribune* later claimed that Sherrod had also maintained that he had "been abused, vilified, and lied upon," perhaps a reference to his rough treatment by English the few weeks before in Paoli, and he talked of the convention being packed and unrepresentative. Some unpleasantness and even anger apparently did take place on Sherrod's part. But the main point was that he and Comingore had caved to the Administration's wishes.[87]

The rest fell neatly into place. As the formal balloting began, Wolfe, claiming he was bound by Harrison County to continue in the race, remained along with English. When the first and only ballot was taken, Harrison County indeed stayed with Wolfe, but it was the only one to do so. Final tabulation showed English nominated, 93 to 17; immediately thereafter Wolfe, in easy gallantry, moved that the nomination be made unanimous. According to the *New Albany Ledger*, this motion was "confirmed amidst tremendous shouting, the immense assemblage exhibiting the greatest enthusiasm." Be that as it may, despite certainly hurt and angry feelings, the general assessment was indeed that English's nomination had become a political necessity. "Mr. Buchanan had manifested his great anxiety that Mr. English should again be endorsed by his constituents," William Lee of the *Jeffersonville Democrat* wrote. "To have repudiated English under these circumstances would have been construed as a repudiation of his great measure of pacification and a rebuke to Mr. Buchanan and his wise and patriotic administration." Of how 'wise and patriotic' the President's administration was Simeon Wolfe was uncertain, but he agreed that English was "the most appropriate at the present time and under existing circumstances." Wolfe concluded that there was much "force" to the argument that a repudiation of [English] by his constituents would be regarded elsewhere as repudiation of the [English] bill, and thereby would have given aid and comfort to the enemy."[88]

---

87. *New Albany Ledger,* July 30, 1858. *New Albany Tribune,* July 29, August 2, 11, 1858. The *Tribune* publically named Democrat William M. Weir, a respected citizen of New Albany, as its source for Sherrod's angry remarks.

88. *New Albany Ledger,* July 30, 1858. *Jeffersonville Democrat,* in *Ledger,* August 9, 1858. *Corydon Democrat,* in *Ledger,* August 5, 1858. Comingore's *Paoli Eagle* simply summarized the convention's proceedings and gallantly (if falsely) claimed that "the best feelings prevailed throughout." Almost two full months before the Paoli convention, Milton Gregg had made the following prediction concerning its prospective proceedings: "[after some criticism of English's longevity of service by Cravens, Sherrod, and Wolfe] Mr. Norman will take his willing bride, Mr. English, by the left hand [and] escort him upon the platform around which the assembled multitude of the democracy are gathered. Mr. Norman will then take the desk, talk, laugh, and joke with the democratic brethren until they are all in perfect good humor, excepting of course the above named anxious to serve personages. These political 'milkmaids,' however, applaud when William rises to speak, and appear in the delightful flow of spirits. [English will speak of his pacification role, and of the]

Wolfe, Cravens, and Sherrod all subsequently declared that they would support the full ticket of the Democratic Party, but Sherrod's unpleasant comments at the district convention would not be forgotten. By September, the disappointed doctor was forced to resign the $1,200 clerkship that English had procured for him. The *New Albany Ledger* attempted to explain that the position itself had been abolished, but if English really wished to help Sherrod, he could no doubt have saved the office. Samuel Crowe had voluntarily resigned his own federal appointment (to become surveyor-general of Nebraska and Kansas—an obvious plum granted by the Administration to English), so if the congressman wished to forgive Sherrod he could easily have shifted him into Crowe's former place. Instead, it went to a Cravens man.[89] William English was a politician who could play hardball when called for.

5.

During the time of the Lecompton battle in Congress, Michael Kerr had written English that the Indiana state Democracy was beyond salvation in 1858; it should instead concentrate on future regeneration. Other Democrats heavy-heartedly agreed. "If elections were held today, a sometime correspondent wrote English on February 22, "we should be badly beaten." Two weeks later, Norman agreed, maintaining that the only way the Democrats could stay in power in the state was "if our opponents act very badly." William Wick noted the great dissension among party editors over Lecompton, and added that the "Germans" were determined to "walk off and leave us." Even after the passage of the English Bill, prospects for the Party appeared dim. On May 8, Wick wrote English that "your bill came too late, and was too indirect to save our foreigners. I much fear that the Germans, immigrants within the last dozen years, will leave us as a body." And a leading anti-Lecompton newspaper, the *Sullivan Democrat,* commented in early May that "we cannot regard the English Bill as a peace measure." Although it agreed that it "disposes of the question for this session of Congress," it saw only future discord when Kansas reapplies next winter.[90]

As the summer approached, however, the Party began to repair its discord. In the first week in May, William Wick had written that "only a partial reconciliation can be expected from the conference bill," but only one week later he more

---

inevitable doom of all the opposition to [Democratic] principles…The exercises will shut up by declaring William the unanimous nominee of the convention." *Tribune,* June 8 1858.

89. S.K. Wolfe to J.B. Norman, August 24, 1858, English Papers. *New Albany Ledger,* August 19, 24, 1858. *New Albany Tribune,* September 11, 1858. *New Albany Ledger,* September 11, 1858.

90. M.C. Kerr to WHE, February 19, 1858; Joshua Huckelberry to WHE, February 22, 1858; J.B. Norman to WHE, March 5, 1858; W.W. Wick to WHE, May 8, 1858, English Papers. *Sullivan Democrat,* n.d., in English Scrapbook, 101.

optimistically wrote to English "under the results of your very skillful effort, we shall not suffer more than a temporary check." Even the "German defections," he admitted had been overestimated. The *Sullivan Democrat*, too, changed its tune. Noting that "the only hope the Republicans had of success in the approaching fall elections was in the dismemberment of the Democratic party," it refused to stand on "hair-splitting technicalities" and advised every Democrat to sacrifice something for the good of the party." Most newspapers likewise fell in line, and the great majority of Democratic county conventions refused to make a party candidate's stand on Lecompton a test for office. Of course, some dissension continued. In the Third District, anti-Lecompton Democrats bolted when Hughes was renominated; and in the Seventh, John G. Davis announced an independent candidacy when Henry Secrest, an anti-Lecomptonite but supporter of the English bill, received the party nomination instead. Hughes had been such an obnoxious Lecomptonite that the Third District bolt was quite understandable. As for Davis, he was the only Indiana Democratic congressman to vote against the English Bill, and for that and his strong anti-Lecomptonism he was in this race supported by the Republicans. Most Democrats, it appeared, remained with Secrest, and Democratic newspapers throughout the state as well deplored Davis's course.[91]

Besides the English Bill, three other factors contributed toward renewed Democratic optimism. One was the final full confirmation of Joseph Wright as ambassador to Prussia. In May the *New Albany Ledger* noted that Wright, who had been serving abroad for one year, would have to return home because Congress would adjourn before he could be confirmed. But on June 14, the last day of the session, Wright was senatorially approved. The *Ledger* hoped that this action would satisfy Wright's friends (practically all of whom were anti-Lecomptonites) "that there is no disposition on the part of the administration to proscribe the Governor." Second, two days before Wright was confirmed, the Republicans lost their challenge against Bright and Fitch in the Senate. Although Douglas voted against the Indiana Democrats and some Wright partisans still fumed over Bright's exclusion of Wright from the cabinet, these two results coming so close together (and likely tied) could only help to unite the Hoosier Democracy.[92]

---

91. W.W. Wick to WHE, May 8, 15, 1858, English Papers. *Sullivan Democrat*, in *New Albany Ledger*, May 8, 1858. English Scrapbook, 101-102. In the Third District John W. Carr ran as a third candidate, an independent anti-Lecompton Democrat without Republican support, thereby hurting Hughes. *Ledger*, June 10, 11, 12, 13, 1858. Concerning the 7th District race, the *Ledger* denounced Davis for his selfishness, noting that Secrest had courageously supported him all along and had been promised the nomination this time around. July 12, 25, 1858.

92. *New Albany Ledger*, May 3, June 17, 1858. *CG, 35-1,* 2981. The *Ledger* showed that it continued to respect, or, more accurately, fear, Bright by publishing his Lecompton speech, complimenting it, and later stating "at every successive trial those petty politicians who sneer at Mr. Bright have been compelled to bite the dust." *Ledger,* April 9, June 2, 1858.

The third factor favoring the Democrats was the continued identity problem of the Opposition. Back in mid-January the Republican State Central Committee announced a state convention would be held on March 4. It invited "all persons without regard to past party designations opposed to the Lecompton policy of the present administration" to come together in order to select "a state ticket in opposition to the one nominated on the 8th inst." Clearly these Republicans were hoping to benefit from the differences among the Indiana Democrats coming out of their own state convention. But not all Republicans agreed with this policy. The more nationally oriented of them, those who stressed the core issue of congressional exclusion of slavery from the territories, were not keen to a call that invited Democrats. Included in this group were not only abolitionists like George Julian, but also Michael Garber of the *Madison Courier* and even the relatively moderate Schuyler Colfax. These men wished not only to relieve the Party from an association with what they considered the pro-slavery Democrats, but they also wanted to cut its ties with the Know-Nothings. As Garber had suggested soon after the 1856 defeat, the only road to Republican victory in Indiana would be to rid the Party of "the debris of fusionism," thereby enhancing its purity. But the more conservative members of the Party, like Henry Lane, Caleb Smith, and, at least then, Oliver P. Morton, would deign to appeal to impurity in order to more certainly win the election. It was they who controlled the Party machinery, like the *Indianapolis Journal.* Although these men were unalterably anti-slavery, they had come to see at least the present usefulness of allowing for genuine popular sovereignty.[93]

At the convention the moderates placed Morton in the Chair, a position, Julian wrote, from which he could rule unfairly against the "radicals." The platform eventually adopted called Lecompton a "gross outrage." It denied the fancy reasoning behind the *Dred Scott* decision as "extra-judicial" *dicta*, and reaffirmed the constitutional right of Congress to exclude slavery from the territories. But it also supported the use of popular sovereignty as a "proper and constitutional method" to restrict slavery as well, and its first resolution declared that all state constitutions must be "fairly and fully submitted" to the voters for ratification. Moreover, it refused to adopt the moral language of the 1856 Republican National Convention, leading Julian to label the platform "a shameless retreat in the face of an overbearing foe." On the other hand, the delegates also refused to include any anti-immigrant planks favored by conservative Know-Nothings, and they also nominated a ticket devoid of nativists. These were designed to cement appeal to anti-slavery Germans. This disregard of Know-Nothingism, combined

---

93. *New Albany Tribune,* January 13, 19, 1858. Stampp, *Indiana Politics,* 24. Carter, "Hoosier History," 128-129, includes Morton among the radicals, but in 1858 the denunciations by Julian and others label him "practical." *Madison Courier,* in *New Albany Ledger,* January 13, 1858. Schuyler Colfax to Charles Heaton, February 10, 1858, in Smith, *Schuyler Colfax,* 101-103. Elbert, "Southern Indiana Politics," 22. *Ledger,* March 8, 1858.

with the fact that enough old-line Whigs still considered the Republicans a threat to the Union, moved many former oppositionists to stand aloof from the Party.[94]

Down in New Albany, Milton Gregg was perched on the horns of a dilemma. To support the convention's work opened him up to criticism from the numerous old-line Whigs and Know-Nothings in the district. But to stand aloof from the Republican organization meant certain victory for the district Democracy. He tried to solve this dilemma by insisting that the Republican state platform was essentially conservative, and consistently published Julian's denunciations of it to prove his point. He extolled popular sovereignty and the Webster climate argument, maintaining that Wilmot-type solutions have proven unnecessary. When the American Party, in leading old-line Whig Richard Thompson's home county, adopted resolutions advising Know-Nothings not to unite with Republicans, Gregg criticized them, claiming that the Republican principles of 1858 were almost identical to those of the American platform of 1857. (Considering the Republican omission of any nativist sentiment and its more pointed antislaveryism than the Americans, Gregg's assertion was just not true.) Summing up his attitude, the *New Albany Tribune* declared "we shall be pleased with [Republican] acts and measures so long as they maintain their present high conservative position and eschew antislavery fanaticism." Yet the *Tribune* refused to put the Republican nominees on its masthead, and when it finally did it simply labeled them the "Anti-Lecompton ticket."[95]

In the central and northern portions of the state, the moderate Republican platform gained acceptance by mid-summer. In these districts, the congressional nominees represented the Party's new core, so much so that the venerable Whig leader, John D. Defrees, was denied nomination in the Sixth District because he was viewed as a "crystallized old fogy." The delegates instead chose the younger, more vibrant, Albert G. Porter. But in the confused state of opposition politics near the Ohio River, the Republican organization was weak. In the First District "pocket," the opposition to the Democracy actually backed Alvin Hovey, the ousted anti-Lecompton Democratic district attorney, to run against William Niblack. Gregg and the Second District opposition would have been overjoyed to find a similarly prominent Democrat to run against English. This was especially the case because the most prominent oppositionists in the district were unavailable. The rivals of Wilson in 1856 had all become disqualified: Ferguson was

94. Peek, "The True and Everlasting Principle," 382-384, 388, 389-401. *New Albany Ledger,* March 6, 1858. Clarke, *George Julian,* 193. *Indianapolis Journal,* March 5, 1858. Clarke, *George Julian,* 192. *New Albany Tribune,* March 24, 1858. Charles Roll, *Colonel Dick Thompson: The Persistent Whig* (Indianapolis: Indiana Historical Bureau, 1948), 154.

95. *New Albany Ledger,* September 2, 1858. *New Albany Tribune,* March 8, February 2, 12, 13, 1858. Roll, *Dick Thompson,* 154. The Know-Nothing 1857 Convention had opposed the extension of slavery, but coupled it with paeans to compromise and unionism. It also, of course, called for restrictions on immigrant suffrage. *Ledger,* February 21, 1857. *Tribune,* March 21, 1858. *Ledger,* November 8, 1858.

dead, Crawford had become a too unabashed Republican, and Laird had actually switched to the Democratic Party. John S. Davis, the perennial favorite, had decided to run as an Independent Whig for the state legislature. Gregg himself had been considered a possible congressional nominee, but he formally declined interest at the end of July. In the same issue of the *Tribune* he wondered whether anyone could be found who was willing to undertake "a run against English."[96] (Quite a tribute to English's political skills.)

John M. Wilson was the only one left. English's 1856 opponent had kept himself politically visible, most recently speaking (to the *Ledger's* disgust) at the Old Settler's picnic in early July. On August 7 he spoke at the Market House in New Albany declaring that he would oppose English if no one else would. Four days later, the *New Albany Tribune* announced him as an "Independent anti-Lecompton Candidate" for Congress. Gregg had sent letters to Oppositionists around the district to come to New Albany on August 9 "in order to consult with others on the subject of bringing out a candidate against Mr. English." Here Wilson was nominated, not by a regular convention, but, as the *Ledger* put it, "the supposed creatures of the New Albany clique." Not only Norman, but many oppositionists as well, were disgusted by these tactics. The *Salem Times* had to be bought out to endorse Wilson, and the *Corydon Argus* remained uncommitted for over two weeks. William French's *Jeffersonville Republican* which had become somewhat enamored of English during his anti-Lecompton heyday, declined to support either the incumbent or the challenger. For a short time there was even another challenge by an unknown anti-Lecompton Democrat, but when he found no support Wilson became the only alternative to English. In due time, most Republicans, Americans, and old-line Whigs fell in behind him.[97]

The Democrats were surprised at the Opposition's selection. "We had supposed," the *Paoli Eagle* pointedly commented, "that Wilson, after his character was shown up in the last canvass in the style it was, could never have suffered his name to come before the people again." But Wilson was the last man standing, and on the same day he was 'nominated' he wrote English to ask the congressman to confer on the issue of joint appointments. Having previously anticipated that Wilson would be the opposition's nominee, Luciene Matthews had already warned English that the congressman should "have nothing to do with him at all." Matthews wrote that Norman agreed with him. Indeed, this appears to have

96. Thornbrough, *Civil War Era*, 81-82. *Indiana True Republican*, August 12, in Carter, "Hoosier History," 135. Elbert, "Southern Indiana Politics," 59-60. Nichols, *Disruption* , 215. *New Albany Tribune*, April 12, 1858. *New Albany Ledger*, December 30. 1856. Woolen, *Eminent and Self-Made Men*, District 1, 29-30. *Tribune*, June 23, 1858. *Ledger*, July 31, 1858. *Tribune*, July 30, 1858.

97. *New Albany Ledger*, July 2, 1858. L. G. Matthews to WHE, August 8, 1858, English Papers. *New Albany Tribune*, August 11, 1858. *Paoli Eagle*, August 26, 1858. *Ledger*, August 26, 30, 1858. *Tribune*, August 17, 1858. *Jeffersonville Republican*, in *Eagle*, April 22, 1858. *Putnam Republican Banner*, in *Ledger*, September 27, 1858. *Corydon Argus*, in *Ledger*, August 11, 1858. *Ledger*, August 25, 1858.

been the general attitude of the district's leading Democrats. Cravens noted not only that Wilson was a rogue, but that he was not properly nominated by a popular convention. English nevertheless conferred with Wilson on a number of occasions in mid-August, without reaching any conclusion as to a joint canvass. In New Albany, on August 22, he closeted with several important Democrats in the offices of the *Ledger*. They tried to persuade him not to make any formal agreement, for besides Wilson's suspect character and suspect selection, he was "without that experience in public matters that could give him position and standing." Still unconvinced, and wishing to do things in the traditional way, English tried to meet with Wilson one more time, but when the challenger failed to show for that appointment, the incumbent finally decided to heed his party's wishes.[98]

What may have been decisive in English's final decision was that his national stature had been considerably enhanced since 1856. It perhaps would not do for so eminent a figure to canvass jointly with so unrecognized (and besmirched) an opponent. As Norman had noted, "*you* can draw crowds, not he." Moreover, despite the well publicized debates between Douglas and Lincoln, joint appearances were rather going out of style. Almost all the congressional races in Indiana that year had abandoned them. For its part, the Opposition naturally denounced what it considered English's ungentlemanly decision. The *Corydon Argus* cited five earlier cases when Whigs, undesignated by a convention, were accorded joint appearances with their Democratic congressional opponents. Throughout the campaign Wilson continued to invite English to share the stump with him, but in all cases the incumbent declined. After a while, Wilson began to show up at English's appointments, seeking to speak when the congressman had finished. To foil this tactic, English traveled with one or two other Democrats who were also scheduled to speak. By the time Wilson was accorded the stage it was usually early evening, and English had long left the scene—as had most of the crowd. Disgusted, Gregg wrote in his *New Albany Tribune* that instead of meeting Wilson head on, English "prefer[red] to sneak around the District under the protecting care of county candidates."[99]

English's refusal to appear jointly with Wilson angered the Opposition more than anything else in the campaign. Yet it was English's course in relation to his celebrated bill that was most politically significant. On August 2, in conformance to the procedures of the conference bill, Kansans went to the polls to vote, tech-

98. *Paoli Eagle,* August 19, 1858. J.M. Wilson to WHE, August 11, 1858; L.G. Matthews to WHE, August 6, 1858; J.A. Cravens to WHE, August 25, 1858, English Papers. *New Albany Ledger,* August 23, 1858. *New Albany Tribune,* August 23, 25, 1858.

99. L.G. Matthews to WHE, August 8, 1858, English Papers. *New Albany Ledger,* August 23, 1858. Smith, *Schuyler Colfax,* 106. *New Albany Tribune,* August 24, 1858. *Corydon Argus,* in *Tribune,* September 2, 1858. J.M. Wilson to WHE, October 1, 1858, English Papers. *Tribune,* August 26, September 6, 9, 14, 23, October 4, 7, 1858. *Ledger,* September 2, 4, 24, October 5, 1858 *Tribune,* September 2, 1858.

nically on the land ordinance, and, 10 days later, English's district learned that "proposition rejected" defeated "proposition accepted" 11,612 to 1,926. With that vote, down went Lecompton. Soon after the *New Albany Tribune* learned of these results, it challenged English to abandon the restrictive population provision. Under great pressure, not only from the *Tribune,* but from Republican newspapers throughout the North, English waffled. Claiming that Kansas's population was already sufficient, he admitted he would vote for its admission "whenever she presents herself with a constitution legally formed and approved by the people of the territory." As the *New Albany Ledger* reported it, English said "that he should look at the question of population as a statesman and not as a pettifogger quibbling about technicalities." In other words, despite the conference bill's wording, no formal census was necessary. In Galesburg, Illinois, during his debate with Lincoln, even Stephen Douglas took notice of English's new stance. "Go to Indiana," he announced, "and there you will find English himself, the author of the English bill, has been forced by public opinion to abandon his own darling project, and to give a promise that he will vote for the admission of Kansas at once."[100]

The Opposition press was eager to display English's infidelity to his own work. Much truth lay in the *Evansville Journal's* statement that English discovered "the people will not tolerate his swindle, and he is backing out of it." At one point, English had even claimed that the population clause was not in the original bill as he framed it, but he included it "for the sake of peaceable adjustment." From Washington, Lewis Jordan wrote him that these sentiments were being widely distributed by the opposition to the Democracy throughout the South, and he wondered whether English was being placed in a "false position."[101] But English's own sense of political survival commanded that he switch his tune once north of the Ohio. No more compelling set of circumstances could more simply illustrate how politically mutable were the English Bill's pretensions toward Democratic harmony.

The August 2 vote and English's own retreat defused the conference bill as a decisive issue in the campaign. The combination of these two factors well satisfied the Democrats, while they reduced the Americans and Republicans into simply labeling English a "trickster." In a certain sense, English's meandering course both in Congress and in the canvass did work somewhat against the favorable perceptions of his character. The Opposition press, apparently wishing to emphasize

---

100. Richard B. Morris, ed., *Encyclopedia of American History* (New York: Harper and Bros., 1953), 224. *New Albany Ledger,* August 12, 1858. *New Albany Tribune,* August 16, 1858. *Ledger,* August 27, September 9, 1858. Robert Johannsen, ed., *The Lincoln-Douglas Debates of 1858* (New York: Oxford University Press, 1965, paperback reprint, 1968), 209.

101. See English Bill in appendix, section 1 for census requirement. *Evansville Daily Journal,* in *New Albany Tribune,* September 14, 1858. *New Albany Ledger,* November 2, 1858. Lewis Jordan to WHE, November 3, 1858, English Papers.

this point, early reminded its readers that in 1856 English and the Democrats had falsely accused Wilson of a number of immoralities. As the *Corydon Argus* remembered it, "these charges English and his friends knew to be false, but they did their work anyway supposing that they could ruin an innocent man." Refusing to let the *Argus* have the last word, the *New Albany Ledger* replied that though it did issue a retraction, "no acknowledgment was ever made that these charges were false." Strictly speaking, Norman was correct, for he had only admitted that some evidence "seemed to indicate" Wilson had been "done an injustice."[102]

Angered by the *Ledger*'s refusal to give the Opposition even this much satisfaction, Gregg prepared to make the character issue central to the canvass. On the last day of August, the *New Albany Tribune* laid before its readers depositions taken in one of Louisville's chancery courts in January 1856. The case concerned the divorce of Eli Vansickle, a ship owner, from his wife Elizabeth. One of the deponents, Pinkney Varble, a pilot working on one of Vansickle's ships, swore that he saw a daguerreotype of Elizabeth and "a man by the name of English" that was shown to him by Elizabeth's husband. "The daguerreotype represented the Defendant sitting alongside of English, he holding his arm around her waist." According to Varble, Elizabeth had told him at one time that "this man English was the only man she ever loved." Varble also saw two letters written from Elizabeth to English. One was directed to Lexington; the other was evidently sent to Indianapolis. (One must assume, at best, these letters were copies.) Both letters requested a meeting between the two alleged lovers. This testimony was supported by another deponent who also swore that Elizabeth had hoped to get out of her marriage by "writing English and getting him to come there and let the Plaintiff catch him there and kill him." The *Tribune* expostulated "such things are generally held to be disgraceful in a young man, but how infinitely more reprehensible in a man who has a wife and family at home." The next day, the *Tribune* quoted Vansickle as remarking in early 1857, "that scoundrel English has ruined my happiness. I thought I would kill him right off, but considered not to do it then."[103]

In truth, Gregg appears to have maliciously and unfairly presented the facts of the association between English and Elizabeth. As the *New Albany Ledger* noted on the same day of the accusation by the *New Albany Tribune*, the daguerreotype mentioned was taken not in 1852, as the *Tribune* led its readers to believe, but considerably earlier. Elizabeth Vansickle was formerly Elizabeth C.K. Lockhart, who knew English from 1839 to at least 1844. She earlier lived in Madison and

---

102. *Corydon Argus*, in *New Albany Tribune*, August 25, 1858. *New Albany Weekly Ledger*, in English Scrapbook, 126. *Ledger*, November 24, 1858.

103. *New Albany Tribune*, August 25, 31, 1858. Louisville Chancery Court, October 3, 1856, Will B. Hovey, Clerk, English Papers. *Tribune*, September 1, 1858. Occupation of Pinkney Varble gained from https://kentuckykindredgenealogy.com/2014/12/16/captain-pink-varble-riverboat-captain/ accessed November 9, 2019.

then in Louisville, once writing English, "William my love I am always willing
to do anything to make you happy." It is not impossible that the daguerreotype
dates from the 1850s, yet it is highly unlikely. It would have been out of keeping
with English's cautious character. As the *Ledger* maintained, "there is no testimony
whatever that Mr. English and Mrs. Vansickle ever met after the marriage of the
latter—no testimony that Mr. English ever wrote to the lady or she to him, excepting a couple of unsigned notes said to be in her handwriting, and addressed
to Mr. E., which were never sent and which Mr. English of course never received."
English himself did not take these charges of infidelity, often repeated, very seriously. At one gathering in Leavenworth (Harrison County) he "advised the modest young men to immediately qualify themselves to vote for him by hunting up
nice *democratic gals* and encircling their arms about their waists."[104]

As Gregg's luck would have it, his attempt to stain English's character rather
comically achieved its denouement with Captain Vansickle's untimely death. Engaged in a quarrel over repairs that one Thomas Nadal made to Vansickle's boat,
the Captain struck Nadal, whereupon Nadal's son "gave the Cap't two or three
blows on the head with a stick of wood." Although Vansickle then walked home
unattended, he died six hours later of the wounds inflicted. The *New Albany
Tribune* lamented that Vansickle's sudden death prevented it from publishing an
affidavit of his "in which the connection of Mr. English with V's divorced wife
would have been fully shown." Perhaps English did continue to associate with
Elizabeth after he was married, but Gregg was never able to even remotely prove
it. Remembering Vansickle's reported threats made against English, Norman eu-
logized the Captain by simply stating that he "was a man of violent and ungov-
ernable temper."[105]

The fact was that a scandal, such as the one Gregg attempted to sow, was
probably the only way a weak candidate in opposition to a now recognized national name, in a district traditionally overwhelmingly Democratic, had any
chance of winning. This was especially true after Kansas rejected the proposed
reduced land ordinance. Now with Vansickle's death, Gregg had only the issue
of English's abandonment of a joint canvass and his vaunted 'trickiness' around
which to build a successful campaign. This was hardly enough. The only unpredictable element that could possibly have cut into English's generally anticipated
great majority was the disaffection of the normally Democratic German vote. In
the spring Norman had written English that "nearly all" of the German immi-

---

104. *New Albany Ledger,* August 31, 1858. See chapter 1, footnote 17, for mention of Elizabeth during En-
    glish's stay in Madison. Elizabeth C. K. Lockhart to WHE, December 23, 1844, English Papers. See also
    Elizabeth to WHE, January 1, November 11, 1844, English Papers. *Ledger,* August 31, 1858. *New Albany
    Tribune,* September 27, 1858.

105. *Louisville Journal,* in *New Albany Ledger,* September 15, 1858. *New Albany Tribune,* September 16, 1858.
    Ledger, September 15, 1858.

grants were anti-Lecompton, and in September the *New Albany Ledger* acknowledged that many had already switched to the Republican Party. In order to try to secure the German vote, the *Paoli Eagle*, at the end of 1856 had begun to allocate a column a week to news in German. But they discontinued that practice in the summer of 1857, and part of the reason was that the German immigrants had begun to switch their readership to the *New Albany Tribune*. It was a strange truth that in the crazy-quilt opposition politics of southern Indiana, recent German emigres aligned with American Party sympathizers to try to dislodge the insufficiently antislavery Democracy.[106]

To keep German defections to a minimum, the Democratic press, toward the end of the campaign, published a crude nativist speech that it alleged was made by Wilson in 1855. It began "no foreigner ever left his native land because of its government being tyrannical; none ever came here for the purpose of adding to the wealth and power of this nation. Their only desire was to further their ambitious schemes, and finally to subvert republicanism in this country." The Irish, he charged, were animals, and the British could not be trusted, but more significantly the Germans snuck away "at the mention of Washington, and vow[ed] eternal enmity and destruction to him who slew [their] Hessian brethren at Trenton." Again: "Look at the Dutchman, smoking his pipe, and if you can see a ray of intelligence in that dirty, idiotic looking face of his, show it to me." Germans he called "lop-eared, wide mouthed [and] mullet-headed, coming [to America] from some hut in the land of Krout." And most significantly Wilson ended his purported speech by claiming that if "I were a candidate for any office, I would tell these paupers and vagabonds, these vile, dirty, filthy, degraded, idiotic foreigners, I did not want their votes, and if I ever am a candidate, I hope to God I will never get them."[107]

Two days after the *New Albany Ledger* printed this alleged speech in full, the *New Albany Tribune* denounced it as "a vile forgery and a slander." It did not deny, and could not deny, that Wilson had made typical nativist remarks in the early days of Know-Nothingism, but the *Tribune* convincingly argued that he would never have been so impolitic. The peroration of the speech was clearly too good for the Democrats to be authentic, and it is difficult to believe the Party would not have used this item in 1856 as well. The *Salem Times* was able to publish an affidavit signed by 14 men who witnessed the original speech declaring that the Democratic version of it was "a gross misrepresentation from beginning to end."

---

106. Gresham, *Walter Q. Gresham*, 76. J.B. Norman to WHE, March 31, 1858, English Papers. *New Albany Ledger*, September 30, 1858. *Paoli Eagle*, December 25, 1856, August 13, 1857. After the election English was told that a certain educated German should be patronized and solicited for the Democratic Party to win back his fellow countrymen. C.T. Nixon to WHE, October 21, 1858, English Papers. *Washington* (County) *Democrat*, September 16, 1858. *Ledger*, September 21, 1858.

107. *Washington* (County) *Democrat*, September 16, 1858. *New Albany Ledger*, September 21, 1858.

They swore that the "spirit and sentiment of Mr. Wilson's speech was wholly different from that represented in [the Democratic version]—that he did not use the low-flung abuse toward the foreign population of this country." The Democrats finally admitted that the published speech was actually reconstructed from notes that two Democratic editors took on that night. But, as the *Ledger* maintained "it is a matter of small importance whether the speech was word for word as published, [for] it is well known that Mr. Wilson was at that time an active and leading K[now] N[othing], and that he was bitterly hostile to 'foreigners'." For good measure, the Democrats translated the speech into German and had it circulated in the district through the columns of the *Louisville Anzeiger*.[108]

The disrespect for the truth that both the Democrats and their opponents exhibited in this campaign may be a function of the political pressure that the slavery issue put upon politics. Or, perhaps, it may simply be understood as a natural tendency of democratic politics in general. Political parties in America have sometimes acted as associations producing religious-like certainty in their members, allowing for unsavory means to achieve victory. At any rate, by Election Day only the most rabid oppositionists could doubt that English would be reelected. Even Gregg admitted that the Opposition goal was more modest than outright victory: "If English falls behind his vote in 1856 two thousand, or even one thousand, it would be really as great a rebuke to the traitor and trickster as if he were defeated." As for the Democrats, the *New Albany Ledger* predicted that English would take every county, and this majority would equal that of 1856. The results proved somewhat disappointing to both sides. English polled a very respectable 55.6 percent of the vote, but that was 1.5 percent lower than two years previously. In every county except one he polled fewer votes than the head of the state Democratic ticket, secretary of state nominee Daniel McClure. Wilson, on the other hand, equaled or exceeded his head of the ticket in all but two counties. One of those he lagged behind was Perry County, which had the highest proportion of German citizens in the district—perhaps 'old' Germans.[109] Neither candidate, in truth, seemed to inspire great enthusiasm.

A couple factors appear to have cut into English's margin of victory. First, there was resentment caused by his succeeding himself so many times. At least this is what the *New Albany Ledger* surmised. It also appears that a sizeable number of anti-Lecompton Democrats refused to vote for him. The *Paoli Eagle* maintained that this was a trend in other congressional districts where Democrats refused to

---

108. *New Albany Tribune*, September 23, 1858. *Salem Times*, in *Tribune*, October 2, 1858. *New Albany Ledger*, September 27, 1858. *Tribune*, October 2, 1858.

109. *New Albany Tribune*, October 12, 1858. *New Albany Ledger*, September 21, October 14, 1858. Dubin, ed., *Congressional Elections*, 176, 181. *Tribune Almanac and Political Register for Year 1859*, (New York: Greeley and McGrath, 1859), 59. Elisha E. Griffith, "The Growth and Decline of the German Element in Indiana" (Master's Thesis, Butler University, 1972), map within.

rally around their party's candidate if he had not criticized Lecompton to their liking. For strong anti-Lecomptonites English fit into this category. It is a curious factor that his worst comparative showing between 1856 and 1858 was in Clark County, the home not only of many recent arriving Germans, but of Amos Lovering. Lovering, a respected common pleas judge who had previously served on the district's Democratic Central Committee, refused to back English because of his compromise. From one angle, the English Bill may be seen to be statesmanlike, especially as a result of the August 2nd Kansas vote. But the great anger that the Lecompton Constitution produced in not a few Democrats made the author of the compromise bill indeed a trickster and traitor. Although such sentiment was not nearly wide enough to defeat English, especially considering both his opponent and the general southern Indiana distrust of Republicanism, it most clearly accounts for his diminished, though still not unimpressive, showing.[110]

In the state as a whole, the Indiana Democracy did suffer a setback. Technically, they lost two congressional seats, but one of them was when Henry Secrest, the official Democratic nominee, was beaten in the Seventh District by anti-Lecompton Democrat John G. Davis, who was aided by Republican support. The other official Democratic loser was James Hughes, who was defeated in a three-way contest in the Third District, which included Madison. Besides English and Niblack, victorious candidates in southernmost Indiana, only William S. Holman, also anti-Lecompton (but, unlike Davis, the official Democratic nominee) won in the Fourth District. Counting Davis, the Democrats, therefore, held four of the state's 11 congressional seats. In both houses of the state legislature, the Republicans held a plurality, only denied majorities by the election of a handful of old-line Whigs (like John S. Davis). Only for state office did the Democrats achieve a victory, though ever so narrowly. Their nominees for secretary of state, auditor, treasurer, attorney general, and superintendent of public instruction were elected on average by a 1 percent margin. Considering the more rapid development of the northern part of the state, this did not augur well for the 1860 gubernatorial and presidential elections.[111]

110. *New Albany Ledger,* October 22, 1858. *Paoli Eagle,* October 28, 1858. Elbert, "Southern Indiana Politics," 74-75. *Indiana State Sentinel,* in *Ledger,* November 27, 1858. *Ledger,* October 23, 1858. Monks, ed., *Courts and Lawyers, vol. 2,* 998. *Ledger,* March 1, 1852.

111. Dubin, ed., *Congressional Elections,* 181. Davis's forthright and consistent anti-Lecompton stand gave him some needed traction in his district. See William Snyder to Davis, April 15, 1858; J.B. Olney to Davis, April 18, 1858, and [Unintelligible] to Davis, April 27, 1858, Davis Papers. As the Opposition *Randolph County Journal* put it, while other northern Indiana Democrats went along with the English Bill, "John G. Davis has stood first to last unobtrusively, unflinching, and unsuspectedly opposed to this great usurpation." *Washington* (County) *Democrat,* May 6, 1858. Shepherd, *Biographical Directory,* 516-518. *Tribune Almanac and Political Register for Year 1857* (New York: Greeley and McGrath, 1857), 58. Barnhart and Carmony, *Indiana, vol. 1,* 412-414.

But it was not in Indiana alone that the Democratic vote declined. Through-out the North, Democratic congressmen went down to defeat. Whereas 53 north-ern Democrats sat in the first session of the 35th Congress (and would continue to sit in the lame-duck second session), the 36th Congress would see that number reduced to 35, only 24 percent of all northern representatives. Only seven north-ern Lecompton Democrats were returned, while 11 of 22 anti-Lecomptonites who voted for the Montgomery substitute were reelected. As for the English Bill, it, too, was accorded an unfavorable hearing. Of the nine anti-Lecompton Demo-crats who supported it, three would see the halls of the 36th Congress. Of the 13 who opposed it, eight were returned.[112] As he prepared to leave for Washington in late November, English must have realized that despite his best efforts the Party as a national force was severely diminished.

6.

English returned to Congress to a mixed reception. On the one hand his solid electoral victory was viewed by administration Democrats as a great relief. Many had actually expected the worst and feared he would be bested. Lewis Jordan wrote him that it was "a grand victory." Even among those who believed he would win, few expected him to do so by more than a few hundred votes. Yet the results around the rest of the nation were indeed sobering to Democrats, and it was quite obvious to all that the English Bill had not prevented the Republicans from capitalizing on the Lecompton fiasco. As the *Albany Evening Journal* remarked, "Buchanan has lost Pennsylvania to keep South Carolina. To retain Florida and Texas he [has forfeited] Indiana and Illinois." In the spring, English's uncle had written his nephew from Louisville that he hoped and believed he would live to see the day English was elected president. But in the autumn of 1858 few elector-ates outside southern Indiana would have chosen him to any position of honor and profit.[113]

The second session of the 35th Congress convened on December 6. A couple of days before its Christmas recess, an incident occurred, which marvelously dis-played the frustration of the previous spring. Strolling down Pennsylvania Avenue after Congress had adjourned, on Saturday, December 18, English encountered William Montgomery, the congressman after whom the Montgomery substitute had been named. They had not yet addressed one another since the lame duck session began, and as he strolled past the Pennsylvanian, English offered a per-functory, "How are you, Montgomery?" Although the first reports of the encoun-

---

112. *CG, 36-1,* 1-2. Dubin, ed., *Congressional Elections,* 181-185. Nichols, *Disruption,* 223-224.

113. Lewis Jordan to WHE, November 3, 1858, English Papers. *Albany Evening Journal,* n.d., in English Scrap-book, 117. S.S. English to WHE, May 4, 1858, English Papers.

ter claimed that Montgomery responded, "I speak to no puppy, sir," it is clear that he simply ignored the Hoosier and continued on his way. Enraged by so obvious a rebuff, English swirled and struck Montgomery on the cheek with his cane, knocking him into the street. When the 200-pound congressman recovered himself he took a step toward the much more diminutive English, apparently to retaliate, but the Indiana congressman was holding a sword that came from inside his cane as he backed away from his dazed but angry victim. Unwilling to engage a swordsman, Montgomery put down a brick he had reflexively picked up and watched as English turned and retreated around a corner. But before English could complete his retreat, Montgomery again picked up the brick, threw it at him, and had it rather harmlessly nick the heel of English's boot.[114]

Immediately thereafter, Montgomery entered a complaint before a magistrate and procured a writ against English for assault and battery. Quickly learning of the writ, English voluntarily entered the courthouse and gave bail for his promised appearance at a possible trial. Montgomery later sent a message to English's quarters challenging him to a fight without weapons, admirable in the sense that it ignored the tradition of pistols, but rather cowardly considering that Montgomery weighed almost 100 pounds more than English and was at least six inches taller. According to one source, English responded that he would fight Montgomery "with anything from a needle to an anchor," but that statement is probably apocryphal. By this time, the story had been picked up by the wire services and spread to the rest of the country. Details differed over whether Montgomery had actually said anything, over whether English's cane had been shattered leaving him inadvertently with the sword in his hand, and over whether English swiftly retreated or "coolly walked away." In general, however, it was asserted that Montgomery had indeed offended English and by some code of honor English was forced to retaliate.[115]

The next day Montgomery procured three witnesses to the incident, and on Monday, December 20, their attested accounts appeared in the *Washington Star*. The two who saw the events from the beginning denied that Montgomery had said anything to English, and they also claimed that English had actually struck Montgomery from behind. All three swore that English was running away when

---

114. *CG*, 35-2, 1. *Washington Daily Intelligencer*, December 18, 1858, in English Scrapbook, 139. *New York Times*, December 18, 1858, in *New Albany Ledger*, December 23 1858. *Louisville Journal*, in *Ledger*, December 22, 1858. Description of Montgomery may be found in Hesseltine, ed., *Three against Lincoln*, 107. English Scrapbook, 141. *Ledger*, December 22, 1858.

115. *Louisville Journal*, in *New Albany Ledger*, December 21. 1858. *Louisville Democrat*, December 21, 1858. When reporting on the congressional melee begun by Keitt and Grow earlier in the year, the *Brookville American* reported that Montgomery shouted to Thomas Bocock, who was trying to restrain the Pennsylvanian from joining the fray, that the Virginian should "'Let go of my arm [fuck]er, or I'll knock you down.'" The newspaper went on to note that "William Montgomery is a very large man," though it also noted that he was a "quiet, gentlemanly person." *American*, February 16, 1858.

Montgomery threw the brick at him. The blow from the cane, one witness remarked, "was a very heavy one, and Montgomery was bleeding profusely from the nose." Though it printed these cards, the *Star* questioned the character of the witnesses. The two principal ones, it claimed, were bartenders, one of them unemployed. *The Star* alleged that it was Montgomery who actually wrote their affidavits, while the two 'witnesses' signed them in an inebriated state. Having read these cards, English privately prepared a statement of his own, while Montgomery found two physicians to swear that he had "incontestably" been struck from behind. On Wednesday, December 22, these new developments were printed in the Washington press.[116]

The *Star* remarked that neither of Montgomery's physicians was a resident of Washington, and it appears that one may have been a medical student from Pennsylvania. As for English's card, here it is in full:

> My attention has been called to the statement inserted in the Washington papers of yesterday at the request of Hon. Wm. Montgomery, purporting to give an account of his recontre with me on Saturday last. I propose saying but a few words in relation to it. I neither know nor care who the parties are who made the statement, as it carries on its face conclusive evidence of its partial and *ex parte* character. That different versions of such an affair should exist might be expected; and that the part that I took in it should be grossly misrepresented, occasions me no surprise whatever.
>
> I shall not hunt up counter statements from hackmen or others; neither shall I engage in newspaper controversies about it, invoke the protection of law, or the intervention of the police. I neither seek, nor have sought, any difficulty with Mr. Montgomery—I shall avoid none. When I met him on Saturday I was not aware (nor am I yet) that I had by word or deed given him any cause for offense; and when in friendly recognition I extended him my hand, I addressed him in terms courteous, polite, and gentlemanly. This friendly salutation was met in a rude and insulting manner, which I resented, on the instant, in the most effective way then in my power. The blow fell as quick as it could reach its object after the insult was given.
>
> For this I was recognizised in court, at the instance and upon the affidavit of Mr. Montgomery, and this is the whole transaction in a nutshell. The details of the recontre or which got the best of it, or whether the blame rests upon one, or both, or neither, are matters about which I shall not bandy words. On my part the collision was wholly unpremeditated

---

116. *Washington Star,* December 20, 22, 1858.

and without malice—an impulse based upon an unprovoked indignity offered me.[117]

Significantly, this rather cultured statement does not declare that Montgomery said anything, and by claiming that his blow "fell as quick as it could reach the object," he does not deny that he struck from behind. But he offers no remorse, and apparently believed that such behavior as Montgomery had exhibited deserved a licking. And one other point remains: did English use the word "unpremeditated" to distinguish his attack from that of Preston Brooks?

One day before English's account appeared, Montgomery had given an interview to the Washington correspondent of the *New York Tribune*. In it, the Pennsylvania congressman claimed that after English struck him, the Hoosier shouted, "God d[amn] you, I will teach you to insult me in that way." More significantly, Montgomery suggested the reason for his rebuff to English's salutations. According to his memory, on the night of the celebration at the White House upon the passage of the English bill that afternoon, English told the crowd that he had only associated with the anti-Lecompton Democrats "to find out their plans to defeat me." Since then, Montgomery argued, not only he, but all anti-Lecompton Democrats "looked upon [English] as a treacherous spy and unfit associate for gentlemen." In the printed version of English's speech no such admission exists, although it may have been purposely omitted. Be that as it may, what truly explains Montgomery's behavior toward English was that the conference bill's passage stole the Pennsylvanian's thunder, and placed him in a politically dangerous position. In his desire to be renominated that summer against an Administration inspired revolt, he had publicly declared the English bill a settlement acceptable to anti-Lecompton Democrats. He even wrote letters to constituents praising Buchanan, and during the canvass for reelection he defended both the president and the conference bill. So angered was Horace Greeley by Montgomery's new found friendliness for the Administration, that he withdrew the *New York Tribune's* support for his candidacy.[118] Essentially, in order to be renominated and reelected, Montgomery took the same route that English did in Congress but for less noble reasons. No wonder he resented one whom he probably considered a Hoosier pipsqueak.

After English's printed response, the controversy hung fire over the Christmas recess. Few newspapers appear to have come to Montgomery's defense beyond noting that he was severely beaten. English, however, continued to receive high praise for upholding his honor. From his district, the *Clark County National Dem-*

117. *Ibid.*, December 22, 1858.

118. *New York Tribune*, December 20, 1858, in *Paoli Eagle*, December 23, 1858. *New Albany Ledger*, May 26, 1858. *Cincinnati Tribune*, in *New Albany Tribune*, June 30, 1858. English Scrapbook, 140. *Ledger*, December 21, 1858. *Washington (Pa.) Examiner*, December 30, 1858, in English Scrapbook, 139.

ocrat declared "we like to see a man resent an insult on the spot, and not wait to have an apology by the interference of personal friends, or a challenge to fight a duel, as we have known some members of congress to do. When a man," the editor went on, "will not be insulted or imposed upon himself, it is a sure sign that he will not permit his constituents to be imposed upon." The *New Albany Ledger*, recounting Montgomery's ill-mannered treatment of secretary of the interior Jacob Thompson only a few days earlier, concluded "it [was] evident that Montgomery required a lesson in manners." But what was more astonishing than the favorable response he received from his own district was the favorable response given English by Pennsylvanians. The *Washington (Pa.) Examiner,* one of Montgomery's anti-Lecompton supporters, admitted that their representative's behavior was not acceptable, "and as a man of spirit [English] could not do less than resent it on the spot." Individual constituents of Montgomery agreed. One wrote English that Montgomery's insult "merited chastisement given to a blackguard and fool." Another told the combative Hoosier that "there is but one sentiment here respecting your treatment of the individual who offered such an indignity: everybody says he deserved what he got." Finally, Joshua Weaver, an apparent devotee of the *lignum vitae,* wrote English that "Mr. Montgomery should follow Charles Sumner to Europe."[119] These men were probably not great admirers of Montgomery to begin with, but the simple fact that they were so moved to write their feelings to his attacker vouches for the popularity of their sentiments.

Ten days after Congress returned from its Christmas recess, the following card appeared in the *Washington Union:*

> The undersigned, Joseph C. McKibbin and G. B. Adrian, friends of the Hon Wm. Montgomery, and Joseph Lane and Wm. E. Niblack, friends of the Hon. Wm. H. English, having by consent of the parties, examined fully the facts and circumstances of the late difficulty between them, have come to the conclusion that while Mr. English evidently acted under the impression that an insult had been offered him calling for resentment, yet the evidence does not allow to show any insult had been offered which authorized the violence he used; and he having expressed to Mr. Montgomery his deep regret for what he had done, we think this apology sufficient, and have mutually accepted the terms as a final adjustment of the difficulty.[120]

119. *Clark County National Democrat,* December 22, 1858. *New Albany Ledger,* December 30, 1858. *Washington (Pa.) Examiner,* n.d., in English Scrapbook, 140. J. W. Spence to WHE, January 21, 1859; E.D. Whitney to WHE, December 25, 1858; Joshua Weaver to WHE, January 6, 1859, English Papers.

120. *Washington Union,* January 13, 1859.

The agreed explanation still allowed English to claim that he had believed he had been insulted, and despite the mediators' rejection of English's rash use of violence, male America had clearly declared him not guilty. As a last comment on the affair, witness the words of one newspaper that apparently saw in the incident a commentary on the integrity of public men. It is not exactly clear whether the editor upheld the *code duello* or not, but where he places his contempt is unmistakable.

> They would have settled a matter of this nature very differently in France, or in phlegmatic England, or even in Spain, whose citizens we are so prone to brand as a nation of cowards. Our prominent men, however, though holding to the *code duello*, with more punctiliousness than any class of similar status in almost any other nation, are nevertheless very content with venting their valor in words, and shrinking from the responsibilities of their code when the emergency comes upon them
>
> It is well for humanity perhaps—it certainly is well for Messrs. English and Montgomery, that their differences were not carried out to a bloody issue. But I put it to [the reader] in all seriousness, whether gentlemen who *believe* in the code of honor are justified in bringing it into *contempt.* They should either fight when a fair occasion offers, or else repudiate the obligations of the code.[121]

English was no doubt surprised that he was called to defend his conference bill on the streets of Washington. He was less surprised when Republicans attacked it in the halls of Congress. One day before the incident with Montgomery, the House Committee on Territories rejected, 5 to 4, a proposed amendment to the Oregon Bill calling for repeal of the population provision of the English measure. On December 23, John Bingham of Ohio introduced a measure on the floor of the House intended to completely repeal the conference bill. Referred to the Committee on Territories Bingham's measure died there. After the Christmas recess, the Republicans caucused and decided to oppose the admission of Oregon "while the English bill of prohibition stands in reference to Kansas." The Republicans knew that Oregon would come in as a Democratic state anyway, and they were determined to have Republican Kansas accompany it.[122]

Before the congressional Republicans could attempt to execute their plan in Washington, the Indiana state legislators almost embarrassed their Second District congressman on their own. Led by anti-Lecompton Douglas Democrats, it

---

121. English Scrapbook, 143.

122. *New Albany Ledger,* December 17, 1858. *CG, 35-2,* 196. *New York Times* dispatch, January 7, 1859, in *Ledger,* January 12, 1859.

introduced a resolution favoring "repeal of that part of the 'English bill,' which requires said territory to have a population equal for representative purposes in congress before her people can hold another convention to form another constitution preparatory to an application for admission of such State." In the Indiana House the measure passed 51 to 10, one Second District Democrat voting for it and the other eight abstaining. But the Republicans in the state Senate tabled it, not because they agreed with the English Bill's population provision, but because they argued that the conference bill, with its clause to immediately admit Kansas had its voters approved the bill's proposition, contained too much of popular sovereignty for their liking. They would rather have voted to pass a resolution completely repealing the bill, and thus the House resolution was tabled in the upper chamber. All Second District Democratic state senators, respecting their congressman, voted with the Republicans as strange bedfellows to help table the bill. They thus helped prevent English from having his own state repudiate his work.[123]

A little over a week later the scene again shifted back to Washington. On February 10, John G. Davis announced his intention to call for recommittal of the Oregon bill with express instructions to add a section repealing the population clause of the Kansas conference measure. In response the next day, English indicated that should Davis actually introduce his amendment he would introduce a substitute of his own that would simply require that no territory could become a state without a population equal to the requirement for one representative in Congress. In this manner, he hoped to take what he considered the high ground. One day later, on February 12, the battle fully commenced on the House floor, but it was begun not by Davis, but by Republican Galusha Grow. The Pennsylvanian introduced an amendment to the Oregon bill that enabled both Kansas *and* Oregon to frame constitutions, and that repealed the first section of the English bill. This amendment supported congressional over territorial power. When English rose to offer his earlier substitute to Davis's measure as a substitute to Grow's, Orr ruled him out of order, but he also ruled Grow's amendment out of order according to the 55th rule: "No motion or proposition on the subject different from that under consideration shall be admitted under color of amendment." Grow protested that the subject under consideration was the admission of states, and he appealed the speaker's ruling. On a motion to table the appeal, only four anti-Lecompton Democrats voted with Grow, and Orr's ruling stood.[124]

After these votes, John G. Davis offered the Oregon recommittal scheme he proposed two days earlier. This time the speaker ruled this particular motion out of order on the grounds that Davis's amendment "is an instruction to one of the committees to do that which the House itself cannot do." Apparently Orr was maintaining that the Oregon bill cannot be amended to repeal part of another

---

123. Ariel and Will H. Draper, *Brevier Legislative Reports* (Indianapolis: Daily Indiana State Sentinel, 1859), 81. Lew Wallace introduced the resolution.

124. *CG, 35-2*, 944, 985-986, 1007.

bill, i.e., the Kansas Conference measure. Like Grow, Davis appealed the speaker's ruling, whereby English, happy to have Orr procedurally fight for his conference measure, moved that the House table Davis's appeal. Again the Administration prevailed, 118 to 95. After that, only one belated attempt was made to repeal the population part of the English bill. On March 2, in a poorly attended House one day before adjournment, Davis asked for unanimous consent to introduce such a bill. English, ever at his post, objected. As Davis's bill was moved without pre-notification, English's objection triggered the House rule requiring Davis's motion to receive a two-thirds majority to pass. In the only vote ever to record a majority against the conference bill the House voted 100 to 87 to allow Davis to introduce his repeal, but that margin was hardly two-thirds. In making his objection English had noted that it was "rather late in the day to introduce a bill of that kind." He was clearly angered by tactics, like Montgomery's rebuff, that he considered ungentlemanly.[125]

Kansas would not be admitted to the Union until late January 1861, as a free state. While the English Bill was certainly controversial, it did have the effect of lowering the political temperature and killing Lecompton itself. After its opponents' attempts to gut it failed in the second session of the 35th Congress, it was essentially left to run its course. It was, in truth, a pacification measure. But events in the next two years, most significantly the northern reaction to John Brown's raid at Harper's Ferry and the subsequent election of a Republican president, made the English conference bill simply a bump in the road to civil war. English had mostly hoped that his bill would bring some harmony to the Democratic Party, but even this moderate goal would not stick. On the last day of the 35th Congress, the Democrats dutifully passed a resolution thanking Orr for the "able, impartial, and dignified manner in which he has discharged the duties as Speaker." The vote on so perfunctory a resolution was revealing: remembering Orr's role in packing the Kansas select investigating group and in choosing English over Montgomery for the conference committee, 15 of the 22 original anti-Lecomptonites abstained. The wound had not yet healed and would not be given time to heal. Perhaps had Alexander Stephens allowed a proposed celebratory dinner to take place upon his announced retirement from Congress, some personal good feeling within the Party may have been restored to a significant degree. Sixty Democratic congressmen signed the invitation, including Douglas, Bright, and English. But the sometimes-testy Georgian declined the invite, eschewing such sentimental transactions, thereby preventing a social gathering between northern and southern Democrats, Lecomptonites and anti-Lecomptonites, that might have had some effect on repairing a fractured party. English could not have been pleased.[126]

---

125. *Ibid.,* 1009, 1594.

126. CG, 35-2, 1671. *Dignitaries Invited to Party for Alexander H. Stephens,* March 1, 1859, Ricks Collection, Illinois State Historical Society, Springfield. Schott, *Alexander Stephens,* 263.

CHAPTER EIGHT

Young America Revisited

P olitically and historically, the Kansas issue was central to the coming of the
Civil War, but in truth it was not high upon the list of everyday concerns of
Second District Hoosiers. Indeed, if southerners had been less aggressive in
promoting the undemocratic Lecompton Constitution, Second District citizens
would have kept muted any anti-southernism, for considering the district's prox-
imity to the Ohio River, these citizens' concern with pecuniary matters would
naturally work to downplay any tensions between North and South. To the more
perspicacious citizens of the district, the slavery issue represented the one consistent threat to an otherwise prosperous and optimistic decade. In the year before
the Civil War the Second District's prosperity had reached heights theretofore
unknown. Agricultural produce increased yearly, the shipbuilding industry flour-
ished, and the New Albany and Salem Railroad shifted north-south traffic in the
state away from Madison and into New Albany. In the middle of the decade it was
confidently predicted that the district's premier city could reach a population of
50,000 by 1860, leading a number of municipal boosters to talk of outstripping
Louisville as the primary Ohio River port west of Cincinnati.[1]

Even in the area of manufacturing the Second District well accounted for itself, partly because it possessed the Cannelton Cotton Mills. Originally projected
to hold over 10,000 spindles and 350 looms, the mill failed to attract sufficient investment to make it a first-rate factory, but it was nevertheless the most profitable
industrial enterprise in southern Indiana, and it continued to operate well beyond
the decade. Although this Perry County mill was clearly the greatest single example of manufacturing in the area, it was Floyd County, because of the sheer size of
New Albany, which produced in the aggregate the most industrial output. Indeed,
it actually ranked fourth in the state in the value of its manufactured products.
Washington and Orange counties, too, had smaller yet profitable steam powered

---

1. Barnhart, *From Frontier to Commonwealth, vol. 1,* 1-5. Crane, "Joseph Wright," 182. *New Albany Ledger,* January
   17, June 2, 9, 1857. *Madison Courier,* in *Ledger,* October 11, 1858. *New Albany Tribune,* December 7, 1854.

saw and grist mills, and geographical surveys of the district located abundant sources of coal and iron. Most believed it would be only a short time before these deposits were significantly exploited. Second District Hoosiers also shared in the period's technological advances. Gas lighting was introduced into New Albany in 1852 and into Jeffersonville in 1860; the magnetic telegraph sped dispatches from Washington to a number of cities as early as 1855, and John Norman introduced a new, state of the art steam press into the offices of the *New Albany Ledger* three years before the end of the decade.[2]

The existence of New Albany also allowed this essentially rural and provincial district to encounter some examples of high culture. Frequent lectures took place in the city's Market House, including ones by Lucy Stone, Oliver Wendell Holmes, and Dorothea Dix. The city also offered concerts and recitals, and although it could never claim to have hosted Jenny Lind, she did angelically sing in nearby Madison in one of its pork houses. As for its religious diversity, New Albany contained not only eight different protestant denominations represented by at least one church, but it also harbored two Catholic churches and one synagogue. In 1858 the *New Albany Ledger* was cosmopolitan enough to even recognize Yom Kippur, though it gruesomely characterized it as the day when "radicals of the Hebrew faith neither eat or drink anything for twenty-four hours and spend the whole day in prayer clothed in their death garments."[3]

But in the midst of what appeared to be a flourishing decade for a confident city and district, a keen observer could locate certain clues of impending decline. These had nothing to do with the recession of 1857, which although it temporarily forced wage cuts and debt even to the *New Albany Ledger*, was short-lived and limited in its consequences. (Unlike every other western bank, the Bank of the State of Indiana did not suspend specie payments, and it may be reasonably argued that Hoosiers suffered less than other northern states.) Instead, the district's decline was simply a matter of demographics. As in Illinois and Ohio, In-

---

2. Kale B. Torrey, "Visions of a Western Lowell." *Indiana Magazine of History* 73, no. 4, (December 1977), *passim.* de la Hunt, *Perry County,* 131-132. *One Hundred and Fifty Years,* 39. Carter, "Hoosier History," 227. Elbert, "Southern Indiana Politics," 8. Carter, "Hoosier History," 219-220. *New Albany Ledger,* August 24, 1858. Barnhart, *From Frontier to Commonwealth, vol. 2,* 8. *History of Orange, Warwick, and Washington,* 401, 403, 692, 761. de la Hunt, *Perry County,* 133. *Ledger,* December 6, 1856, April 2, July 1, 1857, April 16, 1858, May 3, 1857. Baird, *Clark County,* 110. *Ledger,* June 1, 2, 1857.

3. *New Albany Ledger,* November 17, 1853, September 17, December 22, 1855. Carter, "Hoosier History," 355. *Ledger,* November 27, 1855. *New Albany Tribune,* April 24, 1858. *Ledger,* September 18, 1858. The *Tribune* and *Paoli Eagle* lampooned Lucy Stone, Comingore claiming his conception of "women's rights" was "a good looking husband, eight children, and a happy home." *New Albany Weekly Tribune,* May 11, 1855; *Eagle,* April 14, 1854. But the *Ledger* believed Stone had a point: "The system of female education takes it for granted that every woman is to become a wife…Should the woman never marry, should her husband be disabled from labor, should he die and she be left a widow with a family and children, she is, by the wages of society and by education, left resourceless." Norman also believed it a lie that women had "no desire to be recognized as independent elements in the body politic," declaring those who made such an argument were similar to those who claimed that slaves preferred slavery to freedom. *Ledger,* November 18, 1853. As Mrs. A. L. (Ruter) Dufour wrote English, she was that "unenviable character: a political woman." October 6, 1854, English Papers.

diana had witnessed a marked shift in population from its southern regions to its northern and central ones. Between 1850 and 1860, northern Indiana increased its population by 73 percent while the southern counties experienced only a 29 percent rise. The census of 1860 would essentially show that for the first time in the state's history the counties south of the national road would contain less than 40 percent of the state's citizens. The Second District, which contained about 9.5 percent of the state's population in 1850, 10 years later fell almost one full percentage point, to 8.6 percent. And New Albany, which was the state's most populous city in 1850, fell into second place, 6,000 souls behind Indianapolis.[4]

The demographic decline of southern Indiana, especially southeastern Indiana, was most obviously caused by the Great Lake and railroad migration from the East. Ironically, by opening up settlements in the northern and western portions of the state, the New Albany and Salem Railroad itself contributed to this shift. Among the citizens of New Albany who resettled in the town of Brookston in White County were included not only Phineas Kent, but Thomas Smith, the erstwhile stalking horse for William English during the 1856 congressional nominating convention. These were the new lands of Young America, and while the terrain of southern Indiana was by no means worn out or overpopulated, it was to the newer settlements that migrants went to make a name for themselves. Assessing New Albany's fortunes between 1852 and 1857, Norman perceptively noted that "our city has not grown in the same proportionate rapidity as it had from 1847 to 1852," and he hoped that if the *New Albany Ledger* "should be called upon to chronicle events for another five years that they will be more flattering to our growth than the past five." But this was not to be; New Albany and the Second District of the 1850s had seen the height of their influence.[5]

The course of two transportation issues in the late 1850s are examples of New Albany's failure to remain a prominent western city. First there was the case of the New Albany and Sandusky Railroad. In early 1854, about half a year before the completion of the New Albany and Salem project, the New Albany city council pledged itself to raise $300,000 to be used by the directors of the Sandusky Corporation. The council did this to establish New Albany as the western terminus on a railroad projected to run from Lake Erie, in Ohio, southwest to the Ohio River. Such a project was deemed essential if New Albany was to remain competitive with Louisville for trade along the western Ohio, for as it stood in 1854 many shippers west of New Albany crossed the river before they reached the city and used Louisville as a transshipment point eastward. This crossing occurred because

4. *New Albany Ledger,* October 17, 1857. J. M. Morrison to WHE, February 3, 1858, English Papers. Barnhart, *From Frontier to Commonwealth, vol. 2,* 3. *Ledger,* October 13, 1857. Thomas C. Cochran and William Miller, *The Age of Enterprise* (New York: Harper Torchbooks, 1961), 85. Barnhart, *From Frontier to Commonwealth,* vol. 2, 14.

5. Hubbert, *The Older Middle West,* 4-5. *New Albany Ledger,* June 9, May 13, 1857. Ironically, the *Ledger* surpassed the *Indiana State Sentinel* during the decade in daily circulation. This, too, was due to New Albany being a terminus on the New Albany and Salem Railroad. *Ledger,* March, 1857, December 3, 1858. *Paoli Eagle,* May 20, 1858.

shippers could more easily avoid the Ohio Falls on the south side of the river due to the existence of the Louisville and Portland Canal. If they stayed on the north bank they had to take a meandering overland course to Jeffersonville before re-packing their goods on an upriver boat. Thus the New Albany city council figured that a northern railroad near the Ohio, with New Albany as its terminus, would favor its city and keep northern shippers from using Louisville.[6]

The city council's pledge of $300,000 was to be raised not by a tax but by indi-vidual subscriptions. In order to further these subscriptions, the Sandusky Corpora-tion moved its main offices to New Albany, and in a short time prominent citizens of the city became the most important members of the Corporation's board. These included Phineas Kent, Thomas L. Smith, John S. Davis, and John B Winstandley. But despite the removal of its offices and the prestige of these men, it soon became apparent that the money could not be raised by private subscription. Consequently the city council pledged the city itself to buy 8,000 shares of Sandusky stock, the money to be raised primarily by the sale of city bonds on the New York market, and the bondholders to be paid early dividends by a city tax of 1 percent *ad valorem* on all taxables. With this procedure in place, work was begun on the road in 1855.[7]

Shortly after the initial sanding and clearing had begun, a new city council, elected in April 1855, convened for the first time. Unlike the earlier councilors, these men, a majority of whom were Know-Nothings, were hostile to the Sandusky project. They had been influenced by labor and safety problems on the New Albany and Salem, by the fear of influx of Irish laborers, and by the belief that a new rail-road was not worth the cost. In order to discredit the project they passed a 4 percent tax that they claimed was necessary to fund it, though three-quarters of the proceeds of that tax were actually earmarked for other municipal functions. Latching on to the discontent created by the tax, the *New Albany Tribune* led a movement to re-pudiate the whole subscription. In this it was opposed by the *New Albany Ledger*, which continually tried to make clear both the desirability of the road and the chi-canery of the anti-Sandusky politicians. But the anti-railroad faction grew stronger, and in December 1855 the railroad was forced to accept a compromise whereby the city reduced its obligation to 5,000 shares of stock. The *Ledger* argued that such compromise was wholly dishonorable. Although better than full repudiation, it was a "severe blow to New Albany." Fearing that full repudiation was the actual goal of the anti-railroad faction, Norman warned that the railroad was essential to the city's prosperity, and he added that New Albany was "not now in a position where she can afford to throw away any advantage at her command."[8]

---

6. Bogle, "Reaching for the Hinterland," 153, 154.

7. *Ibid.,* 155. *New Albany Ledger,* October 10, 1855.

8. Bogle, "Reaching for the Hinterland," 156. *New Albany Ledger,* July 19, 1854, March 31, April 1, April 2, April 29, October 10, November 9, 10, 11, 15, 26, December 5, 1855. *New Albany Weekly Tribune,* Decem-ber 5, 1855. *Ledger,* December 8, 1857.

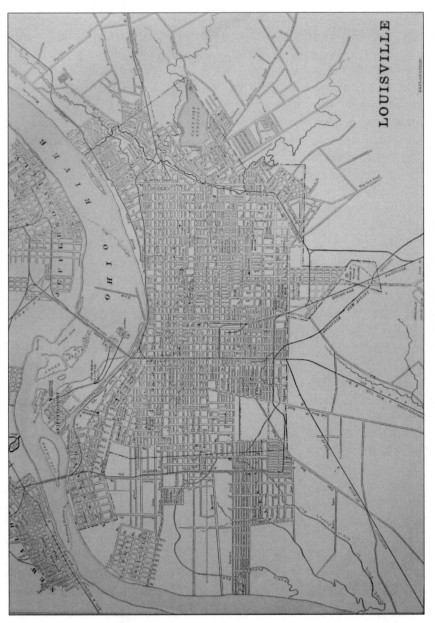

New Albany, the Ohio River, and Louisville

In spring 1856, the pro-Sandusky forces put up a "Citizens Ticket" composed of Democrats and old-line Whigs who opposed the Know-Nothing city council. But the anti-tax and pro-nativist platform of the opponents was far more appealing in a city that normally contained an anti-Democratic majority anyway, and the incumbents were returned to office on April 7. That autumn the anti-Sandusky partisans brought a case into court that challenged the original city council's authority "to subscribe the stock on the part of the city." Even though the case was not decided that term, the Sandusky Corporation was able to read the handwriting on the wall, and in May 1857 it suspended operations. In two years it had only graded 16 miles of land. "We hope they may be able to go ahead and complete the road without the aid of the city," Norman wrote in September. But no more work was ever accomplished.[9]

Given the absence of an east-west railroad the only other way New Albany could possibly compete with Louisville was either to construct its own canal around the Ohio falls, or, at the least, to prevent the improvement of the Louisville and Portland Canal. Actually, as early as the first decade of the century citizens of both Indiana and Kentucky formed canal corporations. In 1818, the Jeffersonville-Ohio Canal Company, backed by investors from Cincinnati, was incorporated by the Indiana state legislature and permitted to use convict labor from the Jeffersonville State Prison. The company did begin work the next year, but the limestone bedrock proved too tough to cut through. In the following decade, another Hoosier company was incorporated, but it never raised enough money to enable it to begin digging. Then to New Albany's dismay, between 1825 and 1831 Kentucky succeeded where Indiana had failed. Probably due to the influence of Henry Clay, a Kentucky corporation, initially supported by capital from Philadelphia, received a major boost in 1825 when the federal government purchased $237,000 worth of its stock. With the national government significantly interested in its success, the Kentucky canal was completed in six years. Although it was only 49 and a half feet wide, and the bridge above it only 52 feet above the water, it allowed over 30,000 steamboats through it in its first 10 years. Innumerable smaller craft also used the canal. By charging 50 cents per ton of cargo, the Louisville and Portland Canal Corporation was able to raise almost $10 million by 1845, quickly allowing the federal government to recoup its initial investment. In essence, the canal enabled Louisville to become the primary city along the western Ohio. But the limitations of the waterway's dimensions did not foreclose the importance of New Albany and Jeffersonville, for the larger and improved steamboats could not fit through the L&P canal and continued to use the Indiana cities as transshipment points. The apparent inadequacy of the Louisville

9. Bogle, "Reaching for the Hinterland," 156. *New Albany Ledger,* February 25, March 29, 31, 1856. *New Albany Weekly Tribune,* April 26, 1856. *Ledger,* November 14, 1856, May 1, 1858, September 8, 1857.

and Portland also spurred renewed Hoosier interest in building a better and larger canal on its own side.[10]

In 1848, the Indiana legislature passed an act to incorporate the Indiana Canal Company. Cincinnati investors subscribed $70,000 to the project, and important Hoosiers, including Richard Thompson, George H. Dunn, James Morrison, and Amos Lovering became officers of the company. But the competing interest in the New Albany and Salem Railroad, combined with the conservative fears of the transshippers, defeated the project before it could commence. Four years later, a joint resolution of the Indiana General Assembly petitioned Congress itself to appropriate money "to build a canal around the falls of the Ohio on the Indiana side." Although Congress ignored the resolution, the idea behind it had gained favor in Cincinnati and Pittsburgh, and in order to counter any chance of its success, Kentucky began to propose that the United States government take over the Louisville and Portland Canal and improve it. Should such a measure pass, it would forever foreclose federal approval of a competing canal on the Indiana side.[11]

In order to effect its purpose, the Kentucky legislature amended the Louisville and Portland charter to allow the company to use its proceeds to buy out all its private stockholders. The amendment then commanded the company to offer the full stock to the United States government, in return for which the federal government would make the canal "equal to the wants of commerce." In 1854, anticipating the general desire of the United States to buy the stock and conform to these conditions, the congressman from Louisville, William Preston, pushed through the House a measure granting the president the right to appoint the canal's commissioners once the purchase occurred. The Hoosiers voting on this measure split 3 to 2 in favor of it. John G. Davis and Norman Eddy, the two opposed to the legislation, neither of whose district was located adjacent to the Ohio, probably voted against it in accordance with Jacksonian maxims against federal power; but William English joined Whig Samuel Parker and soon-to-be Republican Daniel Mace in supporting it.[12] One might think that voting for a bill which would go some way to improving the Louisville and Portland canal would be inimical to Second District Indiana, but English was playing a clever game. Aware that the key to the Kentucky scheme was not the appointment of commissioners but the anticipated law appropriating the federal money for the purchase of the stock,

10. Victor M. Bogle, "New Albany as a Commercial and Shipping Point," *Indiana Magazine of History* 48, no. 4 (December, 1952), 375-378. Esarey, *Internal Improvements,* 66-68, 69. Victor M. Bogle "New Albany within the Shadow of Louisville," *Indiana Magazine of History* 51, no. 4 (December 1955), 304-305. *One Hundred and Fifty Years,* 49.

11. *One Hundred and Fifty Years,* 51. Baird, *Clark County,* 100. Bogle, "Within the Shadow of Louisville," 306-307. *Indiana State Sentinel,* January 23, 1852.

12. *CG, 33-1,* 1676-1677, 1711.

English would save his opposition when a future bill came up for the appropriation of such funds. With the particular measure before him at the moment he was free to comply, especially when it also contained a $190,000 appropriation for the improvement of the Ohio in general.

English's strategy became clear in the next few sessions of Congress. As Preston's successor Humphrey Marshall put it in 1858:

> year in and year out the representative from the city of Louisville has been before Congress with this offer made by the [Louisville and Portland] Company, asking that an appropriation may be made so that the United States might become the proprietor of the work, in conformity with the Kentucky statute, [but] these Indiana gentlemen have proposed to acquiesce in it with the condition that the Government of the United States should [at the same time] appropriate money to build another canal on the Indiana side of the river.

Because Marshall refused to be so blackmailed, English often used his considerable prestige to thwart Kentucky's desires. Meanwhile, John B. Norman used the *New Albany Ledger* to wage a propaganda war against the city of Louisville. Repeatedly drawing his readers' attention to the Louisville election riots of 1855, uniting the Democracy against Know-Nothings like Marshall, Norman wrote that "a community which permits its passions to be played upon to result in such lamentable outbreaks cannot reasonably expect law abiding citizens from other places and other states to contribute to their growth and prosperity." "Let it be given out," he continued, "that New Albany is *the* city of the Falls of the Ohio where the rights of property, of person, and of citizenship are respected and protected." Two years later, claiming the 1855 riots created a continuing atmosphere of "mob rule," Norman labeled Louisville "a disgraced city."[13]

Finally, on March 15, 1858, a week after English made his firm anti-Lecompton speech in the House, he attempted to introduce a resolution calling for an investigation into what had been done with the federal revenue collected from the Louisville and Portland Canal since 1855. He also proposed a second resolution to markedly reduce the canal's tolls. Humphrey Marshall naturally objected to the introduction of these measures, but English was able to gain a two-thirds majority to suspend the rules. Thereupon a debate ensued, and it soon became apparent that a factual dispute existed over whether or not at that time the United States possessed a controlling interest in the canal. According to English, on evidence

---

13. *CG, 35-1*, 1126. See, for example, English's objection to Marshall's bills of August 15, 1856 and February 26, 1857. *CG, 34-1*, 2160; *CG, 34-3*, 913. *New Albany Ledger,* August 11, 1855, May 18, 1857. The *Ledger* conveniently forgot that it claimed that New Albany had suffered some Know-Nothing hooliganism one year earlier, in 1854. (See ch. 3, pp.151–152)

from the secretary of the treasury himself, the United States actually owned 9,995 of the 10,000 shares of the Louisville and Portland stock, yet it had received no more money than that which flowed to it from dividends upon its original 2,700 shares. On the other hand, Humphrey Marshall maintained that the United States had never met the financial conditions of the Kentucky legislature, and that, although the full stock of the canal was held in trust for the United States, it did not actually own it. According to Marshall, the five directors of the canal had used the proceeds to improve and enlarge the waterway on their own, largely because the representatives from Indiana, Ohio, and Pennsylvania had prevented Congress from ever making an appropriation to effect federal ownership.[14]

In stating the facts as they truly were, Marshall refused to remain on the defensive. He accused English of attempting to discredit the Louisville canal in order to gain a new canal on the Indiana side. In this accusation he was correct, but the rules of the House prevented him from long pursuing this tangential line of argument. What especially worked against him in general, and therefore in English's favor, was the apparent ignorance of most representatives on the matter and the Democratic majority in the House. Ignorant of the true state of affairs, Democrats were quite willing to vote for an investigation, especially when it had been cleverly coupled with a request that the tolls be reduced. In vain did Marshall attempt to discourage them. Had English brought this matter up after he began to distance himself from anti-Lecomptonism he probably would not have succeeded. Although Marshall, too, voted against Lecompton, he did so on strong partisan grounds: it was English who needed to be rewarded, ironically because his anti-Lecomptonism was less certain. As do all good politicians, English had chosen his moment well.[15]

In harassing the Louisville and Portland Canal Company, English and his allies prevented the United States from enlarging that waterway sufficiently, so that it became only a secondary throat of commerce. By the time the canal was revamped to fully accommodate the larger steamboats built in the late 1850s, the Civil War had ended, and the railroads had taken over as the primary carriers. But any success that English could claim in halting the advance of Louisville over New Albany was temporary. Despite his efforts, Indiana never built a canal of its own, and by the 1860s New Albany and Jeffersonville began to adapt themselves to the inevitable ascendancy of Louisville on their part of the Ohio.[16] The demographic shift away from southern Indiana, and the rise of Republican dominance in the

---

14. *CG, 35-1*, 1125-1129.

15. *Ibid. New Albany Ledger,* April 1, September 8, 1858.

16. Bogle, "Within the Shadow of Louisville," 307. About one month after the Louisville and Portland debate, the House Commerce Committee denied a petition from the citizens of New Albany and Jeffersonville to establish a federal board of local inspectors in New Albany. Writing for the Committee, Elihu Washburne argued that a new board was unnecessary because one "already exists at Louisville and there is no allegation

statehouse, sealed the Second District's fate. The failure to realize the New Albany and Sandusky Railroad had been the first real symptom of decline; after that, as evidenced by English's congressional politics, New Albany could only stage a brief holding action. And it soon settled, not entirely discontentedly, for the destiny of a provincial little town on the banks of a mighty river.

2.

Although New Albany certainly was in economic and demographic decline, in truth, its urbanity was unrepresentative of the socio-economic environment of the district as a whole. In October 1857, English was invited to speak at the Washington and Orange agricultural fair, held that year in Livonia. The fair had become an annual event since 1853, when governor Wright was the featured speaker, and it had also become an important autumn social event throughout southeastern Indiana. The *Paoli Eagle* proudly announced that this 1857 fair was "to be the most interesting [one] ever held by the Society." The attending dignitaries included not only the district's competent congressman, but also senator Jesse Bright. They came both to celebrate the agricultural abundance of the region as well as to do a little bit of politicking. Railroads and canals were certainly very important to farmers who naturally considered them "handmaidens" to agriculture, but few farmers really cared whether Louisville, Jeffersonville, or New Albany carried their crops to market. And despite the political importance of the New Albany Democratic establishment to English's electoral successes, it was these farmers he had to please if he wished to remain a triumphant politician.[17]

English perhaps had been chosen as the honored speaker because he had recently raised three acres of "fine sorghum" on his lands in Scott County. No doubt hired laborers did the actual farming, but the family had installed a mill to process the grain and press out its juices. The usually unfriendly *Madison Courier* complimented English for his endeavor, noting that the congressman intended "to make a fair trial of making sugar." These were important credentials for any man in antebellum America. Indeed, one-third of English's speech at Livonia detailed his experiments in attempting to produce *sorgo sucre*, a Chinese sugary syrup. He spoke intimately not only of its growth, but of its potential uses and its history. Proudly he noted "how desirable it [was] that every farmer should be able to make, on a small plot of his own farm, the sugar and molasses required for the use of his family." He extolled agriculture as "the most ancient and useful of all

---

that the board at Louisville is not able to inspect promptly all the boats at New Albany and Jeffersonville." *House Report no. 147*, 35-1.

17. Rudolphus Schoonover to WHE, September, 1857, English Papers. *Paoli Eagle*, October 8, 1857. *History of Orange, Warwick, and Washington Counties*, 433. *Eagle*, October 1, 1857. Jesse Bright to WHE, October 9, 1857, English Papers.

industrial pursuits," standing in relation "to the other branches of industry what the root is to the tree, or the sun to the material universe." Although he appears to have made the Copernican mistake of putting the sun at the center of the whole of creation, his argument lost none of its luster before his rural audience.[18]

As befitted his venue, English spoke of the importance of a practical education, one that "correspond[ed] with the essentially utilitarian genius of our age." It was not "dead languages" that required study, but "those branches [of learning] as will increase and diffuse that kind of knowledge which adds to the usefulness of the man, and the prosperity of the country." It is not difficult to see in these phrases the influence of the Smithsonian in general and Joseph Henry in particular. But for English (and probably for Henry as well) such an education fostered more than simply national and individual economic success. It also contributed to the backbone of republican government itself because it helped to promote individual characteristics of economic and social independence. More than any other occupation, he reasoned like a good Jeffersonian, farming promoted a sturdy democracy:

> What other pursuit is there more likely to produce healthy, honest, and patriotic citizens? If independence is essential to happiness, then the farmer should be the most happy of men, for who is so independent as he; who can live so entirely on his own resources? Within his own domain he enjoys a freedom, and an absence of all restraint, unknown to even princes and kings, whereas the man engaged in commerce and trade is sometimes thrown into temptations from which the farmer is fortunately exempt.[19]

Though perhaps necessary in this case, it is of course ironic that a man reared in relative wealth, educated in rhetoric and the law, and occupied in speechmaking and politicking, should so glowingly extol manual labor. For despite his recent foray into the growth of *sorgho sucre*, English was essentially a man divorced from the labors of the soil. His interest in land appears to have been primarily in its

---

18. *Madison Courier,* in *New Albany Ledger,* October 3, 1857. *Address of Hon. William H. English Delivered at Livonia, Indiana before the Washington and Orange District Agricultural Society, October 15, 1857* (Washington: Congressional Globe Office, 1858), 3-5.

19. *Address at Livonia,* 6-7. Stoking some social and cultural fires a bit too vigorously, he noted that "a collegiate course perhaps served no other end than to make a boy a pedant and a fop; and at last he comes home with his native energies all exhausted, and his constitution made feeble and sickly by close application to books and by an entire abstinence from manual labor. He comes, too, very often, with a lurking idea, though he may not express it, that he is rather better than the boys working on the farms around him, and that it would be vulgar for one of his literary pretentions to engage in so *dirty* a business." It may be that his harsh criticisms of the effect of spending a few years at college grew from a subconscious reflection on the fact that he had not completed a full college degree.

value as real estate. Indeed, in the late spring immediately prior to the Livonia fair, English traveled to Kansas not to homestead, but to speculate. "All the world and the rest of mankind are here," John Whitfield wrote him in May. "Money now seems to be the question." English had invited Bright to go along with him, but the senator was tied down with business until June. "You must start sooner [than that]," Bright advised, "if you intend to attend the Kansas land sales." English took his father with him instead. As his later registration of 2,200 acres of Iowa land proved, sometimes he gained title to real estate without ever having to leave his chair. In Scott County alone he bought and sold land worth over $7,000 between 1852 and 1857.[20]

Real estate was only one field of commercial moneymaking in which English engaged. Another arena of speculation was state and federal bonds. Not only was he heavily invested in Texas bonds, but he also speculated in California securities as well. In 1857 he stated he had $16,000 worth of California bonds "on hand." Sometimes his speculating backfired on him. In January 1857 he wrote Mardulia that he would "probably lose several thousand dollars" because the California state legislature had "decided the bonds of that state unconstitutional." Yet he was wise enough (or sufficiently unethical) to understand that not everyone was aware of California's decision, and in anticipation of getting rid of those securities at maximum value he warned his wife to "say nothing about it." He was evidently so well apprised of the true state of speculative affairs that other politicians often sought his advice. For example, John W. Davis asked him what he should do with his California and Texas bonds. "I am greatly inclined to sell them," he admitted, but he would not act until English advised him. English was also touched for loans: "Please lend me either $200 in gold or your check for that sum," Jesse Bright rather commanded his young friend in 1854. His protégé naturally obliged.[21]

As a regent of the Smithsonian, English's expertise in financial matters was put to good use. Ever since he had helped secretary Joseph Henry out of his mess in 1855, the Hoosier wizard had been given more responsibilities within the Institution. He was already on the Building Committee, when at the end of his second congressional session he was named to a special finance committee appointed to discover a better way of investing the Institution's funds. English quickly became the moving force on that group, despite the fact that the other two members, senators Pearce and Mason, both had served as regents for many more years. In June 1856 he presented his plan before the full Board. It called for investing $143,000 of the Smithsonian's funds in the state bonds of Virginia (Mason), Pennsylva-

20. J.M. Whitfield to WHE, May 9, 1857; Jesse Bright to WHE, April 16, 1857; WHE to Mardulia, January 18, 1857, English Papers. For the Iowa purchases see Chapter 7. *Land Records for Scott County*, microfilm, Indiana State Library, Indianapolis.

21. WHE to Mardulia, January 18, 1857; John W. Davis to WHE, December 20, 1857; Jesse Bright to WHE, December 7, 1854, English Papers.

nia (Buchanan), Missouri (John Phelps, Democratic House floor leader), and, of course, Indiana. He not only suggested these particular securities, he also suggested the exact terms of interest the Institution should ask from each state.[22]

Realizing that the Smithsonian would need a broker to purchase these bonds, English had asked the renowned banker W.W. Corcoran to attend this particular meeting of the Board of Regents. Corcoran was Jesse Bright's close friend, and it was probably through the senator that English was first introduced to him. Corcoran had also been a fellow investor in Texas bonds, and the 1855 law that made good the federal government's promise to redeem Texas bondholders was passed largely due to his extensive lobbying. No doubt English had often consulted with Corcoran while that bill was under discussion. At the meeting of the Board of Regents that Corcoran attended, the banker promised to try to purchase the designated securities at the stipulated value, but three weeks later he reported that English's desired rates of interest were too high for the amount he wished to expend per share. Consequently, the regents amended their resolution, allowing Corcoran to purchase the bonds at "market value." Within a year, "with the assistance of the Hon. Mr. English, and under the direction of the Committee on Finance," Corcoran's company already made the Smithsonian $1,000 richer. (Corcoran's own commission is unclear).[23]

English remained on the Smithsonian's Board for his full tenure in Congress, and he continued to monitor the institution's finances during that time. His duties naturally led him to a greater study of investment politics than he had theretofore attempted, so that by the time he retired from Congress, he was thoroughly educated in the field. During one of his congressional campaigns, the *New Albany Tribune* had wondered how English had "become the possessor of [so] large an amount of money" when he had been collecting a politician's salary "for about fifteen years." The implication was, of course, that there was something shady about his accumulation of wealth.[24] But English was the son of a well-to-do farmer and speculator, and he only did what any other ambitious young man of the antebellum era did: he saw his opportunities and he took them. And as long as he publicly worshipped at the altar of husbandry and the agrarian ideal and

---

22. *Ninth Annual Report of the Board of Regents of the Smithsonian Institution* (Washington, D.C.: Government Printing Office, 1855), 317. *Annual Report of the Board of Regents of the Smithsonian Institution, showing the Operations, Expenditures, and Conditions of the Institution for the Year 1856 and the Proceedings of the Board up to January 28, 1857* (Washington, D.C.: Cornelius Wendell, 1857), 86-87.

23. Van der Weele, "Jesse Bright," 161, 295. Holman Hamilton, "Texas Bonds and Northern Profits," *Mississippi Valley Historical Review* 43, no. 4 (March, 1957), 585. *Annual Report for the Board of Regents of the Smithsonian for 1856,* 86-88.

24. *Annual Report of the Board of Regents of the Smithsonian Institution for 1857* (Washington, D.C.: William A. Harris, 1858), *passim. New Albany Tribune,* October 10, 1856.

worked diligently in his role as congressman, his rural constituents could hardly begrudge him the realization of the dreams of a Young American.

3.

It is probably unfair to imply that the accumulation of wealth was English's primary goal in life, for at least as much he desired the perennial success of the Democratic Party. Of course these two ends were hardly mutually exclusive, as English believed Democratic rule would create a healthier economy and more opportunities for wealth. And for the Democratic Party to be successful it needed to promote internal harmony, which dictated not only his course concerning Lecompton but his policy on a whole range of measures that sometimes put him at odds with public opinion back home.

On most economic issues English hewed to the orthodox Democratic position, which aligned well with the majority viewpoint of his own congressional district most of the time. This was certainly the case with the tariff, a principal issue that had generally divided Whigs from Democrats. In the main it continued to divide Democrats from Republicans. With the notable exception of much of Pennsylvania, parts of Ohio, and New York, the Democrats continued to favor a low revenue tariff to their opponent's call for protective rates. In early 1857 the Party once again sought downward revision. With the United States at an apex of prosperity and with a treasury surplus higher than it had ever been before, all the Republicans could do was offer a more conservative version of a lower tariff. In the end, two approaches evolved. The Democratic one significantly enlarged the free list and reduced the rate on all other items to 20 percent. The Republicans, led by Lewis Campbell of Ohio, simply sought to more moderately increase the list of untaxables. In a remarkable show of partisan solidarity, only three Democrats voted against their party's formula, thereby allowing one of the lowest schedules in the nation's history to pass in the House by almost 50 votes. English quite willingly voted both the party line and his district's wishes. Indeed, since Indiana as a whole was the most agrarian oriented state north of the Ohio, even three Hoosier Republicans voted for the Democratic formula.[25]

General satisfaction with a low tariff lasted only as long as prosperity did. When the Panic of 1857 occurred later that year, the Republicans came back to Congress determined to raise the duties for the first time since 1828. Unfortunately for them, even if their sometime allies among the southern Know-Noth-

---

25. *New Albany Ledger*, March 27, 1857. Nevins, *Emergence, vol. 1*, 22. *CG, 34-2*, 742-746, 790. Indiana's ratio of agricultural to industrial investment was nineteen to one, far greater than any other northern state. Keith A. Sutherland, "Congress and Crisis: A Study in the Legislative Process, 1860" (PhD diss. Cornell University, 1966), 174. In all fairness it should be noted that two of the three Indiana Republicans who voted for the Democratic tariff were former Democrats.

ings and Pennsylvania and New York Democrats voted with them, they were still short of a majority on the issue. Consequently, no new tariff was passed in 1858 or 1859. The Indiana Democratic Party officially remained silent on the question in its 1858 platform, but its congressmen continued to vote against protection. It must be remembered that the 1857 Panic hurt Indiana perhaps less than any other free state, and the Hoosier Democrats certainly were not to be swayed by Republican arguments that the low tariff helped bring on what proved at any rate to be a short-lived recession. If one issue strengthened the unification of the Democratic Party, at least in the south and the west, it was probably this one.[26]

If English well represented his essentially agrarian district by his votes on the tariff, he also appeared to reflect rural frugality in his approach to federal appropriations. This too was rather congruent with Democratic orthodoxy. Most consistently did English vote against private claims of relief, appropriations for customhouses, and other such pork-barrel legislation. He was even loath to allow the federal government to aid in the research of medicine, once voting to kill an appropriation of $30,000 to help the army discover the causes and etiology of cholera. Indeed, outside of federal appropriations to improve travel on the Ohio River, very few others received English's sanction. The one glaring exception was when he supported a resolution allowing a number of scientists to use five federal vessels in order to study a lunar eclipse.[27] Perhaps he associated the expedition with the charge of the Smithsonian, or maybe the tides affected the growing habits of *sorgho sucre*.

Sometimes English's thrifty approach to the federal purse put him at odds with the Administration on some important piece of legislation, attesting to his real concern for limiting government spending. The best example of this was his opposition to the Deficiency Bill of 1858. The bill was designed to pay federal contractors for supplying an additional five regiments for a military expedition to Utah to put down a threatened Mormon resistance to federal authority. In April, one day after English served Buchanan by attempting to get the House to agree to a conference with the Senate over Lecompton, he voted with 35 other Democrats (mostly southern, but also seven anti-Lecomptonites) to recommit this bill to the Committee on Ways and Means. He and they wanted that committee to divide the bill into smaller measures to be sent back to full House to be voted upon individually. They almost succeeded, but upon reconsideration the original bill eventually passed 111 to 97. Refusing, perhaps, to vote directly against so important an administration measure, especially in the midst of the Lecompton fight, English discreetly absented himself from this final vote. And, indeed, on the truly

---

26. Nevins, *Emergence, vol. 1*, 223-224. *CG, 35-1*, 2197. *CG, 35-2*, 1197, 1411-1412. *Indiana State Sentinel*, January 9, 1858.

27. *CG, 35-1*, 2406, 2523-2524, 2705, 2616-2617. *CG, 34-2*, 977. *CG, 36-1*, 2889.

significant pieces of financial legislation, Buchanan could almost always count upon his Hoosier friend to support him in the end. In essence, English opposed most appropriations schemes that came before Congress, but he did not allow his general frugality to interfere with what he considered legitimate Administration needs.[28]

But, economically, it was not the traditional issues of the tariff and government spending that would be decisive in the coming elections in Indiana. Two newer measures, both championed by Republicans, became far more prominent by the late 1850s. One of them eventually came to be called the Morrill Land Grant. Named after its original congressional promoter, Justin S. Morrill, Republican of Vermont, it proposed to grant each state an amount of federal land proportionate to its number of electors. The states would then be obliged to sell this land and use the proceeds as endowments for the construction and administration of schools devoted to agricultural study. As a political measure it offered great advantages, for it appealed directly to farmers in both parties. Yet, largely because of the bill's expansive use of federal power, the Administration and the southern and Jacksonian Democrats in Congress opposed it. Williamson R Cobb, the House chairman of the Committee on Public Lands, further argued that the recession had made such an ambitious plan impractical. Nevertheless, despite a Democratic majority, the measure passed the House, 105 to 100, on April 22, 1858.[29]

The bill survived because 17 Democrats voted for it. One argument against the bill had been its tendency to make money for speculators, as most states, including Indiana, had no public federal land left, thus promoting a scheme whereby the federal government would issue government securities to states to sell to private buyers. The states would use the proceeds from these transactions to buy private land upon which to establish the colleges, and the buyers could speculate in these securities backed by the national government. This boon to speculators was thus considered ideologically a problem for many western Democrats. Indeed, Democratic representatives from the northwest voted against the measure, 15 to 1; Foley of Indiana being the only one to favor it. Yet the real cause for opposition appears to have been constitutional, based upon the Jacksonian shibboleth of a federal government both limited and frugal. As the *New Albany Ledger* put it, Morrill's grant was "a gross perversion of a sacred trust." The money, Norman reasoned, would only be "squandered on palace-like buildings and lazy professors." (The latter part of that phrase reprising a certain anti-elitist and anti-intellectual tradition in the 19th Century Democratic Party.) It would be better, Norman reasoned, to follow tradition and allow youngsters to learn agricultural science on the family

---

28. *CG, 35-1,* 1550. Nichols, *Disruption,* 184. *CG, 35-1,* 1551. *CG, 35-2,* 701. *CG, 36-1,* 3254-3255.

29. Dennis W. Johnson, *The Laws that Shaped America: Fifteen Acts of Congress and their Lasting Impact* (New York and London: Routledge, 2009), 83, 86-87. *CG, 35-2,* 1412-1413. *CG, 35-1,* 1842.

farm: "We do not believe the farmers of the country ask or desire any such special favors. They have not petitioned for them." In the end, despite closely passing the Senate as well, the bill was vetoed by president Buchanan.[30]

Norman was confident that he knew the minds of men who resided outside New Albany, and perhaps he did. But what about English? When he spoke at Livonia only a few months before the vote on Morrill, he made the following remarks:

> There is no trouble in this country to find law schools, medical academies, and commercial colleges; yet where can the farmer find a college with a farm attached to it, where his son would not only be educated, but required to devote at least a small portion of his time to manual labor; thus fostering a love of industry, preserving the health of the body—so essential to happiness and mental advancement—and where he could acquire a knowledge of the elements of the soils, the physiology of plants, and all that class of useful information so essential to the proper development and advancement of agriculture?

Despite these sentiments, English voted against the Morrill bill every time it came before the House. It is not perhaps necessary to accuse him of insincerity in the above remarks, or, for that matter, hypocrisy, for he may have been promoting state rather than federal action. And there may well have been another aspect to English's votes on the measure in Congress. It has been rather established that increase in federal power in one area was often viewed by southerners as promoting a possibility that such precedents would tend to support increase of federal power over restrictions on slavery. There is, therefore, the distinct possibility that English, ruing his anti-Lecompton activity, was repairing his relationship with the South by opposing the Morrill land grant. English's votes may simply be chalked up to frugality, but these other motives should not be ruled out. (The Buchanan administration again opposed the bill as well.)[31] Indeed, the ironic effect of his dabbling with anti-Lecomptonism was to actually *increase* his doughface tendencies in a rather delusional effort to prevent disunion. This tendency would appear repeatedly in various forms until he eventually realized its inefficacy.

English's changing position on another measure, the Homestead Bill, which proposed granting 160 acres of land 'for free' should the occupant of the land work it for at least five years, may well be compared to his stance on the Morrill

---

30. *CG, 35-1,* 1742. J. B. Edmond, *The Magnificent Charter: The Origin and Role of the Morrill Land Grant in Colleges and Communities* (Hicksville, NY: Exposition Press, 1978), 15. Johnson, *Laws that Shaped America,* 88. *New Albany Ledger,* March 3, 1859. Johnson, *Laws that Shaped America,* 88-89.

31. *Address at Livonia,* 7. *CG, 35-1,* 37, 1742. *CG, 35-2,* 1067, 1414. *CG, 36-1,* 1025. Nichols, *Disruption,* 236. Johnson, *Laws that Shaped America,* 88.

land grant. In his first years as a congressman, like almost all northwestern Democrats, English enthusiastically favored the Homestead ideal. He directly voted for it twice, and in December of 1854 he even introduced a Homestead resolution of his own. His support was such that in his first re-election campaign the *New Albany Ledger* wrote approvingly that he had always been "an ardent friend" of the principle. But in the 35th Congress English reversed himself. First of all, in early 1859 he joined 14 southern Know-Nothings, 58 southern Democrats, and only four northerners in opposing H 72, Galusha Grow's straightforward measure. Then, a year later, he did it again, this time becoming the only northerner to vote to table HR 280, another Homestead measure sponsored by Grow. He did this despite the contrary instruction of the Indiana legislature and in opposition to all the other Indiana Democrats in the House. When, on March 12, English again reversed himself and voted for the bill, he prefaced his vote by declaring it was cast only because "the legislature of Indiana instructs her representatives in favor of the homestead law." This was obviously not a vote he cast willingly.[32] Why he began to oppose the Homestead principle only in his later years, and why he opposed it so conspicuously, are questions that must be addressed.

It would be reasonable to explain his position as caused by selfish financial reasons. After all, should the measure pass, speculators would have less land to play with. But Stephen Douglas, a prince of speculators, was one of the great proponents of the measure, and supporters also predicted that the homesteader would be an excellent prospect for speculators because he was certain to desire more than the 160 acres guaranteed him by the bill. It is not likely then that English opposed the measure for simply selfish pecuniary considerations. It is also unimaginative simply to declare that he followed his mentor on this one, for he defied him on the far more volatile issue of Lecompton and would certainly have been excused on opposing him here. Moreover, English had become far too influential in his own right to worry about losing the support of a senator who most could see had only a slim hold on his own position by 1859.[33]

In order to understand English's opposition to the Homestead bill, it is necessary first to return to his speech in front of the White House upon the passage of the Kansas conference measure. "There were those who knew so little of me," he said early in that effort, "as for a time to suppose that I had some affinity with the black republican party, but never were men more mistaken." It had not been easy for English to withstand the reproaches of the *Paoli Eagle* and the *Washington Union* for his apparent alliance with Republicanism, and he was determined to

---

32. *CG, 33-2*, 8. *New Albany Ledger,* August 10, 1854. *CG, 35-2,* 727. *CG, 36-1,* 1015, 1115. Leah R. Atkins, "Southern Congressmen and the Homestead Bill" (PhD diss., Auburn University, 1974), 281.

33. Johannsen, *Stephen Douglas,* 691, 723. Atkins, "Homestead Bill," 202.

crush out any continued resentment over his behavior. In the middle of his speech he recounted the following anecdote:

> When the black republicans set this last trap and invited me to come into it, I said to myself I beg to be excused. I had no objection to side up near enough to look into the entrance to it and see what the signs were; but that was as far as I would go. The signs did not suit me. I saw neither fur nor hair [in the trap] but any quantity of wool, and then there was an *odor* not at all agreeable to my olfactories. It reminded me of the home of an animal I need not mention to you. I caught a glimpse of a figure within very much in the semblance of Horace Greeley. It was long, lean, lank, cadaverous, white-livered, and hollow-hearted. I knew that was no place for me, and that I could never become a member of the republican household.

Aside from the racism implicit here, these were extremely uncomplimentary terms English used to describe the opposition. They not only signaled his intention never to be allied with the Republicans again, but they also connoted his anger at having been so abused by the Republican editors once he abandoned them and destroyed their partisan plans. When one considers that the Homestead bill was sponsored by Galusha Grow, the Republican leader, a man not only personally obnoxious to Alexander Stephens, but one who had engaged in more than one bout of fisticuffs with Democrats on the floor of the House, English's opposition perhaps becomes clearer. Not only was he never going to ally with that hateful party on a major piece of legislation again, he would certainly not contribute to the prominence of one of its most loathsome members.[34]

Related to the above was a debt he believed he owed to the southern Democracy, which, almost to a man, opposed the Homestead bill for its anticipated effect to promote free soil settlement of the west. The debt in a sense concerned the southern votes on the English Bill, for when it was first introduced, despite the constitutional arguments made by some southerners, it was clear that in effect the measure submitted Lecompton to a vote of the people of Kansas. Consequently, initial southern reaction to the bill was not especially favorable. Only the assiduous efforts of Stephens, Howell Cobb, and Toombs eventually worked to hold the southern Democrats in line almost as a unit. Although it may be argued that the southern Democracy really had no other choice, it should be kept in mind that most southern Know-Nothings voted against the bill in order to try to illustrate to the southern voters that they were better defenders of southern rights than their counterparts. Because he was a man who appreciated individual political sacrifice

---

34. *Washington Union*, May 2, 1858. Ilisevich, *Galusha Grow*, 77-78.

for the sake of party harmony, English was no doubt impressed (and relieved) by what he must have considered rather courageous support of his essentially free-soil popular sovereignty measure by southern Democrats. Considering that half of the anti-Lecompton Democrats, including Douglas himself, refused to support the conference bill despite its effectual submission of Lecompton, the southern-ers' stance is even more impressive. It was partly to acknowledge their deed that English voted against the Homestead bill.[35]

There is an important corollary to this reasoning. English continued to pro-mote the moderates within the southern Democracy, for without their ascendency the northern Democrats would most assuredly fall to the Republicans. The hope of both the party and the Union depended upon their success. If the defeat of the Homestead bill could deprive their enemies, the southern secessionists, from possessing another weapon by which to capture a greater portion of the southern electorate, it had to be defeated. (In truth, this was why Buchanan opposed the bill as well, along with the lost revenue it would cost the federal government.) It was primarily for this reason that English also voted against the application of the neutrality laws toward William Walker and against an exclusively northern Pa-cific railroad route. Young America had aged since English first entered Congress, largely because of the agitation over slavery on all sides. When English denied his own constituents the possibility of a free 160 acres in the near future, he believed it was a necessary vote to cast for the Union's preservation.[36]

4.

For the most part, when William H. English is remembered at all as a congress-man, it is for the conference bill that bears his name. Yet the greatest quantity of his work in the same 35th Congress that passed his English Bill was actually con-cerned not with the Kansas question but rather with his duties as chairman of the Post Office Committee. As such, he was required to oversee the formation of any new postal routes, offer reforms in the postal system, consider petitions of relief from carriers, and assist the Committee on Ways and Means in such matters as appropriations to the Post Office Department and selection of transatlantic trans-porters. On the committee with him were five other Democrats (four of them

---

35. Ibid., 64; James T. Dubois and Gertrude S. Matthews, *Galusha A. Grow: Father of the Homestead Law* (Boston and New York: Houghton Mifflin Co., 1917), 72-73. Atkins, "Homestead Bill," v, 256-257, 282-283. Cooper, *Liberty and Slavery*, 260, 261-262. Eli Shorter to WHE, [1859], English Papers. It should be noted that besides trying to appear as pro-slavery as the Democrats, southern Know-Nothings also opposed the Homestead bill because it allowed immigrants to take advantage of its provisions. Ilisevich, *Galusha Grow*, 67.

36. Philip S. Klein, *President James Buchanan: A Biography* (University Park, PA: The Pennsylvania State Univer-sity Press, 1962), 346. *CG, 35-2,* 316-318. *CG, 35-1,* 105, 353.

from the South and one from California) and three Republicans. His was the only Democratic voice from the northwest, an area burgeoning with new communities. As the *New Albany Ledger* understood, English's chairmanship at this time was especially significant, for despite the willingness of postmaster-general Aaron Brown to establish as many routes as possible, great areas of the United States were still underaccommodated. English's leadership here could make quite an impact.[37]

English's interest in postal routes dated back to his earliest days as a congressman-elect when he petitioned the department for a number of extra routes in his district (see Chapter 3). Generally successful in those petitions, he continued to address the issue throughout his congressional tenure. In 1855, for example, he persuaded the Postmaster-General to direct the Cincinnati postmaster to send mail bound for New Albany and Jeffersonville directly to those cities; theretofore, such mail was first sent to Louisville for distribution. During his first term in the House eight new post offices had been established in his district, leading one newspaper to truthfully assert that "Mr. English has done more for the people of his district, in the way of mails, than all the members of Congress had ever done before." He continued to serve his constituents in his second term, petitioning both Congress and the Department to establish three new interior post roads coursing through Washington, Orange, and Clark counties. All three were granted, as well as another post office in Scott County. When English was informed that a certain service to and from Orleans, in Orange County, had been suddenly discontinued, he succeeded in getting the postmaster-general to reinstate it; the Department claimed that the "contractor had abandoned it" without authorization.[38]

English's successful efforts to accommodate his own constituents made his selection as committee chairman quite natural and appropriate, and he approached his new duties as energetically as he approached all his official functions. One of the most time consuming aspects of his new job was the review of dozens of petitions received from carriers asking for reimbursement for some service rendered or injury incurred.[39] It must be remembered that in this period the work of the post office was farmed out to hundreds of private contractors, some of whose terms of service were either unclear, unexpectedly onerous, or undercompensated. As examples of instructions lacking clarity, one carrier delivered his mail six days a week in obedience to his contract, which called for "daily mail." Arguing that "daily"

---

37. Alexander, *History and Procedure*, 234. *CG, 35-1*, 31. *New Albany Ledger*, December 23, 1857.

38. *New Albany Ledger*, February 21, June 18, 1855. *Cannelton Mercury,* in *Ledger*, March 9, 1855. *CG, 34-1*, 1159. *Ledger*, September 15, July 15, 1856. *Paoli Eagle*, July 2, 1857.

39. In all, I have located 36 different petitions *formally* entertained by English and his committee in the 35th Congress. Many others were denied without a formal report. *House Reports, 35th Congress, 1st session*, nos. 59, 97, 99, 113, 114, 115, 118, 235, 251, 264, 265, 266, 267, 268, 269, 270, 271, 287, 437, 438, 456. *2nd session*, nos. 124, 129, 135, 195, 196, 251, 252. *CG, 35-1*, 366, 636, 2513, 2918.

meant seven days a week, the Post Office Department deducted approximately one-seventh of his pay every quarter, leading the carrier to petition English's committee for relief. Believing, contrary to the Department, that it was traditional for all routes to be advertised for either three days or six days per week and holding that Sunday delivery was "not customary," the committee unanimously sustained this contractor's petition for restitution. The recommendation passed both houses and became law in the summer of 1858.[40]

An example of unexpectedly onerous duty was a petition from one carrier who proved that he had to employ double the amount of horse-drawn coaches allowed for in his contract because of the unexpected greater bulk of his mail. The committee likewise sustained this appeal. A more significant petition concerned the Turner brothers, who carried mail across Lake Superior originating from Detroit. The compensation to which they had originally agreed, $45 per trip, they later claimed was unreasonably low, and they asked the committee to offer proper remuneration. As it turned out, the Turner brothers were carrying mail to and from Minnesota lands that had been bought by Bright, Douglas, and a number of other important Democratic speculators. Consequently, they were able to present supporting affidavits from both Douglas and George Manypenny, the longtime Democratic Indian Commissioner who used the opportunities his job offered him to buy up choice western territory. In sustaining the brothers' petition, the committee wrote "it will not be denied that the general interest and business of the country demand that these facilities should be offered to the progressive spirit and energies of our people, and that the wise policy of the government in opening such facilities is amply remunerated in the rapid development of our national wealth and prosperity;" $22,000 was offered in compensation. The bill was so favored by the Democratic powers that be that Speaker Orr pretended not to hear objections to it, and it flew through the House and Senate in five days.[41]

The committee's reasoning for upholding the Turner petition was generally applicable to all routes opening up the hinterland, and, in this sense, the work of the Post Office Department could be seen as an indispensable arm of Young America. As chairman of the Post Office Committee, English worked closely with postmaster-general Brown to formulate newer routes, and he was naturally in charge of shepherding the Department's recommendations through the House. The recommendations were contained in the general Post Route bill, considered by every session of Congress. In English's first session as chairman, the bill, like almost all other bills that year, was delayed because of the controversy over Lecompton, and it was not until May 12 that he announced to his congressional

---

40. *House Report no. 266, 35-1. CG, 35-1,* 2776

41. *House Report no. 251, 35-2. CG, 35-2,* 200. *House Report no. 287, 35-1. CG, 35-1,* 2481, 2489, 2490, 2664, 2667, 2677, 2683, 2712, 2776.

colleagues that the routes were just about completed. He advised each member to come to the Post Office Committee room to make certain that his district's routes were properly entered. Because of the great backlog of bills, both public and private, English was delayed day after day from bringing his own measure to a vote. Upset by what he considered the monopolization of the floor by J. Clancy Jones, chairman of the Ways and Means committee (and particular friend of the president), he angrily queried "whether the gentleman from Pennsylvania, because he happens to be the head of a particular committee, has the right to engross the entire attention of the House." English wondered "whether the Chairmen of other Committees have not some rights as well as the Chairman of the Committee on Ways and Means."[42] The contentiousness and length of the session was certainly taking its toll.

Three days after his public outburst, on May 28, English rose as soon as Congress convened to attempt to ram through the route bill. He stated that the measure was certain to be liberally amended by the Senate, necessitating its return to the House, so he wished to pass it quickly to get it over there. "It has been very carefully matured," he assured his colleagues, "and most of the members of the House have had an opportunity of examining it." Unfortunately, Charles Ready of Tennessee (not incidentally a Know-Nothing American), who had just read the bill for the first time, objected; he wished to offer amendments to it. Because the route measure was not part of the regular order of business, Ready's objection would prevent its coming to a vote, so English attempted to persuade him to withdraw it. "I'm sure that if the gentleman from Tennessee will reflect for a moment he will not object," the Post Office chairman patronized. "If he desires amendments to be made to the bill, it can be amended in the Senate." But Ready stood firm, and upon Orr's suggestion, English withdrew the bill for one day to allow additions to be made to it. He warned, however, that the next morning he would again seek to put it upon its passage.[43]

A number of members having added a few routes, the bill was indeed passed by the House the next day. About two weeks later, the Senate passed it, also adding a few amendments of its own. On the same day that the House received the measure back from the upper chamber, English moved that the members quickly concur with the Senate's amendments. John Letcher, fearful the senators had tacked something of substance onto the bill, wanted the clerk to read the Senate's amendments, but English persuaded him that although he himself had not read the senators' additions he had been advised by the chairman of the Senate Post Office committee that they contained only a few new routes. Satisfied, Letcher withdrew his demand, and the House concurred with the Senate's version

---

42. *CG, 35-1,* 2080, 2248, 2552, 2398.

43. *Ibid.,* 2471.

posthaste. The bill then went to the president on June 12, two days before the end of the session. On June 14, Buchanan signed it, and it became law.[44]

On that same day, the last one of the session, Benjamin Stanton of Ohio noticed that one of the Senate's amendments sounded very suspicious. It authorized the postmaster-general "to make such arrangement for the transmission of the great through mails between Portland [Maine] and new Orleans as will insure the most speedy and certain connection, including in its route for one of its daily mails as many of the seaboard commerce cities as may be consistent with the greatest dispatch." What bothered Stanton and other members of the House was that this was a very unusual provision for a post route bill, for it allowed the postmaster-general, without consultation with Congress, to select a carrier for a lucrative route that could easily be traveled by sea as well as land. All water routes were usually authorized under special ocean steamer bills, and such an amendment appeared to violate precedent and the rightful power of the legislature. English, obviously shaken over Stanton's discovery, apologized for having, however inadvertently, deceived the House. Yet he maintained that he was "astonished [to see] that there prevails an idea that this Senate amendment has reference to ocean service between eastern cities and New Orleans." Nothing of the sort was intended, he assured the members (though his assurances now were becoming suspect). The Senate version, he said, "refers to land service, and is therefore legitimately upon the post route road bill." Yet he admitted that "the language may be more indefinite than it should be," and, if the House wished to repeal that section, he would not stand in its way.[45]

The House did indeed wish to repeal it, but before it did one member stated that "a story [was] in circulation that this section was put upon the bill surreptitiously." The implication was that some senators, in concert with postmaster-general Aaron Brown, had already selected the carrier, and that all were to share in the profits. Implicitly tainted by such a charge was English himself, for he had assured the House that all the Senate's amendments were routine. Coming so soon after English's suspected subterfuge over Lecompton, these inferences took on a heightened credibility. "In justification of myself and of the Post Office Committee of the Senate," English responded, "I have received a note from the Chairman of that Committee stating that the Committee never dreamed of such an application or construction being given to this amendment as it seems to have been given to it by many members upon this floor." Considering that the chairman of the Senate committee was David Yulee of Florida, a stout southern defender of slavery, this explanation may not have deeply resonated with all congressmen. Stanton replied that be that as it may a majority of senators themselves were unaware of

44. *Ibid.*, 2510-2511, 3027, 3035

45. *Ibid.*, 3046-3048.

the amendment. Consequently, in this reproachful mood, the House repealed the tainted section by an overwhelming vote.[46]

Right before the repeal passed, Lawrence Keitt wondered whether it would do any good, for only a few hours remained for the Senate to agree and for the president to sign it. In fact, the repeal bill never even got to the president, for the Senate refused to act upon it at all. Consequently, Congress adjourned with the disputed route safely ensconced as law.[47] To all concerned English had either been a villain, a fool, or just plain incompetent. In other words, he either conspired with Yulee, was used by Yulee, or simply abnegated his responsibilities to the House. This was not how chairmen were supposed to act. The post route bill was usually the most ordinary of measures, yet English had mismanaged it at best. It was one of the most embarrassing moments of his congressional career.

The second session of the 35th Congress would also prove itself a challenge for the House post office chairman. Although English's problems in this session revolved around greater issues than the post route bill, even this relatively simple measure did not pass without difficulty. He reported it to the House on February 14, 1859, four days after he gave notice, that it would be on his desk for review by all members. One of its provisions, a section that allowed the postmaster-general to contract for the mails independent of Congress on all routes established between sessions, was defeated and omitted because it granted the cabinet officer too wide powers of discretion. Some members, remembering the fiasco of the first session's post route bill, complained that English was again rushing the measure through; others disliked the overland transcontinental route favored in the bill. Yet the full bill eventually did pass on the same day and was sent to the Senate. This time, when English received the bill back from the upper chamber, he reviewed it carefully. He noticed that the amendments attached to it not only added some new routes, but also touched upon subjects usually reserved for the Post Office Appropriations Bill, e.g., postage rates, the franking privilege, and compensation to postmasters. Consequently, he took the liberty of drawing up a new post route bill that incorporated the Senate's new post route amendments but omitted the appropriation topics. The House approved his initiative and passed the revamped route bill 110 to 66.[48] The bill was then sent back to the Senate where it was temporarily held up while the senators considered how to incorporate its rejected measures in the more sensitive Post Office Appropriations bill.

The whole question of Post Office appropriations was fraught with difficulty. In the first session English was able to get the House to agree to create a fourth

46. *Ibid.,* 3048. For David Yulee, see Robert N. Rosen, *The Jewish Confederates* (Columbia, S.C.: University of South Carolina Press, 2000), 62. Yulee was a Jew who practiced Christianity but did not formally convert. Rosen, 60-61.

47. *Ibid.,* 3048, 3040.

48. *CG, 35-2,* 1020, 941. *New Albany Ledger,* February 14, 1859. *CG, 35-2,* 1020-1023, 1667-1668.

office of assistant postmaster-general. He had noted that he was "as little inclined to increase the number of offices of the General Government as any member of this floor," but he cogently argued that the increased business of the Department had made this necessary. Few disputed him, and the measure passed easily. But in the main the Post Office Department was viewed as profligate, bloated, and mismanaged. It had carried a deficit for each of the years between 1852 and 1857, caused both by the scores of new routes introduced and the reduction of the postage to three cents in 1851. In that first session of the 35th Congress, John Letcher made a meek attempt to return the rate of postage on most letters to five cents. Arguing that the projected $3.5 million deficit was outrageous, Letcher reminded the congressmen that the Department was originally designed to be "self-sustaining." Although the Post Office Appropriations Bill was handled by the Ways and Means Committee, not the Post Office Committee, English was the one to object to Letcher's proposed amendment. He evidently feared that the proposal would jeopardize the chances of the whole Appropriations bill, and he was able to get a ruling from the Chair that it was out of order. But it was left to Horace Maynard, a Know-Nothing from Tennessee, to make the substantive argument against Letcher's proposal. It was foolish, he noted, to expect the department to financially sustain itself in a nation growing so quickly, and it was undemocratic to tax communication so heavily. As an inducement to settlement and industrial enterprise, cheap postal rates were indispensable. This was Young America's argument.[49]

Although Letcher and other Southerners had failed to restrict the Department's general appropriations in that first session, they did defeat English's attempt to gain a principal messenger for each of the Department's assistant postmasters-general at $840 *per annum*. They were able to do so, despite the fact that the assistants of all the other departments had such messengers and despite English's plea that all he asked for was common equity. But the real revolt against the Department took place in the second session. It was then that disgruntled northern Democrats, angered by the Administration's opposition to the Homestead Bill, and dissatisfied southern Democrats, unhappy with an administration supported moderate increase of the tariff, combined to break party ranks. The northern Democrats, many of whom were lame duck congressmen who blamed their 1858 defeat on Buchanan's Lecompton policy, were not reluctant to assist Republicans in gaining revenge on the Administration. As a bloc they held up all the government's appropriation measures in an effort to bargain for one or another of their projects. The Post Office Department was the most inviting target.[50]

49. *CG-1*, 2964-2965. LeRoy R. Hafen, *The Overland Mail, 1848-1869* (Cleveland: The Arthur H. Clark Co., 1926), 31. *CG, 35-1*, 2418-2420.

50. *CG, 35-1*, 2429-2430, 2471, 2965. Elbert B. Smith, *The Presidency of James Buchanan* (Lawrence, Manhattan, and Wichita: The University Press of Kansas, 1975), 126. Klein, *James Buchanan*, 345. Nichols, *Disruption of Democracy*, 227, 236-237, 241.

Consequently, in January 1859, when English reported a bill out from his committee that asked the House to grant the Post Office Department four temporary clerks at $1,200 each per year, it was coolly received. Actually, English's request was merely an extension of the previous year's grant which expired on December 21, 1858, but the rebellious House was in no mood to give the Administration anything extra. John Haskin of New York, one of the staunchest of the anti-Lecompton Democrats, moved to table the measure. "I can see no propriety in increasing the expenses of that Department," he intoned. "It has already cost the Government twice as much as it did under the last Administration." Francis Spinner, the Republican who broke the purported Iowa land scandals involving Bright, English, and Foley in 1858, asked English "how many hours a day the [present] clerks are employed in the Post Office Department?" When another member answered "from 9:00 to 3:00," Spinner responded "that is only six hours, while I work not less than fifteen hours a day." He concluded that "if the[se] clerks cannot accomplish the labor desired in the few hours they are now employed let them work more hours." The House concurred, 103 to 80, 14 northern Democrats and 11 southern Democratic watchdogs of the Treasury joining 78 Republicans and Know-Nothings to table the proposal. The Administration could not cry effects of the recession one moment and necessity the next.[51]

Realizing that because of its deficits the Post Office Department was an easy mark for Republicans and disgruntled Democrats, English tested these congressmen's sincerity by proposing to save the Department money by restricting the franking privilege—something congressmen used freely for political purposes. Specifically, English's bill proposed to allow each member $100 worth of stamps paid for out of the contingency fund of each house. All senators and representatives would be required to use these stamps when sending matter through the mail. If a member should extinguish this allotment he would have to pay his own postage on any further mailings. Such a measure would not only save the Department money, it might actually decrease the bulk of mail coming out from Washington. English reported this bill out of his committee late in January, but it was immediately referred, over English's objection, to the Committee of the Whole. There it languished. Republicans were skeptical over a measure they viewed as saving relatively little money. They were convinced that the real purpose of the bill was to hinder their efforts at effective campaigning in the upcoming presidential contest. Consequently, when English called for a reconsideration of the vote that sent his measure to the Whole, Republicans objected. Claiming that since one of its provisions called for a transfer of funds, they argued that, like all appropriation

---

51. *CG, 35-2,* 588-589.

transfers, this one had to first be discussed by the House in full committee. To English's disappointment, Orr had to agree.[52]

Aware that there was little chance the House would ever reach his bill, English tried to attach an even more complete abolition of the franking privilege to the general Post Office Appropriation Bill. His proposed amendment actually called for the entire abolition of the privilege after July 4, excepting only letters exclusively concerning post office business. But the chair, occupied by George Washington Hopkins of Virginia (a former Post Office Chair and the present Foreign Relations one), was forced to declare the amendment out of order in obedience to an earlier vote concerning the type of amendments allowed. This was the last attempt that English personally made to reduce or abolish the franking privilege; any future attempt would have to come from the Senate.[53]

Meanwhile, all of this bickering paled in comparison to the debate over the full Appropriations Bill itself. A coalition of Republicans and dissatisfied Democrats had actually defeated the measure its first time around the House, but upon reconsideration it passed by four votes. When it arrived in the Senate, Yulee tacked on two amendments favored by the southern Democrats. One was a third revival of an attempt to abolish the franking privilege; this Senate proposal being along the lines of English's more extreme earlier failed amendment. The other, reprising Letcher, called for an increase in the postage from three to five cents. Aaron Brown had actually asked for the latter amendment as finally necessary to do something about the deficit, although he also argued that the only way the Department could become completely self-sustaining would be to cut back services to a point "commensurate with neither the business nor the social wants of the country." When the amended bill arrived back in the House on the evening of March 2, the Republicans objected to removing it from the Speaker's table. They ostensibly reasoned that because the pricing amendment was a revenue measure, it could only be introduced in the House. They proposed instead a resolution returning the bill to the Senate along with this reasoning. John Phelps, chairman of Ways and Means in place of the resigned J. Clancy Jones, at first refused to allow the resolution to come to a vote, but the Republicans threatened, along with their Democratic allies, to kill all appropriations if he maintained his course. Forced to retreat, Phelps saw the anti-administration coalition pass the resolution, 117 to 76, English voting in the negative.[54]

Refusing to acquiesce in the House's judgement, the senators attached the franking amendment to the pork-barrel Civil Appropriations Bill, reasoning that

52. *New Albany Ledger,* January 17, 1859. *CG, 35-2,* 588, 1093. *Ledger,* February 18, 1859. Nichols, *Disruption,* 240.

53. *CG, 35-2,* 1235, 1287. *Biographical Directory of the U.S. Congress,* 1276.

54. Nichols, *Disruption,* 240. *New Albany Ledger,* January 15, 1859. *CG, 35-2,* 1667. Nichols, *Disruption,* 241.

congressmen would be afraid to vote against a bill that appropriated money directly to their districts. Believing this had a much better chance to pass, English called quickly for the yeas and nays when it reached the House. But rather surprisingly it, too, failed 89 to 84. Meanwhile, the Post Office Appropriations Bill languished for complete lack of agreement. Finally, with Congress remaining in session throughout the night and morning of March 3 and 4, a conference was agreed upon that stripped the bill of the Senate amendments and ambiguously asserted that neither House had waived "any constitutional right which they may respectively consider belong to them." At 11:15 am, only 45 minutes before the session was scheduled to end, the House agreed to this version. But the Senate, led by its southern and doughfaced members, refused to accept a report it considered a surrender to the northern dominated House. In the middle of their denunciations, the bell rang, and the raucous Congress ended without any post office appropriation at all.[55]

Congress's failure to pass a post office appropriations bill forced the department to issue promissory notes to its carriers to be payable on January 1, 1860. This policy coincided with the death of postmaster-general Brown just days after Congress adjourned. As his replacement, Buchanan nominated Joseph Holt, a Kentucky politician who believed that the Post Office Department should be administered as a business concern. True to his philosophy, Holt cut back drastically on postal routes, and he abolished a great number of post offices while Congress was out of session. Using the excuse that no appropriation had been made for them, he refused to put into operation the nearly new 700 routes created in the post-route act. Nine post offices were discontinued in Indiana, one of them in Orange County. Moreover, mail delivery between New Albany and the interior was reduced by half, from six to three times per week; the *New Albany Ledger* complained that poor mail service in general was regularly causing late receipt of the newspapers to which it subscribed.[56]

Historian Roy Nichols called the second session of the 35th Congress "a runaway session," and Allan Nevins labeled it a "deadlock."[57] It was clear that the bitterness occasioned over Kansas had spilled over onto simple administrative functions of the government. It was English's misfortune, perhaps, to be chairman of the Post Office Committee when the Post Office Department became one of

55. Nichols, *Disruption,* 242. *CG, 35-2,* 679, 1682, 1684. Nichols, *Disruption,* 244-245. Hafen, *Overland Mail,* 132-134. Sutherland, "Congress and Crisis," 130.

56. Sutherland, "Congress and Crisis," 130. Nichols, *Disruption of Democracy,* 246, Hafen, *Overland Mail,* 134, 138. Smith, *Schuyler Colfax,* 126. *New Albany Ledger,* May 24, June 20, 21, 1859. At first, Buchanan considered calling a special session of congress to deal with the matter, but he probably declined because it would contain all the successful Republicans of the Fall 1858 election, a Congress he had no desire to convene prematurely. *Ledger,* March 5, 14, 21, 1859.

57. Nichols, *Disruption,* 226. Nevins, *Emergence of Lincoln vol. 1,* 427.

the indirect battlegrounds between the sections and even within the Democratic Party. That English himself was considered by not a few congressmen to have played a double game during the Lecompton crisis, only made his situation worse. Moreover, his occasional blunders as chairman may be attributed to the fact that the rules of the game had changed. The representatives seemed less concerned with governing than with gaining political advantage, and although there had always been a decent amount of sparring between parties and sections before, it had now reached a degree of incapacitating the normal functions of government. This was not an easy atmosphere within which conservative congressmen could best work, and it may be one of the reasons why Alexander Stephens retired when he did.[58] By the end of the session, English may have regretted his reelection five months earlier. As it was, he could only go home to Mardulia hoping that the more moderate elements in both parties regained the advantage. In that case, the 36th Congress might be more traditionally manageable, and America could get on with the proper business of its ever-diminishing youth.

---

58. One biographer of Stephens notes that when he retired at the end of the 35th Congress, the Georgia legislator had "given up on his own power to affect the future," was fed up with Buchanan's war on Douglas, and predicted a general "smash up" in the coming congresses. Schott, *Alexander Stephens,* 263-264.

CHAPTER NINE

The Irrepressible Conflict

The summer and fall of 1859 was not a personally pleasant time for William Hayden English. He had been home fewer than three months when he received word that one of his closest childhood friends, Calvin Ruter, had died in New Albany. At the time of his death, Ruter was the most eminent Protestant minister in the district. Raised in Scott County, on a farm adjacent to Elisha's, Ruter had entered Divinity School about the same time that young William had set off for Madison. Since the mid-1840s, he had lived in New Albany, gaining prestige not only as a Presbyterian divine, but also as a local supporter of the Democratic Party. In 1853 English had paid Ruter a high compliment by giving him his first vote for congressional chaplain, and Ruter's death greatly grieved him. Six hundred citizens attended the minister's funeral, half of them Masons who took part in a procession in his honor. Among the mourners, of course, were William, Mardulia, Elisha, and Mahala English, perhaps accompanied by Will, now 8 ½ years old, and Rosalind, now almost 4.[1]

Later that year, in October, English learned that Dr. William M. Daily had been expelled from the Indiana Methodist Episcopal Church. A longtime friend of English's, Daily had been the president of Indiana University from 1853-1858. Competent and well respected by his students, Dr. Daily's tenure as president was a great success, but his Democratic politics were an embarrassment to the Methodist clergy who ran the university. Citing unsubstantiated charges of public intoxication, the university trustees were finally able to suspend Daily; whereupon, in January 1859, he resigned his position in disgrace. Much depressed by this turn of events, he began (or continued) to drink liberally. He was then in due course fully expelled from the Church, but, as the *New Albany Ledger* saw it, his primary fault was that he had "resisted the attempts, so permanently made, of converting the Methodist Church into a political machine for disseminating doctrines which

---

1. *New Albany Ledger*, June 27, 1859. *Scott County Assessor's Book, 1839*, Indiana State Library, Indianapolis. *CG, 33-1*, 12. *Ledger*, June 27, 1859.

already have brought about one division of the Church (and will result in another, both in Church and State)." English no doubt agreed, but he could never locate for Daily a suitable federal appointment, and eventually he saw his friend succumb and drift into the Republican Party.[2]

But the most significant event of 1859, for English as well as for almost everyone else, was political not personal. It occurred on October 16 when John Brown and some 20 other abolitionists, with the intention of instigating a slave rebellion, entered Virginia and raided the federal arsenal at Harper's Ferry. The whole affair went terribly wrong and ended in a shootout with federal troops. Shortly after the capture of Brown and his associates, 10 of them dead, the full story was transmitted by telegraph to the nation, and predictable reactions poured in. In southern Indiana, Brown naturally received little sympathy from Democrats, but he also was rather severely criticized by the political opposition. "The people of the North will rejoice that this conspiracy has been nipped in the bud," the *New Albany Tribune* declared on October 21. Gregg hoped, he continued, that "Brown and his fellow fanatics who survived the late affair may receive the punishment that their high crimes deserve." Indeed, it appears that most Oppositionists in southern Indiana were eager to condemn John Brown in order to disassociate themselves from the extremists in the Republican Party. As Horace Greeley wrote Schuyler Colfax a few days later, "Don't be so downhearted about the Old Brown business…It will probably help us nominate a moderate man for President on our side."[3]

But the Democrats were not willing to allow the Republicans and their allies to so easily avoid association with Brown's actions. As John B. Norman understood it, Brown's raid was the "natural fruit of agitation." Because of its continued and excessive criticism of slavery, the *New Albany Ledger* reasoned, "the Republican party [was] entirely responsible for what occurred at Harper's Ferry." The *Paoli Eagle* heartily agreed, and Henry Comingore printed quoted excerpts from such men as Joshua Giddings, Charles Sumner, Frederick Douglas, Ralph Waldo Emerson, and noted abolitionist Wendell Phillips, to prove that all Brown did was follow the instructions of 'Black' Republican leaders. The Democrats were

---

2. Theophilus A. Wylie, *Indiana University: Its History from 1820, when Founded, to 1890* (Indianapolis: William B. Buford, 1890), 96-97. *New Albany Ledger*, December 25, 28, 1854. Burton D. Myers, *Trustees and Officers of Indiana University, 1820-1950* (Bloomington: Indiana University Press, 1951), 327-328. *Ledger*, January 25, March 30, October 8, October 10, 1859. Wm. Daily to WHE, October 28, 1858, February 9, April 22, December 16, 1859, English Papers. Wylie, *Indiana University*, 97.

3. Nevins, *Emergence of Lincoln, vol. 2*, 79-84. *New Albany Tribune*, October 21, 1858. Elbert, "Southern Indiana Politics," 83. Horace Greeley to Schuyler Colfax, October 29, 1859, in Smith, *Schuyler Colfax*, 121. The Stephen Oates biography of John Brown, *To Purge this Land with Blood*, despite what some might consider a too sympathetic portrait of the man, is generally considered the best historical study of the Harper's Ferry incident. Oates also published a set of essays on aspects of the coming of the Civil War, *Our Fiery Trial: Abraham Lincoln, John Brown, and the Civil War* (Amherst: University of Massachusetts Press, 1979), one of which is a critical discussion of the historiography of Brown and his raid (Chapter three: "John Brown and his Judges.")

well aware that they now had an issue with which to harangue the Republicans, and they were not going to allow them to avoid responsibility. For years, the Democratic Party, North and South, had argued that the agitation of the slavery question would lead to violence and disunion, and the events at Harper's Ferry appeared to sustain that argument. Moreover, Democrats claimed that the anti-Brown Republican sentiment of the moment could not be trusted, for, as the *Ledger* put it, "those Republican editors who today speak of Brown as a fool and a fanatic would have spoken of him as a patriot and a hero had he succeeded."[4]

For their part, the Republicans and many other oppositionists in Indiana naturally denied that the Party was responsible. "As well we might assert that the majority of the people of the South are traitors and disunionists," the *New Albany Tribune* argued, "because a considerable number of their principal speakers and papers openly advocate disunion." Quick analysis illustrates that such an argument used an improper analogy, for no citizen of the South had as yet attempted an insurrection. But even if a majority of Republicans honestly did condemn the raid, that condemnation had eased by December 2 when Brown was executed for treason. All accounts have recorded that on that day, northern church bells clanged in honor of Brown as northern citizens mourned the death of a martyr. Indeed, even in New Albany, as Norman noted, there were "men, professing to be Christians, who do not hesitate to avow themselves 'Brown sympathizers', and to mourn the death of a criminal." While some of that northern reaction was in response to Brown's dignity and speech at his trial, southerners were naturally incensed at the attempt being made to deify so bloody an abolitionist. Because of this northern reaction many southerners became a good deal more convinced that an election of a Republican president in 1860 would be just cause to dissolve the Union.[5]

John Brown's raid, then, was politically helpful to the southern fire-eaters. Yet for conservative and moderate Democrats, North and South, it might also prove helpful in uniting the Democratic Party. They had to reason that, as a result of Brown's raid, northern Democrats would consider it their duty to reassure Southerners of their willingness to consider the South's position as a besieged minority. Pretty doughface stuff, but there it was. Perhaps, for example, northern Democrats could try to find a compromise formula on popular sovereignty that would respect some degree of the South's concern for their slave property. It rather

---

4. *New Albany Ledger,* October 20, 25, 1859. *Paoli Eagle,* October 27, November 3, 1859. *Ledger,* October 20, 1859.

5. *New Albany Tribune,* October 27, 1859. Potter, *Impending Crisis,* 378-380. Nevins, *Emergence of Lincoln, vol. 2,* 98-100. *New Albany Ledger,* December 3, 1859. In a letter to R. M. T. Hunter, one James A. Seddon (ex-Virginia Congressman and later Confederate Secretary of War) blamed Governor Henry A. Wise of Virginia, for Wise's complimentary assessment of Brown's character elevated the abolitionist's "vulgar crime" into a simple political offense. Ambler, *Correspondence of Hunter,* 281. Potter, *Impending Crisis,* 378-384

happened in 1850. Anyway, this attitude would enable Democrats to unite on the 1860 party platform, defeat the Republicans, and thereby prevent secession or civil war—at least for four years.

If the raid actually could work to unite the Party, the Democrats would soon discover it, for the 36th Congress's speakership caucuses began the day after Brown was executed. Most prominently mentioned as Democratic nominees were two southerners: John Phelps of Missouri, a moderate who was last session's Democratic floor leader, and Thomas Bocock, a states'-rights but not extreme Virginian. Interestingly, there was also some talk of William English fulfilling that role. The *Evansville Enquirer* claimed itself "credibly informed" that English was among the favorites for the post, and this time the *New Albany Ledger* did not act surprised. "He is certainly eminently qualified by his long legislative experience to discharge [the speaker's] important duties in a manner creditable to himself and advantageous to the country," Norman wrote. But English himself, ever the harmonizer and well aware that his compromise on Lecompton would certainly cause dissension at the caucus, declined promotion as a candidate. Scotching anything that could lead to a flare-up in intraparty relations, he wrote a public letter, printed in the *New Albany Ledger* on July 9, announcing that he was "not a candidate for that position whatever." He "fully appreciate[d] the kind intentions of those who [had] made favorable mention of my name," but he wished to firmly advise all his supporters to cease their efforts. As the boomlet for him was rather small, and localized to south Indiana, the *Indiana State Sentinel* believed it rather "presumptuous" for English to have taken it so seriously that he felt he needed to publish a disclaimer. Yet considering the tender nature of national party solidarity, the 'presumption' was justified. In fact, the *Sentinel* followed up its sarcasm with a compliment, as the editor saw English's declination as "evidence that we have one public man in these degenerate days who is animated with the same spirit which influenced public men in the early and purer days of the Republic."[6]

Actually, even if English had wanted to become speaker, neither he nor any other Democrat stood a great chance of being selected. Because of the disastrous election of 1858, largely due to the Administration's support of Lecompton, the Democrats were in a decided minority in the 36th Congress's House of Representatives. The party and factional breakdown of the House looked like this:

---

6. Nichols, *Disruption,* 273. *New Albany Ledger,* December 2, 1859. Thomas Bocock to M.R.H. Garnett, November 8, 1859, in Ambler, *Correspondence of Hunter,* 274. *Cincinnati Enquirer,* January 22, 1859. Alexander, *History and Procedure,* 110. Nichols, *The Democratic Machine,* 67. *Evansville Enquirer,* in English Scrapbook, 135. *Ledger,* June 28, July 12, 1859. *Indiana State Sentinel,* July 18, 1859. Walter Q. Gresham's daughter maintained that English was "thoroughly discredited" by the apparent reversal on Lecompton that the English Bill represented, and the *New Albany Tribune* claimed that he was "the most detested man in the House." Although both of these comments were made by Oppositionists, and were no doubt exaggerated, it is not difficult to perceive that English had made too many enemies to be a viable and harmonious candidate. Gresham, *Life of Walter Q. Gresham,* 76-77; *Tribune,* July 2, 1858.

Republicans: 109	Democrats: 101	Americans: 27
	regular: 88	slave state: 23
	anti-Lecompton:13	free state: 4

[7]

With 119 votes needed for a majority in a full House, it was clear that some coalition was necessary for any party to gain the speakership. At the first gathering of the Democratic caucus on December 3, the Party discovered that only five anti-Lecomptonites would caucus with them. These five were from the Illinois delegation, an obvious attempt by senator Douglas to illustrate his harmonious intentions in order to better position himself for the presidential nomination to come. Because the fire-eater James L. Pugh of Alabama also refused to caucus (and Stallworth of Alabama would remain home for two months on a bender) the Democratic caucus contained at most 91 members, 28 shy of a majority. Clearly, if the Party were to succeed it would have to attract some of the non-caucus attending anti-Lecomptonites, as well as some of the Americans. Yet fully aware that the Republicans, too, would be hard-pressed to gain a majority, the Democratic caucus balloted with some hope of success. In the end, they chose Bocock as their nominee, his victory over Phelps somewhat indicative of the present strength of the more ardent elements of the South over the moderates.[8]

The Republicans decided on December 3 that in order to avoid a split between their eastern and western wings, they would allow their members to vote for whomever they wished on the first ballot; whichever Republican received the greatest number of votes would then become the official party nominee going forward. Ten short of a majority, the Republicans also made overtures to two other groups. To appeal to the anti-Lecomptonites they made it clear that John Forney would receive their support for clerk. Forney, a Pennsylvanian, had been a key Democratic supporter of Buchanan early in the president's tenure but refused to support the Administration's Lecompton policy and would soon become a Republican. He had also served as clerk from 1851-1855. To appeal to the North Americans the Republicans were willing to grant them one of the lesser House positions. After John Brown's raid there was no point trying to add the southern Americans to their coalition. As it turned out, however, no Anti-Lecomptonite

---

7. Nichols, *Disruption,* 272. Johannsen, *Stephen Douglas,* 717.

8. Nichols, *Disruption,* 273. Johannsen, *Stephen Douglas,* 717. Victor Hicken, "John McClernand and the House Speakership Struggle of 1859," *Illinois State Historical Society Journal* 53, no. 2 (Summer 1960), 168. Robert Toombs to Alexander Stephens, December 26, 1859, in Phillips, *Toombs, Stephens, and Cobb,* 452. Frank J. Tusa, "Congressional Politics in the Secession Crisis, 1859-1861" (PhD diss., Pennsylvania State University, 1979), 43-44. Thomas Bocock to M.R.H. Garnett, November 8, 1858, in Ambler, *Correspondence of Hunter,* 274.

would vote for a Republican, eight casting a vote for another anti-Lecompton Democrat, and the five Illinoisans voting for Bocock. Two of the North Americans did, however, vote Republican on the first ballot.[9]

On this first ballot, John Sherman of Ohio outpolled Galusha Grow by 20 votes and therefore became the official Republican nominee. The combined vote of the two Republicans was 109, over 20 votes greater than Bocock's, but well short of a majority due to smatterings of votes for Americans and anti-Lecomptonites. Sherman's defeat of Grow was somewhat of a defeat for the more radical elements of the Republican Party. As Alexander Stephens later remarked from Georgia, Sherman was "by no means among the rabid and ultra men of the House." Nevertheless, the election of any Republican was anathema to the southern Democracy, and soon after this first ballot John B. Clark of Missouri proposed a resolution intended to disqualify not only Sherman, but 40 other Republicans as well. In introducing his resolution, Clark noted that Sherman was among 68 Republican congressmen of the previous Congress who endorsed a Republican plan to distribute freely to poor white southerners 100,000 copies of *The Impending Crisis of the South,* a book written by a North Carolinian arguing that slavery was disastrous for the South in that it prevented a progressive diversified economy. What especially offended the southern planter class about the book was its appeal to non-slaveholding whites, an appeal that if successful threatened to divide white southerners on the whole question of slavery's beneficence. Hinton Helper, the author of the book, was denounced as an insurrectionist, and the Republicans who endorsed and promoted his views were accused by Clark of contributing to the destabilization of the South. Clark's resolution maintained that Helper's book was "hostile to the domestic peace and tranquility of the country," and that no House member who endorsed it "is fit to be Speaker."[10]

Immediately after Clark spoke, a number of Republicans rose to challenge the right of any member to offer resolutions before the House was organized. But unlike Forney in 1855, James C. Allen, the holdover Clerk from the 35th Congress, declared that he was not authorized to rule on points of order, thereby allowing Clark's resolution to be debated. During this debate, while Republicans stood silent, one southern Democrat after another took the opportunity to threaten

---

9. Tusa, "Congressional Politics," 44-45. Nichols, *Disruption,* 274. Ilisevich, *Galusha Grow,* 182. Theodore E. Burton, *John Sherman* (Boston and New York: Houghton Mifflin Co., 1906), 61. *New Albany Ledger,* December 5, 1859. *New York Times,* September 20, 1859, in *Ledger,* September 24, 1859. *Ledger,* November 29, 1859. *CG, 36-1,* 1-2.

10. *CG, 36-1,* 2. Ilisivech, *Galusha Grow,* 182-3. Alexander Stephens to J. Henley Smith, February 4, 1860, in Phillips, *Toombs, Stephens, Cobb,* 459. *CG, 36-1,* 3, 16. Potter, *Impending Crisis,* 387. Southerners essentially believed that the election of Sherman would be equal to the incitement of slave rebellion. Shelton F. Leake, for example, congressman from Virginia, demanded that the South not elect a speaker who "is stimulating my negroes at home to apply the torch to my dwelling and the knife to the throats of my wife and helpless children." *CG, 35-1,* 21.

disunion to the delight of some in the galleries. Clark's resolution never directly came to a vote, but a motion to table it the next day failed by a tie. One hundred and eight Republicans could only pick up three of the independent anti-Lecompton Democrats and five Americans; on the other hand, the Democrats added all but one of the southern Americans and four anti-Lecompton Democrats to equal the opposition's total of 116. The vote was a clear indication that the Republicans would have trouble electing Sherman.[11]

No regular northern Democrat voted to table Clark's resolution, and the 25 who voted to keep it alive included three from Indiana, Holman, Niblack, and English. Even John G. Davis, counted among the anti-Lecomptonites, voted with his fellow Hoosiers. English took stock of this and realized that the combined effect of John Brown and Hinton Helper could ironically go a long way toward strengthening the southern moderate Democracy if northern Democrats could continue to illustrate their understanding of southern fears. On December 23, shortly after the 19th ballot for speaker had failed to dislodge Sherman or elect anyone else, English took the floor to respond to Chicago Republican John Farnsworth's assertion that the Republicans considered John Brown's actions extreme. "I heard with surprise," he began, "the statement made by the gentleman from Illinois that he did not believe any of his constituents sympathized with John Brown in his raid into the Commonwealth of Virginia." The reason for his astonishment, English claimed, was an article from the *Chicago Times* reporting the occurrence of a meeting in Farnsworth's district "in which strong sympathy was expressed for John Brown, and approbation for his conduct." English remarked that "there seems to be an unaccountable defect of memory, not only with the gentleman, but upon that side of the House, in reference to the proceedings of this meeting in Chicago, and also in reference to the signing and recommendation of the Helper book…I submit it is a little remarkable that they all have such defective memories."[12]

Farnsworth protested that he never said that his constituents did not sympathize with Brown's intentions, but only that they disapproved of his actions. Indeed, when the *Chicago Times* article was read to the House it became clear that Farnsworth's interpretation of his district's sentiments was correct. The actual resolution that passed read:

> 'Oppression maketh even the wise man mad', and therefore it need not surprise us that the slaves, and sometimes those who remember them in bonds as bound with them, should be driven to rash resistance and revenge, as in the recent insurrection at Harper's Ferry—a rising which

---

11. Sutherland, "Congress and Crisis," 113. *New Albany Ledger,* December 13, 1859. *CG, 36-1,* 19.

12. *CG, 36-1,* 19, 231.

we deplore and a repetition of which we would endeavor to prevent, by concentrating on the benevolent efforts of all good men upon the use of moral and peaceful means for the abolition of slavery.[13]

But while Republicans were able to separate intent from effect, English bargained that everyone else, North and South, realized that one naturally shaded into the other, and any sympathy whatsoever for John Brown was evidence of irresponsible agitation of the slavery issue and not proper conservative behavior. The message was clear: a wide gulf existed between reckless Republicans and law-abiding Democrats. No Democrat, North or South, signed the Helper circular; no Democrat, north or south, sympathized with John Brown.

While English was thinking of the long-term unification of the Party for its upcoming test against Republicanism in 1860, his approach could also affect the speakership contest by convincing the southern Americans to unite with the Democrats on a candidate to challenge Sherman. Indeed, on December 19, three days before English criticized Farnsworth, Bocock withdrew his name from consideration. For the next five ballots the Democrats scattered their votes, English even receiving one from Clement Vallandigham. On the final three of these ballots English voted for John McClernand, a Douglas lieutenant from Illinois. But McClernand, though the highest Democratic vote-getter on this ballot at 28, could not command any southern members. After these inconclusive five ballots, Andrew Boteler of Virginia, the formal American candidate who had been receiving from 25-35 votes throughout the contest, withdrew himself and nominated John Millson, a Democrat but fellow Virginian. This led McClernand to do the same, promoting the English hoped for coalition between the southern Americans and the Democrats. On Millson's first ballot (the 17th on December 20), he received 95 votes, trailing Sherman by only 11 members. Among those votes were 10 southern Americans. However, on that and successive ballots, 13 southern Americans voted for one of their own and Millson was never able to increase his total vote over the next several ballots as both Americans and Democrats began to slip away from him when it became clear he could not be elected. Any wise Democrat could see that the only way to defeat Sherman would be with a southern American candidate, and no matter how much a true Democrat was repelled by the nativist notions still attached to that party, the threat of Republicanism was far worse and far more real. Moreover, on December 22, Buchanan told the Democratic managers that he desired an organization of the House without regard to party lines. Because southern Democrats would never accept a Republican, Buchanan's suggestion was interpreted to mean that the Party choose a southern

---

13. *Ibid.*, 231-232.

American. While southern Democrats began to warm to the idea, most northern Democrats remained steadfastly opposed to it.[14]

One northern Democrat who did not oppose it was William English. He was very aware that the election of a Republican speaker could prove disastrous for Democratic chances in 1860; for in such case the House was certain to promote all sorts of investigations into Kansas and Administration malfeasance. Consequently, on the 20th ballot, after Millson had slipped to 69 votes on the previous one, English joined three other Democrats and one southern American in casting his ballot for Horace Maynard, American from Tennessee. This was a bold step, and although it did not have an immediate effect, five days later 60 other members followed English's lead and also cast their votes for Maynard. This was the first significant move toward a coalition that had to occur for the Democrats to have any chance of defeating the Republicans. But as yet neither Hoosier Democrats Niblack nor Holman could see their way clear to voting for a non-Democrat, and many Democrats in Indiana questioned the wisdom of such a move. Considerably later, the *New Albany Ledger* defended English's vote on the grounds that Maynard had never been a card-carrying Know-Nothing; additionally, the Tennessean already had voted for Democrat Millson three separate times. Yet it was English himself who explained his vote directly to Congress: "Disavowing all sympathy with the peculiar doctrines of the American party, but preferring a national and conservative man upon the slavery question to a sectional man, I will vote for Mr. Maynard of Tennessee."[15]

A few minutes after English made this statement, John Haskin, anti-Lecomptonite from New York, refuted its reasoning. Haskin, who had been rather consistently voting for Sherman, declared that Maynard was no more conservative or Union-loving than Sherman, and, in the end, the New Yorker preferred a conservative northern Republican to a conservative southern American. At this point, English interrupted Haskin. How could he berate the southern Americans, English asked, when Haskin himself had "the other day" cast his vote for John Gilmer, an American from North Carolina? Haskin, quite obviously angered by English's interruption, simply replied that Gilmer was preferable to Maynard because he "stood alongside Mr. Sherman and myself in opposition to the Lecompton policy of the Administration, which Mr. English sought to cover up by a bill which, in my judgement, was the meanest bill offered by the last session." English, having apparently anticipated the substance (and probably tenor)

14. *CG, 36-1*, 188, 189, 197, 198, 206, 209, 219, 220. *Cincinnati Gazette,* December 14, 1859, in *New Albany Ledger,* December 17, 1859. *Cincinnati Gazette,* December 23, 1859, in *Ledger,* December 27, 1859.

15. *CG, 36-1*, 220, 235, 274. *New Albany Ledger,* January 26, 1860. *CG, 36-1*, 275. The *Indianapolis Journal* commented that "perhaps Mr. English has no foreign element in his district and is not afraid [as other Democrats were] that an affiliation with Know-Nothingism will sweep the Democratic party like chaff before the whirlwind." *Journal,* January 2, 1860. Of course there were plenty of Germans in the Second District.

of Haskin's reply, dryly "called the attention of the [House] and the country to the fact that Gilmer himself voted for that English bill." Great laughter and applause met that last riposte, but Haskin was not to be put off so easily. He countered that Gilmer only voted for that bill (a measure, according to Haskin, Gilmer called a "shilly-shally, namby-pamby, nasty kind of bill") because, as a *southern* unionist, he viewed it as acceptable enough under the circumstances. "I, as a northern man," Haskin continued, opposed the bill because "a discrimination was made unjustly to the north." Haskin maintained that he respected Gilmer for his course, one preferable to Maynard's because he had not tried to shove Lecompton down the country's throat.[16] This colloquy was a good example of the anger that strong Democratic anti-Lecomptonites continued to feel for English.

In any event, as it turned out, Maynard could not command enough northern Democrats to ever be elected. The search would have to continue. Meanwhile, apparently stung by Haskin's gratuitous and excessive criticism of the Kansas Conference bill, English prepared a detailed defense of the measure. His remarks, made before the House on January 3, were actually the most extended he ever made on the conference bill in front of his colleagues. He repeated again that the bill was not a bribe, that it was destined to give "peace and prosperity to the oppressed and distressed people of Kansas," (which it did), that it essentially upheld the principle of popular sovereignty (true), and that it was only proper to delay the admission of any state until its population reached the required amount equal to the ratio of one representative. But on the last point, clearly nettled by the imputation that the North was penalized by the bill's partiality, English repeated his declarations made in the recent canvass that an official federal census was not the only way to certify Kansas's population: "The bill indicates the most appropriate method of ascertaining what the population is; but at the same time I do not hold a *technical* adherence to that method to be a *sine qua non* to admission, provided always it is evident that there is the required population." He declared the bill "conservative, rational, and just," its flexibility being a virtue, and its population clause was but "an incidental consideration, forming no essential part of the great Lecompton question, which was referred to the Conference Committee and which patriots everywhere were trying to end." Southern Democrats, perhaps, did not appreciate the diminution of a clause they had considered essential to their support of the measure, but English was clearly so disheartened by the abuse the bill continued to receive at the North that he let himself vent his frustration despite the certainty of southern disapproval.[17]

It is also in this speech that English warned the Democratic Party "not to degenerate into a mere southern sectional party, or a party that tolerates the sen-

---

16. *CG, 36-1,* 275.

17. *Ibid.,* 286, 312-315.

timent of disunion." If it does, he predicted, its days as a successful national party were numbered, and "its mission ended." It was these kinds of statements that continued to mark him as no true doughface, whatever others who are less analytical might think. He admitted that the South had the right, "reserved to every people," to defend their liberties by revolution, but he also noted with remarkable foresight that the North could "muster more men [than the South]" with the "'cartridge box,' so that it was in the best interests of Southerners in the long run to protect their liberties *within the Union.*" He cautiously did not comment on the propriety of the liberties themselves; they would have to be worked out in the political and judicial process. But their due liberties were best protected by the Democratic Party; and if the Party remained true to the "Constitution and the Union," it could defeat the dangerous doctrines of abolitionism and "negro equality."[18] There was a certain self-delusion to the efficacy of this course and clearly a great deal of racism, but it still stopped short of doughfacism.

It is not coincidental that English, in using the words "the Constitution and the Union," used most of the phrase that the Constitutional Union Party would select for its platform the next year. Indeed, to strengthen the moderate and conservative factions of the Democracy, he no doubt welcomed crossovers from the Americans. And, in a sense, a continued promotion of a Democratic-American alliance in the speakership contest was one way of promoting such crossovers. Maynard was evidently not the man to forge this alliance, and it would be three more weeks before another Democratic-American coalition was attempted. In the meantime, the Democracy switched official nominees from Charles Scott of California to Clement Vallandigham of Ohio to Andrew Hamilton of Texas and even back to Bocock.[19] But none of them could come within 10 votes of Sherman (who himself could not pick up enough anti-Lecompton Democrats to succeed), so once again Democrats realized that their only hope of success lay in adopting the nomination of a southern American. On the 39th ballot, then, seven and a half weeks after Congress first convened, the Democrats coalesced around the candidacy of William N.H. Smith, an American from North Carolina who claimed to be primarily a Whig, and who, because he was a freshman congressman, had cast no vote either for or against Lecompton and the English Bill. Both the Illinois Douglasites and the fire-eaters fully supported Smith, and on his first ballot as the Democratic-American coalition candidate, he received 112 votes—six more than

---

18. *Ibid.,* 316-317.

19. *Ibid.,* 338, 348, 360, 373, 386, 408, 409, 587, 603, 607. On the 37th ballot, when Bocock was down to 55 votes, four of the other scattered Democratic votes went to William English. The geography of these votes to some degree illustrates English's geographic appeal. One came from the lower north, George Pendleton of Ohio, two from the upper South, John Phelps of Missouri and Thomas Bocock himself, and a fourth from the lower South, George S. Houston, whose mountain Alabama district was hardly secesh. Parsons, *Congressional Districts,* 78-79, Dubin, *Congressional Elections,* 183; Parsons, 70-71, Dubin, 182; Parsons, 90-91, Dubin, 185; Parsons, 44-45, Dubin, 184.

Sherman, and, as only 227 representatives cast votes on that ballot, two shy of election. He had picked up all the southern Americans, two of the four northern ones, one anti-Lecompton Democrat (two others were absent), and every regular Democrat present but two. If Stallworth could be induced to return from Alabama, and the two recalcitrant Democrats could be won over, Smith stood a real chance of success.[20]

One of the Democrats who voted against Smith was William Holman from Indiana's Fourth District. Whereas English and Niblack supported Smith on the ground that, as English put it, he was an old-line Whig who "hates Republicanism and sympathizes with the national Democracy," Holman claimed he could not vote for any nominee not an official Democrat because a recent resolution of the Indiana Democratic State Convention declared that it was "the imperative duty of every Democrat from Indiana to stand firmly by the regular nominee of the Democratic party." English, incredulous, inquired of Holman who he thought was "the nominee of the Democratic party at this time?" Holman replied, "the gentleman from Virginia [Bocock], for whom I have voted with a good deal of pleasure." "The gentleman from Virginia," English responded, "has been withdrawn as a candidate, and has himself voted for Smith; and I respectfully submit to my colleague to consider whether the fact that a very large majority of the Democratic party has voted for Smith is not equivalent to making him the nominee of the Democratic party." Likely narrowing his eyes, English then asked of Holman, "would not voting for Smith under these circumstances come within the spirit of the Indiana resolution?" Holman replied that his interpretation of the resolution forced Indiana's Democratic representatives to vote only for a formal Democratic nominee, and he would not vote for any American and thereby "embarrass the action of the Democracy of my state."[21]

One can only guess what words English muttered to himself at the end of this colloquy; and if Holman thought he understood the Indiana Democracy's intent better than English, he soon discovered he was wrong. When word of his action reached Indiana, most Hoosier Democrats considered him quite arrogant to assume that he was "better able to judge the action which would advance his party and the public interest than the ninety Democrats who voted for Smith." Phineas Kent wrote English that Holman's "course was anything but satisfactory to his friends, and what was due to the party to which he belongs." James Foley, the man whom Holman succeeded, also understood that his successor was gravely in error, for the contest had narrowed down "to a national man or a Black Republican of the worst stamp." Foley tried to explain his friend's behavior by noting that Holman had been angered by the Know-Nothings in 1854 when they

20. *CG, 36-1*, 611. Johannsen, *Stephen Douglas*, 720.

21. *CG, 36-1*, 611, 614, 615.

destroyed his chances of political preferment. Moreover, there [are] a number of German voters in this district, and being a very selfish man the whole matter is explained."[22] To English, the only explanation could be that that Holman was a naïve political fool.

Duly frightened by the new coalition, the Republicans were finally forced to drop Sherman and look for a more conservative candidate by which to bring as many northerners to their standard as possible. In the end, they selected William Pennington from New Jersey, a man elected to the House by a fusion of old-line Whigs, Americans, and Republicans to his first term. On January 30 the strategy worked well enough to vault Pennington past Smith, 115 to 113, with six votes going to other candidates. The Republican move had brought back three Republicans who were voting for the very conservative Thomas Corwin of Ohio on previous ballots. It also brought over anti-Lecomptonites Garnett Adrian and John H. Reynolds, as well as northern American John T. Nixon. Smith's vote held, but Holman continued to vote for Bocock. Two more ballots on the same day elicited no further movement.[23]

With defeat staring them in the face, the Democrats caucused that evening and decided on a different strategy. As Smith seemed incapable of gaining any more votes, the Party decided to formally try John A. McClernand, who, for a time, had some support in December. Many Democrats apparently hoped that so obvious a Douglas Democrat would at least prevent a Republican victory by stripping that party of its anti-Lecompton support. Perhaps, too, the southern Americans would repay the loyalty Democrats had shown to Smith. Since December, on orders from Douglas, McClernand had been assiduously supporting, whenever there was one, whoever was the official Democratic nominee. McClernand had been so helpful that he was even put on a five-man steering committee designated by the Democratic caucus. So conciliatory was McClernand to the southern Democracy that when English had attempted to nominate him on the floor of the House in early January, McClernand declared that he "did not desire my name to be used in connection with the Speakership." Even at the January 30 caucus, he tried to discourage the Democrats from nominating him, but after "considerable pressure" he acquiesced to their plan. The next day his name was presented.[24]

22. Blake, *The Holmans*, 75. P.M. Kent to WHE, February 4, 1860; James B. Foley to WHE, February 29, 1860, English Papers.

23. Oliver Crenshaw, "The Speakership Contest of 1859-1860," *Mississippi Valley Historical Review 29*, no. 3 (December 1942), 327-328. Robert Toombs to Alexander Stephens, February 10, 1860, in Phillips, *Toombs, Stephens, Cobb*, 461. *CG, 36-1*, 611, 634, 635.

24. *New York Times*, February 1, 1860, in *New Albany Ledger*, February 7, 1860. Hicken, "John A. McClernand," *passim*. Johannsen, *Stephen Douglas*, 717-720. *CG, 36-1*, 338, 348. Hicken, "McClernand," 171-172. *CG, 36-1*, 641.

The balloting showed that the Democrats had greatly miscalculated. Only three non-Illinois anti-Lecomptonites voted for McClernand, while five others remained with Pennington. Moreover, 14 southern Americans stayed away from the Democratic nominee, as did two-thirds of the Democrats from Alabama and all but one of those from South Carolina. The southern Democratic defectors, unable to forget Douglas's stand on Lecompton, voted against McClernand despite being urged to support him by Jefferson Davis. When the balloting was completed, it showed Pennington only one vote away from election, prompting Warren Winslow of North Carolina to move that the House adjourn. A loud "No!" rang up from the Republican side, and it was strangely supported by none other than William English. "I move that we proceed to vote again for Speaker," the tired and frustrated Hoosier began. "It is time that this protracted contest end." So statesmanlike a gesture received short shrift from the rest of his party, and, eventually, the Democrats were able to convince the Republicans that fairness and the late hour of the day demanded an adjournment. But the Democracy could come up with nothing new that evening, and, the next morning, Pennington picked up the vote of American George Briggs of New York City, and he was elected by one vote.[25]

Although the Republicans had succeeded, most Democratic politicians and editors believed that the Democracy had at least claimed a moral victory by forcing Sherman's withdrawal. In a certain sense, this was true, but it soon became clear that such an assessment was overly optimistic. Although Pennington assumed the chair, he did so ineffectively, and the real Republican leadership remained in Sherman's hands as the chairman of the Ways and Means committee and as the one Republican most responsible for the composition of committees in general. Indeed, for the purpose of Democratic unity, the contest had also been a disaster. The anti-Lecomptonites showed little willingness to be mollified, even by McClernand's nomination; the fire-eaters had made clear their antipathy toward Douglas on the last two ballots; and the conservatives had failed to prove that the Republicans could be stopped by any conservative anti-Republican coalition. In truth, English and his ilk could hardly be pleased.[26]

2.

The divisions in the national House, as politically great as they were, could not compete in depth of animosity with the fracture that divided Bright from Douglas Democrats in Indiana. Indeed, simply the organization of the Indiana House

25. *CG, 36-1,* 641. Hicken, "John A. McClernand," 174. *Cincinnati Enquirer,* in *New Albany Ledger,* February 2, 1860. *CG, 36-1,* 645-646, 650. Dubin, *Congressional Elections,* 182; Parsons, *Congressional Districts,* 75.

26. Nevins, *Emergence of Lincoln, vol. 2,* 124. Tusa, "Congressional Politics," 60. Sutherland, "Congress and Crisis," 44. Alexander, *History and Procedure,"* 123. Nichols, *Disruption,* 276. *New Albany Ledger,* February 2, 1860.

elected in the fall of 1858 poignantly illustrated the depth of such animosity. The recorded party breakdown in the House read 50 Democrats, 46 Republicans, 3 Americans, and 1 Independent, apparently giving the Democratic Party a plurality one vote shy of a majority. But because the handful of Douglas anti-Lecompton Democrats refused to caucus with their party and vote for the caucus's nominee, David Turpie, a coalition of one anti-Lecompton Democrat (the other three not voting at all), two Know-Nothings, the Independent Whig (John S. Davis) and all the Republican representatives elected Republicans speaker, assistant clerk, and doorkeeper, while anti-Administration Douglas Democrats were elected principal clerk, agent of state, and state printer. This was not unlike a similar coalition in the 36th Congress that eventually chose Pennington as speaker, Republican Cornelius Wendell as printer, and anti-Lecomptonite John A. Forney as principal clerk. In a special November early session of this legislature, the anger against Bright and Fitch was made evident when the House passed a resolution, 51 to 45, maintaining that the two men were not legally elected to the Senate in 1857. In this case, all four anti-Lecompton Democrats joined two Americans and 45 Republicans to pass the measure.[27]

In the regular session, in January 1859, a House resolution calling for the repeal of the "odious" population provision in the English Bill gained the approval of a plurality of the House members, 48 to 30. But it failed because it did not receive the constitutionally required majority of House members when 11 representatives present in their seats (eight Democrats, two Americans, and John S. Davis) refused to cast a ballot. Later in the session, however, the House polled 51 votes for a resolution that called for their congressmen to vote for the admission of Kansas into the Union "whenever she shall apply to congress with a Constitution…adopted by a vote of the majority of her people, fairly expressed, without regard to what shall be the opinion of her people on the subject of slavery, and without regard to her population." This resolution at least implicitly ran counter to the population provision of the English Bill. Many members from both parties absented themselves from this vote: Republicans because of its clear endorsement of popular sovereignty, and Democrats because it defied the English Bill. The 51-vote majority was composed of 23 Republicans, 21 regular Democrats, 3 anti-Lecompton Democrats, all 3 Americans, and John S. Davis. In any event, it failed to pass the Senate as a joint resolution.[28]

---

27. Shephard, *Biographical Directory,* 516-518. *New Albany Ledger,* November 20, 1858, January 7, 13, 16, 1859. Kettelborough, "Indiana on the Eve of War," 150. Thornbrough, *Civil War Era,* 83. According to the *Ledger,* Norman himself was "urgently solicited to become a candidate for printer, but declined doing so." February 16, 1859. *Journal of the House of Representatives of the State of Indiana during the Special Session of the General Assembly Commencing Saturday, November 20, 1858* (Indianapolis: Joseph J. Bingham, 1858), 47, 50.

28. *Journal of the House of Representatives of the State of Indiana during the Fortieth Regular Session of the General Assembly Commencing on January 5, 1859* (Indianapolis: John C. Walker, 1859), 189-191, 304-306. Draper, *Brevier Reports,* 109.

The Douglas Democrats in the legislature also tried to pass a resolution condemning the Democrats in the United States Senate for stripping Douglas of his chairmanship of the Committee on Territories. Only because the Republicans refused to extol a man who might be their chief rival in the presidential election of 1860 did that resolution fail, but it probably represented the general sentiment of the citizens of the state. The *New Albany Ledger*, which competently had its hand on the pulse of the Indiana Democracy throughout the 1850s, condemned Douglas's removal as indicative of the anachronism of caucus politicians deciding party doctrine at Washington. "The Caucus have had their say, the time for the people to speak will come after a while," it intoned, most likely referring to the 1860 Democratic presidential convention. The *Paoli Eagle*, on the other hand, still representative of the Bright forces, could not "understand how Mr. Douglas or his friends could expect the democrats to retain him as their Chairman of that Committee when he went over to the opposition [on Lecompton and the English Bill] and voted against a large majority of his own party."[29]

For its part, the Bright clique took every opportunity to criticize and humiliate Douglas. Most obnoxious in this regard was John L. Robinson who had long been Bright's premier hatchet man. From his control of the *Rushville Jacksonian*, Robinson lashed out at editors and politicians even if they only inconspicuously promoted Douglas for the presidential nomination of 1860. Both the *New Albany Ledger* and the *Indiana State Sentinel* were at one time or another victims of Robinson's wrath, the *Sentinel* countering by noting that the Marshal's "disagreeable qualities are fast depriving him of whatever political influence he may have possessed." Even the *Lexington National Guard*, the Democratic newspaper published in William English's own home town, was not immune from Robinson's attacks. The degree of hate that seemed to animate Robinson's assaults simply reflected the emotion of Bright himself. Writing to one of his regular correspondents late in 1858, the three-term United States Senator remarked that he would never "regard a set of men in this country who call themselves 'Anti-Lecompton Democrats' in any other light than abolitionists, and most of them rotten in every sense of the term,…from their lying hypocritical Demagogical Monster Douglas, down to the basest puppy in the kennel." As Murat Halstead later remarked, Bright's hatred for Douglas was "the strongest passion of his soul."[30]

Bright's animosity toward Douglas may be traced back to many sources. Its original germ was contained in the natural rivalry between the two caused by each's desire to be the premier Democrat from the Northwest. But Bright's du-

---

29. *New Albany Ledger*, December 27, 18, 1858. *Paoli Eagle*, December 23, 1858.

30. *New Albany Ledger*, December 22, 1858, January 3, 1859. *Indiana State Sentinel*, September 26, 1859. *Ledger*, October 4, 1859. Jesse Bright to Allen Hamilton, December 1858, Hamilton Papers. Hesseltine, *Three against Lincoln*, 17. The attacks were not completely one-sided—the *Paoli Eagle* noted "Douglas" attacks on Bright. See, especially, November 3, 1859.

plicity toward Douglas at the 1856 Democratic National Convention, his vote for Republican Lyman Trumbell for the contested Illinois Senate seat over Douglas Democrat James Shields the next year, and Douglas's returning the favor with his vote on Bright's own contested seat in 1858, increased that animosity. Douglas's brash style and Bright's cloakroom method also clashed with each other. In a certain sense their differences over Lecompton were merely tangential to their dislike for each other, but it was this issue which made Douglas wildly popular in Indiana, and which enabled the Wright clique to transfer its leadership from the exiled ex-governor to the neighboring senator. Douglas's charisma, far greater than Wright's, also helped that clique enhance its power as never before, and in the end it was this that so maddened Bright.[31]

The Indiana Democratic old guard was assisted by the Buchanan Administration in trying to destroy Douglas's influence. Graham Fitch had been one of the staunchest Lecomptonites of the 35th Congress's first session, and on more than one occasion he had become locked in debate with the Illinois senator. In the congressional elections later in 1858 both Fitch and Bright supported Buchanan's policy of formally backing an anti-Douglas Illinois Democrat in that state's senatorial contest. When that strategy failed to deprive Douglas of his seat, Buchanan not only sanctioned the removal of Douglas from his Territorial Committee chairmanship, he also refused to consult with the Illinois senator concerning federal appointments in his own state, preferring instead to take the recommendations of the Lecompton Democracy of Chicago. Naturally Douglas denounced this policy, and in an Executive Session of the Senate on January 22, 1859, he called these presidential nominees incompetent and corrupt. Unfortunately, one of the nominees, the one appointed as United States district attorney for Illinois's northern district, was senator Fitch's son, and immediately the apoplectic father excoriated Douglas for the besmirchment of his family. In reply, Douglas agreed that there were exceptions to his declaration, and Fitch's son was one of those, but Fitch refused to allow Douglas to escape so easily. In unmeasured abuse the Indiana senator denounced his adversary so offensively that Douglas had no recourse but to demand a retraction; and when none was given the much heralded machinery of the code of honor began to creak.[32]

Not long before these events, one observer had remarked that the only way the Administration was going to rid itself of Douglas was to kill him. Fitch, it appeared, was willing to do just that; but, as usual, after three days of correspondence, the matter was settled nonviolently. In essence, Fitch apologized after allowing himself to believe that Douglas was in earnest when he excluded Fitch's

31. Johannsen, *Stephen Douglas*, 380-381, 509-510, 511. Lynch, "Douglas-Buchanan Contest," *passim*. *CG, 34-1*, 584. *CG, 35-1*, 2981. *New Albany Ledger*, January 3, 1859. Van der Weele, "Jesse Bright," 225-226.

32. *Indianapolis News*, November 18, 1930, in "Indiana Biography Series," v. 5, 80-81. Johannsen, *Stephen Douglas*, 689-690. *New Albany Ledger*, January 24, 26, 27, 1859.

son from his denunciation. Despite the settlement, the Bright faction continued to use the affair to heap abuse upon the Little Giant. When a little later Douglas once again voted to unseat the Indiana senators, Comingore was furious, and he wondered why "the *Ledger* has never uttered a word of disapprobation concerning [Douglas's] course." Indeed, not only did the *Ledger* fail to mention Douglas's votes against Bright and Fitch, its comment on the election challenge was suspiciously ambivalent. "However irregular the process by which the sitting senators were chosen," it merely admitted, "that by which [their Republican challengers] were chosen is still more so." No longer did Norman find it necessary to defend the chicanery of the Bright machine.[33]

Alongside the personal differences separating Douglas from the Indiana senators were the obvious political differences on the question of slavery in the territories, and it was essentially these political differences that animated their legions. Bright's forces supported justice Taney's position in *Dred Scott*, also supported by the South, which, again, stated that as a creature of Congress, a territorial legislature cannot deprive a territorial resident from holding slaves in its territory. Douglas's forces either supported his Freeport Doctrine or agreed with Republicans that that part of Taney's opinion was *obiter dicta* and thus not a binding legal conclusion of the Court. As the so-called Freeport Doctrine allowed a territorial legislature to decide not to adopt legislation that would protect slavery in a territory, making its existence untenable, the Bright forces along with their southern allies began to overtly support a federal slave code for the territories that would give the national government the responsibility to promote such protection. This concept eventually became contained in one of senator Jefferson Davis's pro-southern resolutions of February 1, 1860. Although most would consider that this concept certainly sanctioned the very un-Democratic doctrine of federal intervention in the "domestic institutions" of the territories, Southerners and Doughfaces (like Bright) viewed it as necessary in order to counter Douglas and effectuate the true intention of chief justice Taney's opinion in *Dred Scott* (*dicta* or not). This position was first officially staked out in the second session of the 35th Congress, and immediately Douglas Democrats in Indiana denounced it. "We are glad that the monstrous doctrine that Congress shall protect slavery in the territories received the prompt and hearty condemnation of Senators Douglas, Pugh, Bigler, and Stuart," the *New Albany Ledger* declared that winter. "If the South is foolish enough to insist on this demand," Norman continued, "it will be met by the unanimous resistance of the North." "We cannot carry a single Congressional District on that doctrine," Holman wrote Allen Hamilton later that year, and James Foley

---

33. Johannsen, *Stephen Douglas*, 690. *New Albany Ledger*, January 28, 1859. *Appendix to the CG, 35-2*, 147, 148. *Paoli Eagle*, February 3, 24, 1859. *Ledger*, February 15, 1859.

succinctly put it to English that if a territorial slave code was "engrafted onto the Democratic platform at Charleston, the party is gone without hope."[34]

Officially, the Indiana legislature in 1859 passed a joint resolution opposing a federal slave code because it was inimical to the concept of popular sovereignty. The resolution was drafted by senator Lew Wallace, who called the southern position "neither Democracy, nor Republicanism, but Federalism." By "Federalism", Wallace of course meant the ideology of the Federalist Party, an ideology that had excessively (to Democrats) promoted the power of the central government. To all good Jacksonians, Wallace included, centralization was a form of aristocracy, for it refused to trust power to the local, common citizens—territorial citizens, for example. Later that summer, Stephen Douglas himself wrote an elaborate article for *Harper's* entitled "The Dividing Line between Federal and Local Authority." He argued that the territories were, in a certain sense, inchoate states, holding the same relation to the national government as the colonies held toward Great Britain. "While the colonies," he wrote, "ceded to the Imperial government the right to pass all laws which were imperial and not colonial, they claimed for themselves the exclusive right of legislation in respect to their internal polity, slavery included." The American Revolution, he asserted, was fought to preserve this local autonomy, and popular sovereignty was thus commensurate with the founding doctrines of the nation. The unconstitutionality of the Missouri Compromise's restriction on congressional or national power to restrict slavery in the territories does not (as Taney asserted) restrict the territory itself to legislate upon that subject, just like the colonies in the British Empire. In a real sense, Douglas's *Harper's* argument went beyond the so-called Freeport Doctrine because it enabled territories not simply to refuse to enact legislation to effectuate the legal existence of slavery but to actually prohibit slavery by positive legislation. This is what Wallace believed, and this was what Douglas Democrats throughout Indiana believed. Wallace had already called parts of the Taney's *Dred Scott* opinion unsound *dicta*, and the *New Albany Ledger* had argued months earlier that "the Democracy have never looked to the Supreme Court as a guide in *political matters*."[35] Considering Andrew Jackson's general disrespect for the opinions of John Marshal, one might consider the *Ledger's* view orthodox Democratic dogma.

In the Democratic county conventions that met in late 1859 in preparation for the 1860 state convention, Douglas's positions and the senator himself per-

34. Van Der Weele, "Jesse Bright," 240. Nevins, *Emergence of Lincoln, vol. 1*, 452. *New Albany Ledger,* March 1, 1859. William Holman to Allen Hamilton, in Blake, *The Holmans,* 78. James B. Foley to WHE, September 11, 1859, English Papers.

35. Drapers, *Brevier Legislative Reports*. Draft of speech, 1859, Wallace Papers. *Harper's Magazine* 19 (September 1859), 521, 529-533. Johannsen, *The Frontier, the Union, and Stephen A. Douglas,* 125, 127, 128. *Indiana State Sentinel,* in *New Albany Ledger,* October 6, 1859. Draft of Speech, 1859, Wallace Papers. *Ledger,* December 22, 1858.

sonally received overwhelming support. Only a handful of counties and Democratic newspapers refused to sustain either him or his platform, and an invitation signed by Democrats in nearly every county was extended to Douglas to speak at Indianapolis. The massive support for Douglas gave heart to his followers and angered the Bright forces. "The Douglas Haters of Indiana," the *New Albany Ledger* remarked, "are reduced to the last extremity. As the Democratic masses, in county after county, express their admiration of, and confidence in, the gallant senator from Illinois, the bitterness of the revilers increases in intensity." Reports even circulated that anti-Douglasites intended to bolt the state convention if the Democratic delegates to the national convention were instructed to cast Indiana's votes for Douglas as president. In any event, all knew that Bright and his followers would not go down without a fight.[36]

Douglas's preconvention victories even swept counties considered Bright strongholds. Jefferson County, Bright's residence until the mid-1850s (and still the home of his brother Michael and law partner Joseph Chapman) was wrested from Bright's control when the rank and file overturned procedural rulings made by the party leadership. Clark County, where Bright had begun to live after 1855, went for Douglas despite the opposition of the *Clark County National Democrat*. Reports also circulated that Michael Bright had become disenchanted with his brother's tactics and had counseled him in the name of harmony to refrain from attacking Douglas.[37]

William English, too, no doubt believed that the attacks on Douglas were both disharmonious and counterproductive, but it appears he did not go so far as to allow himself to be swept upon the Little Giant's bandwagon. In September 1859, English chaired the Scott County Democratic Convention, and the following was the premier resolution agreed upon at that meeting:

> Resolved: That a people of a Territory, when they come to form a State Constitution [are sovereign]. The question of what laws the people of a territory may constitutionally pass before that time, we consider of secondary importance to the above…[and] we believe it our duty to acquiesce in the decisions of the proper judicial tribunals of the country as to all constitutional questions arising out of the subject.[38]

---

36. Thornbrough, *Civil War Era*, 88. Van Der Weele, "Jesse Bright," 232. *New Albany Ledger,* September 28, October 5, November 30, 1859. W.M. Daily to WHE, December 16, 1859, English Papers. *Ledger,* July 19, November 25, 1859. English Scrapbook, 131. Elbert, "Southern Indiana Politics," 92, fn. 22. *Paoli Eagle,* September 1, 1859. *Ledger,* October 15, 19, November 9, December 28, 1859, January 3, 1860.

37. *New Albany Ledger,* September 28, October 5, 1859. W.M. Daily to WHE, December 16, 1859, English Papers. Elbert, "Southern Indiana Politics," 92, fn. 22. *Ledger,* January 6, 1860, July 15, 1859.

38. English Scrapbook, *131.*

There was a certain, probably intended, lack of clarity to this resolution. Passed in the same month as Douglas's *Harper's* article was printed, it may not have been a direct response to it, but the first sentence implies that Douglas's argument of the internal sovereignty of territories even before they write a state constitution was not supported by this resolution. The second sentence is unclear as to whether it refers to Taney's opinion or to a future decision by the Supreme Court on the subject of territorial authority. Nowhere, however, does the resolution deny the possibility of the constitutionality of the Freeport solution. By refusing to discuss the propriety of a federal slave code, it adds to its general ambiguity and is thus open to some compromise on the great question of the day. It is typically Englishian, i.e., hoping to put off much of the issue for further deliberation in the hope that some agreement can be reached that would unite the Party.

Besides resolving on the question of slavery in the territories, and upon whom the state should place their support for president, local Democrats also made suggestions concerning who should be their party's nominee for governor. Early in 1859, about half a dozen men were mentioned as possibilities. At first prominent among them were James S. Athon, sometime English challenger for nominee to Congress, and Cyrus Dunham, former congressman. But also mentioned as early as one year before the convention was English himself. During the summer, however, he squelched these rumors in the same card in which he declined interest in the speakership. "I desire a small space in your valuable paper," English wrote Norman on July 9, "to say that I am not a candidate for that high office." Underneath the space that the *Ledger* accorded this card, it commented that English's decision "will be regretted by very many Democrats of southern Indiana." In a poorly grammatically written letter to the congressman a couple of months later, James Foley echoed these sentiments: "We have a number of friends in this part of the State [who] would of been pleased to of seen you a candidate."[39] Mardulia probably had something to do with English's declination, but he may have also reasoned that his visibility in the Lecompton debate precluded his nomination in the interests of harmony.

By late summer, Thomas Hendricks, who had most recently been commissioner of the General Land Office, had replaced Athon, and it became clear to all that only Dunham or Hendricks stood any chance of nomination. Contrary to tradition, both of them canvassed the state heavily before the convention, leading the *New Albany Ledger* to remark that it "saw the symptoms of a more animated contest for this nomination than [were] consistent with the harmony and efficiency of the Democratic organization." It appears that Bright indeed favored Dunham, but he also may have realized that the ex-southern Indiana congressman

---

39. *New Albany Ledger,* March 8, 1859; W.M. Daily to WHE, December 16, 1859, English Papers. *Ledger,* July 12, 1859. James B. Foley to WHE, September 11, 1859, English Papers.

was a beaten man. On October 16, 1859, Bright had asked English to come to his home in Jeffersonville to agree "upon a plan of operation as to how we are to proceed to close matters with Dunham." He agreed with English that whatever they decided to do should be done before they both left for Washington. Hendricks had been one of Bright's most powerful associates for most of the 1850s, but after he formally broke with the Administration in 1859, Bright rather distrusted him. "In point of popularity," Lew Wallace wrote, Hendricks "surpassed" the senator, and Bright may have wondered whether the Shelby County politician had decided that 1860 was the year the mantle of party control would fall to him.[40]

Such were the extensive preliminaries to the great transitional Democratic State Convention of 1860, which met on January 11 while Congress was still deadlocked over the speakership. Much of the old guard was on Bright's side, including governor Ashbel Willard, marshall John L. Robinson, Bright's law partner and judge of Indiana's first circuit Joseph W. Chapman, ex-congressman and now secretary of state (by appointment) Cyrus Dunham, and the one relative newcomer U.S. district attorney for Indiana Daniel Voorhees. Prominent within the Douglas faction were ex-_Sentinel_ publisher Austin Brown (founder of a new Douglas sheet called the _Indiana Democrat_), state senator Lew Wallace, Aquilla Jones (who prompted the famous Wallace resolution of 1858 by his piqued withdrawal as nominee for state treasurer), and Supreme Court reporter Gordon Tanner. Both factions knew that the Convention of 1858 had not completely satisfied anyone, and both looked to the gathering in 1860 as decisive.[41]

A full day before the convention was scheduled to begin, Norman, an official member of the Floyd delegation, reported that there was "an immense crowd of delegates already here." Their number caused the Central Committee to exclude all persons from the Convention's floor except those "regularly accredited." Because of the hostility between the two major factions, the traditional meeting in

---

40. _New Albany Ledger,_ June 17, August 31, October 6, November 10, 25, August 1, September 8, 1859. Jesse Bright to WHE, October 16, 1859, English Papers. Elbert, "Southern Indiana Politics," 93. Van Der Weele, "Jesse Bright," 253. It appears that Hendricks broke with the Administration over its positions on slavery and on the Homestead bill, as well as its use of the Land Office as a patronage dispensary. Gray, "Thomas Hendricks," 128. Wallace, _Autobiography,_ 236. Hugh McCulloch wrote that Hendricks, "without being an orator, was one of the most effective speakers of the day. His aim was to convince, [and] he rarely failed to impress his own convictions on those who listened to him." McCulloch, _Men and Measures,_ 73. Hendricks was also very cagey. For example, in reply to Joseph Wright's plea that he come home to Indiana in 1857 to attend the Democratic Senatorial Caucus, Hendricks answered that he could not make the trip, but he hoped that "patriotic considerations would govern the politicians." Hendricks to Wright, December 9, 1856, in Crane "Joseph A. Wright," 234.

41. Van Der Weele, "Jesse Bright," 233. For Chapman see Shepherd, _Biographical Directory,_ 62. Cyrus Dunham was appointed in 1859 upon the resignation of Daniel McClure. Woolen, _Biographical and Historical Sketches,_ 321. For Vorhees, see _Congressional Biographical Directory,_ 2095. For Austin Brown see _Indiana Biographical Series,_ vol. 7, 49. Irving McKee, _"Ben-Hur" Wallace: The Life of General Lew Wallace_ (Berkeley: University of California Press, 1947), 30. For Tanner see David Stevenson, _Indiana's Roll of Honor_ (Indianapolis: A. D. Straight, 1864), 501.

the State House on the eve of the convention was cancelled, and most observers expected a real party squabble. On January 9, two days before the conclave convened, Jesse Bright himself arrived from Washington. He was accompanied by one of his trusty lieutenants, Finley Bigger, and it was rumored that they carried $8,000 with which to bribe the delegates. A correspondent of John G. Davis's later wrote that "Bright was coldly received—all were mad at his coming," and the editor of the *Indiana State Sentinel* wrote that "if Mr. Bright had a regard for the harmony and success of the Democracy in Indiana, he would have confined his attention to his public duties in Washington, or else have taken a trip to [his property] in the salubrious region of Lake Superior."[42] For a couple of days before the Convention opened, the senator had mapped out his strategy with two of his supporters—Robinson and governor Willard. Already they were prepared to contest the delegates from seven separate counties—one-seventh of the Convention's vote. If they could win all those protests, they stood an outside chance of stopping the Douglasites. Much depended on the selection of the permanent chairman, for it was he who traditionally appointed the Credentials Committee. Considering that the challenged county delegates could not vote for that office, if the Bright forces selected a popular man, they might win. At any rate, whether they captured the permanent chairmanship of not, their strategy on the presidential nomination would be to prevent the convention from instructing the national delegates for Douglas. Because of the strength of the Douglasites, it would be impossible to instruct for someone else, so the best they could hope for was a free delegation, unobstructed, as well, perhaps, by the unit rule.[43]

At 10 a.m. on January 11, Joseph Chapman, a member of the Central Committee, called the Convention to order. Immediately, the struggle for permanent chairman commenced. Lew Wallace nominated judge Robert Lowry, a prominent Douglas Democrat ever since the 1858 convention; Robinson, the floor leader of the Bright forces throughout, nominated Samuel E. Perkins. Perkins was a wise choice, for he was a highly respected figure, having served on the State Supreme Court since 1845. Moreover, he had conspicuously supported Douglas for the presidency in 1856, and Robinson no doubt believed that he might be the man to divide the opposition. Indeed, Perkins almost succeeded, falling 16 votes short of defeating Lowry. But as close as they had come, the Bright forces knew that this was a significant defeat. Robinson tried to get the Convention to take the power to appoint the Credentials Committee from the chairman, but the delegates would have none of it. A few minutes later, Lowry predictably appointed a

42. *New Albany Ledger,* January 11, 1860. *Indiana State Sentinel,* January 12, 1860. *Indianapolis Journal,* January 12, 1860. *Ledger,* January 11, 1860. Kettleborough, "Eve of the Civil War," 152. Ezra Read to J.G. Davis, January 15, 1860, in Elbert, "Southern Indiana Politics," 95. *Sentinel,* January 10, 1860.

43. *Indianapolis Journal,* January 11, 1860. Kettleborough, "Eve of the Civil War," 151. *Indianapolis Journal,* January 12, 1860. *New Albany Ledger,* January 11, 1860.

majority of Douglas men to sit as the arbiters of delegate challenges. When the Credentials Committee returned, all but one of the counties were decided in favor of the Douglas men, and that one—Spence County—was allowed one-half vote for each of the two sets of delegates. As the Convention adjourned after its first day, things indeed looked dark for the Indiana senior United States senator.[44]

On the second day, the delegates immediately began consideration of Indiana's delegation to the Democratic National Convention. At every step of the way, Robinson and Willard tried to thwart the Douglasites; at every step they were defeated. First of all, Robinson's attempt to take from the chairman the power to appoint the committee to report Charleston delegates was voted down, 239 to 156. The 26 delegates who were finally selected (two from each congressional district and four at-large) included John B. Norman and Simeon K. Wolfe, and only four of the delegates could be considered unfavorable to Douglas. Once these procedures were completed, John C. Walker moved that the delegation be instructed to vote for Douglas, and that all their ballots be cast as a unit. Immediately, Robinson was on his feet, moving an amendment to Walker's motion that substituted Joseph Lane for Douglas; but in his speech that followed, he primarily spoke against the whole principle of instruction, advancing the concept that at least the congressional district delegates ought to be free to vote as they pleased. This caused a general debate, as the Convention had reached the most significant point of its deliberations.[45]

As Norman realized even a year earlier when Lane's name was first suggested, the Bright men were clearly using this favorite son to draw off support from the Little Giant. But the Douglas men were too committed to their man for this tack to work, and the Convention easily rejected Robinson's amendment. Thereupon governor Willard offered another amendment to instruct only the at-large delegates, leaving the district delegates uninstructed and allowing the state delegation to cast its vote as the majority determined. This 'compromise' ploy was also defeated, and, in the end, the Convention voted 265 to 129 to bind the whole delegation to Douglas "so long as his name was before the Convention." On all other questions that might come before the national convention, a majority of the Indiana delegates were free to determine how the state would cast its vote—thus allowing wiggle room on the platform planks, for example. On these motions the Second District voted 27 to 10 with the Douglas majority, but the 10 anti-Douglas votes came from significant areas: four from Clark, four from Orange, and two

44. *New Albany Ledger*, January 12, 1860. Woolen, *Eminent and Self-Made Men*, District 4, 169. Perkins was the judge who handed down the decision overturning the 1855 liquor law. Thornbrough, *Civil War Era*, 68-69. *Indianapolis Journal*, January 12, 1860.

45. *New Albany Ledger*, January 13, 1860. Hesseltine, *Three against Lincoln*, 283. *Ledger*, January 13, 1860. Norman received the approval of 27 of the 37 Second-District delegates as one of their choices as Charleston delegate. J.B. Norman to WHE, January 17, 1860, English Papers.

from Scott, reflecting the influence of Bright, Comingore, and English. Though the latter was unable to attend the Convention because of the speakership battle, Elisha was there, and there is little doubt that English's home county at least partially reflected his position at this point.[46]

At one point, Lafe Devlin (one of the four Bright delegates selected to the national convention) protested the "tyranny" of these instructions, and he even suggested that he could not obey them if his congressional district was not in favor of Douglas. But his idle threats were ignored, and in a more accommodating manner the Bright forces allowed the Charleston decisions of the state convention to repass unanimously. State officers and final resolutions were still to be decided, and they no doubt hoped this accommodating attitude might gain them something in these upcoming areas. On the question of resolutions they were not entirely incorrect, for the Convention refused to take any specific ultra-Douglas stance. They instead wrote an ambiguous set of planks that reaffirmed the general principle of federal "non-intervention" in territorial affairs and accepted the decisions of the Supreme Court "as the best evidence of the true meaning of the Constitution," declaring that the Party "would respect and maintain them with the fidelity we owe to the Constitution itself." On the other hand, the delegates also resolved that the "Federal Government is one of limited power, [and that such power] ought to be strictly construed by all departments and agents of the government, and that it is inexpedient and dangerous to exercise doubtful constitutional power." The latter resolution, the first plank of the platform, was clearly, though interestingly not directly, intended as a criticism of the senatorial resolutions sanctioning a federal slave code.[47]

The late Bright-led accommodation also allowed the Douglas forces to oblige their opponents on the nominees for state officers. In the months before the convention, the Bright forces had feared that the majority was only going to allow men of their own presidential preference to be state nominees, but in victory also came the majority's realization that their brotherly enemies would be needed for final triumph that fall. In the end, it turned out that almost half the state nominees were non-Douglas men, leading even the *Paoli Eagle* to declare that the ticket was a "good" one, "one that the party can and will support." Among the Douglasites on the ticket was Michael Kerr, who replaced Bright's ultra-critic Gordon Tanner as the nominee for Supreme Court reporter. As for the gubernatorial nomination, Dunham took the whole suspense out of it when he withdrew as a candidate just before the balloting. "I am satisfied that my continuance as a candidate will not contribute to the peace and harmony of the Convention," he said in removing

---

46. *New Albany Ledger,* March 19, 1859, January 13, 1860. *Indiana State Sentinel,* January 13, 1860. *Paoli Eagle,* January 26, 1860.

47. *New Albany Ledger,* January 13, 14, 1860. *Indiana State Sentinel,* January 13, 1860.

his name. But it was clear anyway that Hendricks was the overwhelming favorite of the delegates. "Hendricks' nomination was one of the most flattering things I ever witnessed," Winston B. Pierce wrote John G. Davis two days later. "[T]he tumult was overpowering—shouting, waving of handkerchiefs, hats, and rising from seats to do it told the intense satisfaction which was enhanced by the fact that everything else had been finished, and this was the *crowning act.*" As for Dunham, he took his frustrations out on colonel Allen May, a delegate who had rudely interrupted him when he made his withdrawal speech. On the night the Convention adjourned *sine die,* the ex-congressman met the colonel on the streets of Indianapolis and gave him "a severe lick on May's forehead over the eye...a large and ugly looking cut." The Convention had ended with a bang.[48]

"Mr. Bright thought he had it all fixed when he compromised with Joseph Wright and sent him to Berlin," William Wick wrote R.M.T. Hunter late that spring. "In this he is in error," Wick concluded, "[for] 100,000 Joseph Wrights have sprung from the ashes of his weak and despised self-immolation." "It is a complete triumph of the *popular will* over the designing and crafty *office-holders,*" William Daily wrote Douglas a week after the Convention adjourned; and Austin M. Puett, Wright's son-in-law, simply noted that "the State of Indiana [was] entirely out of Jesse's Breeches pocket." More sober observers tried to downplay this great shift in Indiana's political bedrock. "To be a friend of Mr. Douglas is not necessarily to be an enemy of Senator Bright," wistfully declared the *New Albany Ledger,* and Norman "deeply regret[ted]" that some "so-called 'Douglas' papers" had crowed over what they were labeling "the defeat of Willard, Robinson, Voorhees, and Co." David Turpie later noted, not incorrectly, that while the "State Convention of 1860 met under circumstances of much excitement and confused activity," it "adjusted its differences, deliberated, and acted in Unity." But it was difficult to keep the Douglasites from celebrating the apparent transfer of power. "Glory enough, is it not," wrote Winston Pierce. "Our friends are wild with exultant enthusiasm."[49]

How English, in the midst of the speakership battle, received the news from Indianapolis is not hard to discern. Since December 1859, he had been serving as Indiana's representative on the Democratic National Committee,[50] a position he

48. *Paoli Eagle,* December 22, 1859; *New Albany Ledger,* December 24 1859. *Ledger,* January 14, July 2, 1860. *Eagle,* January 19, 1860. Ebert, "Southern Indiana Politics," 94. *Ledger,* January 17, 1860. Winston S. Pierce to J.G. Davis, January 14, 1860, in "Some Letters to John G. Davis," *Indiana Magazine of History* 24, no. 3 (September 1928), 209.

49. W.W. Wick to R.M.T. Hunter, May 6, 1860, in Ambler, "Correspondence of R.M.T. Hunter," 324. William Daily to Stephen Douglas, January 18, 1860, in Van Der Weele, "Jesse Bright," 236. A.M. Puett to J.G. Davis, January 15, 1860, "Some Letters to John G. Davis," 209. *New Albany Ledger,* January 16, 1860. Turpie, "Typewritten *Sketches,*" 140. W.S. P[ierce] to J.G. Davis, January 14, 1860, "Some Letters to J.G. Davis," 209.

50. *New Albany Ledger,* December 8, 1859.

and the other Committee members (excluding, perhaps, John A. Logan) acquired for their general support of the Administration. Most of the northern Democrats on the Committee, though they might be able to support Douglas if he were nominated (as Vallandigham of Ohio and Cochrane of New York eventually did),[51] did not believe that the Illinois senator's nomination was in the best interests of the Party's harmony. English shared this understanding, and he was no doubt unhappy with Indiana's instructions, as foreordained as they might have been. But, on the other hand, he had to notice that the Indiana Convention's resolutions refrained from explicitly stating Douglas's understanding of popular sovereignty, adopting instead resolutions that closely resembled the Scott County language. This was a sure sign that the Douglasites were somewhat willing to compromise on the platform; now the only task was to get them to compromise on the candidate as well. It would be a tricky business, but harmony at the national level, English must have believed, might yet be achieved.

Not all Hoosier non-Douglasites could see their way to such moderation. One especially, John L. Robinson, was downright bitter. Immediately after the Convention, he went home to Rushville and spewed out his venom from the columns of the *Jacksonian*. The earlier rumors that he would refuse to support Douglas were revived, and his behavior made moderates on both sides almost despair of harmony. At one point, Robinson attacked the integrity of the Credentials Committee, an assault that Norman, a member of that committee, resented vigorously. A few days later, on March 17, the *New Albany Ledger* reported that Robinson had become ill with "inflammation of the stomach," and Norman may well have wondered if the Marshal's attitude had not internalized itself in his own body. Five days later, to the shock of all, Robinson died. The *Ledger* announced his death in a touching editorial, and on the day of his funeral all business in Rushville was suspended.[52] The death of no other figure, aside from Bright himself, could have better symbolized the impending demise of the Bright Democracy.

3.

Three weeks after the Indiana State Democratic delegates completed their tasks, the House speakership battle also ended, and from that time until the National Democratic Convention in Charleston, two and a half months later, Congress operated less as a legislature than as a cauldron of presidential politics. Presiding over this charged atmosphere, on the House side, was the dignified, poised, honest, but incompetent William Pennington. When Alexander Stephens heard about Pen-

51. James L. Vallandigham, *A Life of Clement L. Vallandigham* (Baltimore: Trumbull Brothers, 1872), 137. Hesseltine, *Three against Lincoln*, 20, 21.

52. Stampp, *Indiana Politics*, 21. *New Albany Ledger,* January 30, March 17, 22, 30, 1860.

nington's victory in February he wrote J. Henley Smith that "so far as the duties of the chair are concerned Sherman would have made a better Speaker. Pennington, I fear, will make an inefficient officer—[He will fall] far below any of his late predecessors." A week later, Toombs wrote Stephens himself that, indeed, "poor Pennington seems wholly incompetent to discharge the duties of the chair," and it was Sherman who functioned as the real leader of the body. Whether a more competent speaker could have lent more cohesion to a fractured and contentious House is problematic, but Pennington's indecisiveness only exacerbated the situation. Yet as the storm swirled about him, the speaker remained outwardly cheerful. "He goes on with great *Bohommy*," congressman Charles Sedgwick wrote Israel Washburn of Maine. "He says he has stopped drinking, but his nose is a plain denial of his speech."[53]

An inebriated chief officer and a politically intoxicated House made for a migraine of a session. Through their control of the committees and the flow of business, Republicans continually sought to embarrass the Democracy. Most significant in this regard was the formation of two House investigating committees essentially formed to locate corruption emanating from the Administration. Of the two, the one chaired by representative John Covode of Pennsylvania was the more politically damaging. It was this committee that heard testimony inculpating Buchanan of using the Administration's largesse to influence the outcome on Lecompton. English, of course, and all the other regular Democrats (including two of the Illinois five) consistently voted to hamper the Committee's proceedings, but a coalition of Republicans, anti-Lecompton Democrats, and Americans just as consistently outvoted them. Indeed, it was on the eve of the Charleston convention that Covode dug up Buchanan's original letter to ex-Kansas governor Robert Walker, and later testimony suggested widespread corruption in the Navy and Post Office departments.[54]

Substantively, the most politically charged issue was still Kansas; this time it concerned its admission as a free state. In the summer of 1859, despite the fact that no official census had yet put the population of Kansas over 90,000, the Republican dominated territorial legislature authorized the election of a constitutional convention. The delegates selected convened in Wyandotte County and wrote a constitution that not only prohibited slavery, but encouraged integrated schools, allowed some mixed-race people to vote, and essentially did not exclude trial by jury in fugitive slave cases. Ex-congressional Kansas delegate John Whitfield wrote

---

53. Alexander, *History and Procedure*, 88-89. Alexander Stephens to J. Henley Smith, February 4, 1860, in Phillips, *Toombs, Stephens, Cobb*, 459-460. Robert Toombs to Alexander Stephens, February 10, 1860, *Toombs, Stephens, Cobb*, 461. Charles B. Sedgwick to Israel Washburn, in Hunt, *Israel, Elihu, and Cadwallder Washburn*, 92.

54. Nichols, *Disruption*, 285-286. Nevins, *Emergence of Lincoln, vol. 2*, 196-198. *New Albany Ledger*, February 11, 1860. *CG, 36-1*, 1440, 1624.

English that the Convention was controlled by the "Beecher-Seward-Giddings" type of Republicans and was chaired by "a true disciple of Wendell Phillips." Whitfield also complained that the Convention shamefully allowed women to attend common schools with men, and he was shocked to report that "the naked" (this word begs deconstruction) "question of allowing females all political rights enjoyed by males received eight of the thirty-three Republican votes." To Whitfield, Kansas barely avoided a social revolution; even as the constitution was, it was much too racially and sexually egalitarian. Agreeing with Whitfield, Samuel Medary, the Administration-appointed governor of the territory, declared that the Wyandotte Constitution "is crowded with infamous provisions for the vilest partisan purposes, and from sheer ignorance and desire of experiment." In other words, a Yankee nightmare.[55]

Both Whitfield and Medary also complained that the Republicans had defined the boundaries of their new state with the express purpose of having another one carved out of the territory. "You are aware, perhaps," Whitfield wrote English, "that there was a strong effort upon the part of the Democrats to annex Southern Nebraska, but it was defeated by the Republicans." Whitfield explained Republican behavior by the fact that "if Kansas was admitted by the boundaries as fixed by this Constitution, the Pike's Peak region and Nebraska would both soon be applying for admission as separate states, thus making three instead of one free state." Medary noted that he had not conversed "with a single person who is not opposed to our boundaries" and both he and Whitfield maintained that without the Pike's Peak region, Kansas fell over 8,000 citizens short of the amount required in the English bill. The Convention's haste and boundary designations were clearly intended, they believed, to maximize Republican power nationally. Both commentators wished that the Democrats in Congress would delay the matter, as each believed that, in a few years, the area would contain a Democratic majority.[56]

One day after Congress convened in December 1859, Kansas, having completed the Constitution, held an election to select the prospective governor and state legislature. Because, according to Whitfield, the Wyandotte legislative districts were "so arranged that we [Democrats] could not possibly elect more than

55. Tusa, "Congressional Politics," 162. *New Albany Ledger,* October 19, 1859. Beecher refers to Lyman Beecher, the abolitionist minister of the Plymouth Church in Brooklyn. Rifles sent to anti-slavery Kansans during the territorial civil war were called "Beecher Bibles." Seward was William Seward, anti-slavery senator from New York and front-runner for the Republican presidential nomination. Giddings was Joshua Giddings, abolitionist and free-soil congressman. The Wyandotte Constitution can be found at https://www.kansasmemory.org/item/90272/text. J.M. Whitfield to WHE, November 25, 1859; S. Medary to WHE, December 12, 1859, English Papers.

56. J.M. Whitfield to WHE, November 25, 1859; S. Medary to WHE, December 12, 1859, English Papers. In late February 1860, Medary vetoed a bill abolishing slavery, which the legislature had passed 30 to 7. *New Albany Ledger,* February 28, 1860.

30 of the 100 members," the Republicans swept to victory in the Assembly. They also captured the governorship by electing the former leader of the Topeka forces (but actually rather moderate) Charles L. Robinson. This was the situation when Congress received Kansas's application for admission; action upon it was delayed, however, until the House was organized. When debate finally did begin it became clear that conservative northern Democrats felt politically impotent to deny the obvious desire of their constituents to ratify Kansas's application. Opposition, thus, came almost entirely from southerners, who argued, like Whitfield and Medary, that Kansas's population was insufficient and its boundaries were improper. In the midst of this debate, however, the population argument was somewhat undercut when the Administration-appointed Chief Justice of the Kansas territory, John Pettit, the ex-Hoosier senator, declared that he believed the territory had more than 100,000 inhabitants, an estimate confirmed by the unofficial census taken in each county prior to the December election.[57]

When the admission bill finally came to a vote on April 12, the House passed it overwhelmingly, 134 to 73. Every northern Democrat but three supported it. In voting for admission, William Niblack of the First District in southwestern-most Indiana, "frankly concede[d] that such an enumeration of the inhabitants of the Territory as is contemplated by the English bill has not been taken," but "from other sources of information" he was "satisfied that Kansas has a sufficient population to entitle her to admission under the bill." Consequently, he was "violating no fundamental principle [while] reflecting the wishes of an overwhelming majority of the people of the district from which I came." This was the rationale of all northern Democrats who voted for Kansas's admission. Two of the three free state Democrats who voted against admission had their own peculiar reasons. Charles Scott of California represented the southern politicians of that hybrid state (and, indeed, he himself later fought for the Confederacy), and Dan Sickles of New York was Buchanan's close personal friend. But for the most part, as they did on the Homestead Bill, northern Democrats just could not afford to vote against the manifest desire of their constituents.[58]

The third northern Democrat who voted against Kansas's admission was William English. As the reputed author of the great conference measure, he could perhaps be excused for doing so on the grounds that no official territorial-wide census had yet been taken. But in his last congressional campaign, and even in Congress early in the year, he had made it crystal clear that despite the measure's

57. J.M. Whitfield to WHE, December 3, 1859: S. Medary to WHE, December 12, 1859, English Papers. Nevins, *Emergence of Lincoln, vol. 2*, 196. *New Albany Ledger*, February 22, 6, 18, 1860. *Biographical Directory of U.S. Congress*, 1729. The Constitution was ratified by an almost two-to-one margin; Etcheson, *Bleeding Kansas*, 206.

58. *CG*, 36-1, 1672, 1665. For Scott see *Biographical Directory of U.S. Congress*, 1878. For Sickles, see Klein, *James Buchanan*, 226.

language, he would not insist upon such officiality. He made manifest numerous times during the late canvass that he would accept as sufficient a general understanding that Kansas has met the minimum population requirement. Voting now formally against the admission of Kansas because of a lack of an official population count would clearly lead anyone to denounce him for having then lied to his constituents in order to get elected, a tactic, indeed, of a 'trickster'. Indeed, in this case, when explaining his vote against Kansas's admission he did not even refer to the population argument. His full explanation, which speaks the proverbial volumes, was simply this: "More than two-thirds of my political friends have voted against the bill, I shall vote the same way."[59] That was it. By 'political friends' he certainly meant Democrats, which sounds at least somewhat reasonable until one realizes that those two-thirds (except for Scott and Sickles) were all composed of southerners. So why did English appear to betray his constituents in so brazen and flippant a manner?

One could maintain, that like Medary and Whitfield, he disagreed with the socially liberal Wyandotte provisions concerning women and blacks, but voting against Kansas's admission because he disagreed with sections of its popularly ratified constitution would deny the basic idea of popular sovereignty. An easy answer would be that he was simply a doughface,[60] but though he certainly respected the southern viewpoint, we have seen that he often chastised southern congressmen for their overly protective attitude concerning their peculiar institution, especially when it threatened the harmony of the Democratic Party or denounced the concept of popular sovereignty. And whatever one might think of his willingness to confer with the Senate over Lecompton as an example of doughfacism, the fact is that the English Bill *did essentially* submit the Lecompton constitution to the voters of Kansas and *it did* result in its defeat, which was an essential defeat for the South. This leaves us then to look for other, more complex, reasons. We may start with the reasonable assumption that English had decided not to seek re-election to the House next time around; indeed, this was pretty well understood at the

---

59. *CG, 36-1*, 1672.

60. I have tried to show throughout this work that William English should be best understood as more of a party-loving union Democrat that an unalloyed doughface. A typical, rather recent, example of a work that concluded English was simply a typical doughface is Michael Todd Landis, *Northern Men with Southern Loyalties: The Democratic Party and the Sectional Crisis* (Ithaca and London: Cornell University Press, 2014.) To my way of thinking, its fault, at least in relation to English, is that it rather ignores gradations of accommodation to the South and the reasons for such accommodation. He also makes some key errors, e.g., claiming that voting for the proposition of the Lecompton conference bill would grant Kansas "more land than it requested" (p. 197), and he completely ignores the eventual Kansas vote against the proposition of the conference bill, which English expected to occur, and for all intents and purposes killed bringing Kansas into the Union as a slave state. Throughout the Lecompton controversy and elsewhere English fell short of a true doughface. Though understanding of the southern position and devoted to the Democracy, he was not a man of southern loyalties or principles.

Democratic district convention of 1858, the main reason for his final nomination being to legitimize his compromise measure. Having no fear of facing the electorate in 1860, he was free to pursue an independent course. But the reason he *substantively* chose to 'independently' at this time vote *against* the admission of Kansas has, as always, to do with his perception of what was needed for the success of the Democratic Party—beyond merely the 1860 presidential election. He believed fervently, iterating many times previously, that in order to prevent the dissolution of the Party, he had to promote the more moderate attitude in its southern part. It, therefore, was incumbent upon him, as the author of a conference bill that guaranteed a free Kansas, to oppose the restricted boundaries of the state and to implicitly illustrate that the population provision of the bill that favored the South should be fully respected, i.e., that the honor of the South would not be breached.

From English's perspective, however quixotic and self-deluded the idea might have been, if the southern Democrats were given some signs of respect from their northern brethren there was still the possibility of finding a way to harmonize at the upcoming national convention in Charleston and possibly, though unlikely, defeat the Republicans. This high-minded perspective was well abetted by his disappointment with the unfair attitude of many anti-Administration Democrats toward his fair-minded English Bill. That attitude had led him closer to Buchanan and Bright and necessarily, therefore, away from Douglas. Perhaps, like with the conference committee, he also thought of himself as among the few who could prevent the feared party breach, and he needed to burnish his credentials as a peacemaker with this vote.

His belief in his growing influence in the Party is aptly illustrated by a curious episode right before the vote on Kansas. Upon the death of John L. Robinson the post of United States marshal for Indiana was eagerly sought by a number of Democrats. English himself received at least one letter from the former Whig Allen Hamilton asking him to use his influence to gain the position for one F.P. Randall. Bright and Fitch no doubt received other requests. The frontrunner, it appears, and the man supported by both Indiana senators, was Cyrus Dunham. The *New Albany Ledger,* among other newspapers, declared that such an appointment would be highly appropriate. But no sooner had Dunham become confident of receiving the post, when Buchanan instead appointed none other than Elisha English, William's father. On March 28, William himself had gone to the White House to ask the president for this favor. Perhaps it was simply hardly possible for the president to refuse so personal a request from the Party's great savior of 1858, but Elisha's appointment also illustrates that William had likely eclipsed Bright in political influence. As the *Indianapolis Journal* put it, while Elisha's appointment may have been proper considering his "active and faithful service" in the Indiana legislature, his commission was primarily due to "his son's influence with the President."[61]

Although many Democratic sheets subsequently applauded the president's decision, it soon became clear that one Indianan was hardly pleased at being so blithely bypassed and so obviously disregarded. In his somewhat typically choleric manner, Graham Fitch reportedly declared that in protest he would never enter the White House again. He also vowed to defeat Elisha's nomination, and he proposed as a substitute not Dunham, but one of the anti-Douglasites of Indiana's delegation to the National Convention, Lafe Devlin. When Elisha's appointment reached the Senate, Fitch used all the powers of his position to hold it up. Some observers speculated that his great obstinacy turned upon the fact that Fitch believed Elisha would use the influence of his new post to help William defeat him for the next Democratic nomination for United States senator. In mid-April Samuel Crowe wrote English that he supposed Fitch opposed Elisha's appointment because "his salvation depend[ed] upon the patronage of that office." Crowe, however, considered Fitch a "doomed man," and he was certain that his opposition could be overcome. In a few weeks, Crowe's prediction proved well founded, and Elisha was in his new office by the end of May.[62]

It is certainly possible that English wanted his father in the marshal position to promote his own senatorial ambitions. The United States marshals had great patronage power that might be used in this manner. Some even speculated that Buchanan allowed the appointment with this express goal in mind. But the greater significance of soliciting the appointment was to illustrate that *he* was now the conservative force in Indiana to be reckoned with and not Bright. This changing of the guard was necessary to be recognized if he was to have any real influence at the Democratic National Convention later that year. Unlike Bright, who was the template of a doughface, English's plan for the Party was to promote harmony by getting the southern delegates to abandon their federal slave code panacea in exchange for the northern delegates to abandon their firm attachment to Douglas as the nominee. He was, as with the English Bill, attempting to thread the needle, and he believed, perhaps delusionally, that this was the way to do it. It is ironic that Orr and Stephens, both who at this point generally shared English's outlook within the Democratic Party, did not expressly oppose Douglas's nomination,[63] but English more deeply understood that specific concessions from both sections

61. Allen Hamilton to WHE, March 23, 1860, English Papers. *New Albany Ledger,* March 24, 30, 1860. James Buchanan to WHE, March 28, 1860, English Papers. *Indianapolis Journal,* in *Ledger,* May 25, 1860.

62. English Scrapbook, 148. *New Albany Ledger,* April 2, 4, 1860. S.S. Crowe to WHE, April 17, 1860, English Papers. *Ledger,* May 25, 1860.

63. For Orr's and Stephens's willingness to support Douglas as the nominee, see Johannsen, *Stephen Douglas,* 743.

were necessary if the Party was to have any chance of holding together. And he needed to burnish his credentials to promote his scheme.

Back home, Norman was disappointed that English differed with him on the presidential nomination, and he was quick to point out that "in regard to the action of our district in Indianapolis, it so *happens* that *your* most active and zealous friends were for Douglas, while the Clark and Orange men, who denounced you most bitterly [in 1858 for his anti-Lecomptonism] were exceedingly hostile to D." Norman further wrote that he " care[d] nothing about Douglas as an individual; never saw him but for a moment, never spoke to him or corresponded with him, nor am I aware that he knows of the existence of so humble a person as myself. But he is the man for the times." He went on, "and about the only Democrat who could carry Indiana and be elected President."[64] But English might fairly argue that it wasn't the presidency that mattered most, rather it was the longer term viability of the Democratic Party as a national force and the prevention of its sectional dissolution. To be sure, he would fight the Republicans to the end, but only a skillful and nuanced approach at the Convention would make victory possible.

While English might be correct that a Douglas nomination could well split the Party, as Norman implied no other nominee appeared able to carry the essential states of Indiana, Illinois, and Pennsylvania, two of which must be carried if the Democracy was to repeat its triumph of 1856. Although some Democrats believed that a good moderate southern man, like R.M.T. Hunter or John Breckinridge of Kentucky, could both unify the Party and carry two of those states, more sober Democrats knew that no southerner stood a chance of carrying any electoral votes north of the Ohio. Considering that fact, English-like opponents of Douglas were compelled to seek a northerner around whom to concentrate. Politicians mentioned, for example, were Horatio Seymour and Daniel S. Dickinson of the rich electoral state of New York. And for a time Joseph Lane, the former Hoosier who had been territorial governor of Oregon as well as its congressional delegate and first U.S. senator, was prominent. From Indiana Foley wrote English that "unless Douglas or Joe Lane is nominated for President, the man that makes the race in this state will have a hard time." English probably agreed, for a letter he wrote back in 1859 defended Lane as a "firm, consistent, vigilant representative [who] stood very high here [in Washington] and many think will be on the next presidential ticket." But as Oregon delegate, Lane had made a speech in Congress that was emphatically pro-Lecompton, and that cancelled him out in the North.[65]

---

64. J.B. Norman to WHE, January 25, 1860, English Papers.

65. For examples of Hunter's northern Democratic support see Henry Fitzhugh to Hunter, March 26, 1860; John M. Johnston to Hunter, April 4, 1860; Thomas L. Kane to Hunter, March 30, 1860, in Ambler, *Correspondence of R.M.T. Hunter,* 308, 313, 309-310. See also Nichols, *Disruption,* 294. For the waxing and waning of Hunter's presidential prospects see Richard Randall Moore, "In Search of a Safe Government: A Biography of RMT Hunter of Virginia" (PhD diss., University of South Carolina, 1993), 237-265. James

It should be made clear that English's opposition to Douglas, unlike Buchanan's and Bright's, was political and not personal. Indeed, in early 1860, English wrote Douglas a complimentary letter accompanying a request that the Illinois senator read the speech English delivered before the House on January 2. Douglas promised to do so, and he replied that he "cordially reciprocated the kind sentiments expressed in your private note." The Little Giant also agreed to "confer" with English upon the subject of his speech, but whether this actually occurred is unknown. That English still had a high regard for Douglas is unquestionable, he just didn't think his nomination was good for the Party. Norman had noted to English a few weeks after the Indiana Convention, "I very much regret that the course of the *Ledger* or of the Democrats in Indianapolis should have compromised you with the administration or its friends." Indeed, despite the congressman's strategy, it was probably true that the animosity between the Democratic factions had so widened that no two legs of even such a trimmer as William English could bestride them both.[66]

4.

As a gesture of friendship to the southern delegates who had ironically (as things turned out) supported Douglas in 1856, the victorious Buchanan managers that year had agreed that Charleston, South Carolina would be the convention site in 1860. To hold the 1860 convention in a fire-eating citadel was a fateful decision, and early in the year many northerners began to feel uneasy at the prospect. English, as a member of the Democratic National Committee, received at least two letters from northern Democrats requesting he use his influence to convince the Party to change the Convention's venue, preferably to Baltimore. The correspondents cited Charleston's great distance, poor accommodations, and inflated prices, but in between the lines one could easily read that the real fear was that Douglas's chances at a southern center of the 'slavocracy' would not be as good as elsewhere. Despite these pleas, the Party refused to alter its decision. Consequently, on March 30, the Indiana Democratic Executive Committee announced that it had made special arrangements for those Hoosiers traveling to the Convention. Anyone so desiring could take advantage of a group rate: $50 for round

---

Foley wrote English on February 20 that "if we have to take a southern man, Hunter is my man. And William H. English is the mate." English Papers. For Administration support of Joseph Lane, see the *New Albany Ledger*, August 31, 1859, January 7, 1860; Nichols, *Disruption*, 294; Howell Cobb to John B. Lamar, May 22, 1860, in Phillips, *Toombs, Stephens, Cobb*, 480. General support for Lane as early as 1859 can be found in the *Ledger*, July 8, 1859, and James L. Burnet to Hunter, May, 18, 1859, in Ambler, *Correspondence of Hunter*, 272. James B. Foley to WHE, September 11, 1859, English Papers. WHE to Joseph Donthill, February 16, 1859, Lane Papers. *CG, 35-1*, 1394-1396.

66. Stephen A. Douglas to WHE, January 20, 1860; J.B. Norman to WHE, January 25, 1860, English Papers.

trip travel by rail and accommodations in a large tent able to hold 500 persons in all. Norman and Wolfe, the two delegates from the Second District, declined the offer, choosing instead to travel at a more leisurely pace and to stay at a nearby hotel. By April 20, all the Indiana delegates had arrived at Charleston, and they immediately sought out the other northwestern delegations in order to plan how best to nominate their hero.[67]

Although neither was a delegate, both Bright and English attended the Convention. Despite the refusal of the House to adjourn, English left Washington on April 23, and as a National Committeeman he was accorded the right to the Convention's floor. Bright operated from outside the Convention as part of a senatorial cabal determined to deny Douglas the nomination. It was part of English's strategy to avoid a confrontation on the platform by allowing the Douglasites their conservative formula on territorial power resembling the Scott County resolutions, but then to work for another candidate more amenable to the South. The senators, on the other hand, while they harmonized with English on the idea of dropping Douglas (in favor of Lane, Hunter, or Breckinridge), they differed with him on how to do so; they believed that the adoption of a federal slave code resolution would more easily prevent Douglas's nomination because he would have to refuse to run on such a platform. Because the Committee on Resolutions was to be composed of one delegate from each state, and because anti-Douglasite William Gwin controlled California and the Lane delegates Oregon, the senators could be assured of at least 17 of the 33 votes.[68]

Neither of these plans stood much chance of success, but of the two, English's was more realistic. As it turned out, the Douglas delegates, holding a majority in the Convention, could overrule any platform that committed the Party to support the possibility of a congressional slave code. In other words the senatorial resolutions could never be adopted, so why exacerbate the differences between North and South by having them reported? If instead the Committee on Resolutions could be persuaded to initially recommend the more conservative version as possible of Douglas's position, the harmony of the Party might yet be saved; for despite their *simple* majority, the Douglas delegates still needed a two-thirds majority to nominate their favorite, and if their opponents held firm, Douglas himself,

---

67. Nichols, *Disruption,* 291. Johannsen, *Stephen Douglas,* 747. Ovette O. Ross to WHE, March 17, 1860; C.B. Bentley to WHE, March 20, 1860, English Papers. *New Albany Ledger,* March 30, April 14, 1860. Nichols, *Disruption,* 291, 193. Johannsen, *Stephen Douglas,* 750.

68. *CG, 36-1,* 1759. Nichols, *Disruption,* 293-295. Van der Weele, "Jesse Bright," 241. The Senatorial resolution, proposed by Jefferson Davis in Congress did not call for a federally adopted slave code unless a territorial legislature refused, by unfriendly or unprotective legislation, and ineffective judicial or executive action, to assure the effective ability of citizens to exercise their right to possess slaves in that territory. Only then would Congress act with a federal law. *CG, 36-1,* 658. The *New Albany Ledger* had predicted back in March that "all prominent politicians [of Indiana] who opposed Douglas will be on hand at Charleston to work against the man for whom their own state has expressed a preference." *Ledger,* March 13, 1860.

having prevented a southern victory on the platform, would eventually withdraw from contention. As subsequent events showed, the Douglas delegates were indeed willing to compromise to a certain degree on the platform, and Douglas did eventually, though unsuccessfully, send a note to his managers to withdraw his candidacy to "preserve...the unity and ascendancy of the Democratic party."[69]

Yet even English's plan disregarded some fundamental forces operating within the party by 1860. In the first place, many southerners were simply unwilling to acquiesce in another platform capable of dual construction. Alabama and Mississippi had already declared that they would walk out of any convention that did not positively assert the undisputed right of a slave owner to hold his slave property in a territory. The majority of delegates in Louisiana, South Carolina, Florida, and Texas agreed. As Murat Halstead reported one Alabama delegate's opinion, "he was for southern principles, and if the Democratic party was not for them it was against them—and...the sooner it was destroyed and sent to the devil the better." Even Robert Toombs realized that a Douglas platform referring to the Supreme Court a territory's right to follow the Freeport Doctrine was patently unfair. "I certainly do not feel bound to surrender the judicial question," he wrote Alexander Stephens from Washington, "when it has been determined in principle in my favor" [i.e., Taney's opinion]. "Certainly," he went on, "we are entitled to require Douglas and all others to stand by interpretations of the power of the people of the territories as expounded by the Supreme Court. But Mr. Douglas's whole position in the Harper article is adverse to the principles laid down by the court on that point."[70]

A second problem with English's plan was that Douglas's northern delegates, especially the northwesterners, were adamant that Douglas be the candidate. He was the only Democrat, most believed, who could carry their states. "To succumb would be destructive to us at home," one wrote, concluding that the Douglasites of the Northwest would refuse even to give "a complimentary vote" for anyone else. Indeed, when Douglas at one point sent a telegram to his convention manager, William Richardson, that the time was at hand to withdraw, Richardson disregarded its instructions and denied its existence. Had he been inclined to follow his principal's wishes it is likely that the northwesterners would have refused to follow it anyway. The northern Democrats had tired of fighting southern battles up North only to be treated with disdain by their southern colleagues. As one of

---

69. Nichols, *Disruption*, 293, 303. Hesseltine, *Three against Lincoln*, 81-82. Bain, *Convention Decisions*, 63-65. Johannsen, *Stephen Douglas*, 770. William Wick basically agreed with English's approach. "Mr. Douglas," he wrote R.M.T. Hunter on April 27, "is *not*, as *I* well know, ambitious for the Presidency, *just now*; but is convinced that his ideas are right, and that unless they are adopted formally or acted upon informally we can no longer carry the North West." Wick went on to say that the South should not risk everything for an abstract right they would never realize. Ambler, *Correspondence of R. M. T. Hunter*, 321-322.

70. Nichols, *Disruption*, 295. Hesseltine, *Three against Lincoln*, 6. Robert Toombs to Alexander Stephens, May 12, 1860, in Phillips, *Toombs, Stephens, Cobb*, 477-478.

their delegates put it after Douglas had not been abandoned, "there is one thing of which we can't be accused of any more—there was not a doughface shown in the Northwest."[71]

In sum, English's plan underestimated the divergence of purpose that had come to animate the behavior of southern and northern Democrats. Five days before the Convention, a Hoosier, a Kentuckian, and two delegates from Mississippi came together in a tavern in Atlanta. When one of the Mississippians proposed a toast to the prospective nominee's health, the Hoosier inquired whether that included Douglas. The Mississippian replied it did not, because the Illinois senator had no chance to be nominated. The Hoosier thereupon demanded that Douglas be included, and intimated that if he was nominated he deserved the support of all the delegates, including "Southern fanatics and fire-eaters, such as Jeff Davis." The Mississippi man, greatly angered, denied that Davis was in any way fanatical and asserted that he demanded only "the rights of the South." He scorned the Hoosier's assurances that Indiana and the rest of the North would fight the South's battles, and refused to thank them for so imperfectly upholding its rights so far. "The South was able to fight its own battles," he declared, "and to protect her rights out of the Union if not in it." When the Hoosier appealed to love of party the Mississippian responded "damn the party if it were not placed squarely on principle." As Murat Halstead summed up this confrontation, "my Indiana friend was, I think, astonished to find a real live specimen of fire-eater—and was rather embarrassed by his discovery."[72]

English's plan, then, was probably doomed from the outset. Indeed, it was an example of a certain amount of wishful thinking and self-deception, difficult for him to abandon as a natural compromiser. It quickly began to break down when the Committee on Resolutions' majority report forwarded two resolves to the assemblage the Douglas convention majority could never accept. One denied a territorial legislature the right to prohibit slavery in its jurisdiction or "impair" its existence; the other strongly implied that it was the "duty of the Federal Government" to protect slavery in these same territories should, essentially, the first plank be transgressed. After much acrimonious debate and clever procedural moves continuing over several days the convention, in frustration, substituted a resolution on territories simply reiterating the Cincinnati platform of 1856. Had the Resolutions Committee originally reported out this evasive solution, or had it reported out as a majority plank the original Douglas scheme to refer all territorial questions to the courts, the convention might have avoided the animosity caused from overturning the southern plank. As it was, the Senatorial strategy had given false hope to the southern radicals, and their disappointment helped compel them

---

71. Nichols, *Disruption,* 290. Johannsen, *Stephen Douglas,* 746-747, 770. Hesseltine, *Three against Lincoln,* 263.

72. Hesseltine, *Three against Lincoln,* 4-5.

to walk out of the convention. (These included all the delegates from Alabama, Mississippi, Louisiana, Texas, and Florida, and some from Georgia, Arkansas, and Delaware.) Had English's plan been followed, it is possible there might have been enough goodwill left in the convention to have promoted the Gulf states to remain.[73]

The limited southern walkout occurred on Monday, April 30, one week after the Convention had commenced, but by the previous Friday, English could clearly see that the disruption was imminent. Accordingly, he returned to Washington that weekend to make one more plea for Democratic harmony in a forum in which his credentials to speak were unquestioned. He had hoped to address the House on Monday, but because it had already scheduled itself for other business, his speech was delayed; on Tuesday he graciously yielded the floor to his Indiana Republican colleague, James Wilson of Crawfordsville, because the latter was scheduled to leave the city at 3 pm. Finally, on May 2, the same day that the Douglas forces decided to recess the Charleston Convention for six weeks to reconvene in Baltimore and three days after the Gulf states had formed their own "Constitutional Democratic Convention" at Military Hall in the same city, English rose to address this fractured Democracy. It should be understood that at this point the Party's breach was not yet irreparable. The seceding delegates, along with the Buchanan Administration, had originally expected the Dougalsites at the Charleston Convention to compromise on a candidate once it became clear that the Illinois senator could not receive a two-thirds majority. Chastened by the determination of the Douglasites not to give in, their general tactic now was to attempt a reentry into the Baltimore Convention, allow a compromise platform, and gain a candidate other than Douglas—the exact plan English urged from the beginning. Indeed, if any group was obstinate now, it was understandably the Douglasites.[74]

English began his speech by directly addressing the "events which are transpiring at Charleston." He immediately denounced both sides in the controversy. On the one hand, he held "little sympathy with those who imperiously demand "Caesar or nobody;" on the other he castigated that "rule or ruin" spirit that clearly animated many southern delegates. It was these attitudes that had created "whatever difficulty now exist[s]," and he correctly predicted that if "disaster or serious trouble ensues, the masses of the Democratic party never will forgive, as they never ought to forgive, those who will have needlessly precipitated this state of affairs on the country." English spoke here not only of the disruption of the Democratic Party, but of the disruption of the Union itself, clearly understand-

---

73. Nichols, *Disruption*, 297-302. Bain, *Convention Decisions*, 63-66, Appendix. Hesseltine, *Three against Lincoln*, 45-88. Throughout the proceedings Indiana cast its 13 votes solidly each time for the Douglas position. Bain, *Convention Decisions*, Appendix. Hesseltine, 212.

74. *CG, 36-1*, 1888, 1890, 1903. Nichols, *Disruption*, 306-312.

ing that one was practically tantamount to the other. Having said this, he then chose to take a more optimistic view of future events, preferring to believe that "whatever storms may have prevailed at Charleston were necessary for the purity and healthfulness of the political atmosphere." And he expressed an "abiding faith that these clouds will soon break away, [leaving] the glorious sun of Democracy shining brighter than ever."[75]

But English had not sought the floor to speak for long about the Party's schism. Even before Charleston had physically divided the Democracy, it was clear to all that the Party was fundamentally at odds with itself. As one who dreaded the destruction of the Democracy more than almost any other Democrat, English had for some time been planning a foundation upon which all Democrats could unite. In early December, he and seven other National Committeemen had been placed upon a resident Washington committee to "superintend the printing and publishing of documents." In this capacity, English had sent confidential queries to selected Democrats in Republican controlled states generally asking them to furnish him information that tended to prove that "the Republican party are in favor of establishing equality between Negroes and white people." Such questions he asked concerned whether any effort had been made "in your State" to restrict black immigration, whether or not blacks voted there (and if so, what ticket they supported), whether blacks could (and did) hold office, whether they could testify in judicial cases "where white persons are parties," whether blacks could be jurors or lawyers, and whether they could (and did) "intermarry with whites?" "If they do any of those things," English wrote, he also requested his correspondents to "furnish striking examples, and [state] by the action of what party the authority [was] given?" He also requested these Democrats to "state any and all facts in addition tending to show that party to be in favor of equalizing the two races—such as speeches and declarations of leading Republicans, &C—enclosing extracts and documents as far as convenient." As an afterthought he also wished to know "what is the general character of your colored population as to improvidence, immorality, pauperism, and crime? Is it not generally true, that they work only when employed in menial capacities under the eye and direction of white persons?"[76]

Clearly English was attempting to unite and strengthen the Democracy around all the racial fears, prejudices, and ignorance so prevalent in antebellum America. It has been rather well documented that despite the rise of antislavery (in many ways a form of anti-southernism), racial prejudice had become more pronounced in the North during the second quarter of the 19th Century. English sought to nakedly use this attitude in an attempt to remind Democrats that their party, *all* of their party, was united in this attitude as opposed to what he consid-

---

75. *Appendix to the CG, 36-1*, 281.

76. *New Albany Ledger*, December 18, 1859. WHE to Nahum Capen, February 1, 1860, English Papers.

ered the Republican tendency toward "negro-equality." To label the Republicans in this manner was not original—Douglas had used it in his debates with Lincoln almost two years earlier—but it was here used not to simply increase the Democratic vote but to fundamentally unite the Party around an emotional attitude not deeply shared, indeed often denied, by the common enemy. "Even those Democrats who may think our best man has not been selected for the presidency," English reminded the Douglasites and their Democratic opponents, "will still have the consolation of knowing that he is better than the best one the Republicans are likely to present us, and that any Democratic platform is infinitely preferable to theirs." This racist tactic, certainly abhorrent today, and even abhorrent to many then, was to what English would resort to try to achieve the salvation of the Democratic Party.[77]

He began his argument by citing statements made by prominent Republicans tending not only to elevate the black race but to debase the white one. For example, Horace Greeley was quoted as declaring that a particular black man he met while traveling through Virginia was "a gentleman in his bearing, as most negroes and some of the white men in that state were known to be." From Illinois the *Freeport Journal* was cited as "believ[ing] that the negro is superior, in all requirements necessary for citizenship to a majority of the Irish 'cattle' who disgrace our soil." And the speakership contest of 1855 was used again to show that Nathanial Banks had stated, during the "catechism," he could not be certain which race was superior, believing it was left only to time to determine that point. Moving to the actions of Republican dominated states, English accused all of them of allowing blacks to immigrate without restriction, attend schools with whites, and give testimony in court against a white party. In "nearly all," blacks were allowed to hold office and vote, and "in more than half," they were permitted to intermarry with whites. On the other hand, English noted, Indiana, *"because it is a Democratic State [is] a white man's government."* As for his own Second District, English "thank[ed] God that my constituents are white freemen; and I glory in the belief that they will never consent to be placed on an equality with the negro."[78]

"As a general thing," English went on to say, the black man was "unfit to govern himself. The inferior being we find him, the Almighty, for some wise purpose, seems to have designed him. A negro he made him, and it is not in the power of all the Abolitionists and Republicans on earth to make him anything else." English then offered the findings of one "gentleman who has possessed better opportunities for forming a correct judgment than, perhaps, any man in the United States." Although the "scholar" remained anonymous, English probably was referring to

---

77. Leon Litwack, *North of Slavery* (Chicago: University of Chicago Press, 1961), 66-103, 113-120, 153-168, 263-264, 270-272. George Fredrickson, *The Black Image in the White Mind* (New York: Harper and Row, Inc., 1971), 41. *Appendix to the CG, 36-1*, 281.

78. *Appendix to the CG, 36-1*, 282-285.

Josiah Nott, whose *Types of Mankind* was the reigning tome on black inferiority. Nott argued the theory called "polygenesis," which maintained that blacks were a distinct species from whites. English repeated this notion, and maintained in conformity with it that intelligent blacks, "have invariably been confined to mulattoes." In order to deflect the point that such an argument might be used to encourage miscegenation, English noted that the 'mulatto' "is less prolific than either the white or black, and, after arriving at puberty, gradually becomes sickly, inclining to consumption; and a very large portion of this class die before reaching middle age." His "firm belief" was that considering "the manifest differences of the mental structure of the two races, they can not dwell together in one community on an equality." Repeating the basic position held by many whites at that time, he declared that if blacks are "ever to be elevated, so as to be fit for self-government, it will be while [they are] subject to the legal direction of the white race, under such prudent restrictions as humane white legislators will ever provide."[79]

Getting carried away, reflecting his own deep prejudice divorced from his present political purpose, he actually began to defend slavery as a just and humane institution. "It may be that slavery is the instrument by which and through which Africa is at last to be lifted up from her deeply degraded and barbarous condition," he crooned. Of course this notion runs counter to his earlier polygenetic argument. At all events, he noted, slavery was impossible to eradicate "without producing greater mischief than the evils complained of." Even compensated emancipation would bankrupt the United States treasury, and even if it somehow could be accomplished, English wished to know what would happen if 4 million blacks were suddenly thrust into the national mainstream. He predicted "it would all end in a war of the races, and a degradation of the white man too horrible for the mind to contemplate." The problem of slavery, he concluded, "will be worked out in God's own good time; and no doubt to the advancement of his glory and the welfare of the human family. Our true policy is to let well enough alone."[80]

Consequently, Republican policy was foolish policy, based upon the mistaken belief in the black man's capacities and tending to lead to unnecessary conflict among whites. To those who argued that the Republicans did not, as a rule, believe in the equality of the races, English did admit that the true animus of the Party was to break down the Democracy "for the sake of getting into office or accomplishing party ends." But because "revolutions never go backward, if that party succeeds, the boldest and most ultra will get the lead, and the rest, with but few exceptions, will gradually, but certainly follow." William Wilberforce, English noted by example, began only by claiming it was his desire to end the slave trade. It was the duty of all Americans, but Democrats especially, to forget

---

79. *Ibid.,* 284-286. For Josiah Nott's fame and acceptance see Fredrickson, *The Black Image,* 79-81.

80. *Appendix to CG, 36-1,* 286-287.

their differences and unite against the advancing foe. Rather prescient, as he was sometimes wont to be, English maintained that if the Republican Party were allowed continued success it would produce a "terrible explosion [resulting] in the downfall of the great American republic." That Party must not only be defeated, but "annihilated...crushed out by the people." It was thus the duty of the Democratic Party to unite around their common racial understanding and accomplish that essentially patriotic task.[81]

With little doubt, even considering what may be judged its laudatory goal, this speech marked the lowest point in an otherwise respectful congressional career. And despite some effort for a few to get behind it, it was completely nugatory. With both Democratic conventions in recess, English had hoped that his speech would have some effect in helping to unite the Party, but it was just a lost footnote in a hopeless cause. John B. Norman did print it in full in his *New Albany Ledger*, but he very qualifiedly counseled his readers to "give it a careful perusal and then hand it to your neighbors." For its widest possible circulation, the Democratic National Committee reprinted hundreds of copies, and one Hoosier even wrote English for a German translation, but it appears to have left no actual mark. For their part, the Indiana Republicans resented English's implication that a radical racial equality had taken over their party, and the frontrunner for their presidential nomination, though often perceived as too loquaciously anti-slavery, was hardly a rabid abolitionist. Probably the most discouraging reaction that English received came from one O.C. Gibson of Griffin, Georgia. Gibson wrote as if all of English's racist appeals to harmony were superfluous, maintaining that the issue was still one of equal rights vs. squatter sovereignty. "I will venture to advise you that your worst fears are more than realized," he lamented; "our party is hopelessly gone and our country on the brink of ruin. I talked freely with the friends of Mr. Douglas at Charleston," he continued, "and fully satisfied myself that they were thorough abolitionist, to a fanatical state...And I have not the remotest idea that they will yield to the claims of the slave states made at Charleston." "I know," he concluded, "we will never fraternize with any one who thus wrongs us."[82]

Gibson's prediction of Douglasite intransigence was fairly on the mark. Determined to nominate their hero, the northern majority refused to admit into their Baltimore convention those delegates who had previously bolted at Charleston. This led to a new secession from the convention that included the vast majority of delegates from Virginia, North Carolina, Tennessee, Kentucky, Missouri, Arkansas, California, and Oregon, whose delegates joined the original seceders in the same city over at Market Hall. After that the rump Baltimore convention

---

81. *Ibid.*, 282.

82. *New Albany Ledger*, May 26, 9, 1860. W.H. Schlater to WHE, May 13, 1860, English Papers. *CG, 36-1*, 1903-1904. O.C. Gibson to WHE, May 21, 1860, English Papers.

nominated Douglas on its second ballot. Over at Market Hall Breckinridge and Joe Lane were nominated on a federal slave code platform. Appeals to harmony, like English's, even on the basis of race, had become inoperative by this late date. To save their own states, and in defiance of the long arrogant southern dictators, the northwestern delegates especially refused to surrender the Little Giant. Offered a full dose of the arrogance they were used to administering, the South refused to succumb. The only hope for the Democracy now lay in a fractured election thrown constitutionally into the House of Representatives. And in the canvass upon them, every Democrat, as English had predicted in his May speech, must "be ready to do his duty according to the circumstances which may surround him." "I shall certainly," he concluded, "endeavor to do mine."[83]

5.

It was of course with glee that Republicans witnessed the events at Charleston and Baltimore. Although some worried that perhaps the Democratic schism foreshadowed the disruption of the Union, most simply rejoiced in the fact that the Democracy's troubles made the election of a Republican president even more probable. The National Republican Convention had met between the Democratic adjournment at Charleston and its resumption at Baltimore. It naturally excoriated the Buchanan Administration in general, Taney's *Dred* Scott opinion in specific, maintained that "the normal condition of all the Territory of the United States is that of freedom," and denied "the authority of Congress, of a Territorial Legislature, or of any individuals, to give legal existence to slavery in any Territory of the United States." This implication that popular sovereignty was unconstitutional if it allowed for slavery was backed up by an explicit declaration of the "deception and fraud" involved in its practice. The crackup of the Democratic Party also enhanced the prospects of the Party's state tickets in the North, especially when the Buchanan administration got up electors for the Breckinridge ticket. In Indiana the opposition had their best chance since the 1840s to capture the state's administration. Already by the Charleston Convention, the Democracy's opponents had selected a strong ticket and platform with which to face their foes. Headed by the very popular ex-Whig Henry S. Lane as the gubernatorial nominee, the Indiana Republicans opposed the extension of slavery "by all constitutional means," disputed the "dicta" of Taney's *Dred Scott* opinion, called for Kansas's admission into the Union "without delay," condemned John Brown's

---

83. Nichols, *Disruption*, 312-316. See also Hesseltine, *Three against Lincoln*, 213, 243, 271. *Appendix to the CG, 36-1*, 281. Even before the formal nominations were made English's New Liberty, Kentucky uncle, J.B. English, stated that both eventual Democratic nominees were unsatisfactory: "Douglas I have no patience with," and Breckinridge could not be counted on to be loyal unless it serves his interest. J.B. English to WHE, April 1, 1860.

raid into Virginia as a "lawless invasion of a state," and promoted the "immediate passage" of the Homestead bill. Every one of these planks could even be acceptable to most Indiana Democrats, and the Republicans attempted to shake off any lingering nativism by passing a resolution clearly opposing changes in the naturalization laws.[84]

In making a call for a state convention, the Party's central committee had omitted the word "Republican" in order to achieve as widespread an adherence as possible. Nevertheless, all the Republican newspapers of the state wrote of the upcoming convention as a "Republican" one, and a complete lack of obeisance to the Americans validated such a description. Besides passing the above mentioned anti-nativist plank, the delegates placed no ex-Fillmore men on the Central Committee. Moreover, the convention formally adopted the word "Republican" for the Party's name, and there was absolutely no problem passing a resolution to send a delegation to the Republican National Convention in June—among those chosen were also no Fillmore men. To be sure, the state platform was somewhat conservative and most of the state ticket and eventual nominees to the national convention were not radical abolitionists; George Julian, for example, was rather disgusted with the Party's condemnation of John Brown and its seeming willingness to use popular sovereignty (and not demand congressional restriction) to achieve its goal of prohibition of slavery in new states. But it was a Republican conservatism, untainted by a coalition with Know-Nothings or temperance "fanatics."[85]

Down in the Second District, the *New Albany Tribune* appeared unsure of how to react to the convention's course. This had been its problem in 1856, and this would be the problem for all Fillmoreites in 1860. It was no longer a problem for editor Milton Gregg, however, as he had died a year earlier. Gregg had reported in 1858 that for the last two years he had been suffering from persistent headaches; perhaps, these were predictive of his demise. Norman and the *Ledger* genuinely lamented Gregg's death, though in an obituary they labeled his talents simply "above mediocrity." In the event, his editorship passed to his sons, Orlando and Dennis, whose skills did not quite match their father's. In first reacting to the Republican state convention, the brothers lashed out, calling it "a sham and a cheat." They complained that the Fillmore Americans were "rope[d] in," only to be denied the spoils, and they angrily denounced the adoption of the name "Republican" as the Party's standard. "If to beat the Democracy," the Greggs wrote,

84. Hesseltine, *Three against Lincoln,* 157. Thornbrough, *Civil War Era,* 86-87. *Indianapolis Journal,* February 23, 1860. Zimmerman, "Origins of Republican Party in Indiana," no. 4, 377-380, 383, 385. Peek, "The True and Everlasting Principle," 416-417.

85. *New Albany Ledger,* January 24, 1860. *New Albany Tribune,* February 27, 1860. Elbert, "Southern Indiana Politics," 108. Thornbrough, *Civil War Era,* 86. Zimmerman, "Origins of the Republican Party in Indiana," no. 4, 384-385. Julian unsuccessfully sought the nomination to Congress in his district. *Ledger,* February 27, 1860.

"the Americans and Old Whigs must become Republicans, there are thousands who will take no part in the coming contest. They will stand aloof and allow the Republicans and the Locofocos to fight it out among themselves." But in the same issue they declared that for a Republican platform this one was essentially conservative, and one that "will be generally acceptable to all who oppose the Democracy."[86]

For the next few days, the *Tribune* continued its ambiguous course. It refused at first to put the ticket on its masthead and declared that it could only support "a portion" of it (Henry Lane, Joseph Lange—an "educated" German—and James G. Jones, the only 1856 Fillmoreite on the ticket). Most obnoxious to the brothers was the selection of Oliver P. Morton as Lane's running mate. Morton, the standard bearer in 1856, was considered too "ultra" for southern Indiana, and partly for that reason he had withdrawn himself as a candidate for governor in favor of Lane. But his withdrawal was only nominal, for the two agreed that if the ticket were elected—and the Republicans captured the legislature—Lane would become the Party's nominee for senator, making Morton the governor. This appalled the editors of the *Tribune* and the New Albany opposition in general, and for some time it operated to distance the *Tribune* from the state ticket. It was only in the crucible of the canvass that the Greggs finally decided to fully endorse the Republican state campaign, relenting only in the last month to put the ticket on its masthead, and even then refusing to label it Republican.[87]

Much of the *New Albany Tribune's* ambiguity eventually revolved around the fact that one of the brother-editors, Dennis Gregg, wound up supporting the fourth candidate in the presidential contest, John Bell of the newly formed relatively southern conservative Constitutional Union Party, while the other brother, Orlando, backed Republican nominee Abraham Lincoln. Dennis actually attended the new party's April state convention, composed primarily of old-line Whigs and defunct Americans, which selected delegates to the Constitutional Union national gathering set for May 9. He, himself, was both put on the state central committee and selected as a delegate to the National Convention in Baltimore. On the other hand, Orlando followed the lead of Thomas C. Slaughter, English's opponent in 1854, declaring himself for the eventual Republican nominee should he prove to be conservative. The Indiana delegation to the Republican convention in Chicago, with the blessing of the *Tribune*, had first set out to support Edward Bates of Missouri or Supreme Court *Dred Scott* dissenter Justice John McLean, but the greater strength of Lincoln, both as an anti-Seward can-

---

86. *New Albany Tribune*, June 23, 1858. *New Albany Ledger*, January 5, 1860. *Tribune*, February 27, 1860.

87. *New Albany Tribune*, February 28, 29, 1860. Zimmerman, "Origins of the Republican Party in Indiana," no. 4, 381-382. For New Albany's opposition to Morton see W.T. Otto to Henry Lane, January 31, 1860, in Elbert, "Southern Indiana Politics," 107. One of the few New Albanians who actually had no trouble with Morton was John M. Wilson. *Paoli Eagle*, March 9, 1860.

didate and as a former Hoosier, quickly inclined the delegates toward his nomination. Soon after Lincoln was nominated and the Republican convention safely adjourned, the *Tribune* declared that the Republican Party had shown its true conservative hues, and from then on both Greggs believed it acceptable to work hard for Republican success on the state level.[88]

The nomination of Lincoln proved to be a masterstroke of Republican strategy. Located right in the center of the Party, he could, in Indiana, appeal to both conservatives and radicals, and even the Constitutional Unionists only saw Bell as preferable because of the Southern threats to secede should Lincoln be elected. But Lincoln's most significant feat in the state was that he united the opposition to the Democracy around the state ticket. On August 15, a Constitutional Union State Convention was held to name presidential electors but at no time was it suggested to field a separate state ticket. Throughout the campaign, Richard Thompson, the foremost Bell man in Indiana, worked directly for the success of the Republican state candidates, a fact of extreme importance because in 1856 as a Fillmore elector he had refused to do so. Consequently, despite differing on the presidential question, on the state level the opponents of the Democrats became completely united.[89]

Much less harmonious were the two wings of the state's Democracy. Partly this was a function of the wrenching events at Charleston, but it was more directly caused by Jesse Bright's prodigious effort to defeat Stephen Douglas. Despite Bright's attempts to convince the Indiana delegation to abandon Douglas during the Democratic Convention's recess, the delegates ignored his pleas and stuck with the Illinois senator throughout the renewed contest at Baltimore. Unwilling to support his arch-enemy, Bright, along with most of the southern senators and the Administration, backed the candidate nominated by the seceders from Baltimore and Charleston, vice president John C. Breckinridge. It was probably true, Bright's enemies charged, that he worked for Breckinridge not because he had any real affinity for the Kentuckian, but simply as a means to help defeat Douglas. Indeed, as the *New York Tribune* reported in mid-July, Bright even preferred the election of Lincoln to the success of Douglas.[90]

---

88. *New Albany Ledger,* April 14, 1860. *Paoli Eagle,* April 19, 1860. Hesseltine, *Three against Lincoln,* 289. Elbert, "Southern Indiana Politics," 100. Hesseltine, 294. *Ledger,* March 2, April 18, 1860. Stampp, *Indiana in the Civil War,* 36-37. *New Albany Tribune,* June 6, August 2, 1860.

89. Thornbrough, *Civil War Era,* 90-91. *Indianapolis Journal,* August 16, 1860. *New Albany Ledger,* October 10, 1860.

90. Elbert, "Southern Indiana Politics," 116. *New Albany Ledger,* June 1, 1860. Elbert, 125. Nichols, *Disruption,* 335-336. *Cincinnati Enquirer,* in *Ledger,* July 19, 1860. *Ledger,* August 17, 1860. *New York Tribune,* in *Ledger,* July 14, 1860. According to one historian, Norman himself was not averse to surrendering Douglas during one point of the Baltimore convention. Warren Wesley Woolen maintains that Norman and Simeon K. Wolfe, the Second District delegates, tried to get the Indiana delegation to sign a paper requesting his withdrawal, a rather interesting fact if true considering it conformed to English's position. Woolen, *Eminent*

Senator Bright held a seat on Breckinridge's National Committee, but his most effective work was done inside Indiana. On July 17, his faction began publication of a thrice-weekly newspaper, the Indianapolis *Old Line Guard*. Its slogan was "The Constitution, the Union, and the Equality of the States," and it claimed that between the two, Breckinridge, not Douglas, was the regular nominee of the Democratic Party. In practical terms, it also argued that only Breckinridge was able to defeat the Republicans because "there is no probability of Mr. Douglas receiving a solitary electoral vote in the United States." (Douglas, indeed, would only receive 12.) Even a week before the appearance of this sheet, Bright had issued a call for a mass state convention to select Breckinridge electors to meet at Indianapolis on July 31. According to the Republican *Indianapolis Journal*, about 3,000 people attended that day, and Bright sat on the platform with ex-senator Pettit and Orange County favorite, William F. Sherrod. By the end of the day, Sherrod had accepted the position as elector for the Second District, and, because of this act, he was later removed from the same position by the regular Democrats who had placed him there in January. Other supporters of Breckinridge included Fitch, delegate-to Charleston W. H. Talbott (who became chairman of the Breckinridge State Central Committee), James Hughes, and Phineas Kent; but governor Ashbel Willard, Lafe Devlin, Cyrus Dunham, and a host of other Administration Democrats refused to associate with their erstwhile allies. All in all, only seven newspapers in the state came out unalterably for Breckinridge.[91]

Naturally, the Douglas regular Democrats resented Bright's organization and decried his factionalism. Norman remarked that "before Mr. Bright came to the State there was no disposition among any considerable portion of the Democracy to disrupt the party or get up bolting tickets," and the *Cannelton Reporter* declared that "three times a week [the *Indianapolis Old Line Guard*] traduces Stephen A. Douglas, assails the National Democracy, kneels like a camel [to] receive the burden which Bright and Fitch place upon its back, carries 'aid and comfort' to the ranks of the Black Republicans, and all this for 50 cents." All attempts by the much weaker Bright forces to wedge some of their electors into a joint electoral ticket with the regular Democracy were scorned by the Douglas men, the *Indiana State Sentinel* maintaining that such compromises were offered only because Bright knew they would be rejected. In the Second District, only the *Paoli Eagle* counseled that the regular Democrats accept a joint ticket, and Comingore used

and Self-Made Men, District 3, 45-46. Back in January, Norman had written English that he was for "The Democratic ticket" and for the man who could beat the Black Republicans, be it Douglas, Breckinridge, Lane, or who else." J.B. Norman to WHE, January 17, 1860.

91. Nichols, *Disruption,* 335. Indianapolis Old Line Guard, July 17, 1860. *Indianapolis Journal,* August 1, 1860. New Albany Ledger, August 1, 1860. *Old Line Guard,* August 28, 1860. H.L. Duncan, "James Hughes," 91. Kent's support may be inferred from comments he wrote English declaring that Douglas supporters were not true Democrats. P.M. Kent to WHE, February 4, 1860, English Papers. *Ledger,* June 28, 20, 1860. English Scrapbook, page devoted to 1860 election.

all his influence to get the Orange County Democrats to formally call for accommodation. By the end of the campaign, Comingore finally made it clear that he favored Breckinridge, but the enthusiasm for Douglas was so great among Democrats in southern Indiana that for the most part he simply took a middle course.[92]

In essence, the Democratic old guard actually wished to defeat the Party in order to recapture it four years later. As Bright admitted through his press organ late in the campaign:

> We are connected with the only national organization of the Democratic party now in existence—we have every prospect of becoming, in 1864, the successful party, if we do not succeed at this election…The November election will finish Douglas' career with the Democracy and with his defeat, his followers will see that he is not the man they have taken him for. They will then return to the true Democratic fold…Our friends abroad in every state in the Union will then place confidence in us, as Democrats tried in the crucible, and whether successful or not in November next, we shall be regarded as the *true blues* in every part of the Union, and our delegates will be received in the National Democratic Convention of 1864 as the representatives of the only Democratic organization in Indiana.

Such sentiments led most Douglas Democrats to believe that Bright wished to defeat the state ticket as well. Indeed, although it put the January-selected state ticket on its masthead, the *Indianapolis Old Line Guard* did note that it had "expressed no opinion as to the duty of our friends to support the State Ticket. We suppose that each Democrat will act in the premises as he thinks best, and vote in October with a due regard to the effect of that election on the November election." At one point, Bright actually favored the idea of coming out with a competing state ticket, but upon reflection he declared it "inexpedient." In any event, it is almost certain that the senator wished defeat upon the Democracy in October as well as November—partly because positive October results would hearten Douglas supporters in November, and partly because he simply wished to recapture the Indiana Democracy from his enemies.[93]

Few detested the great rupture in the Democratic Party more than William H. English. For six years, since the Kansas-Nebraska imbroglio, by way of speechmaking, letter writing, and legislative politicking, he had faithfully sought to prevent it. Yet now it was upon him, and it comes as no surprise that he was hardpressed to choose one side or the other. On the one side was a majority of his

---

92. *New Albany Ledger*, July 18, 1860. *Cannelton Reporter*, September 20, 1860, in Elbert, "Southern Indiana Politics," 131. *Indianapolis Old Line Guard*, July 18, 1860. *Paoli Eagle*, July 12, 19, August 2, 9, 23, 1860.

93. *Indianapolis Old Line Guard*, October 6, 1860. *New Albany Ledger*, September 5, September 29, 1860. *Old Line Guard*, September 17, 20, 18, 1860.

Democratic constituents; on the other, just as in the Lecompton controversy, were Bright and Buchanan. But unlike with Lecompton, Douglas's position this time was not unassailable. If the Illinois senator had his principles, so did the southerners, and in fairness to the latter, Taney's *Dred Scott* opinion, taken to be the main opinion of the Court, did imply that their principles were at least as constitutional as Douglas's. One could argue that to support Breckinridge made no practical sense, since only Douglas could capture the state; but as wise a political observer as English was he no doubt realized that neither Breckinridge nor Douglas could capture Indiana, for it was Lincoln and the united Republicans who were destined for victory in both the state and national elections. Consequently, whether English chose to support Breckinridge or Douglas depended less on principles or practical politics than on other factors he found more compelling.

English had returned to Indiana soon after Congress adjourned, sometime in the last week in June. At no time from then until the election in November did he ever utter a word publicly, and maybe not privately, concerning his preference. Evidently the Douglas forces, aware of his disapprobation of Indiana's fervor for the Little Giant, made no attempt to solicit his support. They no doubt hoped he would join them, but he was never in their inner circle, and he was not necessary to their cause. Senator Bright, on the other hand, assiduously sought his services. On July 30 Bright persuaded English to come to Indianapolis to confer with the Breckinridge forces one day before their state convention. Along with Pettit, Bright himself, and other Administration Hoosiers, English checked into the Bates House and allowed himself to listen to the plans of the senator. Yet on the day of the convention, English was nowhere to be found. The *Indianapolis Journal* and the *Indianapolis Old Line Guard*, which both published the most detailed reports of the proceedings, make no mention of him at all. He was definitely not on the rostrum, nor was he an officer of the gathering, nor chosen an elector, nor on the central committee. He neither spoke to the "delegates" (as Bright and Fitch did) nor took any official part in the proceedings. It is possible that he attended, but the *Journal* appears to have named all the prominent Democrats it could locate and English was not among them. In all probability, he had conferred with the Breckinridge forces, made certain suggestions of his own, and then left the city.[94]

For the next three weeks he maintained what the *New Albany Ledger* called "an impenetrable silence." Sometime earlier, aware that he could not truly support either wing of the Party, he had resigned his position on the Democratic National Committee, but he never offered a public explanation for his resignation. Even Norman, who had for the longest time been a closer political confidante than anyone else, had completely lost touch with him. "We are frequently asked what is the position occupied by Hon. W. H. English in the present canvass," the *Led-*

---

94. *Indianapolis Journal,* July 30, August 1, 1860. *Indianapolis Old Line Guard,* August 1, 1860.

ger noted on August 20, and it declared that it could not answer: "If he intends to make his bed with those who have heretofore traduced him and opposed his aspirations [i.e., Comingore, Sherrod in 1858]," Norman peevishly added, "his former friends want to know it, and the sooner the better." If such a public declaration was intended to shake the 'impenetrable silence', it failed in its mission. English primarily remained in Lexington and corresponded with no one.[95]

Yet only three days after Norman tried to smoke English out, the editor received what he thought was a definitive answer from another quarter. On August 23, the *Indianapolis Old Line Guard* announced that Bright, Fitch, Sherrod, Alexander Morrison, and William English would make 14 joint appearances around the state between September 18 and October 3. Norman's only comment upon the news was "so be it," but the pithiness of that remark spoke volumes of disappointment and anger. For almost a decade Norman had promoted English's elevation faithfully and had defended the congressman ably. He had not, of course, gone unrewarded, but still, he was unable to understand why English would "make his bed" with those who not only had castigated him on Lecompton, but who clearly did not have the bulk of the Party behind them. Perhaps English sensed Norman's chagrin, for two days later he showed up in New Albany. The exact reason for his trip may never be known, but it is not unlikely that he came to explain his behavior, off the record, to his many friends there. Whatever he said, his strategy soon became clear, for at none of those 14 advertised gatherings did he actually appear. Bright showed up at every one of them, Fitch came to a few, Sherrod spoke at New Albany, but nowhere did English join them. Even when asked to speak at Paoli and his own home town, English declined. In his last public loyalty to Bright, he had loaned his name to the Breckinridge forces, but nothing else.[96]

Nominated congressman Daniel Voorhees later noted that "in the presidential election of 1860, the majority of younger Democratic leaders in Indiana, such as Hendricks, [David] Turpie, [Joseph E.] McDonald and William English" supported Douglas. Voorhees was correct concerning at least the first two, and it is quite possible that most insiders knew that English did not wish the Breckinridge forces well. On September 23, after English had failed to present himself at the

---

95. *New Albany Ledger,* June 27, August 20, 1860.

96. Norman actually first learned of the 14 advertised meetings from the *Indiana State Sentinel. New Albany Ledger,* August 23, 1860. *Indianapolis Old Line Guard,* September to early October 1860. *Ledger,* August 25, 1860. *Wabash Plain Dealer,* September 22, 1860; *Wabash Intelligencer,* September 20, 1860; *Putnam Republican Banner,* September 22, 1860; *Vincennes Weekly Sun,* September 29, 1860. *Ledger,* September 27, 1860; *Seymour Times,* October 4, 1860; *Richmond Palladium,* October 4, 1860; *Franklin Democrat,* October 5, 1860. The Breckinridge Committee of Orange County invited English to speak to its citizens on October 3, but he never showed. Breckinridge Committee of Orange Co. to WHE, August 25, 1860, English Papers; *Paoli Eagle,* August 30, September 5, 1860. *The Old Line Guard* made no mention of English at the mass rally of Breckinridge supporters in Lexington, October 4, 1860. English was also invited to speak by the Douglasites in Kosciusko County. E.V. Long to WHE, August 28, 1860, English Papers.

first five scheduled appearances advertised in the *Guard,* Bright frantically wrote him that he "must meet us at [the two scheduled appearances in] New Albany on Sept. 26 and Seymour on Sept. 27. I tell you now," he practically commanded, "it is *important* that you should." But English did not go, blithely disregarding his mentor's instructions. It is quite possible that Bright had taken it upon himself to list English as a speaker before he gained his protégé's consent; or, it is also possible that English, having once given his consent out of personal loyalty to Bright and to the president, had reconsidered his options (maybe during his trip to New Albany) and decided against it. Significantly, despite his continued political prominence until his death in 1896, the Republicans never accused English of supporting Breckinridge in 1860, and it is quite probable that only his intimate friendship with Bright prevented him from outwardly assisting the Douglasites.[97]

While English rather sat on the sidelines in relation to the presidential contest, he was much less passive in promoting James A. Cravens as his successor for the Democratic nomination to Congress. As early as the 1858 campaign, English had once again announced that he would not be a candidate for reelection, and this time he stuck to his promise. One historian maintains that the "bitterness" of the 1858 canvass had led English to make such a decision; others maintain that he forsook the House to "commence a hopeless scramble for the Senatorship." At any rate, as Cravens had done twice before, he wrote English early to solicit his support for the nomination. In particular, he hoped that English would use his influence to let his friends know that he preferred Cravens to succeed him. Actually, English had already decided to support the Washington County farmer in gratitude for his helpful withdrawal in 1858. As Lewis Jordan had written after the convention that year, "the delegates who were strong for you swear that Cravens ought to have the nomination next time for withdrawing." Consequently, throughout May and June, English informed his followers to do all they could for the perennial also-ran.[98]

---

97. Leonard S. Kenworthy, *The Tall Sycamore of the Wabash: Daniel Wolsey Voorhees* (Boston: Bruce Humphries, Inc., 1936), 34. J.D. Bright to WHE, September 23, 1860, English Papers. E.D. Elbert and Wayne Van Der Weele both assumed that English was a Breckinridge supporter from his name being advertised in the *Old Line Guard.* Elbert "Southern Indiana Politics," 135.; Van Der Weele "Jesse Bright," 256. When English ran as the Democratic nominee for vice president in 1880 the Republicans did attack him for his support of Kansas-Nebraska and the English Bill, maintaining such amounted to his being pro-slavery, but they never mentioned anything about 1860. See William H. English, "His Record as a Civilian," reprinted in Indiana State Library Collection, Indianapolis, Indiana.

98. *New Albany Tribune,* August 25, 1858. Gresham, *Walter Q. Gresham,* 77. *Cincinnati Gazette,* in *Ledger,* June 12, 1860. English Scrapbook, 146. J. A. Cravens to WHE, January 27, March 5, 1860; Lewis Jordan to WHE, August 2, 1858; Frank Gwin to WHE, May 30, 1860; Lewis Jordan to WHE, June 2, 1860; David McClure to WHE, June 3, 1860, English Papers. The *Cincinnati Gazette* had suggested John B. Norman as English's successor, "if ability and party service may dictate the man." Luciene Matthews published these sentiments in the *New Albany Ledger* while Norman was in Charleston. *Ledger,* April 24, 1860. During 1859, Cravens had served as Indiana's agent of state, declining reappointment later that year for personal

English's endorsement of Cravens narrowed the field from five candidates to two. At first, politicos John I. Morrison (falsely promised future English support in 1858), Ballard Smith (former state legislator, 1856 contingent Buchanan elector, Indiana judge, and Douglas supporter), and Simeon K. Wolfe had declared themselves available, but once they realized they could not gain English's support, they soon withdrew. This left, once again, only Sherrod to face Cravens; as the convention neared, it was clear that the doctor could only rely on the undivided support of Orange County. Cravens, on the other hand, had the full support of Washington, Floyd, Harrison, and Crawford. In Scott County, English's home, no attempt had been made to instruct the delegates. When English heard of this he wrote what must have been a rather scathing letter to David McClure, the county's perennial representative to the Indiana House, for McClure proudly replied that "under the circumstances you ought not to be offended when I act in the present case as my judgment may dictate, and my honor and manhood requires." Yet, realizing English's power, he apologetically added that he did not know "you were for Cravens, and neither did many of our mutual friends." As it turned out, the Lecompton Democrats from Scott sent a large contingent to the congressional convention that handed the county to Sherrod. It is perhaps significant that after that McClure held no official positions until 1864, at which time he decided to move to Jeffersonville.[99]

Because the district congressional convention was held in early June while Congress was still in session, English did not attend, but his political friends had things well in hand. Although Sherrod was able to pick up Scott, and a portion of the delegate count from Clark and Perry, the caucuses before the first ballot revealed that had the ballot been held he would have been handily defeated. Consequently, he bitterly withdrew, declaring that "if there were two Democratic candidates for President, there would be two Democratic candidates for Congress." He never made good on this threat, but he did categorically refuse to support Cravens. Once Cravens was nominated, the delegates passed resolutions, and one of these expressed the

> respect and esteem we entertain for our present member, Hon. Wm. H. English, and our confidence in him as a public officer. In his retirement, in accordance with his well known wishes, from the position of representative, which he has so long filled with credit to himself and benefit to

---

reasons—no doubt to remain home to gather the congressional nomination. *Ledger*, January 18, March 15, December 6, 1859.

99. *New Albany Ledger*, May 3, May 21, May 28, 1860. *New Albany Tribune*, June 6, 1860. *Ledger*, May 29, 1860. David McClure to WHE, June 3, 1860, English Papers. *Tribune*, June 8, 1860. Shepherd, *Biographical Directory*, 247.

the country, we heartily greet him with the plaudit, 'Well done good and faithful servant.'

John Menaugh wrote English that this resolution "was got up by a few of your friends, [and although] it is not just what I wished nor just what you may have desired," it was adopted with "great satisfaction and by acclamation."[100] English might have hoped for a more effusive endorsement, one that perhaps could have been used to boost his senatorial chances, but considering the divisions within the Party and the many years he had been around to make enemies, the resolution was all that could have been reasonably expected.

For the first time in nearly a decade, the Democratic opposition was not faced with William English as candidate, and its partisans could hardly contain their joy when they found out who had succeeded him. "Major Cravens is the weakest man [the Democrats] could have nominated," the *New Albany Tribune* gleefully announced. "He is exceedingly illiterate, and devoid of force or shrewdness." Indeed, the Greggs were not far off the mark. The *New Albany Ledger* extolled Cravens as exhibiting the "sterling traits of character peculiar to the plain, hardworking farmer," a Jacksonian through and through, and even Norman admitted that he was not a "cultivated" speaker. In truth, Sherrod, Wolfe, or Morison would probably have made a more effective candidate. With an opportunity facing them such as they had not had in almost 15 years, the Republicans and Americans tried manfully to bury their differences and select a strong opponent. A convention held in New Albany on June 20 illustrated that this would not be easy. The most popular man with the opposition was still John S. Davis, who continued to cling to his Whig antecedents, but for just that reason the Republican delegates refused to vote for him. For his own part, Davis himself refused to accept the nomination "at the hands of this convention or any other," declaring that if he did run it would be as an independent candidate. Unable to decide what to do, whether to support Davis's independent candidacy or to nominate another man, the convention adjourned for three weeks to meet in Salem on July 19.[101]

By the time they reconvened, the animosities between the two factions had actually grown worse. Floyd County even sent two sets of delegates, and only after much discussion was it finally decided to select the "Davis men." Eventually, as illustrated by the result in Floyd, enough Republicans saw the efficacy in nominating Davis. They allowed him to style himself an Independent, but they did gain from him a promise that should he be elected he would cooperate with the Republican Party in Congress, and in the canvass he must make clear that Lincoln

---

100. J. A. Cravens to WHE, June 11, 1860; J.B. Norman to WHE, June 7, 1860, English Papers. *New Albany Ledger,* June 8, 1860. *Paoli Eagle,* June 14, 1860. *Ledger,* June 8, 1860. J.L. Menaugh to WHE, June 11, 1860, English Papers.

101. *New Albany Tribune,* June 8, 1860. *New Albany Ledger,* June 7, 28, 29, 1860.

was at worst his second choice for the presidency. With these stipulations he was nominated, 51 to 4; one county bolting, and one unrepresented. After the convention, the Clark County Republicans refused to endorse him, and it was generally understood that many other Republicans were dissatisfied. But, as the canvass progressed, these Republicans forgot their antagonism, and it soon became clear that the Opposition had made a clever and effective choice.[102]

Along with Davis's superiority as an orator and his fine reputation as a criminal lawyer, he could also count on numerous alliances made through his railroad promotions and service in both the state legislature and on the New Albany Council. But what especially made him a formidable candidate was his early declaration that he would support Lincoln over Bell simply because the latter had no chance in Indiana. This effectively brought the Republicans fully to his standard, and he even made a bid for the Breckinridge voters by claiming he preferred the Kentucky statesman over Douglas. The *Paoli Eagle* commented (perhaps from its disappointment with Cravens's selection over Sherrod) that "through the agency of his wealth, and a fair share of political cunning, [Davis] has managed to carry his points generally." As the campaign progressed, the *New Albany Ledger* truly began to worry about the outcome. It continually reminded Democrats that Davis was "one of the most violent traducers of Judge Douglas anywhere to be found," and it hinted darkly of a deal made between him and Jesse Bright. Yet it was obvious that many Democrats simply considered Davis far more intelligent and capable than Cravens. He had never been a Know-Nothing, nor a Republican, and some Democrats no doubt remembered that, when he was a state legislator in 1858, he refused to vote for the Republican resolution to unseat Bright and Fitch. In the end, the *Ledger* was forced to resort to party discipline. "In voting for a member of Congress, personal considerations should have no weight whatever with Democrats," Norman intoned. "The 2nd district is largely Democratic, and should be represented by a Democrat." Indeed, considering Davis's superiority, it was well for the Party that the candidates followed English's precedent of 1858 and held no joint canvass.[103]

Even after the Bell forces put together a complete Indiana electoral ticket, Davis continued to favor Lincoln. In this he was joined by John M. Wilson and most of the opposition who clearly understood that a vote for Bell was a vote for Douglas. The *Louisville Journal*, the Bell organ of northern Kentucky, agreeing that their man could not capture Indiana, actually tried to convince the Indiana Oppositionists to vote for Douglas on the grounds that if Lincoln was denied a

102. *New Albany Ledger*, July 19, 20, 1860. *New Albany Tribune*, July 20, 1860. *Paoli Eagle*, July 26 1860. *Ledger*, July 31, August 4, 1860. *Eagle*, August 2, 1860. *Ledger*, September 25, 1860.

103. Woolen, *Eminent and Self-Made Men*, District 3, 9. Shepherd, *Biographical Directory*, 94. *History of Ohio Falls Cities*, 159. Hargrave, *Pioneer Railroad*, 17. *New Albany Ledger*, July 28, August 10, 26, 1860. *Paoli Eagle*, August 2, 1860. *New Albany Ledger*, September 25, 1860.

national majority Bell could be chosen as a compromise candidate by the House. But even Richard Thompson, Indiana's foremost old-line Whig, would have none of it. Hoosier oppositionists were apparently satisfied that the ex-Whig, ex-Hoosier Lincoln was duly conservative, and in no way would they for a moment promote Douglas's prospects. Encouraging these sentiments were a slew of Republican speakers who traversed the district as they had never done before. Carl Schurz, Thomas Corwin, and even abolitionist Cassius Clay spoke to large audiences in New Albany. On the other hand Dennis Gregg tried and failed to get the foremost Whig-American senator John Crittenden of Kentucky to speak in that city in early October. As Comingore later remarked, he had never seen the Republicans so thoroughly organized.[104]

For the Democrats, Douglas himself came to the state in late September. He made a whirlwind whistle-stop tour of Indiana between September 27 and September 29, the most publicized effort being a speech in Indianapolis to thousands of cheering partisans on the 28th. According to one historian, 400 people greeted him at 2 AM in Bloomington, and as he did at most of his stops he spoke for about 15 minutes from the train's platform. After he left Indiana, his running mate, Georgia governor Herschel Johnson, appeared for a couple days to keep the Democratic juices flowing. But it soon became apparent that even these gallant efforts were not enough to combat the seemingly limitless speakers the Republicans were importing into the state. In truth, the most effective weapons that the Democrats used, taking a page from William English's speech to Congress in May, were not the husky tones of the Little Giant, but the shrill warnings of race amalgamation. The *New Albany Ledger* predicted that a Republican triumph would make the United States a replica of Canada, where "negroes have used their power as voters to tyrannize, insult, and oppress the original settlers. Lazy and improvident, they have become the pests of every community in which they dwell, filling the poor houses and jails." The *Paoli Eagle* published stories such as one headlined "Practical Black Republicanism—A White Woman Eloping with a Nigger." In a humorous and equally racist riposte, the *New Albany Tribune* noted that "the big dark complected editor of the *Paoli Eagle* talks about negro-equality. Why, Comingore, we thought after looking at you the other day that you ought to be in favor of it." In fact, the *Tribune* blunted much of the effect of the racial equality charge by highlighting Lincoln's support for the Fugitive Slave Law and his 1858 pronouncements against social equality. Such sentiments were echoed by the Republican gubernatorial nominee Henry Lane.[105]

---

104. *New Albany Ledger*, August 10, 16, 23, September 21, October 6, September 3, July 30, October 5. *Paoli Eagle*, October 11, 1860. See also Thornbrough, *Civil War Era*, 94-95.

105. *New Albany Ledger*, September 29, October 1, 1860. Johannsen, *Stephen Douglas*, 795. Elbert, "Southern Indiana Politics," 129. *Ledger*, October 2, January 26, 1860. *New Albany Weekly Tribune*, in *Eagle*, August 23, 1860. Thornbrough, *Civil War Era*, 91.

Finally, on October 9, Hoosiers went to the polls to cast their ballots for state offices and Congress. The result was rather a smashing victory for the Republicans. Not only was Lane elected, but the Republicans captured the state legislature and maintained their seven to four advantage in Congress. In the Second District the Republicans were naturally not as successful as elsewhere, but even there Lane captured 46 percent of the vote, up 3 percent from Morton's poll in 1856, and he actually carried Perry County. But the greatest surprise was in the congressional race. Although he only gained a majority in two counties (Perry and Floyd), Davis barely missed capturing Scott and Crawford, and only Washington County's 500 plurality for Cravens prevented the Opposition from a stunning upset. When all the votes were counted Cravens had recorded a slim 51.3 percent, a smaller majority than in any of English's elections, even the one in 1854 when he faced the powerful fusion assembled from the opposition to the Kansas-Nebraska act. The result was certainly a testimony to Davis's popularity, but another key factor may not be dismissed. On the day before the election Bright made a speech in New Albany apparently intended to counsel Breckinridge Democrats to sit on their hands the following day. "This Anti-Lecompton Douglas-Democratic party," he was reported to have said, "must be defeated, and you may begin tomorrow [as] you will find no better time." Similar statements the senator made in Jeffersonville as well, and by comparing the votes of October with November it certainly appears that the Breckinridge men (unlike the Bell men) refused to vote. Bright later formally denied that he ever voted for Lane, but he never denied having abandoned the Democratic state tickets.[106]

Cravens was incensed. "I cannot but think that Bright's conduct is inexcusable," he wrote to English, "after I have worked as long as I have for him." English wrote back that he sincerely believed Bright had actually voted for Cravens, but the Washington County farmer would not be moved: "As for Bright's voting for me I wish I could believe [it] but I do not." In fact, Cravens was probably right, and English did not again try to persuade him otherwise. Actually both the congressman-elect and the *New Albany Ledger* breathed a collective sigh of relief that they had prevailed at all. "I think this District was much too neglected by our pubic speakers," Cravens wrote the incumbent late in October. "The Republicans flooded the District with Speakers and Documents whilst I had neither, and then, Bright, Fitch, and Sherrod to contend with." The *Ledger* agreed, and added that, as Davis was "one of the most adroit and untiring men who ever undertook to

106. Thornbrough, *Civil War Era*, 95. PItchell, *Indiana Votes*, 8-10. Dubin, *Congressional Elections*, 187. *Tribune Almanac and Political Register for Year 1861* (New York: Greeley and McGrath, 1861), 62. *Tribune Almanac and Political Register for Year 1857 (New York: Greeley and McGrath, 1857)*, 62. [Both Tribune Almanacs bound in *Tribune Almanac, 1857-1862*, Indiana State Library, Indianapolis, Indiana.] *Whig Almanac for year 1855*, 61. Kettleborough, *Eve of the Civil War*, 181. *Jeffersonville Democrat*, in *New Albany Ledger*, October 15, 1860. *Ledger*, October 12, 26, 1860. *Paoli Eagle*, November 1, 1860.

make a canvass," Cravens's victory was substantial. Neither mentioned what role English had played in the congressional canvass, but Cravens's continued friendly correspondence with the lame duck congressman attests to the fact that English had assisted him beyond the district convention.[107]

The results in October, especially when combined with similar Republican victories in Ohio and Pennsylvania, greatly disheartened the Democrats in the month before the presidential ballots. Yet ever gamely, the *New Albany Ledger* continued to battle. It especially tried to capture the Bell men by focusing on what it considered the extreme ideology of Lincoln and Hamlin, predicting that "their election would be the triumph of the most ultra enemies of the South." "Abolitionism has for 20 years been the curse and bane of the country," Norman wrote two weeks before the November vote. "It has destroyed its peace—has divided several of the most prominent churches—has broken up the old Whig party—created dissensions between friends and neighbors, and will cause dissolution of the Union." Such warnings were echoed by Democrats throughout the state, but they had been heard so often that their effect was muted. Indeed, on election day, Lincoln actually carried a clear majority of Indiana's vote, while Douglas, his closest competitor by far, fell almost 25,000 votes behind him, capturing only 42.55 percent of the electorate. Even together, Breckinridge and Douglas only attained 47 percent of the vote, down over three percentage points from Buchanan's total in 1856.[108] Having lost the governorship, both houses of the state legislature, and all of Indiana's electoral votes, the Indiana Democrats, in one election, had allowed the opposition to accomplish three feats it had not done singly for 17 years.

6.

One facet of the election returns that all parties could read was that Breckinridge and his platform found little sympathy in Indiana. In the state as a whole he received less than 5 percent of the vote, over 100,000 votes fewer than Douglas. In the Second District, home of many active supporters, Breckinridge and Hoosier Joseph Lane actually polled fewer votes than Bell and his running mate, Edward Everett. In Perry County they only gained six ballots, and in Crawford County only eight. In only three counties, Scott, Orange, and Clark, did they receive over 100 votes; but even in Clark, the home of Jesse Bright, Breckinridge finished behind the other three candidates. Even more appalling to the Bright-Breckinridge

---

107. J.A. Cravens to WHE, October 21, November 25, 1860, English Papers. *New Albany Ledger*, October 13, 1860.

108. Nichols, *Disruption*, 343-344. *Paoli Eagle*, October 25, 1860. *New Albany Ledger*, October 15, May 19, October 23, 1860. Thornbrough, *Civil War Era*, 96. PItchell, *Indiana Votes*, 8-10. The total Indiana presidential tally was Lincoln—139,033; Douglas—115,509; Breckinridge—12,294; Bell—5,306. Burnham, *Presidential Ballots*, 390.

forces, despite their best efforts, Douglas still received 11,013 Second District votes, which constituted a clear majority of the district's electorate. No politician of any stamp could have any doubt that the Democracy of southeast Indiana was a Douglas one, and, concomitantly, that Jesse Bright was finished. Repudiated, suffering from rheumatism, he crept back to Washington a thoroughly beaten politician.[109]

It was not only in Indiana that the Breckinridge ticket fared so poorly. Of the 35 million votes cast in the free states, the Kentuckian received fewer than 100,000, or 2.9 percent. That fact, combined with the majority given Lincoln in the same states, easily gaining him a majority of the electoral votes and thereby the presidency, convinced many southerners that they could not remain in the Union. Immediately after the election the South Carolina legislature unanimously voted to call a state convention to decide whether to secede from the United States. Before November was out, the governments of Georgia, Mississippi, Florida, and Alabama had scheduled similar conventions. Louisiana and Texas followed suit in December. Consequently, before the 36th Congress had barely settled into its second session, seven states had decided that the results of the presidential election were dire enough at least to demand a formal debate on whether or not to stay in the United States. As the increasingly immoderate Robert Toombs explained earlier that year, "I deeply lament that any portion of our people should hug to their bosoms the delusive idea that we should wait for some 'overt act'. I shall consider our ruin already accomplished when we submit to a party whose every principle, whose daily declarations and acts are an open proclamation of war against us."[110]

About the same day English left Indiana for his final congressional session in Washington, Cravens wrote him that "the election of Lincoln [had] open[ed] a wide field for the patriotic efforts of the true men of stature in Congress to save the Union." No doubt Cravens considered English among those 'true men'. And, indeed, while English was certainly willing to seek an accommodation, he was however firmly set against the right of secession, at least in these circumstances. He had already stated his firm anti-secessionist stance in his speech earlier that year in January, and in May he had warned the South that only a "corporal's guard of the Democratic party of the North" would allow for secession "simply because

---

109. Burnham, *Presidential Ballots*, 390, 392, 394, 396, 398, 404, 406, 410. The exact totals for the Second District were Douglas—11,013; Lincoln—8,804; Bell—1,023; Breckinridge—882. *Paoli Eagle,* December 20, 1860.

110. Burnham, *Presidential Ballots*, 246-250, 256. Lincoln received 55 percent of the free state vote and 39.8 percent of the total popular vote for 180 electoral votes; Douglas received 29.5 percent of the national popular vote, and 12 electoral votes: Breckinridge received 18.1 percent of the total popular vote and 72 electoral votes; Bell received 12.6 percent of the total popular vote and 39 electoral votes. Nichols, *Disruption,* 367-373. Robert Toombs to Alexander Stephens, February 10, 1860, in Phillips, *Toombs, Stephens, Cobb,* 466.

of the mere election of an objectionable man to the Presidency."[111] Consequently, he believed he had no choice but to attempt, along with the outnumbered southern moderates and northern Democrats, to thread the ever decreasing eye of the needle and come up with some plan to calm the South while satisfying the majority of the North.

The basic plan in the House of Representatives was to form a select committee of 33 congressmen, one from each state. These men would hear suggestions from other congressmen, and they would take those suggestions, discuss them, and eventually report back to the House resolutions designed to hold the nation together. On December 4, the second day of the session, the House agreed to this procedure, English voting in the majority along with 144 other congressmen. Generally basing his appointments from each state on the party that held the most congressmen in each state's delegation, speaker Pennington (with Sherman's assistance) composed a committee of 16 Republicans, 14 Democrats, and 3 southern Americans. But in composing the committee in this manner there was not one northern Democrat on it, and only two southern Democrats could have been called moderates. This was not an auspicious beginning.[112]

At the end of the first week of Congress, and about a week before the Committee of Thirty-Three properly organized itself, a southern caucus was held to try to agree on resolutions to present to the aforementioned committee. The proposals coming out of this caucus were an admixture of radical and moderate suggestions. They moderately maintained that states be admitted to the Union only when their population was sufficient to entitle them to a congressman, that a territory was to be admitted as a state with or without slavery as its constitution directed, and that the cost of recapturing fugitive slaves should be paid by the state to which they escaped. As well, no mention was made of reinstating the African Slave Trade, a popular radical idea at the moment. But while these proposals could reasonably be debated by the sections, two others attached to them were deal breakers. One called for the 'common territories' of the United States to be open to all citizens with assurances that the property they take there would be protected—in other words, the Breckinridge platform—and the other required that Congress could never legislate against the existence of slavery in the territories, an essential denial of the effectuation of the Republican platform. In all likelihood southern radicals realized that at least these last two resolutions could never be accepted by the Committee of Thirty-Three or the full House, and the rejection of them would

---

111. J.A. Cravens to WHE, November 25, 1860, English Papers. *CG, 36-1,* 317, 1912. For the breakdown in congress and the possible existence of a middle group, see Nichols, *Disruption,* 388-393.

112. Nichols, *Disruption,* 393-394. *CG, 36-2,* 6, 22. Nichols, 394-395. According to the Pennington/Sherman formula for party representation from each state, Illinois should have gotten a Democrat, as the delegation was five to four in that party's favor. When a state's congressional delegation was equally divided, that state's presidential preference was apparently taken into consideration.

further their goal of secession. Nevertheless, this is the best the moderate southerners could produce.[113]

On Monday December 12, a slew of congressmen presented their own suggested resolutions. These included William English, whose formula typically denoted a middle-ground that took some elements from past experience:

1. The territories of the U.S. to be equitably divided between the slaveholding and non-slaveholding sections, slavery to be prohibited in that portion set apart for the non-slaveholding, and to be recognized in that portion set apart for the slaveholding section, the status of each upon the subject of slavery to remain unchanged during the territorial condition; but when the population in any portion of the territory set apart to either section shall equal or exceed the ratio required for a representative in Congress, and the people shall have formed and ratified a constitution, and asked admission into the Union as a state, such state shall be admitted with or without slavery, as such constitution may prescribe.

2. The rights of property in slaves in the slaveholding States, and in the portion of the Territory set apart for the slaveholding section, shall not be destroyed or impaired by legislation in Congress, in the Territories or in the non-slaveholding states; and whenever a fugitive slave shall be rescued from his master, while *in transitu,* through any non-slaveholding state, city, county or township in which such rescue is made shall be liable to the master in double the value of the slave, recoverable in U.S. courts.[114]

The most striking feature of English's proposals was the essential restoration of the Missouri Compromise-like solution to the territories, that is, the right of Congress to legislate upon the status of slavery in the territories. In doing so, he essentially contradicted the solution of popular sovereignty. This was a remarkable turnabout. He also clearly noted that no state could enter the Union without the people of that entering state voting upon their constitution, an anti-Lecompton position. For the South, he promised land open to slavery, at least during the territorial stage in parts of the West, and made illegitimate personal liberty laws. To be sure this compromise would satisfy neither the majority of Republicans, whose platform demanded the non-extension of slavery in any of the territories, nor the majority of southern representatives, who demanded the protection of slavery in *all* the territories. Its chances of being adopted, then, were less than slim. But it did illustrate English's ability to change his stance to meet the crisis, somewhat

---

113. Nichols, *Disruption,* 397.

114. *CG, 36-2,* 78.

reminiscent of the Lecompton conference committee. While it was the defeat of the Democracy in 1860 that produced his flexibility, it was still a legitimate attempt to compromise and should be commended, even taking into account his virulent racism expressed the previous May.

But eight days after English's proposal, and obviously before the Committee of Thirty-Three could recommend any compromise resolutions, South Carolina formally seceded from the Union. The focus then shifted to Mississippi, Alabama, and Florida, where conventions were scheduled in the second week of January. Between these two time periods, a number of congressmen curiously took an extended Christmas holiday– among them was English. Aware that the Committee of Thirty-Three would not report its resolutions out for a couple of weeks and responsibly paired with Republican Clark B. Cochrane of New York, English returned to Indiana to get a sense of the sentiment of his constituents. While there he essentially found, especially among Democrats, a strong willingness to yield much to the South. As early as mid-November, the *New Albany Ledger* had urged Republicans to heed the crisis by repealing all personal liberty laws and abandoning their doctrine of congressional restriction of slavery in the territories. (Both were congruent with English's plan.) Later that month the city of New Albany held a "Union meeting," ostensibly bipartisan but actually attended far more by Democrats than Republicans. It "deprecated any hasty ill-considered action by the South," called for a faithful obedience to the Constitution, and repeated Norman's request that personal liberty laws should be repealed. But most significantly, it resolved in case of war,

> we, as citizens of Indiana, feeling that our proper destiny is with neither of the extremes of a dismembered confederacy, and knowing that we have no cause or quarrel with our immediate neighbors, should deem it a solid duty to so act as to prevent our soil becoming a theatre of bloody strife, except in defense of our own honor and rights.

Putting it another way, a week after South Carolina seceded, Norman wrote that although northern Democrats desired the preservation of the Union, "they do not feel under any obligation to assist in deluging the land with blood merely to preserve the Chicago [Republican] platform, which has been condemned by a majority of more than a million of the people's votes." Norman's last sentence, of course, somewhat misleadingly referred to the fact that in the four-way presidential contest Lincoln received only 39 percent of the total nation's vote. Of course Lincoln was not even on the ballot in eight southern states. Douglas, his closest popular vote competitor, received 29.5 percent, Breckinridge only 18 percent.[115]

---

115. Nichols, *Disruption,* 407-409. *CG, 36-2,* 171, 279. *New Albany Ledger,* December 28, 1860. Hubbart, *Older Middle West,* 150. *Ledger,* November 17, 1860. Elbert, "Southern Indiana Politics," 175-176. *Ledger,* November 30, December 28, 1860. Burnham, *Presidential Ballots,* 246, 888.

What English gleaned from such expressions was that while all terms of compromise might not be acceptable, coercion was out of the question. Possessing both economic and familial ties with the South and fully sympathetic with its anti-Republican ideals, Second District Democrats wanted no part of a civil war. Even as far north as Indianapolis, the *Indiana State Sentinel* advocated that the state maintain "a separate sovereignty" should the nation divide. The most extreme statement, one which opened southern Indiana to charges of treason, was that made by citizens of Perry County meeting on New Year's Day in Cannelton. After calling typically for "honorable concessions" and the repeal of personal liberty laws, the citizens resolved

> that if no concessions and compromises can be obtained and a disunion shall unfortunately be made between the Northern and Southern States, then the commercial, manufacturing, and agricultural interests of the people of this County require us to say that we can not consent that the Ohio River shall be the boundary line of the contending nations, and we earnestly desire that if a line is to be drawn between the North and the South that line shall be found north of us.

The vote was 99 to 55 in favor of this resolution, reflecting the basic division at the meeting between Democrats and Republicans. A few days later, Washington County passed a similar statement, and the *New Albany Ledger* apparently did not disapprove.[116]

In truth, many Hoosier Republicans were also unwilling to support a policy of coercion. The *Indianapolis Journal* even went so far as to abandon the Republican Chicago platform by advocating the restoration of the Missouri Compromise line and extending it to California, essentially one of English's proposals. It also stated that "the people of the North will never raise an army to force any state to stay in the Union." In the Second District, one of the quickest rising Republicans of New Albany, Walter Q. Gresham, warned governor-elect Lane that he would never fight in any "domestic war." But at least as many Indiana Republicans felt otherwise. Led by Oliver Morton, they consistently denied that any state had the right to secede and warned that South Carolina would leave the Union only "at the point of a bayonet." As 1860 turned into 1861, it was these Republicans who appeared to have the upper hand in the state party, and the *Indianapolis Journal* slowly came around to that position. Unfortunately, primarily because of the death of Orlando Gregg just before the previous October election, the *New Albany Tribune* suspended publication throughout the winter, so it is difficult to

116. Elbert, "Southern Indiana Politics," 182-183. *Indiana State Sentinel,* December 3, 1860. de la Hunt, *Perry County,* 207-208; Hubbart, *Older Middle West,* 164. *New Albany Ledger,* January 12, 1861.

truly ascertain how the Second District opposition to the Democrats generally felt. Most likely, though, it was closer to Gresham than Morton.[117]

Apprised of the conciliatory stance at least among his Democratic constituents, English returned to Washington no later than January 7. While he was gone, the Democratic controlled Senate, in their own special Committee of Thirteen, had come up with what eventually became known as the "Crittenden Plan," named after its chairman and successor to Henry Clay's seat. It proposed a series of constitutional amendments, themselves unamendable, here summarized and commented upon:

1. The restoration of the Missouri Compromise line to California "in all territories now held or hereafter acquired." *Comment*: the 'hereafter acquired' phrase begs southern expansion into Mexico or the Caribbean.

2. The federal protection of slavery in the territories south of the Compromise line. *Comment:* this provision essentially adopts the Breckinridge slave code plank for "half" the territories.

3. The automatic congressional admittance of states when they have the requisite population, with or without slavery as their constitution maintained. *Comment*: this provision did NOT include the necessity for popular ratification, something English's proposal did.

4. No congressional limitation on slavery in states or territories where it is legal.

5. Congress cannot limit slaveholding in Washington, D.C. without a vote of the inhabitants of the District, just compensation to slaveholders, and only if Virginia or Maryland abolishes slavery in either state.

6. The United States would pay compensation to a fugitive slave owner the amount he paid for the slave if he is unable to take hold of the duly convicted fugitive slave because of the execution of state personal liberty laws or violent prevention of such possession. NOTE: A law was proposed in con-

---

117. Stampp, *Indiana in the Civil War,* 52. Kettleborough, "Eve of the Civil War," 186-189. *New Albany Ledger,* January 5, 1861. *Indianapolis Journal,* November 10, 1860. Gresham, *Walter Q. Gresham,* 136. Stampp, 60. *Ledger,* January 19, 1861. Elbert maintains that southern Indiana Republicans were actually more attuned to Morton's stance than the more peaceful position. "Southern Indiana Politics," 165.

nection to this amendment that would nullify the 1850 law's discrepancy of payment to the judicial commissioner in such cases (whereby he would have gotten $10 for declaring the alleged slave a fugitive and $5 for declaring him free) and ensure that payment would be equal in either case. Moreover, a *posse comitatus* would only be formed in cases of "resistance or danger of resistance or rescue" of the alleged slave.

These amendments were almost exclusively concessions to the South and, in truth, would have a difficult time passing the House of Representatives. Indeed, the first and second points above would nullify planks in the Republican platform. Lincoln himself made clear that the first two amendments were unacceptable in a private letter to senator of Illinois Lyman Trumbull: "Let there be no compromise on the question of *extending* slavery. If there be, all our labor is lost and, ere long, must be done again." That these amendments were to be constitutionally unamendable further made them anathema to most Republicans.[118]

Those in the House, like English, who supported the Crittenden Compromise, had Emerson Etheridge, a southern American, present the measures to the House on January 7. The Tennessee congressman had to move a suspension of the rules in order to introduce it, requiring, thus, a two-thirds approval. Rather surprisingly, largely because the southern disunionists abstained from voting, his motion gained a majority of the representatives but fell short of the necessary two-thirds. In the Indiana delegation, English and the rest of the Democracy supported Etheridge, while all the seven Republicans either opposed him or refused to vote. The Democrats back in the state charged that the Hoosier Republican congressmen did not truly represent their rank and file; the *New Albany Ledger* argued that the people of Indiana supported the Crittenden Compromise two to one. But the only official word of the Indiana Republicans, coming from the legislature in Indianapolis, pledged them "to sustain the incoming administration in enforcing the laws and preserving the Union."[119]

Reflecting his district's antipathy toward coercion, English, on January 9, voted against a Republican sponsored resolution calling for an investigation into South Carolina's seizure of most of the federal property in Charleston harbor. Half of the northern Democratic congressmen who voted, including two from Indiana, supported the resolution. The Republicans had been taken aback by the

118. *CG, 36-2,* 279, 114. Nichols, *Disruption,* 433. Smith, *Schuyler Colfax,* 145-146. *New Albany Ledger,* January 7, 1861. Abraham Lincoln to Lyman Trumbull, December 10, 1860, in Philip van Doren Stern, ed., *The Life and Writings of Abraham Lincoln* (New York: The Modern Library, 1940), 616.

119. Nichols, *Disruption,* 434. *CG, 36-2,* 279. *New Albany Ledger,* January 12, 1861. Stampp, *Indiana in the Civil War,* 63. On January 8, the Indiana Democracy, in convention, approved the Crittenden Compromise. *Ledger,* February 10, 1861.

popularity of the Crittenden Compromise, and they clearly intended by this resolution to remind the North that much southern behavior, abetted by the free state
Democracy, was treasonous. Indeed, on January 9, 10, and 11, Mississippi, Florida, and Alabama followed the Palmetto state out of the Union. On January 14, at
the last meeting of the House Committee of Thirty-Three, that Republican controlled group countered Crittenden with its own report. Refusing substantially to
yield the Chicago platform, it did allow for the repeal of the personal liberty laws,
the faithful execution of the Fugitive Slave Law (with, however, an amendment
that allowed a jury trial for the alleged fugitive), the immediate admission of New
Mexico with its slave code as a state into the Union after it wrote a state constitution (Republicans believed it would actually write a free state constitution), and,
perhaps most significantly, a constitutional amendment guaranteeing the rights of
slaveholders in the slave states.[120]

As the Committee put its finishing touches on these resolutions, English
gained the floor in the House. He attempted to introduce a resolution recommending the Crittenden plan "as an equitable and honorable compromise," and
instructing the Committee of Thirty-Three "to carry that plan into practical effect." When Owen Lovejoy of Illinois, the brother of an abolitionist editor who
was murdered decades earlier, objected to this motion, English moved to suspend
the rules. But because the morning hour had not yet expired, Pennington ruled
that such a motion could not be entertained. English thereupon gave notice that
he would "endeavor to get the floor hereafter" for the same purpose, but when
he did, the House refused to accede to his motion, 79 to 71. Exactly why he attempted such a futile gesture probably had to do with simple politics, that is, to
show the Republicans up as lacking concern for the breakup of the Union. At any
rate, the next day Thomas Corwin, Chairman of the Committee of Thirty-Three,
made the Committee's report the special order for January 21, six days hence.
In the meantime, Georgia also seceded, making five states that declared themselves out of the Union and 25 representatives who were no longer attending the
House.[121]

On the appointed day for debate concerning the House Committee's report,
English rose again to introduce the Crittenden program as a basis for settlement.
Sherman asked his colleague if his resolution was "introduced simply for reference [to the House Committee]." English responded that it was not; that it was
introduced as "an expression of the opinion of the House, and I wish to have it
voted upon now." He added that he hoped "the other side of the House will give
us an opportunity of voting on this proposition." But the Republicans were hardly
going to put themselves on record against Crittenden if they could help it, and

---

120. *CG, 36-2*, 296. Nichols, *Disruption*, 445. Nevins, *Emergence of Lincoln, vol. 2*, 408-409.

121. *CG, 36-2*, 362, 365, 378.

his motion to introduce was brusquely defeated, 90 to 62. (One must remember, now, that the Republican margin of victory would be continually strengthened as the seceding states' southern representatives resigned their seats and went home.) After the vote English stated that he "wish[ed] to call the attention of the country to the fact that the Republican side of the House will not ever allow us to have a vote on the proposition." So markedly a statement for pure political consumption did not go unanswered, and Galusha Grow haughtily responded that "the Republican side of the House will vote when it pleases them." Soon after, Dan Sickles's more direct motion to substitute the Crittenden Compromise for the Committee's report was similarly brushed aside.[122]

A few days later, English received another solicitation from congressman-elect Cravens to "do all you can to save the Union," but little it appeared could be done along any lines but Republican ones. For the next few weeks English's constituents busied themselves by passing resolution after resolution supporting Crittenden; some even demanding that it be put to a national referendum. In Congress, English presented three of these resolutions, one from the Common Council of New Albany, one from 180 citizens of Orange County, and one from 110 citizens from rural Floyd. In the meantime, Louisiana and Texas had joined the five other lower South states in leaving the Union, and together these seven states provisionally formed the Confederate States of America in Montgomery, Alabama on February 4. Eight slave states still formally remained in the United States, and a Peace Conference trying to repair the breach was convened in the nation's capital on the same day that the provisional government in Montgomery was formed. In the end, the 21 states that sent delegates to the conference succeeded in primarily endorsing the Crittenden Compromise; the crucial provision extending the Missouri Compromise line passed by simply one vote. Oliver Morton, now governor when Henry Lane was voted into the Senate, allowed Indiana to participate in the conference, but kept the appointment of representatives in his own hands. Consequently, each Hoosier delegate was a Republican, and all of them (excluding perhaps Thomas Slaughter from the Second District) chiefly wished to keep the conference in session long enough to prevent the upper South from seceding before Lincoln's inauguration.[123]

---

122. *Ibid.*, 498, 499, 502.

123. J.A. Cravens to WHE, January 20, 1861, English Papers. Examples of such Indiana "Union" meetings can be found in the *New Albany Ledger*, January 21, 27, 29, 31, February 12, 22, 23, 1861, and in the *Paoli Eagle*, January 24, February 7, 1861. *CG, 36-2*, 194-5. Robert Gray Gunderson, *Old Gentlemen's Convention: The Washington Peace Conference of 1861* (Madison: University of Wisconsin Press, 1961), 6, 9-10, 86-87, 89. States *not* represented at the Peace Conference were the seven seceded states, the western states of Oregon and California, and Arkansas, Michigan, and Minnesota. Nevins, *Emergence of Lincoln, vol. 2*, 411. On Indiana's participation see *Ledger*, February 2, 4, 5, 1861; Thornbrough, *Civil War Era*, 102. Elbert, "Southern Indiana Politics," 174. Indiana's Peace Commissioners were Slaughter, E.W. H. Ellis, Godlove Orth, Caleb Smith, and P.A. Hackelman.

In the last week of February, as the Peace Conference concluded its ineffective labors, and the Confederate government ended its first month of existence, the House finally got around to voting on the Report of the Committee of Thirty-Three. Directly preceding these votes were a couple of last-ditch attempts at Democratic substitutes. One proposal called for the gathering of a national convention to amend the Constitution in order to "afford more sufficient guarantees to the diversified and growing interests of the government." Even English understood that such a proposal merely grasped at straws. He averred that he was "in favor of a convention if no better mode can be agreed on for settling our difficulties," but still having his heart set on the Crittenden amendments he voted against the convention. It went down to defeat easily, 108 to 74, despite the fact that some Republicans were disposed to support it. But the key vote on February 27 was the one that finally was taken to substitute the Crittenden resolutions for the Committee's report, a vote that English, Millson, Sickles, and all other Democratic compromisers had been hoping to force all along. They finally had their day, but the depleted ranks of the Democracy were no match for the Republicans. Every southerner left in Congress voted for Crittenden except three, as did all the northern Democrats but two, yet it buckled under the united weight of the Republican congressmen. The final tally showed 80 votes for it and 113 against, every single Republican congressman on the floor voting against it except William Millward of Pennsylvania and Charles H. Van Wyck of New York.[124]

Once the Crittenden formula was defeated, the massaged proposals of the Committee of Thirty-Three became the next order of business. Although English considered the Republican program hardly conciliatory enough to satisfy even the upper South, he overcame his disappointment and patriotically got behind it. The first formal resolution combined two provisions that were pro-southern (that each state repeal its personal liberty laws and a provision making unlawful invasions into other states) with two pro-northern stipulations (that there was no sufficient cause for secession and that the federal government had a duty to "enforce Federal Law and protect Federal property"). This hodgepodge resolution passed the House, 136 to 53, only radical Republicans and southern Democrats voting against it. Except for Charles Case of Fort Wayne, every Hoosier congressman supported it. Next up was the constitutional amendment prohibiting the federal government from interfering with slavery in the slave states. At first this failed the necessary two-thirds for a proposed constitutional amendment, but the next day it was reconsidered and passed by three votes, 133 to 65. This time while Democrats Niblack, Holman, Davis, and English all continued to vote with the

---

124. *CG, 36-2,* 1258, 1261.

Committee, three of the Indiana Republicans—Case, Pettit, and James Wilson—broke away. They could not accept perpetual slavery in the United States.[125]

For a Republican-dominated committee, these above provisions were remarkably even-handed. But the whole compromise attempt foundered when the Committee's proposed bill to admit New Mexico directly upon the territory's writing a constitution was tabled 115 to 71. English, of course, voted to keep it alive. It failed because it was clever by half. Despite the existent slave code in New Mexico, southern Democrats voted 20 to 13 to table it because the able among them understood that once it came to writing a constitution, slavery would be prohibited there. And a vast majority of Republicans voted to table it (75 to 23) because they could not go back on the Chicago platform's promise to essentially oppose popular sovereignty. In truth, these Republicans voted against the measure for the same reason they voted against Crittenden: they had won the 1860 election, and the extension of slavery would not be permitted, however unlikely it would be in the New Mexico case. After refusing to hold the olive branch out on New Mexico, the Republicans then went ahead and passed a change in the Fugitive Slave Law that would have allowed the accused fugitive a jury trial. (No recorded vote was shown for English on this bill.) In the end, despite the Committee's prodigious efforts, there wasn't enough "give" in the full proposal to satisfy the South or the non-moderate Republicans. Predictably, only the northern Democrats could support it. (The Senate eventually voted for the amendment prohibiting the federal government from interfering with slavery in the slave states, 24 to 12, the minimum possible approval, but events within seven weeks would make any ratification impossible.)[126]

On the last full day of the session English cast his final vote for continued conciliation when the Republicans proposed to suspend the rules in order to allow introduction of a bill providing for the collection of import duties in the face of anticipated "unlawful obstruction." The measure allowed for the president to move customs houses to a "secure place," even upon a naval vessel, and it authorized him to use force in his application of the law. All the Indiana Republicans, along with Democrat William Holman, supported the measure, but English, Niblack, and even J.G. Davis continued to oppose any semblance of coercion to the last. They still hoped for a peaceful accommodation, and upon this they were at one with their constituents. But the House adjourned *sine die* later in the day having accomplished really nothing to avert the present and coming crisis. Two days later, at 12 PM, the remaining representatives drifted into the noonday sun to hear the new president deliver his inaugural address.[127]

---

125. *Ibid.,* 1263, 1264, 1285.

126. *Ibid.,* 1327, 1328-1336. Nevins, *Emergence of Lincoln, vol. 2,* 407-410. CG, 36-2, 1403.

127. *Ibid.,* 1422-1423, 1433.

7.

William English entered Congress as a young man of 31. Now, after four consecutive terms, he was about to retire to Indiana, never to return to Washington as an official representative of his constituents. He had served his district, his party, and his nation for eight years, and, in the process, he had received a certain measure of national prominence. He was still only 38, but from all he had been through, he must have felt considerably older. In no similar span of American history has crisis upon crisis followed one another with such methodical consistency. From the introduction of the Kansas-Nebraska Bill a mere 30 days after English assumed his duties, to the formation of the Confederate States of America some 30 days before he ended them, he found himself in the midst of a bubbling cauldron he could neither cool nor control. To be sure, it was not for want of trying, but the historical force of antislavery unleashed too much heat for both him and his party. Having always appealed to the conservative self-interest of individual white Americans, he was ill-equipped to combat the superior strength of awakened morality and understandably perceived injustice.

As he stood in the crowd before Willard's Hotel awaiting the president-elect's arrival, he probably doubted that war could be averted. He had already read Lincoln's comments made at Indianapolis on February 11 that appeared to support a policy of coercion. "From what source came the right of a state, a small part of the whole, to break up the nation and play tyrant over the rest," Lincoln asked his Hoosier audience on that day, rhetorically wondering "whether holding the forts and other federal property and collecting the revenues [could possibly] constitute invasion or coercion." In his congressional speech a year ago, English had warned that the South could not expect secession to go unchallenged, and it appeared that the president-elect was bearing out this warning. Yet some of Lincoln's pre-inaugural statements had sounded a bit more conciliatory, so it was with keen anticipation that English awaited the address. If he had hoped that the new president would reconcile his apparent ambiguities, he was sadly mistaken. On the one hand, Lincoln reiterated his authority "to hold, occupy, and possess the property and places belonging to the government, and to collect the duties and imposts"; on the other, he averred that he would not go "beyond what may be necessary for those objects...there will be no invasion—no use of force against or among the people anywhere."[128] English, a man who had also chosen words carefully to find some moderate ground between the extremes, may well have wondered if Lincoln, like he, deceived himself with their power.

However English felt, back in the Second District the Democrats wasted little time criticizing the inaugural. It "will sadly disappoint the hopes of those who be-

---

128. Nevins, *Emergence of Lincoln, vol. 2,* 457. Stampp, *Indiana in Civil War,* 68. Harold Syrett, *American Historical Documents* (New York: Barnes and Noble, 1960), 271.

lieved he would take a position that would preserve the peace of the country and avoid the horrors of Civil War," the *New Albany Ledger* intoned. "His message, though abounding in soft words, breathes warlike *acts.*" A week later Norman wrote concerning the surrounded Fort Sumter, one of only two forts in the seceded states still flying the American flag:

> It is quite certain that the fort cannot be reinforced or provisioned without a collision with the South Carolina troops, and it is a question whether the barren honor of holding a fort in a State which has ceased her connection with the Union will outweigh in value the blood which will inevitably be shed to accomplish that end, involving, as it undoubtedly would, collisions elsewhere.

And on March 19, the *Ledger* continued to counsel conciliation, arguing that a policy of accommodation would prevent further secession "and eventually build up a party in the seceded states sufficiently strong to bring them back into the Union." (Interestingly, for a time this was close to Lincoln's own position.) The *Paoli Eagle* predictably agreed, though it was less concerned with the ultimate preservation of the Union. "If the difficulties between the North and South can not be amicably settled," Comingore wrote on March 7, "the people of the North will never consent that the South shall be forced to remain in the Union." Two weeks later he suggested that "the administration should withdraw from the forts, as it would meet with the approval of the masses of the American people of all parties."[129]

Although the *Paoli Eagle* appeared a bit extreme, the *New Albany Ledger*, as usual, generally reflected Democratic opinion around the state. In the state legislature, the Democratic Party had for two months been trying to commit Indiana to a course congruent with the Crittenden resolutions, and lately it had been attempting to limit governor Morton's authority over the state militia. On March 8, state senator Stosenberg, a Democrat from Floyd, introduced three resolutions unanimously agreed upon in the party's caucus. They basically proposed that the president reconvene Congress and call for a national convention with authority to propose and consider constitutional amendments. Initially these ideas received scant consideration from the Republican majority, but on March 11, the Republicans did allow a resolution to pass that stated that although the Constitution appeared sufficient to meet the crisis, "inasmuch as a misunderstanding exists relative to its interpretation," a convention might be helpful. Even this, however, Morton opposed.[130]

---

129. *New Albany Ledger,* March 5, 12, 19, 1861. *Paoli Eagle,* March 7, 21, 1861.

130. *New Albany Ledger,* March 8, 12, 1861.

Early in April, while still in Washington, English addressed a letter to Cravens asking the new congressman what Indiana might do in event of war. Many Democrats had been suggesting a neutral attitude and even the formation of a Northwestern Confederacy; others, reflecting the Perry County resolution of January, were actually prepared to join the South. Cravens responded that he did not know, but he curiously added that he wouldn't mind creating a new state out of the southern halves of Indiana and Illinois in order to avoid being dragged into a war with the South. "I cannot obviate the fact that our interest is with the South, and I cannot reconcile to separation, and it will be the last day in the [unintelligible] before I consent to fight them." In this response to English, Cravens gave credence to the suspicions that he was not up to the demands of his new office, but it may well be that his sentiments received widespread approbation in southern Indiana. "I am ready to recognize the Southern confederacy as a government de facto," he wrote English on April 9, "and to treat it as such, amicably adjusting all questions at issue affecting the rights of person and property."[131]

Eerily, despite the crisis of the moment, venal politics went on as usual, for having won the federal administration for the first time, the Republicans were eager for the patronage. In the Second District this meant especially the postmastership of New Albany, a position that in February attracted 13 suitors. The Republican who would be appointed would not be replacing longtime loyal English Democrat Frank Gwin, for he had died at only 30 years of age on January 6. W.J. Newkirk, a Breckinridge man English at best did not oppose, was appointed Gwin's short successor. The *New Albany Ledger,* not completely happy with this appointment, soon sarcastically noted that Newkirk's unfamiliarity with his duties had forced him to hire an assistant fully versed in post office work. English, having once been a friend of Newkirk's, probably allowed the appointment because of its obviously brief tenure. As usual, he saved himself for more important matters. In this case it was the reappointment of his uncle, Sam S. English, as the surveyor of the port of Louisville. A strong Douglas man, Sam had been replaced by the Buchanan administration late in its tenure, and English had fought to have him reinstated. Despite Buchanan's high regard for his young friend, he could not impose his will on the Breckinridge Democrats in Kentucky, and for quite some time English's appeals went unheeded. It is quite possible that English acquiesced in the appointment of Newkirk in exchange for the reinstatement of his uncle, for in February Sam English received his position back. In a letter to his nephew later that month, Sam thanked him for his assistance, adding that the Republicans had promised to keep him in office. To the last, English played politics competently.[132]

---

131. J.A. Cravens to WHE, April 9, 1861, English Papers. Elbert, "Southern Indiana," 175, 177-178, 181-190.

132. *New Albany Ledger,* February 13, 1861. Frank Gwin died of inflammation of the bowels. *Ledger,* January 7, 1861. *Ledger,* January 30, February 24, 1861. Jesse Bright to WHE, August 19, 1857; S.S. English to

Although the Republicans worked with the Douglas Democrats in the loyal slave states once in power, they had no such intentions in southern Indiana. To the definite dismay, but not surprise, of the Second District Democracy, the successor to Newkirk was none other than John M. Wilson, English's opponent in the congressional elections of 1856 and 1858. Wilson had slowly but certainly left his Know-Nothing antecedents behind, and by 1861 he was one of the staunchest Morton Republicans in the state. Backed by both the governor and senator Lane, he was officially appointed on March 29, although two weeks earlier it was clear that his appointment was inevitable when "his office was crowded all day by the faithful of the Party, anxious to know what course to pursue to obtain a share of the spoils." During the same period, English received an even more personal reminder of the transfer of power when, on March 14, senator Lane penned him a note requesting that he immediately notify his father to send in his resignation as United States marshal. Some faithful Republican, of course, had to be appointed in his stead.[133]

These preoccupations with the patronage, along with the general pro-southern or neutral spirit of the Second District Democracy, substantially dissolved when reports reached Indiana of the southern bombardment of Fort Sumter. Norman, who as late as April 9 had been burned in effigy by New Albany Republicans, quickly used his *Ledger* to rally the district around Lincoln's call for volunteers. "The indications throughout the North are that the people intend to sustain the government in the position they have taken for maintaining the integrity of the Union, the *Ledger* noted on April 18. "Whatever differences may have originally existed, it is now the manifest duty of every citizen to do all he can to maintain the honor of the country." "There is no party," Norman concluded, "this is not the time for party." In Clark County, resolutions were passed by Democrats committing themselves to loyally sustain the government, and in Washington County, John I. Morison presided over a meeting that resolved that "secession was treason, that the South was responsible for the War, and that the government should be commended and respected for its call to arms." Even Horace Heffren, the most obstinate of Democrats in the state legislature, completely turned around and devoted himself to the Union; his newspaper, the *Salem Democrat*, did likewise.[134]

Historians have generally argued that the South's attack on the American flag put everything in a different perspective; and many Democrats who formally

WHE, February 2, 1861, English Papers. *Ledger,* February 27, 1861. Mott to WHE, February 20, 1861; S.S. English to WHE, February 26, 1861, English Papers.

133. The *New Albany Ledger,* on March 9, 1860, made note of Wilson's complete adoption of Republican principles. *Cincinnati Commercial,* in *Ledger,* March 16, 1861. *Ledger,* March 28, 12, 1861. Henry S. Lane to WHE, March 14, 1861, English Papers.

134. *New Albany Ledger,* April 17, 18, 22, May 9, 1861. *History of Orange, Warwick, and Washington,* 513. Elbert, "Southern Indiana Politics," 198.

criticized coercion now saw the issue as one of defense of the Union's honor. Not all Second District Democrats, however, were so eager to follow the government. Some who sustained its policy nevertheless hoped that an all out conflict could still be avoided; others, like Comingore, argued that it was Lincoln's attempted reinforcement of Fort Sumter, even with non-military provisions, enabling it to hold out, that constituted the real initiation of hostilities. Some of these Democrats found their way into the Knights of the Golden Circle, a southern Indiana group based in Orange County that blatantly opposed the United States throughout the war. But in the main, partly because Kentucky remained loyal, southeastern Indiana Democrats faithfully supported the government. Much like with Pearl Harbor 80 years later, the nation became unified upon attack. As William Holman wrote Allen Hamilton the day after Sumter was bombarded, "I would not *coerce a State* (what fool ever thought or talked of doing so) but I would defend the property of the American people wherever it may be, and sustain the American flag, wherever it rightfully waves at every hazard."[135] These sentiments may not have been deeply analyzed, but they were strongly and emotionally held.

Of all of the Second District Democrats who declared their fealty to the Union, no one was more influential than William H. English. On April 20, in Lexington, at a grand Union meeting of Scott County, he made a decisive speech in support of the government. He told the crowd that he completely disapproved of secession and could never support it, and that although he still opposed Republican doctrines, as a native Hoosier his complete allegiance was to Indiana and the United States. He stated that he hoped that peace could soon be regained, but so long as the war lasted it must be closely pressed. When the county resolved to form a Home Guard, English enlisted as a private, and when the Stars and Stripes were raised atop a tall hickory pole, Scott County's first citizen helped pull the cord. He left no doubt where he stood, the compromises, moderation, and appeals to sectional harmony having come to an end.[136]

During that summer English liberally donated his money to the Union cause. The full first company of the district, from Washington County, was partially outfitted by his $200 contribution. Then, in late August, he became the first Hoosier to lend money to the national government under its call for subscriptions. He mailed $5,000 to the secretary of the treasury, understandably boasting to Indiana's designated collector that he "made the tender even before the government's appeal to the public." Such patriotic generosity could hardly go unnoticed, and on

---

135. In Clark and Harrison counties Democrats held meetings disavowing enmity toward Kentucky. *New Albany Ledger,* April 27, 30, 1861. *Paoli Eagle,* April 18, 1861. Throughout May and June the *Eagle* continued to call for compromise. On the Knights of the Golden Circle, see Dillard, *Orange County Heritage,* 178, 196, 199, and Perry, *Indiana in the Mexican War,* 334. Holman to Allen Hamilton, April 13, 1861, in Blake, *The Holmans,* 96.

136. *Madison Courier,* in *New Albany Ledger,* April 25, 1861.

October 3, the *Madison Courier* wished to honor one whom it so often attacked. "The sympathizers with rebellion are ferocious in their denunciations of patriotic Democrats who have in this crisis determined to sink their party affiliation and to support the President," Garber began, noting that in their denunciations that

> no man has been more abused than Hon. W. H. English. Like all his Party, he seemed willing to grant almost anything but the Constitution and the Union for the sake of peace, and to maintain the integrity of the party; but the Union he would not give up; and now, by precept and example he is sustaining the President of the United States. He talks for the Union, works for it, and subscribes liberally of his means to the public loan.

The time for accommodation had ended, and in the words of a Scott County Democratic resolution of September 7, "the war must be vigorously prosecuted until an honorable peace can be obtained."[137]

---

137. English Scrapbook, 159. WHE to William Ray, September 8, 1861, English Papers. *Madison Courier* October 3, 1861, in English Scrapbook, 162. *New Albany Ledger,* September 13, 1861.

Epilogue

Although he remained active in Democratic politics for the rest of his life, after 1861 William English never again held public office. Instead, not yet 40 years old, he prematurely began to serve as one of the Party's respected elder statesmen. A clear "War Democrat," governor Morton offered English a command of an Indiana regiment, but, as his expertise was not in military affairs, he turned that offer down. He did, however, accept appointment as provost marshal for the Second Congressional District and in this position was most likely responsible for the physical security of the area. As the war progressed, he continued to preach what many considered the fundamental precepts of the northern Democracy. "Let us firmly stand together under the old flag and in the old organization, fighting secession to the bitter end," he counseled his fellow Democrats in 1862, "[but] it should not be forgotten that a generous support of the administration in all proper and legitimate measures is one thing, and a blind adherence to ruinous fanaticism and monstrous corruptions is quite another." He fought to the last the policy of slave emancipation, warning that it would only lead to "negroes…being turned loose amongst us to compete with and cheapen labor of white men and women, to fill our poor houses and jails, and demoralize our people." If he had the power, he would have restored "the old Government as it was, leaving the people of the several states to regulate and determine for themselves their own domestic institutions."[1]

These remarks were made in an open letter English wrote to his former constituents on June 23, 1862. He had once again been conspicuously solicited to become a candidate for Congress, and the above comments were contained in a firm note of declension that appeared in the *New Albany Ledger*. His political

---

1. *Commemorative Biographical Sketches of Prominent and Representative Men of Indianapolis and Vicinity, containing Biographical Sketches of Business and Professional Men and of many of the Early Settled Families* (Chicago: J.H. Beers & Co., 1909), 13. English letter of June 23, 1862, printed in *New Albany Ledger,* English Papers. Woolen, *Eminent and Self-Made Men,* District 7, 221. Later English was contacted to help make certain that conscription was "fairly" conducted. Fred Matthis to WHE, March 6, 1863, English Papers.

ambitions, however, were not yet completely quenched. In January of 1863, the Indiana legislature was scheduled to select a United States senator to replace Jesse Bright, and as early as the preceding August, English began to line up support for himself. (Largely because of the Emancipation Proclamation, the Democrats had regained a healthy majority in both houses of the Indiana General Assembly.) As one of his correspondents wrote him, "you are the natural political representative of this section of the State." Unfortunately, during the Civil War, southern Indiana was not a politically advantageous place from which to hail. After two ballots, English, among others, was defeated by the 1860 Democratic nominee for governor, Thomas Hendricks. English had solidly received the votes of two districts, the Second and Ninth, but a combination of forces from northern Indiana sealed his fate. Never again would he seek the Party's nomination for any office bestowed by Hoosiers.[2]

The Senatorial defeat closed the chapter in English's life devoted to holding direct political power; and almost immediately it was followed by what may perhaps be described as his most successful period. Ever since the same month that he had completed his duties as congressman, William had begun to investigate the possibilities of entering the banking field. In the spring of 1861, he had toyed with the idea of taking control of the branch of the state bank at Jeffersonville. He received the cautious support of Hugh McCulloch, the president of the Indiana State Bank; and Jesse Bright pledged at least $25,000 in stock should English give his "sole and personal attention to the transaction of [its] business." But the events at Fort Sumter discouraged him, and it was actually not until 1863 that English finally and firmly decided to enter the banking world. It was in that year, on February 25, that Congress, in order to better finance the war, passed the National Banking Act. It authorized the establishment of national banks, which were required to invest one-third of their funds in United States securities. In return, these banks were allowed to issue notes up to 90 percent of these holdings. English immediately recognized both the financial and patriotic potential of such institutions, and using the contacts he had made while a regent of the Smithsonian, he soon raised the money to establish the First National Bank of Indianapolis. English administered this bank as president for 14 years, turning an original capital of $150,000 into $1 million by 1877, and, incidentally, keeping it open and functioning during the Recession of 1873.[3]

---

2. George S. Bicknell to WHE, August 22, 1862; "N" to WHE, January 14, 1863; English Papers. Thornbrough, *Civil War Era*, 122. Shepherd, *Biographical Directory*, 521-523. Bicknell to WHE, August 22, 1862; David Turpie to WHE, January 23, 1863, English Papers.

3. Hugh McCulloch to WHE, March 27, 1861; Jesse Bright to WHE, March 31, April 14, 1861, English Papers. Morris, ed., *Encyclopedia of American History*, 239. Woolen, *Eminent and Self-Made Men*, District 7, 221-222. *Commemorative Biographical Sketches*, 13.

Already wealthy before the war (his assets in Scott County alone were worth well over $100,000), English was probably the richest man in Indianapolis by the mid-1870s. His investments obliged him to pay taxes to 10 other states besides Indiana, the total amounting to about $10,000 a year. Such investments were primarily in real estate, but he had also acquired the controlling interest in all railway lines in Indianapolis. Having financially conquered about all that he could, he resigned as Bank president on July 25, 1877, the other stockholders naturally expressing their regret. Within three years he completely liquidated his assets; his wealth then exceeding several million dollars.[4]

Although from 1863 English resided at Indianapolis, he continued to own land in Scott County for a decade, and at least until the end of the Civil War, he remained active in district politics. In 1864, for example, he was instrumental in denying John A. Cravens a third term, promoting instead the successful candidacy of his young New Albany friend, Michael C. Kerr. (Kerr would be elected speaker of the House to the 44th congress in 1875.) In 1864, English also supported the presidential bid of Democratic nominee George B. McClellan. It appears, however, that his business responsibilities increasingly cut into the time he could devote to political activity, so that for the next 13 years he became somewhat of a political spectator. Indeed, his only public political pronouncement in this period occurred in 1876, when he was moved to preside at an Indianapolis meeting ratifying the presidential nomination of Samuel J. Tilden. He had been apparently led to speak out in order to chastise the greenbackers in the Indiana Democracy who were dissatisfied with Tilden's conservative economics. "I contend there is nothing in the St. Louis platform upon the subject of finances about which Democrats should differ," he declared,

> It repudiates a changeable standard of values, and advocates that standard which is recognized in our Constitution as well as by the whole civilized world. It proposes to secure to our own people real dollars, that shall have as much purchasing power as the dollars of other nations. It secures to the farmer, the mechanic and the laborer, a dollar that will have as great a purchasing power as the dollar of the bond-holder. It secures to the manufacturer and the men of business that reasonable degree of certainty as to the financial future which will enable him to make investments and engage in business with some intelligence and feeling of security, which he never can have with a changeable standard of values. In short, it but reaffirms the old and time-honored doctrine of the Democratic party in favor of a currency of specie, and paper convertible to specie on demand.

---

4. 1860 Census, Lexington Township, Scott County, June 20, 1860, Microfilm, Indiana State Library, Indianapolis, Indiana. *Indianapolis People,* December 29, 1872, in English Scrapbook, 163. Wilson, *Lexington,* 126. Woolen, *Eminent and Self-Made Men,* District 7, 222, 224.

It is true the platform places the Democratic party fairly and squarely upon the road to specie payments, but it does not propose to accomplish it by such hasty and inconsiderate legislation as will be unnecessarily oppressive to creditors or injurious to business.

Conservative as a young Democratic politician on the issue of slavery in the 1850s, he remained conservative as the older Democratic banker on the monetary issue in the 1870s and beyond.[5]

Just prior to the time when English had resigned his Bank presidency, great changes occurred within his family. First, on November 14, 1874, his father, Elisha Gale, died from hemorrhaging during surgery. He had been active until the last day of his life. Refusing to forsake politics, he was again elected to the State Senate in 1865. In 1867, William appointed him vice president of the Street Railway Company and a director of the First National Bank, and he held both these posts until the day he died. As late as 1872, when he was 74 years of age, he continued to make frequent horseback excursions between Lexington and Indianapolis, a 100-mile trek. When asked why he taxed his body so violently, he replied that it "was just for the fun of the thing…and to show the boys what an old man can do." Andrew Jackson, no doubt, would have approved.[6]

Elisha Gale lived a full life, well over the three score and 10 allotted in the Old Testament. But this was not the case with Elisha's daughter-in-law. Exactly two years later, on November 14, 1876, Emma Mardulia Jackson English expired after a long sickness. One English biographer claims that she was "universally loved and respected by all who knew her," but whether she achieved any real measure of happiness or accomplishment is not easy to determine. Quite likely she had difficulty in dealing with her husband's darker side, for even after nine years of marriage, he continued to apologize for the "harsh and unkind" acts he committed when "crossed or misjudged." More significantly, she may have come to resent his energetic pursuit of wealth and power to the exclusion of attention paid to her. But this is sheer speculation. Of what we are certain is that she died before reaching 50 years of age. Fortunately, her last days were made happy by the knowledge that her daughter Rosalind had made a good match, marrying one Willoughby Walling, a well educated physician born in Louisville of Virginia stock. He was also, of course, a Democrat. On Mardulia's grave, William inscribed an epitaph atypically incomplete:

---

5. English Scrapbook, page on 1864 election. *Congressional Biographical Directory,* 1377. Woolen, *Eminent and Self-Made Men,* District 7, 223-224.

6. Wilson, *Lexington,* 124. *Indiana Daily Journal,* November 16, 1874. Shepherd, *Biographical Directory,* 119. Wilson, 123-124.

There was no sorrow on this earth
but touched her heart;
And in a gentle, child-like mirth
she bore her part.[7]

Two other individuals, unrelated by blood, also deserve mention. Between the time of the deaths of Elisha and Mardulia, Jesse Bright died in Baltimore on May 20, 1875. Thirteen years earlier he had been expelled from the United States Senate for having, on March 1, 1861, recommended to Jefferson Davis (whom he then addressed as "His Excellency, President of the Confederation of States") a purveyor of firearms. After failing to regain his Senate seat in 1863, he left Indiana and settled in Kentucky for 11 years. The senatorial contest of 1863, in which both he and English were candidates, appears somewhat to have strained their relationship. English no doubt believed Bright's candidacy divisive and inimical to his own chances and the interests of southern Indiana. After that, although they appear to have patched up their differences, they were no longer on intimate terms. The ex-senator made two trips to Indianapolis in the 1870s, but no evidence exists to show that he called on his former protégé. Because he died and was buried in Maryland, quite likely English did not even attend the funeral.[8]

Finally, there is the tale of the demise of John B. Norman. After their differences in the election of 1860 English and Norman no longer corresponded, though naturally their paths would have crossed at the Democratic congressional conventions of 1862 and 1864. Unlike English, Norman remained in southeastern Indiana the rest of his life, and he continued to edit the *New Albany Ledger* until his death. Tragically that occurred only a few years after the end of the Civil War, on October 30, 1869. The cause was reported to have been an "apoplectic fit." Luciene Matthews, the co-owner of the *Ledger,* edited it solely for the next three years; but, in 1872, he sold it to Josiah Gwin (Frank's brother) and James Kelso, who merged it with the *New Albany Standard,* a newly formed Democratic sheet. Norman's illustrious but now completely forgotten career as editor spanned 20 years. For the standards of the 19th Century he had been exceptionally objective, but, of course, a Democrat through and through.[9]

---

7. Woolen, *Eminent and Self-Made Men,* District 7, 224. WHE to Mardulia, November 18, 1857, English Papers. *The National Cyclopedia of American Biography, vol.* 18 (New York: James T. White and Co., 1922), 209. Mardulia is buried in Crown Heights Cemetery, Indianapolis.

8. Van Der Weele, "Jesse Bright," 305, 265-293. Jesse Bright to WHE, December 31, 1862, January 27, 1863, English Papers. Van Der Weele, 300, 303.

9. Miller, *Indiana Newspaper Biography,* 108.

Neither Elisha, nor Mardulia, nor Bright, nor Norman would thus witness English's last moment in the political sun. In 1879, now two years retired, the incredibly wealthy ex-congressman and ex-banker was selected as chairman of the Democratic State Central Committee. For all his political talents, it was nevertheless no doubt his access to funds that placed him on top of the state party. He was thus Indiana's party chairman when the Democratic National Convention convened at Cincinnati in 1880. At that gathering, Indiana's delegates stood as a unit, casting all their ballots for their former governor, Thomas A. Hendricks. Four years earlier Hendricks, at the end of his gubernatorial term, had received the party's vice-presidential nomination, partly because he was Samuel Tilden's closest competitor and partly because Indiana was a clear swing state. But Hendricks's moment had passed, and besides Indiana's 30 votes on the two ballots conducted in 1880, he only received 19.5 votes more. Yet the convention was not unmindful of the importance of carrying so doubtful and geographically pertinent a state as Indiana, and in a move clearly orchestrated by the party chieftains, William H. English instead was nominated by acclamation for vice president.[10]

English's nomination was thus a function of wealth, geography, his conservative political economy, and Hoosier disappointment. Officially informed of it at his running mate's residence on July 13, 1880, he officially responded with an acceptance letter written from Indianapolis two weeks later. In that letter he fundamentally argued that after 20 years of Republican rule, it was time for a change. "The continuance of that party in power four years longer," he noted, "would not be beneficial to the public, or in accordance with the spirit of our republican institutions." Of the basic policy interests that English saw dividing the two parties, none stood so clearly delineated as the old constitutional one. The Republican Party, he asserted, practiced

> the constant assumption of new and dangerous powers by the general government; the interference of home rule [*the phrase used to 'liberate' the white south*], and with the administration of justice in the courts of the several states; the interference with the elections through the medium of paid, partisan, federal office-holders interested in keeping their party in power [*especially in the South*], and caring more for that than fairness in elections; in fact, the constant encroachments which have been made by that party upon the clearly reserved rights of the people and the states will, if not checked, subvert the liberties of the people and the government of limited powers created by the fathers, and end in a great, consol-

10. Shepherd, *Biographical Directory*, 119. Roseboom, *Presidential Elections*, 109. Bain, *Convention Decisions*, Appendix. Thornbrough, *Civil War Era*, 297. Bain, 120. For the most detailed story of English's nomination and canvass see Handfield, "William H. English," *passim*.

idated central government , 'strong', indeed, for evil and the overthrow of republican institutions.

Realizing that such pronouncements opened the Democracy to the charge of supporting the now-military-defeated notion of state sovereignty and its connection to secession, English added that "in resisting the encroachments of the general government upon the reserved rights of the people and the States, I wish to be distinctly understood as favoring the proper exercise of the general government of the powers rightfully belonging to it under the Constitution." And he hastened to add that "the legitimate results of the war for the Union will not be overthrown or impaired should the Democratic ticket be elected." Concerning the newer issues, he noted that the Democrats supported a "sound currency of honest money," were committed to "encouraging [the] labor, manufacturing, commercial, and business interests of the country in every legitimate way," and were pledged to the "proper restriction" of Chinese immigrants in order to "protect the toiling millions of our own people…from [their] destructive competition." That last point, and the following one that stated that the success of the Democratic Party would "bury, beyond resurrection, the sectional jealousies and hatreds, which have so long been the chief stock in trade of pestiferous demagogues," rather hearkened back to his congressional days in the 1850s.[11]

But English was four years too early, for in 1880 the North was not quite ready to trust the Democracy again. Consequently, the Party suffered defeat, though in some ways quite narrowly. Out of 8,899,368 votes cast for the major party candidates, Republicans James Garfield and Chester Arthur outpolled General William Hancock and English by only 9,464 votes, or .1 percent. But in the Electoral College the result was a healthy 214 to 155, the Democrats only able to carry two states outside the South. Even Indiana went to the Republicans, albeit by a small margin. After this defeat, English retired from electoral politics for the final time. Yet by no means did he remain idle. In the same year he ran for vice president he completed his great Hotel and Opera House situated in the heart of downtown Indianapolis where today's famous Monument Circle presides. In the center of the circle is the grand State Soldiers' Monument that grew out of a resolution English penned suggesting its construction. When the resolution was approved by the city, English became the president of the committee that oversaw its construction. Then, in the last 16 years of his life, he began what may be considered a third career, that of a historian. Diligently collecting correspondence

---

11. Woolen, *Eminent and Self-Made Men*, District 7, 226-227. *Official Proceedings of the National Democratic Convention, Held in Cincinnati, O., June 22d, 23d,* and 24th, *1880 at* https://babel.hathitrust.org/cgi/pt?id=mdp.39015030799442;view=1up;seq=195, 166, 167. No doubt English believed the most pestiferous of those Republican demagogues was Oliver Morton, now senator, and in one year dead.

and material from Indiana's early years, he completed three books on its history. One, *The Conquest of the Northwest,* received special commendation, but he also wrote *The Life of George Rogers Clark* and *History of Indiana,* which were both well received. In this period he also helped establish the Indiana Historical Society and became its first president. In that role he collected short biographies of almost all men who served in the state General Assembly, used later as the basis for a thoroughly researched book on such members.[12]

This complete life lasted just about as long as his father's. On February 7, 1896, having been declared one of the two richest men in the entire state, William H. English finally breathed his last. Even in death he looms above the rest, for he is buried on a small hill in Crown Heights Cemetery surrounded by almost a score of his relatives. His death was recognized by hundreds of statesmen and businessmen, including a condolence from president Grover Cleveland. One day after he died, his body lay in state in the Capitol building in Indianapolis, where 15,000 people came by to pay their respects. He is memorialized by two statues of his likeness, one in Crawford County in English, Indiana, and the other in Scottsburg (formerly Lexington) in Scott County. Vice president Charles Fairbanks, in 1907, attended the unveiling of the statue in Scott County.[13]

Having died five months before the Democratic National Convention later that July, he was spared the indignity of having to witness his party's nomination of William Jennings Bryan, any economic-conservative Democrat's nightmare. One can only speculate that if he had lived until then, that act alone would have killed him. Two other ironies he was spared as well. One was the socialism of one of his grandsons and namesake, William English Walling. While his other grandson, Willoughby George, quite properly became a conservative banker and a "well-known businessman," his own namesake became famous as a founder of the NAACP and a fervent supporter of the presidential hopes of Eugene V. Debs. Finally, however, the ultimate irony concerned English's own son, Will Elisha. While English lived, Will dutifully rose in Democratic politics, elected first to the Indianapolis City Council, then to the state legislature, and finally followed his father into Congress in 1882. During the same year his father died, Will continued to keep the faith, attending the Democratic National Convention as a Grover Cleveland delegate. But after serving gallantly in the Spanish-American War, he

12. *Guide to U.S. Elections,* vol. 1, 6th ed., (Washington, D.C., CQ Press: 2012), 753, 859. For pictures of the Opera House, demolished in 1948, see 1911 photos posted by Joan Hostetler at https://historicindianapo-lis.com/then-and-now-english-hotel-and-opera-house-120-monument-circle. *Commemorative Biographical Sketches,* 15, 17. *The National Cyclopedia of American Biography,* vol. 9, 377.

13. Shepherd, *Biographical Directory,* 119. The only other Hoosier perhaps richer than English was Clement Studebaker. Paul W. Gates, "Hoosier Cattle Kings," *Indiana Magazine of History* 44, no. 1 (March 1948), 10. *Commemorative Biographical Sketches,* 18.

emerged from that conflict a thoroughgoing imperialist, and in admiration for Theodore Roosevelt, he shocked his family and friends by switching his allegiance to the Republican Party. He remained in that party until his death, and if there really is an afterlife, one can only hope that Will has used it to steer clear of his father.[14]

14. Richard Hofstadter, *The Age of Reform* (New York: Vintage Books, 1955), 240, n. 249. Berry Craig, "William English Walling: Kentucky's Unknown Civil Rights Hero," *Register of the Kentucky Historical* Society 96, no. 4 (Autumn 1998), 352. Ray Ginger, *Eugene V. Debs: A Biography* (New York: Collier Books, repr., 1962, orig: 1949), 314. *The National Cyclopedia*, v. 10, 182. When Will English was still a Democrat he stood for election to the U.S. House of Representatives for the district surrounding Indianapolis. On the initial vote tabulation he was beaten by 87 votes out of over 35,000 cast, but he appealed this narrow verdict to the House of Representatives itself. Subsequently, the House, with a Democratic majority margin of 63 members, appointed the Elections Committee to investigate. Dubin, *Congressional Elections,* 258, 263; *Congressional Record, 48-1,* 4157-4158. After a majority (pro-English) and minority report were submitted, furious debate occurred on May 22, 1884, at the end of which Will was successful in his challenge, though by a mere three votes (130-127), with 66 representatives not voting. *Ibid.,* 4400-4407. He was immediately sworn in, but literally seconds later a resolution was introduced to inquire "whether or not the Hon. William H. English, an ex-member of this House, has violated a privilege thereof in the contested election case of English v. Peelle." The basis of the resolution was the charge that William H. had influenced the outcome with some personal conversations with one or more members on the floor of the House. The resolution to investigate was passed, but not before it was amended to include any malfeasance by any ex-member and that the speaker appoint a select committee, as opposed to the matter going the regular route to the Elections Committee. *Ibid.,* 4407-4408. Speaker John G. Carlisle of Kentucky, a few days later, dutifully appointed a committee with a four to three majority of Democrats. *Ibid.,* 4677. That committee's report exonerated English primarily on the grounds that any conversations he had with members of the House was *not on the floor itself.* The charges against English were laid on the table, 137 to 72, with 115 members not voting. *Ibid,* 5969-5977.

William H. English as depicted on the cover of Harper's Magazine, May 1858

Emma Mardulia Jackson English, painted in the late 1850s; Indiana Historical Society M0098

Emma English with her and William H. English's daughter Rosalind, c. 1858; Indiana Historical Society M0098

Phineas M. Kent, master politician and supporter of William English, after he moved to Brookston; Indiana Historical Society M0098

Jesse Bright, most significant mentor to William H. English; U.S. Senator from Indiana between 1845 and 1862; Indiana Historical Society M0098

Joseph A. Wright, governor of Indiana from 1849-1857; great Democratic Party rival of Jesse Bright

Alexander Stephens, Georgia Whig turned Democrat, sometime ally of William H. English in the U.S. House of Representatives.

William Montgomery, House of Representatives' sponsor of the anti-Lecompton bill bearing his name; fought with English on the streets of Washington, D.C."

Elisha English, father of William, soon before his death; Indiana Historical Society M0098

William Hayden English, around the time he was nominated for vice president

Appendix

Text of the English Bill

Whereas the people of the Territory of Kansas did, by a convention of delegates assembled at Lecompton, on the 7th day of November, 1857, for that purpose form for themselves a constitution and State government, which constitution is republican; and whereas at the same time and place, said convention did adopt an ordinance, which said ordinance asserts that Kansas, when admitted as a State, will have an undoubted right to tax the lands within her limits belonging to the United States, and proposes to relinquish said asserted right if certain conditions set forth in said ordinance be accepted and agreed to by the Congress of the United States; and whereas, the said constitution and ordinance have been presented to Congress by order of said convention, and admission of said Territory into the Union theron, as a State, requested; and whereas, said ordinance is not acceptable to Congress, and it is desirable to ascertain whether the people of Kansas concur in the changes in said ordinance hereinafter stated, and desire admission into the Union as a State as herein proposed: Therefore,

Be it enacted by the Senate and House of Representatives of the United States of America in Congress assembled, That the State of Kansas be, and is hereby, admitted into the Union on an equal footing with the original States in all respects whatever, but upon this fundamental condition, precedent, namely; that the question of admission with the following proposition in lieu of the ordinance framed at Lecompton be submitted to a vote of the people of Kansas, and assented to them or a majority of the voters voting at an election to be held for that purpose, namely; that the following propositions be, and the same are hereby, offered to the people of Kansas for acceptance or rejection, which, if accepted, shall be obligatory on the United States, and upon the said state of Kansas, to wit: First, that sections numbered sixteen and thirty-six in every township of public lands in said State, or, where either of said sections or any part thereof has been sold or otherwise disposed of, other lands equivalent thereto, and as contiguous as may be, shall be granted to said State for the use of schools. Second, that seventy-two sections of land shall be set apart and reserved for the support of a State university, to be selected by the Governor of said State, subject to the approval of the Commissioner of the General Land Office, and to be appropriated and applied in such manner as the legislature of said State may prescribe for the purpose aforesaid, but for no other purpose. Third, that ten entire sections of land, to be selected by the Governor of said State, in legal subdivisions, shall be granted to said State for the purpose of completing the public buildings, or for the erection of others at the seat of government, under the directions of the Legislature thereof. Fourth, that all salt springs within said State, not exceeding twelve in number, with six sections of land adjoining or as contiguous as may be to each, shall be granted to said State for its use, the same to be selected by the Governor thereof, within one year after the admission of said State, and when so selected to be used or disposed of on such terms, conditions, and regulations as the Legislature may direct: *Provided*, That no salt spring or land, the right whereof is now vested in any individual or individuals or which may hereafter be confirmed or adjudged to any individual or individuals, shall, by this article, be granted to said State. Fifth, that five per centum of the net proceeds of the sales of all public lands, lying within said State, which shall be sold by Congress after the admission of said State into the Union, after deducting all the expenses incident to the same, shall be paid to said State for the purpose of making public roads and internal improvements, as the Legislature shall direct. *Provided*, The foregoing propositions herein offered are on the condition that said State of Kansas shall never interfere with the primary disposal of the lands of the United States, or with any regulations which Congress may find necessary for securing the title in said soil to *bona fide* purchasers thereof, and that no tax shall be imposed on lands belonging to the United States, and that in no case shall non-resident proprietors be taxed higher than residents. Sixth, and that said State shall never tax the lands of property of the United States in that State. At the said election the voting shall be by ballot, and by indorsing on this ballot, as each voter may please, "proposition accepted," or "proposition rejected." Should a majority of the votes cast be for "proposition accepted," the President of the United States, as soon as the fact is duly made known to him, shall announce the same by proclamation, and thereafter and without any further proceeding on the part of Congress, the admission of the State of Kansas into the Union upon an equal footing with the original States in all respects whatever, shall be complete and absolute, and said State shall be entitled to one member in the House of the Representatives, of the Congress of the United States, until the next census be taken by the Federal Government. But should a majority of the votes cast be for "proposition rejected," it shall be deemed and held that the people of Kansas do not desire admission into the Union with said constitution under the conditions set forth in said proposition, and in that event the people of said Territory are hereby authorized and empowered to form for themselves a constitution and State government by the name of the State of Kansas, according to the Federal Constitution, and may elect delegates for that purpose, whenever, and not before, it is ascertained, by a census, duly and legally taken, that the population of said Territory equals or exceeds the ratio of representation required for a member of the House of Representatives of the Congress of the United States, and whenever thereafter such delegates shall assemble in convention, they shall first determine by a vote whether it is the wish of the people of the proposed State to be admitted into the Union at that time, and if so, shall proceed to form a constitution, and take all necessary steps for the establishment of a State government in conformity with the Federal Constitution, subject to such limitations and restrictions as to the mode and manner of its approval or ratification by the people of the proposed State as they may have prescribed by law, and shall be entitled to admission into the Union as a State under such constitution thus fairly and legally made with or without slavery, as said constitution may prescribe.

Sec. 2. And be it further enacted, That, for the purpose of insuring, as far as possible, that the election authorized by this act may be fair and free, the Governor, United States district attorney, and Secretary of the Territory of Kansas, and the presiding officers of the two branches of its Legislature, namely, the President of the Council and the Speaker of the House of Representatives, are hereby constituted a board of commissioners to carry into effect the provisions of this act, and to use all the means necessary and proper to that end. Any three of them shall constitute a board, and the board shall have power and authority to designate and establish precincts for voting, or to adopt those already established; to cause the polls to be opened at such places as it may deem proper in the respective counties and election precincts of said Territory; to appoint, as judges of election, at each of the several places of voting, three discreet and respectable persons, any two of whom shall be competent to act; to require the sheriffs of the several counties, by themselves or deputies, to attend the judges at each of the places of voting, for the purpose of preserving peace and good order; or the said board may, instead of said sheriffs and their deputies, appoint, at their discretion, and in such instances as they may choose, other fit persons for the same purpose. The election hereby authorized shall continue one day only, and shall not be continued later than sundown on that day. The said board shall appoint the day for holding said election, and the said Governor shall announce the same by proclamation; and the day shall be as early a one as is consistent with due notice thereof to the people of said Territory, subject to the provisions of this act. The said board shall have full power to prescribe the time, manner, and places of said election, and to direct the time and manner of the returns thereof, which returns shall be made to the said board, whose duty it shall be to announce the result by proclamation; and the said Governor shall certify the same to the President of the United States without delay.

Sec. 3. And be it further enacted, That in the election hereby authorized, all white male inhabitants of said Territory, over the age of twenty-one years, who possess the qualifications which were required by the laws of said Territory for a legal voter at the last general election for members of the Territorial Legislature, and none others, shall be allowed to vote; and this shall be the only qualification required to entitle the citizens to the right of suffrage in said election; and if any person not so qualified shall vote or offer to vote, or if any person shall vote more than once, at said election, or shall make or cause to be made any false, fictitious, or fraudulent returns, or shall alter or change any returns of said election, such person shall, upon conviction thereof before any competent court of jurisdiction, be kept at hard labor for not less than six months and not more than three years.

Sec. 4. And be it further enacted, That the members of the aforesaid board of commissioners, and all persons appointed by them to carry into effect the provisions of this act, shall, before entering upon their duties, take an oath to perform faithfully the duties of their respective offices, and on failure thereof they shall be liable and subject to the same charges and penalties as are provided in like cases under the territorial laws.

Sec. 5. And be it further enacted, That the officers mentioned in the preceding section shall receive for their services the same compensation as is given for like services under the territorial laws.[1]

---

1. CG, 35-1, 1765-1766

Works Cited

Primary Sources

Manuscript Collections

Jesse D. Bright Papers. Lilly Library, Bloomington, Indiana

Linn Boyd Papers. The Filson Club, Louisville, Kentucky

James Buchanan Papers. Historical Society of Pennsylvania, Philadelphia

Howell Cobb Papers. University of Georgia, Athens

Schuyler Colfax Papers, Indiana Historical Society, Indianapolis

James A. Cravens Papers. Lilly Library, Bloomington, Indiana

John G. Davis Papers. Indiana Historical Society, Indianapolis

Stephen Douglas Letter, Indiana Historical Society, Indianapolis

William H. English Papers. Indiana Historical Society, Indianapolis

Allen Hamilton Papers. Indiana Historical Society, Indianapolis

Phineas M. Kent Papers. Indiana Historical Society, Indianapolis

Joseph Lane Papers. Oregon State Historical Society. Microfilmed copies in Lilly Library, Bloomington, Indiana

Ricks Collection, Illinois State Historical Society, Springfield

Alexander Stephens Papers, Manhattanville College Library, Purchase, New York

Lew Wallace Papers. Indiana Historical Society, Indianapolis

James Whitcomb Papers, Indiana Historical Society, Indianapolis

Joseph Wright Papers, Indiana Historical Society, Indianapolis

Joseph A. Wright Papers, Indiana State Library, Indianapolis

John Zulauf Papers. Indiana Historical Society, Indianapolis

Newspapers and Magazines: All Indiana unless noted

Brookville American

Cannelton Express

Cannelton Reporter

Corydon Argus

Evansville Daily Democrat

Franklin Democrat

Harper's Weekly (NYC)

Indiana Locomotive

Indiana State Sentinel

Indiana Statesman

Indiana Weekly Express

Indianapolis Journal

Indianapolis Old Line Guard

Jeffersonville Weekly Democrat

Lafayette Argus

Madison Courier

New Albany Democrat

New Albany Ledger

New Albany Tribune

New York (NY)Tribune

Paoli American Eagle

Putnam Republican Banner

Randolph County Journal

Richmond Palladium

Seymour Times

Vincennes Weekly Sun

Wabash Intelligencer

Wabash Plain Dealer

Washington Democrat

Washington (D.C.) Star

Washington (D. C.)Union

Published Public Documents

Address of Hon. William H. English Delivered at Livonia, Indiana before the Washington and Orange District Agricultural Society, October 15, 1857. Washington: Congressional Globe Office, 1858.

Annual Report of the Board of Regents for the Smithsonian Institution for 1856. Washington, D.C.: A. O. P. Nicholson, 1857.

Annual Report of the Board of Regents for the Smithsonian Institution for 1857. Washington, D. C.: William A. Harris, 1858.

Congressional Globe, 31st Congress, 1st session through 36th congress, second session. Washington, D.C.: John C. Rives, 1850-1861. Online at http://memory.loc.gov/ammem/amlaw/lwcglink.htms

Darlington, Jane Eaglesfield, transcriber. *Scott County, Indiana Assessor's Book for 1839.* Indiana State Library, 1981.

1850 Census: The Seventh Census of the United States: Online at https://wwwcensus.gov/library/publications/1853/dec/1850a.html.

1860 Census, Lexington Township, Scott County, Microfilm, Indiana State Library.

Eighth Annual Report of the Smithsonian Institution. Washington, D.C.: A.O.P. Nicholson, 1854.

Indiana Census Records, 1820-1850. Online at https://indianagenealogy.org/census.

Journal of the Convention of the People of the State of Indiana to Amend Their Constitution, Assembled at Indianapolis, October, 1850. Indianapolis: Austin H. Brown, 1851.

.*Journal of the House of Representatives of the State of Indiana during the Twenty-Eighth Session of the General Assembly.* Indianapolis: Dowling and Cole, 1843 (actually printed n 1844).

Journal of the House of Representatives of the State of Indiana during the Twenty-Ninth Session of the General Assembly. Indianapolis: J. P. Chapman, 1844 (actually printed in 1845).

Journal of the House of Representatives of the State of Indiana during the Thirty-Sixth Session of the General Assembly. Indianapolis: J. P. Chapman, 1851 (actually printed in 1852)

Journal of the House of Representatives of the State of Indiana during the Special Session of the General Assembly Commencing on Saturday, November 20, 1858. Indianapolis: Joseph J. Bingham, 1858.

Journal of the House of Representatives of the State of Indiana during the Fortieth Regular Session of the General Assembly Commencing on January 5, 1859. Indianapolis: John C. Walker, 1859.

Ninth Annual Report of the Smithsonian Institution. Washington, D.C.: Beverly Tucker, 1855.

Reports of the Debates and Proceedings of the Convention for the Revision of the Constitution for the State of Indiana, 1850, 2 vols. Indianapolis: Austin H. Brown, 1851.

Report of the Secretary of Interior in Compliance with a resolution of the Senate of March 10, 1853, calling for a statement of the amounts paid as annuities, under the different treaties with the Choctaw Indians. Executive Document No. 64, Congressional Session 33-2.

Scott County Assessor's Book (1839). Indiana State Library, Indianapolis.

Scott County Land Records, Indiana State Library, Indianapolis (microfilm).

Tenth Annual Report of the Smithsonian Institution. Cornelius Wendell, 1856.

Unpublished Records and Collections

William H. English Scrapbook of Newspaper Clippings. Indiana State Library. Indianapolis

Indiana Biography Series. Microfilm. Indiana State Library, Indianapolis

Lexington Township, Scott County. 1860 Census. Microfilm. Indiana State Archives. Indianapolis

Indiana Land Records, Scott County. Microfilm. Indiana State Library. Indianapolis

EXCLUSIVELY ONLINE CITATIONS: Public and Political

American Presidency Project. www.presidency.ucsb.edu/ws/?pid=29575

Carol O. Rogers, "Black and White in Indiana," *Indiana Business Review.* https://www. ibrc.indiana.edu/ibr/2005/summer/article1.html

Congressional Record. 48th congress. https://www.govinfo.gov/app/collection/crecb/_ crecb/Volume%20016%20(1885)

Douglas/Buchanan argument first reported by New York Times. www.nytimes. com/1860/10/22/ archives/the-lecompton-constitution-was=mr-douglas–its-autor-his-speech—at. html.

Dred Scott opinion by Chief Justice Roger Taney. http://www.loc.gov/resource/llst.022.

Hanover College book of William Alfred Willis. https://history.hanover.edu/texts/millis/ millistc.html.

Indiana Census Records, 1820-1850. https://indianageneolgy.org/census.

The Indiana Constitution of 1850. http://secure.in.gov/history/2838.htm.

Indiana state population statistics. https://en.wikipedi.org/wiki/Indiana#Population

Indiana statistical vote on "Negro Exclusion Clause." https://en.wikipedia.org/ wikiINiana#population.

John Calhoun's "Southern Address." https://www.hist.furman.edu/~benson/docs/ calhoun.htm

Kansas-Nebraska bill, January 4th version. http://memory.loc.gob/cgi-bin/ ampage?collid=llsb&fileName=033/lisb033.db&recNum=71.

Lecompton Constitution. https://www.kansasmemory.org/item/90818.

Official Proceedings of the National Democratic Convention, Held in Cincinnati, O., June 22d, 23d, and 24th. https://babel.hathitrust.org/cgi/ pt?id=mdp.390150307799442;view=1up;seq=195

Population congressional apportionment in 1850. https://en.wikipedia.org/wiki/United_States_congressional_apportionment

Smithsonian Institution, Board of Regents Minutes, 1854. https://siarchives.si.edu/collections/siris 14323.

South Carolina Encyclopedia article on William Aiken, by Matthew A. Byron, April 26, 2016. http://www.scencyclopedia.org/sce/entries/aiken=william-jr/.

State of Massachusetts Archives. https://archives.lib.state.ma.us/bitstream/handle/2452/297079/1855acts0256.txt?sequence=1&isAllowed=y.

United States. Bills and Resolutions, 1774-1875. https://www.memory.loc.gov/ammem/amlaw/lawhom.html

U. S. Chinese Commissioners. http://history.state.gov/deartmenthistory/eople/chiefsofmission/china.

United States Senate party breakdown. https://www.senate.gov/history/partydiv.html.

United States Statutes at Large, 1774-1875. https://www.memory.loc.gov/ammem/amlaw/lawhome.html

Willoughby Walling, husband of William H. English's daughter. https://www.myheritae.com/names/willoughbywalling.

Wyandotte Constitution. https://www.kansasmemory.org/item/90272/test.

Secondary And Edited Works

Alexander, D. Stanwood. History and Procedure of the House of Representatives. 1916. Reprint, New York: Lennox Hill Publishing Co., 1970.

Ambler, Charles H., ed. Correspondence of R.M.T. Hunter, 1826-1876. 1918. Reprint, New York: De Capo Press, 1971.

Anbinder, Tyler G. Nativism and Slavery. New York and Oxford: Oxford University Press, 1992.

Atkins, Leah R. "Southern Congressmen and the Homestead Bill." PhD diss., Auburn University, 1974.

Bain, Richard C. and Judith H. Parris, eds. Convention Decisions and Voting Records, 2nd ed. Washington, D.C.: The Brookings Institution, 1960.

Baird, Lewis C. Baird's History of Clark County, Indiana. Indianapolis: B. F. Bowen and Co., 1919.

Baker, Jean H. Affairs of Party: The Political Culture of the Northern Democrats in the mid-Nineteenth Century. Ithaca and London: Cornell University Press, 1983.

Banta, R. E. *Indiana Authors and Their Books.* Crawfordville, IA: Haddon Craftsman, Inc., 1949.

Barnhart, John D. and Carmony, Donald F. *Indiana: From Frontier to Industrial Commonwealth,* 2 vols. New York: Lewis Historical Publishing Co., 1954.

Basler, Roy P. *The Collected Works of Abraham Lincoln, vol.3.* New Brunswick, N.J.: Rutgers University Press, 1953.

Beeler, Dale. "The Election of 1852 in Indiana (part 1)." *Indiana Magazine of History* 11, no. 4 (December, 1915): 301-312.

Beeler, Dale. "The Election of 1852 in Indiana (part 2)." *Indiana Magazine of History* 12, no. 1 (March, 1916): 34-52.

Berwanger, Eugene H. *The Frontier Against Slavery.* Urbana: University of Illinois Press, 1967.

Biographical Directory of United States Congress, 1774-2005. Washington, D.C., United States Government Printing Office, 2005. Online version: www.http//bioguide.congress.gov/scripts/biodisplay.pl?index=L000141.

Biographical and Historical Souvenir for the Counties of Clark, Crawford, Floyd, Harrison, Jefferson, Jennings, Scott, and Washington. Chicago: Chicago Printing Co., 1889.

Blake, Israel G. *The Holmans of Veraestau.* Oxford, Ohio: Mississippi Valley Press, 1943.

Bogle, Victor M. "New Albany as a Commercial and Shipping Point." *Indiana Magazine of History* 48, no. 4 (December, 1952): 369-379.

Bogle, Victor M. "New Albany: Reaching for the Hinterland." *Indiana Magazine of History* 50, no. 2 (June, 1954): 145-166.

Bogle, Victor M. "New Albany within the Shadow of Louisville." *Indiana Magazine of History* 51, no. 4 (December, 1955): 303-316.

Bogle, Victor M. "New Albany's Attachment to the Ohio River." *Indiana Magazine of History* 49, no. 3 (September, 1953): 249-266.

Boone, Richard. *A History of Education in Indiana.* 1892. Reprint, Indianapolis: Indiana Historical Bureau, 1941.

Bordewich, Ferguson M. *Bound for Canaan: the Underground Railroad and the War for the Soul of America.* New York: Harper Collins, 2005.

Brand, Carl F. "The History of the Know-Nothing Party in Indiana." *Indiana Magazine of History* 18, nos. 1, 2, 3 (March, June, September, 1922): 47-81, 177-206, 266-305.

Brooke, John L. "Party, Nation, and Cultural Rupture: The Crisis of the American Civil War." In *Practicing Democracy: Popular Politics in the United States from the*

Constitution to the Civil War, edited by Daniel Pearl and Adam J. P. Smith, 72-95. Charlottesville: University of Virginia Press, 2015.

Buley, R. Carlyle. "Indiana in the Mexican War," *Indiana Magazine of History* 16, no. 1 (March, 1920): 46-68.

Burnham, Walter Dean, ed. *Presidential Ballots, 1836-1892.* Baltimore: Johns Hopkins University Press, 1955.

Burt, John. *Lincoln's Tragic Pragmatism: Lincoln, Douglas, and Moral Conflict.* Cambridge, Mass., and London: The Belknap Press of Harvard University Press, 2013.

Burton, Theodore E. *John Sherman.* London and New York: Houghton Mifflin Co.,, 1906.

Byron, Matthew A. "William Aiken, jr." In *South Carolina Encyclopedia*, edited by Walter Edgar. Columbia: University of South Carolina Press, 2006. Updated Online, August 26, 2016. http://www.scencyclopedia.org/sce/entris/ aiken-william-jr.

Camp, Charles E. "Temperance Movement and Legislation in Indiana." *Indiana Magazine of History* 16, no. 1 (March, 1920): 3-35.

Campbell, Tracy. *Deliver the Vote: A History of Electoral Fraud, an American Political Tradition—1742-2004.* New York: Carroll and Graf Publishers, 2005.

Carmony, Donald F. *Indiana, 1816-1850: The Pioneer Era.* Indianapolis: Indiana Historical Bureau and Indiana Historical Society, 1988.

Carter, Harvey L. "A Decade of Hoosier History." PhD diss., University of Wisconsin, 1939.

Childers, Christopher. "Interpreting Popular Sovereignty: A Historiographical Essay." *Civil War History* 57, no. 1 (March, 2013): 48-70.

Clark, Minnie B. "The Old College of Livonia." *Indiana Magazine of History*, 23, no. 1 (March, 1927), 73-81.

Clarke, Grace Julian. *George W. Julian.* Indianapolis: Indiana Historical Commission, 1923.

Cochran, Thomas C. and Miller, William. *The Age of Enterprise.* (New York: Harper Torchbooks, 1961).

Cole, Arthur C. *The Whig Party in the South.* Washington, D.C.: American Historical Association, 1913.

Collins, Bruce. "The Ideology of the Antebellum Northern Democrats." *Journal of American Studies* 11, no. 1 (April, 1977): 105-120.

Commemorative Biographical Record of Prominent and Representative Men of Indianapolis and Vicinity, containing Biographical Sketches of Business and Professional Men and of Many of the Early Settled Families. Chicago: J. H. Beers & Co., 1909.

Cooper, William J. *Liberty and Slavery: Southern Politics to 1860.* New York: Alfred A. Knopf, 1983.

Cotton, Fasset A. *Education in Indiana.* Bluffton, Indiana: The Progress Publishing Co., 1934.

Cox, Samuel S. *Three Decades of Federal Legislation, 1855-1885.* Providence, R. I.: J. A. and R. A. Reid, 1885.

Craig, Berry. "William English Walling: Kentucky's Unknown Civil Rights Hero." *The Register of the Kentucky Historical Society* 96, no. 4 (Autumn, 1998): 351-376.

Crane, Philip. "Onus with Honor: The Political History of Joseph A. Wright, 1808-1857." Master's thesis, Indiana University, 1961.

Craven, Avery O. *The Coming of the Civil War,* 2d. ed. Chicago and London: The University of Chicago Press, 1947.

Craven, Avery O. *The Growth of Southern Nationalism, 1848-1861.* Baton Rouge: Louisiana State University, 1953.

Crenshaw, Oliver. "The Speakership Contest of 1859-1860." *Mississippi Valley Historical Review* 29, no. 3 (December, 1942).

Davis, William C. *Breckinridge: Statesman, Soldier, Symbol.* Baton Rouge: Louisiana State University Press, 1974.

de la Hunt, Thomas J. A. *Perry County: A History.* Indianapolis: W. K. Stewart, 1916.

Dillard, Arthur L., ed. *Orange County Heritage.* Paoli, Indiana: Stout's Print Shop, 1971.

Dix, Morgan. *Memoirs of John Adams Dix, volume 1.* New York: Harpers and Bros., 1883.

Draper, Ariel and Will H. *Brevier Legislative Reports.* Indianapolis: Daily Indiana State Sentinel, 1859.

Dubin, Michael J., ed. *United States Congressional Elections, 1788-1997.* Jefferson, North Carolina and London: McFarland and Co., Inc., 1998.

Dubois, James T. and Matthews, Gertrude S. *Galusha A. Grow: Father of the Homestead Law.* Boston and New York: Houghton Mifflin Co., 1917.

Duncan, H. L. "James Hughes." *Indiana Magazine of History* 5, no. 3 (September, 1909): 85-98.

Dunn, Jacob P., ed. *Indiana and Indianans, vol. 5.* Chicago: The American Historical Society, 1919.

Earle, Jonathan H. *Jacksonian Antislavery and the Politics of Free Soil, 1824-1854*. Chapel Hill and London: The University of North Carolina Press, 2004.

Edmond, J. B. *The Magnificent Charter: The Origin and Role of the Morrill Land-Grant Colleges and Universities*. Hicksville, New York: Exposition Press, 1978.

Elbert, Elmer Duane. "Southern Indiana Politics on the Eve of the Civil War." PhD diss., Indiana University, 1967.

Esarey, Logan. *History of Indiana*, 2 vols. Indianapolis: B. F. Bowen, 1915. 1918.

Esarey, Logan. *Internal Improvements in Early Indiana*. Indianapolis: Edward J. Hicker, 1912.

Esarey, Logan. *State Banking in Indiana, 1814-1873: Indiana University Studies, no. 15*. Bloomington: Indiana University, 1912.

Etcheson, Nicole. *Bleeding Kansas: Contested Liberty in the Civil War Era*. Lawrence: University Press of Kansas, 2004.

Etcheson, Nicole. *The Emerging Midwest: Upland Southerners and the Political Culture of the Old Northwest, 1787-1861*. Bloomington: Indiana University Press, 1996.

Fackler, Jon B. "An End to Compromise: The Kansas-Nebraska Bill of 1854." PhD diss., Pennsylvania State University, 1969.

Fehrenbacher, Don E. *The Dred Scott Case: Its Significance in American Law and Politics*. New York: Oxford University Press, 1978.

Feller, Daniel. *The Jacksonian Promise: America, 1815-1840*. Baltimore and London: The Johns Hopins University Press, 1995.

Finkelman, Paul. "The Appeasement of 1850." In *Congress and the Crisis of the 1850s*, edited by Paul Finkelman. Athens: Ohio University Press, 2012: 36-79.

Foner, Eric. *Free Soil, Free Labor, Free Men: The Ideology of the Republican Party before the Civil War*. London: Oxford University Press, 1970.

Foner, Eric. "The Wilmot Proviso Revisited." *Journal of American History* 56, no. 2 (September, 1969): 262-279.

Forbes, Robert P. *The Missouri Compromise and its Aftermath: Slavery and the Meaning of America*. Chapel Hill: University of North Carolina Press, 2007.

Foulke, William Dudley. *Life of Oliver P. Morton, Including His Important Speeches*. Indianapolis and Kansas City: The Bowen-Merrill Co., 1899.

Fredrickson, George. *The Black Image in the White Mind*. New York: Harper and Row, Inc., 1971.

Freeman, Joanne B. *The Field of Blood: Violence in Congress and the Road to the Civil War*. New York: Farrar, Straus, Giroux, 2018.

Gates, Paul W. "Hoosier Cattle Kings." *Indiana Magazine of History* 44, no. 1 (March, 1948): 1-24.

Gienapp, William E. *Origins of the Republican Party, 1852-1856.* New York and Oxford: Oxford University Press, 1979.

Ginger, Ray. *Eugene V. Debs: A Biography.* 1949. Reprint, New York: Collier Books, 1962.

Goodwin, T. A. *Seventy-Six Years Tussle with the Traffic.* Indianapolis: Carlton and Hollenbeck, 1883.

Gray, Ralph D. "Thomas A. Hendricks: Spokesman for the Democracy." In *Gentlemen from Indiana: National Party Candidates, 1836-1940,* ed. by Ralph D. Gray. Indianapolis: Indiana Historical Bureau, 1972: 117-139.

Greeley, Horace. *Recollections of a Busy Life.* New York: J. B. Ford and Company, 1868.

Gresham, Matilda. *The Life of Walter Q. Gresham, 1832-1895, vol. 1.* Chicago: Rand McNally and Co., 1910.

Griffith, Elisha E. "The Growth and Decline of the German Element in Indiana." Master's Thesis. Butler University, 1972.

Grinnell, Josiah B. *Men and Events of Forty Years: Autobiographical Reminiscences of an Active Career.* Boston: D. Lothrop, 1891.

Guide to U.S. Elections, 6th ed., vol. 1. Washington, D.C.: CQ Press, 2010.

Gunderson, Robert Gray. *Old Gentlemen's Convention: The Washington Peace Conference of 1861.* Madison: University of Wisconsin Press, 1961.

Hafen, LeRoy R. *The Overland Mail, 1848-1869.* Cleveland: The Arthur H. Clark Co., 1926.

Hamilton, Holman. *Prologue to Conflict: The Crisis and Compromise of 1850.* 1964. Reprint, New York: W. W. Norton & Co., 1966.

Hamilton, Holman. "Texas Bonds and Northern Profits: A Study in Compromise, Investment, and Lobby Influence." *Mississippi Valley Historical Review* 43, no. 4 (March, 1957): 575-594.

Handfield, F. Gerald, Jr. "William H. English and the Election of 1880." In *Gentlemen from Indiana: National Party Candidates, 1836-1840,* edited by Ralph D. Gray. Indianapolis: Indiana Historical Bureau, 1972: 83-116.

Hargrave, Frank L. *A Pioneer Indiana Railroad.* Indianapolis: Wm. M. Buford Printing Co., 1932.

Harrington, Fred H. "The First Northern Victory." *Journal of Southern History* 5, no. 2 (May, 1939): 186-205.

Heck, Frank H. *Proud Kentuckian: John C. Breckinridge 1821-1875*. Lexington: The University Press of Kentucky, 1976.

Hesseltine William B., ed. *Three Against Lincoln: Murat Halstead Reports the Caucuses of 1860*. Baton Rouge: Louisiana State University Press, 1960.

Hesseltine, William B. and Fischer, Rex G. *Trimmers, Trucklers, and Temporizers: Notes of Murat Halstead from the Political Conventions of 1856*. Madison: State Historical Society of Wisconsin, 1961.

Hicken, Victor. "John McClernand and the House Speakership Struggle of 1859." *Illinois State Historical Society Journal 53*, no. 2 (Summer, 1960): 163-178.

Hill, N.N. *History of the Ohio Falls Cities and Their Counties*. Cleveland: L.A. Williams and Co., 1882.

History of Orange, Warwick, and Washington County, Indiana. 1884. Reprint, Paoli, Indiana: Stout's Print Shop, 1961.

Hodder, Frank H. "Some Aspects of the English Bill for the Admission of Kansas." *Annual Report of the AHA for the Year 1905, vol. 1*. Washington, D.C.: Government Printing Office, 1908.

Hoffer, Williamjames Hull. *The Caning of Charles Sumner: Honor, Idealism, and the Origins of the Civil War*. Baltimore: The Johns Hopkins University Press, 2010.

Hofstadter, Richard. *The Age of Reform*. New York: Vintage Books, 1955.

Holcombe, John W. and Skinner, Hubert M. *Life and Public Services of Thomas A. Hendricks*. Indianapolis: Carlon and Hollenbeck, 1888.

Hollandsworth, James G., Jr. *Pretense of Glory: The Life of Nathaniel P. Banks*. Baton Rouge: Louisiana State University Press, 1998.

Hollcroft, Temple R., ed. "A Congressman's Letters on the Speaker Election in the Thirty Fourth Congress." *Mississippi Valley Historical Review* 43, no. 3 (December, 1956): 444-458.

Hollister, O. J. *Life of Schuyler Colfax*. New York: Funk and Wagnalls, 1886.

Holt, Michael F. *The Fate of Their Country: Politicians, Slavery Extension, and the Coming of the Civil War*. New York: Hill and Wang, 2006.

Holt, Michael F. *Franklin Pierce*. New York: Henry Holt and Co., 2010.

Holt, Michael F. *The Political Crisis of the 1850s*. New York and London: John Wiley and Sons, 1978.

Holt, Michael F. *The Rise and Fall of the American Whig Party: Jacksonian Politics and the Onset of the Civil War*. New York and Oxford: Oxford University Press, 1999.

Howe, Daniel Walker. *The Political Culture of American Whigs*. Chicago: University of Chicago Press, 1970.

Hubbart, Henry C. *The Older Middle West, 1840-1880: Its Social, Economic, and Political Life and Sectional Tendencies before, during and after the Civil War.* 1884. Reprint, New York: Russel & Russel, 1973.

Hunt, Gallard. *Israel, Elihu, and Cadwallder Washburn: A Chapter in American Biography.* New York: MacMillan & Co., 1925.

Huston, James L. *Stephen A. Douglas and the Dilemmas of Democratic Equality.* New York and Toronto: Rowman and Littlefield Publishers, Inc., 2007.

Ilisevich, Robert D. *Galusha A. Grow: The People's Candidate.* Pittsburgh: University of Pittsburgh Press, 1988

Illustrated Atlas and History of Harrison County, Indiana. Corydon, Indiana: F. A. Bulleit, 1906.

Johannsen, Robert W. *The Frontier, the Union, and Stephen A. Douglas.* Urbana and Chicago: University of Illinois Press, 1989.

Johannsen, Robert W., ed. *The Letters of Stephen A. Douglas.* Urbana: The University of Illinois Press, 1961.

Johannsen, Robert W., ed. *The Lincoln-Douglas Debates of 1858.* New York: Oxford University Press, 1965, paperback reprint, 1968.

Johannsen, Robert W. *Stephen A. Douglas.* New York: Oxford University Press, 1973.

Johnson, Allen. *Stephen A. Douglas: A Study in American Politics.* 1908. Reprint. New York: De Capo Press, 1970.

Johnson, Dennis, W. *The Laws that Shaped America: Fifteen Acts of Congress and their Lasting Impact.* New York and London: Routledge, 2009.

Johnson, Hadley. "How the Kansas-Nebraska Line was Established." *Transactions and Reports, Nebraska State Historical Society, vol. 2,* 1887.

Johnston, Richard M. *Autobiography of Col. Richard Malcolm Johnston.* Washington, D.C.: The Neale Co., 1901.

Johnston, Richard M. and Browne, William H., eds. *Life of Alexander Stephens.* Philadelphia: J. B. Lippincott and Company, 1878.

Julian, George W. *Political Recollections: 1840-1872.* Chicago: Jansen, McClung, and Co., 1884.

Kenworthy, Leonard. *The Tall Sycamore of the Wabash: Daniel Wolsey Voorhees.* Boston: Bruce Humphries, Inc., 1936.

Kettleborough, Charles. "Indiana on the Eve of the Civil War." *Indiana Historical Society Publications, vol. 6.* Indianapolis: the Bobbs-Merill Co., 1919.

Klein, Philip S. *President James Buchanan: A Biography.* University Park, PA: Pennsylvania State University Press, 1962.

Kleppner, Paul. *The Third Electoral System, 1853-1892*. Chapel Hill: University of North Carolina Press, 1979.

Klunder, Willard Carl. *Lewis Cass and the Politics of Moderation*. Kent, Ohio and London: The Kent State University Press, 1996.

Knupfer, Peter B. *The Union As It Is: Constitutional Unionism and Sectional Compromise, 1787-1861*. Chapel Hill and London: The University of North Carolina Press, 1991.

Kutler, Stanley I., ed. *The Dred Scott Decision: Law or Politics?* Boston: Houghton, Mifflin Co., 1967.

Landis, Michael Todd. *Northern Men with Southern Loyalties: The Democratic Party and the Sectional Crisis*. Ithaca and London: Cornell University Press, 2014.

Leemhuis, Roger P. *James L. Orr and the Sectional Conflict*. Washington, D.C.: University Press of America, 1979.

Litwack, Leon. *North of Slavery*. Chicago: University of Chicago Press, 1961.

Lynch, William O. "Indiana in the Douglas-Buchanan Contest of 1856." *Indiana Magazine of History* 30, no. 2 (June, 1934): 119-133.

MacPherson, James M. *Ordeal by Fire: The Civil War and Reconstruction, 2nd ed.* New York, et al.: McGraw Hill, Inc., 1992.

Maizlish, Stephen E. "The Meaning of Nativism and the Crisis of the Union: The Know-Nothing Movement in the Antebellum North." In *Essays on American Antebellum Politics, 1840-1860*, edited by Stephen E. Maizlish, 166-198. College Station: Texas A &M University press, 1982.

Malavasic, Alice. *The F Street Mess: How Southern Senators Rewrote the Kansas-Nebraska Act*. Chapel Hill: The University of North Carolina Press, 2017.

May, Robert E. *John A. Quitman: Old South Crusader*. Baton Rouge and London: Louisiana State University Press, 1985.

McCulloch, Hugh. *Men and Measures of Half a Century*. Charles Scribner's Sons, 1880.

McDonald, Daniel D. *A History of Freemasonry in Indiana from 1806 to 1898*. Indianapolis: Grand Lodge, 1898.

McKee, Irving. *"Ben Hur" Wallace: The Life of General Lew Wallace*. Berkeley: University of California Press, 1947.

Merck, Frederick. *Manifest Destiny and Mission in American History*. New York: Alfred A. Knopf, Inc., 1963.

Miller, John W. *Indiana Newspaper Bibliography*. Indianapolis: Indiana Historical Society, 1982.

Milton, George Fort. *The Eve of Conflict: Stephen A. Douglas and the Needless War.* Boston and New York: Houghton-Mifflin, 1934.

Monks, Leander J. , ed. *Courts and Lawyers of Indiana,* 3 vols. Indianapolis: Federal Publishing Co., 1916.

Moore, A. Y. *Life of Schuyler Colfax.* Philadelphia: T. B. Peterson and Bros., 1868.

Moore, Glover. *The Missouri Controversy: 1819-1821.* Lexington: University of Kentucky Press, 1953.

Moore, John B. *The Works of James Buchanan: Comprising his Speeches, State Papers, and Private Correspondence, vol. 10.* 1911. Reprint, New York: Antiquarian Press Ltd, 1960.

Moore, Richard Randall. "In Search of a Safe Government: A Biography of RMT Hunter of Virginia." PhD diss., University of South Carolina, 1993.

Morris, Richard B. *Encyclopedia of American History.* New York: Harper and Brothers, 1953.

Morrison, Chaplain. *Democratic Politics and Sectionalism: The Wilmot Proviso Controversy.* Chapel Hill: The University of North Carolina Press, 1967.

Morrison, Michael A. *Slavery and the American West.* Chapel Hill and London: The University of North Carolina Press, 1997.

Myers, Burton D. *Trustees and Officers of Indiana University, 1850-1920.* Bloomington: Indiana University Press, 1951.

The National Cyclopedia of American Biography, vols. 9, 10, 18. New York: James T. White and Co., 1899, 1900, 1922.

Neely, Mark E. "The Kansas-Nebraska Act in American Political Culture." In *The Nebraska-Kansas Act of 1854,* edited by John R. Wunder and Joann M. Ross. Lincoln and London: University of Nebraska Press, 2008: 13-42.

Nevins, Allan. *The Emergence of Lincoln, 2 vols.,* 1950. Reprint, New York and London: Charles Scribner's Sons, 1975.

Nevins, Allan. *Ordeal of the Union: A House Dividing, 1852-1857, 2 vols.,* 1947. Reprint, New York and London: Charles Scribner's Sons, 1975.

Nichols, Alice. *Bleeding Kansas.* New York: Oxford University Press, 1954.

Nichols, Roy F. *Blueprints for Leviathan: American Style.* New York: Athenum, 1963.

Nichols, Roy F. *The Democratic Machine, 1850-1854.* 1923. Reprint, New York: AMS Press, Inc., 1967.

Nichols, Roy F. *The Disruption of American Democracy.* New York: The Free Press, 1948.

Nichols, Roy F. *Franklin Pierce: Young Hickory of the Granite Hills*, 2nd edition. Philadelphia: University of Pennsylvania Press, 1958.

Nichols, Roy F. "The Kansas-Nebraska Act: A Century of Historiography." *Mississippi Valley Historical Review* 43, no. 2 (September, 1956): 187-212.

Niven, John. *Martin van Buren: The Romantic Age of American Politics*. New York and Oxford: Oxford University Press, 1983.

Nowland, John H. B., *Early Reminiscence of Indianapolis*. Indianapolis: Indianapolis Sentinel, Inc., 1870. Microfiche, LH 11832, Indiana State Library.

One Hundred and Fifty Years: An Exhibit Commemorating the Sesquicentennial of Indiana Statehood. Bloomington: Indiana University, The Lilly Library, 1966.

Overdyke, W. Darrell. *The Know-Nothing Party in the South*. Baton Rouge: Louisiana State University Press, 1950.

Parsons, Stanley B., Beach, William W., Dubin, Michael. *United States Congressional Districts, 1843-1883*. New York: Greenwood Press, 1986.

Pease, Theodore Calvin, ed. *The Diary of Orville Hickman Browning, vol. 1*. Chicago: Blakely Printing Co., 1927.

Peckham, Howard H. *Indiana: A Bicentennial History*. New York: W. W. Norton & Co., 1978

Peek, Gregory. "The True and Everlasting Principle of States Rights and Popular Sovereignty: Douglas Democrats and Indiana Republicans Allied, 1857-1859." *Indiana Magazine of History* 111, no. 4 (December, 2015): 381-421.

Perry, Oran, ed. *Indiana in the Mexican War*. Indianapolis: Wm. H. Buford, 1908.

Persinger, Carl. "The Bargain of 1844 as the Origin of the Wilmot Proviso." *American Historical Association Reports, 1911, vol. 1*. Washington, D.C.: Government Printing Office, 1913.

Peters. Pamela R. *The Underground Railroad in Floyd County, Indiana*. Jefferson, North Carolina and London: McFarland & Company, 2001.

Phillips, Ulrich B., ed. *The Correspondence of Robert Toombs, Alexander Stephens, and Howell Cobb*. 1913. Reprint, New York: De Capo Press, 1970.

Phillips, Ulrich B. *The Life of Robert Toombs*. New York: Burt Franklin, 1913.

Pitchell, Robert J. *Indiana Votes*. Bloomington: Bureau of Government Research, 1970.

Pleasant, Hazen Hayes. *A History of Crawford County, Indiana*. Greenfield, Indiana: William H. Mitchell Printing Co., 1926.

Poore, Benjamin Perley. *Perley's Reminiscence of Sixty Years in the National Metropolis, vol. 1*. Philadelphia: Hubbard Brothers, 1886.

Porter, Robert B., ed. *Abstract of the Eleventh Census.* 2nd ed. Washington, D.C.: Government Printing Office, 1890.

Potter, David. *The Impending Crisis.* New York, Hagerstown, San Francisco, London: Harper and Row, 1976.

Quitt, Martin H. *Stephen A. Douglas and Antebellum Democracy.* New York, Cambridge, *et al.:* Cambridge University Press, 2012.

Rayback, Joseph G. *Free Soil: The Election of 1848.* Lexington: The University Press of Kentucky, 1970.

Rhodes, James Ford. *History of the United States from the Compromise of 1850 to the McKinley-Bryan Campaign of 1896, vol. 2.* Port Washington, NY: Kennikat Press, Inc., 1892.

Richards, Leonard L. *The Slave Power: The Free North and Southern Domination, 1780-1860.* Baton Rouge: Louisiana University Press, 2000.

Riker, Dorothy, and Thornbrough, Gayle, eds. *Indiana Election Returns, 1816-1851.* Indianapolis: Indiana Historical Bureau, 1960.

Roll, Charles. *Colonel Dick Thompson: The Persistent Whig.* Indianapolis: Indiana Historical Bureau, 1948.

Roseboom, Eugene H. *A Short History of Presidential Elections.* New York: Collier Books, 1967.

Rosen, Robert N. *The Jewish Confederates.* Columbia, S.C.: University of South Carolina Press, 2000.

Russel, Robert R. "The Issues in the Congressional Struggle over the Kansas-Nebraska Bill." *Journal of Southern History* 29, no. 2 (May, 1963): 187-210.

Schott, Thomas E. *Alexander H. Stephens of Georgia: A Biography.* Baton Rouge and London: Louisiana State University Press, 1988.

Seigenthaler, John. *James K. Polk.* New York: Henry Holt and Company, 2003.

Shade, William G. *Banks or No Banks: The Money Issue in Western Politics, 1832-1865.* Detroit: Wayne State University Press, 1972.

Shepherd, Rebecca A., Calhoun, Charles W., Shanahan-Shoemaker, Elizabeth, January, Alan F., eds. *A Biographical Directory of the Indiana General Assembly*, vol. 1, 1819-1899. Indianapolis: Indiana Historical Society Bureau, 1980.

Shockley, Ernst V. "County Seats and County Seat Wars in Indiana." *Indiana Magazine of History* 10, no. 1 (March, 1914): 1-46.

Silbey, Joel H. *The American Political Nation, 1838-1883.* Stanford, California: Stanford University Press, 1991.

Silbey, Joel H. *The Partisan Imperative: The Dynamics of American Politics before the Civil War.* New York and Oxford: Oxford University Press, 1985.

Silbey, Joel H. *Party over Section: The Rough and Ready Presidential Election of 1848.* Lawrence, Kansas: The University Press of Kansas, 2009.

Silbey, Joel H. "The Southern National Democrats, 1845-1861." *Mid-America,* vol. 47 (July, 1965): 176-190.

Silbey, Joel H. "The Surge of Republican Power: Partisan Antipathy, American Social Conflict, and the Coming of the Civil War." In *Essays on American Antebellum Politics, 1840-1860,* edited by Stephen E. Maizlish. College Station: Texas A&M University Press, 1982: 199-229.

Smith, Earl and Hattery, Angela J. *Interracial Intimacies: An Examination of Powerful Men and Their Relationships across the Color Line.* Durham, North Carolina: Carolina Academic Press, 2009.

Smith, Elbert B. *The Presidency of James Buchanan.* Lawrence, Manhattan, Wichita: The University Press of Kansas, 1975.

Smith, Willard H. *Schuyler Colfax: The Changing Fortunes of a Political Idol.* Indianapolis: Indiana Historical Bureau, 1952.

"Some Letters to John G. Davis." *Indiana Magazine of History* 24, no. 3 (September, 1928): 201-213.

Spurgeon , Ian Michael. *Man of Douglas Man of Lincoln: The Political Odyssey of James Henry Lane.* Columbia, Missouri: University of Missouri Press, 2008.

Stampp, Kenneth. *America in 1857: A Nation on the Brink.* Oxford and New York: Oxford University Press, 1990.

Stampp, Kenneth. *Indiana Politics during the Civil War.* Indianapolis: Indiana Historical Bureau, 1949.

The State of Indiana Delineated. New York: J. H. Colton, 1838.

Stegmeier, Mark J. *Texas, New Mexico, and the Compromise of 1850.* Kent, Ohio: Kent State University Press, 1966.

Stephenson, Wendell Holmes. *The Political Career of General James H. Lane.* Topeka: Kansas State Printing Office, 1930.

Stern, Philip van Doren, ed. *The Life and Writings of Abraham Lincoln.* New York: The Modern Library, 1940.

Sternberg, Richard R. "The Motivation of the Wilmot Proviso." *Mississippi Valley Historical Review* 18, no. 3 (March, 1932): 535-541.

Stevenson, David. *Indiana's Roll of Honor.* Indianapolis: A. D. Strait, 1864.

Stoler, Mildred C. "Insurgent Democrats of Indiana and Illinois in 1854." *Indiana Magazine of History*, 33, no. 1 (March, 1937): 1-33.

Summers, Mark W. *The Plundering Generation: Corruption and the Crisis of the Union, 1849-1861.* New York and Oxford: Oxford University Press, 1987.

Sutherland, Keith A. "Congress and Crisis: A Study in the Legislative Process, 1860." PhD diss., Cornell University, 1966.

Syrett, Harold. *American Historical Documents.* New York: Barnes and Noble, 1960.

Thornbrough, Emma Lou. *Indiana in the Civil War Era, 1850-1880.* Indianapolis: Indiana Historical Society, 1965.

Thornbrough, Emma Lou. *The Negro in Indiana.* Indianapolis: Indiana Historical Bureau, 1957.

Torrey, Kale B. "Visions of a Western Lowell." *Indiana Magazine of History* 73, no. 4 (December 1977): 276-304.

Tribune Almanac, 1838-1868. Bound copies of years inclusive. Indiana State Library, Indianapolis, Indiana.

Tribune Almanac and Political Register for Year 1857. New York: Greeley and McGrath, 1857.

Tribune Almanac and United States Register for Year 1859. New York: Greeley and McGrath, 1859.

Tribune Almanac and United States Register for Year 1861. New York: Greeley and McGrath, 1862.

Turpie, David. "Typewritten Copy of *Sketches of My Own Time.*" Indiana State Library, Indianapolis, Indiana

Tusa, Frank. "Congressional Politics in the Secession Crisis, 1859-1861." PhD diss., Pennsylvania State University, 1979.

Vallandigham, James L. *A Life of Clement L. Vallandigham.* Baltimore: Turnbull Brothers, 1872.

Van Bolt, Roger H. "Fusion out of Confusion." *Indiana Magazine of History* 49, no. 4 (December, 1953): 353-390.

Van Bolt, Roger H. "The Hoosiers and Eternal Agitation, 1848-1850." *Indiana Magazine of History* 48, no. 4 (December, 1952): 331-368.

Van Bolt, Roger H. "The Hoosier Politician of the 1840s." *Indiana Magazine of History* 48, no. 1 (March, 1952): 23-36.

Van Bolt, Roger H., "Hoosiers and the Western Program, 1844-1848." *Indiana Magazine of History* 48, no. 3 (September, 1952): 255-271.

Van Bolt, Roger H. "Indiana in Political Transition, 1851-1853." *Indiana Magazine of History* 49, no. 2 (June, 1953): 130-160.

Van Bolt, Roger H. "The Rise of the Republican Party in Indiana." *Indiana Magazine of History* 51, no. 3 (September, 1955): 185-220.

Van Bolt, Roger H. "Sectional Aspects of Expansion." *Indiana Magazine of History* 48, no 2 (June, 1852): 119-140.

Van Der Weele, W. J. "Jesse David Bright: Master Politician from the Old Northwest." PhD diss., Indiana University, 1958.

Von Abele, Rudolf. *Alexander H. Stephens: A Biography.* New York: Alfred A. Knopf, Inc., 1946.

Voss-Hubbard, Mark. *Beyond Party: Cultures of Antipartisanship in Northern Politics before the Civil War.* Baltimore and London: The Johns Hopkins University Press, 2002.

Waldrup, Carole Chandler. *The Vice-Presidents: Biographies of the 45 Men Who Had Held the Second Highest Office in the United States.* Jefferson, North Carolina and London: McFarland & Co., 1996.

Walker, Francis A., ed. *The Statistics of the Population of the United States.* Washington, D.C.: Government Printing Office, 1971.

Wallace, Lew. *An Autobiography,* vol. 1, 1906. Repint, New York and London: Garnett Press, Inc., 1969.

Wallner, Peter A. *Franklin Pierce: Martyr for the Union.* Concord, New Hampshire: Plainswede Publishing, 2007.

Walsh, Justin E. *The Centennial History of the Indiana General Assembly, 1816-1978.* Indianapolis: Indiana Historical Bureau, 1987.

Walter, Scott. "'Awakening the Public Mind': The Dissemination of the Common School Idea in Indiana, 1787-1852." In *Hoosier Schools: Past and Present,* edited by William J. Reese. Bloomington and Indianapolis: Indiana University Press, 1998: 1-28.

Walther, Eric. *William Lowndes Yancey and the Coming of the Civil War.* Chapel Hill: University of North Carolina Press, 2006.

Whig Almanac and United States Register for Year 1845. New York: Greeley and McGrath, 1846.

Whig Almanac and United States Register for Year 1853. New York: Greeley and McGrath, 1853.

Whig Almanac and United States Register for Year 1855. New York: Greeley and McGrath, 1855.

White, William Alfred. *The History of Hanover College from 1827-1927.* Hanover, Indiana: Hanover College, 1927

"William H. English: His Record as a Civilian," repr., Indiana State Library Collection, Indianapolis.

Wilson, Major L. *Space, Time, and Freedom: The Quest for Nationality and the Irrepressible Conflict, 1815-1861.* Westport, Connecticut and London: Greenwood Press, 1974.

Wilson, Mary and Asher, Sharon Y. *Lexington.* Typed manuscript in Indiana State Library.

Wood, Gordon S. *Revolutionary Characters: What Made the Founders Different.* New York: The Penguin Press, 2006

Woolen, William Wesley. *Biographical and Historical Sketches of Early Indiana.* Indianapolis: Hammond and Co., 1883.

Woolen, William Wesley. *A Biographical History of Eminent and Self Made Men of the State of Indiana*, 2 vols. Cincinnati: Western Biographical Publishing Co., 1889.

Wolff Gerald W. "The Kansas-Nebraska Bill and Voting Behavior In the Thirty-Third Congress." PhD diss., University of Iowa, 1969.

Wylie, Theophilus A. *Indiana University: Its History from 1820, when Founded, to 1890.* Indianapolis: William B. Buford, 1890.

Zimmerman, Charles. "The Origin and Rise of the Republican Party in Indiana from 1854 to 1860." *Indiana Magazine of History* 13, no. 3 and no. 4 (September, 1917, December 1917): 211-269, 349-412.

Index